(a)

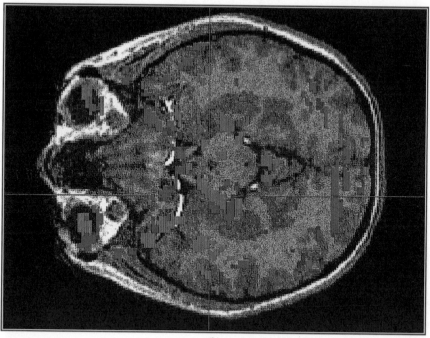

(b)

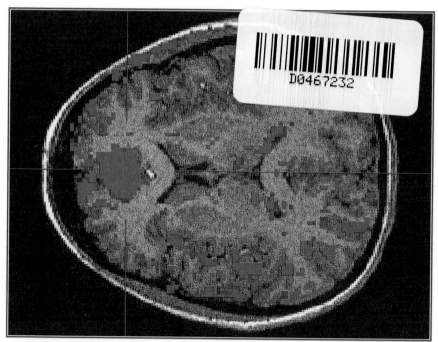

fMRI scans of a subject practicing a complex task studied by Fincham, Schneider, and Anderson. Red indicates activation early in practice, and green indicates activation late in practice.
(a) An oblique axial scan of a slice through the upper part of the brain showing large anterior cingulate activation early in practice.
(b) An oblique axial scan of a slice through the medial part of the brain showing large hippocampal activation late in practice.

COGNITIVE PSYCHOLOGY
AND ITS
IMPLICATIONS

COGNITIVE PSYCHOLOGY
AND ITS
IMPLICATIONS

FIFTH EDITION

John R. Anderson
Carnegie Mellon University

Worth Publishers

Cognitive Psychology and Its Implications, Fifth Edition

Copyright © 2000, 1995, 1990, 1985, 1980 by Worth Publishers and W. H. Freeman

Printed in the United States of America.

Library of Congress Catalog Card Number: 99–066922

ISBN: 0-7167-3678-0

Printing: 5 4 3

Year: 04 03 02

Sponsoring editor: Jessica Bayne
Text and cover design: Cambraia (Magalhães) Fernandes
Production editor: Tracey Kuehn
Production manager: Sarah Segal
Illustration coordinator: Lou Capaldo
Line art: Nugraphic Design, Inc.
Composition: Progressive Information Technologies
Printing and binding: R. R. Donnelley & Sons

Worth Publishers
41 Madison Avenue
New York, New York 10010
www.worthpublishers.com

To Gordon Bower

◆ Contents

◆ Preface

This is the fifth edition of my book. It was over twenty years ago that I undertook the writing of the first edition. A generation has passed and a lot has happened in cognitive psychology since that time, and a lot has happened to me and my perspectives on the field and its teaching.

The first edition was written when the field of cognitive psychology had just reached maturity. In the 1950s, a number of true pioneers broke with the behaviorist tradition and laid the foundations for cognitive psychology. In the 1960s psychologists worked hard to establish experimental paradigms and theoretical models for the new discipline. When I entered the field at the beginning of the 1970s, I was able to take full advantage of the previous two decades of effort. In the 1970s there was an amazing blossoming of research, and by the end of the decade, it became apparent to me that there was a coherent structure to the field that could be communicated in a textbook. The first edition of this book was published in 1980.

Since 1980 cognitive psychology has matured substantially. Almost every area has broadened in its empirical bases and in the detail of its theoretical interpretations. It has become increasingly difficult to choose exactly what to discuss in the book, but I continue to strive to provide the student with the big picture of the current state of the field. There have been new areas of research, most notably studies of human expertise and research on the neural basis of cognition. Some of the research on expertise is presented in Chapter 9, which was new in the second edition. Probably, the most significant difference between this current edition and the fourth edition is the increased use of data from cognitive neuroscience. Such data is starting to substantially determine our understanding of the mind.

In response to a publishing merger, my book is now being published by Worth. This has been a relatively painless transition for me, and I appreciate the effort at Worth to make it so. Among their many activities, they arranged for an extensive set of reviews. I appreciate the many comments and suggestions of these reviewers: Charles K. Allan, University of Montana; James Beale, Grand Valley State University; Stephen Blessing, University of Florida; Bruce Britton, University of Georgia; Gregory Burton, Seton Hall University; Robert Calfee, Stanford University; Nick Chater,

University of Warwick, United Kingdom; David Elmes, Washington and Lee University; K. Anders Ericsson, Florida State University; Dorthea Halpert, Brooklyn College; Lorna Hernandez-Jarvis, Hope College; Robert Hoffman, University of West Florida; Earl Hunt, University of Washington; Philip Johnson-Laird, Princeton University; Karen J. Mitchell, Kent State University; John D. Murray, Georgia Southern University; E. Slater Newman, North Carolina State University; Thomas Palmeri, Vanderbilt University; Joseph Thompson, Washington and Lee University; Roman Traban, Texas Tech University; Patricia deWinstanley, Oberlin College; Charles A. Weaver, Baylor University; Larry Wood, Brigham Young University.

I would also like to thank the people who read the first four editions of my book, as much of their earlier influence remains: Jim Anderson, Irv Biederman, Liz Bjork, Lyle Bourne, John Bransford, Pat Carpenter, Bill Chase, Micki Chi, Bill Clancy, Chuck Clifton, Lynne Cooper, Gus Craik, Bob Crowder, Martha Farah, Ronald Finke, Susan Fiske, Michael Gazzaniga, Ellen Gagné, Rochel Gelman, Lynn Hasher, Geoff Hinton, Kathy Hirsh-Pasek, Buz Hunt, Laree Huntsman, Lynn Hyah, Marcel Just, Stephen Keele, Walter Kintsch, Dave Klahr, Steve Kosslyn, Al Lesgold, Clayton Lewis, Beth Loftus, Marsha Lovett, Maryellen MacDonald, Brian MacWhinney, Dominic Massaro, Jay McClelland, Al Newell, Don Norman, Gary Olson, Allan Paivio, Nancy Pennington, Jane Perlmutter, Peter Polson, Jim Pomerantz, Mike Posner, Roger Ratcliff, Lynne Reder, Steve Reed, Russ Revlin, Phillip Rice, Lance Rips, Roddy Roediger, Miriam Schustack, Terry Sejnowski, Bob Siegler, Ed Smith, Kathy Spoehr, Bob Sternberg, Charles Tatum, Dave Tieman, Tom Trabasso, Henry Wall, and Maria Zaragoza.

Finally, I would like to thank my secretary Helen Borek, who also worked on the previous two editions. She has become a veteran of the book writing process whose accumulated knowledge is essential to the success of the project.

John R. Anderson

COGNITIVE PSYCHOLOGY
AND ITS
IMPLICATIONS

1

The Science of Cognition

Our species is referred to as *homo sapiens*, or "human, the intelligent." This term reflects the general belief that intelligence is what distinguishes us from other animals. The goal of cognitive psychology is to understand the nature of human intelligence and how it works. Subsequent chapters in this book discuss what cognitive psychologists have discovered about various aspects of human intelligence. This chapter attempts to answer the following preliminary questions:

- Why do people study cognitive psychology?

- Where and when did cognitive psychology originate?

- What are the methods of cognitive psychology as a science?

Motivations

Intellectual Curiosity

One reason for studying cognitive psychology is the same one that motivates any scientific inquiry—the desire to know. In this respect, the cognitive psychologist is like the tinkerer who wants to know how a clock works. The human mind is a particularly interesting device that displays remarkable adaptiveness and intelligence. We are often unaware of the extraordinary aspects of human cognition. Just as we can easily overlook the enormous accumulation of technology that permits coverage of a news event that we see on television to be broadcast live from anywhere in the world, so too can we forget how sophisticated our mental processes must be to enable us to understand that news event. One would like to understand the mechanisms that make such intellectual sophistication possible.

The inner workings of the human mind are far more intricate than the most complicated systems of modern technology. Researchers in the field of **artificial intelligence** (AI) have been attempting to develop programs that will enable computers to display intelligent behavior. Although this field has been an active one for more than forty years and there have been many notable successes, AI researchers still do not know how to create a program that matches human intelligence. No existing program can recall facts, solve problems, reason, learn, and process language with human facility. This lack of success has occurred not because computers are inferior to human brains, but rather because we do not yet know in sufficient detail how intelligence is organized in the brain.

It does not appear that there is anything magical about human intelligence that would make it impossible for it to be modeled on a computer. Consider scientific discovery, for instance. This is often considered to reflect the ultimate feats of human intelligence, in which scientists supposedly make great leaps of intuition in order to explain a puzzling set of data. To formulate a novel scientific theory is supposed to require both great creativity and special deductive powers. Herbert Simon, who won the 1978 Nobel prize for his theoretical work in economics, has spent the last forty years studying cognitive psychology and has more recently focused on the intellectual accomplishments involved in "doing" science. He and his colleagues (Langley, Simon, Bradshaw, & Zytkow, 1987) have built computer programs that simulate the problem-solving activities involved in such scientific feats as Kepler's discovery of the laws of planetary motion, Ohm's law for electric circuits, and the laws of chemical reactions. These programs are among the most impressive accomplishments of artificial intelligence. Simon has also examined the processes involved in his own now-famous scientific discoveries (Simon, 1989). In all cases, he finds that the processes of scientific discovery can be explained in terms of the basic cognitive processes that are being studied in cognitive psychology. He writes that many of the activities involved are just well-understood problem-solving processes (we will study these in Chapters 8 and 9). He adds,

> *Moreover, the insight that is supposed to be required for such work as discovery turns out to be synonymous with the familiar process of recognition; and other terms commonly used in the discussion of creative work—such terms as "judgment," "creativity," or even "genius"—appear to be wholly dispensable or to be definable, as insight is, in terms of mundane and well-understood concepts. (p. 376)*

Thus, Simon's basic argument is that when we look in detail at human genius we find that it involves basic cognitive processes operating together in complex ways to produce the brilliant results.[1] Most of this book will be devoted to describing what we know about those basic processes.

◆
Basic cognitive processes underlie great feats of intelligence such as scientific discovery.

Implications for Other Fields

Students and researchers interested in other areas of psychology or social science have another reason for following developments in cognitive psychology. The basic mechanisms governing human thought that cognitive psychology attempts to understand are important in understanding the types of behavior studied by other social sciences. For example, understanding how humans think is important to understanding why certain thought malfunctions occur (clinical psychology), how people behave with other individuals or in groups (social psychology), how persuasion works (political science), how economic decisions are made (economics), why certain ways of organizing groups are more effective and stable than others (sociology), or why natural languages have certain features (linguistics). Cognitive psychology is thus the foundation on which all other social sciences stand, in the same the way that physics is the foundation for other physical sciences.

Nonetheless, much social science has developed without a grounding in cognitive psychology. Two facts account for this situation. First, cognitive psychology is not that advanced. Second, researchers in other areas of social science have managed to find higher-order principles unrelated to cognitive mechanisms to explain the phenomena in which they are interested. Thus, for instance, economists discuss rational decision making without re-

◆

[1]Weisberg (1986) in *Creativity: Genius and other myths* comes to a similar conclusion.

ally considering how humans make decisions (a topic of Chapter 10). However, much is unknown or poorly understood in these other social sciences. If we knew how these higher-order principles were explained in terms of cognitive mechanisms and how to apply cognitive mechanisms directly to higher-order phenomena, we might have a firmer grasp on the phenomena in question. For instance, if we understood human decision making better, we could understand deviations from the economist's prescription for rational decision making.

◆
Cognitive psychology can provide the foundation for many other areas of social science.

Practical Applications

The desire to understand is an important motivation for the study of cognitive psychology, as it is in any science, but the practical implications of the field constitute another important motivation. If we really understand how people acquire knowledge and intellectual skills and how they perform feats of intelligence, then we will be able to improve their intellectual training and performance accordingly.

The knowledge of the mind that cognitive psychologists are developing will prove beneficial to both individuals and society. Many of our problems derive from an inability to deal with the cognitive demands made on us. These problems are being exacerbated by the "information explosion" and the technological revolution we are presently experiencing. Cognitive psychology is just beginning to make headway on these issues, but some clear and positive insights with direct application to everyday life have already emerged. There have been applications of cognitive psychology to law (e.g., Loftus, 1979, on the reliability of eyewitness testimony), to the design of computer systems (e.g., Card, Moran, & Newell, 1983, on using word processors, or Pirolli & Card, in press, on surfing the Web), and to instruction (Gagné, Yekovich, & Yekovich, 1993, on classroom practice). Cognitive psychology is also making important contributions to our understanding of brain disorders that reflect abnormal functioning, such as schizophrenia (Cohen & Servan-Schreiber, 1992) or that are the result of brain damage such as amnesia (Baddeley, Wilson, & Watts, 1995).

At many points in this book, research in cognitive psychology will be shown to have implications for study skills. Students who read this text and learn the lessons it has to offer will improve the capacity of their intellects, at least modestly. In our own laboratory (Anderson, Corbett, Koedinger, & Pelletier, 1995), we have merged the knowledge of cognitive psychology and the techniques of artificial intelligence to create "intelligent" computer tutors that have substantially enhanced students' performance, as will be discussed in Chapter 9.

So another reason for studying cognitive psychology and for encouraging its development as a field is to enable people to be more effective in their intellectual pursuits. In the next subsection, we will give a down payment on this claim. We will summarize some of the implications of cognitive psychology for effective study of a textbook like this.

◆

The results from the study of cognitive psychology have implications for improving intellectual performance.

How to Study This Book

One of the contributions of cognitive psychology is that it has identified methods that enable one to read and remember a text like this. This research will be described in Chapter 7 on memory and in Chapter 12 on language processing. It would be an aid to you as students, however, to be told the basic gist of these techniques now so that you will be able to apply these methods to the book. The key idea is that it is critical to identify the main points of each section of a text like this and to try to understand how these main points are organized. I have tried to help you do this by following each significant section with a short summary sentence identifying its main point. I recommend that you use the following study technique to best help you remember the material. This is a variant of the PQ4R method discussed in Chapter 7:

1. Preview the chapter. Read the section headings and summary statements to get a general sense of where the chapter is going and how much material will be devoted to each topic. Try to understand each summary statement and ask yourself whether this is something you knew or believed before reading the text.

Then for each section of the book, go through the following steps:

2. Make up a study question. From the section heading make up a related question that you will try to answer while reading the text. For instance, in the section, "Intellectual Curiosity," you might ask yourself, "What is there to be curious about in cognitive psychology?" This will give you an active goal to pursue while you read the section.

3. Read the section to understand it and answer your question. Try to relate what you are reading to situations in your own life. In the section, "Intellectual Curiosity," for example, you might try to think of scientific discoveries you have read about that seemed to require creativity.

4. At the end of each section, read the summary and ask yourself if that is the main point you got out of the section and why it is the main point. Sometimes you may be required to go back and reread some parts of the section.

At the end of the chapter, you should engage in the following review process:

5. Go through the text, mentally reviewing the main points. Try answering the questions you made up (step 2), plus any other questions that occur to you. Often, when preparing for an exam, it is a good idea to ask yourself what kind of exam questions you would make up for the chapter.

As we will review in later chapters, such a study strategy does lead to better memory for the text.

◆

Memory for a text can be improved if you read the text in multiple passes, asking yourself questions as you do so.

The History of Cognitive Psychology

Early History

In Western civilization, interest in human cognition can be traced to the ancient Greeks. Plato and Aristotle, in their discussions of the nature and origin of knowledge, speculated on memory and thought. These early discussions, which were essentially philosophical in nature, eventually developed into a centuries-long debate. The two positions were **empiricism,** which held that all knowledge comes from experience, and **nativism,** which held that children come into the world with a great deal of innate knowledge. The debate intensified in the seventeenth, eighteenth, and nineteenth centuries, with such British philosophers as Berkeley, Locke, Hume, and Mill arguing for the empiricist view and such continental philosophers as Descartes and Kant propounding the nativist view. Although these arguments were at their core philosophical, they frequently slipped into psychological speculations about human cognition.

During this long period of philosophical debate, such sciences as astronomy, physics, chemistry, and biology developed markedly. Curiously, however, no concomitant attempt was made to apply the scientific method to the understanding of human cognition; such an undertaking did not take place until the end of the nineteenth century. Certainly, there were no technical or conceptual barriers preventing the study of cognitive psychology earlier. In fact, many cognitive psychology experiments could have been performed and understood in the time of the Greeks. But cognitive psychology, like many other sciences, suffered because of our egocentric, mystical, and confused attitude about ourselves and our own nature. Before the nineteenth century it had seemed inconceivable that the workings of the human mind also could be subjected to scientific analysis. As a consequence, cognitive psychology as a science is only about 125 years old, and lags behind many other sciences in sophistication. We have spent much of the first one hundred years freeing ourselves of the pernicious misconceptions that can arise when people engage in such an introverted enterprise as a scientific study of human cognition. It is the case of the mind studying itself.

◆
Only in the last 125 years has it been realized that human cognition could be the subject of scientific study rather than philosophical speculation.

Psychology in Germany

The date usually cited as marking the beginning of psychology as a science is 1879, when Wilhelm Wundt established the first psychology laboratory in Leipzig, Germany. Wundt's psychology was cognitive psychology (in contrast to other major divisions of psychology, such as comparative, clinical, or social), although he had far-ranging views on many subjects. The method of inquiry used by Wundt, his students, and a large number of the early psychologists was **introspection.** In this method, highly trained observers reported the contents of their own consciousnesses under carefully controlled conditions. The basic belief was that the workings of the mind should be open to self-observation. Drawing on the empiricism of the British philosophers, Wundt and others believed that very intense self-inspection would be able to identify the primitive experiences out of which thought was constituted. Thus, to develop a theory of cognition, a psychologist had only to account for the contents of introspective reports.

Let us consider a sample introspective experiment. Mayer and Orth (1901) had their subjects perform a free-association task. The experimenters spoke a word to the subjects and then measured the amount of time the subjects took to generate responses to this word. Subjects then reported all their conscious experiences from the moment of stimulus presentation until their response was generated. To get a feeling for this method, try to generate an association to each of the following words; after each association try to introspect on the contents of your consciousness during the period between reading the word and making your association:

coat

book

dot

bowl

In Mayer and Orth's experiment, many reports were given of rather nondescribable conscious experiences. Whatever was in consciousness, it did not always seem to involve sensations, images, or other things that subjects in these laboratories were accustomed to reporting. This result started a debate on the issue of imageless thought—whether conscious experience could really be devoid of concrete content. As we will see in Chapters 4 and 5, modern cognitive psychology has made real progress on this issue.

◆

At the turn of the century, German psychologists tried to use introspection to study the workings of the mind.

Psychology in America

Wundt's introspective psychology was not well accepted in America. Early American psychologists engaged in what they called "introspection" but it was not the intense analysis of the contents of the mind practiced by the Germans. Rather, it was largely an armchair avocation, in which the only self-inspection was casual and reflective rather than intense and analytic. William James's (1890) *Principles of Psychology* reflects the best of this tradition, and many of the proposals in this work are still relevant and cogent today. The mood of America was determined by the philosophical doctrines of pragmatism and functionalism. Many psychologists of the time were involved in education, and the demand was for an "action-oriented" psychology that was capable of practical application. The intellectual climate in America was not receptive to a psychology focused on such questions as whether or not the contents of consciousness were sensory.

One of the important figures of early American scientific psychology was Edward Thorndike, who developed a theory of learning that was directly applicable to school situations. Thorndike was interested in such basic questions as the effects of reward and punishment on the rate of learning. To him, conscious experience was just excess baggage that could be largely ignored. As often as not, his experiments were done on animals such as cats. Research on animals involved fewer ethical constraints than research on humans. Thorndike was probably just as happy that such subjects could not introspect.

While introspection was being ignored at the turn of the century in America, it was getting into trouble on the continent. Different laboratories were reporting different types of introspections—each type matching the theory of the particular laboratory from which it emanated. It was becoming clear that introspection did not give one a clear window into the workings of the mind. Much that was important in cognitive functioning was not open to conscious experience. These two factors, the "irrelevance" of the introspective method and its apparent contradictions, set the groundwork for the great behaviorist revolution in American psychology that occurred around 1920. John Watson and other behaviorists led a fierce attack, not only on introspectionism, but also on any attempt to develop a theory of mental operations. **Behaviorism** held that psychology was to be entirely concerned with external behavior and was not to try to analyze the workings of the mind that underlay this behavior:

> *Behaviorism claims that consciousness is neither a definite nor a usable concept. The Behaviorist, who has been trained always as an experimentalist, holds further that belief in the existence of consciousness goes back to the ancient days of superstition and magic. (Watson, 1930, p. 2)*

> *The Behaviorist began his own formulation of the problem of psychology by sweeping aside all medieval conceptions. He dropped from his scientific vocabulary all subjective terms such as sensation, perception, image, desire, purpose, and even thinking and emotion as they were subjectively defined. (Watson, 1930, pp. 5–6)*

The behaviorist program and the issues it spawned pushed research on cognition into the background of American psychology. The rat supplanted the human as the principal laboratory subject, and psychology turned to finding out what could be learned by studying animal learning and motivation. Quite a bit was discovered, but little was of direct relevance to cognitive psychology. Perhaps the most important lasting contribution of behaviorism is a set of sophisticated and rigorous techniques and principles for experimental study in all fields of psychology, including cognitive psychology.

Behaviorism was not as dominant in Europe. Psychologists like Frederick Bartlett in England, Alexander Luria in Russia, and Jean Piaget in Switzerland were pursuing ideas that are important in modern cognitive psychology. Cognitive psychology was an active research topic in Germany, but much of it was lost in the Nazi turmoil. A number of German psychologists emigrated to America and brought Gestalt psychology to America.

Some of them became quite prominent, such as the Gestalt psychologist Wolfgang Kohler, who was elected to the presidency of the American Psychological Association. In America, however, the Gestalt psychologists received most attention for their claims about animal learning and were the standard targets for the behaviorist critiques. Edward Tolman was an American psychologist who anticipated many ideas of modern cognitive psychology, but he also did his research on animal learning and spoke the language of behaviorism. Again, he served as a foil for the dominant behaviorist psychologists.

In retrospect, it is hard to understand how American behaviorists could have taken such an antimental stand and clung to it for so long. Just because introspection proved to be unreliable did not mean that it was impossible to develop a theory of internal mental structure and process. It only meant that other methods were required. In physics, for example, a theory of atomic structure was developed, although that structure could only be inferred, not be directly observed. But behaviorists argued that a theory of internal structure was not necessary to an understanding of human behavior, and in a sense they may have been right (see Anderson & Bower, 1973, pp. 30–37). A theory of internal structure, however, makes understanding human beings much easier. The success of cognitive psychology during the later part of the twentieth century in analyzing complex intellectual processes testifies to the utility of postulating mental structures and processes.

In both the introspectionist and the behaviorist programs, we see the human mind struggling with the effort to understand itself. The introspectionists held a naive belief in the power of self-observation. The behaviorists were so afraid of falling prey to subjective fallacies that they refused to let themselves think about mental processes. Modern cognitive psychologists seem to be much more at ease with their subject matter. They have a relatively detached attitude toward human cognition and approach it much as they would any other complex system.

◆

Behaviorism, which dominated American psychology in the first half of the century, rejected the use of mental constructs in explaining behavior.

The Emergence of Modern Cognitive Psychology

Cognitive psychology, as we know it today, took form in the two decades between 1950 and 1970. Three main influences account for its modern development. The first was research on human performance, which was given a great boost during World War II, when practical information was badly needed on how to train soldiers to use sophisticated equipment and how to deal with problems like breakdown of attention. Behaviorism offered no help with such practical issues. While the work during the war had a very applied bent, the issues it raised stayed with psychologists when they went back to their academic laboratories after the war. The work of the British psychologist Donald Broadbent at the Applied Psychology Research Unit in Cambridge was probably most influential in integrating ideas from human performance with new ideas that were developing in an area called information theory. Information theory was an abstract way of analyzing the processing of information. Broadbent and other psychologists such as George Miller, Fred Attneave, and Wendell Garner initially developed these ideas with respect to perception and attention, but such analyses now pervade all of cognitive psychology. The characteristics of the information-processing approach are discussed later in this chapter. Although other types of analysis in cognitive psychology exist, information processing is the dominant viewpoint and the main one presented in this book.

Second and closely related to the development of the information-processing approach were developments in computer science, particularly **artificial intelligence (AI),** which tries to get computers to behave intelligently. Allen Newell and Herbert Simon at Carnegie Mellon University spent forty years educating cognitive psychologists on the implications of artificial intelligence (and educating workers in artificial intelligence about the implications of cognitive psychology). The direct influence of computer-based theories on cognitive psychology has always been minimal. The indirect influence, however, has been enormous. A host of concepts have been taken from computer science and used in psychological theories. Probably more important, observing how we can analyze the intelligent behavior of a machine has largely liberated us from our inhibitions and misconceptions about analyzing our own intelligence.

The third field of influence on cognitive psychology is linguistics. In the 1950s, Noam Chomsky, a linguist at the Massachusetts Institute of Technology, began to develop a new mode of analyzing the structure of language. His work showed that language was much more complex than had previously been believed and that many of the prevailing behavioristic formulations were incapable of explaining these complexities. Chomsky's linguistic analyses proved critical in enabling cognitive psychologists to fight off the prevailing behavioristic conceptions. George Miller, at Harvard University in the 1950s and early 1960s, was instrumental in bringing these linguistic analyses to the attention of psychologists and in identifying new ways of studying language.

Cognitive psychology has grown rapidly since the 1950s. A very important event was the publication of Ulric Neisser's *Cognitive Psychology* in 1967. This book gave a new legitimacy to the field. It consisted of six chapters on perception and attention and four chapters on language, memory, and thought. This contrasts sharply with this book, which has only two chapters on perception and attention but has ten on language, memory, and thought. My chapter division reflects the growing emphasis on higher mental processes. Following Neisser's work, another important event was the beginning of the journal *Cognitive Psychology* in 1970. This journal has done much to give definition to the field.

More recently a new field, called *cognitive science,* has emerged which attempts to integrate research efforts from psychology, philosophy, linguistics, neuroscience, and artificial intelligence. This field can be dated from the appearance of the journal *Cognitive Science* in 1976. The fields of cognitive psychology and cognitive science overlap. It is not profitable to try to define precisely the differences, but cognitive science makes greater use of methods such as computer simulation of cognitive processes and logical analysis, while cognitive psychology relies heavily on experimental techniques for studying behavior that grew out of the behaviorist era. This book draws on all methods but, as its title suggests, it makes most use of cognitive psychology's experimental methodology.

The field of cognitive neuroscience has grown rapidly in the last two decades as advances have been made in its theoretical and experimental techniques. We will review these developments at the end of the chapter. The ability to more firmly anchor cognitive phenomena in brain mechanisms is having a major impact on the field, as we will describe throughout the book. It has served to consolidate cognitive psychology's break with behaviorism. Criticisms like Watson's against postulating mental structures sound very hollow today when we can localize these mental structures in the brain.

◆ Cognitive psychology broke away from behaviorism in response to developments in information theory, artificial intelligence, linguistics, and neuroscience.

Information-Processing Analyses

The various factors described in the previous subsection converged in a particular approach to studying human cognition—the **information-processing approach**—which has become dominant in cognitive psychology. It attempts to analyze cognition into a set of steps in which an abstract entity called information is processed. Probably the best way to explain this approach is to describe what is probably the most famous example of it.

In 1966, Saul Sternberg described an experimental paradigm and proposed a theoretical account of it that proved to be quite influential. In what has come to be called the **Sternberg paradigm,** subjects are shown a small number of digits, such as "3 9 7," that they must keep in mind. Then they are asked whether a particular probe digit is in the memory set, and they must answer this question as quickly as they can. Sternberg varied the number of digits in the memory set from 1 to 6 and looked at the speed with which subjects could make this judgment. Figure 1.1 shows his results

Figure 1.1 Time needed to recognize a digit increases with the number of items in the memory set. The straight line represents the linear function that fits the data best. (From Sternberg, 1969.)

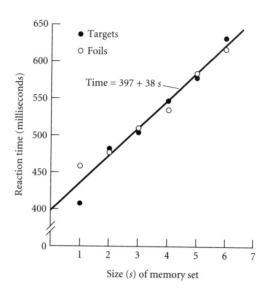

as a function of the size of the memory set. Data are plotted separately for positive probes, or targets (9 would be a positive probe for the set above), and for negative probes, or foils (6 would be a negative probe). Subjects can make these judgments quite fast, with their latencies varying between 400 milliseconds (ms) (a millisecond is a thousandth of a second) and 600 ms. Sternberg found a nearly linear relationship between the size of the memory set and judgment time. As shown in Figure 1.1, subjects take about 38 ms extra to judge each digit in the set.

Sternberg developed a very influential account of how subjects made these judgments. This account exemplifies what an abstract information-processing theory is like. His explanation is illustrated in Figure 1.2. Sternberg assumed that when subjects saw a probe stimulus such as a 9, they went through the series of information-processing stages illustrated in that figure. First, the stimulus has to be encoded. Then, the stimulus would be compared to each digit in the memory set. He assumed it took 38 ms to complete each one of these comparisons, which accounted for the slope in Figure 1.1. Then the subject had to decide on a response and finally generate it. Sternberg showed that different variables would influ-

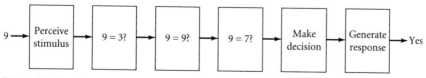

Figure 1.2 Sternberg's analysis of the sequence of information-processing stages in his task.

ence each of these information-processing stages. Thus, if he degraded the stimulus quality, subjects took longer to make their judgments, but this did not affect the slope in Figure 1.1. This is because it affected only the stage of stimulus perception in Figure 1.2. Again, if he biased subjects to say yes or no, this would affect the decision-making stage but not other stages.

It is worth noting the ways in which Sternberg's theory exemplifies an abstract information-processing account:

1. There is discussion of the information processing that is going on without any attempt to conceptualize it in terms of brain location or brain processes.

2. The processing of the information had a highly symbolic character. Thus, we speak of the system as comparing the symbol 9 against the symbol 3. There is no consideration of possible neural representations of these symbols.

3. Sternberg called upon the computer metaphor in justifying his theory of information processing. He thought information processing in this task could be compared to the way computers do high-speed scanning.

4. Measurement of time to make a judgment is a critical variable. This is because the information processing is conceived of as taking place in discrete stages. Flowcharts such as the one in Figure 1.2 have been a very popular means of expressing the steps of information processing. Flowcharts are themselves imported from computer science.

◆ Information-processing analysis decomposes a cognitive task into a set of abstract information-processing steps.

Cognitive Psychology Since the 1970s

Theories like the Sternberg model reflected much of the state of the field of cognitive psychology through the 1970s. That is, precise and accurate information-processing models were being proposed for various aspects of human cognition. However, a number of concerns that were being expressed about such models in the 1970s really set the direction for the last two decades of cognitive psychology research in the twentieth century. Read over the description of the Sternberg model again and ask yourself what concerns cognitive psychologists might have had about such models. Three questions, discussed on the next pages, became dominant.

1. Relevance: This is a study and theory of a laboratory task. Is cognition really like this in the real world? Neisser, whose book a decade earlier had helped define the field, wrote another book in 1976 that was highly critical of the relevance of laboratory research. In 1982, Neisser wrote, "If X is an interesting or socially significant aspect of memory, then psychologists have never studied X." One of the ways in which cognitive psychology has answered this concern has been to see if laboratory research generalizes to practical applications. As we noted earlier, there have been very successful extensions of such research to areas like education and human-computer interaction. This research has confirmed that the basic cognitive processes uncovered in the laboratory do extend to real-world phenomena. However, the concern with practical applications has not left the field of cognitive psychology unchanged. For instance, it has helped generate new areas of research, such as the nature of expert problem solving (discussed in Chapter 9).

2. Sufficiency: The Sternberg model is a theory of how people do a very simple task. Will theories like this ever add up to explain anything so complex as human cognition? Newell in 1973 wrote an influential paper in which he criticized cognitive psychologists for playing 20 questions with nature and claimed they would never understand human cognition unless they worked on theories that encompassed more of human cognition. Psychologists have tried to develop much more comprehensive theories of cognition in response to this issue (Anderson, 1983; Rumelhart & McClelland, 1986b; Newell, 1991). These theories are called **cognitive architectures** because they describe how a complete cognitive system functions. For instance, I work in what is called the ACT-R architecture, which not only has been used to explain how people perform in the Sternberg task but also in a wide variety of other situations, from understanding metaphors to designing psychology experiments (see Anderson & Lebiere, 1998).

3. Necessity: While the Sternberg model adequately predicts the data, is there any reason to believe that this is actually the way the human brain does the task? James Anderson in 1973 wrote an article in which he criticized the Sternberg model and other information-processing models as being incompatible with what we know about how the brain does things. There has been an increasing concern with having theories that are compatible with what is known about brain functioning. Also, more cognitive psychologists are studying the brain processes that occur during cognition. In the last decade of the twentieth century, **cognitive neuroscience** has become a major area of research. One cannot follow the research on human cognition anymore without understanding some basic facts about brain structures and processes. Therefore, in recent editions of this textbook I have concluded this introductory chapter with a basic overview of the nervous system.

◆

Since the 1970s, cognitive psychology has displayed a greater concern with cognition in a real-world setting, with large-scale theories of cognition, and with the brain mechanisms underlying cognition.

The Nervous System

The nervous system refers to more than just the brain. It refers to the various sensory systems that gather information from parts of the body and to the motor system that controls movement. In some cases, the information processing that takes place outside the brain is considerable. From an information-processing point of view, the most important components of the nervous system are the neurons.[2] A **neuron** is a cell that accumulates and transmits electrical activity. The human brain itself contains roughly 100 billion neurons, each of which may have roughly the processing capability of a small computer.[3] A considerable fraction of the 100 billion neurons are active simultaneously and do much of their information processing through interactions with one another. Imagine the information-processing power in 100 billion interacting computers! According to this view of the brain, there is more computational power in one 3-pound brain than in all the computers in the world. Lest you become overwhelmed by the brain, we must point out that it is not good at doing some things the computer does well. There are many tasks, like finding square roots, at which a simple hand calculator can outperform all 100 billion neurons. To understand the strengths and weaknesses of the human nervous system is a major goal in understanding the nature of human cognition.

◆

[2]Neurons are by no means the majority of cells in the nervous system. There are many others, such as glial cells, whose main function is thought to be supportive of the neurons.

[3]For instance, according to one view, each neuron computes on the order of 1000 multiplications and additions of real numbers every 10 milliseconds.

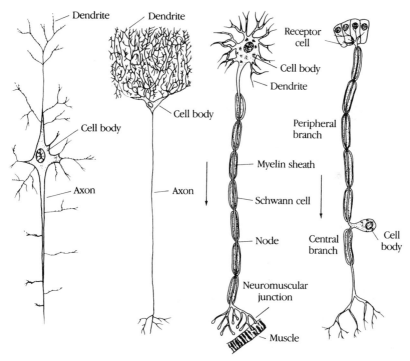

Figure 1.3 Some of the variety of neurons. (From Keeton, 1980.)

The Neuron

Neurons come in a wide variety of shapes and sizes, depending on their exact location and function. (Figure 1.3 illustrates some of the variety.) There is, however, a generally accepted notion of what the prototypical neuron is like, and individual neurons match up with this prototype to greater or lesser degrees. This prototype is illustrated in Figure 1.4. The main body of

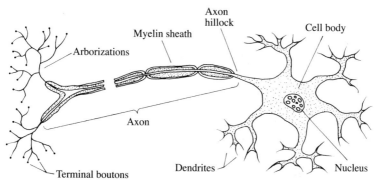

Figure 1.4 A schematic representation of a typical neuron. (From Katz, 1952.)

the neuron is called the soma. Typically, the soma is 5 to 100 micrometers (mm — millionths of a meter) in diameter. Attached to the soma are a set of short branches called **dendrites,** and extending from the soma is a long tube called the **axon.** The axon can vary in length from a few millimeters to a meter.

Axons provide the fixed paths by which neurons communicate with one another. The axon of one neuron extends toward the dendrites of other neurons. At its end, the axon branches into a large number of terminal arborizations. Each arborization ends in terminal boutons that almost make contact with the dendrite of another neuron. The gap separating the terminal bouton and the dendrite is typically in the range of 10 to 50 nanometers (a nanometer is one-billionth of a meter). This near contact between axon and dendrite is called a **synapse.** The most typical means of communication between neurons is that the axon terminal on one side of the synapse releases chemicals, called **neurotransmitters,** that act on the membrane of the receptor dendrite to change its polarization, or electric potential. The inside of the membrane covering the entire neuron tends to be 70 millivolts (mV; a millivolt is one-thousandth of a volt, or 0.001 V) more negative than the outside, due to the greater concentration of negative chemical ions inside and positive ions outside. Particularly important to understanding the functioning of the neuron is the existence of a greater concentration of positive sodium ions on the outside. Depending on the nature of the neurotransmitter, the potential difference can decrease or increase. Synaptic connections that decrease the potential difference are called **excitatory,** and synapses that increase the difference are called **inhibitory.**

The average soma and dendrite have about 1000 synapses from other neurons, and the average axon synapses to about 1000 neurons. The change in electrical potential due to any one synapse is rather small, but the individual excitatory and inhibitory effects can sum (the excitatory effects being positive in the summation, and the inhibitory effects being negative). If there is enough net excitatory input, the potential difference in the soma can drop sharply. If the reduction in potential is large enough, a depolarization will occur at the axon hillock, where the axon joins the soma (see Figure 1.4). This depolarization is caused by a rush of positive sodium ions into the inside of the neuron. The inside of the neuron momentarily (for a millisecond) becomes more positive than the outside. This sudden change, referred to as an **action potential** (or spike), will propagate down the axon. That is, the potential difference will suddenly and momentarily change down the axon. The rate at which this change travels can vary from 0.5 meters per second (m/s) to 130 m/s, depending on the characteristics of the axon — such as the degree to which the axon is covered by a myelin sheath (the more myelination, the faster the transmission). When the nerve impulse reaches the end of the axon, it will cause neurotransmitters to be released from the terminal boutons, thus completing the cycle.

To review, potential changes accumulate on a cell body, reach threshold, and cause an action potential to propagate down an axon. This pulse in turn causes neurotransmitters to be transmitted from the axon terminal to the body of a new neuron, causing changes in its membrane potential. It should be emphasized that this sequence is almost all there is to neural information processing, yet intelligence arises from this simple system of interactions. A major challenge to cognitive science is to understand how.

The time for this neural communication to complete that path from one neuron to another is roughly 10 milliseconds—definitely more than 1 millisecond and definitely less than 100; the exact speed depends on the characteristics of the neurons involved. This is much slower than the millions of operations that can be performed in 1 second by a computer. There are, however, billions of these activities occurring simultaneously throughout the brain.

◆ ──

Neurons communicate by accumulating electric potential changes from other neurons on their dendrites and cell bodies and by sending signals down their axons that reflect these changes.

───

Neural Representation of Information

Information in the brain is represented in terms of continuously varying quantities. There are two such quantities. First, the membrane potential can range more or less negative. Second, the axon can vary in terms of the number of nerve impulses it transmits per second. This is referred to as its **rate of firing.** It is usually thought that the number, not the pattern, of impulses along a single axon is important. There can be upward of 100 nerve impulses per second. The greater the rate of firing, the more effect the axon will have on the cells to which it synapses. Information representation in the brain is to be contrasted with information representation in a computer, where individual memory cells, or bits, can have just one of two values—off and on, or 0 and 1. There is not a continuous variation in a typical computer cell as there is in a typical neural cell.

There is a general way to conceptualize the interactions among neurons that captures the many specific variations on information transfer in the nervous system. This is to think of a neuron as having an activation level that corresponds roughly to its firing rate on the axon or to the degree of depolarization on the dendrite and soma. Neurons interact by driving up the activation level of other neurons (excitation) or by driving down their activation level (inhibition). All neural information processing takes place in terms of these excitatory and inhibitory effects; they are what underlies human cognition.

It is an interesting question just how these neurons represent information. There is evidence that individual neurons respond to specific features of a stimulus. For instance, the next chapter will describe neurons that are maximally active when there is a line in the visual field at a particular angle. There is some evidence that neurons exist that respond to more complex sets of features. For instance, there are neurons in the monkey brain that appear to respond maximally to faces (Bruce, Desimone, & Gross, 1981; Desimone, Albright, Gross, & Bruce, 1984; Perrett, Rolls, & Caan, 1982). However, it is not possible that we have single neurons encoding all the concepts and shades of meaning we possess. Moreover, a single neuron's firing cannot represent the complexity of structure in a face.

If a single neuron cannot represent the complexity of our cognition, how is it represented? How can the activity of neurons represent our concept of baseball; how can they result in our solution of an algebra problem; how can they result in our feeling of frustration? Similar questions can be asked of computer systems, which have been shown to be capable of answering questions about baseball, solving algebra problems, and displaying frustration. Where in the millions of off-and-on bits in a computer does the concept of baseball lie? How does a change in a bit result in the solution of an algebra problem or in a feeling of frustration? The answer in every case is that these questions fail to see the forest for the trees. The concepts of baseball, problem solution, and emotion occur in large patterns of bit changes. Similarly, human cognition is achieved through large patterns of neural activity. In one study, Mazoyer, Tzourio, Frak, Syrota, Murayama, Levrier, Salamon, Dehaene, Cohen, and Mehler (1993) compared subjects hearing random words to subjects hearing words that made nonsense sentences to subjects hearing words that made coherent sentences. Using methods that will shortly be described, the researchers measured brain activity. They found activity in more and more regions as subjects went from hearing words to hearing sentences to hearing meaningful stories. This indicates that our understanding of a meaningful story involves activity in many regions of the brain.

It is informative to consider how the computer stores information. Consider a simple case: the spelling of words. Most computers have codes by which individual patterns of binary values (1's and 0's) represent letters. Table 1.1 illustrates the use of one coding scheme, called ASCII; it contains a patterns of 0's and 1's that codes the words *cognitive psychology.*

Similarly, information in the brain can be represented in terms of patterns of neural activity rather than simply as cells firing. The code in Table 1.1 includes certain redundant bits that allow the computer to correct errors should certain bits be lost (note that each column has an even number of 1's). Like the computer case, it seems that the brain codes information redundantly so that even if certain cells are missing, it can still determine what the pattern is encoding. It is generally thought that the brain uses

Table 1.1 Coding of Cognitive Psychology in ASCII

1	1	1	1	1	1	1	1	1
0	0	0	0	0	0	0	0	0
0	0	0	0	0	1	0	1	0
0	1	0	1	1	0	1	0	0
0	1	1	1	0	1	0	1	1
1	1	1	1	0	0	0	1	0
1	1	1	0	1	0	1	0	1
1	1	0	0	1	1	1	0	1

1	1	1	1	1	1	1	1	1	1
0	0	0	0	0	0	0	0	0	0
1	1	1	0	0	0	0	0	0	1
0	0	1	0	1	1	1	1	0	1
0	0	0	0	0	1	1	1	1	0
0	1	0	1	0	1	0	1	1	0
0	1	1	1	0	1	0	1	1	1
0	0	0	1	0	1	1	1	0	0

very different schemes for encoding information and achieving redundancy than the computer. It also seems that the brain utilizes a much more redundant code than the computer. This is because individual neurons are not particularly reliable in their behavior.

So far we have talked only about patterns of neural activation. Such patterns, however, are transitory. The brain does not maintain the same pattern for minutes, let alone days. This means that these patterns cannot encode our permanent knowledge about the world. It is thought that memories are encoded by changes in the synaptic connections among neurons. By changing the synaptic connections, the brain can enable itself to reproduce specific patterns. There is not much growth of new synapses in the adult, but synapses can change in their effectiveness in response to experience. There is evidence that synaptic connections do change during learning with both increased release of neurotransmitters (Kandel & Schwartz, 1984) and increased sensitivity of dendritic receptors (Lynch & Baudry, 1984). We will discuss some of this research in Chapter 6 on memory.

◆

Information is represented in patterns of activation across many neurons and in the interconnections among neurons that allow these patterns to be reproduced.

Organization of the Brain

Having reviewed some of the basic principles of neural information processing, we will look at the overall structure of the central nervous system, which

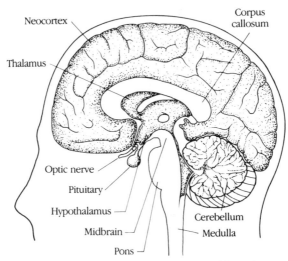

Figure 1.5 A cross-sectional view of the brain showing some of its major components. (From Keeton, 1980.)

consists of the brain and the spinal cord. The major function of the spinal cord is to carry neural messages from the brain to the muscles and sensory messages from the body back to the brain. Figure 1.5 shows a cross section of the brain with some of the more prominent neural structures labeled. The lower parts of the brain are evolutionarily more primitive. The higher portions are well developed only in the higher species.

Correspondingly, it appears that the lower portions of the brain are responsible for more basic functions. The medulla controls breathing, swallowing, digestion, and heartbeat. The cerebellum plays an important role in motor coordination and voluntary movement. The thalamus serves primarily as a relay station for motor and sensory information from lower areas to the cortex. The hypothalamus regulates expression of basic drives.

A particularly important area for memory proves to be the limbic system, which is at the border between the cortex and the lower structures. The limbic system contains a structure called the **hippocampus,** which appears critical to human memory. Unfortunately, it is not possible to show the hippocampus in a cross-section like Figure 1.5 because it is a structure that occurs in the right and left halves of the brain between the surface and the center.

The cerebral cortex, or neocortex, is the most recently evolved portion of the brain. Although it is quite small and primitive in many mammals it accounts for a large fraction of the human brain. In the human, this cerebral cortex can be thought of as a rather thin neural sheet with a surface area of about 2500 cm^2. To fit this neural sheet into the skull, it has to be

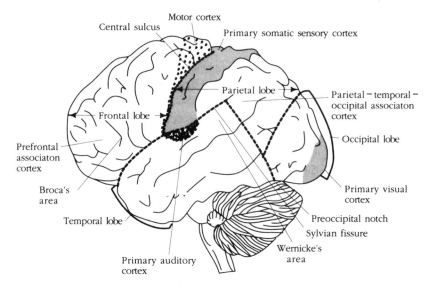

Figure 1.6 A side view of the cerebral cortex with the major components identified. (From Kandel & Schwartz, 1984. Reprinted by permission of the publisher. Copyright © 1984 by Elsevier Science Publishing Co., Inc.)

highly convoluted. The amount of folds and wrinkles on the cortex is one of the striking physical differences between the human brain and those of lower mammals.

The neocortex is divided into left and right hemispheres. One of the interesting curiosities of anatomy is that the right part of the body tends to be connected to the left hemisphere and the left part of the body tends to be connected to the right hemisphere. Thus, motor control and sensation in the right hand are controlled by the left hemisphere. The right ear is most strongly connected to the left hemisphere. The neural receptors in either eye that receive input from the left part of the visual world are connected to the right hemisphere.

Each hemisphere can be divided into four lobes: frontal, parietal, occipital, and temporal (see Figure 1.6). Major folds or fissures on the cortex separate the areas. The **frontal lobe** is involved in two major functions. The back portion of the frontal lobe is primarily involved with motor functions. The front portion, called the **prefrontal cortex,** is thought to be involved in higher-level processes like planning. The **occipital lobe** contains the primary visual areas. The **parietal lobe** is concerned with some sensory functions, particularly those involving spatial processing. The **temporal lobe** has the primary auditory areas and is also involved in the recognition of objects. The hippocampus, which could not be shown in the view of Figure 1.5, cannot be shown in this view either: It is found within the temporal lobe.

Brodman (1909) identified 52 distinct regions of the human cortex, based on differences in the cell types in various regions. Many of these regions proved to have functional differences as well. The figure on the front inside cover is a "color map" of the brain illustrating those of the 52 Brodman areas that can be seen from the surface (others are to be found in the folds of the cortex). We will have occasion to refer to a number of these areas throughout the book.

◆
The brain is organized into a number of distinct areas, which serve different types of functions.

Localization of Function

We are now beginning to understand where higher-level cognitive functions occur in the brain. It appears that the two hemispheres are somewhat specialized for different types of processing. In general, the left hemisphere seems more associated with linguistic and analytic processing, while the right hemisphere is more associated with perceptual and spatial processing. Much of the evidence for the difference between the hemispheres comes from research with "split-brain" patients. The left and right hemispheres are connected by a broad band of fibers, called the **corpus callosum.** The corpus callosum has been surgically severed in some patients to prevent epileptic seizures. Such patients are referred to as **split-brain patients.** The operation is typically successful, and patients seem to function fairly well. However, careful psychological research has found profound differences between such patients and subjects who have not had this surgery. In one experiment, the word *key* was flashed on the left side of a screen the patient was looking at. This stimulus should be handled by the right, nonlanguage hemisphere. When asked what was presented on the screen, he was not able to say because the language-dominant hemisphere did not know. However, the patient's left hand (but not the right) was able to pick out a key from a set of objects hidden from view.

By studying such split-brain patients, psychologists have been able to identify the separate functions of the right and left hemispheres. The research has shown a linguistic advantage for the left hemisphere. For instance, commands can be presented to the patients in their right ears (and hence to their left brains) or in their left ears (and hence to their right brains). The right hemisphere can comprehend only the simplest linguistic commands, whereas the left hemisphere displays full comprehension. A quite different result is obtained when the ability of the right hand (hence the left hemisphere) to perform manual tasks is compared with that of the left hand (hence the right hemisphere). In this situation, the right hemisphere clearly outperforms the left hemisphere.

Research with other types of patients who have had damage to specific brain regions indicates that there are areas in the left cortex, called **Broca's area** and **Wernicke's area** (see Figure 1.6), that seem critical for speech, since damage to them results in **aphasia,** which is severe impairment to speech. They may not be the only neural areas involved in speech, but they certainly are important. Different language deficits appear depending on whether the damage is to Broca's area or Wernicke's area. People with Broca's aphasia (i.e., damage to Broca's area) speak in short, ungrammatical sentences. For instance, when one patient was asked whether he drives home on weekends, he replied:

> *Why, yes . . . Thursday, er, er, er, no, er, Friday . . . Bar- ba-ra . . . wife . . . and, oh, car . . . drive . . . pumpike . . . you know . . . rest and . . . teevee. (Gardner, 1975, p. 61)*

In contrast, patients with Wernicke's aphasia speak in fairly grammatical sentences that are almost devoid of meaning. Such patients have difficulty with their vocabulary and generate "empty" speech. The following is the answer given by one such patient to the question "What brings you to the hospital?"

> *Boy, I'm sweating, I'm awful nervous, you know, once in a while I get caught up, I can't mention the tarripoi, a month ago, quite a little, I've done a lot well. I impose a lot, while, on the other hand, you know what I mean, I have to run around, look it over, trebbin and all that sort of stuff. (Gardner, 1975, p. 68)*

◆
Different specific areas of the brain support different cognitive functions.

Topographic Organization

In many areas of the cortex, information processing is organized spatially in what is called a **topographic organization.** For instance, in the visual area at the back of the cortex, adjacent areas represent information from adjacent areas of the visual field. Figure 1.7 illustrates one piece of evidence for this (Tootell, Silverman, Switkes, & De Valois, 1982). Monkeys were shown the bull's-eye pattern represented in part a of the figure. Part b shows the pattern of activation that was recorded on the occipital cortex using a method of injecting a radioactive material that marks locations of maximum neural activity. We see that the bull's-eye structure is reproduced

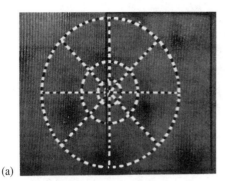

(a)

Figure 1.7 (a) The stimulus presented to the monkey. (b) Pattern of brain activation produced by the visual stimulus. (From Tootell, Silverman, Switkes & De Valois, 1982. Copyright © 1982 by the AAAS.)

(b)   1 cm

with only a little distortion. A similar principle or organization governs the representation of the body in the motor cortex and the somatosensory cortex along the central fissure. Adjacent parts of the body are represented adjacently in the neural tissue. Figure 1.8 illustrates the representation of the body along the somatosensory cortex. Note that the body is distorted, with certain areas receiving a considerable overrepresentation. It turns out that the overrepresented areas correspond to those that are more sensitive. Thus, for instance, we can make more subtle discriminations among tactile stimuli on the hands and face than on our back or thigh. Also, in the visual cortex there is an overrepresentation of the visual field at the center of our vision, where we have the greatest visual acuity.

It is thought that the reason for topographic maps is so that neurons processing similar regions can interact with one another (Crick & Asanuma, 1986). This may be related to an aspect of neural information processing called coarse coding. If one records the neural activity from a single neuron in the somatosensory cortex, it does not just respond when a single point of the body is stimulated but rather responds when any point on a large patch of the body is stimulated. How, then, can we know exactly what point has been touched? That information is recorded quite accurately but not in the response of any particular cell. Rather, different cells will respond to different overlapping regions of the body, and any point will

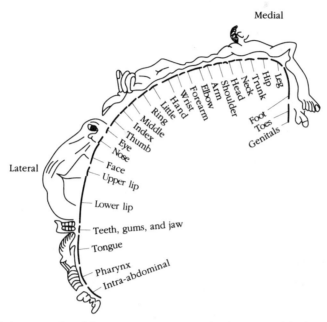

Figure 1.8 A cross section of the somatosensory cortex, showing a map of the human body. (From Kandel & Schwartz, 1984. Reprinted by permission of the Publisher. Copyright © 1984 by Elsevier Science Publishing Co., Inc.)

evoke a different set of cells. Thus, the location of a point is reflected by the pattern of activation. This reinforces the idea that neural information tends to be represented in patterns of activation.

◆

Adjacent cells in the cortex tend to process sensory stimuli that are close to one another.

Methods in Cognitive Neuroscience

How does one go about understanding the neural basis of cognition? Much of the past research in neuroscience has been done on animals. Some research has involved surgically removing various parts of the cortex. By observing the deficits these operations have produced, it is possible to infer the function of the region. Other research has recorded the electrical activity in particular neurons or regions of neurons. By observing what activates these neurons, one can infer what these do. However, the difference between the cognitive potential of humans and most other animals is enormous. With the possible exception of other primates like chimpanzees, it is difficult to get other animals even to engage in the kinds of cognitive processes that humans engage in. This has been the great barrier to understanding the neural basis of human cognition.

Until recently, the principal basis for understanding the role of the brain in human cognition has been to study patient populations. We have already described some of this research, such as that with the split-brain patients or with patients who have suffered strokes that cause language deficits. It was research with patient populations that indicated that the brain is lateralized, with the left hemisphere specialized for language processing. Such hemispheric specialization does not occur in other species.

More recently there have been major advances in non-invasive methods of imaging the functioning of the brains of normal subjects engaged in various cognitive activities. These advances in neural imaging are among the most exciting developments in cognitive neuroscience. While not as precise as recording from single neurons, which can almost never be done with humans for ethical reasons, these methods have achieved dramatic improvements in precision.

Electroencephalography (EEG) involves recording the electrical potentials that are present on the scalp. When large populations of neurons are active they will result in distinctive patterns of electrical potential on the scalp. The typical methodology involves a subject wearing a cap of many electrodes. The electrodes detect rhythmic changes in electrical activity and record them on what are called electroencephalograms. Figure 1.9 illustrates some recordings typical of various cognitive states. When EEG is used to study cognition, the subject is asked to respond to some stimulus, and researchers are interested in what impact processing this stimulus has on general activity. To average out the effects not due to the stimulus, many trials are averaged together, and what remains is the activity produced by the stimulus. For instance, Kutas & Hillyard (1980a) found that there was a large negative amplitude wave about 400 milliseconds after subjects heard an unexpected word in a sentence (this will be discussed more in Chapter 12 on language). Such averaged EEG responses aligned to a particular stimulus are called **event-related potentials** or ERPs. ERPs are very good in terms of their temporal resolution, but it is difficult to infer the location in the brain of the neural activity that is producing the scalp activity. The next two methods we talk about, **PET (positron emission tomography)** and **fMRI (functional magnetic resonance imaging),** are relatively good in terms of their abilities to localize neural activity but rather poor in their abilities to trace out the time course of neural activity.

Neither PET nor fMRI measure neural activity directly. Rather they measure metabolic rate or blood flow in various areas of the brain, relying on the fact that more active areas of the brain require greater metabolic expenditures. PET involves injecting a radioactive tracer into the bloodstream (the radiation exposure in a typical PET study is equivalent to two chest X-rays and is not considered dangerous). Subjects are placed in a PET scanner that can detect the variation in concentration of the radioac-

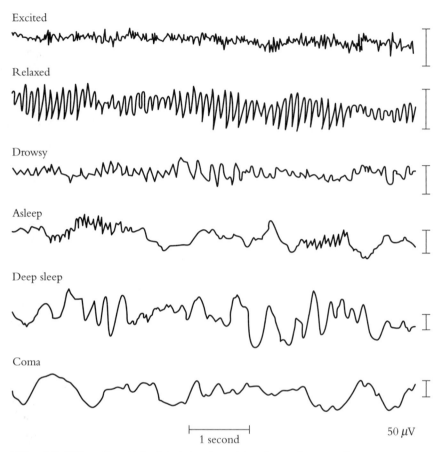

Figure 1.9 EEG profiles obtained during various states of consciousness. (From Kolb and Whishaw, 1986, after Penfield and Jaspers, 1954.)

tive element. Current methods allow a spatial resolution of 5 to 10 mm. For instance, Posner, Peterson, Fox, and Raichle (1988) used PET to localize the different components of the reading process, by looking at what areas of the brain are involved in reading a word. Figure 1.10 illustrates their results. The triangles on the cortex represent areas that were active when subjects were just passively looking at concrete nouns. The squares are areas that became active when subjects were asked to engage in the semantic activity of generating uses for these nouns. The triangles are located in the occipital lobe, while the squares are located in the frontal lobe. Thus, the data indicate that the processes of visually perceiving a word take place in a different part of the brain from the processes of thinking about the meaning of a word.

The fMRI methodology offers even better spatial resolution than PET and is less intrusive. fMRI uses the same MRI equipment that is now

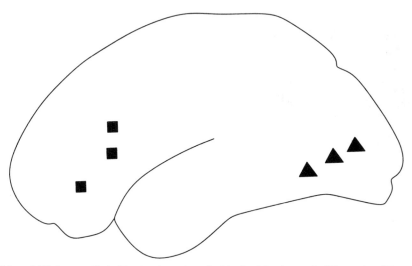

Figure 1.10 Areas activated in visual word reading in the lateral aspect of the cortex. Triangles refer to the passive visual task while squares refer to the semantic task. (From Posner, Peterson, Fox, & Raichle, 1988. Copyright © 1988 by the AAAS.)

standardly used in hospitals to image various structures, including patients' brain structures. With minor modification, it can be used to image the functioning of the brain. It does not require injecting the subject with a radioactive tracer, but rather counts on the fact that there is more oxygenated hemoglobin in regions of greater neural activity. Radio waves are passed through the brain, and these cause the iron in the hemoglobin to produce a local magnetic field that is detected by magnetic sensors surrounding the head. The magnetic signal is stronger in areas of greater activity. The methodology is so tractable that even I have gotten involved in fMRI studies of cognitive function. The inside of the cover shows some results of a study that we (Jon Fincham, Walter Schneider, and I) have done with fMRI, comparing a subject performing a complex problem-solving task (Anderson & Fincham, 1994) initially or after much practice. These are cross sections of the brain—the top one relatively high and the bottom one relatively low. Red indicates areas active early in practice, and green indicates areas active later in practice. The top section shows a large area in a frontal region called the anterior cingulate gyrus, indicating that it is highly active early in practice. The lower section shows large green areas in a region of the brain called the hippocampus, indicating that it is late in practice. As we will see in later chapters, the anterior cingulate gyrus is associated with complex problem solving, and the hippocampus with memory. What is happening in this experiment is that with practice the subject is memorizing problems and no longer has to solve them but rather retrieves the answers from memory. The change in brain activation patterns reveals this switch. Later chapters will present other imaging research showing the impact of practice on brain function.

◆
──
Brain imaging allows researchers to identify what brain structures are most active in the performance of a cognitive task.
──

Connectionism

The preceding section has given you some sense of where we are in understanding the neural bases of cognition. We know quite a bit about how basic neural elements operate; we have fairly good ideas about how they might be put together to perform relatively low-level processes such as basic vision (as will be discussed in the next chapter); and we are now beginning to study how more advanced cognitive processes are organized and localized in the brain. However, there are great gaps in our knowledge The contrast is glaring between what we know about how we perceive a line versus how we can remember facts about people and judge their character. In the first case, we can present relatively detailed neural models; in the second case we cannot.

Traditionally, in cognitive psychology the more advanced aspects of human cognition have only been discussed in terms of abstract information-processing models, but there has been an effort to try to develop models of higher-level processes that are better grounded in our understanding of neural processing. Given that our knowledge of the relevant facts of the brain is still thin, these attempts start, not by asking how the brain actually achieves the higher processing, but by asking how it might do so. These efforts start from our general knowledge of how neurons work and ask the question: How could higher-level function be achieved by connecting together basic elements like neurons? This approach is therefore called **connectionism** because it is concerned with ways of connecting neural elements together to account for higher-level cognition. Connectionist models have had some degree of success in accounting for various aspects of human cognition, which we will discuss in later chapters. Here, I would just like to present an example of how such models are developed.

Jay McClelland and David Rumelhart have developed one of the existing frameworks for such connectionist models. They call their framework **parallel distributed processing**, or **PDP** for short. Parallel distributed processing takes very seriously the idea that information is represented in patterns of activation among neural elements. To understand cognition in a PDP model, it is necessary to understand how neural elements simultaneously interact with one another. McClelland, Rumelhart, and Hinton (1986) describe a PDP model of the following situation: Imagine living in an unsavory neighborhood dominated by two gangs, called the Jets and the Sharks,

TABLE 1.2 Characteristics of a Number of Individuals Belonging to Two Gangs, the Jets and the Sharks

	Name	Age	Education	Marital Status	Occupation
Jets					
	Art	40s	J.H.	Sing.	Pusher
	Al	20s	J.H.	Mar.	Burglar
	Sam	20s	Col.	Mar.	Bookie
	Clyde	40s	J.H.	Sing.	Bookie
	Ralph	30s	J.H.	Sing.	Pusher
	Jim	20s	H.S.	Div.	Burglar
	Lance	20s	J.H.	Sing.	Burglar
	John	20s	H.S.	Mar.	Burglar
	Doug	30s	J.H.	Sing.	Pusher
Sharks					
	Phil	30s	Col.	Mar.	Pusher
	Ike	30s	J.H.	Mar.	Burglar
	Nick	30s	Col.	Sing.	Bookie
	Don	40s	H.S.	Sing.	Pusher
	Ned	30s	H.S.	Mar.	Bookie
	Karl	50s	H.S.	Div.	Pusher
	Ken	20s	J.H.	Mar.	Pusher
	Earl	40s	H.S.	Mar.	Burglar
	Rick	30s	H.S.	Div.	Burglar

From *Retrieving General and Specific Knowledge from Stored Knowledge of Specifics,* by J.L. McClelland, 1981. Proceedings of the Third Annual Conference of the Cognitive Science Society, Berkeley, CA.

and meeting the people described in Table 1.2. McClelland et al. propose a neurallike model of how one might represent such knowledge and answer questions about the individuals in the neighborhood. They suggest that someone might set up a network of neural elements to represent these people, such as that illustrated in Figure 1.11 (which represents only part of the information—McClelland et al. actually built a structure representing all of Table 1.2). One might think of each element as a neuron and the links between elements as connections among neurons. Each element in the central "cloud" represents what they call an instance unit that stands for one of the gang members. It is linked by excitatory connections to units that represent all of that fellow's properties. Although not shown in Figure 1.11, within each cloud there are inhibitory links among the units such that the most active unit tends to inhibit the activation of the remaining units. Thus, each cloud tends to have a single active unit.

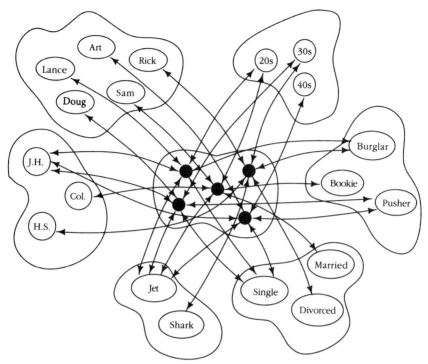

Figure 1.11 Some of the units and interconnections needed to represent the individuals shown in Table 1.2. The units connected with double-headed arrows are mutually excitatory. All the units within the same "cloud" are mutually inhibitory. (From Retrieving General and Specific Knowledge from Stored Knowledge of Specifics by J. L. McClelland, 1981. Proceedings of the Third Annual Conference of the Cognitive Science Society. Berkeley, CA. Copyright © 1981 by J. L. McClelland. Reprinted by permission.)

Suppose one wants to retrieve information about Lance. Note that there is one element in the central cloud connected to the name *Lance*, the age *20*, the occupation *burglar*, the status *single*, the gang *Jets*, and the educational level *junior high*. To retrieve information about Lance in such a network, one would start with activating the unit corresponding to Lance's name. This would in turn activate the instance unit for Lance, which would then activate the other properties for Lance, thereby creating a pattern of activation over the neural network corresponding to Lance. In effect, one has retrieved a representation of Lance from the neural network.

One can answer questions such as "Who do you know who is a Shark and in his twenties?" This would be done by activating the *Sharks* and *20s* units and observing the pattern of activation that results. As it turns out, Ken (not shown in Figure 1.11 but in Table 1.2) is the only individual who fits this description, and his name unit would be most active in the network and could be retrieved as the answer.

This model has a number of features that enable it to display a certain degree of intelligence. For instance, suppose we ask it who is 20 years old, a Shark, married, and a bookie. Inspection of Table 1.2 will reveal that no person matches this description, but that Sam, Ken and Ned come closest. This system would most activate the Sam, Ken and Ned units, and would retrieve one of them as an answer. Thus, it can make judgments about the closeness of a match of a description to an individual.

Such a system can also make inferences based on similarity. For instance, suppose we do not know Lance's profession (that is, suppose it was not represented in the network). If we ask what Lance's profession is, we can activate the *Lance* unit, which will in turn activate the properties we know about Lance—such as that he is in his twenties and that he is a Jet and has a junior high education. These properties will in turn activate other people who share these properties and activate their profession. It turns out that all Jets in their twenties with junior high education are burglars. Correspondingly, this network will most activate burglar and make the reasonable inference that this is Lance's profession, even if it was not represented in the network. Such a network also allows us to make generalizations about categories. So if we ask what Jets are like, the nodes for *single, 20s,* and *junior high* will become active because most Jets have these features. So the system is capable of making spontaneous judgments about the character of various groups.

What McClelland et al. have provided for us, then, is a demonstration of how neural mechanisms might underline some of the subtle memory judgments one might make. In many cases, the behavior produced by such mechanisms also corresponds to the behavioral details of how people actually make these judgments. We will review a number of such situations in later chapters. Right now such connectionist models are regarded in cognitive psychology as displaying considerable promise as a way to help bridge the gap that has existed between the brain and higher-level cognition.

◆

Connectionist models process information by neurallike elements that accumulate activation and send inhibitory and excitatory influences to other units.

Remarks and Suggested Readings

In Anderson (2000), I review in greater detail some of the issues separating the behaviorist and cognitivist approaches. Boring's (1950) book is a classic review of the early history of psychology. Boden (1996) is a book on artificial intelligence. O'Nuallain, McKevitt, & MacAogain (1997) discuss consciousness and cognitive science. Kandel, Schwartz, & Jessell (1991) offer a thorough discussion of the nervous system and the neural basis of learning and behavior. A two-volume series by McClelland and Rumelhart (1986) and Rumelhart and McClelland (1986b) provides a good discussion of connectionism. For examples of connectionist models other than PDP, read Schneider and Oliver (1991) and Grossberg (1987). Banich (1997) and Gazzaniga, Ivry, & Mangun (1998) are two texts devoted to cognitive neuroscience. Posner & Raichle (1994) wrote a book summarizing research based on PET, ERP, and lesion studies.

There are a great many journals containing research relevant to cognitive psychology, but particularly important are the journals *Cognition; Cognitive Neuroscience; Cognitive Psychology; Cognitive Science; Journal of Experimental Psychology: General; Journal of Experimental Psychology: Learning, Memory, and Cognition; Journal of Experimental Psychology: Human Perception and Performance; Journal of Memory and Cognition;* and *Quarterly Journal of Experimental Psychology. Psychological Review* publishes theoretical papers from all areas of psychology.

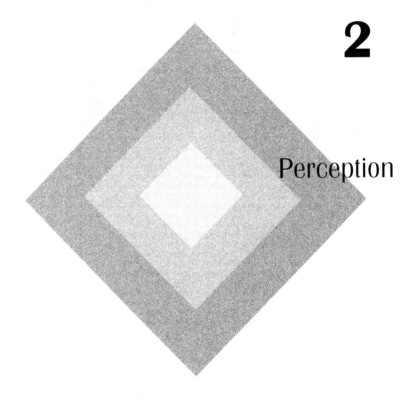

2

Perception

Our bodies are literally bristling with sensors to detect sights, sounds, smells, and physical contact. Billions of neurons are processing sensory information and delivering what they find to the higher centers in the brain. This enormous information-processing system creates a problem for higher-level cognition, which is to decide what to attend to from all the sensory information being processed. This problem will be the topic of the next chapter on attention, but the current chapter focuses on how these sensory systems identify what is in the outside world. We will concentrate on visual perception, and, to a lesser extent, speech, which are the two most important perceptual systems for the human species.

Perception involves more than simply registering the information that arrives at our eyes and ears. A major issue concerns placing some sort of interpretation on that information. An interesting demonstration of this

Figure 2.1 The patient was able to copy this anchor but was unable to recognize it. (From Ellis & Young, 1988. Reprinted by permission of Quarterly Journal of Experimental Psychology.)

fact concerns a soldier who suffered brain damage due to accidental carbon monoxide poisoning. He could recognize objects through their feel, smell, or sound, but was unable to distinguish a picture of a circle from a square or recognize faces or letters (Benson & Greenberg, 1969). On the other hand, he was able to discriminate light intensities and colors, and to tell in what direction an object was moving. Thus, his system was able to register visual information, but somehow his brain damage resulted in a loss of the ability to combine visual information into perceptual experience. This case shows that perception is much more than simply the registering of sensory information.

The patient suffers from what is called **visual agnosia,** an inability to recognize visual objects that is neither a function of general intellectual loss nor a loss of basic sensory abilities. Generally, visual agnosias are broken down into **apperceptive agnosias** and **associative agnosias** (for a review, read Farah, 1990). Benson and Greenberg's patient above is described as having apperceptive agnosia. Such patients are unable to recognize simple shapes such as circles or triangles, or draw shapes that are shown. In contrast, patients with associative agnosia are able to recognize simple shapes and can successfully copy drawings of even complex figures. However, they are unable to recognize such objects. Figure 2.1 shows the original drawing of an anchor and a copy of it made by a patient studied by Ratcliff and Newcombe (1982). Despite being able to produce a relatively accurate drawing, the patient could not recognize this as an anchor (he called it an umbrella). It is generally believed that patients with apperceptive agnosia have problems with information processing relatively early in the visual system, whereas patients with associative agnosia have intact early processing but have difficulties with pattern recognition, which occurs later in information processing.

Figure 2.2 offers an opportunity for a person with normal perception to appreciate the distinction between early and late visual process. If you have not seen this image before, it will strike you as just a bunch of ink blobs. You would be able to judge the size of the various blobs and repro-

Figure 2.2 A scene in which we initially only perceive low-level visual details (blobs) and then the pattern of a dog. (From Ronald James.)

duce these blobs just as could the patient studied by Ratcliff and New-combe, but you will not see any patterns. If you keep looking at it, how-ever, you may suddenly see a dog in the center of the picture. Now your pattern perception capabilities have succeeded, and you have placed an interpretation on what you have seen. This chapter begins with a discussion of how visual information is processed before pattern recognition. Then, we discuss the processes of pattern recognition.

◆

Visual perception can be divided into an early phase, in which shapes and objects are extracted from the visual scene, and a later phase, in which the shapes and objects are recognized.

Visual Information Processing

Early Visual Information Processing

A fair amount is known about the neural underpinnings of very early visual information processing. Figure 2.3 is a schematic representation of the eye. Light passes through the lens and the vitreous humor, and falls on

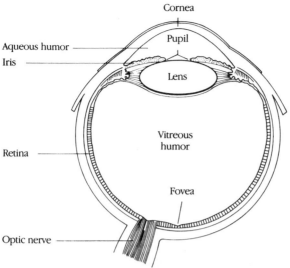

Figure 2.3 A schematic representation of the eye. Light enters through the cornea, passes through the aqueous humor, pupil, lens, and vitreous humor to strike the retina, which is stimulated by the light. (From Lindsay & Norman, 1977.)

the retina at the back of the eye. The retina contains the light-sensitive cells that actually respond to the light. Light is scattered slightly in passing through the vitreous humor, so the image falling on the back of the retina is not perfectly sharp. One of the functions of early visual processing is to sharpen that image.

Light is converted into neural energy by a photochemical process. There are two distinct types of photoreceptors in the eye—rods and cones. Cones are involved in color vision and show high resolution and acuity. Less light energy is required to trigger a response in the rods, but they are associated with poorer resolution. As a consequence, they are principally responsible for the less acute, black-and-white vision we experience at night. Cones are especially concentrated in a small area of the retina called the **fovea.** When we fixate on an object, we move our eyes so that the object falls on the fovea. This enables us to maximize the high resolution of the cones in perceiving the object. Foveal vision is concerned with detection of fine details, while the rest of the visual field, the periphery, is responsible for detection of more global information, including movement.

The receptor cells synapse onto bipolar cells and these onto ganglion cells, whose axons leave the eye and form the optic nerve, which goes to the brain. Altogether there are about 800,000 ganglion cells in the optic nerve from each eye. Each ganglion cell encodes information from a small region of the retina. The amount of neural firing on a ganglion axon will

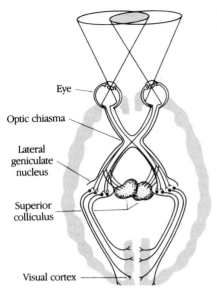

Figure 2.4 Neural paths from the eye to the brain. (From Keeton, 1980.)

Eye

Optic chiasma

Lateral geniculate nucleus

Superior colliculus

Visual cortex

typically encode the amount of light stimulation in that region of the retina.

Figure 2.4 illustrates the neural paths from the eye to the brain. The optic nerves from both eyes meet at the optic chiasma, and the nerves from the nasal side of the retina cross over and go to the other side of the brain, while the nerves from the outside of the retina continue to the same side of the brain as the eye. This means that the right halves of both eyes are connected to the right brain. As Figure 2.4 illustrates, the lens focuses the light so that the left side of the visual field falls on the right half of each eye. Thus, information about the left part of the visual field goes to the right brain; similarly, information about the right side of the visual field goes to the left brain. This is one instance of the general fact, discussed in the previous chapter, that the left hemisphere processes information about the right part of the world and the right hemisphere processes the left part.

Once inside the brain, the fibers from the ganglion cells synapse onto cells in various subcortical structures. Two of these structures are the lateral geniculate nucleus and the superior colliculus illustrated in Figure 2.4. Both are areas below the cortex in the brain. It is thought that the lateral geniculate nucleus is part of the neural pathway that is important in perceiving details and recognizing objects, while the superior colliculus is involved in the localization of objects in space. This is referred to as the "what-where" distinction. Both neural structures are connected to the primary visual cortex (Brodman's Area 17 in the brain map on the inside front cover), the first cortical area that receives visual input; however, there are many other visual areas, including Areas 18 and 19, surrounding it. There are similar what-where divisions in the cortex, with certain areas of the temporal lobe responsible for recognizing what an object is and other areas of the parietal lobe responsible for recognizing where an object is.

◆
Light energy is converted by a photochemical process into neural activity. This information progresses by various neural tracks to the visual cortex.

Information Coding in Visual Cells

Kuffler's (1953) research showed how information is encoded by the ganglion cells. These cells generally fire at some spontaneous rate even when no light is being received by the eyes. For some ganglion cells, if light falls on a small region of the retina, there will be an increase in these spontaneous rates of firing. If light is presented in the region just around this sensitive center, however, the spontaneous rate of firing will go down. Light farther from the center elicits no response at all. These are known as on-off cells. There are also off-on ganglion cells, where light at the center suppresses the spontaneous rate of firing, and light in the surrounding areas increases the rate of firing. Figure 2.5 illustrates the receptive fields of these cells. Cells in the lateral geniculate nucleus respond in the same way.

Huble and Wiesel (1962), in their study of the primary visual cortex in the cat, found that visual cortical cells responded in a more complex manner than these lower cells. Figure 2.6 illustrates four of the patterns that have been observed in cortical cells. As can be seen, all these receptive fields have an elongated shape, in contrast to the on-off cells. The types shown in parts a and b are **edge detectors.** They respond positively to light on one side of a line and negatively to light on the other side. They will respond maximally if there is an edge of light lined up so as to fall at the boundary point. The types shown in parts c and d are **bar detectors.** They respond positively to light in the center and negatively to light at the periphery, or vice versa. Thus, a bar with a positive center will respond maximally if there is a bar of light just covering its center.

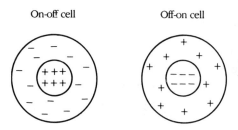

Figure 2.5 On-off and off-on receptive fields of ganglion cells and the cells in the lateral geniculate nucleus.

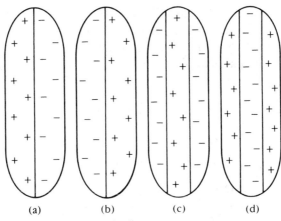

Figure 2.6 Response patterns of cortical cells.

Both edge and bar detectors are specific with respect to position, orientation, and width. That is, they respond only to stimulation in a small area of the visual field, to bars and edges of a small range of orientations, and to bars and edges of certain widths. Thus, a striped pattern like the one in Figure 2.7 will excite a particular bar detector to the degree that the stripes are of the appropriate orientation and width for that detector. However, different detectors seem tuned to different widths and orientations, and so some subset of bar detectors would be maximally stimulated by any such pattern.

Figure 2.8 illustrates how a number of on-off and off-on cells might combine to form bar or edge detectors. Note that no single on-off cell is sufficient to stimulate a detector. Rather, the detector is responding to *patterns* of the on-off cells, and so even at this low level we see the nervous system processing information in terms of patterns of neural activation, a theme emphasized in the previous chapter.

Figure 2.7 A pattern that excites detectors of a particular width and orientation.

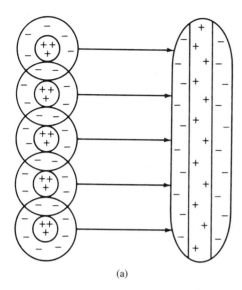

Figure 2.8 Hypothetical combinations of on-off and off-on cells to form (a) bar detectors and (b) edge detectors.

(a)

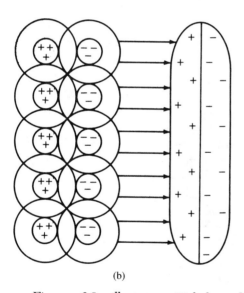

(b)

Figure 2.9 illustrates Hubel and Wiesel's (1977) hypercolumn representation of cells in the primary visual cortex. They found that the visual cortex was divided into 2 × 2 mm. regions, which they called hypercolumns. Each hypercolumn represents a particular region of the receptive field. As we noted in Chapter 1, the organization of the visual cortex is topographic, and so adjacent areas of the visual field are represented in adjacent hypercolumns. Figure 2.9 shows that each hypercolumn is itself parceled into a two-dimensional organization. Along one dimension, there are alternating rows receiving input from the left and right eye. Along the other dimension, the cells vary in what orientation they are most sensitive to. Adjacent regions represent similar orien-

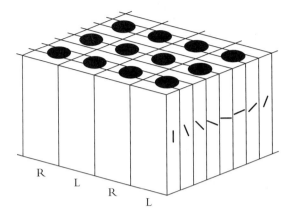

Figure 2.9 Representation of a hypercolumn in the visual cortex — organized in one dimension according to orientation of line and in the other dimension according to eye. (Based on Horton, 1984.)

tation. This should impress upon us how much information is encoded about the visual array. We have hundreds of regions of space separately represented for each eye, and within these regions we have many different orientations represented. Also, but not shown, different cells will code for different sizes and widths of line. Thus, an enormous amount of information has been extracted from the visual signal by the time it reaches the first cortical areas.

In addition to this rich representation of line orientation, the visual system extracts other information from the visual signal. For instance, we can also perceive the color of objects and whether they are moving. Livingstone and Hubel (1988) have proposed that these various dimensions (form, color, and movement) are all processed separately by the visual system. There are many different visual pathways and many different areas of the cortex devoted to visual processing (32 in the count by van Essen and DeYoe, 1996). Different pathways have cells that are differentially sensitive to color, movement, and orientation. It seems that the visual system analyzes the stimulus into many independent features and represents the locations of these features. Such spatial representations of features are called **feature maps** (Wolfe, 1994). Thus, if a vertical red bar is moving at a particular location, there are separate feature maps representing that it is red, vertical, and moving in that location, and these maps may be in different visual areas of the brain.

◆

The ganglion cells encode the visual field in terms of on-off and off-on cells, which are combined by higher visual processing to form various features.

Perceiving Depth and Surfaces

Even after the visual system has identified edges and bars in the environment, a great deal of information processing must still be performed before the visual system is able to perceive the world. One of the problems it must solve is deciding where those edges and bars are in space. The fundamental problem is that the information that is laid out on the retina is inherently two-dimensional (2-D), while we need to construct a three-dimensional (3-D) representation of the world. There are a number of cues that the visual system processes to infer distance. One of these is texture gradient. Elements tend to appear more closely packed together as the distance from the viewer increases. Consider Gibson's (1950) classic examples in Figure 2.10. Even though this is a flat surface the change in the texture gives the appearance of distance. Another cue to depth is stereopsis, which refers to the fact that the two eyes receive slightly different views of the world. Three-dimensional glasses, which one finds in a few movies and other demonstrations, depend on this fact. They filter the light coming from a single 2-D source (like a movie screen) such that different light information reaches the two eyes. The perception of a three-dimensional structure resulting from stereopsis can be quite compelling.

A third compelling source of information about three-dimensional structure comes from what is called motion parallax. As more distant points move they will move more slowly across the retina than closer points. Similarly, as one moves one's head, objects that are more distant will move more slowly across the retina than closer objects. An interesting demonstration is to look at the leaves of a nearby tree or bush with one eye closed. Denied stereopic information, you will have the sense of a very flat image in which it is hard to see the position of the many leaves relative to one another. Then, move your head. Suddenly, the three-dimensional structure of the tree becomes quite compelling, and it is easy to appreciate the position of leaves and branches relative to one another.

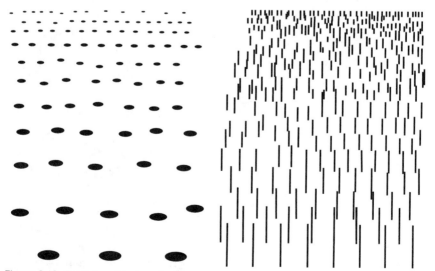

Figure 2.10 Examples of texture gradient. (From Gibson, 1950.)

Although it is easy to demonstrate the importance of cues like texture gradient, stereopsis, and motion parallax to depth perception, it is quite a difficult matter to understand how the brain actually processes such information to enable such compelling demonstrations. A number of researchers in the area of computational vision have worked on the problem of how this is actually done. For instance, David Marr (1982) has been quite influential in his proposal that these various sources of information work together to create what he called a $2\frac{1}{2}$-**D sketch** that identified where various visual features are relative to the viewer. However, he recognized how far this representation was from an actual perception of the world. In particular, such a representation only represents parts of surfaces and does not yet identify how these go together to form objects out in the environment (the problem we had with Figure 2.2). He used the term **3-D model** to refer to a representation of objects in the scene.

◆

Cues such as texture gradient, stereopsis, and motion parallax combine to create a representation of the locations of surfaces in three-dimensional space.

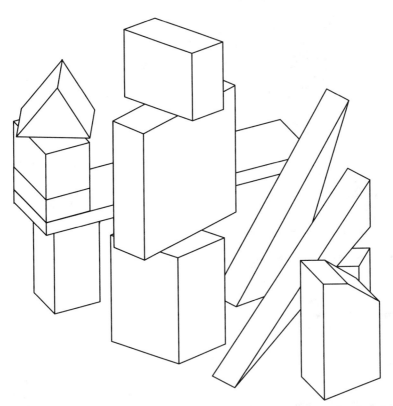

Figure 2.11 An example of how we can aggregate the perception of many broken lines into the perception of solid objects. (From Winston, 1970.)

Object Perception

A major problem in calculating such a representation of the world is object segmentation. Knowing where the lines and bars are in space is not enough. We need to know which ones go together to form objects. Consider the scene in Figure 2.11. Many lines go this way and that, but somehow we put them together to come up with the perception of a set of objects.

We tend to organize objects into units according to a set of principles called the **gestalt principles of organization** after the gestalt psychologists who first proposed them (e.g., Wertheimer, 1912). Consider the various parts of Figure 2.12. In part a we perceive four pairs of lines rather than eight separate lines. This picture illustrates the principle of proximity: elements close together tend to organize into units. Part b illustrates the principle of similarity. We tend to see this array as rows of O's alternating with rows of X's. Objects that look alike tend to be grouped together. Part c illustrates the principle of good continuation. We perceive two lines, one from A to B and the other from C to D, although there is no reason why this sketch could not represent another pair of lines, one from A to D and the other from C to B. However, the line from A to B displays better continuation than the line from A to D, which has a sharp turn. Part d illustrates the principles of closure and good form. We see the drawing

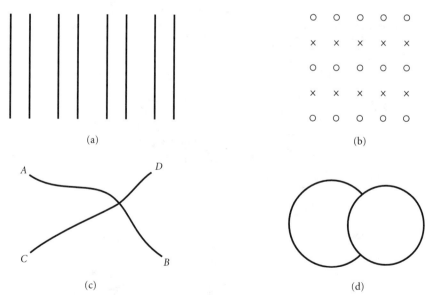

Figure 2.12 Illustrations of the gestalt principles of organization: (a) the principle of proximity, (b) the principle of similarity, (c) the principle of good continuation, (d) the principle of closure.

(a)   (b)   (c)   (d)   (e)

Figure 2.13 Examples of stimuli used by Palmer (1977) for studying segmentation of novel figures: (a) the original stimulus that subjects saw; (b) to (e) the subparts of the stimulus presented for recognition. Stimuli shown in (b) and (c) display good subparts; (d) and (e) give bad subparts.

as one circle occluded by another, although the occluded object could have many other possible shapes.

These principles will tend to organize even completely novel stimuli into units. Palmer (1977) studied subjects' recognition of figures such as the ones in Figure 2.13. He first showed subjects stimuli such as the one shown in part a and then asked them to decide whether fragments b to e were part of the original figure. The stimulus in part a tends to organize itself into a triangle (closure) and a bent letter *n* (good continuation). Palmer found that subjects could recognize the parts most rapidly when they were the segments predicted by the gestalt principles. So, the stimuli in parts b and c were recognized more rapidly than those in parts d and e. Thus, we see that recognition critically depends on the initial segmentation of the figure. Recognition can be impaired when this gestalt-based segmentation contradicts the actual pattern structure. FoRiNsTaNcEtHiSsEnTeNcEiShArDtOrEaD. The reasons for the difficulty are that the gestalt principle of similarity makes it difficult to see adjacent letters of different case together and that by removing the spaces between words the proximity cues have been eliminated.

These ideas about segmentation can be extended to describe how more complex three-dimensional structures are segmented. Figure 2.14 illustrates a proposal by Hoffman and Richards (1985) for how gestalt-like principles can be used to segment an outline representation of an object

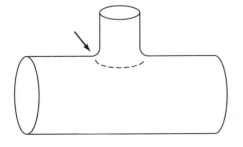

Figure 2.14 Segmentation of an object into subobjects: the part boundary can be identified with a contour that follows points of maximum concave curvature. (Stillings et al., 1987; based on Hoffman & Richards, 1985.)

into subobjects. They observe that where one segment joins another, there is typically a concavity in the line outline. Basically, people exploit the gestalt principle of good continuation: the lines at the points of concavity are not good continuations of one another, and so they do not group these parts together.

We have discussed visual information processing to the point where the position and shape of objects are identified in three-dimensional space. The current view is that the visual processing that underlies this ability is largely innately specified. Young infants appear to be capable of recognizing objects and their shape, and of appreciating where these objects are in three-dimensional space (i.e., Granrud, 1986, 1987).

◆

Gestalt principles of organization are used to segment visual scenes into objects.

Visual Pattern Recognition

Our discussion of visual information processing has gotten us to the point where we organize the visual world into objects. However, this still leaves us a major step from seeing the world. We have to identify what these objects are. This is the task of pattern recognition. Much of the research on this topic has focused on the question of how we recognize the identity of letters. For instance, how do we recognize a presentation of the letter A as an instance of the pattern A? We will first discuss pattern recognition and then move on to a more general discussion of object recognition.

Template-Matching Models

Perhaps the most obvious way to recognize a pattern is by means of **template matching.** The template-matching theory of perception assumes that a retinal image of an object is faithfully transmitted to the brain and that an attempt is made to compare it directly to various stored patterns. These patterns are called templates. The basic idea is that the perceptual system tries to compare the letter to the templates it has for each letter and reports the template that gives the best match. Figure 2.15 illustrates various attempts to make template matching work. In each case, an attempt is made to achieve a correspondence between the retinal cells stimulated by the A and the retinal cells specified for a template pattern.

The diagram in Figure 2.15a shows a case in which a correspondence is achieved and an A is recognized. The second diagram, in part b, shows that no correspondence is reached between the input of an L and the template pattern for an A. But L is matched in the diagram in part c by the L template. However, things can go wrong very easily with a template. The diagram in part d shows a mismatch that occurs when the image falls on the wrong part of the retina, and the diagram in part e shows the problem when the image is a wrong size. The diagram in part f shows what happens when the image is in a wrong orientation, and the diagrams in parts g and h show the difficulty when the images are nonstandard A's. There is no known way to correct templates for all these problems.

A common example of template matching involves the account numbers printed on checks, which are read by check-sorting machines used by bank computers. Figure 2.16 shows one of my blank checks (from a former account). The account number is the row of numbers at the very bottom of the check. A great deal of effort has gone into making the characters in this

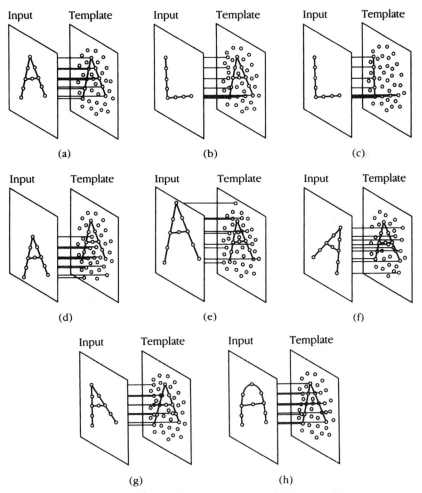

Figure 2.15 Examples of template-matching attempts: (a) and (c) successful template-matching attempts; (b) and (d) to (h) failed attempts. (Adapted from Neisser, 1967.)

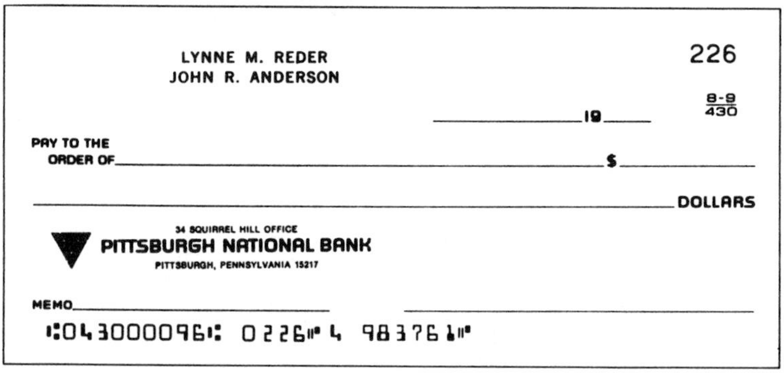

FIGURE 2.16 A typical blank check, with account numbers specially designed to permit successful template matching.

number maximally discernible. To ensure standardization of size and position, they must be printed by machine; a check sorter would not recognize hand-printed numbers. The fact that a very standardized character system is needed for template matching to work reduces the credibility of this process as a model for human pattern recognition. In humans, pattern recognition is very flexible. We can recognize LARGE characters and small characters; characters in the wrong place, in strange o^{r}i^e^{n}t$_a$ti$_o$ns and in unusual SHa$\mathcal{P}$e**s**; blurred or broken characters; and even with some efforts, ꞑbɐꞁpꞁɘ qoʍɥ characters.

◆

Template matching involves trying to measure the exact correspondence between a pattern and a stimulus.

Feature Analysis

Partly because of the difficulties posed by template matching, psychologists have proposed that pattern recognition occurs through **feature analysis.** In this model, stimuli are thought of as combinations of elemental features. The features for the alphabet might consist of horizontal lines, vertical lines, diagonal lines, and curves. Thus, the capital letter A can be seen as consisting of two lines at 30° angles (/ and \) and a horizontal line (–). The pattern for the letter A consists of these lines plus a specification as to how they should be combined. These features are very much like the output of edge and bar detectors in the visual cortex (discussed earlier).

You might wonder how feature analysis represents an advance beyond the template model. After all, what are the features but minitemplates? However, the feature model has a number of advantages over the template model. First, since the features are simpler, it is easier to see how the system might try to correct for the kinds of difficulties caused by template models. Indeed, to the extent that features are just line strokes, the bar and edge detectors we discussed earlier can extract such features. A second advantage of the feature-combination scheme is that it is possible to specify those relationships among the features that are most critical to the pattern. Thus, for A the critical point is that there are three lines, two diagonals (in different directions) and one horizontal, at certain positions relative one to another. Many other details are unimportant. Thus, all the following patterns are A's: A, A, **A**, *A*, A. A final advantage is that use of features rather than larger patterns will reduce the number of templates needed. In the feature model, we would not need a template for each possible pattern but only for each feature. Since the same features tend to occur in many patterns, this would mean a considerable savings.

There is a fair amount of behavioral evidence for the existence of features as components in pattern recognition. For instance, if letters have many features in common—as with C and G—evidence suggests that subjects are particularly prone to confuse them (Kinney, Marsetta, & Showman, 1966). When such letters are presented for very brief intervals, subjects often misclassify one stimulus as the other. So, for instance, subjects in the Kinney et al. experiment made 29 errors when presented with the letter G. Of these errors, 21 involved misclassification as C, 6 misclassifications as O, 1 misclassification as B, and 1 misclassification as 9. No other errors occurred. It is clear that subjects were choosing items with similar feature sets as their responses. Such a response pattern is what we would expect if a feature-analysis model were used. If subjects could extract only some of the features in the brief presentation, they would not be able to decide among stimuli that shared these features.

Another kind of experiment that yields evidence in favor of features involves stabilized images. The eye has a very slight tremor, called *psychological nystagmus,* which occurs at the rate of 30 to 70 cycles per second. Also, the eye's direction of gaze slowly drifts over an object. Consequently, the retinal image of the object on which a person tries to fixate is not perfectly constant; its position changes slightly over time. There is evidence that this retinal movement is critical for perception. When techniques are used to keep an image on the exact same position of the retina regardless of eye movement, parts of the object start to disappear. It seems that if the exact same retinal and nervous pathways are constantly used they become fatigued and stop responding.

The most interesting aspect of this phenomenon is the way the stabilized object disappears. It does not simply fade away or disappear all at once. Rather, different portions drop out over time. Figure 2.17 illustrates the fate of one of the stimuli in an experiment by Pritchard (1961). The left-hand item was the image presented; the four others are

Figure 2.17 The disintegration of an image that is stabilized on the eye. On the left is the original display. The partial outlines on the right show different patterns reported as the stabilized image begins to disappear. (From Pritchard, 1961.)

various fragments that were reported. Two points are important to note First, whole features such as "vertical bar" seemed to be lost. This finding suggests that features are the important units in perception. Second, the stimuli that remained tended to constitute complete letter or number patterns. This result indicates that these features are combined together to define the recognized patterns. Thus, even though our perceptual system may extract features, what we perceive are patterns composed from these features. The feature-extraction and feature-combination processes underlying pattern recognition are not available to conscious awareness; what we are aware of are the patterns.

◆

Feature analysis involves separately recognizing the features that make up a pattern and then their combination.

Object Recognition

While feature analysis does a satisfactory job of describing how we recognize simple objects like the letter A, one might wonder how it extends to explaining how we recognize more complex objects that might seem to defy description in terms of a few features. One of the exciting developments in the field of perception is the increasing evidence that the same processes might underlie the recognition of such familiar categories of objects as horses or cups. The basic idea is that a familiar object can be seen as a known configuration of simple components. Figure 2.18 (on page 54) illustrates a proposal by Marr (1982) as to the way familiar objects can be seen as configurations of simple pipelike components. For instance, an ostrich has a horizontally oriented torso attached to two long legs and a long neck.

Biederman (1987) has proposed a theory of object recognition, **recognition-by-components theory.** It proposes that there are three stages in our recognition of an object as a configuration of simpler components:

> **1.** The object is segmented into a set of basic subobjects. This reflects the output of the early visual processing that we discussed earlier in the chapter.

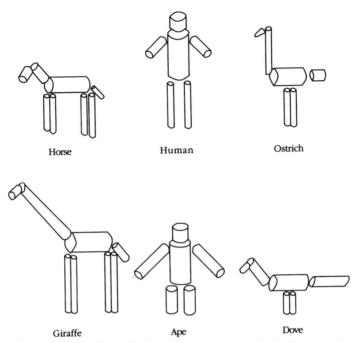

Figure 2.18 Segmentation of some familiar objects into basic cylindrical shapes. (Adapted from Marr & Nishihara, 1978.)

2. Once an object has been segmented into basic subobjects, one can classify the category of each subobject. Biederman (1987) argues that there are thirty-six basic categories of subobjects, which he calls **geons** (an abbreviation of "geometric ions"). Figure 2.19 shows some examples. We can think of the cylinder as being created by a circle as it is moved along a straight line (the axis) perpendicular to its center. We can generalize this basic cylinder shape to other shapes by varying some of the properties of its generation. We can change the shape of the object we are moving. If it is a rectangle rather than a circle that we move along the axis we get a block rather than a cylinder. We can curve the axis and get objects that curve. We can vary the size of the shape as we are moving it and get objects like the pyramid or wine glass. Biederman proposes that altogether there are about thirty-six geons which can be generated in this manner and that they serve as an alphabet for composing objects, much as letters serve as the alphabet for building up words. Recognizing a geon involves recognizing the features that define it where

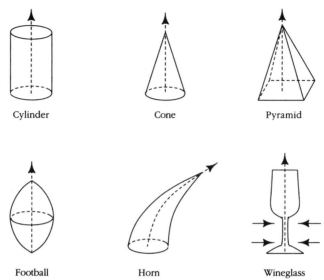

Figure 2.19 Generalized cylinders. In each object the dashed line represents the central axis of the object. The objects can be described in terms of the movement of a cross-sectional shape along an axis. Cylinder: a circle moves along a straight axis. Cone: a circle contracts as it moves along a straight axis. Pyramid: a square contracts as it moves along a straight axis. American football: a circle expands and then contracts as it moves along a straight axis. Horn: a circle contracts as it moves along a curved axis. Wineglass: a circle contracts then expands, creating concave segmentation points marked by arrows. (From Biederman et al., 1985.)

these features describe elements of its generation such as the shape of the object and the axis along which it is moved. Thus, recognizing a geon is like recognizing a letter.

3. Having identified the pieces out of which the object is composed and their configuration, one recognizes the object as the pattern composed from these pieces. Thus, recognizing an object is like recognizing a word.

As in the case of letter recognition there are many small variations on the underlying features or geons that should not be critical for recognition. For example, one need only determine whether an edge is straight or curved (in discriminating, say, a brick from a cylinder) or whether edges are parallel or not (in discriminating, say, a cylinder from a cone). It is not necessary to determine precisely how curved an edge might be. Only edges are needed to define geons. Color, texture, and small detail should not matter. This predicts that schematic line drawings of complex objects that allow the basic geons to be identified should be

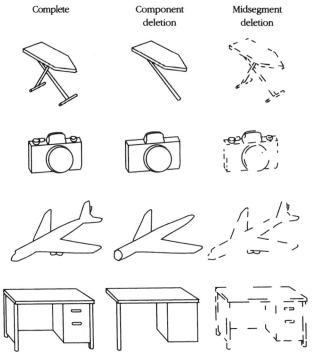

Complete   Component   Midsegment
                deletion   deletion

Figure 2.20 Sample stimuli used by Biederman et al. (1985) with equivalent proportion either of contours removed at midsegments or of whole components removed. (Copyright © 1985 by the American Psychological Association. Adapted by permission.)

recognized just as quickly as detailed color photographs of the objects. Biederman and Ju (1988) confirmed that this is true—that is, schematic line drawings of objects like telephones provide all the information needed for quick and accurate recognition.

The critical assumption in this theory is that object recognition is mediated by recognition of the components of the object. Biederman, Beiring, Ju, and Blickle (1985) performed a test of this prediction with objects such as those in Figure 2.20. Whole components of some objects were deleted while in other objects all the components were present but segments of these components were deleted. They presented these two types of degraded figures to subjects for various brief intervals and asked them to identify the objects. The results are shown in Figure 2.21. At very brief presentations (65 to 100 milliseconds), subjects were more accurate at the recognition of figures with component deletion than segment deletion; this reversed for the longer, 200-millisecond presentation. Biederman et al. reasoned that at the very brief intervals, subjects were not able to identify the components with segment deletion and so had difficulty in recognizing the objects. With 200-millisecond exposure, however, subjects were

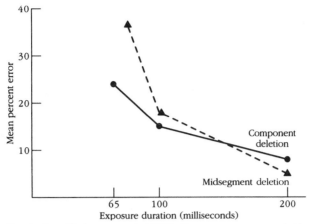

Figure 2.21 Results from Biederman et al. (1985): Mean percent errors of object naming as a function of the nature of contour removal (deletion of midsegments or of entire components) and exposure duration. (Copyright © 1985 by the APA. Adapted by permission.)

able to recognize all the components in either condition. Since there were more components in the condition with segment deletion, they had more information as to object identity.

◆

Objects like horses and cups are recognized as configurations of a simple set of subobjects.

Speech Recognition

Up to this point, we have considered only visual pattern recognition. An interesting test of the generality of our conclusions is whether they extend to speech recognition. Although we will not discuss details of early speech processing, it is worth noting that similar issues arise. A major problem for speech recognition is segmentation of the objects to be recognized. Speech is not broken up into discrete units the way printed text is. Although well-defined gaps seem to exist between words in speech, this is often an illusion. If we examine the actual physical speech signal, we often find undiminished sound energy at word boundaries. Indeed, a cessation of speech energy is as likely to occur within a word as between words. This property of speech is particularly compelling when we listen to someone speaking in an unknown foreign language. The speech appears to be a continuous stream of sounds with no obvious word boundaries. It is our familiarity with our own language that leads to the illusion of word boundaries.

Within a single word, even greater segmentation problems exist. These intraword problems involve the identification of **phonemes.**

Phonemes are the basic vocabulary of speech sounds; it is in terms of them that we recognize words.[1] A phoneme is defined as the minimal unit of speech that can result in a difference in the spoken message. To illustrate, consider the word *bat*. This word is analyzed into three phonemes: [b], [a], and [t]. Replacing [b] by the phoneme [p], we get *pat;* replacing [a] by [i] we get *bit;* replacing [t] by [n], we get *ban.* Obviously, a one-to-one correspondence does not always exist between letters and phonemes. For example, the word *one* consists of the phonemes [w], [ə], and [n]; *school* consists of the phonemes [s], [k], [ú], and [l]; and *knight* consists of [n], [ī], and [t]. It is the lack of perfect letter-to-sound correspondence that makes English spelling so difficult.

A segmentation problem arises when the phonemes composing a spoken word need to be identified. The difficulty is that speech is continuous, and phonemes are not discrete, in the way letters are on a printed page. Segmentation at this level is like recognizing a written (not printed) message, where one letter runs into another. Also, as in the case of writing, different speakers vary in the way they produce the same phonemes. The variation among speakers is dramatically clear, for instance, when a person first tries to understand a speaker with a strong and unfamiliar dialect—as when an American listener tries to understand an Australian speaker. However, examination of the speech signal will reveal that, even among speakers with the same accent, considerable variation exists. For instance, the voices of women and children normally have a much higher pitch than those of men.

A further difficulty in speech perception involves a phenomenon known as coarticulation (Liberman, 1970). As the vocal tract is producing one sound, say the *b* in bag, it is moving toward the shape it needs for the [a]. As it is saying the *a*, it is moving to produce the *g*. In effect, the various phonemes overlap. This means additional difficulties in segmenting phonemes, and it also means that the actual sound produced for one phoneme will be determined by the context of the other phonemes.

It is thought that speech perception involves specialized mechanisms that go beyond the mechanisms in general auditory perception. We will be discussing in subsequent subsections some of the ways that speech perception is special. It is also the case that a number of patients have been identified who, as the result of injury to their left temporal lobe, have lost just the ability to hear speech (Goldstein 1974, for a review). Their ability to detect and recognize other sounds is intact as is their ability to speak. Thus, their deficit is specific to speech perception. Sometimes, these patients have some success if speech is very slow (e.g., Okada,

◆
----

[1]Massaro (1996) presents a frequently proposed alternative that the basic perceptual units are consonant-vowel and vowel-consonant combinations.

Hanada, Hattori, & Shoyama, 1963), suggesting that some of their problem might be in segmenting the speech stream.

◆

Speech recognition involves segmenting phonemes from the continuous speech stream.

Feature Analysis of Speech

Feature-analysis and feature-combination processes seem to underlie speech perception much as they do visual recognition. As with individual letters, individual phonemes can be analyzed as consisting of a number of features. It turns out that these features refer to aspects of how the phoneme is generated. Among the features for phonemes are the consonantal feature, voicing, and the place of articulation (Chomsky & Halle, 1968). The **consonantal feature** is the quality in the phoneme of having a consonantlike property (in contrast to vowels). **Voicing** is the sound of a phoneme produced by the vibration of the vocal cords. For example, compare the ways you produce *sip* and *zip*. The [s] in *sip* is voiceless, but the [z] in *zip* is voiced. You can detect this difference by placing your fingers on your larynx as you generate these sounds. The larynx will vibrate for the voiced consonant.

Place of articulation refers to the place at which the vocal track is closed or constricted in the production of a phoneme. (It is closed at some point in the utterance of most consonants.) For instance [p], [m], and [w] are considered bilabial because the lips are closed during their generation. The phonemes [f] and [v] are considered labiodental because the bottom lip is pressed against the front teeth. Two different phonemes are represented by [th]—one in *thy* and the other in *thigh*. Both are dental because the tongue presses against the teeth. The phonemes [t],[d],[s],[z],[n],[1], and [r] are all alveolar because the tongue presses against the alveolar ridge of the gums just behind the upper front teeth. The phonemes [sh], [ch], [j], and [y] are all palatal because the tongue presses against the roof of the mouth just behind the alveolar ridge. The phonemes [k] and [g] are velar because the tongue presses against the soft palate, or velum, in the rear roof of the mouth.

Consider the phonemes [p], [b], [t], and [d]. All four share the feature of being consonants. However, the four can be distinguished according to

---

◆

Table 2.1 The Classification of [b], [p], [d], and [t] According to Voicing and Place of Articulation

	Voicing	
Place of Articulation	*Voiced*	*Voiceless*
Bilabial	[b]	[p]
Alveolar	[d]	[t]

voicing and place of articulation. Table 2.1 classifies these four consonants according to these two features.

Considerable evidence exists for the role of such features in speech perception. For instance, Miller and Nicely (1955) had subjects try to recognize consonants such as [b], [d], [p], and [t] when presented in noise. Actually, subjects were presented with the sounds ba, da, pa, and ta. Subjects exhibited confusion, thinking they had heard one sound in the noise when in reality another sound had been presented. The experimenters were interested in what sounds subjects would confuse with what. It seemed likely that subjects would most often confuse consonants that were distinguished by just a single feature, and this prediction was confirmed. To illustrate, when presented with [p], subjects more often thought that they had heard [t] than that they had heard [d]. The phoneme [t] differs from [p] only in terms of place of articulation, whereas [d] differs both in place of articulation and in voicing. Similarly, subjects presented with [b] more often thought they heard [p] than [t].

This experiment is an earlier demonstration of the kind of logic we saw in the Kinney, Marsetta, and Showman study on letter recognition. When the subject can identify only a subset of the features underlying a pattern (in this case the pattern is a phoneme), the subject's responses will reflect confusion among the phonemes sharing the same subset of features.

◆

Phonemes are recognized in terms of features involved in their production, such as place of articulation and voicing.

Categorical Perception

The features of phonemes refer to properties by which they are articulated. What are the properties of the acoustic stimulus that encodes these articulatory features? The issue has been particularly well researched in the case of voicing. In the pronunciation of such consonants as [b] and [p],

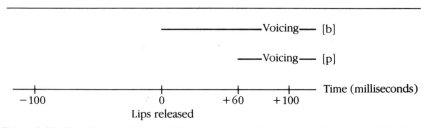

Figure 2.22 The difference between [b] and [p], the delay between the release of the lips and voicing in the case of [p]. (From Psychology and Language by Herbert H. Clark and Eve E. Clark. Copyright by Harcourt Brace Jovanovich. Reproduced by permission of the publisher.)

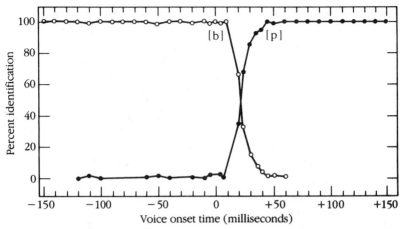

Figure 2.23 Percentage identification of [b] versus [p] as a function of voice-onset time. A sharp shift in these identification functions occurs at about 25 milliseconds. (From Lisker & Abramson, 1970.)

two things happen: The closed lips are opened, releasing air, and the vocal cords begin vibrating (voicing). In the case of the voiced consonant [b], the release and the vibration of the vocal cords are nearly simultaneous. In the case of the unvoiced consonant [p], the release occurs 60 milliseconds (ms) before the vibration begins. What we are detecting when we perceive a voiced versus an unvoiced consonant is the presence or absence of a 60-ms interval between release and voicing. This period of time is referred to as the voice-onset time. The difference between [p] and [b] is illustrated in Figure 2.22. Similar differences exist in other voiced-unvoiced pairs, such as [d] and [t]. Again, the factor controlling the perception of a phoneme is the delay between the release of closure and vibration of the vocal cords.

Lisker and Abramson (1970) performed experiments with artificial (computer-generated) stimuli in which the delay between release of closure and voicing was varied from −150 ms (voicing 150 ms before release) to +150 ms (voicing 150 ms after release). The task was to identify which sounds were [b]'s and which were [p]'s. Figure 2.23 plots the percentage of [b] identifications and [p] identifications. Throughout most of the continuum, subjects agreed 100 percent on what they heard, but there is a sharp switch from [b] to [p] at about 25 ms. At a 10 ms voice onset, subjects are in nearly unanimous agreement that the sound is a [b]; at 40 ms they are in nearly unanimous agreement that the sound is a [p]. Because of this sharp boundary between the voiced and unvoiced phoneme, perception of this feature is referred to as categorical.

Categorical perception refers to the perception of stimuli as belonging in distinct categories and the failure to perceive the gradations among stimuli within a category.

Other evidence for categorical perception of speech comes from discrimination studies (see Studdert-Kennedy, 1976, for a review). Subjects are very poor at discriminating between a pair of [b]'s or a pair of [p]'s that differ in voice-onset time. However, they are good at discriminating pairs that have the same difference in voice-onset time but where one is identified as a [b] and the other is identified as a [p]. It seems that subjects can identify only the phonemic category of a sound and are not able to make acoustic discriminations within that phonemic category. Thus, subjects are able to discriminate two sounds only if they fall on different sides of a phonemic boundary.

There are at least two views of what exactly is meant by categorical perception. The weaker view is that we experience stimuli as coming from different categories. There seems to be little dispute that perception of phonemes is categorical in this sense. A stronger viewpoint is that we cannot discriminate among stimuli within a category. Massaro (1992) has taken issue with this viewpoint, and he has argued that there is some residual ability to discriminate within categories. He further argues that the poor discrimination within a category may reflect a bias of subjects to say that stimuli within a category are the same even when there are discriminable differences.

Another line of research showing evidence for use of the voicing feature in speech recognition involves an adaptation paradigm. Eimas and Corbit (1973) had their subjects listen to repeated presentations of *da*. This sound involves a voiced consonant [d]. The experimenters reasoned that this constant repetition of the voiced consonant might fatigue, or adapt, the feature detector that responded to the presence of voicing. They then presented subjects with a series of artificial sounds that spanned the acoustic continuum—such as that between *ba* and *pa* (as in the Lisker and Abramson study mentioned earlier). Subjects had to indicate whether each of these artificial stimuli sounded more like *ba* or more like *pa*. (Remember that the only feature difference between *ba* and *pa is* voicing.) Eimas and Corbit found that some of the artificial stimuli that subjects would normally have called the voiced *ba,* they now called the voiceless *pa.* Thus, the repeated presentation of *da* had fatigued the *voiced* feature detector and raised the threshold for detecting voicing in *ba,* making many former *ba* stimuli sound like *pa.*

◆
  People tend to perceive phonemes as coming from distinct categories even when they differ on a single continuous dimension.

Context and Pattern Recognition

So far, we have considered pattern recognition as if the only information available to a pattern recognition system was the information in the physical stimulus to be recognized. However, this is not the case. Objects occur in context, and we can use those contexts to help object recognition. Consider the example in Figure 2.24. We perceive the symbols as *THE* and *CAT*, even though the specific symbols drawn for *H* and *A* are identical. The general context provided by the words forces the appropriate interpretation. When context or general world knowledge guides perception, we refer to the processing as **top-down** processing, because high-level general knowledge contributes to the interpretation of the low-level perceptual units. A general issue in perception concerns how such top-down influences are combined with the **bottom-up** information from the stimulus.

One important line of research on top-down effects comes from a series of experiments on letter identification, starting with those of Reicher (1969) and Wheeler (1970). Subjects were given a very brief presentation of either a letter (such as *D*) or a word (such as *WORD*). Immediately afterward, they were given a pair of alternatives and instructed to report which alternative they had seen. (The initial presentation was sufficiently brief that subjects made a good many errors in this identification task.) If they had been shown the letter *D*, subjects might be presented with *D* or *K* as alternatives. If they had been shown *WORD*, they might be given *WORD* or *WORK* as alternatives. Note that the two word choices differ only in the *D* or *K* letter. Subjects were about 10 percent more accurate in the word condition. Thus, they more accurately discriminated between *D* and *K* in the context of a word than as letters alone, even though, in a sense, they had to process four times as many letters in the word context. This phenomenon is known as the **word superiority effect.**

Rumelhart and Siple (1974) and Thompson and Massaro (1973) provided one explanation as to why subjects are more accurate when dealing with the word condition. Suppose subjects are able to identify the first three letters as *WOR*. Now consider how many four-letter words are consistent with a *WOR* beginning: *WORD, WORK, WORM, WORN, WORT*. Suppose subjects only detect the bottom curve in the fourth letter. In the *WOR* context, they know the stimulus must have been *WORD*. However,

TAE CAT

Figure 2.24 A demonstration of context. The same stimulus is perceived as an H or an A, depending on the context. (From Selfridge, 1955.)

when the letter is presented alone and subjects detect the curve, they will not know whether the letter was *B, D, C, O,* or *Q,* since each of these letters is consistent with the curve feature. Thus, in the *WOR* context subjects need only detect the curved feature to identify the fourth letter as *D,* but when the letter is presented alone they need to detect more features to be able to uniquely identify the letter. Note that this analysis implies that perception is a highly inferential process. It is not that the subject sees the *D* better in the context of *WOR;* rather the subject is better able to infer that *D* is the fourth letter. However, the subject is not conscious of these inferences; rather the subject is said to make unconscious inferences in the act of perception. Note in particular that the subject in this example does not have conscious access to the fact that the bottom curve was detected or it would have been possible to choose between *D* and *K.* Rather, the subject has conscious access only to the word or letter that the perceptual system has inferred.

This example illustrates the redundancy of many complex stimuli such as words. These stimuli consist of many more features than are required to distinguish one stimulus from another. Thus, perception can proceed successfully when only some of the features are recognized, with context filling in the remaining features. In language, this redundancy exists on many levels besides the feature level. For instance, redundancy occurs at the letter level. We do not need to perceive every letter in a string of words to be able to read it. To xllxstxatx, I cxn rxplxce xvexy txirx lextex of x sextexce xitx an x, anx yox stxll xan xanxge xo rxad xt—ix wixh sxme xifxicxltx. (This example is adapted from Lindsay & Norman, 1977.)

◆

Word context can be used to supplement feature information in the recognition of letters.

Context and Speech

Equally good evidence exists for the role of context in the perception of speech. A nice illustration is the **phoneme-restoration effect,** demonstrated in an experiment by Warren (1970). He asked subjects to listen to the sentence "The state governors met with their respective legislatures convening in the capital city," with a 120-millisecond tone replacing the middle *s* in legislatures. However, only one in twenty subjects reported hearing the pure tone, and that subject was not able to locate it correctly.

An interesting extension of this first study is an experiment by Warren and Warren (1970). They presented subjects with sentences such as the following:

It was found that the *eel was on the axle.

It was found that the *eel was on the shoe.

It was found that the *eel was on the orange.

It was found that the *eel was on the table.

In each case, the * denotes a phoneme replaced by nonspeech. For the four sentences above, subjects reported hearing *wheel, heel, peel,* and *meal,* depending on context. The important feature to note about each of these sentences is that the sentences are identical through the critical word. The identification of the critical word is determined by what occurs after it. Thus, the identification of words is often not instantaneous but can depend on the perception of subsequent words.

◆

Contextual information can be used to supplement feature information in the recognition of speech.

Context and the Recognition of Faces and Scenes

So far, our discussion has focused on the role of context in the perception of printed and spoken material. When we process other highly over-learned patterns, such as faces, the same kind of interaction that occurs with linguistic stimuli seems to take place between features and context. Consider Figure 2.25, which is derived from work by Palmer (1975). He pointed out that in the context of a face, very little feature information is required for recognition of the individual parts, such as nose, eye, ear, or lips. In contrast, when these parts are presented in isolation, considerably more visual detail is required to permit their recognition.

Context also appears to be important for perception of complex visual scenes. Biederman, Glass, and Stacy (1973) have looked at perception of

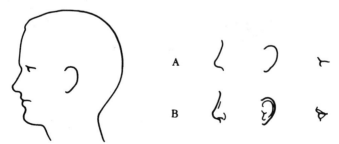

Figure 2.25 Facial features in the context of a face and out of context. Minimal information is necessary in context, but the same minimal features are not easily recognized in row A. More of the features' internal structure must be provided to permit recognition, as in row B. (Adapted from Palmer, 1975.)

(a)

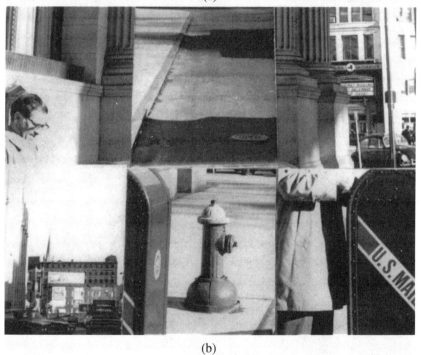

(b)

Figure 2.26 Scenes used in the study by Biederman et al. (1973): (a) a coherent scene; (b) a jumbled scene. It is harder to recognize the fire hydrant in the jumbled scene. (From Biederman et al., 1973. Copyright © 1973 by the APA. Reprinted by permission.)

objects in novel scenes. Figure 2.26 illustrates the two kinds of scenes presented to their subjects. Part a of the figure shows a normal scene; in part b the same scene is jumbled. The scene was briefly presented to subjects on a screen, and immediately after the presentation an arrow pointed to a position on the now blank screen where an object had been moments before. Subjects were asked to identify the object that had been in that position in the scene. So, in the example scene, the object pointed to what might have been the fire hydrant. Subjects were considerably more accurate in their identification with the coherent than with the jumbled pictures. Thus, as with their processing of written text or speech, subjects are able to recruit context in a visual scene to help their identification of an object.

◆
Context information can be used to supplement feature information in the recognition of faces and scenes.

Massaro's FLMP Model for Combination of Context and Feature Information

We have reviewed the effect of context on pattern recognition in a variety of perceptual situations, but the question of how to conceive of these effects still remains. Two main alternatives have been proposed. One proposal is that the context and stimulus provide two independent sources of information as to what the pattern actually is. Massaro's (1979) experiment on letter recognition provides evidence for this perspective. Figure 2.27 shows examples of the material he used in a test of recognition of the letter *c* versus the letter *e*. The four quadrants represent four possibilities in terms of amount of contextual evidence: only an *e* can make a word, only a *c* can make a word, both letters can make a word, or neither can. As one goes down within a quadrant, the letter provides more evidence for letter

Figure 2.27 Items used by Massaro (1979) to study how subjects combine stimulus information from a letter with context information from the surrounding letters.
(Reprinted by permission of the APA.)

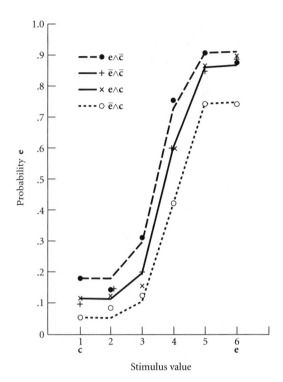

Figure 2.28 Probability of an e response as a function of the stimulus value of the test letter and the orthographic context (from Massaro, 1979). The lines reflect the predictions of Massaro's FLMP model.

e and less for letter *c*. Subjects were briefly exposed to these stimuli and had to identify the letter. Figure 2.28 shows the results as a function of context and stimulus information. As can be seen, as the letter provides more evidence for an *e*, the probability of the subject saying an *e* goes up. Similarly, the probability increases as the context provides more evidence.

Massaro argues that these data reflect an independent combination of evidence from the context and evidence from the letter stimulus. He assumes that the letter represents some evidence L_c for the letter *c* and that the context also provides some evidence C_c for the letter *c*. He assumes that these evidences can be scaled on a scale of 0 to 1 and can be thought of basically as probabilities, which Massaro calls "fuzzy truth values." Since probabilities sum to 1, the evidence for *e* from the letter is $L_e = 1 - L_c$, and the evidence from the context is $C_e = 1 - C_c$. Given these probabilities, then, the overall probability for a *c* is

$$P(c) = \frac{L_c \times C_c}{L_c \times C_c + L_e \times C_e}$$

The lines in Figure 2.28 illustrate the predictions from his theory. In general, Massaro's theory (called **FLMP** for **fuzzy logical model of percep-**

tion) has done a very good job of accounting for the combination of context and stimulus information in pattern recognition.

One might wonder in exactly what sense the equation above qualifies as independently combining stimulus and context information. This can be justified in terms of the Bayesian theory of statistical inference. That theory proposes that if there are two sources of evidence for a hypothesis (in this case the hypothesis that the letter is a *c*) and the two sources of evidence are probabilistically independent, then they should be combined as in the above equation. Probabilistic independence means that the evidence provided by the stimulus feature does not depend on the context. This independence assumption would be violated, for instance, if the way one printed an *e* depended on the word it was part of.

◆

Massaro's FLMP model of perception assumes that contextual information combines independently with stimulus information to determine the pattern perceived.

A PDP Model of Letter Recognition

McClelland and Rumelhart (1981) proposed what seems to be a very different model for the combination of stimulus and context information in pattern recognition. Figure 2.29 (on page 70) illustrates just part of the pattern-recognition network that McClelland and Rumelhart have implemented to model our use of word structure to facilitate recognition of individual letters. In this model, individual features like a vertical bar are combined to form letters, and individual letters are combined to form words. This is a connectionist model like the one we discussed in Chapter 1. It depends heavily on excitatory and inhibitory activation processes. Activation spreads from the features to excite the letters and from the letters to excite the words. Alternative letters in the same position inhibit each other as do alternative words. Activation can also spread down from the words to excite the component letters. In this way, a word can support the activation of a letter and hence promote its recognition. For example, a horizontal bar in the third position supports interpretation of an *A* over an *I* which in turn supports perception of *TRAP* over *TRIP*. To the extent that there is evidence for *TRAP*, this will support perception of the individual letters *T, R, A,* and *P* in the appropriate positions and the features that form them.

In such a system, activation will tend to accumulate at one word, and it will repress the activations of other words through inhibition. The dominant word will support the activation of its component letters, and these letters will repress activation of alternative letters. The word superiority effect is due to the support a word gives to its component letters. The computation proposed by McClelland and Rumelhart's interactive activation model is extremely complex, as is the computation of any model

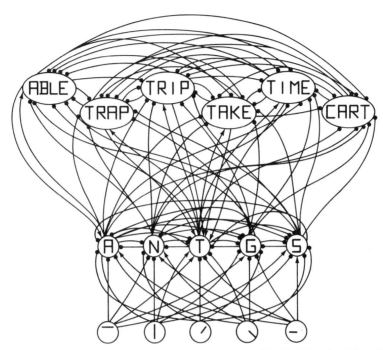

Figure 2.29 Part of the pattern-recognition network proposed by McClelland and Rumelhart (1981) to perform word recognition by performing calculations on neural activation values. Connections with arrowheads (→) indicate excitatory connections from the source to the head. Connections with rounded heads (–•) indicate inhibitory connections from the source to the head.

that simulates neural processing. However, they are able to reproduce many of the results on word recognition in their system.

This model predicts that top-down influences from the context can affect the actual sensitivity to the letters. This is quite different from Massaro's FLMP model, which argues that effects of context and stimulus information combine independently. Massaro (1989) argued that the PDP model was too insensitive to effects of stimulus information that contradicted the information from the context. He made this argument with respect to the effect of context on speech perception. In one of his experiments subjects heard a phoneme that varied in a continuum from an [r] to an [l] in a syllable that began either with a [t] or an [s]. In English, only an [r] may follow a [t] and only an [l] may follow an [s]. As in previous research, subjects showed influence of both sound and context, tending more to think that the phoneme was an [r] the more it sounded like an [r] and when it occurred in the context of a [t].

Figure 2.30 shows the results in a rather stylized form. McClelland and Elman (1986) had proposed a PDP model for this task which they called the TRACE model. Figure 2.30 also shows a stylized version of the kind of results that it produced. As can be seen, it also shows effects of stimulus information and context. However, it shows much stronger effects of context than is shown in the data. In the context of an [s], the TRACE model sticks with the hypothesis of an [l] at very high levels of evidence for an [r] and then abruptly switches. In contrast, subjects change sooner but more gradually. The TRACE curve for the *t* context shows the opposite effect. Massaro concludes "interactive-activation models are nonoptimal because they allow the processing system to distort the environmental input more than is reasonable (p. 420)."

McClelland (1991) showed that this problem with the interactive activation model could be easily remedied by assuming that the activation values would randomly vary a little from moment to moment. Then, the model predicts the gradual switch from perception of one letter to another and is able to predict how subjects combine stimulus and context information. Massaro and Cohen (1991) have responded to McClelland by pointing out other features that this revised model still has difficulty predicting. Massaro's FLMP model does a very good job of describing how stimulus

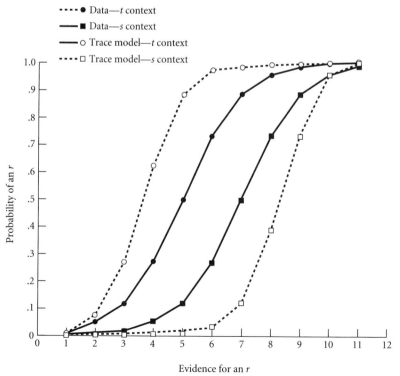

Figure 2.30 A stylized representation of subjects' performance in a phoneme recognition task, and a stylized representation of the predictions of McClelland and Elman's TRACE model.

information and context are integrated. However, the FLMP model is at a higher level of description than the PDP models and does not commit to details such as how processing of adjacent letters determine our perception of each one. It is a fair conclusion to say that a connectionist model like the PDP model can produce such effects, and the model in Figure 2.29 does give us an idea of how this might take place, but we are quite a distance from being able to understand exactly how the processing takes place in such a network.

The advantage of the detail in the PDP model is apparent in the way it analyzes how the context exerts its influence. The context for recognizing the letter *D* in the word condition involves a set of letters like *WOR__*. These letters have to be processed at the same time as the target letter *D* is being perceived. The presence of a *D* in the fourth position will influence the perception of these letters just as their presence influences the perception of *D*. One cannot separately assess the context and the evidence for the letter as is done in Massaro's FLMP model. One of the places where such interactive effects occur is in the perception of regular nonwords like *MAVE* (McClelland & Johnston, 1977). It turns out that recognition of the letter *A* is almost as good in such a context as when it occurs in the context of a word like *CAVE*. The reason is that there are a lot of words similar to *MAVE* like *MAKE* and *SAVE* with the *A* in that position. Each of these words facilitates the perception of the letter *A*. Thus, even though the context *M__VE* is not consistent with the letter *A*, *MAVE* is similar to a lot of words with *A* in second position and this facilitates perception of the *A*. This example makes the point that we do not really have a context and a stimulus but rather four letters that can mutually influence perception of each other.

◆

PDP models show how neural computations might combine stimulus and contextual information to determine pattern recognition.

Conclusions

Figure 2.31 is an attempt to sketch out abstractly the overall flow of perceptual information processing in the case of vision. Perception begins with light energy from the external environment. Receptors, such as those on the retina, transform this energy into neural information. Early sensory processing is concerned with making initial sense of the information. Figure 2.31 illustrates three stages proposed in Marr's model (1982). Features are extracted to yield what Marr called the **primal sketch.** These features are combined with depth information to get a representation of the location of surfaces in space; this is what Marr called the $2\frac{1}{2}$-D sketch. The principles of organization are applied to segment the elements into objects; this is the 3-D model. Finally, the features of these objects and

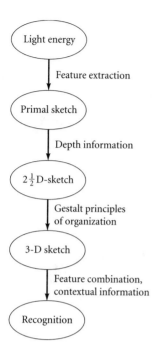

Figure 2.31 The flow of information from the environment to its perceptual representation. The information indicated in the circles is operated upon by the sensory and perceptual processes indicated in the boxes.

the general context information are combined to recognize these objects. The output of this level is what we are consciously aware of in perception, which is a representation of the objects and their locations in the environment. This information is the input to the higher-level cognitive processes. One of the points that Figure 2.31 illustrates is that there is a lot of information processing that needs to take place before we are consciously aware of the objects that we are perceiving.

Remarks and Suggested Readings

The topics covered in this chapter are easily expanded into a full course on perception; most colleges offer at least one course on this material. Such courses focus particularly on what is known about the elemental sensory processes. A fair amount of physiological evidence is available about these processes, and direct connections can be made between physiology and psychological experience. Among the standard texts providing extensive surveys of the research on sensation and perception are those of Goldstein (1999), and Blake and Sekuler (1994). A number of chapters in the book edited by Kosslyn and Osherson (1995) review various aspects of the cognitive science of perception. Plaut and Farah (1990) provide a review of the physiology of object recognition. James Gibson (e.g., 1950, 1966, 1979) developed a very influential theory of perception, quite different from the one presented here.

3

Attention and Performance

The previous chapter described the enormous parallelism that characterizes human perception. Our eyes and other sensory systems are simultaneously processing information from all over their sensory fields. However, one of the fundamental facts of human cognition is that this parallelism does not continue throughout the system. This chapter will document the evidence for a bottleneck in the auditory and visual systems—that there comes a point at which we can only attend to one spoken message or one thing on our visual field.

There is also strong evidence for limits to parallelism on the motor side. For instance, while most of us can perform separate actions at the same time when they involve different motor systems, such as walking and chewing gum, we have difficulty in getting one motor system to do two things at once. Thus, even though we have two hands, we have only one system for moving our hands, so it is hard to get our two hands to move in different ways simultaneously. Think of the familiar problem of trying to pat your head while rubbing your stomach. Inevitably, it seems, one of the movements dominates, and we wind up rubbing our heads or patting our stomachs. The many motor systems that make up human beings—one for moving feet, one for moving hands, one for moving eyes, and so on—can and do work independently and separately, but it is difficult to get any one of these systems to do two things at the same time.

Psychologists have proposed that there exists a **serial bottleneck** in human information processing, the point at which it is no longer possible to continue processing everything in parallel. It is pretty uncontroversial that there is a bottleneck by the time we get to motor action. The question that has occupied psychologists is how much earlier that bottleneck occurs—does it occur before we perceive the stimulus, after we perceive the stimulus but before we think about it, or only before motor action? Common sense suggests that there is a certain amount of seriality to thought even before motor action. For instance, we find it basically impossible to add two digits and multiply them simultaneously. Still, there remains the issue of just where the bottlenecks are in information processing. Different theories about when that selection occurs are referred to as **early selection** or **late selection** theories, depending on how early or late they think the bottleneck is. This is one of the questions studied by psychologists interested in attention. Wherever there is a bottleneck, our cognitive processes need to select which pieces of information to attend to and which to ignore. Another research question concerns *how* we select what to attend to. Many of these issues have been extensively studied in the domain of auditory attention. This is where we will begin our discussion.

◆
There occur serial bottlenecks in information processing at which point it is no longer possible to do things in parallel.

Auditory Attention

Much of the research in auditory attention has centered on the **dichotic listening task.** In a typical dichotic listening experiment, illustrated in Figure 3.1, subjects wear a set of headphones. They hear two messages at the same time, one entering each ear, and are asked to "shadow" one of the two messages (i.e., repeat back the words from one message only). Most subjects are able to attend to one message and tune out the other.

Psychologists (e.g., Cherry, 1953; Moray, 1959) have discovered that very little about the unattended message is processed in a shadowing task. After hearing the messages, subjects report that they can tell whether the unattended message was a human voice or a noise; whether the human

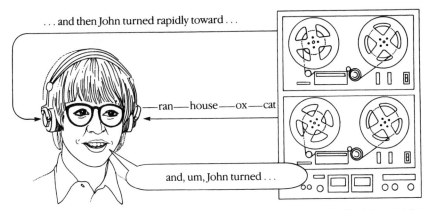

FIGURE 3.1 A typical shadowing task. Different messages are presented to the left and right ears, and the subject attempts to "shadow" one ear. (From Lindsay & Norman, 1977.)

voice was male or female; and whether the sex of the speaker changed during the test. However, this limited information is about all they can report. They cannot tell what language was spoken or remember any of the words spoken, even if the same word was repeated over and over again. An analogy is often made between performing this task and being at a cocktail party, where a guest tunes in to one message (a conversation) and filters out others. This research basically supports an early selection theory in that information is being selected before the message has undergone virtually any processing.

The Filter Theory

Broadbent (1958) proposed a particular early selection theory called the **filter theory** to account for these results. The basic assumption was that sensory information comes through the system until some bottleneck is reached. At this point, a person chooses which message to process on the basis of some physical characteristic. The person is said to filter the other information out. In the case of a dichotic listening task, it was assumed that the messages to both ears were registered but that at some point the subject selected one ear to listen with. In the case of the cocktail party, we pick which voice to follow on the basis of physical characteristics, such as the pitch of the speaker.

A critical feature of Broadbent's original filter model is that it proposed that we select a message to process on the basis of physical characteristics such as ear or pitch. This made a certain amount of neurophysiological sense. Messages coming from the two ears come on different nerves. Different nerves also carry different frequencies from each ear. Thus, we might imagine the brain, in some way, selecting certain nerves to "pay attention to." There are cells in the auditory cortex that are active only when an animal is paying attention to an auditory stimulus (Hubel, Henson, Rupert & Galambos, 1959). These might be viewed as the cells that are "paying attention."

Early auditory areas of the cortex (the part of the temporal cortex buried in the Sylvian fissure — Brodmann's areas 41 and 42 — see front inside cover of the book) show enhanced response to auditory signals coming from the ear the listener is attending to. Through ERP and ERF recording, Woldorff, Gallen, Hampson, Hillyard, Pantev, Sobel, and Bloom (1993) have shown that these responses occur between 20 and 50 milliseconds after stimulus onset. The enhanced responses occur much sooner in auditory processing than the point at which things like the speaker's voice or the meaning of the message can be identified. It seems that listeners can enhance the auditory signal coming from the ear to which they have chosen to attend.

Results like these clearly indicate that people can choose to attend to a message on the basis of its physical characteristics. However, there is evidence that we can also select messages to process on the basis of their semantic content. For instance, at a cocktail party we may be following one conversation, but suddenly our attention will switch when we hear our name mentioned in another conversation (Moray, 1959). In a number of experimental demonstrations, subjects have shown that they are able to choose which message to follow on the basis of semantic content.

In one study, Gray and Wedderburn (1960), who at the time were a couple of undergraduates at Oxford, demonstrated that subjects were quite

FIGURE 3.2 An illustration of the shadowing task in the Gray and Wedderburn experiment. The subject follows the meaningful message as it moves from ear to ear. (Adapted from R. L. Klatzky, Human memory, 1st Edition, W. H. Freeman and Co. Copyright © 1975.)

successful in following a message that jumped back and forth between ears. Figure 3.2 illustrates the subjects' task in their experiment. Suppose that part of the meaningful message that subjects were to shadow was *dogs scratch fleas.* The message to one ear might be *dogs six fleas,* while the message to the other might be *eight scratch two.* Instructed to shadow the meaningful message, subjects will report *dogs scratch fleas.* Thus, subjects are capable of shadowing a message on the basis of meaning rather than on the basis of what each ear physically hears.

Treisman (1960) looked at a situation (see Figure 3.3) in which subjects were instructed to shadow a particular ear. The message in the to-be-shadowed ear was meaningful until a certain point, when it turned into a random sequence of words. Simultaneously, the meaningful message switched to the other ear—the one to which the subject had not been attending. Some subjects switched ears, against instructions, and continued to follow the meaningful message. Other subjects continued to follow the shadowed ear. Thus, it seems that sometimes people use the physical ear to select which message to follow, and sometimes they choose semantic content.

◆

Broadbent's filter model proposes that we use physical features to select one message to process, but it has been shown that subjects are also able to use semantic content.

FIGURE 3.3 An illustration of the Treisman experiment. The meaningful message moves to the other ear, and the subject sometimes continues to shadow it against instructions. (Adapted from R. L. Klatzky, <u>Human memory,</u> 1st Edition, W. H. Freeman and Co. Copyright © 1975.)

The Attenuation Theory and Late Selection Theory

To deal with these kinds of results, Treisman (1964) proposed a modification of the Broadbent model, which has come to be known as the **attenuation theory**. This model assumed that certain messages would be weakened but not filtered out entirely on the basis of their physical properties. Thus, in a dichotic listening task, subjects would minimize the signal from the unattended ear but not eliminate it. Semantic selection criteria could apply to all messages, whether they were attenuated or not. If the message was attenuated, it would be harder to apply these selection criteria, but it would still be possible, as in the Gray and Wedderburn experiment. Treisman (personal communication) emphasizes that in her 1960 experiment most subjects actually continued to shadow the prescribed ear. It was easier to follow the nonattenuated message than to apply semantic criteria to switch attention to the attenuated message.

An alternative explanation was offered by Deutsch and Deutsch (1963) in their **late selection theory**. They proposed that all the information was processed completely unattenuated. Rather than there being any capacity limitations in the perceptual system, their proposal was that the capacity limitation was in the response system. They claimed that people can perceive multiple messages, but that they can shadow only one message at a time. Thus, subjects need some basis for selecting which message to shadow. If subjects use meaning as the criterion (either according to or in contradiction to instructions), they will switch ears to follow the message. If subjects use ear of origin in deciding what to attend to, they will shadow the proper ear.

The difference between the two theories is illustrated in Figure 3.4 from Treisman and Geffen (1967). Both models assume that there is some filter or bottleneck in processing. Treisman's theory (in part a) assumes that the filter selects which message to attend to, while Deutsch and Deutsch's theory (in part b) assumes that the filter occurs after the perceptual stimulus has undergone analysis for verbal content. Treisman and Geffen (1967) tried to address the difference between these two theories. They used a dichotic listening task in which subjects had to shadow one message but also had to process both messages for a target word. If they heard the target word, they were to tap. According to the late selection theory, messages from both ears would get through and subjects should have been able to detect the critical word equally well in either ear. In contrast, the attenuation theory predicted much less detection in the nonshadowed ear because the message would be attenuated. In fact, subjects detected 87 percent of the target words in the shadowed ear and only 8 percent in the nonshadowed ear. Other evidence consistent with the attenuation theory is reported by Treisman and Riley (1969) and by Johnston and Heinz (1978).

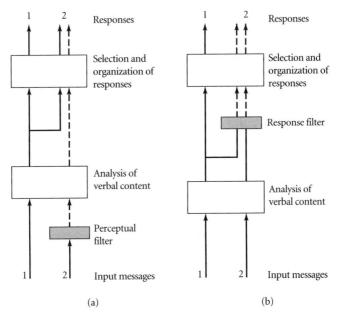

FIGURE 3.4 Treisman and Geffen's (1967) illustration of attentional limitations produced by (a) a perceptual filter and (b) a response filter. (Reprinted by permission of the Quarterly Journal of Experimental Psychology.)

While it is the case that unattended auditory information is not processed well, it appears that subjects are capable of maintaining such information for brief periods of time. Glucksberg and Cowan (1970) presented subjects with two spoken messages, one to each ear. Subjects were required to shadow the message that was being said in one ear. From time to time, the experimenter would say a digit to the ear that was not being shadowed. They would stop the subjects and ask whether a digit had occurred. This was like the Treisman and Geffen selection experiment except that subjects were explicitly cued to recall the target item from the unattended ear. Glucksberg and Cowan found that if they asked subjects right after the digits were said, subjects could still detect the digit with some success. They were able to recall the digits over 25 percent of the time if cued immediately, whereas the spontaneous detection rate was only 5 percent. Performance dropped off dramatically over the first two seconds and after five seconds reached the point at which subjects' ability to detect the digit was not greater than their spontaneous detection rate. The researchers thus concluded that the information in the unattended message is available for a short period of time but is lost within five seconds. Neisser (1967) has called the system that maintains unprocessed auditory information the echoic memory. Unless the material in this memory is attended quickly, it will be lost.

◆

We can select which auditory message to process on the basis of its physical properties. Unless we quickly attend to the message, it will be lost.

Conclusion

To summarize this discussion of auditory attention, we appear to select what to attend on the basis of physical properties of the message such as location or ear. The physiological evidence is that we enhance this message and so, in effect, attenuate the alternative messages. The alternative messages are not totally blocked out and so have the ability to grab attention if they are physically striking (a loud noise), particularly important (our name), or consistent with the message we are processing (switching ears to follow a meaningful message).

Visual Attention

The bottleneck in visual information processing is even more apparent than that in auditory information processing. As we reviewed in the previous chapter, the retina varies in its acuity, with maximal acuity in a very small area called the fovea. Although our eyes register a large part of the visual field, our fovea only registers a small fraction of that field. Thus, in choosing where to fixate, we also choose to give maximal visual processing resources to a particular part of the visual field and "attenuate" the resources given over to processing other parts of the visual field. Usually, it is the case that we are attending to that part of the visual field which we are fixating. For instance, as we read, we move our eyes so that we are fixating the words we are attending.

However, it is not the case that the focus of visual attention is always identical with the part of the visual field being processed by the fovea. Subjects can be instructed to fixate on one part of the visual field (so that is where the fovea is) and to attend to another nonfoveal region of the visual field. In one experiment, Posner, Nissen, and Ogden (1978) had subjects fixate on a constant point and then presented them with a stimulus either 7 degrees to the left or right of the fixation point. On some trials, subjects were given a warning as to which side the stimulus was likely to occur on, but on other trials there was no such warning. When there was a warning, it was correct 80 percent of the time, but 20 percent of the time the stimulus appeared on the unexpected side. Posner et al. monitored eye movements, and included only those trials in which the eyes had stayed on the fixation point. Figure 3.5 shows time to judge the stimulus if it appears in the expected location (80 percent), if the subject has not been given a cue (50 percent), or if the stimulus is in the unexpected location (20 percent). Subjects are able to shift attention from where their eyes are fixated such that

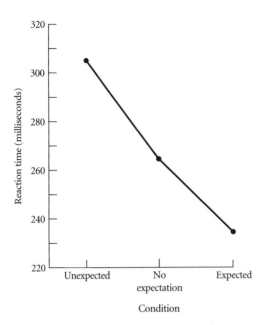

FIGURE 3.5 Reaction time to expected, unexpected, and neutral (no expectation) signals that occur 7 degrees to the left or right of fixation. (Posner, Nissen, & Ogden, 1978.)

their responses to the stimuli are faster when the stimulus appears in the expected location and slower when it appears in the unexpected location.

Posner, Snyder, and Davidson (1980) found that subjects can attend to positions as far as 24 degrees from the fovea. While, in experiments like these, visual attention can be moved without accompanying eye movements, subjects usually move their eyes so that their fovea processes the portion of the visual field to which they are attending. Posner (1988) points out that successful control of eye movements requires that we attend to places outside the fovea. That is, we must attend to and identify an interesting nonfoveal region so that we can guide our eyes to fixate on that region to achieve maximal acuity in processing that location. Thus, a shift of attention frequently precedes the corresponding eye movement.

◆ We attend to a single part of the visual field, and we usually (but not always) fixate the portion of the visual field we are attending.

The Spotlight Metaphor

One type of theory treats visual attention as if it were a spotlight that we can move around to focus on various parts of our visual field. Research on the size of this spotlight suggests that it can span varying degrees of visual angle (Erikson & St. James, 1986; Erikson & Yeh, 1987). The more of the visual field it spans, the less well it can process any part of the visual field. The spotlight can be focused, however, so that it spans only a few degrees of visual angle (Erikson & Erikson, 1974; Erikson & Hoffman, 1972). Narrowing of the spotlight gives maximal processing to that part of the visual field, but if the person wants to process material in other parts of the visual field, it is necessary to move the spotlight, and this takes time. Thus, the reason subjects take longer in the 20 percent unexpected condition of Posner et al. (see Figure 3.5) is that the subjects have to shift their attention from the focused position to the other position.

An experiment by LaBerge (1983) illustrates the consequences of focusing on one part of the visual array. He presented subjects with a string of five letters that subtended approximately 1.77 degrees of visual angle. Subjects usually saw a set of letters like LACIE and were asked to judge if the middle letter came from the beginning (which the C does in this case) or end of the alphabet. In this way, the subject's attention was kept centered on the middle letter. However, the visual angle was so small that all of the letters were within the fovea. Occasionally, subjects saw a stimulus like + 7 + + + which consisted of four pluses and a single item. Subjects were to judge if this item was 7 or one of two distractors (T and Z). These were critical trials, and LaBerge was interested in speed of judgment as a function of distance from the center of attention. Figure 3.6 shows his results. Subjects were fastest for items at the center and about 50 milliseconds (ms) slower for items at the periphery. Remember that all these items were within the fovea, but attention was differentially distributed over the area.

To process a complex visual situation, it is necessary to move our attention around in the visual field to track the visual information. This is

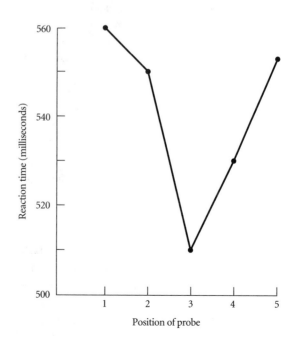

FIGURE 3.6 Results from LaBerge (1983): Reaction time to a probe when attention is focused on the third letter of a letter string.

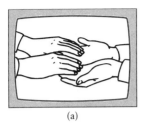  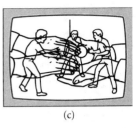

      (a)   (b)   (c)

FIGURE 3.7 Frames from the two films used by Neisser and Becklen (1975). (a) The "hand-game" film; (b) the basketball film; and (c) the two figures superimposed. (From Neisser & Becklen, 1975. Reprinted by permission of Academic Press.)

like shadowing a conversation. Neisser and Becklen (1975) performed the visual analog of the auditory shadowing task. They had subjects observe two videotapes superimposed over one another. One was of two people playing a hand-slapping game, and the other was of some people playing a ball game. Figure 3.7 shows what the situation looked like to the subjects. They were instructed to pay attention to one of the two episodes and to monitor for odd events such as the two players of the hand-slapping game pausing and shaking hands. They were able to monitor one episode quite successfully and reported filtering out the other episode. When asked to monitor both episodes for odd events, the subjects experienced great difficulty and missed a great many of the critical events.

As Neisser and Becklen note, this situation involved an interesting combination of the use of physical cues and content cues. Subjects moved their eyes and their attention such that the critical aspects of the to-be-followed event fell on their foveas and the center of their attentive spotlight. On the other hand, they knew how to move their eyes to follow one event only, by making reference to the content of the event they were processing. Thus, physical cues facilitate processing of the critical episode, which in turn facilitates knowing where to move one's eyes to obtain more physical cues to process the episode and so on.

◆

Subjects can focus their attention on a few degrees of area in their visual field and move their focus of attention over the visual field to process a meaningful event.

Neural Basis of Visual Attention

It appears that the neural mechanisms underlying visual attention are very similar to the neural mechanisms underlying auditory attention. Just as auditory attention directed to one ear enhances the cortical signal from that ear, so it appears that visual attention directed to a spatial location enhances the cortical signal from that location. If a person attends to a

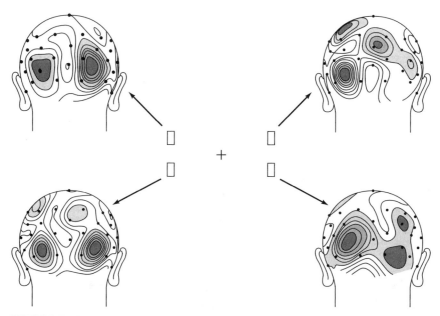

FIGURE 3.8 ERP density maps for stimuli in each of the four quadrants pointed to by the arrows (Mangun, Hillyard & Luck, 1993).

particular spatial location, there appears a distinct neural response (using ERP records) in the visual cortex within 70–90 milliseconds (ms) after the onset of the stimulus. On the other hand, when a subject is attending to a higher-order feature (attending to chairs not tables), we do not see a response for more than 200 ms.

Mangun, Hillyard, and Luck (1993) had subjects judge the length of bars presented in different positions from fixation (upper left, upper right, lower left, lower right). They recorded how much the ERP recording was affected at various locations across the back of the scalp. Figure 3.8 shows the distribution of scalp activity when a subject is attending to different regions of the visual array (while fixating the center of the screen). Consistent with the topographic organization of the visual cortex, we see greatest activity over the side of the scalp that is opposite the side of the visual field where the object appears. Recall that the visual cortex (at the back of the head) is topographically organized, with each visual field (left or right) represented on the opposite hemisphere. Thus, it appears that there is enhanced neural processing in the portion of the visual cortex corresponding to the location of visual attention.

It seems that the electrophysiological data are consistent with the early selection model. Subjects appear to select stimuli to attend to, either in the visual or auditory domain, on the basis of physical properties and, in particular, on the basis of location. How do subjects then find an object with particular higher-order properties such as the face of a friend in a crowd?

In this case, they appear to have to search through locations looking for one that has the desired properties. Much of the research on visual attention has been concerned with how people perform such searches. In later sections of this chapter, we will discuss this search process.

◆ When people attend to a particular location there is enhanced neural processing in portions of the visual cortex corresponding to that location.

Visual Sensory Memory

Earlier, we reviewed the evidence that we can attend to one visual location at a time. If we are presented with a visual array of items like the letters in Figure 3.9 and try to encode them, most people report that they have to look through the array one location at a time. It appears as if our attention is stepping through this array one letter at a time. What if the array is flashed only briefly? Many studies have been done with brief presentations of arrays like Figure 3.9, and they shed light on how people encode such information. A typical trial in such an experiment begins with having the subject fixate on a dot in a blank white field. By having the subject fixate in this way, the experimenter can control where the subject is focusing during stimulus presentation. The stimulus is visually projected where the subject is looking. After a brief exposure (e.g., 50 milliseconds), the stimulus is removed. In such experiments, a display of letters, such as that shown in Figure 3.9, is presented briefly, after which subjects are asked to report as many items as they can recall. Usually, subjects are able to report three, four, five, or at most six items. Subjects report that they were aware that there were more items but that the items faded away before they could attend to them and report them.

An important methodological variation on this task was introduced by Sperling (1960). He presented arrays consisting of three rows of four letters, such as the one shown in Figure 3.9. Immediately after this stimulus was turned off, the subject was cued to attend to just one row of the display and had to report only the letters in that row. The cues were in the form of differential tones (high tone for top row, medium for middle, and low for bottom). Sperling's method was called the **partial-report procedure** in contrast to the **whole-report procedure**, which was what had been used until then. Subjects were able to recall all or most of the items from a row

X	M	R	J
C	N	K	P
V	F	L	B

FIGURE 3.9 An example of the kind of display used in a visual-report experiment. This display is presented briefly to subjects, who are then asked to report the letters it contains.

of four. Because subjects did not know beforehand which row would be cued, Sperling argued that they must have had most or all of the items stored in some sort of short-term visual memory. Given the cue after the visual display went off, they could attend to that row in their short-term visual memory and report the digits in that row. The reason the subjects could not report more items in the full-report procedure was that these items had faded from this memory before the subjects could attend to them. Thus, visual attention can be applied to this brief memory of the experience as well as to the perceptual experience itself.

In the procedure just described, the tone cue was presented immediately after offset of the display. Sperling also varied the length of the delay between the offset of the display and the tone. The results he obtained, in terms of numbers of letters recalled, are presented in Figure 3.10. As the delay increases to one second, the subjects' performances decay back to what would be expected from the original whole-report level of four or five items. That is, subjects are reporting about one-third as many items from the cued row as they can report from three rows in the whole-report procedure. Thus, it appears that the memory of the actual display decays very rapidly and is essentially gone by the end of one second. All that is left after a second is what the subject has had time to attend to and convert to a more permanent form.

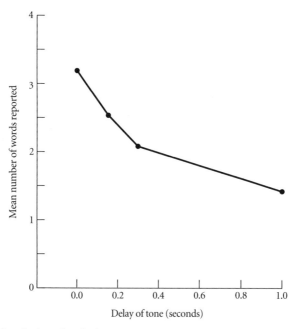

FIGURE 3.10 Results from Sperling's experiment. As the tone that signals the row to report is delayed, the number of items reported decreases. (Adapted from Sperling, 1960.)

Sperling's experiments indicate the existence of a brief **visual sensory store**—a memory that can effectively hold all the information in the visual display. While information is being held in this store, the subject can attend to it and report it. This sensory store appears to be particularly visual in character. In one experiment showing the visual character of the sensory store, Sperling (1967) varied the post-exposure field (the visual field after the display). He found that when the post-exposure field was light, the sensory information remained for only one second, but when the field was dark, it remained for a full five seconds. Thus, a bright post-exposure field tends to "wash out" memory for the display. Further, following a display with another display of characters effectively "overwrites" the first display and so destroys the memory for the first set of letters. The brief visual memory revealed in these experiments was called an **icon** by Neisser (1967). Unless information in this display was attended to and processed further, it would be lost. This iconic memory is like the echoic memory for the auditory system. That is, it briefly holds information so that the information can be accessed if attended to.

Iconic memory seems quite sensory in character and may even reflect activation of the neural systems responsible for early visual processing. For instance, Sakitt (1976) argued that the icon is predominantly located in the photoreceptors of the retina of the eye. She showed that many of the timing and sensitivity properties of the iconic image mirror those of the rods, the photoreceptors in the eye responsible for night vision. Thus, under her analysis the icon is very much like the afterimage we have at night for a bright light. Haber (1983) has questioned the relevance of the icon for normal visual perception because we do not usually perceive the world in such brief flashes. To make his point amusing, he argued that the icon would only be relevant to reading in a lightning storm. Others have argued that the neural processes that underlie the icon go beyond the retina. Coltheart (1983) argues that icons are obtained when there are no rod-based afterimages and that these icons do play an important role in everyday information processing.

The Sperling paradigm is most often thought of in terms of the information it provides about the duration of visual iconic memory. However, it is at least as significant in terms of the information it provides about how fast attention can move through iconic memory and encode the objects. Visual attention must move through this visual icon, focusing on different locations to encode the letters. If we assume that iconic memory lasts about one second and that four items can be encoded in this one second, a time of about 1/4 = .25 seconds to shift attention among items is implied.[1]

---

[1]This is probably an overestimate of both the duration of the icon and the time to encode the letter. See Anderson, Matessa, and Lebiere (1997).

◆

Visual information is held in a brief visual sensory memory where we can attend to items that it contains and process them.

Pattern Recognition and Attention

Treisman (e.g., Treisman & Gelade, 1980) in her **feature-integration theory**, has proposed that people must focus attention on a stimulus before they can synthesize its features into a pattern. This would be why attention must shift among the items in the Sperling paradigm. One experiment demonstrating this was performed by Treisman and Gelade (1980). They instructed subjects to try to detect a T in an array of thirty I's and Y's (see Figure 3.11a). They reasoned that subjects could do this by simply looking for the cross-bar feature of the T that distinguishes it from all

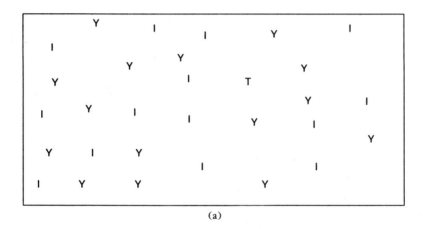

(a)

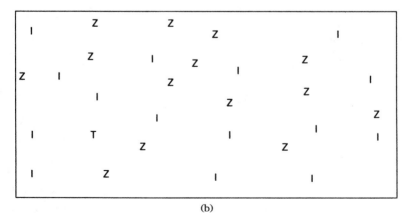

(b)

FIGURE 3.11 Stimuli used by Treisman and Gelade (1980). Subjects find it easier to detect a T in an array like that shown in (a) than in an array like the one shown in (b).

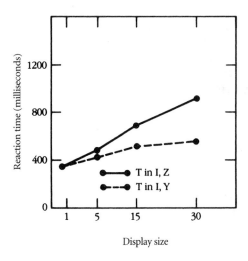

FIGURE 3.12 Results from Treisman and Gelade: Reaction time to detect a target as a function of number of distractors and whether the distractors contain separately all the features of the target. (Adapted from Treisman & Gelade, 1980.)

I's and Y's. Subjects took about 400 milliseconds (ms) to make this decision. Treisman and Gelade also asked subjects to detect a T in an array of I's and Z's, such as in Figure 3.11b. In this condition, they could not use just the vertical bar or just the horizontal bar of the T; they would have to look for the conjunction of these features and perform the feature combination required in pattern recognition. It took subjects more than 800 ms to make their decisions. Thus, a condition requiring them to recognize the conjunction of features took about 400 ms longer than one in which perception of a single feature was sufficient. Moreover, when Treisman and Gelade varied the size of the display, they found that subjects were much more affected by display size in the condition that required recognition of the conjunction of features. Figure 3.12 shows these results.

It might seem surprising that attention is required to detect the patterns of features that define common letters. We have the experience of automatically recognizing letters. It should be noted, however, that for familiar letters the deficit in perception of feature conjunctions only becomes apparent with large displays, when the processing load gets large enough to expose attention deficits.

It appears that it is necessary to fixate on a location in order to be able to determine what conjunctions of features are present. Treisman and Gelade found that subjects could detect the presence of a single feature (like a vertical bar) without knowing where it was in the display. On the other hand, they were able to detect a conjunction of features only if they were able to report the location of those features—subjects must attend to a specific location in order to confirm that there is a conjunction of features there.

Treisman and Gelade's study also provides information about how fast subjects can scan arrays. Subjects take about 600 ms longer to find the target when there are thirty items in the I,Z display than when there is one.

On average they would have to search about half of the display (or fifteen items) before they found the target. Thus, it takes approximately 600/15 = 40 ms to consider and reject an item. This is a lot faster than the scanning time estimate from the Sperling task, but in this experiment subjects are not identifying (but only rejecting) the items they are scanning.

Treisman and Schmidt (1982) looked at what happened to feature combinations when the stimuli were out of the focus of attention. Subjects were asked to report the identity of two black digits flashed in one part of the visual field. This was their primary task, and it was where their attention was focused. In another part of the visual field, letters in various colors were presented. Thus, subjects might be presented with a pink T, a yellow S, and a blue N in the unattended portion of the field. After they reported the numbers, subjects were asked to report any letters they had seen and the colors of these letters. Subjects reported seeing illusory conjunctions of features (e.g., a pink S) almost as often as they reported seeing correct combinations. Thus, it appears that we are able to combine features into an accurate perception only when our attention is focused on the object. Otherwise, we perceive the features but may well combine them into a perception of objects that were never there.

In the previous chapter, we discussed how the visual array is separately analyzed into different feature maps that encode information such as line orientation and color. People can choose to attend to a particular feature map, like that for vertical lines or that for the color pink. They can then restrict their search to all positions that possess this feature. They must serially look through all such locations, looking for a particular target pattern. In each place they look, they can synthesize all of the features there into a perception. There is some controversy about whether subjects can only use a single feature to direct attention (Duncan & Humphreys, 1989; Treisman, 1991). Wolfe (1994) has developed a computer simulation model that is like Treisman's proposal except that subjects can use multiple features to direct attention (i.e., they can direct their attention to look for a bar that is both red and vertical). Wolfe argues that such conjunction-directed searches are noisier and less accurate than single-feature searches. However, in his model as in Treisman's, one must direct attention to a location before one can recognize the object in that location.

◆
Feature information must be in the focus of attention in order for it to be synthesized into a pattern.

Neglect of the Visual Field

Earlier in the chapter, we discussed the evidence that visual attention to a location results in enhanced activation in the appropriate portion of the primary visual cortex. However, the evidence is that the neural structures that control this shift of attention are located elsewhere than the primary visual cortex. Three areas of the monkey brain have been shown to be involved in controlling attention (Peterson, Robinson, & Morris, 1987; Wurtz, Goldberg, & Robinson, 1980). These areas are the superior colliculus, the posterior parietal lobe, and a midbrain area known as the pulvinar. Damage to these areas in human patients, particularly the parietal lobe, has been shown to result in deficits in visual attention. For instance, Posner, Walker, Friedrich, and Rafal (1984) showed that patients with parietal lobe injuries have difficulty in disengaging attention from one side of their visual field. If they have right parietal lobe damage, they find it difficult to disengage attention from something in the right visual field to attend to something in their left visual field (which goes to their damaged right parietal lobe). Patients with left parietal lobe damage show the symmetrical deficit.

Figure 3.13 shows data describing attention deficit in a patient with right parietal damage (Posner, Cohen, & Rafal, 1982). Using the same paradigm as in Figure 3.5, the patient was either cued to expect a stimulus to the left or right of the fixation point, and 80 percent of the time that is where the stimulus was present. However, 20 percent of the time the stimulus appeared in the unexpected field. Figure 3.13 shows time to detect the stimulus as a function of which visual field it was presented in and which field had been cued. When it is presented in the right field, subjects show only a little disadvantage if they are inappropriately cued. However, if they are inappropriately cued for a stimulus that appears in the right visual

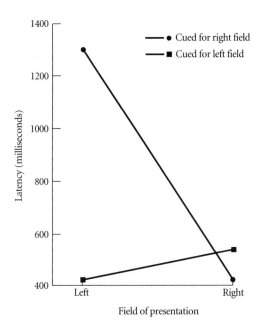

FIGURE 3.13 Deficit that a patient with right parietal lobe damage shows in switching attention to the left field. (From Posner et al., 1982.)

field, they show a large deficit if it appears in the left field. Since the right parietal lobe processes the left visual field, this implies that damage to that right lobe impairs its ability to draw attention back to the left visual field once attention is focused on the right visual field.

Posner et al. (1984) note that this experimental result is like the clinical phenomenon called visual extinction, observed in patients with damage to the parieto-occipital cortex. Patients with damage to the right hemisphere do not have difficulty attending to single objects in the left visual field (which go to this damaged hemisphere); however, when a competing object is presented to the right visual field, the patients fail to note the object in the left visual field. Again, the deficit is symmetrical for patients with damage to the left hemisphere.

A more extreme version of this attentional disorder is called **unilateral visual neglect**. Patients with right hemisphere damage ignore the left side of the visual field, and patients with left hemisphere damage ignore the right side of the field. Figure 3.14 shows the performance of a patient with left field damage (Albert, 1973). She had been instructed to put slashes through all the circles. As can be seen, she ignored the circles in the left part of her visual field. Such patients will often behave quite peculiarly. For instance, one patient failed to shave half of his face (Sacks, 1985).

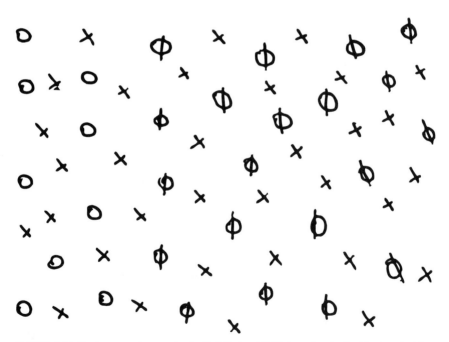

FIGURE 3.14 Performance by a patient with left visual field damage who had been asked to put slashes through all the circles. (From Ellis & Young, 1988. Reprinted by permission of Lawrence Erlbaum Associates Ltd., Hove, UK.)

Patients with damage to a parietal lobe on one side of the cortex suffer difficulty attending to the half of the visual field processed by that cortical area.

Object-Based Attention

Up to this point, we have discussed attention as if it were focused on certain regions of space. However, there is also evidence that we also sometimes focus our attention on particular objects rather than regions of space. This would make a lot of sense in the real world, because particular objects do not always occupy the same region of our visual space as we move or they move. The eyes can smoothly track objects as they move through our visual field. While our eyes do generally follow the object we are attending to, eye movement is not required for attention to track an object.

An experiment by Behrmann, Zemel, and Mozer (1998—one of a series of follow-ups of an original experiment by Duncan, 1984) provides one line of evidence that subjects sometimes find it easier to attend to an object than to a location. Figure 3.15 illustrates some of the stimuli used in the experiment. Subjects were asked to judge whether the number of "bumps" on the two ends of objects were the same. The stimuli in the left column are examples of positive instances, and the stimuli in the right col-

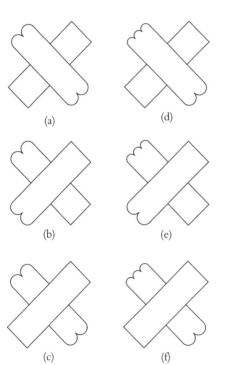

(a) (d)

(b) (e)

(c) (f)

FIGURE 3.15 Stimuli used in an experiment by Behrmann, Zemel, and Mozer (1998). The left and right columns indicate same and different judgments, respectively, and the rows from top to bottom indicate the single-object, two-object, and occluded conditions, respectively.

umn are instances of negative stimuli. Subjects are faster to make these judgments when the bumps are on the same object (first and third row in Figure 3.15) than when they are on different objects (middle row). This is despite the fact that when they are on different objects they are closer together in location, which should facilitate judgment. Behrmann et al. argue (as did Duncan) that subjects can shift attention to one object at a time and not one location at a time. Therefore, when the bumps are all on the same object, subjects are saved the need of shifting attention between objects.

Other evidence for object-centered attention involves a phenomenon called **inhibition of return**. If we have looked at a particular region of space, we find it harder to return our attention to that region. This also makes sense. If we are searching for something and have already looked at a location, we would prefer if our visual system found other locations to look at rather than return to an already searched location. If humans move their eyes to location A and then to location B, they are slower to return their eyes to location A than some new location, C. This is also true when they move their attention without moving their eyes (Posner, Rafal, Chaote, & Vaughn, 1985).

Tipper, Driver, and Weaver (1991) performed one demonstration of this inhibition of return that also provided evidence for object-based attention. In their experiments, subjects saw objects consisting of three squares, as in Figure 3.16. The subjects' attention was drawn to one of the outer squares by flickering it. Two hundred milliseconds later, attention was drawn back to the center square by flickering that square. A probe was then presented in one of the two outer positions. Subjects were slower to press a key indicating that they had seen the probe when it occurred at the outer square that had been flickered (now on the right in Figure 3.16e) than when it occurred at the outer square (now on the left)—in one case taking about 460 ms and in the other case 420 ms. This 40 ms advantage is an example of a spatially defined inhibition of return. Subjects are slower to move their attention to a location where it has already been.

In another condition the objects moved after the flicker so that they rotated around the screen. By the end of their motion, the object that had been flickered on one side was now on the other side, and in fact the two outer objects had traded positions. For instance, the object on the right might have rotated so that it was now on the left. The question of interest was whether subjects would be faster to detect a target on the right (where the flickering had been) or on the left (where the flickered object had gone to). The answer is that they were about 20 ms slower to detect an object in the location that had not been flickered but which contained the object that had been flickered. Thus, their visual systems had an inhibition to return to the same object, not the same location.

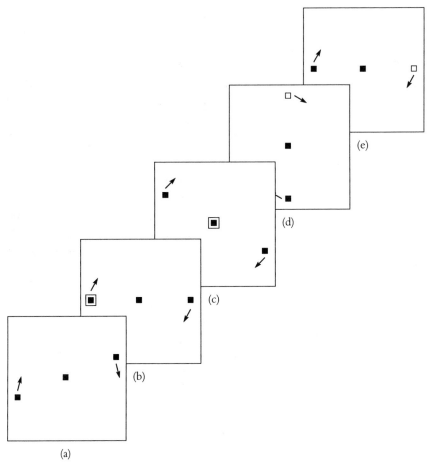

FIGURE 3.16 Examples of frames used in the moving condition of a demonstration by Tipper, Driver, and Weaver (1991 – arrows represent motion). (a) Display onset, with no motion for 500 milliseconds. After two moving frames, the 3 filled squares were horizontally aligned (b) whereupon the cue appeared. Clockwise motion then continued, with central cueing for the initial three frames (c). The outer squares continued clockwise until horizontal alignment (e), where a probe was presented, as before.

Another example of object-based attention comes from studies of visual neglect. Earlier, we noted with respect to examples like Figure 3.14 that some patients have difficulty detecting information in the left side of the visual field. A number of patients have been identified who neglect the left side of objects regardless of which visual field these objects occur in (Behrmann & Moscovitch, 1994; Driver, Baylis, Goodrich, & Rafal, 1994).

◆
Visual attention can be directed toward objects independent of their location.

A Central Bottleneck

So far we have looked at how subjects allocate attention within a single modality like vision or audition, and we have seen evidence that they focus their attention on one stimulus and neglect others. This sort of evidence indicates that there are bottlenecks in the various perceptual modalities. That is, it seems we can only process one thing in a modality at a time. However, what if we are presented with a visual stimulus and an auditory stimulus? Can we process these in parallel? These issues have been explored in a number of dual-task studies. For instance, Karlin and Kestenbaum (1968) asked subjects to perform two tasks:

> *Task 1.* A digit was presented visually. If the digit was a 1, the subjects responded by pressing a key with the little finger of their left hand, and if it was a 2, they responded by pressing a key with their ring finger.

> *Task 2.* In this task, subjects heard a tone. If it was a low tone (600 Hz), they responded with the middle finger of their right hand, and if it was a high tone (3000 Hz), they responded with their right index finger.

Subjects were supposed to do the first task first, and the delay between the two stimuli (called the stimulus onset asynchrony—SOA) was manipulated from 90 ms to 1150 ms. Figure 3.17 displays the time taken to perform the two tasks as a function of SOA. Subjects are taking just under 400 ms to perform the first task independent of SOA. This makes sense, since they were told to complete this task first and as quickly as possible.

The interesting pattern of data concerns how long it took them to perform the second task. If there were no bottlenecks in the performance of the two tasks, one might expect there would be no effect of SOA on time to perform the second task. Subjects would do it in parallel with the second

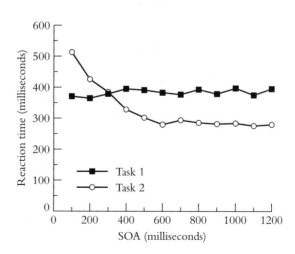

FIGURE 3.17 Results from the Karlin and Kestenbaum (1968) experiment: time to perform Task 1 and Task 2 as a function of the delay between the two tasks.

task. This is clearly not the case. At short SOAs, they are delayed in performing the second task by the need to complete the first task. It is only at long SOAs, after they have completed the first task, that subjects perform the second task without any interference. Thus, the first task interferes with the second.

One might suppose that subjects would have to complete the first task before they could begin the second task. Consider what this predicts for their time to perform the second task at the shortest SOA, which is 90 ms. It takes 383 ms to complete the first task. Thus, when the tone is presented for the second task they still have the $383 - 90 = 293$ ms left to do on the first task. Thus, the time to do the second task should be this time plus the 284 ms that the second task takes: $293 + 284 = 577$ ms. However, they take only 514 ms at the shortest SOA. So subjects are able to overlap more than 60 ms for processing.

Thus, subjects are neither able to perform the two tasks entirely in parallel nor do they have to complete all of one task before doing any of the other. It is conventionally assumed that, since these two tasks involve different sensory systems that the subject can attend to the auditory stimulus while performing the first visual task. The 60+ ms saved in performance of the second task reflects the fact that they were encoding the auditory stimulus while doing the first task. However, once the subjects encode the auditory stimulus, they reach a central bottleneck and can do nothing further with the second task until they have completed the first task.

The central bottleneck occurs when the subject must do the thinking for each task. One cannot think about multiple things at once. However, as long as the modalities do not conflict, one can process multiple stimulus sources at a time. One can also engage in multiple actions at a time such as driving and talking at the same time. The ability to do this depends on the fact that one of these processes is highly automated (in this case, driving) and does not make much demand on central cognition. However, when the driving gets difficult, one often finds it difficult to carry on the conversation in parallel. Next, we turn our discussion to the issue of automaticity and its implications for performing multiple tasks in parallel.

◆──

   People can process multiple perceptual modalities at once or execute multiple actions at once, but they cannot think about two things at once.

──

Automaticity

In Chapter 9 we will discuss at some length how people become expert with practice. The general impact of practice is to reduce the central cognitive component. When one has practiced this central cognitive component of a task so much that the task requires little or no thought, we say that doing the task is automatic. A nice demonstration of the way practice affects attentional limitations is the study reported by Underwood (1974) on the psychologist Neville Moray, who had spent many years studying shadowing. During that time, Moray practiced shadowing a great deal. Unlike most subjects, he had a good ability to report what was contained in the nonattended channel. Through a great deal of practice, the process of shadowing had become partially automated for Moray, and he had capacity left over to attend to the nonshadowed channel.

Spelke, Hirst, and Neisser (1976) provide an interesting demonstration of how a highly practiced skill ceases to interfere with other ongoing behaviors. (This is a follow-up of a demonstration pioneered by the writer, Gertrude Stein, when she was at Harvard University.) Their subjects had to perform two tasks—read a text silently for comprehension while simultaneously copying words dictated by the experimenter. At first, these tasks were extremely difficult to do simultaneously. Subjects read much more slowly than normal. However, after six weeks of practice, the subjects were reading with normal speed. They had become so skilled that their comprehension scores were the same as for normal reading. For these subjects, reading while copying had become no more difficult than reading while walking. It is of interest that subjects reported no awareness of what it was they were copying. Much as with driving, the subjects lost their awareness of the automated activity.[2]

Another example of automatic processing is transcription typing. The typist is simultaneously reading the text and executing the finger strokes for typing. In this case, we have three systems operating in parallel: perception of the text to be typed, central translation of the earlier perceived letters into keystrokes, and the actual typing of still earlier letters. Skilled transcription typists often report little awareness of what they are typing, since this has become so automated. It is also the case that skilled typists find it impossible to immediately stop typing. If suddenly told to stop, they will hit a few more letters before quitting (Salthouse, 1985, 1986).

The various perceptual systems (e.g., vision and audition), the various motor systems (e.g., speech and manual movements), and central cognition are independent systems that progress in parallel. However, each system is itself serial—one can only attend to one region of space, execute one pattern of hand movement, or think one thought. Central cognition is often the bottleneck because so many tasks require it for coordination. Automaticity occurs when practice eliminates most of the need for central cognition. Then, most of the task performance involves different parallel perceptual and motor systems, and there is little conflicting demand placed on the same system. In Chapter 9 on expertise, we will discuss further research on the role of practice in automating skills.

◆———————————

[2]When given further training with the intention of remembering what they were transcribing, subjects were also able to recall this information.

◆

As tasks become practiced, they become more automatic and require less and less central cognition to execute.

The Stroop Effect

Automatic processes not only require little or no central cognition to execute, but they also appear to be difficult to stop from executing. A good example is word recognition for practiced readers. It is virtually impossible to look at a common word and not read it. This strong tendency for words to be automatically recognized has been studied in a phenomenon known as the **Stroop effect** after J. Ridley Stroop who first demonstrated it (Stroop, 1935). The task requires subjects to say the ink color that words are printed in. The word whose ink color they have to name may be a color word like *red* or a neutral word like *bed*. If the word is a color word, it may either be printed in that ink color or in a different ink color. Figure 3.18 shows the results from an experiment by Dunbar and MacLeod (1984). Compared to the control condition of a neutral word, subjects are somewhat faster in the congruent condition of naming the ink color when the word is the name of that color. They are much slower in the conflict condition at naming the ink color of the word when the word is the name of a different color. That is, for instance, they have great difficulty in saying that the ink

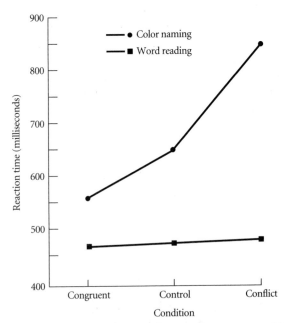

FIGURE 3.18 Performance data for the standard Stroop task. (From Dunbar & MacLeod, 1984.)

FIGURE 3.19 The task is to say aloud the number of characters in each row. This is a variation of the Stroop task. (From Glass & Holyoak, 1986. Reprinted by permission of McGraw-Hill.)

```
        5   5   5
      1   1   1   1
              2
    3   3   3   3   3
          4   4
          5   5   5
    4   4   4   4   4
      5   5   5   5
              3
          4   4   4
    2   2   2   2
          3   3
          4   4   4
    1   1   1   1
              3
          2   2   2
```

color of the word *red* is green. Figure 3.18 also shows the times subjects took to name the words in these three conditions. The effects are asymmetrical. That is, subjects do not experience the same facilitation or interference in reading the word as a function of its ink color. Of course, they are also much faster at reading a word than naming its ink color, reflecting the highly automatic character of reading.

Subjects are not only much slower at naming the ink color in the conflict condition; they also make many more errors that involve intruding the name of the color word rather than its ink color. Reading is such an automated response that they are often unable to inhibit reading the word, even though they are instructed not to read the word but to say the color. Figure 3.19 presents an analog of the Stroop effect developed by Flowers, Warner, and Polansky (1979) which we can demonstrate in a black-and-white text. You should process it row by row saying as fast as possible the number of characters in each row. You should find it very difficult to resist saying the numbers that make up the row rather than counting the numbers. This is because number recognition is much more automated than counting.

MacLeod and Dunbar (1988) looked at the effect of practice in a Stroop task. They used an experiment in which the subjects had to learn the color names for random shapes. The experimenters then presented the subjects with test geometric stimuli in which subjects had to say either the color name associated with the shape or the actual ink color of the shape. As in the original Stroop experiment, there were three conditions:

- Congruent: The random shape was in the same ink color as its name.

- Control: White shapes were presented when subjects were to say the color name for the shape, or colored squares were pre-

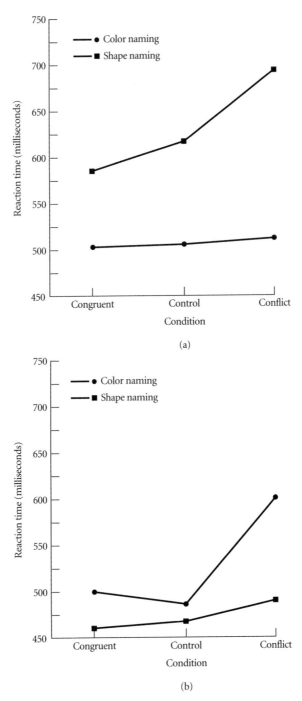

FIGURE 3.20 Data from MacLeod and Dunbar (1988): time required to name shapes and colors as a function of color-shape congruence at (a) initial performance; (b) after 20 days of practice.

sented when they had to name the ink color of the shape. (The square shape was not associated with any color.)

- Conflict: The random shape was in a different ink color from its name.

Figure 3.20a shows the results from this task. Color naming was much more automatic than shape naming and was relatively unaffected by the congruence with the shape, whereas shape naming was impacted by congruence with the ink color. Then, MacLeod and Dunbar gave the subjects twenty days' of practice at naming the shapes. Figure 3.20b shows the results then obtained. Subjects had gotten much faster at shape naming, and doing so interfered with color naming rather than vice versa. Thus, the consequence of the training was to make shape naming automatic, like word reading, so that it impacted on color naming.

◆

Reading a word is such an automatic response that it is difficult to inhibit, and it will interfere with processing other information about the word.

Conclusions

There has been a gradual shift in the way the field of cognitive psychology has perceived the issue of attention. For a long time, the implicit assumption of the field was captured by this famous quote from William James (1890) over a century ago:

> *Everyone knows what attention is. It is the taking possession by the mind, in a clear and vivid form, of one out of what seem several simultaneously possible objects or trains of thought. Focalization, concentration of consciousness are of its essence. It implies withdrawal from some things in order to deal effectively with others. (pp. 403–404)*

Two features of this quote reflect once-held conceptions about attention. One is that attention is strongly related to consciousness—that we cannot attend to one thing unless we are conscious of it. The second is that attention, like consciousness, is a unitary system. The field is more and more coming to recognize that the association of attention with consciousness has been unfortunate (e.g., Shiffrin, 1997) since many attentional phenomena seem quite unconscious. For instance, people are often not conscious of where they have moved their eyes. Along with this realization has come the realization that attention is not just one factor (e.g., Pashler, 1995). We have seen that it makes sense to separate auditory attention from visual attention, attention in perceptual processing from attention in response generation. The brain consists of a number of parallel-processing systems for the various perceptual systems, motor systems, and central cognition. Each of these parallel systems seems to suffer bottlenecks at which it must focus its processing on a single thing. Attention is best conceived as the processes by which each of these systems is allocated to potentially competing information-processing demands. The amount of interference one gets among tasks is a function of the overlap in the demands that these tasks make on the same systems.

Remarks and Suggested Readings

A biannual Conference on Attention and Performance results in a book of the same name that contains the leading new research in the field. Treisman and Sato (1990) provide a discussion of the role of attention in perception of feature conjunctions. A 1992 issue of the *American Journal of Psychology* presented a number of views about the connection between automaticity and attention. Wolfe (1994) describes a computer simulation of attention that is heavily built on Treisman's ideas. A text by Wickens (1992) presents a couple of detailed and up-to-date chapters on the topic of attention. Pashler (1998) presents his views on the nature of attention and performance, including the psychological refractory period (PRP). Meyer and Kieras (1997) present a recent model that disputes whether there really is a fundamental bottleneck in PRP tasks.

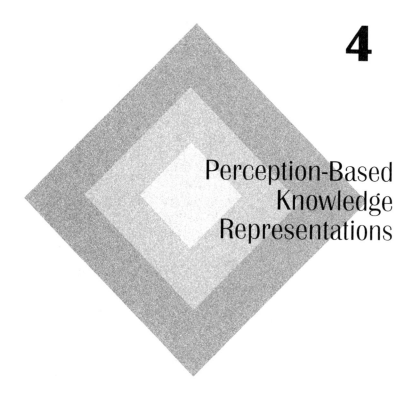

4

Perception-Based Knowledge Representations

The previous two chapters were concerned with information processing on the periphery of the cognitive system—largely with the perceptual system and to some degree with the response system. Now we turn to the issue of the way information is processed once it has been perceived and has entered the cognitive system. It turns out that the answer to this question depends on the way information is represented in the system. Some types of **knowledge representation** tend to preserve much of the structure of the original perceptual experience. This chapter will focus on such **perception-based representations**; Chapter 5 will focus on **meaning-based representations**, which are quite abstracted from the perceptual details and encode the meaning of the experience.

Perhaps more than anything else, the field of cognitive psychology is distinguished from the earlier behaviorism by its claim that there are internal representations of knowledge on which the mind operates. Partly reflecting the turmoil and confusion created in the separation of cognitive psychology from behaviorism, there has been a great deal of controversy about the nature of knowledge representations. There were debates about what sorts of knowledge representations the mind has and exactly what is meant by various claims about knowledge representation. With respect to perception-based knowledge representations, which are the focus of this chapter, these debates have largely subsided as the connection between these knowledge representations and the perceptual systems became clear. The previous two chapters were largely concerned with the perceptual processing of visual and verbal information. Correspondingly, in this chapter we will be concerned with the way visual and verbal information is represented and processed in the absence of an external perceptual stimulus. Processing of such internal perceptual information is called perceptual imagery, and many of us can report vivid phenomenological experiences of images as we process such information. For instance, when people imagine themselves "confronting the boss" they often "see" vivid details of the imagined event and "hear" the words spoken. Kosslyn (1995) has argued that the real function of imagery is not these compelling phenomenological experiences but rather to prepare us to process external perceptual stimuli and take action in the world. Thus, this imagery may help prepare us to actually meet the boss.

◆ The study of knowledge representations is concerned with how we organize and use information in long-term memory.

The Dual-Code Theory

Paivio (e.g., 1971, 1986) has long championed the **dual-code theory**, which claimed that there are separate representations for verbal and visual information. Much of his evidence came from research showing that human memory is better if we encode it both visually and verbally. For instance, researchers have found that memory for verbal material is greatly enhanced if one can develop visual images corresponding to the material. For instance, subjects given the sentence *The dog chased the bike* will better remember the sentence if they develop a corresponding image of the sentence (Anderson & Bower, 1973, Chap. 10). In later chapters, we will discuss such memory data in detail. Here, we will consider some experiments that more directly illustrate the difference between the two types of representations.

Comparisons of Verbal versus Visual Processing

An experiment by Santa (1977) nicely illustrates the difference between visual and verbal representations. The two conditions of Santa's experiment are illustrated in Figure 4.1. In the geometric condition (part a), subjects studied an array of three geometric objects: two geometric objects above and one below. As the figure shows, this array had a facelike property—without much effort we can see eyes and a mouth. After subjects studied it, this array was removed, and subjects were immediately presented with one of a number of test arrays. The subjects' task was to verify that the test array contained the same elements, although not necessarily in the same spatial configuration, as the study array. Thus, subjects should respond positively to the first two test arrays and negatively to the other two arrays. Interest was focused on the contrast between the two positive test arrays. The first array is identical to the study array (same-configuration condition), but in the second array the elements are displayed linearly (linear-configuration condition). Santa predicted that subjects would make a positive judgment more quickly in the first case, where the configuration was identical since, he hypothesized, the visual memory for the study stimulus would preserve spatial information. The results for the geometric condition are displayed in Figure 4.2. As can be seen, Santa's predictions were confirmed. Subjects were faster when the geometric test array preserved the configuration information in the study array.

The results from the geometric condition are more impressive when they are contrasted with the results from the verbal condition, illustrated in Figure 4.1b. Here, subjects studied words arranged in spatial configurations identical with geometric objects in the geometric condition. However, because it involved words, the study stimulus did not suggest a face or have any pictorial properties. Santa speculated that subjects would encode the word array according to normal reading order, that is, left to right and top to bottom. So, given the study array, subjects would encode it *triangle, circle, square*. Following the study, one of the test arrays was presented. Subjects had to judge whether the words were identical. All the test stimuli involved words, but otherwise they presented the same possibilities as the tests in the geometric condition. In particular, the two positive stimuli exemplify the same-configuration condition and the linear-configuration condition. Note that the order of words in the linear array is the same as that in which Santa assumed subjects would encode the study stimulus. Santa predicted that, since subjects had encoded the words linearly from the study array, they would be fastest when the test array was linear. As Figure 4.2 illustrates, his predictions were again confirmed. The verbal and the geometric conditions display a sharp interaction.

108 ◆

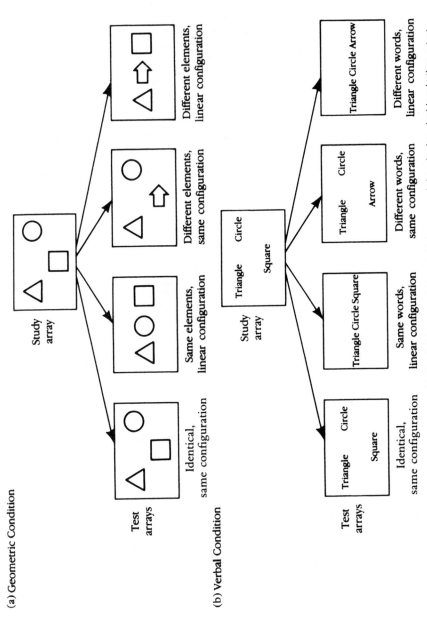

Figure 4.1 Procedure in Santa's experiment (1977). Subjects studied an initial array and then had to decide whether a test array contained the same elements.

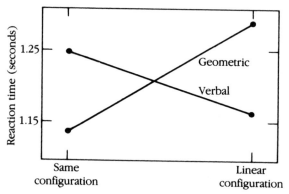

Figure 4.2 Reaction times for Santa's experiment (1977), showing an interaction between type of material and test configuration.

In conclusion, Santa's experiment indicates that some visual information, such as geometric objects, tends to be stored according to spatial position, whereas other information, such as words, tends to be stored according to linear order.

A very different sort of data for the difference between visual and verbal representations comes from the research of Roland and Friberg (1985). These investigators had subjects either mentally rehearse a word jingle or mentally rehearse finding their way from their house and around streets in their neighborhood. Roland and Friberg measured changes in blood flow in various parts of the cortex. Figure 4.3. shows the regions of the left

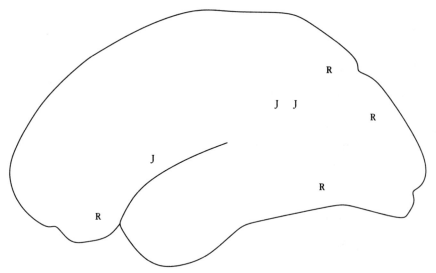

Figure 4.3 Results from Roland and Friberg (1985) showing regions of the left cortex with increased blood flow when imagining a verbal jingle (J) and when imagining a spatial route (R).

cortex that were activated by one mental process versus the other. Rs indicate areas with increased activity in the spatial route task, and Js indicate areas with increased activity during the verbal jingle task. It is apparent that different neural regions are involved when we process verbal versus spatial information. Moreover, these neural regions appear to be the ones that are involved in the actual processing of spoken and seen (rather than imagined) material. The occipital areas involved in the route-finding task are the same areas involved in vision. Among the areas involved in the jingle task is Broca's area, which, as we saw in Chapter 1, has a major role in the processing of speech. Thus, when we imagine information in one of the two modalities, we are using the same neural regions as would be used in the perception of these materials, as Paivio's dual-code hypothesis claimed.

◆
Verbal and visual information are processed by different parts of the brain in different ways.

Nature of Knowledge Representations

Thus, we see that different types of information are represented in different locations in the brain. Although issues of brain localization are important, the principal reason why psychologists are concerned with knowledge representation is because the way in which information is represented can affect the way it is processed. The Santa study illustrates the very different ways various types of information are processed.

There is a strong temptation to take a very literal interpretation of the way such perceptual images are represented. One might imagine that there are pictures in the head that some internal being in the brain looks at or that there is speech in the head that the same internal being listens to. The mythical internal being in the brain that sees and hears is infamous in cognitive psychology and is known as the homunculus. Use of such a concept is recognized as a failure of scientific explanation because we have simply replaced understanding human cognition with understanding homunculus cognition. Of course, this can lead to infinite regress where there is a homunculus inside the homunculus that sees pictures and hears words and so on.

There is evidence that might be interpreted as indicating that there really are "pictures in the head." For instance, as we noted in the first chapter, the visual area in the cortex maintains a topographic representation of the visual stimulus. The activity in the cortex will correspond to the spatial structure of the stimulus (e.g., see Figure 1.7). However, there is no homunculus looking at the image on the back of the brain. As we discussed in Chapter 1, the reason for topographic representation is so that neural areas processing adjacent information can better interact because they will be directly connected.

The second chapter gave us some ideas about the way visual information might be represented in perception. For instance, we saw that there were particular cells that represented lines in specific locations and orientations. A scene was represented by a pattern of activation over such cells, where the cells encoded various features of the scene. One might speculate that when subjects are imagining a visual scene, there would be a similar representation in terms of a pattern of activation over feature cells. We will discuss in this chapter some neural evidence that is consistent with this conjecture. Kosslyn (1995) argues that when we engage in such imagery we are basically evoking the same mechanisms to process internally generated information that we use in perception to process externally presented information.

◆
Imagined information is represented and processed in the ways that perceptual information is represented and processed.

Visual and Spatial Imagery

Many times when we are thinking about a scene or an object no longer present, we experience an image of that scene or object. People often refer to this as "seeing it in their mind's eye." There has been a great deal of research during the last forty years on the nature of the knowledge representations that underlie such visual imagery; these representations are typically referred to as **mental images**. The term "imagery" is often used as synonymous with visual imagery, although one can have auditory or tactile imagery as well. Therefore, we call this section visual and spatial imagery. We add the modifier spatial because, as we will see, some of our imagery is not tied to the visual modality but is concerned more generally with the location of things in space.

Mental Rotation

Among the most influential research on mental images is the long series of experiments on **mental rotation** performed by Roger Shepard and his colleagues. The first experiment was that of Shepard and Metzler (1971). Subjects were presented with pairs of two-dimensional representations of three-dimensional objects, like those in Figure 4.4. Their task was to determine if the objects were identical except for orientation. The two figures in part a are identical to each other, and the two figures in part b are identical to each other; they are just presented at different orientations. Subjects report that to match the two shapes they rotated one of the objects in each pair mentally until it was congruent with the other object. Part c is a foil pair: There is no way of rotating one object so that it is identical with the other.

The graphs in Figure 4.5 show the time required for subjects to decide that the members of pairs, such as those in Figure 4.4a and b, were iden-

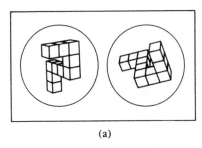

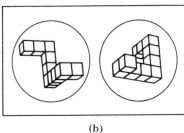

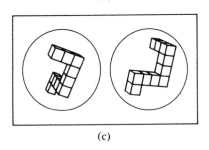

Figure 4.4 Stimuli in the Shepard and Metzler study on mental rotation (1971): (a) the objects differ by an 80-degree rotation in the picture plane; (b) the objects differ by an 80-degree rotation in depth; (c) the pair cannot be rotated into congruence. (From Metzler & Shepard, 1974).

(a)

(b)

(c)

tical. The reaction times are plotted as a function of the angular disparity between the two objects presented to the subjects. This angular disparity represents the amount one object would have to be rotated in order to match the other object in orientation. Note that the relationship is linear—for every equal increment in amount of rotation, an equal increment in reaction time is required. Reaction time is plotted for two different kinds of rotation. One is for two-dimensional rotations (Figure 4.4a), which can be performed in the picture plane (i.e., by rotating the page); the other is for depth rotations (Figure 4.4b), which require the subject to rotate the object into the page. Note that the two functions are very similar. Processing an object in depth (in three dimensions) does not appear to take longer than processing in the picture plane. Hence, subjects must be operating on three-dimensional representations of the objects in both the picture-plane condition and the depth condition.

These data might seem to indicate that subjects rotate the object in a three-dimensional space within their heads. The greater the angle of disparity between the two objects, the longer subjects take to complete the rotation. Of course, subjects are not actually rotating an object in their

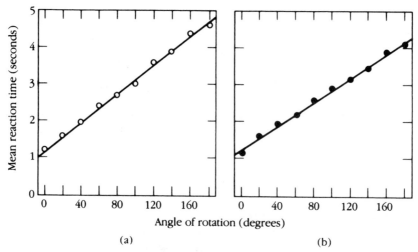

Figure 4.5 Mean time to determine that two objects have the same three-dimensional shape as a function of the angular difference in their portrayed orientations. (a) Plot for pairs differing by a rotation in the picture plane. (b) Plot for pairs differing by a rotation in depth. (From Metzler & Shepard, 1974.)

heads. However, whatever the actual mental process is, it appears to be analogous to physical rotation.

Neural recording from monkeys have provided some evidence about the neural representation during mental rotation. Georgopoulos, Lurito, Petrides, Schwartz, and Massey (1989) had monkeys perform a task in which they had to move a handle at an angle to a given stimulus. For instance, if monkeys had to move the handle 90 degrees to the left and the stimulus appeared at 12 o'clock, they would have to move the handle to 9 o'clock. If the stimulus appeared at 6 o'clock, they had to move to 3 o'clock. The greater the angle, the longer it took the monkeys to initiate the movement, suggesting that this task involved a mental rotation process. Georgopoulos et al. recorded from cells in the motor cortex that fire when a monkey makes a particular movement. When the monkey does not have to transform the direction but just moves in a particular direction different cells will fire for movements in different directions. When the monkey has to transform the direction, Georgopoulos et al. found that different cells fired at different times during the transformation. At the beginning of a transformation trial, when the stimulus is presented, they found that the cells that fired most were associated with a move in the direction of the stimulus. However, by the end of a transformation trial, when the monkey moved the handle, they found maximum activity in cells associated with the movement. Between the beginning and the end of the trial, cells representing intermediate directions were maximally active. This suggests that mental rotation involves gradual shifts of firing from cells that encode the initial stimulus to cells that encode the transformed stimulus. We saw in

Chapter 2 that visual cells are location- and direction-sensitive. Rotation may involve a gradual shift in the activity of cells representing various positions.

It might seem strange to make a connection between activity of cells in the motor cortex, which is where Georgopoulos et al. were recording, and rotation of a visual image. However, Deutsch, Bourbon, Papanicolaou, and Eisenberg (1988) have found that when humans engage in mental rotation there is activation in frontal and parietal areas of the cortex associated with motor planning and execution. Kosslyn (1995) suggests that mental rotation is normally done in preparation for motor actions when one has to deal with an object in a non-standard position. For instance, if we see a knife we need to imagine how to rotate our hand in reaching for it in order to grasp the handle. Kosslyn argues that the reason why the mental image must go through the intermediate positions is that our limbs must go through these intermediate locations in dealing with the objects.

◆

When subjects must transform the orientation of a mental image to make a comparison, they rotate it through the intermediate positions until it achieves the desired orientation.

Image Scanning

Something else we often do with mental images is to scan them looking for some critical information. For instance, when people are asked how many windows there are in their houses, many report visually going through the house as they count the windows. Researchers have been interested in the degree to which people are actually scanning perceptual representations in such tasks versus just retrieving abstract information.

Brooks (1968) performed an important series of experiments on the scanning of visual images. He had subjects scan imagined diagrams such as the one in Figure 4.6. For example, the subject was to scan around an

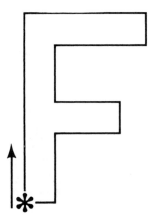

Figure 4.6 An example of a simple block diagram used by Brooks (1968) to study the scanning of mental images. The asterisk and arrow showed the subject the starting point and the direction for scanning the image. (Copyright ©1968 by the Canadian Psychological Association. Reprinted by permission.)

Figure 4.7 A sample output sheet of the pointing condition in Brooks (1968) for mental image scanning. The letters are staggered to force careful visual monitoring of pointing. (Copyright ©1968 by the Canadian Psychological Association. Reprinted by permission.)

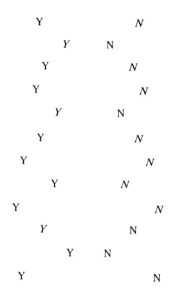

imagined block F from a prescribed starting point and in a prescribed direction, categorizing each corner as a point in the extreme top or bottom (assigned a yes response) or as a point in between (assigned a no response). In the example, the correct sequence of responses is yes, yes, yes, no, no, no, no, no, no, yes. For a nonvisual contrast task, Brooks also gave subjects sentences such as *A bird in the hand is not in the bush.* Subjects had to scan through such a sentence while holding it in memory, classifying each word as a noun or not. A second experimental variable was the way subjects made their responses. Subjects either (1) said yes and no; (2) tapped with the left hand for yes and with the right hand for no, or (3) pointed to successive *Y*'s or *N*'s on a sheet, such as that in Figure 4.7. The two variables of stimulus material (diagram or sentence) and output mode were crossed to yield six conditions.

Table 4.1 gives the results of Brooks's experiment in terms of the mean time spent in classifying the sentences or diagrams in each output condition. The important result for our purposes is that subjects took much longer for diagrams in the pointing condition than in any other condition. This was not the case for sentences. Apparently, scanning a sheet like the

Table 4.1 Mean Classification Times in Brooks, 1968

| Stimulus Material | *Output, in seconds* | | |
	Pointing	Tapping	Vocal
Diagrams	28.2	14.1	11.3
Sentences	9.8	7.8	13.8

one in Figure 4.7 conflicted with scanning a mental array. Thus, this result strongly reinforces the conclusion that when subjects are scanning a mental array, they are scanning a representation that is analogous to a physical array. Requiring the subject to simultaneously engage in a conflicting scanning action on an external physical array causes great interference to the mental scan.

It is sometimes thought that Brooks's result was due to the conflict between engaging in a visual pointing task and scanning a visual image. However, subsequent results make it clear that the interference is not due to the visual character of the task per se. Rather, the problem is spatial and not specifically visual, arising from the conflicting directions in which subjects had to scan the physical array versus the mental image. For instance, in another experiment, Brooks found evidence of similar interference when subjects had their eyes closed and indicated yes or no by scanning an array of raised Y's and N's, as in Figure 4.7, with their fingers. In this case the actual stimuli were tactile, not visual. Thus, the conflict is spatial, not visual per se.

Baddeley and Lieberman (reported in Baddeley, 1976) performed an experiment that strongly supports the view that the nature of the interference in the Brooks task is spatial rather than visual. Subjects were required to perform two tasks simultaneously. All subjects performed the Brooks letter-image task. However, subjects in one group simultaneously monitored a series of stimuli of two possible brightnesses. Subjects had to press a key whenever the brighter stimulus appeared. This task involved the processing of visual but not spatial information. Subjects in the other condition were blindfolded and seated in front of a swinging pendulum. The pendulum emitted a tone and contained a photocell. Subjects were instructed to try to keep the beam of a flashlight on the swinging pendulum. Whenever they were on target, the photocell caused the tone to change frequency, thus providing auditory feedback. This test involved the processing of spatial but not visual information. The spatial auditory tracking task produced far greater impairment in the image scanning task than did the brightness judgment task. This result also indicates that the nature of the impairment in the Brooks task was spatial, not visual.

◆ People suffer interference in scanning a visual image if they have to engage simultaneously in conflicting processing of a spatial structure in their environment.

Comparison of Visual Quantities

A fair amount of research has focused on the way subjects judge the visual details of objects in their mental images. One line of research has asked subjects to discriminate between objects on some dimension such as size. This research has shown that, when subjects try to discriminate between two objects, the time it takes for them to make this discrimination decreases continuously as the difference in size between the two objects increases.

Moyer (1973) performed an experiment illustrating such a latency effect on size judgment. He was interested in the speed with which subjects could judge the relative size of two animals from memory. For example, *Which is larger, moose or roach?* and *Which is larger, wolf or lion?* Many people report that in making these judgments, particularly for the items that are similar in size, they experience images of the two objects and seem to compare the size of the objects in their images.

Moyer also asked subjects to estimate the absolute size of these animals. He plotted the reaction time for making a mental-size-comparison judgment between two animals as a function of the difference between the two animals' estimated sizes. Figure 4.8 reproduces these data. The individual points represent comparisons between pairs of items. In general, the judgment times decrease as the difference in estimated size increases. The graph shows that a fairly linear relation exists between the scale on the abscissa and the scale on the ordinate. Note, however, that on the abscissa the differences have been plotted logarithmically. That is, if S_1 is the size of the larger animal (animal 1) and S_2 is the size of the smaller animal (animal 2), what is plotted on the abscissa is $\log(S_1 - S_2)$. A log-difference scale makes the distance between small differences large relative to the same distances between large differences. Thus, the linear relationship in the figure means that increasing the size difference has a diminishing effect on reaction time.

Significantly, very similar results are obtained when subjects make comparisons of actual physical magnitudes. For instance, Johnson (1939) asked subjects to judge which of two simultaneously presented lines was

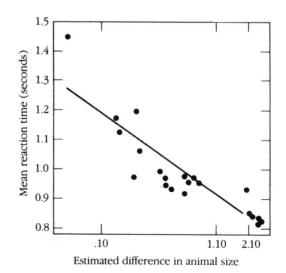

Figure 4.8 Results from Moyer (1973): Mean time to judge which of two animals is larger as a function of the estimated difference in size of the two animals. The difference measure is plotted on the abscissa in a logarithmic scale.

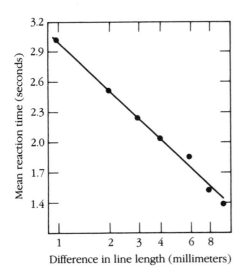

Figure 4.9 Results from Johnson (1939): Mean time to judge which of two lines is longer as a function of the difference in line length. The difference measure is plotted on the abscissa in a logarithmic scale.

longer. Figure 4.9 plots subject judgment time as a function of the log difference in line length. Again, a linear relation is obtained. It is reasonable to expect perceptual judgments to take longer the more similar the quantities being compared are, since discriminating accurately is more difficult in such circumstances. The fact that similar functions are obtained when mental objects are compared indicates that making mental comparisons involves difficulties of discrimination similar to those involved in perceptual comparisons.

◆─────────────────────────────

Just as with pictures, subjects experience greater difficulty in judging the relative size of two images that are similar in size.

─────────────────────────────

Two Types of Imagery

We have reviewed the Brooks research that indicates that people are sensitive to the spatial structure of their images and the Moyer research that indicates people process visual details like size. The distinction between spatial and visual attributes of imagery has proved important in recent research. Spatial representations are not tied to the visual modality but can be accessed tactually or auditorily. There seems to be common spatial representation that can receive information from any modality. On the other hand, certain aspects of visual experience, such as color, are unique to the visual modality and seem quite different from spatial information. Intuitively, imagery seems to involve both the spatial and the visual components.

Farah, Hammond, Levine, and Calvanio (1988) have provided evidence that there may be both kinds of imagery—that involving visual properties and that involving spatial properties. In Chapters 1 and 2, we noted that tasks that involved recognition of visual objects and patterns seemed to be performed in the temporal lobe, whereas visual or tactile tasks that involved the location of objects tended to be performed in the parietal lobe. Farah et al. argue that these same cortical regions are used in imagery tasks that do not involve any external stimuli. They also argue that imagery tasks that involve spatial judgments will be performed in the parietal regions and will not show modality-specific effects. In contrast, imagery tasks that require access to visual details will be performed in the temporal region and will show modality-specific effects.

Farah et al. provide some supportive data that was collected from a subject who had suffered bilateral temporal damage. They compared his performance on a wide variety of imagery tasks to that of normal subjects. They found that he had problems only on a subset of these tasks: tasks where he had to make judgments about color (What is the color of a football?), where he had to judge sizes (Which is bigger, a popsicle or a pack of cigarettes?), where he had to judge lengths of animals' tails (Does a kangaroo have a long tail?), and where he had to judge whether two states in the United States had similar shapes. In contrast, he did not show any deficit on tasks that seemed to involve a substantial amount of spatial processing—mental rotation, image scanning, letter scanning (as in Figure 4.7), or judgments of where one state was relative to another state. Thus, temporal damage seemed only to affect those imagery tasks that required access to visual detail and not those that required spatial judgments. It would seem that spatial information can be represented in a modality-free way during imagery but that we have a separate imagery system that comes into play when we have to process distinctly visual information.

◆
Neuropsychological evidence suggests that different areas of the brain may be responsible for supporting the spatial and visual aspects of imagery.

Are Visual Images Like Visual Perception?

A significant issue concerns the degree to which visual images are similar to visual perception. In one experiment, Finke, Pinker, and Farah (1989) asked subjects to create mental images and then engage in a series of transformations of these images. Here are a couple of examples of the problems that they read to their subjects:

- Imagine a capital letter N. Connect a diagonal line from the top right corner to the bottom left corner. Now rotate the figure 90 degrees to the right. What do you see?

- Imagine a capital letter D. Rotate the figure 90 degrees to the left. Now place a capital letter J at the bottom. What do you see?

Subjects closed their eyes and tried to imagine these transformations as they were read to them. The subjects were able to recognize their composite images just as if they had been presented with them. In the first case above they saw an hourglass, in the second case an umbrella. The ability to perform such tasks illustrates an important function of imagery in enabling us to construct new objects in our minds and inspect them. It is just this sort of visual synthesis that structural engineers or architects must perform as they design new artifacts.

The Finke et al. study shows that we can make judgments on imagined objects and come to the same conclusions as the judgments we could make on seen objects. However, are these imagined objects really the same as seen objects? Researchers have been doing studies to see if subtle properties associated with visual perception are also reproduced for mental images. For instance, Wallace (1984) did an experiment that involved presenting subjects with the stimuli either in Figure 4.10a or 4.10b. In part b they were asked to imagine an inverted V superimposed over the two horizontal lines so that their mental image had the same components as the physical stimulus in part a. Subjects in both conditions were to rate the length of the two horizontal lines. Subjects in part a rated the top line as longer, even though it is not. This replicates a classical illusion in visual perception known as the Ponzo illusion (Berbaum & Chung, 1981). Subjects in the imagery condition, shown only the two visual lines in part b, rated the top line longer and by the same amount. Thus, it appears that the imagery system can reproduce a detailed visual illusion, supporting the apparent equivalence between the imagery and perception.

Chambers and Reisberg (1985) reported a study that seemed to indicate that there were differences between having an image and actually seeing the object. Their research appears to involve processing reversible figures like the duck-rabbit figure shown in Figure 4.11. Subjects were briefly shown the figure and asked to form an image of it. Subjects had only enough time to form one interpretation of the picture before it was removed, but they were asked to try to find a second interpretation of the image. Subjects were not able to do this. Then, they were asked to draw the image on paper to see if they could then reinterpret it. In this

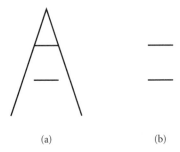

(a) (b)

Figure 4.10 Figures used by Wallace (1984) to study the Ponzo illusion in imagery. (Reprinted by permission of the Psychonomic Society, Inc.)

Figure 4.11 The ambiguous duck-rabbit figure. (From Chambers & Reisberg, 1985. Reprinted by permission of the APA.)

circumstance, they were successful. This suggests that visual images differ from pictures in that they are committed to a particular interpretation.

However, more recently Peterson, Kihlstrom, Rose, and Gilsky (1992) were able to get subjects to reverse images by giving them more explicit instructions. For instance, subjects might be told how to reverse another figure or given the instructions to consider the back of the head of the animal in their image as the front of the head of another animal. Thus, it seems that it may be more difficult to reverse an image than a picture but both are capable of being reversed. In general, it seems harder to process an image than the actual stimulus. If given a choice, people will almost always choose to process an actual picture of a situation rather than imagine it. For instance, players of Tetris prefer to rotate shapes on the screen to find an appropriate orientation rather than rotate them in their head (Kirsh & Maglio, 1994).

In addition to the behavioral data that we have reviewed indicating the similarity between perception and imagery, there is now neural imaging data. For instance, Kosslyn, Alpert, Thompson, Maljkovic, Weise, Chabris, Hamilton, Rauch, and Buonanno (1993) compared imagery and perception. They had subjects either view block letters or image them. They measured activity in the primary visual cortex (area 17 in the brain-map in the inside cover) using the PET methodology described in Chapter 1. This is the area where visual information first reaches the brain from subcortical structures and is involved in relatively low-level perception. In another study, they asked subjects to imagine large versus small letters. In the small condition, activity in the visual cortex occurred in a more posterior region closer to where the center of the visual field is represented (recall that the visual field is topographically represented). This would make sense because a small image would be more concentrated at the center of the visual field.

Le Bihan, Turner, Zeffiro, Cuenod, Jezzard, and Bonnerot (1993) found similar evidence using the fMRI technology also described in Chapter 1. Subjects were alternatively shown patterns or asked to imagine them. They recorded from the same primary visual cortex that Kosslyn et al. studied.

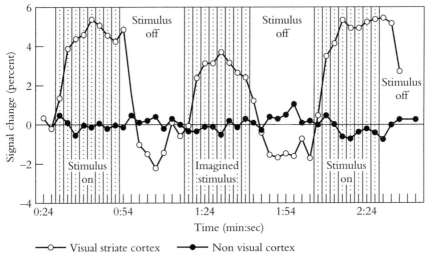

Figure 4.12 Plot of activity over time in striate cortex measured by MRI, as a function of the subject's activity. The amount of activation when the stimulus is imagined is very similar to the amount of activation when the stimulus is present.

Figure 4.12 shows the results in terms of amount of cortical activity measured by fMRI. When subjects imagine the stimulus there is almost as much activation as when the stimulus is present. Both this study and the study of Kosslyn et al. point to the involvement of basic visual processing in mental imagery.

◆

Visual images share many properties with the products of visual perception, but it is not as easy to reinterpret visual images as actual pictures.

Hierarchical Structure of Images

Complex mental images tend to be organized into pieces where each piece represents part of the whole structure. Consider Figure 4.13a, which illustrates this point. Reed presented subjects with such forms and asked them to hold images of the forms in their minds (Reed, 1974; Reed & Johnsen,

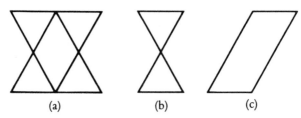

Figure 4.13 Forms used by Reed in his studies concerning the components of images. Forms (b) and (c) are all contained in form (a). However, subjects appear to see form (b) as part of form (a) more easily than they can see form (c) as part of form (a). (From Reed, 1974.)

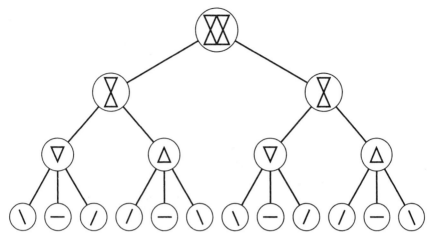

Figure 4.14 One possible hierarchical decomposition of Figure 4.13a.

1975). The form was removed, and the subjects were presented with parts of the form, as shown in 4.13b and c. Subjects were able to identify form b as part of form a 65 percent of the time but were successful with form c only 10 percent of the time. The reason for the difference was that subjects' image of form a consisted of parts such as form b but not form c. As we noted earlier with respect to the experiment of Palmer (see Figure 2.13), the input from visual perception has a similar hierarchical organization.

Complex images can be formed from a hierarchy of units. For instance, Figure 4.14 illustrates one of the possible hierarchical decompositions of the Figure 4.13a. It can be considered to be composed of two hourglass figures, and these to be composed of two triangles. Moreover, the images of the triangles themselves consist of units—namely, lines. The term **chunk** is frequently used in cognitive psychology to refer to a unit of knowledge representation like the triangle (e.g., Miller, 1956; Simon, 1974). At one level, a chunk combines a number of primitive units. At another level, it is a basic unit in a larger structure. Subjects who had such a hierarchical representation of the figure would be able to quickly recognize Figure 4.13b because it is a subchunk of their image.

In another research effort showing evidence for hierarchical organization of spatial images, McNamara, Hardy, and Hirtle (1989) had subjects come into a 20 x 22 foot room and try to memorize the location of the twenty-eight objects illustrated in Figure 4.15. By various measures they were able to show that subjects broke up the overall room into subareas and formed separate subimages of the objects in a particular subarea. For instance, subjects were more rapidly able to recall seeing an object from a subarea if they had just recalled another object from that subarea than if they had recalled an object the same distance away but from another subarea. Subjects were idiosyncratic in their methods of breaking up the

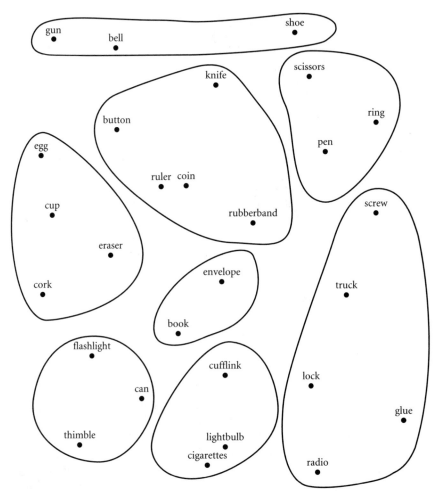

Figure 4.15 A layout used in the experiment by McNamara et al. (1989). The circles indicate hierarchical organization imposed by one subject on this array. Circles enclose objects in the same chunk.

room into subimages. Figure 4.15 shows the organization imposed by one subject.

◆

Visual images are organized hierarchically, with image parts or chunks organized within larger image parts or chunks.

Cognitive Maps

Another important function of visual imagery is in reasoning about the spatial structure of our environment. The imaginal representations that we have of our world are often referred to as **cognitive maps**. In the case

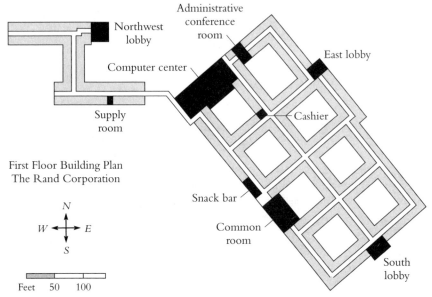

Figure 4.16 The floor plan for part of the Rand building used in a study by Thorndyke and Hayes-Roth (1982).

of cognitive maps, the connection between imagery and action is particularly apparent. We often find ourselves imagining our environment as we plan how we will get from one location to another.

There is evidence (Hart & Moore, 1973) that as children develop, their cognitive maps progress from what are called **route maps** to **survey maps**. Adults often show the same sequence in learning about a new area. A route map is a path that indicates specific places but contains no two-dimensional information. Thus, with a pure route map, if your route from location 1 to location 2 were blocked, you would have no general idea of where location 2 was, and so you would be unable to construct a detour. Also, if you knew (in the sense of a route map) two routes from a source, you would have no idea whether these routes formed a 90° angle or a 120° angle with respect to each other. A survey map, in contrast, contains this information.

Thorndyke and Hayes-Roth (1982) investigated secretaries' knowledge of the Rand building (illustrated in Figure 4.16), a large, mazelike building, in Santa Monica, California. They found that secretaries quickly acquired an ability to find their ways from one specific place in the building to another—for example, from the supply room to the cashier. This knowledge represents a route map. However, typically, secretaries had to have years of experience in the Rand building before they were capable of making such survey-map determinations as the direction of the lunch room from the photocopy room.

◆

With experience, route-map representations of our environment evolve into survey-map representations.

Map Distortions

Subjects' mental maps appear to have the hierarchical structure associated with other spatial images. Consider your mental map of the United States. It is probably divided into regions, and these regions into states, and cities are presumably pinpointed within the states. It turns out that certain systematic distortions arise because of the hierarchical structure of these mental maps. Stevens and Coupe (1978) documented a set of misconceptions people have about North American geography. Consider the following questions taken from their research:

- Which is farther east: San Diego or Reno?
- Which is farther north: Seattle or Montreal?
- Which is farther west: The Atlantic or the Pacific entrance to the Panama Canal?

The first choice is the correct answer in each case, but most people hold the wrong opinion. Reno seems to be farther east because Nevada is east of California, but this reasoning does not account for the curve in California's coastline. Montreal seems to be north of Seattle, since Canada is north of the United States, but the border dips in the east. And the Atlantic is certainly east of the Pacific, but consult a map if you need to be convinced about the Panama Canal. The geography of North America is quite complex, and subjects resort to abstract facts about relative locations of large physical bodies (e.g., California and Nevada) to make judgments about smaller locations (e.g., San Diego and Reno).

Stevens and Coupe were able to demonstrate such confusions with experimenter-created maps. Figure 4.17 illustrates the maps that different groups of subjects learned. The important feature of the incongruent maps is that the relative location of the Alpha and Beta Counties is inconsistent with the X and Y cities. After learning the maps, subjects were asked a series of questions about the locations of cities, including *Is X east or west of Y?* for the left-hand maps, and *Is X north or south of Y?* for the right-hand maps. Subjects were in error 18 percent of the time on the X-Y question for the congruent maps and 15 percent for the homogeneous maps, but they were in error 45 percent of the time for the incongruent maps. Subjects were using information about the location of the counties to help them remember the city locations. This reliance on "higher-order" information led them to make errors, just as

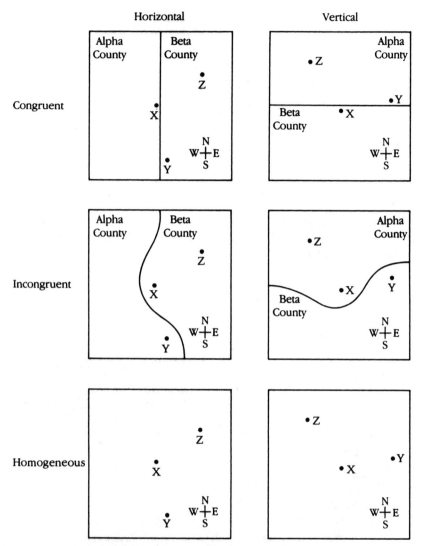

Figure 4.17 Maps studied by subjects in the experiments of Stevens and Coupe (1978), which demonstrated the effects of "higher-order" information (location of county lines) on subjects' recall of city locations.

similar reasoning can lead to errors in questions about North American geography.

◆

When people have to reason about the relative position of two locations, they will often reason in terms of the relative positions of larger areas that contain these two locations.

Translating from Words to Images

Another important use of spatial cognition occurs when we hear a textual description of a spatial structure and have to come up with an image of the situation described. For instance, this happens when we process directions, a description of an event, or hear a sportscast. The British psychologist Alan Baddeley reported that he was not able to drive while trying to follow an American football game on the radio because of the conflicting imagery. As an example of the task of constructing a spatial image, try reading the description in Table 4.2. Franklin and Tversky (1990) presented subjects with such stories. After reading the stories, subjects were asked to reorient themselves with descriptions like

> *As you remain where you are on the balcony, you turn your body 90 degrees to your right, and you now face the lamp. You look again at the short, rigid pole by which it is fixed to the wall. Perhaps this is a precautionary feature in case of earthquake.*

Table 4.2

You are hob-nobbing at the opera. You came tonight to meet and chat with interesting members of the upper class. At the moment, you are standing next to the railing of a wide, elegant balcony overlooking the first floor. Directly behind you, at your eye level, is an ornate lamp attached to the balcony wall. The base of the lamp, which is attached to the wall, is gilded in gold. Straight ahead of you, mounted on a nearby wall beyond the balcony, you see a large bronze plaque dedicated to the architect who designed the theatre. A simple likeness of the architect, as well as a few sentences about him, are raised slightly against the bronze background. Sitting on the shelf directly to your right is a beautiful bouquet of flowers. You see that the arrangement is largely composed of red roses and white carnations. Looking up, you see that a large loudspeaker is mounted to the theatre's ceiling about 20 feet directly above you. From its orientation, you suppose that it is a private speaker for the patrons who sit in this balcony. Leaning over the balcony's railing and looking down, you see that a marble sculpture stands on the first floor directly below you. As you peer down toward it, you see that it is a young man and wonder if it is a reproduction of Michelangelo's *David*.

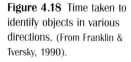 **Figure 4.18** Time taken to identify objects in various directions. (From Franklin & Tversky, 1990).

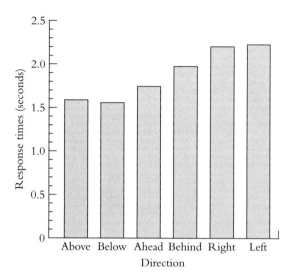

Then they were asked to judge what was in a specific direction. For instance, they might be asked to judge what is above them. On different trials they would be asked what is to their right, to their left, above, below, behind, and in front of them.

Figure 4.18 shows the times that subjects took to make their judgments in the various directions. As can be seen, subjects were fastest to make above-below judgments and slowest to make right-left judgments. Franklin and Tversky point out that such results make sense if we assume that subjects are constructing a spatial framework while reading the description. The up-down vertical axis and the front-back horizontal axis are both quite salient when we navigate in the real world. In contrast, we suffer many left-right confusions because of the bilateral symmetries of the body. We have similar confusions about left and right in our images.

In another experiment Taylor and Tversky (1992) compared the relative effectiveness of three types of spatial information: what they called route descriptions, what they called survey descriptions, and actual maps. The route descriptions described a mental tour through the environment while the survey descriptions gave a bird's-eye description of the environment. Then subjects had to verify route or survey statements about the environment. A survey might be:

Horseshoe Drive runs along the northern shore of Pigeon Lake.

A route statement might be:

Driving from the Town Hall to the gas station, you pass Maple Street on your right.

Subjects were asked to judge whether these sentences were true of the environment. They were equally fast at judging such questions whether they had studied route descriptions, or survey descriptions, or actual maps. From this result, Taylor and Tversky conclude that people are quite effective in constructing cognitive maps from verbal descriptions.

◆
We can convert verbal descriptions into rich cognitive maps of our environment.

Representation of Verbal Information

The second type of knowledge representation in Paivio's dual-code scheme was the verbal. As was the case with visual images, there is evidence for different types of verbal images. For instance, one might want to distinguish between representations of the sound of words versus their printed forms. In addition, there is one component of verbal representations—that having to do with their serial order—which seems to apply to more than verbal material. Words are only one kind of object that are capable of being ordered serially. One can think about the serial order of events or files in a drawer. It is thought in cognitive psychology that we have some general capacity for reasoning about serial order independent of the kind of thing being ordered. Thus, the situation with respect to representation of verbal information is quite analogous to the situation with respect to visual imagery. There, we saw evidence that there were separate representations of amodal spatial information and of pictorial information. Correspondingly, there appear to be separate representations of amodal serial order and the sound or sensory properties of verbal material. With respect to sensory properties, the same string of words will be represented quite differently depending on whether it is written or heard.

Much of the research on verbal memory comes from presenting subjects with a series of verbal items and asking them to repeat them back. For instance, subjects might be presented with a sequence of letters and asked to repeat them back. One of the pieces of evidence pointing to acoustic representation is the existence of acoustic confusions on subjects' recall. Conrad (1964) found that when subjects misremembered letters they often intruded a sound-alike letter. For instance, if asked to remember the sequence of letters HBKLMW, subjects are much more likely to misrecall B as the sound-alike V than as an S. As a non-laboratory example of an acoustic confusion, my wife reports she said the Pledge of Allegiance as a child as "I pledge allegiance to the flag of the United States of America. And to the republic for which it stands, one nation, under God, INVISIBLE, with liberty and justice for all." Perhaps you can recall similar errors from your childhood.[1]

◆
[1]Raised as a Canadian, I was denied such memories of the Pledge of Allegiance.

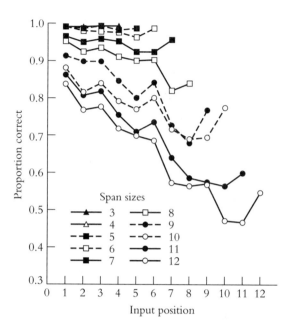

Figure 4.19 Probability of correct positional recall for items in serial lists of various lengths. (From Anderson, Bothell, Lebiere & Matessa, 1998.)

Experiments also provide evidence for the representation of serial-order information. While much of this research is done with letters, words, or other verbal stimuli, similar results can be obtained when one looks for memory in the order of pictures or events. A typical experiment presents a sequence of elements and looks at subjects' accuracy in reproducing the items from the list. A striking phenomenon in this research is what is referred to as front anchoring. Subjects are much better at reproducing the first elements of the list. Figure 4.19 shows some data of ours from an experiment (Anderson, Bothell, Lebiere, & Matessa, 1998) where we looked at subjects' memories for sequences of digits varying in length from three to twelve items. The figure plots the probability of correct recall of an item as a function of where it occurred in the list. The data shows high recall for the first items in the list; recall then falls off until the very end, when there is a small upturn for the last item. The advantage for early items in a list turns out not just to be true for humans. Chen, Swartz, and Terrace (1997) have shown a similar front-anchoring advantage when monkeys reproduce lists of items. On the other hand, some other species do not show these effects. For instance, pigeons can remember sequences of items and reproduce these by pecking. In such tasks, pigeons show best memory for the last elements in a sequence and no advantage for the first item.

An experiment by Sternberg (1969) also shows the importance of front anchoring in a serial ordering. He asked subjects to memorize strings of up to seven digits and then to generate the next item in the string after a probe digit. Thus, a subject might be given 38926 and be asked

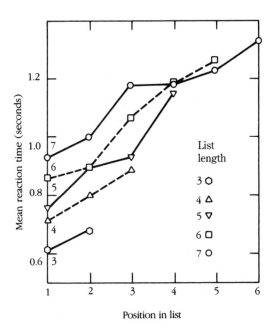

Figure 4.20 Time to generate the next digit in a string of digits as a function of the ordinal position in the string and the length of the list. (From Sternberg, 1969.)

for the digit after 9, in which case the answer would be 2. Figure 4.20 illustrates the results from his experiment as a function of the position of the probe digit in the sequence of digits for lists of varying lengths. Note that subjects are fastest to access the first digit and that they get progressively slower toward the end of the string. It has been suggested that subjects answer such questions by starting at the beginning of the string, searching forward until they find the probe, and then generating the next digit.

◆

Serial-order information is represented in a way such that information about the beginning elements is most available and such that we can serially search through the information.

Hierarchical Encoding of Serial-Order Information

So far we have discussed the representation of rather short sequences of elements. What happens with longer sequences? There is considerable evidence that subjects store long sequences hierarchically, with sub-sequences as units in larger sequences. This is similar to the hierarchical representation for mental images (e.g., Fig 4.14). So, for instance, consider how people might represent the order of the twenty-six letters in the alphabet. A possible hierarchical representation, based on the "Alphabet Song," is illustrated in Figure 4.21. This song is in turn based on the rhythm and melody of "Twinkle, Twinkle Little Star," and this correspondence is also illustrated in the figure. Thus, the alphabet is a hierarchical structure

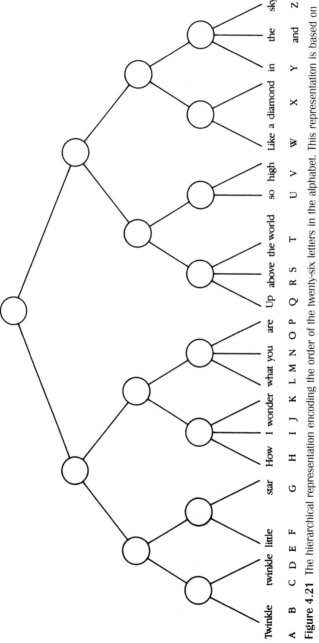

Figure 4.21 The hierarchical representation encoding the order of the twenty-six letters in the alphabet. This representation is in turn based on the hierarchical structure of "Twinkle, Twinkle, Little Star."

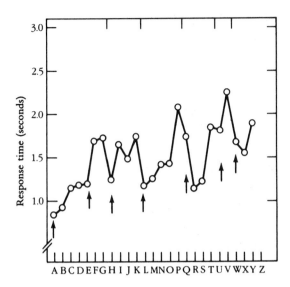

Figure 4.22 Time to generate the next letter in the alphabet. Arrows indicate beginning of new major constituents in the hierarchical encoding. (From Klahr et al., 1983. Copyright ©1983 by the APA. Adapted by permission.)

whose major constituents are ABCD, EFG, HIJK, LMNOP, QRST, UV, WXYZ.[2] In the "Alphabet Song" there are pauses, as indicated here by the commas, between the sublists.

Klahr, Chase, and Lovelace (1983) did an experiment to look for effects of this hierarchical structure on time to generate the next letter in the alphabet. A subject in this experiment might be given K and asked to generate the next letter (L). Figure 4.22 shows the generation times for each letter in the alphabet. Note that generation times are fastest at the beginning of a major constituent and get progressively slower toward the end of the constituent. Thus, within a constituent, subjects' judgment times show the same front-anchoring effect found by Sternberg. Klahr et al. theorize that subjects have access to the beginning of a sublist and search forward for the target letter.

The research of Johnson (1970) provides more evidence for the reality of the hierarchical structure of long lists. He had subjects commit to memory random strings of letters, but used spacing to encourage a particular hierarchical organization. So he might present his subjects with the following string to memorize:

DY JHQ GW

He assumed that subjects would set up hierarchies in which the individual phrases would be strings like JHQ, as dictated by the spacing. He looked at subjects' later recall of these strings and found that they tended to recall

---

[2]Another variant of the "Alphabet Song" segments it as QRS, TUV.

these substrings as units. If subjects recalled the first letter of a substring, there was only a 10 percent probability of failing to recall the next letter. For instance, if they recalled the J, they would very likely recall the H. There was not the same tendency across unit barriers. For instance, if the subjects recalled Y in the foregoing string, they would fail 30 percent of the time to recall the J that follows.

◆

Subjects organize long sequences of items hierarchically with sub-sequences as elements of higher-order sequence units.

Conclusions about Perceptual Knowledge Representations

We have seen that people can process imagined information very much like the way in which they process perceptual information. In many cases, similar neural areas seem to be involved in imaginal processing as in perceptual processing. This is remarkable because there is no incoming perceptual input to stimulate these areas. In some cases, such as the mental synthesis tasks (e.g., Finke, Pinker, & Farah, 1989), there never was an original perceptual experience. Rather, these imagined experiences are being generated by higher-level cognition. Also remarkable is the fact that, while there are rare controversial reports of occasional confusion of imagery and perception (Perky, 1910), we are largely able to keep what we imagine separate from what we perceive.

Remarks and Suggested Readings

Paivio (1971, 1986) should be consulted for a description of his dual-code theory and particularly his theory of visual imagery. Kosslyn and Koenig (1992) present Kosslyn's view of visual cognition and imagery, and the evidence from cognitive neuroscience. Farah (1995) reviews the research on the neural basis of imagery. Tversky (in press) reviews research on cognitive maps. Reisberg (1992) has edited a book on auditory imagery.

5

Meaning-Based Knowledge Representations

Recall a wedding you attended a while ago. Presumably, you can remember who married whom, probably where the wedding was, many of the people at the wedding, and some of the things that happened. However, you would probably be hard pressed to say exactly what all the participants wore, the exact words that were said, the number of steps that the bride took walking down the aisle, and so on—although you probably registered all of these details. It seems we have the ability to remember the gist of an event without recalling many of its exact details.

The previous chapter was concerned with knowledge representations that retain much of the detail of the original event. Unfortunately, this detail can often get in the way of what we are likely to need to remember. It is much more likely that we will want to remember if a friend was at the wedding than simply what the friend wore. We will probably want to remember that the bride's mother said to us that she did not originally like the groom more than the exact words she used to communicate this or whether she was sitting or standing while saying this. In addition we are inclined to want to remember whether a priest or a rabbi performed the ceremony rather than what his or her name was. Fortunately, our minds have an ability to best remember what is most important. This chapter is concerned with how such information is encoded in what are called **meaning-based representations**.

A fair amount of research in cognitive psychology has been devoted to documenting the importance of such meaning-based memories and establishing that they are different from perception-based memories. We will review that research and then consider two types of meaning-based representations: propositional structures that encode the significant information about a particular event (such as who married whom in the wedding) and schemas that represent categories of events and objects in terms of their typical properties (such as what typically happens at a wedding).

Memory for Meaningful Interpretations of Events

Memory for Verbal Information

In the last chapter we discussed verbal images that can store information about the exact order of words. There is no doubt that we use such representations to encode some verbal information. That is, sometimes we can remember verbatim lines from poems, songs, plays, and speeches. However, considerable doubt exists as to whether all or even most of our memory for verbal communication can be accounted for in terms of memory for the verbatim message.

An experiment by Wanner (1968) illustrates circumstances in which people do and do not remember information about exact wording. Wanner asked subjects to come into the laboratory and listen to tape-recorded instructions. For one group of subjects, the warned group, the tape began this way:

> The materials for this test, including the instructions, have been recorded on tape. Listen very carefully to the instructions because you will be tested on your ability to recall particular sentences which occur in the instructions.

The second group received no such warning and so had no idea that they would be responsible for the verbatim instructions. After this point the instructions were the same for both groups. At a later point in the instructions, one of four possible critical sentences occurred:

1. *When you score your results, do nothing to correct your answers but mark carefully those answers which are wrong.*

2. *When you score your results, do nothing to correct your answers but carefully mark those answers which are wrong.*

3. *When you score your results, do nothing to your correct answers but mark carefully those answers which are wrong.*

4. *When you score your results, do nothing to your correct answers but carefully mark those answers which are wrong.*

Immediately after presentation of one of these sentences, all subjects (warned or not) heard the following conclusion to the instructions:

To begin the test, please turn to page 2 of the answer booklet and judge which of the sentences printed there occurred in the instructions you just heard.

On page 2 they found the critical sentence they had just heard plus a similar alternative. Suppose they had heard sentence 1. They might have to choose between sentences 1 and 2 or between sentences 1 and 3. Both pairs differ in the ordering of two words. However, the difference between 1 and 2 does not contribute critically to the meaning of the sentences; the difference is just stylistic. On the other hand, sentences 1 and 3 clearly do differ in meaning. Thus, by looking at subjects' ability to discriminate between different pairs of sentences, Wanner was able to measure their ability to remember the meaning versus the style of the sentence and to determine how this ability interacted with whether or not they were warned. The relevant data are in Figure 5.1.

The percentage of correct identifications of sentences heard is displayed as a function of whether subjects had been warned. The percentages are plotted separately for subjects who were asked to discriminate a meaning-ful difference in wording and for those who were asked to discriminate a stylistic difference. If subjects were just guessing, they would have scored 50 percent correct by chance; thus we would not expect any values below 50 percent.

The implications of Wanner's experiment are clear. First, memory is better for changes in wording that result in changes of meaning than for changes in wording that result just in changes of style. The superiority of memory for meaning indicates that people normally extract the meaning from a linguistic message and do not remember its exact wording. More-over, memory for meaning is equally good whether subjects are warned or not. (The slight advantage for unwarned subjects does not approach

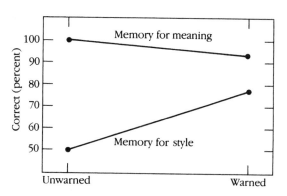

Figure 5.1 Ability of warned versus unwarned subjects to remember a wording difference that affected meaning versus style. (Adapted from Wanner, 1968.)

statistical significance.) Thus, subjects retain the meaning of a message as a normal part of their comprehension process. They do not have to be especially cued to remember the sentence.

The second implication of these results is that the warning did have an effect on memory for the stylistic change. Subjects were almost at chance in remembering stylistic change when unwarned, but they were fairly good at remembering it when warned. This result indicates that we do not naturally retain much information about exact wording, but that we can do so when we are especially cued to pay attention to such information. Even with such a warning, however, memory for stylistic information is poorer than memory for meaning.

◆

After processing a linguistic message, people normally remember just its meaning and not its exact wording.

Memory for Visual Information

On many occasions, our memory capacity seems much greater for visual information than for verbal information. Paivio used this differential memorability as part of the evidence for his dual-code theory—see discussion of this theory in Chapter 4. A representative experiment was reported by Shepard (1967) in which he had subjects study a set of magazine pictures one picture at a time. After studying the pictures, subjects were presented with pairs of pictures consisting of one they had studied and one they had not studied. The subjects' task was to recognize which picture of each pair had been studied. This task was contrasted with a verbal situation in which subjects studied sentences and were similarly tested on their abilities to recognize studied sentences when presented with pairs containing one new and one studied sentence. Subjects exhibited 11.8 percent errors in the sentence condition but only 1.5 percent errors in the picture condition; in other words, recognition memory was fairly high in the sentence condition, but it was virtually perfect in the picture condition. There have been a number of experiments like Shepard's. His experiment involved 600 pictures. Perhaps the most impressive demonstration of visual memory is the experiment by Standing (1973), who showed that subjects had only a 17 percent error rate after studying 10,000 pictures.

While subjects show very good memory for pictures, what they seem to be remembering is some interpretation of the picture rather than the exact picture. That is, it proves useful to distinguish between the meaning of a picture and the physical picture, just as it proves important to distinguish between the meaning of a sentence and the physical sentence. A number of experiments point to the utility of this distinction with respect to picture memory and to the fact that we tend to remember an interpretation of the picture, not the physical picture.

For instance, consider an experiment by Mandler and Ritchey (1977). The experimenters asked subjects to study pictures of scenes, such as the classroom scenes in Figure 5.2. After studying eight such pictures for ten seconds each, subjects were tested for their recognition memory. They were presented with a series of pictures and instructed to identify which

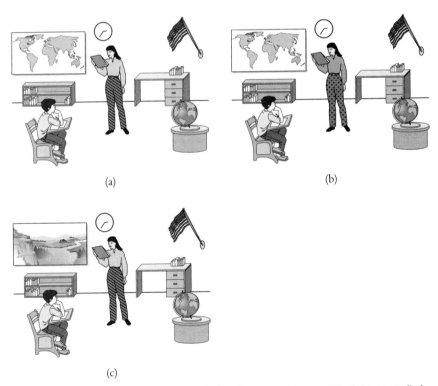

(a)

(b)

(c)

Figure 5.2 Pictures similar to those used by Mandler and Ritchey (1977). Subjects studied the target picture (a). Later they were tested with a series of pictures that included the target (a) along with token distractors such as (b) and type distractors such as (c). (Copyright © 1977 by the APA. Reprinted by permission.)

pictures they had studied in the series. The series contained the exact pictures they had studied as well as distractor pictures. A distractor such as that in part b in the figure was called a token distractor. It differs from the target only with respect to the pattern of the teacher's clothes, a visual detail relatively unimportant to most interpretations of the picture. In contrast, the distractor in part c involves a type change—from a world map to an art picture used by the teacher. This visual detail is relatively more important to most interpretations of the picture, since it indicates the subject being taught. All eight pictures shown to subjects contained possible token changes and type changes. In each case, the type change involved a more important change to the picture's meaning than did the token change. There was no systematic difference in the amount of physical change involved in a type versus a token change. Subjects were able to recognize the original pictures 77 percent of the time, reject the token distractors only 60 percent of the time, but reject the type distractors 94 percent of the time.

The conclusion in this study is very similar to that in the Wanner experiment reviewed earlier. Just as Wanner found that subjects were much more sensitive to meaning-significant changes in a sentence, so Mandler and Ritchey found that subjects are sensitive to meaning-significant changes in a picture. It may be that subjects have better memory for the meanings of pictures than for the meanings of sentences, but they have poor memory for the physical details of both.

Bower, Karlin, and Dueck (1975) reported an amusing demonstration of the fact that people's good memory for pictures is tied to their interpretation of these pictures. Figure 5.3 illustrates some of the material they used. These investigators had subjects study such pictures, called droodles, with

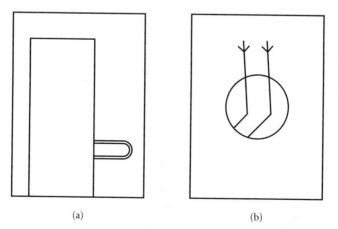

(a)   (b)

Figure 5.3 Recalling "droodles." (a) A midget playing a trombone in a telephone booth. (b) An early bird who caught a very strong worm. (From Bower, Karlin, & Dueck, 1975.)

or without an explanation of their meaning. After subjects had studied the pictures, they were given a memory test in which they had to redraw the pictures. Subjects who had been given labels with which to study the pictures showed better recall of these pictures (70 percent correctly reconstructed) than subjects who were not given the verbal labels (51 percent). Thus, memory for these drawings depended critically on subjects' ability to place a meaningful interpretation on the pictures.

◆

When people see a picture, they tend to remember a meaningful interpretation of the picture.

Retention of Detail versus Meaning

There is evidence that subjects initially encode many of the perceptual details of a sentence or a picture but that they tend to forget this information quickly. Once the perceptual information is forgotten, subjects retain memory for their interpretation of the picture. Memory for orientation of a picture is one of the visual details that appears to decay rapidly, as demonstrated in an experiment by Gernsbacher (1985). Subjects were shown pictures such as the ones in Figure 5.4. After studying one of these

Figure 5.4 Example picture from an experimental story displayed in one orientation (top) and the reverse (bottom). (From Gernsbacher, 1985. Original illustration from <u>One Frog Too Many</u> by Mercer and Mariana Meyer. Copyright © 1975 by Mercer and Mariana Meyer. Reprinted by permission of the publisher, Dial Books for Young Readers.)

pictures, the subjects were asked to judge which of the pair they had seen. At a 10-second delay, subjects displayed 79 percent accuracy in making their judgments, showing a considerable retention of information about left-right orientation. However, after 10 minutes their accuracy in judgment had fallen to 57 percent (50 percent would reflect chance guessing). On the other hand, their memory for what the picture was about remained high over that period of time.

An experiment by Anderson (1974b) made the same point in the verbal domain. Subjects listened to a story that contained various critical sentences that would be tested; for instance:

- The missionary shot the painter.

Later, subjects were presented with one of the following sentences and asked whether it followed logically from the story they had heard. They were also asked to judge which sentence they had actually heard:

1. The missionary shot the painter.

2. The painter was shot by the missionary.

3. The painter shot the missionary.

4. The missionary was shot by the painter.

The first two sentences require a positive response to the logical judgment, and the last two require a negative response. Subjects were tested either immediately after hearing the sentence or at a delay of about 2 minutes.

The delay had little effect on the accuracy of their logical judgment (e.g., 1 or 3 above)—98 percent immediately and 96 percent at a delay. However, when they were asked to judge which sentence they had heard (e.g., 1 or 2 above) there was a dramatic effect of the delay. Subjects were 99 percent correct immediately but only 56 percent correct after a delay.

◆

Memory for detail is available initially but is forgotten rapidly, whereas memory for meaning is retained.

Implications of Good Memory for Meaning

As we have shown above, people tend to have relatively good memory for meaningful interpretations of information. This implies that when people are confronted with some material to remember, it will facilitate their memory if they can place some meaningful interpretation on it. Unfortunately, many people are unaware of this fact, and their memory performance suffers as a consequence. I can still remember the traumatic experience I had in my first paired-associate experiment. It was part of a sophomore class on experimental psychology. For reasons I have long since forgotten, we had designed a class experiment that involved learning sixteen pairs, such as DAX-GIB. That is, our task was to be able to recall GIB when prompted with the cue DAX. I was determined to outperform other members of my class. My personal theory of memory at that time, which I intended to apply, was basically that if you try hard and intensely, you can remember anything well. In the impending experimental situation, this meant that during the learning period I should say (as loud as was seemly) the paired associates over and over again, as fast as I could. My theory was that by this method the paired associates would be forever burned into my mind. To my chagrin, I wound up with the worst score in the class.

My theory of "loud and fast" was directly opposed to the true means of improving memory. I was trying to commit a meaningless verbal pair to memory. But the material in this chapter suggests that we have best memory for meaningful information, not meaningless verbal information. I should have been trying to convert my memory task into something more meaningful. For instance, DAX is like *dad* and GIB is the first part of *gibberish*. So I might have created an image of my father speaking some gibberish to me. This would have been a simple **mnemonic** (memory-assisting) **technique** and would have worked quite well as a means of associating the two.

We do not often have the need to learn pairs of nonsense syllables outside the laboratory situation. However, in many situations we have to associate various combinations of terms that do not have much inherent meaning. We have to learn shopping lists, names for faces, telephone numbers, rote facts in a college class, vocabulary items in a foreign language, and so on. In all cases, we can improve memory if we transform the task into one of associating the items meaningfully.

◆
    It is easier to remember less meaningful material if it is converted into more meaningful material.

Propositional Representations

One frequently finds in cognitive psychology the use of various sorts of notation to represent the meaning of sentences and pictures. That is, these notations represent the meaningful structure that remains after the perceptual details have been abstracted away. The most common notation is some variant of what is called a **propositional representation**. In the 1970s, a number of proposals for such propositional representations appeared, including theories by Anderson and Bower (1973), Clark (1974), Frederiksen (1975), Kintsch (1974), and Norman and Rumelhart (1975). Such representations have become a common method of analyzing meaningful information in cognitive psychology. The concept of a **proposition**, borrowed from logic and linguistics, is central to such analyses. A proposition is the smallest unit of knowledge that can stand as a separate assertion; that is, the smallest unit about which it makes sense to make the judgment true or false. Propositional analysis most clearly applies to linguistic information, and it is with respect to such information that the topic is developed here. Consider the following sentence:

- Lincoln, who was president of the USA during a bitter war, freed the slaves.

The information conveyed in this sentence can be communicated by the following simpler sentences:

A. Lincoln was president of the USA during a war.

B. The war was bitter.

C. Lincoln freed the slaves.

If any of these simple sentences were false, the complex sentence would not be true. These sentences closely correspond to the propositions that underlie the meaning of the complex sentence. Each simple sentence expresses a primitive unit of meaning. One condition that our meaning representations must satisfy is that each separate unit in them correspond to a unit of meaning.

However, the propositional-representation theory does not claim that a person remembers simple sentences such as A through C. Past research indicates that subjects do not remember the exact wording of such underlying sentences any more than they remember the exact wording of the original sentence. For instance, Anderson (1972) showed that subjects would demonstrate poor ability to remember whether they had heard sentence C or the sentence:

- The slaves were freed by Lincoln.

Thus it seems that information is represented in memory in a way that preserves the meaning of the primitive assertions but does not preserve any information about wording. A number of propositional notations represent information in this abstract way. One, used by Kintsch (1974), represents each proposition as a list containing a **relation** followed by an ordered list of **arguments**. The relations organize the arguments and typically correspond to the verbs (in this case, free), adjectives (bitter), and other relational terms (president of). The arguments refer to particular times, places, people, and objects and typically correspond to the nouns (Lincoln, war, slaves). The relations assert connections among the entities referred to by these nouns. As an example, sentences A through C would be represented by these lists:

A′. (president-of, Lincoln, USA, war)

B′. (bitter, war)

C′. (free, Lincoln, slaves)

Kintsch represents each proposition by a parenthesized list consisting of a relation plus arguments as above. Note that various relations take different numbers of arguments: *president-of* takes 3, *free* takes 2, and *bitter* takes 1. Whether a person heard the original complex sentence or

- The slaves were freed by Lincoln, the president during a bitter war,

the meaning of the message would be represented by lists A′ through C′.

An interesting demonstration of the psychological reality of propositional units was provided by Bransford and Franks (1971). In this experiment, subjects studied twelve sentences, including the following:

- The ants ate the sweet jelly which was on the table.
- The rock rolled down the mountain and crushed the tiny hut.
- The ants in the kitchen ate the jelly.
- The rock rolled down the mountain and crushed the hut beside the woods.
- The ants in the kitchen ate the jelly which was on the table.
- The tiny hut was beside the woods.
- The jelly was sweet.

These sentences are all composed from two sets of four propositions. One set of four propositions can be represented:

A. (eat, ants, jelly, past)

B. (sweet, jelly)

C. (on, jelly, table, past)

D. (in, ants, kitchen, past)

The other set of four propositions can be represented:

E. (roll-down, rock, mountain, past)

F. (crush, rock, hut, past)

G. (beside, hut, woods, past)

H. (tiny, hut)

Bransford and Franks looked at subjects' recognition memory for the following three kinds of sentences:

- Old: The ants in the kitchen ate the jelly.
- New: The ants ate the sweet jelly.
- Noncase: The ants ate the jelly beside the woods.

The first kind of sentence was actually studied, the second was not but is a combination of propositions that were studied, while the third consists of words that were studied but cannot be composed from the propositions studied. Bransford and Franks found that subjects had almost no ability to discriminate between the first two kinds of sentences and were equally likely to say that they had actually heard either. On the other hand, subjects were quite confident that they had not heard the third noncase sentence.

The experiment shows that although subjects remember quite well what propositions they encounter, they are quite insensitive to the actual combination of propositions. Indeed, subjects were most likely to say they heard a sentence consisting of all four propositions, such as:

- The ants in the kitchen ate the sweet jelly which was on the table,

even though they had in fact not studied this sentence.

◆
Propositional analyses represent memory for complex sentences in terms of memory for simple, abstract propositional units.

Propositional Networks

In the cognitive psychology literature, one sometimes finds propositions represented in a network form like those in Figure 5.5, which illustrates the structure of a propositional network that encodes the sentence *Lincoln, who was president of the USA during a bitter war, freed the slaves.* In this **propositional network**, each proposition is represented by an ellipse, which is connected by labeled arrows to its relation and arguments. The propositions, the relations, and the arguments are called the **nodes** of the network, and the arrows are called the **links** because they connect nodes. For instance, the ellipse in Figure 5.5a represents proposition A′ from the earlier Kintsch analysis. This ellipse is connected to the relation *president-of* by a link labeled *relation* (to indicate that it is pointing to the relation node), to *Lincoln* by an *agent* link, *USA* by an *object* link and to *war* by a *time* link. The three network structures in parts a to c of the figure represent the individual propositions A′ through C′ listed on page 146. Note

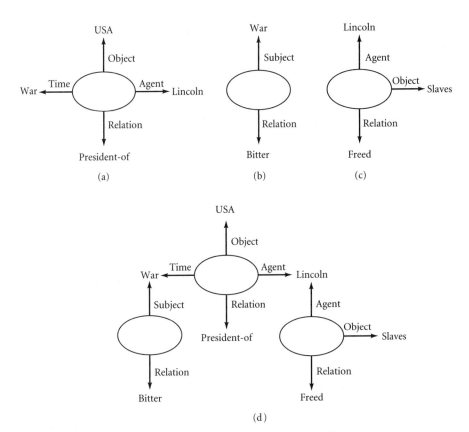

Figure 5.5 Network representations for the proposition underlying *Lincoln, who was president of the USA during a bitter war, freed the slaves.*

that these different networks contain the same nodes; for example, parts a and b both contain *war*. This overlap indicates that these networks are really interconnected parts of a larger network, which is illustrated in part d. This last network represents all the meaningful information in the original complex sentence on page 145.

The spatial location of elements in a network is totally irrelevant to the interpretation. A network can be thought of as a tangle of marbles connected by strings. The marbles represent the nodes, and the strings represent the links between the nodes. The network represented on a two-dimensional page is that tangle of marbles laid out in a certain way. We try to lay the network out in a way that facilitates its understanding, but any layout is possible. All that matters is which elements are connected to which, not where the components lie.

We now have two ways of representing the same propositional information: with a set of linear propositions, as in propositions A′ through C′, or with a network, as in Figure 5.5. Since the information represented is abstract, either notational convention will work. The linear representation is somewhat neater and more compact, but the network representation reveals the connections among elements. As we will see, this connectivity proves useful for understanding certain memory phenomena.

One of the important features about propositions is that, like spatial images and linear orderings, they can enter into hierarchical relationships in which one proposition occurs as a unit within another proposition. Parts a and b of Figure 5.6 illustrate the propositional representations for the following two sentences:

- John bought some candy because he was hungry.

- John believed Russia would invade Poland.

Note in Figure 5.6 that both the proposition *John bought some candy* and the proposition *John was hungry* occur as arguments within a larger proposition that asserts that the first proposition is caused by the second. Similarly, the proposition *Russia would invade Poland* occurs as the object of the proposition about John's believing.

It is useful to think of the nodes in such networks as ideas and to think of the links between the nodes as associations between the ideas, as a number of experiments suggest. Consider an experiment by Weisberg (1969) that used a constrained association task. In this experiment, subjects studied and committed to memory such sentences as *Children who are slow eat bread that is cold*. The propositional-network representation for this sentence is illustrated in Figure 5.7. After learning a sentence, subjects were administered free-association tasks in which they were given a word from the sentence and asked to respond with the first word from the sentence

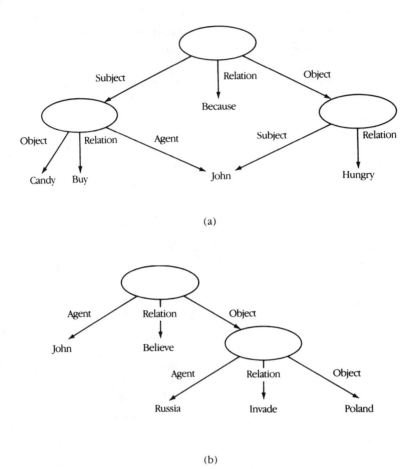

(a)

(b)

Figure 5.6 Propositional representations for (a) John bought some candy because he was hungry and (b) John believed Russia would invade Poland.

that came to mind. Subjects cued with *slow* almost always free-associated *children* and almost never *bread*, although *bread* is closer to *slow* in the sentence than *children*. However, the figure shows that *slow* and *children* are nearer each other (two links) than *slow* and *bread* (four links). Similarly, subjects cued with *bread* almost always recalled *cold* rather than *slow*,

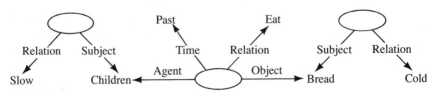

Figure 5.7 A propositional-network representation of the sentence Children who are slow eat bread that is cold.

although in the sentence *bread* and *slow* are closer than *bread* and *cold*. This is because *bread* and *cold* are closer to each other (three links) in the network than are *bread* and *slow* (five links). (A similar point was made in an experiment by Ratcliff and McKoon, 1978.)

◆

Propositional information can be represented in networks that display the relations among concepts.

Conceptual Knowledge

The topic of this chapter is meaning-based knowledge representations. The fundamental characteristic of such representations is that they involve some significant abstraction away from the experiences that originally gave rise to the knowledge. In the case of propositional representations, the principal topic of the preceding portion of this chapter, the abstraction involved deletion of many of the perceptual details and retention of the important relationships among the elements. In the same way, the subjects in the Mandler and Ritchey experiment forgot what the teacher wore but remembered the subject she taught.

There are other possible abstractions. One kind of abstraction is from specific experiences to general categorizations of the properties of that class of experiences. This sort of abstraction creates conceptual knowledge involving categories, for example, chairs and dogs. Once we have created such categories, we can use these to represent specific experiences abstractly. For instance, rather than just remembering that we were licked by a four-legged furry object that weighed about 50 pounds and had a wagging tail, we will remember that we were licked by a dog. What does the cognitive system gain by categorizing the object as a dog? Basically, we gain ability to predict. Thus, we can have expectations about what sound this creature might make and what would happen if we threw a ball (it might chase it and stop licking us). Because of this ability to predict, categories give us great economy in representation and communication. For instance, we can tell someone "I was licked by a dog," and the person can predict the number of legs on the creature, approximate size, and so on.

Research on categorization is concerned both with how these categories are formed in the first place and how they are used to interpret experience. It has also been concerned with notations for representing this categorical knowledge. We will consider in this section a number of notations that have been proposed for representing conceptual knowledge. We will start by describing two early theories. One theory is about semantic networks, which are similar to the propositional networks just considered. The other is about what are called schemas. Both theories have been closely allied to certain empirical phenomena that seem central to conceptual structure. Later in this section, after describing more empirical phenomena, we will describe two other theories of the nature of concept representation, exemplar theory and a connectionist network model.

Semantic Networks

Network representations have also been used to encode conceptual knowledge. Quillian (1966) proposed that subjects stored information about various categories such as canaries, robins, fish, and so on, in a network structure like that shown in Figure 5.8. In this figure, we represent a hierarchy of categorical facts, such as that a canary is a bird and a bird is an animal, by linking nodes for the two categories with **isa links**. Associated with the categories are properties that are true of them. Properties true of higher-level categories are also true of lower-level categories. Thus, since animals breathe, it follows that birds breathe and canaries breathe. Note that Figure 5.8 can also represent information about exceptions. For instance, even though most birds fly, the figure does represent that ostriches cannot fly.

Collins and Quillian (1969) did an experimental test of the psychological reality of such networks by having subjects judge the truth of assertions about concepts such as the following:

1. Canaries can sing.

2. Canaries have feathers.

3. Canaries have skin.

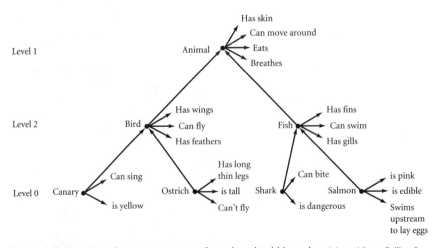

Figure 5.8 Hypothetical memory structure for a three-level hierarchy. (Adapted from Collins & Quillian, 1969. Reprinted by permission of Academic Press.)

Subjects were shown facts such as these as well as false assertions, such as *Apples have feathers*. They were asked to judge whether a statement was true or false by pressing one of two buttons. The time from presentation of the statement to the button press was measured.

Consider how subjects would answer such questions if Figure 5.8 represented their knowledge of such categories. The information to confirm sentence 1 is directly stored with *canary*. However, the information for sentence 2 is not directly stored at the *canary* node. Rather, the *have feathers* property is stored with *bird*, and sentence 2 can be inferred from the directly stored facts that *a canary is a bird* and *birds have feathers*. Again, sentence 3 is not directly stored with *canary*; rather, the *have skin* predicate is stored with *animal*. Thus, sentence 3 can be inferred from the facts *a canary is a bird* and *a bird is an animal* and *animals have skin*. Thus, with sentence 1, all the requisite information for its verification is stored with *canary*; in the case of sentence 2, subjects must traverse one link from *canary* to *bird* to retrieve the requisite information; and in sentence 3, subjects would have to traverse two links from *canary* to *animal*.

If our categorical knowledge were structured like Figure 5.8, we would expect sentence 1 to be verified more quickly than sentence 2, which would be verified more quickly than sentence 3. This is just what Collins and Quillian found. Subjects required 1310 milliseconds to make judgments about statements like sentence 1; 1380 milliseconds for sentences like 2; and 1470 milliseconds for sentences like 3. Subsequent research on the retrieval of information from memory has somewhat complicated the conclusions drawn from the initial Collins and Quillian experiment. The frequencies with which facts are experienced have been observed to have strong effects on retrieval time (e.g., Conrad, 1972). Some facts, such as *Apples are eaten*—for which the predicate could be stored with an intermediate concept such as food, but which are experienced quite frequently—are verified as fast as or faster than facts such as *Apples have dark seeds*, which must be stored more directly with the apple concept. It seems that if a fact about a concept is frequently encountered, it will be stored with that concept even if it could also be inferred from a more general concept. The following statements about the organization of facts in semantic memory and their retrieval times seem to be valid conclusions from the research:

1. If a fact about a concept is frequently encountered, it will be stored with that concept even if it could be inferred from a more superordinate concept.

2. The more frequently encountered a fact about a concept is, the more strongly that fact will be associated with the concept. And

the more strongly associated facts are with concepts, the more rapidly they are verified.

3. Verifying facts that are not directly stored with a concept but that must be inferred takes a relatively long time.

Thus, both the strength of the connections between facts and concepts (determined by frequency of experience) and the distance between them in the semantic network have effects on retrieval time. We will have much more to say about the strength factor in Chapter 6, which discusses the effects of practice on memory.

◆ When a property is not stored directly with a concept, people can retrieve it from a higher-order concept.

Schemas

Consider our knowledge of what a house is like. We know many things about houses, such as the following:

- Houses are a type of building.
- Houses have rooms.
- Houses can be built of wood, brick, or stone.
- Houses serve as human dwellings.
- Houses tend to have rectilinear and triangular shapes.
- Houses are larger than 100 square feet and smaller than 10,000 square feet.

The importance of a category is that it stores predictable information about instances of a category such as the above. So, when someone mentions a house we have a rough idea of the size of the object being referred to.

Semantic networks, which just store properties with concepts, cannot capture the approximate nature of our knowledge about a house, such as its typical size or shape. Researchers in cognitive science (e.g., Rumelhart & Ortony, 1976) proposed a particular way for representing such knowledge in cognitive science that seemed more useful than the semantic-network representation. This representational structure is called a **schema**. The concept of a schema was articulated in artificial intelligence and computer science. Readers who have experience with modern programming languages should recognize its similarity to various types of data structures (e.g., records in Pascal) that are used. The question for the psychologist is what aspects of the schema notion are appropriate for understanding how people reason about concepts. We will describe some of the properties associated with schemas and then discuss the psychological research bearing on these properties.

Schemas represent categorical knowledge according to a *slot* structure, where slots specify values that members of a category have on various attributes. So, we have the following partial schema representation of a house:

House
- *Isa*: building
- *Parts*: rooms
- *Materials*: wood, brick, stone
- *Function*: human dwelling
- *Shape*: rectilinear, triangular
- *Size*: 100–10,000 square feet

In this representation, terms like *materials* or *shape* are the attributes or **slots**, and terms like *wood, brick*, or *rectilinear* are the values. Each pair of a slot and a value specifies a typical feature. The fact that houses are typically built of materials like wood and brick does not exclude such possibilities as cardboard. Thus, the values listed above are called **default values**. For instance, the fact that we represent that birds can fly as part of our schema for birds does not prevent us from seeing ostriches as birds. We simply overwrite this default value in our representation for an ostrich.

Note that certain of these features, such as that houses serve as human dwellings, are basically propositional, whereas other features, such as that about shape and size, are basically perceptual. Thus, as noted earlier, schemas are not simply an extension of propositional representations. Rather, they are ways of encoding regularities in categories, whether these regularities are perceptual or propositional. They are abstract in the sense that they encode what is generally true rather than what is true about a specific instance. Thus, our schema is for houses in general, not a particular house. Hence, we do not represent information that is true only of a specific house, whether its color is white or whether it is located in Pittsburgh. So, whereas propositions can represent what is important about specific things, schemas can represent what specific things tend to have in common.

A special slot in each schema is its *isa* slot, which is like the *isa* link in a semantic network, and points to the superset. Basically, unless contradicted, a concept inherits the features of its superset. Thus, stored with the schema for *building*, the superset of *house*, we would have features such as that it has a roof and walls and that it is found on the ground. This information is not represented in the above schema for *house* because it can be inferred from *building*. As illustrated in Figure 5.8, these *isa* links can create a hierarchy called a generalization hierarchy.

Schemas have another type of hierarchy, called a part hierarchy. Thus, parts of houses, such as walls and rooms, have their own schema definitions. Stored with schemas for *walls* and *rooms*, these parts have windows and ceilings. Thus, using the part relationships, we would be able to infer that houses have windows and ceilings.

Schemas are abstractions from specific instances that can be used to make inferences about instances of the concepts they represent. If we know something is a house, we can use the schema definition to infer that it is probably made of wood or brick and that it has walls, windows, and the like. However, the inferential processes for schemas must be able to deal with exceptions. So, we can still understand what a house without a roof is. Also, it is necessary to understand the constraints between the slots of a schema. So if we hear of a house that is underground, we can infer that it will not have windows.

◆

Schemas represent concepts in terms of supersets, parts, and other attribute-value pairs.

Psychological Reality of Schemas

One property of schemas is that they have default values for certain schema attributes. This provides schemas with a useful inferential mechanism. If you recognize an object as being a member of a certain category, you can infer—unless explicitly contradicted—that it has the default values associated with that concept's schema. Brewer and Treyens (1981) provided an interesting demonstration of the effects of schemas on memory inferences. Thirty subjects were brought individually to the room shown in Figure 5.9. They were told that this was the office of the experimenter, and they were asked to wait there while the experimenter went to the laboratory to see if the previous subject had finished. After 35 seconds, the experimenter returned and took the waiting subject to a nearby seminar room. Here, the subject was asked to write down everything he or she could remember about the experimental room. What would you be able to recall?

Brewer and Treyens predicted that their subjects' recall would be strongly influenced by their schema of what an office contains. Subjects would do very well recalling items that are part of that schema; they should do much less well at recalling office items that are not part of the schema; they should falsely recall things that are part of the typical office but not of this one. This is just the pattern of results that Brewer and Treyens found. For instance, twenty-nine of the thirty subjects recalled that the office had a chair, a desk, and walls. However, only eight subjects recalled that it had

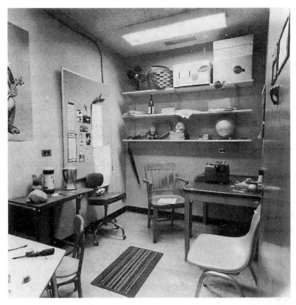

Figure 5.9 The experimental room used in the memory experiment of Brewer and Treyens (1981).

a bulletin board or a skull. On the other hand, nine subjects recalled that it had books, which it did not. Thus, we see that a person's memory for the properties of a location is strongly influenced by that person's default assumptions about what is typically found in the location. A schema is a way of encoding these default assumptions.

◆
People will infer that an object has the default values for its category, unless they explicitly notice otherwise.

Degree of Category Membership

One of the important features of schemas is that they allow variation in the objects that might fit a particular schema. There are constraints on what typically occupies various slots of a schema, but there are few absolute prohibitions. This suggests that if schemas encode our knowledge about various object categories, we ought to see a shading from less typical to more typical members of the category as the features of the members better satisfy the schema constraints. There is now considerable evidence that natural categories like *birds* have the kind of structure that would be expected of a schema.

Early research documenting such variation in category membership has been done by Rosch. In one experiment (Rosch, 1973), she instructed subjects to rate the typicality of various members of a category on a 1 to 7 scale, where 1 meant very typical and 7 meant very atypical. Subjects consistently rated some members as more typical than other members. In the bird category, *robin* got an average rating of 1.1, and *chicken* a rating of 3.8. In reference to sports, *football* was thought to be very typical (1.2), whereas *weight lifting* was not (4.7). *Murder* was rated a very typical crime (1.0), whereas *vagrancy* was not (5.3). *Carrot* was a very typical vegetable (1.1); *parsley* was not (3.8).

Rosch (1975) also asked subjects to judge actual pictures of objects. Subjects are faster to judge a picture as an instance of a category when it presents a typical member of the category. For instance, apples are more rapidly seen as fruits than are watermelons, and robins are more rapidly seen as birds than are chickens. Thus, typical members of a category appear also to have an advantage in perceptual recognition.

Rosch (1977) demonstrated another way in which some members of a category are more typical. She had subjects compose sentences for category names. For *bird*, subjects generated sentences such as these:

- I heard a bird twittering outside my window.

- Three birds sat on the branch of a tree.

- A bird flew down and began eating.

Rosch replaced the category name in these sentences with a typical member (robin), a less central member (eagle), or a peripheral member (chicken) and asked subjects to rate the sensibleness of the resulting sentences. Sentences involving central members got high ratings, sentences with less central members got lower ratings, and sentences with peripheral members got the lowest ratings. So, the evidence is that when people think of a category member, they generally think of typical instances of that category.

Failing to have a default or typical value does not disqualify an object from being a member of the category. People should have great difficulty and should be quite inconsistent in judging whether items at the periphery of a category are actually members of that category. McCloskey and Glucksberg (1978) looked at people's judgments as to what were or were not members of various categories. They found that although subjects did agree on some items, they disagreed on many. For instance, whereas all thirty subjects agreed that *cancer* was a disease and *happiness* was not, sixteen thought *stroke* was a disease and fourteen did not. Again, all thirty subjects agreed that *apple* was a fruit and *chicken* was not, but sixteen thought *pumpkin* was and fourteen disagreed. Once again, all subjects agreed that a *fly* was an insect and a *dog* was not, but thirteen subjects thought a *leech* was and seventeen disagreed. Thus, it appears that subjects do not always agree among themselves. McCloskey and

Glucksberg tested the same subjects a month later and found that many had changed their minds about the disputed items. For instance, eleven out of thirty reversed themselves on *stroke*, eight reversed themselves on *pumpkin*, and three reversed themselves on *leech*. Thus, disagreement as to category boundaries does not just occur *among* subjects. Subjects are very uncertain *within* themselves exactly where the boundaries of a category should be drawn.

Figure 5.10 illustrates a set of materials used by Labov (1973). He was interested in studying which items subjects would call *cups* and which they would not. Which do you consider to be *cups* and which do you consider *bowls*? The interesting point is that these concepts do not appear to have clear-cut boundaries. In one experiment, Labov used the series of items 1 through 4 and a fifth item, not shown. These items reflect an increasing ratio of width of the cup to depth. For the first item that ratio is 1, whereas for item 4 it is 1.9. The ratio for the item not shown was 2.5. Figure 5.11 shows the percentage of subjects calling each of the five objects a cup and the percentage calling it a bowl. The solid lines indicate the classifications when subjects were simply presented with pictures of the objects (the neutral context). As can be seen, the percentages of *cup* responses gradually decreased with increasing width, but there is no clear-cut point where subjects stopped using *cup*. At the extreme 2.5 width ratio, about 25 percent of the subjects still used the *cup* response, while another 25 percent used *bowl*. (The remaining 50 percent used other responses.) The dotted lines give classifications when subjects were asked to imagine the object filled with mashed potatoes and placed on a table. In this context, fewer *cup* responses and more *bowl* responses were given, but the data show the same gradual shift from *cup* to *bowl*. Thus, it appears that subjects' classification behavior varies continuously not only with the properties of an object but also with the context in which the object is imagined or presented. These influences of perceptual features and context on categorization judgments are very much like the similar influences of these features on perceptual pattern recognition (see Chapter 2).

◆
Different instances are judged to be members of a category to different degrees, and more central members of a category have an advantage in processing.

Event Concepts

It is not only objects that have a conceptual structure. We also have concepts of various kinds of events such as going to a movie. Schemas have been proposed as ways of representing such categories. We can encode our knowledge about stereotypic events according to their parts—for instance, going to a movie involves going to the theater, buying the ticket, buying refreshments, seeing the movie, and returning from the theater. Schank

Figure 5.10 The various cuplike objects used in the experiment by Labov (1973) studying the boundaries of the cup category. (Reprinted with permission from W. Labov, "The boundaries of words and their meanings." In <u>New ways of analyzing variations in English,</u> edited by C.-J. N. Bailey and R. W. Shuy. Washington, DC: Georgetown University Press, page 354. Copyright © 1973 by Georgetown University Press.)

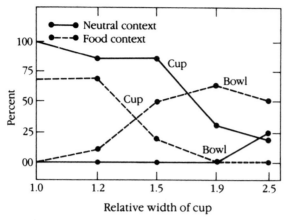

FIGURE 5.11 The percentage of subjects who used the terms cup or bowl to describe the objects shown in Figure 5.10 as a function of the ratio of cup width to cup depth imagined. The solid lines are for the neutral-context condition; the dotted lines are for the food-context condition. (Reprinted with permission from W. Labov, "The boundaries of words and their meanings." In New ways of analyzing variations in English, edited by C.-J. N. Bailey and R. W. Shuy. Washington, DC: Georgetown University Press, page 356. Copyright © 1973 by Georgetown University.)

and Abelson (1977) proposed versions of event schemas that they call *scripts*. They pointed out that many circumstances involve stereotypic sequences of actions. For instance, Table 5.1 shows their hunch as to what stereotypic aspects of dining at a restaurant might be, and represents the components of a script for such an occasion.

Bower, Black, and Turner (1979) report a series of experiments in which the psychological reality of the script notion was tested. They asked subjects to name what they considered the twenty most important events in an episode, such as going to a restaurant. With thirty-two subjects, they failed to get complete agreement on what these events were. No particular action was listed as part of the episode by all of the subjects. However, considerable consensus was reported. Table 5.2 lists the events named. The items in roman were listed by at least 25 percent of the subjects. The italicized items were named by at least 48 percent of the subjects, and the items in capitals were given by at least 73 percent. Using the 73 percent as a criterion, we find the stereotypic sequence was *sit down, look at menu, order, eat, pay bill*, and *leave*.

Bower et al. went on to show a number of the effects of such action scripts on memory for stories. They had subjects study stories that included some but not all of the typical events from a script. Subjects were then asked to recall the stories (in one experiment) or to recognize (in another experiment) whether various statements came from the story. When recalling these stories, subjects tended to report statements that were parts of

---

Table 5.1 The Schema for Going to a Restaurant, According to Schank & Abelson

Scene I: Entering
Customer enters restaurant
Customer looks for table
Customer decides where to sit
Customer goes to table
Customer sits down

Scene 2: Ordering
Customer picks up menu
Customer looks at menu
Customer decides on food
Customer signals waitress
Waitress comes to table
Customer orders food
Waitress goes to cook
Waitress gives food order to cook
Cook prepares food

Scene 3: Eating
Cook gives food to waitress
Waitress brings food to customer
Customer eats food

Scene 4: Exiting
Waitress writes bill
Waitress goes over to customer
Waitress gives bill to customer
Customer gives tip to waitress
Customer goes to cashier
Customer gives money to cashier
Customer leaves restaurant

---

the script but that had not been presented as parts of the stories. Similarly, in the recognition test, subjects thought they had studied script items that had not actually been in the stories. However, subjects showed a greater tendency to recall actual items from the stories or to recognize actual items than to falsely recognize foils not in the stories, despite the distortion in the direction of the general schema.

In another experiment, these investigators read to subjects stories composed of twelve prototypical actions in an episode. Eight of the actions occurred in their standard temporal position, but four were rearranged.

Table 5.2 Empirical Script Norms at Three Agreement Levels

Open door
Enter
Give reservation name
Wait to be seated
Go to table
BE SEATED
Order drinks
Put napkins on lap
LOOK AT MENU
Discuss menu
ORDER MEAL
Talk
Drink water
Eat salad or soup
Meal arrives
EAT FOOD
Finish meal
Order dessert
Eat dessert
Ask for bill
Bill arrives
PAY BILL
Leave tip
Get coats
LEAVE

Adapted from Bower et al. (1979).

Thus, in the restaurant story the bill might be paid at the beginning and the menu read at the end. In recalling these stories, subjects showed a strong tendency to put the events back in their normal order. In fact, about half of the statements were put back. This experiment serves as another demonstration of the powerful effect of general schemas on memory for stories.

These experiments indicate that new events are encoded with respect to these general schemas and that subsequent recall is influenced by the schemas. We have talked about these effects as if they were "bad"; that is, as if subjects were misrecalling the stories. However, it is not clear that these results should be classified as acts of misrecall. Normally, if a certain standard event such as paying a check is omitted in a story, we are supposed to assume it occurred. Similarly, if the storyteller says the check was paid at the beginning of the restaurant episode, we have some reason to doubt the storyteller. Scripts or schemas exist because they encode the predominant sequence of events in a particular kind of situation. Thus, they can serve as valuable bases for predicting missing information and for correcting errors in information.

◆
Scripts are event schemas that people use to reason about prototypical events.

Abstraction versus Instance Theories

We have already described semantic networks and schemas as two ways of representing conceptual knowledge. It is fair to say that, while each has merits, the field has concluded they are inadequate. We already noted that semantic networks do not capture the graded character of categorical knowledge. While schemas can do this, it has never been clear in detail how to relate them to behavior. The field is currently struggling between two alternative ways of theorizing about conceptual knowledge. One type of theory holds that we have actually abstracted general properties from the instances we have studied, while the other type of theory holds we actually store only specific instances with the more general inferences emerging from these instances. We will call these the **abstraction** and the **instance theories**.

The schema theory we have considered is an abstraction theory but others have been more successful. One alternative assumes that people store a single prototype of what an instance of the category is like and judge specific instances in terms of their similarity to that prototype (e.g., Reed, 1972). Other models assume that subjects store a representation that also encodes some idea of the allowable variation around the prototype (e.g., Hayes-Roth & Hayes-Roth, 1977; Anderson, 1991).

Instance theories could not be more different. They hold that we store no central concept but only specific instances. When it comes time to judge how typical a specific object is of birds in general, we compare it to specific birds and make some sort of judgment of average difference. Instance theories include those of Medin and Schaffer (1978) and Nosofsky (1986). Given that such theories differ so widely in what they propose the mind does, it is surprising that they generate such similar predictions over a wide range of experiments. For instance, both types of theories predict better processing of central members of a category. Abstraction theories predict this because central instances are more similar to the abstract representation of the concept. Instance theories predict this because central instances will be more similar, on average, to other instances from a category.

There appear to be subtle differences between the predictions of the two types of theories. Instance theories predict that subjects should be influenced by studying specific instances similar to a test instance and that such influences should go beyond any effect of some representation of the central tendency. Thus, while we may think that dogs in general bark, we may have experienced a peculiar-looking dog that did not and we would then tend to expect that another similar-looking dog would also not bark. Such effects of specific instances can be found in some experiments (e.g., Medin & Schaffer, 1978; Nosofsky, 1991). On the other hand, some research has shown that subjects will infer tendencies that are not in the specific instances (Elio & Anderson, 1981). For instance, if one has encountered many dogs who chase balls and many dogs who bark at the postman, one might consider a dog who both chases balls and barks at the postman to be particularly typical. However, we may never have observed any specific dog who both chased balls and barked at the postman.

One of the other peculiarities of the difference between instance and abstraction models is that connectionist models have been proposed to instantiate both. The network for the Jets and Sharks described in Chapter 1 is a system that represents individual instances and makes generalizations from these. Kruschke (1992) describes a much more thoroughly developed model of this variety. On the other hand, Gluck and Bower (1988) have described an influential connectionist model that extracts central tendencies and does not represent specific instances. We will describe the Gluck and Bower model in the next subsection.

◆

The effects of categorical structure can be explained either by assuming that subjects extract the central tendency of categories or that they store specific instances of categories.

Learning Schemas in a Neural Network

Gluck and Bower applied their theory to a task where subjects studied records of fictitious patients who suffered from four symptoms (bloody nose, stomach cramps, puffy eyes, and discolored gums) and made discriminative diagnoses as to which of two hypothetical diseases the patients had. One disease was three times more common than the other. Figure 5.12 illustrates one way to conceive of the neural network model that Gluck and Bower were proposing to underlie these judgments. The four symptoms are inputs that synapse onto two output neurons that represent the common disease and the rare disease. For each patient, the input neurons corresponding to that patient's symptoms would be active, and the goal would be to have the output neuron corresponding to that patient's disease active. Basically, one can think of a unit of activation coming in on the active inputs and no activation on the inactive inputs, and the goal is to have activation only go out on the output neuron that corresponds to the correct disease. To achieve this goal, the network has to learn strengths of synaptic connections among the neurons. Since there are 4 input neurons and 2 output neurons, there are $4 \times 2 = 8$ synaptic associations being learned.

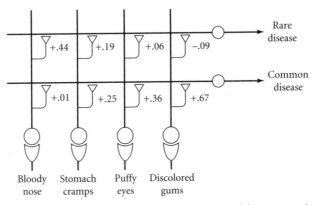

Figure 5.12 A neural net representing the Gluck and Bower model in an experiment where subjects are associating symptoms with diseases.

Gluck and Bower used a popular neural learning rule called the **delta rule** to learn these associations. The delta rule is stated as

$$\Delta A_{ij} = \alpha A_i (T_j - A_j)$$

where ΔA_{ij} is the change in the strength of synaptic connections between input i and output j; A_i is the level of activation of input neuron i; A_j is the level of activation of output neuron j; and T_j is the target or desired activity of j. The parameter α in this equation controls rate of learning. This rule is basically an error-correction rule and tries to change the strengths of association among neurons to minimize the difference between the actual output and the desired output.

Subjects in the Gluck and Bower experiment saw hundreds of patients reflecting different combinations of symptoms. Each combination had a different probability of each disease. The subjects were supposed to learn from this experience how to predict a disease given a pattern of symptoms. Figure 5.12 illustrates the final strengths of association that were learned in accordance with the delta rule. These strengths of association did an excellent job of predicting subjects' classification behavior and the way they rated each symptom as to whether it was diagnostic of the rare disease or the common disease.[1] As can be seen from the synaptic weights

---

[1]Gluck and Bower's model actually has a single output that varies from +1 to −1 depending on probability of the rare disease. The model in Figure 5.12 is formally equivalent. In this model, each disease is predicted separately in a 0 to 1 scale and the maximum strength of association s 1. The Gluck and Bower values can be gotten by subtracting the strength of the common disease from the strength of the rare disease.

in Figure 5.12, bloody nose is treated as more symptomatic of the rare disease (.44 strength versus .01 strength) while the other three symptoms are treated as more symptomatic of the common disease. In their ratings of the symptoms after the experiment, subjects agreed that only bloody nose was predictive of the rare disease.

This model illustrates just one of many mechanisms that have been proposed to achieve schema abstraction. It is interesting in that the schema representation is essentially in the synaptic strengths. The synaptic strength of the connection between an input and an output is essentially a measure of how typical that symptom is of that disease.

◆
<hr>

The delta rule can learn synaptic associations that encode the feature structure of a category.
<hr>

Categories in the Brain

The connectionist model in the previous section offers an abstract model of how concepts might be implemented by neural computation. However, this chapter has been silent on the actual brain structures behind semantic memory. While there is relatively little evidence on this issue, there is some data from patients that provides evidence about the neural basis of certain object categories. It has been found that patients with damage to the temporal lobe suffer deficits in their knowledge about biological categories such as animals, fruits, and vegetables (Warrington & Shallice, 1984; Saffran & Schwartz, 1994). These patients are unable to recognize objects like ducks, and when one was asked what a duck was, the patient was only able to say "an animal." These patients are relatively unaffected in their knowledge of artifacts such as tools and furniture. On the other hand, patients with frontoparietal lesions are impaired in their processing of artifacts and unaffected in their processing of biological categories. Table 5.3 compares example descriptions of biological categories versus artifact categories by two patients with impaired knowledge of living things. These types of patients are more common than patients with deficits in their knowledge of artifacts.

It has been suggested (e.g., Warrington & Shallice; Farah & McClelland, 1991) that dissociation occurs because biological categories are more associated with perceptual categories like shape, while artifacts are more associated with the actions that we perform with them. Farah and McClelland (1991) offer a connectionist model of this dissociation that learns associations among words, pictures, visual semantic features, and functional semantic features. By selectively damaging the visual features in their computer simulation, they were able to produce a deficit in knowledge of living things and by selectively damaging the functional features

Table 5.3 Performance of Two Patients with Impaired Knowledge of Living Things on Definitions Task: Examples of Definitions

Living Things		Artifacts
JBR	Parrot: don't know	Tent: temporary outhouse, living home
	Daffodil: plant	Briefcase: small case used by students to carry papers
	Snail: an insect animal	Compass: tools for telling direction you are going
	Eel: not well	Torch: hand-held light
	Ostrich: unusual	Dustbin: bin for putting rubbish in
SBY	Duck: an animal	Wheelbarrow: object used by people to take material about
	Wasp: bird that flies	Towel: material used to dry people
	Crocus: rubbish material	Pram: used to carry people, with wheels and a thing to sit on
	Holly: what you drink	Submarine: ship that goes underneath the sea
	Spider: a person looking for things, he was a spider for his nation or country	

Adapted from Farah & McClelland, 1991.

they were able to produce a deficit in knowledge of artifacts. Thus, loss of categorical information in such patients seems related to loss of the featural information that defines these categories.

◆ Deficits in knowledge of different categories are produced by the occurrence of damage to different brain areas.

Summary

We have reviewed two types of meaning-based representations. Propositions represent the atomic units of meaning and can be used to encode the meaning of sentences and pictures. The interconnections among propositions define a network that can be profitably used to understand memory phenomena. In this chapter, we discussed a few examples of how these networks can be used to understand memory phenomena (e.g., Weisberg's constrained association task). The next two chapters on memory will make extensive use of such network representations.

However, certain reports of our knowledge cannot be represented simply by the network structures defined by propositions. Certain sets of facts cohere together in larger-order categorical units. For instance, part of our knowledge about restaurants is not just that certain events happen there, but that they tend to occur together in certain sequences. We discussed various mechanisms to represent this knowledge about how features tend to go together to define object categories or how events tend to go together to define episode categories. This knowledge about what tends to occur with what is very important to our ability to predict what we will encounter in our environment.

Remarks and Suggested Readings

The exact details of the propositional network given in this chapter differ from those described in any of the specific proposals in the literature. See Anderson (1976), Anderson and Bower (1973), Kintsch (1974), and Norman and Rumelhart (1975) for some of these specific proposals about how propositional information is represented. Read Kintsch (1998) for his more recent proposals about knowledge representation. For current discussions of issues in representing conceptual knowledge, consult Estes (1991), Medin & Heit (in press), Medin & Ross (1996), and Nosofsky, Palmeri, & McKinley (1994). During the 1970s, there was a debate between dual-code theorists who believed only in spatial and verbal codes, and the propositional theorists who believed only in propositional codes. Key papers in this debate include those of Pylyshyn (1973), Kosslyn & Pomerantz (1977), Palmer (1978), Paivio (1975), and Anderson (1978a). Researchers are now moving to a more eclectic viewpoint, which allows all representations.

6

Human Memory: Encoding and Storage

The first rigorous experimental investigation of human memory was performed by Ebbinghaus in 1885 (Ebbinghaus, 1885). No pools of subjects were available when Ebbinghaus was doing his research. Therefore, he used himself as his sole subject. He taught himself series of nonsense syllables, consonant-vowel-consonant trigrams such as DAX, BUP, and LOC. In one of his many experiments, Ebbinghaus required himself to learn lists of thirteen syllables to the point of being able to repeat the lists twice in order without error. Then he tested his retention for these lists at various delays. He counted the amount of time he took to relearn the lists, using the same criterion of two perfect recitations. He measured how much faster the second learning was than the first. In one case it took him 1156 seconds to learn the list initially and only 467 seconds to relearn the list. This meant he had saved $1156 - 467 = 689$ seconds in the relearning.

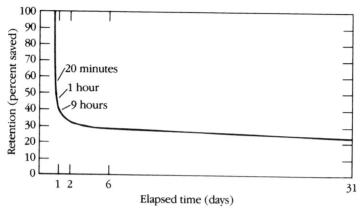

Figure 6.1 The forgetting function of Ebbinghaus (1885). Retention of nonsense syllables is measured by savings in relearning. Retention decreases as the retention interval (the time between initial learning and the retention time) increases, but the rate of forgetting slows down.

This savings can be expressed as a percentage of the original learning: 689 / 1156 = 64.3 percent. Ebbinghaus used percent-savings scores as the standard measure of his retention. Figure 6.1 plots these percent-savings scores as a function of retention intervals. As this figure shows, rapid forgetting occurs initially, but some forgetting still occurs up to 30 days following the learning of the material.

Using a 24-hour retention interval, Ebbinghaus considered what would happen if, after learning the list to the criterion of two perfect recitals, he rehearsed it thirty additional times. Without this overlearning, Ebbinghaus achieved a savings score of 33.8 percent, but with this amount of overlearning, his savings on a subsequent 24-hour retention test was 64.1 percent. Thus, the additional study trials resulted in increased savings on a subsequent retention test.

Over the decades, the basic experimental results of Ebbinghaus have been reproduced by many other researchers using a large variety of techniques and measures. There was a big surge in research on human memory when cognitive psychology completed its separation from behaviorism in the 1960s, for two reasons. First, since research in the behaviorist tradition had focused on learning in animals, there were a great many questions about human memory that were ripe for answering, given the new freedom in theory and research. Second, human memory proved to have a number of research paradigms that were useful for addressing questions about cognition that were not about memory per se. For instance, in the previous two chapters, there were experiments on knowledge representation (such as the one in Figure 5.9) that used a memory paradigm. Subsequent chapters will review the use of memory experiments to pursue issues of problem solving and language processing. Thus, other areas of cognition have made considerable use of human memory paradigms.

In this chapter and the next, we will focus on the understanding of the core human memory system that has emerged from that research. In this chapter, we consider research on the way information gets into the human memory system, and in the next chapter we will consider research on how information is retained and retrieved. This distinction is a little artificial, since any memory experiment will involve encoding, retention, and retrieval. However, the experiments considered in this chapter will mainly inform us about the initial encoding process.

◆
Research on human memory has had a long history but has greatly intensified since the end of the behaviorist era.

The Rise and Fall of the Theory of Short-Term Memory

A very important event in the history of cognitive psychology was the development of a theory of **short-term memory** in the 1960s. It clearly illustrated the power of the new cognitive methodology to account for a great deal of data in a way that had not been possible with previous behaviorist theories. Broadbent (1958) had anticipated the theory of short-term memory, and Waugh and Norman (1965) gave an influential formulation of the theory. However, it was Atkinson and Shiffrin (1968) who gave the theory its most systematic development. It has had an enormous influence on psychology, and, while few researchers still accept the original formulation, similar ideas play a crucial role in some of the modern theories that we will be mentioning, including SAM (Gillund and Shiffrin, 1984; later in this chapter) and Kintsch and van Dijk (1978; in Chapter 12). It is being presented here both because of its influence and because many sources still describe it as the current theory of memory.

Figure 6.2 illustrates the basic theory. We have already reviewed in Chapter 3 how information coming in from the environment tends to be held in transient sensory stores (iconic and auditory memories) from which it is lost unless attended. The theory of short-term memory proposed that attended information went into an intermediate short-term memory where it had to be rehearsed before it could go into a relatively permanent long-term memory. Short-term memory had a limited capacity to hold information. At one time, its capacity was identified with the memory span. **Memory span** refers to the number of elements one can immediately repeat back. Ask a friend to test your memory span. Have that friend make up lists of digits of various lengths and read them to you. See how many digits you can repeat back. You will probably find you are able to repeat back around seven or eight perfectly but not more. The size of the memory

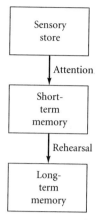

Figure 6.2 The model of memory involving an intermediate short-term memory.

span is convenient, given that phone numbers tend to be seven digits. One view was that short-term memory had room for about seven elements, although other theorists (e.g., Broadbent, 1975) proposed that its capacity was smaller and that memory span depended on other stores as well as short-term memory.

In a typical memory experiment it was assumed that subjects rehearsed the contents of short-term memory. For instance, in a memory span experiment, one might rehearse the digits by saying them over and over again to oneself. Every time an item was rehearsed, it was assumed that there was a probability that the information would be transferred to a relatively permanent long-term memory. However, if the item left short-term memory before a permanent long-term memory representation was developed, it would be lost forever. One could not keep information in short-term memory forever since new information would always be coming in and would push out old information from the limited short-term memory.

The experiment by Shepard and Teghtsoonian (1961) is a nice illustration of these ideas. They presented subjects with a long sequence of 200 three-digit numbers. The subject's task was to identify when a number was repeated. Shepard and Teghtsoonian were interested in subjects' ability to recognize a repeated number as a function of how many numbers intervened between the first appearance of the number and its repetition. This variable is referred to as the "lag." If the subject tended to keep only the most recent numbers in short-term memory, memory for the last few numbers would be good, but memory would get progressively worse as the numbers were pushed out of short-term memory. The results are presented in Figure 6.3. Note that recognition memory drops off rapidly over the first few numbers, but then the drop-off slows down to the point where it appears to be reaching some sort of asymptote of about 60 percent. The rapid dropoff can be interpreted as reflecting the decreasing likelihood that

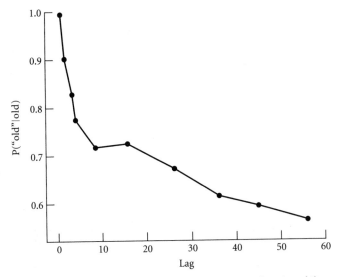

Figure 6.3 The probability of an "old" response to old items as a function of the number of intervening presentations since the last presentation of a stimulus. (From Shepard & Teghtsoonian, 1961. Reprinted by permission of the APA.)

the numbers are being held in short-term memory. The 60 percent level of recall for the later numbers reflects the amount of information that got into long-term memory.[1]

One of the reasons for believing in a theory of short-term memory was the very rapid forgetting that is displayed in data like that in Figure 6.3. This is much more rapid than the forgetting function displayed from long-term memory in Ebbinghaus's function in Figure 6.1. This led people to believe that there was something very different about the memory system involved in this task. The memories involved in such short-term memory tasks appeared to be particularly transient. However, later research and analysis (as we will describe in the next chapter) have led researchers to question whether there really are fundamental differences in such forgetting functions. The rate at which the information is lost is basically a function of how well it is learned. Ebbinghaus learned his material much better, and so the memory losses in his retention function are delayed, but they are of the same character. Both functions are negatively accelerated in that they both show rapid loss initially and slower loss later.

Another reason for believing in the theory of short-term memory was evidence that the amount of rehearsal controlled the amount of informa-

---

[1]This level of memory is not really 60 percent because subjects were falsely accepting over 20 percent of new items as repeated.

tion transferred to long-term memory. For instance, Rundus (1971) asked subjects to rehearse out loud and showed that the more subjects rehearsed an item, the more likely they were to remember it. Data of this sort was perhaps most critical to the theory of short-term memory because it was a reflection of the fundamental property of short-term memory—that it was a necessary halfway station to long-term memory. Information had to "do time" in short-term memory to get into long-term memory, and the more time done, the more remembered.

In an influential article, Craik and Lockhart (1972) argued that what was critical was not how long information was rehearsed but rather the depth to which it was processed. This theory, called **depth of processing**, held that rehearsal improved memory only if the material was rehearsed in a deep and meaningful way. Passive rehearsal does not result in better memory. A number of experiments were performed that showed that passive rehearsal resulted in little improvement in memory performance. For instance, Glenberg, Smith, and Green (1977) had subjects study a four-digit number for 2 seconds, then rehearse a word for 2, 6, or 18 seconds, and then recall the four digits. Subjects thought that their task was to recall the digits and that they were just rehearsing the word to fill the time. However, they were given a final surprise test for the words. Subjects recalled 11, 7, and 13 percent of the words that they had rehearsed for 2, 6, or 18 seconds. Their recall was poor and showed little relationship to amount of rehearsal.[2] On the other hand, as we reviewed in the previous chapter on semantic processing, subjects' memories can be greatly improved if they process material in a deep and meaningful way. Thus, it seems that there may be no short-term, halfway station to long-term memory. Rather, what is critical is that we process information in a way that is conducive to setting up a long-term memory trace. Information may go directly from sensory stores to long-term memory.

◆

A once-popular view in cognitive psychology was that information had to be rehearsed in a limited-capacity short-term memory in order to be deposited in long-term memory.

Rehearsal and Working Memory

Although the evidence appears to be against a separate short-term memory, there remains the empirical observation that people have limits on the

---

◆

[2]While recall memory tends not to be improved by amount of positive rehearsal, Glenberg et al. did show that recognition memory is improved. Recognition memory may depend on a kind of familiarity judgment that does not require explicit creation of new memory traces.

amount of information that they can rehearse at one point in time. This limitation shows most clearly in the memory span studies. What controls the amount of information that we can reproduce in a memory span test? The short-term memory explanation might be that we have a fixed number of elements we can hold in short-term memory (say, seven). In contrast, Baddeley (1986) has proposed that what controls the length of the memory span is the speed at which we can rehearse the information. With respect to verbal material, his proposal is that we have an **articulatory loop** in which we can keep however much information we can rehearse in a fixed duration.

One of the most compelling pieces of evidence for the existence of the articulatory loop concerns the word-length effect (Baddeley, Thomson, & Buchanan, 1975). Read the five words below and then try to repeat them back without looking at the page:

- wit, sum, harm, bay, top

Most people can do this. Baddeley et al. found that subjects were able to repeat back an average of 4.5 words out of 5 such one-syllable words. Now read and try to repeat back the following five words:

- university, opportunity, aluminum, constitutional, auditorium

Subjects were able to recall only an average of 2.60 words out of 5 such 5-syllable words. The crucial factor appears to be how long it takes to say the word. Vallar and Baddeley (1982) looked at recall for words that varied from one to five syllables. They also measured how many words of the various lengths subjects could say in a second. Figure 6.4 shows the results. Note that the percent correct exactly mirrors the reading rate.

Trying to maintain information in working memory is analogous to the circus act that involves spinning plates on a reed. The circus performer will get one plate spinning on one reed, then another on another reed, then another, and so on. Then he runs back to the first before it slows down and falls off. He respins it and then respins the rest. He can keep only so many plates spinning at the same time. Baddeley proposes that it is the same situation with respect to working memory. If we try to keep too many items in working memory, by the time we get back to rehearse the first one it will have decayed to the point where it takes too long to retrieve and re-rehearse. Baddeley proposes that we can keep about 1.5 to 2.0 seconds worth of material rehearsed in the articulatory loop.

There is considerable evidence that this articulatory loop truly involves speech. We discussed some of this research in Chapter 4 under the topic of verbal memory. For instance, there was the research of Conrad (1964) in which he showed that subjects suffered more confusion when trying to re-

Figure 6.4 Mean reading and percentage correct recall of sequences of five words as a function of length. (From Baddeley, 1986.)

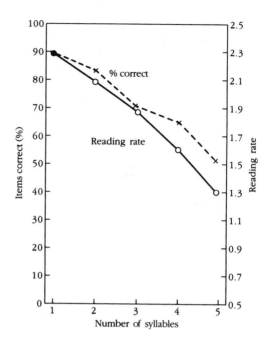

member spans that had a high proportion of rhyming letters (such as BC-THVZ) than ones that did not (such as HBKLMW).

The articulatory loop is not the only mechanism we have for rehearsing material. Baddeley also proposes that we have what he calls a **visuospatial sketchpad** for rehearsing images of the kind we discussed in Chapter 4. He argues that these are two separate "slave" systems for maintaining information in working memory and speculates that there might be more. Figure 6.5 illustrates Baddeley's overall conception of how these various slave systems interact. A **central executive** controls the use of various slave systems, such as the visuospatial sketchpad and the phonological loop (same as articulatory loop). The central executive can put information into

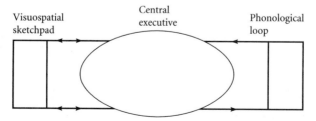

Figure 6.5 Baddeley's theory of working memory in which a central executive coordinates a set of slave systems. (From Baddeley, 1986. Reprinted by permission of Oxford University Press.)

any of these slave systems or retrieve information from the systems. It can also translate information from one system to the other. Baddeley claims that the central executive needs its own transient store of information to make decisions about how to control the slave systems.

One might wonder what is the difference between short-term memory and something like Baddeley's phonological loop. The critical difference is that information does not have to spend time in the phonological loop to get into long-term memory. Rather, the phonological loop is just an auxiliary system for keeping information available.

Consider how these systems are involved in performing a multiplication task like finding the product of 37×28. Try calculating the answer in your head and observe what you do. You might try to hold a visual image of the multiplication, which will eventually look like

$$
\begin{array}{r}
37 \\
\times 28 \\
\hline
296 \\
+740 \\
\hline
1036
\end{array}
$$

You might also find yourself verbally rehearsing information to help you retain it. Thus, you might well be using both your phonological loop and visuospatial sketchpad to help you perform the task. But there is information which you need to access that is in neither store. You have to remember that your task is multiplication, and you must keep track of where you are in the multiplication, of facts like $7 \times 8 = 56$, and of temporary carries such as the 5 from 56. All this information is held by the central executive and used to determine the course of solving the problem and the use of the slave systems.

◆
———————————————————————————————————————
Baddeley proposed that we have an articulatory loop and a visuospatial sketchpad, both of which are controlled by a central executive.
———————————————————————————————————————

Frontal Cortex and Primate Working Memory

The frontal cortex plays a major role in working memory, at least in primates. The frontal cortex shows a major enlargement as one goes from lower mammals, like the rat, to higher mammals, like the monkey, and shows a proportionately greater development as one goes from the monkey to the human. It has been known for some time that the frontal cortex plays an important role in tasks that can be thought of as working-memory tasks. The task that has been most studied in this respect is the delayed match-to-sample task, which is illustrated in Figure 6.6. The monkey is shown an item of food that is placed in one of two identical wells (Figure 6.6a). Then,

Figure 6.6 Examples of delayed memory tasks: (a) Food is placed in well on the right and covered; (b) curtain is drawn for delay period; and (c) curtain is lifted and monkey can lift cover from one of the wells. (From Goldman-Rakic, 1987.)

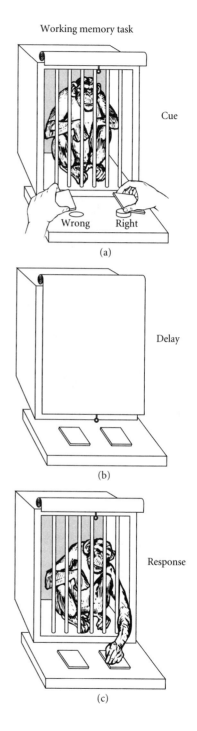

Working memory task

Cue

Wrong   Right

(a)

Delay

(b)

Response

(c)

the wells are covered, and the monkey is prevented from looking at the scene for a delay period—typically 10 seconds (Figure 6.6b). Finally, the monkey is given the opportunity to retrieve the food but must remember in which well it was hidden (Figure 6.6c). Monkeys with lesions to the frontal cortex cannot perform this task (Jacobsen, 1935, 1936). Human infants cannot perform similar tasks successfully until their frontal cortices have matured somewhat, usually at about one year (Diamond, 1991).

A particular area of the frontal cortex is involved when the monkey must remember where in space this object has been placed (Goldman-Rakic, 1988). This small region, called area 46 (see Figure 6.7), is found on the side of the frontal cortex. Lesions to this specific area produce deficits in this task. It has been shown that neurons in this region fire only during the delay period of the task, as if they are keeping information active during that interval. They are inactive before and after the delay. Moreover, different neurons in that region seem tuned to remembering objects in different portions of the visual field (Funahashi, Bruce, & Goldman-Rakic, 1991).

Goldman-Rakic (1992) has examined monkey performance on other tasks that require maintaining different types of information over the delay interval. For instance, she examined a task in which monkeys had to remember different objects. Thus, the animal would have to remember to select a red circle after an interval and not a green square. It appears that a different region of the prefrontal cortex is involved in this task. Different neurons in this area will fire when a red circle is being remembered rather than a green square. Goldman-Rakic speculates that the prefrontal cortex is parceled into many small regions, each of which is responsible for remembering a different kind of information.

Smith and Jonides (1995) have used PET scans to see if there were similar areas of activation in human subjects. When human subjects held visual information in working memory there was activation in area 47 which is adjacent to area 46. The monkey brain and the human brain are not identical (see Figure 6.7), and we would not necessarily expect a direct correspondence between regions of the two brains. Smith and Jonides also looked at a task in which subjects were rehearsing verbal labels; they found that area 8 was active in this task. This is a region of the prefrontal cortex that is associated with linguistic processing (Petrides, Alivsatos, Evans, & Meyer, 1993). Thus, these results are consistent with Goldman-Rakic's proposal that different regions of the prefrontal cortex are parceled out to provide working memory for different types of material.

◆ Different areas of the frontal cortex appear to be responsible for maintaining different types of information in working memory.

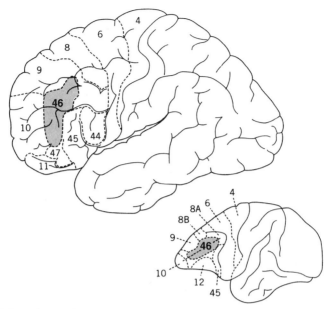

Figure 6.7 Lateral view of human (top) and monkey (bottom) cerebral cortex. Area 46 is the area shown in stippling. (From Goldman-Rakic, 1987. Reprinted by permission of the American Physiological Society.)

Activation and Long-Term Memory

So far, we have discussed how information from the environment comes into working memory and is maintained by rehearsal. However, there is another source of information besides the environment—this is long-term memory. A number of theories have appeared, which assume that different pieces of information in long-term memory can vary from moment to moment in terms of how available they are to working memory. Different theories use different words to describe the same basic idea. The language I use in this chapter is similar to my **ACT** theory (Anderson, 1983; Anderson & Lebiere, 1998). I will talk of memory traces becoming active when associated concepts are presented. However, another well-known theory, **SAM** (Gillund & Shiffrin, 1984; Raaijmakers & Shiffrin, 1981), speaks of images (read memory traces) becoming more or less familiar (read active) as a function of the cues in the context.

Activation determines both the probability of access to memory and the rate of access. Immediately after thinking about information in long-term memory, it is highly active but its activity decreases with the passage of time. An experiment by Loftus (1974) nicely illustrates this. She looked at the time subjects required to retrieve well-learned information about categories such as fruit. She had subjects retrieve instances of a category that began with a certain initial letter. For instance, subjects might have to retrieve a fruit beginning with the letter *p*. She found that they took an average of 1.53 seconds to perform this task the first time they were asked about a category. Then, after varying delays she asked subjects to retrieve from the same category another member beginning with a different letter. Thus, she might ask subjects to retrieve a fruit beginning with *b*. She manipulated delay by inserting tests on other unrelated categories between the two tests on the repeated category. For instance, when there is a two-item delay, subjects might be asked to retrieve a fruit that begins with a *p*, a breed of dog that begins with *c*, a country that begins with *r*, and then a fruit that begins with *b*. Looking at zero, one, and two intervening items, she found retrieval times of 1.21 seconds, 1.28 seconds, and 1.33 seconds, respectively. The first time they were tested, subjects took 1.53 seconds to generate an associate. So, relative to this initial retrieval time, we see strong facilitation if the category is tested again immediately, when the information about the category is still active in working memory. With increasing delay, however, the activation decays, producing longer and longer retrieval times.

Two factors determine the level of activation of a memory. One is how recently we have used the memory, as in the Loftus experiment. The other factor is how much we have practiced the memory. An experiment from my laboratory (Anderson, 1976) illustrates how speed of retrieval varies with both recency and frequency of practice. In the first phase of this experiment, subjects committed to memory facts about locations of various people. For instance, they might learn the following sentences:

The sailor is in the park.
The lawyer is in the church.

Later, they were presented with sentences and asked to say whether each was among the sentences they had studied. Thus subjects might see:

The sailor is in the park.

This would require a positive response. Negative items were created by recombining people and locations in ways that had not been studied. For example, subjects might be presented with the following negative test item:

The sailor is in the church.

Subjects had not studied this sentence and therefore were required to give a negative response. Since they knew the material well enough to be correct almost all the time, we were interested only in the speed with which they made their correct recognition judgments.

We were interested in two variables. One variable was the difference in the amount of study applied to the different sentences before testing.

◆

Table 6.1 Effects of Delay of Repetition and Frequency of Exposure on Recognition Time for Second Presentation of a Sentence

Degree of Study	Delay	
	Short (0 to 2 intervening items)	Long (3 or more intervening items)
Less study	1.11 seconds	1.53 seconds
More study	1.10 seconds	1.38 seconds

From Anderson, 1976.

Some sentences were studied twice as frequently as others. We would expect frequency to be related to the strength of the encoding of a sentence, and hence we assumed that more frequently encountered information would be retrieved more quickly from long-term memory. The second variable was the delay between any two presentations of a particular sentence. We compared the situation in which zero to two items intervened between repetitions (thus, the sentence was still likely to be active) with the situation in which three or more items intervened (thus, the sentence probably had to be reactivated). We were interested in the effect of this delay between tests on recognition time for the second presentation of a sentence.

Table 6.1 displays judgment times for the second sentence in a repetition classified according to these two variables. As can be seen, subjects were faster to recognize sentences that they had just recently encountered, and they were faster to recognize sentences that had received more practice. These factors appear to interact in such a way that the amount of study has little effect for items tested at a short interval.

◆

Speed and probability of accessing a memory is determined by its level of activation, which in turn is determined by how frequently and how recently we have used the memory.

Spreading Activation

It is informative to think about the activation concept within the network framework developed in Chapter 5. **Spreading activation** is the proposal that activation spreads along the paths of such a network. Consider Figure 6.8, which illustrates part of the propositional network surrounding the concept of dog. Note that *dog* is connected to the concept of bone. Thus, when the word *dog* is presented to the subject, not only will that concept become active, but activation should spread to the concepts surrounding

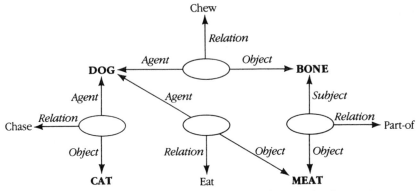

Figure 6.8 A representation of <u>dog</u> in memory and some of its associated concepts.

dog, so that terms such as *bone* become active as well. An unpublished experiment by Perlmutter and Anderson illustrates the kind of evidence that exists for this spreading activation process. Subjects were presented with a sequence of words and asked to generate associates that began with specific letters such as *c* and *m*. We were interested in contrasting sequences such as the following two:

Priming	*Control*
dog—c	gambler—c
bone—m	bone—m

In the first case, the priming condition, the subject might generate *cat* as the associate to *dog* and then be presented with *bone* and generate *meat* as an associate. In the second case, the control condition, the responses might be *card* and *meat*. The important feature of the priming condition is that an already existing associative path leads from *dog* to *bone* and from *dog* to *meat*. Therefore, activating the network structure to answer the first associate should help activate the structure needed to answer the second. The first associate task (dog—c) serves to prime the second (bone—m). In contrast, no priming connection exists in the control case. Therefore, subjects were expected to generate the second associate faster in the priming condition. This expectation was confirmed: Subjects took 1.41 seconds to generate an associate in the priming case, as contrasted with 1.53 seconds in the control case.

Note that the spread-of-activation process is not entirely under an individual's control. For example, when subjects generated an associate to *dog* in the Perlmutter and Anderson experiment, they had no reason to *want* to activate the *bone-meat* association. Still, some activation spread to this part of the network and helped to prime knowledge of the connection between *bone* and *meat*. Many experiments in cognitive psychology have

Table 6.2 Examples of the Pairs Used to Demonstrate Associative Priming

| Positive Pairs | | Negative Pairs | | |
| | | Nonword | Nonword | Both |
Unrelated	Related	First	Second	Nonwords
Nurse	Bread	Plame	Wine	Plame
Butter	Butter	Wine	Plame	Reab
940 ms	855 ms	904 ms	1087 ms	884 ms

From Meyer and Schvaneveldt, 1971.

demonstrated this unconscious priming—called **associative priming**—of knowledge through spreading activation.

Meyer and Schvaneveldt (1971) performed what has become a classic demonstration of associative priming. They asked subjects to judge whether or not pairs of items were words. Table 6.2 shows examples of the materials used in their experiments and subjects' judgment times. The items were presented one above the other. If either item in a pair was a nonword, subjects were to respond no. It appears from examining the negative pairs that subjects judged first the top item and then the second. When the top item was a nonword, subjects were faster to reject the pair than when only the second item was a nonword. (When the top item was not a word, subjects did not have to judge the second item and so could respond sooner.) The major interest in this study was in the positive pairs. There were unrelated items such as *nurse* and *butter*, and pairs with an associative relation such as *bread* and *butter*. Subjects were 85 milliseconds (ms) faster on the related pairs. This result can be explained from a spreading activation analysis. When the subject read the first word in the related pair, activation would spread from it to the second word. This would make more active information about the spelling of the second word and make that easier to judge. The implication of this result is that the associative spreading of activation through memory can facilitate the rate at which words are read. Thus, we can read material that has a strong associative coherence more rapidly than incoherent material in which the words are unrelated.

Ratcliff and McKoon (1981) report a rather different priming demonstration of spreading activation. They had subjects commit to memory sentences such as *The doctor hated the book*. After committing these sentences to memory, subjects were transferred to a word-recognition paradigm where they saw nouns from the sentences and had to recognize whether the nouns came from the studied sentences. So, if subjects saw a word such as *book*, which was in the memorized sentences, they would respond yes.

Sometimes, before presenting the target (e.g., *book*), Ratcliff and McKoon presented a prime noun that came from the same sentence (i.e., *doctor*). They found subjects faster at recognizing the target in this primed condition, compared to a control condition that did not have the prime noun. Subjects took 667 ms in the control condition compared to 624 ms in the primed condition. These results can be explained by assuming that activation spread along the learned association to the target noun. Since the target noun was more active, it could be recognized more rapidly.

Ratcliff and McKoon varied the delay between the prime (*doctor*) and the target (*book*) from 50 to 300 ms. Because all these intervals were too short for subjects to develop any conscious expectations, we are looking at the effects of automatic spread of activation. Figure 6.9 shows how reaction time in the priming condition decreased over this interval. Subjects are somewhat faster in the primed condition than in the control condition, even when there are just 50 ms between prime and target. The priming essentially reached asymptotic levels in 200 ms. This decrease in latency can be taken to reflect the rate at which activation spreads through the network.

Thus, we see in this section that activation will spread from presented material to activate associated material. The more that activation spreads to material, the more rapidly it can be retrieved. It turns out that the amount of activation spread to a memory depends on the strength of that memory. As will be described in the next section, the more a memory is practiced, the stronger it will become, and the more successfully it can be retrieved.

◆
Activation spreads through a network from presented items to activate associated memories.

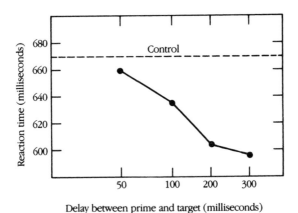

Figure 6.9 Difference between primed and control conditions as a function of the interval between the priming word and the target word. (From Ratcliff & McKoon, 1981.)

Practice and Strength

There are two separate quantities that are required to describe a memory trace: activation and strength. We have already discussed that the activation level of the trace determines how accessible that memory is. The activation level of a memory trace can undergo rapid shifts. For instance, in the Ratcliff and McKoon experiment a trace became fully active in a fifth of a second. Traces also can rapidly lose activation. In this section, we will discuss **strength**, which is a much more gradually changing quantity. Each time we use a memory trace, it will increase a little in its strength. The strength of a trace determines in part how active it can get and hence how accessible it will be. Strength of a trace can be gradually increased by repeated practice.

The effects of practice on memory retrieval are extremely regular and very large. In one study, Pirolli and Anderson (1985) had subjects practice sentences like *The sailor is in the park* and looked at the effects of this practice on the time it took to recognize a sentence. Figure 6.10a illustrates the result of this manipulation. As can be seen, subjects sped up from about 1.6 seconds to 0.7 seconds, cutting their retrieval time by more than 50 percent. The figure also shows that the rate of improvement decreases with more practice. The data are nicely fit by a power function of the form

$$T = 1.40 \, P^{-0.24}$$

where T is the recognition time and P is the number of days of practice. This is called a **power function** because the amount of practice P is

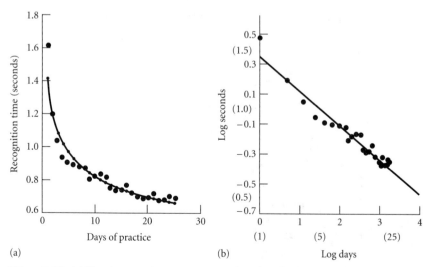

(a)   (b)

Figure 6.10 (a) Time to recognize sentences as a function of number of days of practice; (b) log-log transformation of data in (a) to reveal power function. The dots are average times for individual days, and the curves are the best-fitting power function. (From Pirolli & Anderson, 1985.)

being raised to a power. This power relationship between performance (measured in terms of response time and a number of other measures) and amount of practice is a ubiquitous phenomenon in learning. One way to easily see that data correspond to a power function is to plot log time against log practice. If we have a power function in normal coordinates, we should get a linear function in log-log coordinates:

$$\log T = 0.34 - 0.24 \log P$$

Figure 6.10b shows the data so transformed. As can be seen, the relationship is quite close to a linear function.

Newell and Rosenbloom (1981) refer to the way that memory performance improves as a function of practice as the **power law of learning**. Figure 6.11 shows some data from Blackburn (1936) who looked at the effects for two subjects of practicing addition problems for 10,000 trials. This is plotted in log-log terms, and there is a linear relationship. On this graph and on some others in this book, the original numbers (i.e., those given in parentheses in Figure 6.10b) are plotted on the logarithmic scale rather than expressed as logarithms. Blackburn's data show that the power law of learning extends to amounts of practice far beyond what was given in Figure 6.10. Figures 6.10 and 6.11 reflect the gradual increase in trace strength with practice. As memory traces become stronger, they can receive more activation and so can be more rapidly retrieved.

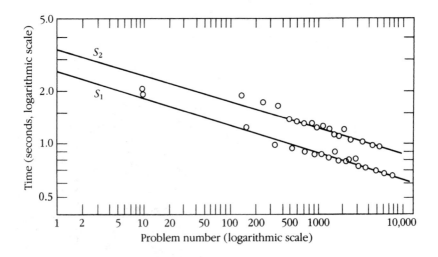

Figure 6.11 Improvement with practice in time taken to add two numbers. Data are given separately for two subjects. Both time and problem number are plotted on a logarithmic scale. (Plot by Crossman, 1959, of data from Blackburn, 1936.)

◆ As a memory is practiced, it is strengthened according to a power function.

Long-Term Potentiation and the Power Law

One might well wonder what really underlies the power law of practice. There is some evidence that it may be related to basic neural changes involved in learning. One kind of neural learning that has attracted much attention is called **long-term potentiation (LTP)**, which occurs in the hippocampus and cortical areas. It is a form of neural learning that seems related to behavioral measures of learning. When a pathway is stimulated with high-frequency electric current, there is increased sensitivity of cells along that pathway to further stimulation. Barnes (1979) looked at this phenomenon in rats, measuring the percent increase in excitatory postsynaptic potential (EPSP) over its initial value.[3] Barnes stimulated the hippocampus of her rats each day for eleven successive days and measured the growth in LTP as indicated by this percent of increase. Figure 6.12a displays her results, plotting percent of change against day of practice. There appears to be a diminishing increase with amount of practice. To see whether there is

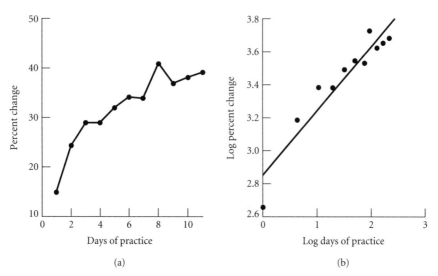

Figure 6.12 Growth in long-term potentiation as a function of number of days of practice: (a) in normal scale; (b) in log-log scale. (Barnes, 1979.)

---

[3]As discussed in Chapter 1, as the dendrite and cell body of a neuron become more excited, there is a decrease in the difference in electric potential between the outside and inside of the cell. EPSP is said to "increase" when this difference decreases.

a power function here, Figure 6.12b plots log percent of change against log of practice. The relationship does appear approximately linear. Thus, it does appear that neural activation changes with practice just as do behavioral measures.

Note that the activation measure in Figure 6.12a is increasing more and more slowly, whereas recognition time (see Figure 6.10a) is decreasing more and more slowly. The assumption is that a performance measure like recognition time is an inverse reflection of the growth of strength that is happening internally. As the strength of the record increases (reflected in Figure 6.12), the performance measures get better (which means shorter times and fewer errors).

◆

Long-term potentiation is a form of neural learning, which appears to follow a power law.

Factors Influencing Memory

A reasonable inference from the preceding discussion might be that the only thing that determines memory performance will be how much we study and practice the material to be remembered. However, we have already reviewed some of the evidence that mere study of material will not lead to better recall. It is important how one processes the material while studying it. We have already seen from the previous chapter that more meaningful processing of material results in better memories. Earlier in this chapter we reviewed, with respect to Craik and Lockhart's depth-of-processing proposal, the evidence that shallow study results in little memory improvement. As a different demonstration of the same point, Nelson (1979) had subjects read paired associates that were either semantic associates (e.g., tulip-flower) or rhymes (e.g., tower-flower). Better memory (81 percent) was obtained for the semantic associates than the rhymes (70 percent). Presumably, subjects were more inclined to process the semantic associates meaningfully. The previous chapter also showed that subjects display better retention for more meaningful information. In this section we will review some other factors, besides depth of processing and meaningfulness of the material, that determine our level of memory.

Elaborative Processing

There is evidence that more elaborative processing results in better memory. **Elaborative processing** involves embellishing a to-be-remembered item with additional information. As an example of an experiment demonstrating the importance of elaboration, consider Anderson and Bower

(1972), who had subjects try to remember simple sentences like *the doctor hated the lawyer*. In one condition subjects just studied the sentence, while in another condition they were asked to generate an elaboration of their choosing like *because of the malpractice suit*. Later, subjects were presented with the subject and verb of the original sentence (e.g., *The doctor hated*) and were asked to recall the object (i.e., *the lawyer*). If subjects just studied the original sentences they were able to recall 57 percent of the objects, but when they generated the elaborations their recall rose to 72 percent. Anderson and Bower proposed that this advantage was because of the redundancy created by the elaboration. If the subjects could not originally recall *lawyer* but could recall the elaboration *because of the malpractice suit* they might then be able to recall *lawyer*.

A series of experiments by Stein and Bransford (1979) also show why self-generated elaborations are often better than experimenter-provided elaborations. In one of these experiments, subjects were asked to remember ten sentences, such as *The fat man read the sign*. There were four conditions of study. In the base condition, subjects studied just the sentence. In the self-generate condition, subjects were asked to generate an elaboration of their own. In the imprecise elaboration condition, subjects were presented with a continuation of the sentence, such as *that was two feet tall*. In the precise elaboration condition, they were presented with a continuation, such as *warning about the ice*. After studying the material, subjects in all conditions were presented with sentence frames like *The _____ man read the sign*, and they had to recall the missing adjective. Subjects recalled 4.2 of the 10 adjectives in the base condition and 5.8 when they generated their own elaboration. Obviously, the self-generated elaborations had helped. They could recall only 2.2 of the adjectives in the imprecise elaboration condition, replicating the typical inferiority found for experimenter-provided elaborations relative to self-generated ones. However, subjects recalled the most—7.8—adjectives in the precise elaboration condition. So, by careful choice of elaboration, experimenter elaborations can be made better than subject elaborations. (For further research on this topic read Pressley, McDaniel, Turnure, Wood, & Ahmad, 1987.)

Thus, it appears that the critical factor is not whether the subject or the experimenter generates the elaborations. Rather, it is whether the elaborations are such that they constrain the to-be-recalled material. Subject-generated elaborations are quite effective because these elaborations reflect the idiosyncratic constraints of the particular subject's knowledge. However, as Stein and Bransford demonstrate, it is possible for the experimenter to construct elaborations that are even more precise in their constraints.

◆

Good memory for material results when it is processed more elaborately.

Techniques for Studying Textual Material

Frase (1975) has found evidence for the benefit of elaborative processing with text material. He compared two groups of subjects on their memories for a text: one that had been given topics to think about before reading the text and a control group that simply studied the text without advance topics. Sometimes called advance organizers (Ausubel, 1968), the topics were in the form of questions that the subjects had to answer. The subjects were to find answers to the advance questions as they read the text. This requirement should have forced them to process the text more carefully and to think about its implications. The advance-organizer group answered 64 percent of the questions correctly in a subsequent test, while the control group answered 57 percent correctly. The questions in the test could be divided into those relevant to the advance organizers and those not relevant. For instance, if a test question was about an event that precipitated America's entry into World War II, it would be considered relevant if the advance questions directed the subject to learn why America entered the war. Such a test question would be considered not relevant if the advance question directed students to learn about the economic consequences of World War II. The advance-organizer group answered 76 percent of the relevant questions correctly and 52 percent of the irrelevant. Thus, they did only slightly worse than the control group on those topics for which they had not been given advance warning, but much better on topics for which they had been given advance warning.

Many college study-skills departments as well as private firms offer courses designed to improve students' memory for text material. These courses mainly teach study techniques for texts such as those used in the social sciences, not for the denser texts used in the physical sciences and mathematics or for literary materials such as novels. The study techniques from different programs are fairly similar, and their success has been documented to some extent. As one example of such a study technique, consider the PQ4R method (Thomas & Robinson, 1972).

The PQ4R method derives its name from the six phases it advocates for studying a chapter in a textbook:

1. **Preview.** Survey the chapter to determine the general topics being discussed. Identify the sections to be read as units. Apply the next four steps to each section.

2. **Questions.** Make up questions about the section. Often, simply transforming section headings results in adequate questions.

3. **Read.** Read the section carefully, trying to answer the questions you have made up about it.

4. Reflect. Reflect on the text as you are reading it, trying to understand it, to think of examples, and to relate the material to prior knowledge.

5. Recite. After finishing a section, try to recall the information contained in it. Try answering the questions you made up for the section. If you cannot recall enough, reread the portions you had trouble remembering.

6. Review. After you have finished the chapter, go through it mentally, recalling its main points. Again try answering the questions you made up.

A slight variation on this technique was recommended in Chapter 1 as a method for studying this book. The central feature of the PQ4R technique is the question-generating and question-answering characteristics. There is reason to suspect that the most important aspect of these features is that they encourage deeper and more elaborative processing of the text material. At the beginning of this subsection, we reviewed the experiment by Frase that demonstrated the benefit of reading a text with a set of advance organizers in mind. It seems that the benefit of that activity was specific to test items related to the questions.

Another experiment by Frase (1975) compared the effects of making up questions with the effects of answering them. He asked pairs of subjects to study a text that was divided into halves. For one half, one subject in the pair read the passage and made up study questions during the process. These questions were given to the second subject, who then read the text while trying to answer them. The subjects switched roles for the second half of the text. All subjects answered a final set of test questions about the passage. A control group, who just read without doing anything special, answered correctly 50 percent of the set of questions that followed. Experimental subjects, when they read in order to make up questions, answered correctly 70 percent of the test items that were relevant to their questions and 52 percent of the irrelevant test items. When they read to answer questions, experimental subjects answered correctly 67 percent of the relevant test items and 49 percent of the irrelevant items. Thus, it seems that both question generation and question answering contribute to good memory. If anything, question making contributes the most. T. H. Anderson (1978), in a review of the research literature, finds further evidence for the particular importance of question making.

Reviewing the text with the questions in mind is another important component of the PQ4R technique. Rothkopf (1966) compared the benefit of reading a text with questions in mind with the benefit of considering a set of questions after reading the text, which enabled subjects to review the text. Rothkopf instructed subjects to read a long text with questions interspersed every three pages. The questions were relevant to the three pages either following or preceding the questions. In the former condition, subjects were supposed to read the subsequent text with these questions in mind. In the latter condition, they were to review what they had just read and answer the questions. The two experimental groups were compared with a control group, which read the text without any special questions. This control group answered 30 percent of the questions correctly in a final test of the whole text. The experimental group whose questions previewed the text, answered correctly 72 percent of the test items relevant to their questions and 29 percent of the irrelevant items—basically the same results as those Frase obtained in comparing the effectiveness of relevant and irrelevant test items. The experimental group whose questions reviewed the text, answered correctly 72 percent of the relevant items and 42 percent of the irrelevant items. Thus, it seems that reviewing the text with questions in mind may be more generally beneficial.

◆
Study techniques involving question generation and question answering lead to better memory for text material.

Meaningful versus Nonmeaningful Elaborations

While the research just reviewed indicates meaningful processing leads to better memory, other research indicates that other sorts of elaborative processing also result in better memory. For instance, Kolers (1979) has looked at subjects' memory for sentences that are read in normal form versus sentences that are printed upside down, and he has found that subjects can remember more about the upside-down sentences. He argues that the extra processing involved in reading the typography of upside-down sentences provides the basis for the improved memory. It is not a case of more meaningful processing but one rather of more extensive processing.

The study by Slamecka and Graf (1978) demonstrated separate effects of elaborative and meaningful processing on memory. They contrasted a "generate" condition with a "read" condition. In the generate condition, subjects either had to generate a synonym of a word that began with a particular letter (e.g., What is a synonym of *sea* that begins with the letter o? Answer: *ocean*.) or generate a rhyme of a word that began with a particular letter (e.g., What is a rhyme of *save* that begins with the letter c? Answer: *cave*.). In the read condition, they just read the rhyme pair or the synonym pair; then they were tested for their recognition of the second word. Figure 6.13 shows the results. Subjects performed better with synonyms, and they

Figure 6.13 Probability of recognition as a function of type of elaboration and whether it was generated or read. (From Experiment 2 of Slamecka & Graf, 1978.)

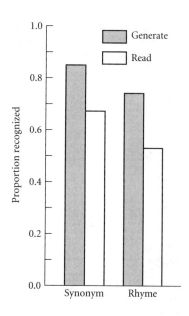

were better when they generated. Thus, there appears to be effects of both semantic processing and elaborative processing.

◆

More elaborate processing will result in better memory, even if that processing is not focused on the meaning of the material.

Incidental versus Intentional Learning

So far, we have talked about factors that affect memory. Now, we will turn to a factor that does not affect memory despite people's intuitions to the contrary: It does not seem to matter whether people intend to learn the material; rather, what is important is how they process the material. This is illustrated in an experiment by Hyde and Jenkins (1973). Subjects saw groups of twenty-four words presented at the rate of 3 seconds per word. One group of subjects was asked to check whether each word had a letter e or a letter g. The other group of subjects was asked to rate the pleasantness of the words. These two tasks were called orienting tasks. It is reasonable to assume that the pleasantness rating involved more meaningful and deeper processing than the letter-verification task. Another manipulation was whether subjects were told that the true purpose of the experiment was to learn the words. Half the subjects in each group were told the true purpose of the experiment. These subjects were said to be in the intentional-learning condition. The other half in each group, who thought the true purpose was to rate the words or check for letters, were said to be

Table 6.3 Percentage of Words Recalled as a Function of Orienting Task and Whether Subjects Were Aware of Learning Task

Learning-Purpose Conditions	Orienting Task	
	Rate Pleasantness	Check Letters
Incidental	68%	39%
Intentional	69%	43%

Adapted from Hyde and Jenkins, 1973.

in the incidental-learning condition. Thus, there are altogether four conditions: pleasantness-intentional, pleasantness-incidental, letter checking-intentional, and letter checking-incidental.

After studying the list, all subjects were asked to recall as many words as they could. Table 6.3 presents the results from the Hyde and Jenkins experiment in terms of percentage of the twenty-four words recalled. Two results are noteworthy. First, subjects' knowledge of the purpose of studying the words (of whether they would be tested for recall) had relatively little effect. Second, a large depth-of-processing effect was demonstrated; subjects showed much higher recall in the pleasantness rating condition, independent of whether they expected to be tested on the material later. In rating a word for pleasantness, subjects had to think about its meaning, which gave them an opportunity to elaborate upon the word.

The Hyde and Jenkins experiment illustrates an important finding that has been proven over and over again in the research on intentional versus incidental learning: Whether a person intends to learn or not really does not matter (see Postman, 1964, for a review). What matters is how the person processes the material during its presentation. If the individual engages in identical mental activities when not intending to learn as when intending, he or she gets identical memory performance in both conditions. People typically show better memory when they intend to learn because they are likely to engage in activities more conducive to good memory, such as rehearsal and elaborative processing. The small advantage for subjects in the intentional learning condition in the Jenkins and Hyde experiment may reflect some small variation in processing. Experiments in which great care is taken to control processing find that intention to learn or amount of motivation to learn has no effect (see Nelson, 1976).

There is an interesting everyday example of the relationship between intention to learn and type of processing: Many students claim they find it easier to remember material from a novel, which they are not trying to remember, than from a textbook, which they are trying to remember.

The reason is that students find a typical novel much easier to elaborate, and a good novel invites such elaborations (e.g., why did the suspect deny knowing the victim?).

◆

Level of processing, and not whether one intends to learn, determines the amount remembered.

Flashbulb Memories and the Self-Reference Effect

While it does not appear that intention to learn has an effect on memory, various sets of data point to the conclusion that people display better memory for events that are important to them. One class of research involves what are called **flashbulb memories**. Brown and Kulik (1977) proposed that certain events are so important that they effectively burn themselves into memory forever. The event they pointed to was the assassination of President Kennedy in 1963, which was a particularly traumatic event for Americans of their generation. They found that most people had vivid memories of the event thirteen years later. However, the interpretation of this result is problematic because Brown and Kulik did not really have any way of assessing the accuracy of the reported memories.

Since the Brown and Kulik proposal, a number of studies have been done to determine what subjects remembered about a traumatic event immediately after it occurred and then testing memory later. This research has a little of the flavor of ambulance chasing. For instance, McCloskey, Wible, and Cohen (1988) did a study surrounding the Challenger explosion in 1986. Many people at that time felt this was a particularly traumatic event that they had watched with horror on television. McCloskey et al. interviewed subjects one week after the incident and then nine months later. They found that although subjects reported vivid memories nine months later, their memory reports were in fact quite inaccurate. Palmer, Schreiber, and Fox (1989, 1991) came to a somewhat different conclusion in a study of memories for the 1989 San Francisco earthquake. They compared people who had actually experienced the earthquake firsthand with subjects who only watched it on TV. The subjects who experienced it firsthand showed much superior long-term memory. Conway, Anderson, Larsen, Donnelly, McDaniel, McClelland, Rawles, and Logie (1994) have argued that the negative result of the study by McCloskey et al. was because these subjects did not have "true" flashbulb memories. They argued that what was critical was that the event be consequential for the individual person. Hence, there were only flashbulb memories for people who actually experienced the San Francisco earthquake and not for those who saw it on TV. They studied memory for Margaret Thatcher's resignation as prime minister of the United Kingdom in 1990. They compared subjects from the United Kingdom, the United States, and Denmark, all of whom had followed the news events. It turned out that 60% of the subjects from the United Kingdom showed perfect memory for the events surrounding the resignation eleven months later while only 20% of the non–U.K. subjects showed perfect memory. Conway et al. argue that this is because the Thatcher resignation was only really consequential for the U.K. subjects.

A similar sort of phenomena seems to surround what is called the **self-reference effect**, which refers to the fact that people tend to remember more about information that refers to themselves. Rogers, Kuipers, and Kirker (1977) found that subjects showed better memory for words that they had been asked to relate to themselves. Greenwald and Banjeri (1989) showed that people also showed better memory for words they related to friends. Thus, the result does not just hold for oneself but for people that are close to oneself.

It is not entirely clear what mechanisms underlie these effects of the importance of the information to be learned. It has been argued, particularly for the self-reference effect, that we are better able to elaborate information about ourselves and our friends because we know so much about ourselves and our friends. Thus, the mechanism for these importance effects may be the elaborateness of processing mentioned earlier in this section.

◆
Information that people regard as important to them tends to be better remembered.

Neural Correlates of Encoding

There is evidence that better memory occurs for items that receive stronger brain processing at the time of study. For instance, it has been shown that words that evoke a stronger ERP response (see discussion of ERP's in Chapter 1) have a higher probability of being recalled at a later point in time. Similarly, Kapur et al. (1994), using PET methodology, found greater activity in left frontal Areas 45, 46, and 47 in tasks that required deeper processing.

A number of studies have found that left frontal activation correlates with deeper processing of verbal material and that verbal items that evoke stronger left frontal activation show better memory. Since the left hemisphere is specialized for verbal processing, these results suggest that what is important is verbal processing of the material.

As we will discuss in more detail in the next chapter, there is a great deal of evidence that another structure, the hippocampus, which is located within the temporal cortex, plays a critical role in the storage of memory. Patients who have suffered damage to their hippocampal regions have very poor memories. It has been shown that these patients, when trying to remember material, show extensive left frontal activation (Buckner, personal communication). However, they show poor memory. Thus, it seems

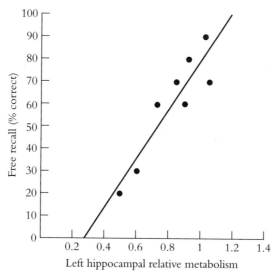

Figure 6.14 Scatterplot relating later level of activation in the left hippocampus at study to free recall a day later. From Alkire, Haier, Fallon & Cahill (in press).

that activity in the left frontal region may be a necessary condition for remembering verbal material but is not a sufficient condition.

Curiously, not all studies find activation in the hippocampal region during the learning of material (Buckner & Koustal, 1998). However, some research has found such activation. Wagner et al. (1998), using fMRI imaging, found greater activation in both the left frontal region and the left hippocampal region during deeper processing of verbal material. He also found greater fMRI activation in both of these regions for words that were subsequently recalled than for words that were not. Similar results have been reported by Alkire, Haier, Fallon, and Cahill (in press) using a PET methodology. They argue that the reason why some research has not found increased hippocampal activation is that these studies have only looked at short-term retention over a few minutes. Alkire et al. looked at the relationship between the increase in activation in the hippocampus at study and how it related to probability of recall twenty-four hours later. Figure 6.14 shows their results. Each dot represents one of their eight subjects. As can be seen, those subjects who showed the greatest increase in hippocampal activation showed the best memory. This is strong evidence for hippocampal activity as a predictor of good long-term memory.

Better memory for verbal material is correlated with greater activation in the left frontal cortex and the left hippocampal region.

Encoding versus Retrieval

This chapter has focused on the processes involved in getting information into memory. However, one cannot talk about any memory experiment without considering what is involved in getting that information out— which is the topic of the next chapter. We will see there that many of the issues considered in this chapter are considerably complicated by retrieval issues. This is certainly true for the effects of elaborative processing that we have just discussed. There are important interactions between how a memory is processed at study and how it is processed at test. Even in this chapter, we were not able to discuss the effects of factors like practice without discussing the activation-based retrieval processes that are facilitated by these processes. The next chapter will also have more to say about the activation of memory traces.

Remarks and Suggested Readings

Anderson (2000), Baddeley (1998), and Neath (1998) are textbooks devoted to memory. Healy and McNamara (1996) review research relevant to the legacy of the theory of short-term memory. The March 1993 issue of the journal *Memory & Cognition* contains a number of articles on issues concerned with short-term memory. A relatively recent exchange on spreading activation occurred between Ratcliff and McKoon (1992a, 1994) and McNamara (1992, 1994). The power law of learning is examined in Anderson and Schooler (1991), Heathcote, Brown, and Mewhort (in press), and Newell and Rosenbloom (1981). There were *Scientific American* articles discussing the role of the prefrontal cortex in working memory (Goldman-Rakic, 1992) and the nature of long-term potentiation in the hippocampus (Kandel & Hawkins, 1992) as well as other kinds of neural learning.

7

Human Memory:
Retention and Retrieval

The previous chapter discussed the process of encoding information in memory. However, most people's principal complaint about their memory is not that they have difficulty initially learning material but rather that they have forgotten so much of what they have learned. There are two obvious reasons why we may later be unable to recall what we have committed to memory. One is that the memory has disappeared, and the other is that the memory is still there but we cannot retrieve it. It is not always easy to distinguish these two possibilities. As we will see, things that we appear to forget in one context may become available in another context.

Of the two possibilities, the more interesting is that we never do really lose our memories—that forgotten memories are still there but we cannot retrieve them. The results reported by Penfield (1959) are consistent with this notion. As part of a neurosurgical procedure, Penfield electrically stimulated portions of patients' brains and asked them to report what they experienced (patients were conscious during the surgery but the stimulation technique was painless). In this way, Penfield determined the functions of various portions of the brain. Stimulation of the temporal lobes led to reports of memories that patients were unable to report in normal recall—for instance, events from their childhood. It was as if Penfield's stimulation activated portions of the memory network that spreading activation could not reach. Unfortunately, it is hard to know whether the patients' memory reports were accurate, since going back in time to check on whether the events reported actually occurred was impossible. Therefore, although suggestive, the Penfield experiments are generally discounted by memory researchers.

A better experiment, conducted by Nelson (1971), also indicates that "forgotten" memories still exist. He had subjects learn twenty number-noun paired associates; they studied the list until they reached a criterion of one errorless trial. Subjects returned for a retest two weeks later, recalling 75 percent of the items on this retention test. However, interest focused on the 25 percent of the items for which the subjects were unable to recall the noun response to the number stimulus. Subjects were given new learning trials on the twenty paired associates. The paired associates they had missed were either kept the same or changed. In the changed cases, a new response was associated with an old stimulus. If subjects had learned 43-*dog* but failed to recall the response to *43*, they might now be trained on either 43-*dog* (unchanged) or 43-*house* (changed). They were tested after studying the new list once. If subjects had lost all memory for the forgotten pairs, there should be no difference between changed and unchanged pairs. However, subjects correctly recalled 78 percent of the unchanged items formerly missed but only 43 percent of the changed items. This large advantage for unchanged items indicates that subjects had retained something about the paired associates, even though they had been unable to recall them initially. This retained information was reflected in the savings displayed in relearning.

Nelson (1978) also looked at the situation in which the retention test involved recognition. Four weeks after learning, subjects failed to recognize 31 percent of the paired associates they had learned. As in the previous experiment, Nelson asked subjects to relearn the missing items. For half the stimuli, the responses were changed, and for the other half they were left unchanged. After one relearning trial, subjects recognized 34 percent of the unchanged items but only 19 percent of the changed items. The initial recognition-retention test should have been very sensitive to whether subjects have anything in memory. However, even when subjects fail this sensitive test, there appears to be some evidence that a record of the item is still in memory—the evidence that relearning was better for the unchanged than the changed pairs. The implication of the Nelson studies is that if we can come up with a sufficiently sensitive measure, we can show that apparently forgotten memories are still there.

These experiments do not prove that everything is remembered. They just show that appropriately sensitive measures can find evidence for remnants of some of the memories that appear forgotten. In this chapter, we will first discuss how memories become less available with time. Then we will discuss some of the factors that determine our success at retrieving these memories.

◆ ───

Even when subjects appear to have forgotten memories, sensitive tests can find evidence of some of these memories.

The Retention Function

Figure 6.1 of the previous chapter described Ebbinghaus's retention function for lists of nonsense syllables. A fair amount of research has studied the form of the retention function. Much of this research has been done by Wickelgren. In one recognition experiment (Wickelgren, 1975), he presented subjects with a sequence of words to study and then looked at the probability of their recognizing the words after delays ranging from one minute to fourteen days. Figure 7.1 shows performance as a function of delay. The performance measure Wickelgren used is called d', which is derived from probability of recognition. Wickelgren interprets it as a measure of memory strength.

We see that performance systematically deteriorates with delay. However, these changes are *negatively accelerated*—that is, the rate of change gets smaller and smaller with delay. In Figure 7.1b, I have replotted the data, plotting the logarithm of the performance measure and the logarithm of delay. Marvelously, the function becomes linear. Log performance is a linear function of the log of the delay T; that is,

$$\log(d') = A - b \log T$$

This equation can be transformed to become

$$d' = CT^{-b}$$

where $C = 10^A$. That is, these performance measures are power functions of delay. Interestingly, the Ebbinghaus retention function in Figure 6.1 can also be shown to be a power function. In a review of research on forgetting, Wixted and Ebbesen (1991) concluded that retention functions are generally power functions. This is called the **power law of forgetting**. Recall

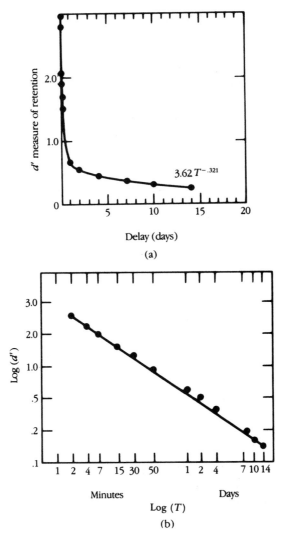

Figure 7.1 (a) Success at word recognition as measured by d′ as a function of delay T; (b) the data in (a) replotted on a log-log scale. (Adapted from Wickelgren, 1975).

from the previous chapter that there is also a power law of learning—practice curves are described by power functions. Both functions are negatively accelerated, but with an important difference. Practice functions show diminishing improvement with practice, whereas retention functions show diminishing loss with delay.

The negatively accelerated character of the retention function is important with respect to the proposed difference between short-term memory and long-term memory. Recall that one argument for short-term memory was predicated on the rapid drop-off of memory performance over the first few seconds followed by relatively stable memory (e.g., Figure 6.3). The fact that all retention functions have this characteristic suggests that there is nothing special about the short-term memory function. As noted earlier, Ebbinghaus's function shows this pattern over a period of days. The reason some memories show rapid decay over a period of seconds and others over days has to do with the strength of encoding of the memory traces. Anderson and Schooler (1991) show that all retention functions (including the purported short-term memory ones) are power functions. Degree of practice just postpones the point of their visible decay.

A very dramatic example of the retention function was produced by Bahrick (1984), who looked at subjects' retention of English-Spanish vocabulary items anywhere from immediately to 50 years after they had completed courses in high school and college. Figure 7.2 plots their scores out of fifteen items as a function of the logarithm of the time since course completion. Separate functions are plotted for students who had one, three, or five courses. The data show a slow decay of knowledge combined with a substantial practice effect. In Bahrick's data, the retention functions are nearly flat between three and twenty-five years (as would be predicted by a power function), with some further drop-off from twenty-five to forty-nine years (which is more rapid than would be predicted by a power function). Bahrick (personal communication) suspects that this final drop-off is probably related to physiological deterioration in old age.

There is some evidence that the explanation of these decay functions may be in the neural processes. Recall from the previous chapter that long-term potentiation is an increase that occurs in neural responsiveness as a

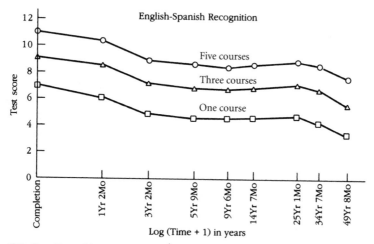

Figure 7.2 The effect of level of training on the retention of recognition vocabulary. (From Bahrick, 1984. Copyright © 1984 by the American Psychological Association. Reprinted by permission.)

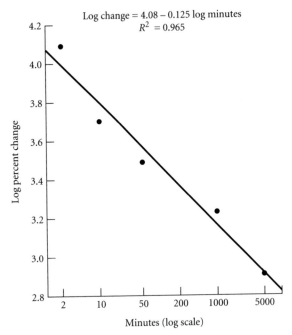

Figure 7.3 Data from Barnes (1979): Percent long-term potentiation as a function of log delay.

function of prior electrical stimulation. We saw in the previous chapter that long-term potentiation mirrored the power law of learning. Figure 7.3 shows some data from Barnes (1979) showing decrease in long-term potentiation with delay. She manipulated the retention interval from two minutes to one week. Figure 7.3 is plotted in log-log scale and is approximately a linear function, implying that the function in the original scale is a power function. Thus, the time course of this neural forgetting mirrors the time course of behavioral forgetting just as the neural learning function mirrored the behavioral learning function. In terms of the strength concept introduced in the previous chapter, the assumption is that the strength of the memory trace decays away with time. The data on long-term potentiation suggest that the locus of this strength decay involves changes in synaptic strength. Thus, there may be a direct relationship between the concept of strength defined at the behavioral level and strength defined at the neural level.

The idea that memory traces simply decay in strength with time is one of the common explanations of forgetting; it is called the **decay theory** of forgetting. We will review one of the major competitors of this theory next: the **interference theory** of forgetting.

◆ The strength of a memory trace decays as a power function of the retention interval.

Interference Effects

The discussion to this point might lead one to infer that the only factor that affects loss of memories is the passage of time. However, it turns out that retention is strongly impacted by another factor—interfering material. Much of the original research on interference has involved learning of paired associates where the interest has focused on how the learning of one list of paired associates would impact on the memory for another list. In the typical interference experiment, two critical groups are defined (illustrated in Table 7.1). The A-D experimental group learns two lists of paired associates, the first list designated A-B and the second designated A-D. These lists are so designated because they share common stimuli (the A terms). For example, among the pairs that the subject studies in the A-B list might be *cat-43* and *house-61*, and in the A-D list *cat-82* and *house-37*. The C-D control group also first studies the A-B list, but then studies a different second list, designated C-D, which does not contain the same stimuli as the first list. For example, in the second C-D list subjects might study *bone-82* and *cup-37*. After learning their respective second lists, both groups are retested for their memory of their first list, in both cases the A-B list. Often, this retention test is administered after a considerable delay, such as twenty-four hours or a week. In general, the A-D group does not do as well as the C-D group with respect to both rate of learning of the second list and retention of the original A-B list (see Keppel, 1968, for a review). Particularly important from the point of view of retention is the observation that learning the A-D list interferes with the A-B list and causes it to be forgotten.

More generally, this research shows that it is difficult to maintain multiple associations to the same stimuli. It is harder both to learn new items and to retain old ones. This might seem to have rather dismal implications for our ability to remember information. It would seem to imply that it would become increasingly difficult to learn new information about a concept. Every time we learned a new fact about a friend, we would be in danger of forgetting an old fact about that friend. Fortunately, there are important additional factors that ameliorate such interference. However,

Table 7.1 Experimental and Control Groups Used in a Typical Interference Paradigm

A-D Experimental		C-D Control	
Learn	A-B	Learn	A-B
Learn	A-D	Learn	C-D
Test	A-B	Test	A-B

before discussing these, we need to examine in more detail the basis for such interference effects. It turns out that a rather different paradigm has been helpful in identifying the cause of the interference effects.

◆
Learning additional associations to a stimulus can cause old ones to be forgotten.

The Fan Effect

The interference effects we have studied can be understood in terms of the amount of activation that is spread to activate a memory structure. The basic idea is that when subjects are presented with a stimulus like *cat*, activation will spread from it to all of its associates. There is a limit on the amount of activation that can be spread from such a source; the more things associated with that source, the less activation that will spread to any particular memory structure. In one experiment illustrating these ideas (Anderson, 1974a), I asked subjects to memorize twenty-six facts, again of the form *A person is in a location*. Some persons were paired with only one location, and some locations with only one person. Other persons were paired with two locations, and other locations with two persons. For instance, suppose that subjects studied these sentences:

1. The doctor is in the bank. (1-1)

2. The fireman is in the park. (1-2)

3. The lawyer is in the church. (2-1)

4. The lawyer is in the park. (2-2)

Each statement is followed by two numbers, reflecting the number of facts associated with the subject and the location. For instance, sentence 3 is labeled 2-1 because its subject occurs in two sentences (sentences 3 and 4) and its location occurs in one (sentence 3). Subjects were drilled on this material until they knew it quite well. Before beginning the reaction-time phase, subjects were able to recall all the locations associated with a particular type of person (e.g., doctor) and all the persons associated with a particular location (e.g., park). Thus, unlike the interference experiments reviewed earlier, all the material was memorized and interest focused on the speed with which it could be retrieved. After memorizing the material, subjects performed in a speed-recognition phase of the experiment, during which they were presented with sentences and had to judge whether they recognized the sentences from the study set. New foil sentences were created by the re-pairing of people and locations from the study set. The reaction times involving sentences such as those listed above are displayed

Table 7.2 Mean Recognition Time for Sentences as a Function of Facts Learned about Person and Location

Number of Sentences Using a Specific Location	Number of Sentences about a Specific Person	
	1 Sentence	2 Sentences
1 Sentence	1.11 seconds	1.17 seconds
2 Sentences	1.17 seconds	1.22 seconds

From Anderson, 1947a.

in Table 7.2, which classifies the data as a function of the number of facts associated with a person and a location. As can be seen, recognition time increases as a function of both the number of facts studied about the person and the number of facts studied about the location. These effects of slowed retrieval are not large but they can add up, as any student knows who has taken a time-pressured test. Taking a little more time to answer each question can mean not finishing the test.

These interference effects can be explained by use of the concepts of spreading activation applied to propositional networks, such as described in Chapter 5. Figure 7.4 shows the network representation for sentences 1 through 4. By applying the activation concept to this representation, we can nicely account for the increase in reaction time. Consider how the subject might recognize a probe such as *A lawyer is in the park*. According

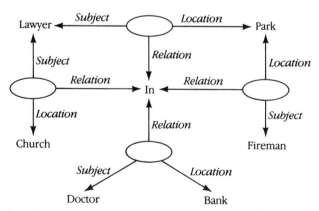

Figure 7.4 Network representations for four sentences used in the experiment of Anderson (1974a). The sentences are: The doctor is in the bank; The fireman is in the park; The lawyer is in the church; and The lawyer is in the park.

to the spreading activation theory, recognizing this proposition involves the following discrete steps:

1. Presentation of the probe will activate the representation of the terms *lawyer*, *in*, and *park* in this network. These are the sources of activation.

2. Activation will spread from these sources along the various paths leading from the nodes. A critical assumption is that these sources have a fixed capacity for emitting activation; thus, the more paths there are leading from a source, the less activation will go down any one path.

3. Activation coming down various paths will converge at proposition nodes. These activations will sum to produce an overall level of activation of the proposition node.

4. The proposition will be recognized in an amount of time that is inversely related to its level of activation.

So, given a structure like Figure 7.4, subjects should be slower to recognize a fact involving *lawyer* and *park* than one involving *doctor* and *bank* because more paths emanate from the first set of concepts. That is, in the *lawyer* and *park* case two paths point from each of the concepts to the two propositions in which each was studied, whereas only one path leads from each of the *doctor* and *bank* concepts. The **fan effect** is the name given to this increase in reaction time related to an increase in the number of facts associated with a concept. It is so named because the increase in reaction time is related to an increase in the fan of facts emanating from the network representation of the concept.

◆
> The more facts associated with a concept, the slower retrieval of any one of the facts.

Interference with Preexperimental Memories

Do such interference effects occur with material learned outside of the laboratory? As one way to address this question, Lewis and Anderson (1976) investigated whether the fan effect could be obtained with material the subject knew before the experiment. We had subjects learn fantasy facts about public figures—for example, *Napoleon Bonaparte was from India*. Subjects studied from zero to four such fantasy facts about each public figure. After learning these "facts," they proceeded to a recognition test phase. In this phase, they saw three types of sentences: (1) statements they

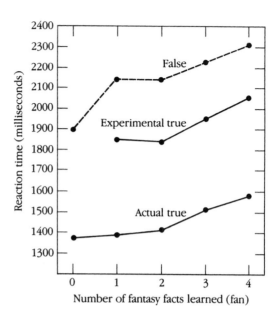

Figure 7.5 Reaction time from Lewis and Anderson (1976). The task was to recognize true and fantasy facts about a public figure and to reject statements that were neither true nor fantasy facts. This figure shows that the time subjects took to make all three judgments increased as they learned more fantasy facts about public figures.

had studied in the experiment; (2) true facts about the public figures (such as *Napoleon Bonaparte was an emperor*); and (3) statements about the public figures that were false both in the experimental fantasy world and in the real world. Subjects had to respond to the first two types of facts as true and to the last type as false.

Figure 7.5 presents subjects' reaction times in making these judgments as a function of the number or fan of the fantasy facts studied about the person. Note that reaction time increased with fan for all types of facts. Also note that subjects responded much faster to actual facts than to experimental facts. The advantage of actual facts can be explained, because these true facts would be much more strongly encoded in memory than the fantasy facts. The most important result to note in Figure 7.5 is that the more fantasy facts subjects learned about an individual such as Napoleon Bonaparte, the longer subjects took to recognize a fact that they already knew about the individual; for example, *Napoleon Bonaparte was an emperor*. Thus, we can produce interference with preexperimental material. For further research on this topic, see Peterson and Potts (1982).

◆

Material learned outside of the laboratory can be interfered with by material learned in the laboratory.

Interference and Decay

We have seen two mechanisms that can produce forgetting. One is decay of trace strength, and the other is interference from other memories. There has been some speculation in psychology that what appears to be decay may really reflect interference. That is, the reason why memories appear to decay over a retention interval is that they are interfered with by additional memories that the subjects have learned. This led to research that studied whether material was better retained over an interval during which subjects slept or during which they were awake. The reasoning was that there would be fewer interfering memories learned during sleep. Ekstrand (1972) reviews a great deal of research consistent with the conclusion that less is forgotten during the period of sleep. However, it seems that the critical variable is not sleep but rather the time of day during which material is learned. Hockey, Davies, and Gray (1972) found that subjects better remembered material that they learned at night, even if they were kept up during the night and slept during the day. It seems that early evening is the period of highest arousal (at least for typical undergraduate subjects) and that retention is best for material learned in a high arousal state. See Anderson (2000) for a review of this literature on effects of time of day.

There has been a long-standing controversy in psychology about whether retention functions, such as those illustrated in Figures 7.1 and 7.2, reflect decay in the absence of any interference or whether they reflect interference from unidentified sources. Objections have been raised to decay theories because they do not identify the psychological factors producing the forgetting, but rather assert that forgetting occurs spontaneously with time. It may be possible, however, that there is no explanation of decay at the purely psychological level. The explanation may be physiological, as we saw with respect to the long-term potentiation data (see Figure 7.3). Thus, it seems that the best conclusion, given the available data, is that both interference and decay effects contribute to forgetting.

◆ Forgetting is produced both by decay in trace strength and by interference from other memories.

Interference and Redundancy

There is a major restriction on the situations in which one gets interference effects: Such interference occurs only when one is learning multiple memories that have no intrinsic relationship to one another. Interference does not occur when the memories are somewhat redundant. An experiment by Bradshaw and Anderson (1982) illustrates the contrasting effects of redundant versus irrelevant information. These researchers looked at subjects' ability to learn some little-known information about some famous people. In one condition they had subjects study just a single fact:

• Newton became emotionally unstable and insecure as a child.

In the irrelevant condition they had subjects learn a target fact plus two unrelated facts about the individual:

- Locke was unhappy as a student at Westminister.

plus

- Locke felt fruits were unwholesome for children.
- Locke had a long history of back trouble.

In the third, relevant condition subjects learned two additional facts that were causally related to the target fact:

- Mozart made a long journey from Munich to Paris.

plus

- Mozart wanted to leave Munich to avoid a romantic entanglement.
- Mozart was intrigued by musical developments coming out of Paris.

Subjects were tested for their ability to recall the target facts immediately after studying them and at a week's delay. They were presented with names like Newton, Mozart, and Locke and asked to recall what they had studied. The results are displayed in Table 7.3. Comparing the irrelevant condition with the single condition, we see the standard interference effect, which is that recall is worse when there are more facts to be learned about an item. However, the conclusion is quite different when we compare the relevant condition to the single condition. Here, particularly at a week's delay, recall is better when the subject had to learn additional facts causally related to the target facts.

Table 7.3 Percentage of Recall as a Function of Condition and Time Intervals

	Immediate Recall	Recall at a Week
Single fact	92	62
Irrelevant facts	80	45
Relevant facts	94	73

From Bradshaw and Anderson, 1982.

To understand why the effects of interference are eliminated or even reversed when there is redundancy among the materials to be learned requires that we move on to discussing the retrieval process and, in particular, the role of inferential processes in retrieval.

◆
Learning redundant material does not interfere with a target memory and may even facilitate the target memory.

Retrieval and Inference

Often, when subjects cannot remember a particular fact, they are able to retrieve related facts and so infer the target fact on the basis of that. Thus, in the case of the Mozart facts given above, even if the subjects could not recall that Mozart made a long journey from Munich to Paris, if they could retrieve the other two facts, they would be able to infer this target fact. There is considerable evidence that people make such inferences at the time of recall and are not even aware that they are making inferences rather than recalling what was actually studied.

Bransford, Barclay, and Franks (1972) reported another experiment that demonstrates how inference can lead to incorrect recall. They had subjects study one of the following sentences:

1. Three turtles rested beside a floating log, and a fish swam beneath them.

2. Three turtles rested on a floating log, and a fish swam beneath them.

Subjects who had studied sentence 1 were later asked whether they had studied this sentence:

3. Three turtles rested beside a floating log, and a fish swam beneath it.

Not many subjects thought they had studied this. Subjects who had studied sentence 2 were tested with:

4. Three turtles rested on a floating log, and a fish swam beneath it.

Sentence 4 was judged as studied much more often by these subjects than was sentence 3 by the other group of subjects. Of course, sentence 4 is implied by sentence 2, whereas sentence 3 is not implied by sentence 1.

Thus, subjects thought that they had actually studied what was implied by the studied material.

A study by Sulin and Dooling (1974) provides an illustration of how inference can bias subjects' memory for a text. They asked subjects to read the following passage:

Carol Harris's Need for Professional Help
Carol Harris was a problem child from birth. She was wild, stubborn, and violent. By the time Carol turned eight, she was still unmanageable. Her parents were very concerned about her mental health. There was no good institution for her problem in her state. Her parents finally decided to take some action. They hired a private teacher for Carol.

A second group of subjects read the same passage except that the name *Helen Keller* was substituted for *Carol Harris*.[1] A week after reading the passage, subjects were given a recognition test in which they were presented with a sentence and asked to judge whether it had occurred in the passage. One of the critical sentences was *She was deaf, dumb, and blind.* Only 5 percent of the subjects who read the Carol Harris passage accepted this sentence, but a full 50 percent of the Helen Keller subjects thought they had read the sentence. This is just what we would expect. The second group of subjects had elaborated the story with facts they knew about Helen Keller. Thus, it seemed reasonable to them at test that this sentence had appeared in the studied material, but in this case their inference was wrong.

It is interesting to inquire whether such an inference as *She was deaf, dumb, and blind* was made while the subject was studying the passage or only at the time of the test. This is a subtle issue, and subjects certainly do not have reliable intuitions about the matter. However, a couple of techniques seem to yield evidence that the inferences are being made at test. One technique is to determine whether the inferences increase in frequency with delay. With delay, subjects' memory for the studied passage should deteriorate, and if subjects are making inferences at test, they will have to do more reconstruction, which in turn will lead to more inferential errors. Both Dooling and Christiaansen (1977) and Spiro (1977) have found evidence for increased inferential intrusions with increased delay of testing.

Dooling and Christiaansen used another technique with the Carol Harris passage to show that inferences were being made at test. They had the subjects study the passage and told them a week later, just before test, that Carol Harris really was Helen Keller. In this situation, subjects also

---

[1]Helen Keller was well known to subjects of the time, famous for overcoming both deafness and blindness as a child.

made many inferential errors, accepting such sentences as *She was deaf, dumb, and blind*. Since they did not know Carol Harris was Helen Keller until test, they must have made such inferences at test. Thus, it seems that subjects do make such reconstructive inferences at time of test.

◆
In trying to remember material, people will use what they can remember to infer what else they might have studied.

Plausible Retrieval

In the foregoing analysis, we spoke of subjects as making errors when they recalled or recognized facts that were not explicitly presented. In real life, however, such acts of recall would often not be regarded as errors, but as intelligent inferences. Reder (1982) has argued that much of recall in real life involves plausible inference rather than exact recall. For instance, in deciding that Darth Vader was evil in *Star Wars*, a person does not search memory for the specific proposition that Darth Vader was evil, although it may have been directly asserted in the movie. The person infers that Darth Vader was evil from memories about his behavior.

Reder has demonstrated that subjects will display very different behavior, depending on whether they are asked to engage in exact retrieval or plausible retrieval. She had subjects study passages such as the following:

> *The heir to a large hamburger chain was in trouble. He had married a lovely young woman who had seemed to love him. Now he worried that she had been after his money after all. He sensed that she was not attracted to him. Perhaps he consumed too much beer and french fries. No, he couldn't give up the fries. Not only were they delicious, he got them for free.*

Then she had subjects judge sentences such as the following:

1. The heir married a lovely young woman who had seemed to love him.

2. The heir got his french fries from his family's hamburger chain.

3. The heir was very careful to eat only healthy food.

The first sentence was studied; the second was not studied, but is plausible; and the third was neither studied nor plausible. Subjects in the exact condition were asked to make exact recognition judgments, in which case they were to accept the first sentence and reject the second two. Subjects in the plausible condition were to judge whether the sentence was plausible given

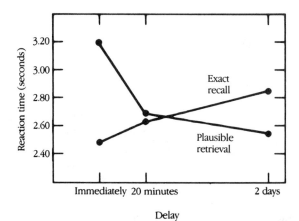

Figure 7.6 Time to make exact versus plausible recognition judgments of sentences as a function of delay since study of a story. (From Reder, 1982.)

the story, in which case they were to accept the first two and reject the last. Reder tested subjects immediately after studying the story, twenty minutes later, or two days later.

Reder was interested in judgment time for subjects in the two conditions, exact versus plausible. Figure 7.6 shows the results from her experiment as a function of delay. Plotted in the figure are the average judgment times for sentence types 1 and 2. As might be expected, subjects get slower with delay in the exact condition. However, they actually get faster in the plausible condition. They start out slower in the plausible than in the exact condition, but this is reversed after two days. Reder argues that subjects get worse in the exact condition because the exact traces are getting weaker. However, a plausibility judgment is not dependent on any particular trace, and so is not similarly vulnerable to forgetting. Subjects get faster in the plausible condition with delay because they no longer try to use inefficient exact retrieval, but use plausibility, which is faster.

Reder and Ross (1983) compared exact versus plausible judgments in another paradigm. They had subjects study sentences such as the following:

Alan bought a ticket for the 10:00 A.M. train.

Alan heard the conductor call "All aboard."

Alan read a newspaper on the train.

Alan arrived at Grand Central Station.

They manipulated the number of sentences that subjects had to study about a particular person such as Alan. Then they looked at subjects' times to recognize sentences such as:

1. Alan heard the conductor call "All aboard."

2. Alan watched the approaching train from the platform.

3. Alan sorted his clothes into colors and whites.

In the exact condition subjects had to judge whether the sentence had been studied. So, given the foregoing material, subjects would accept test sentence 1 and reject test sentences 2 and 3. In the plausible condition, subjects had to judge whether it was plausible that Alan was involved in the activity, given what they had studied. Thus, subjects would accept sentences 1 and 2 and reject 3.

In the exact condition, Reder and Ross found that subjects took longer the more facts they studied about Alan. This is basically a replication of the fan effect discussed earlier in the chapter. In the plausible condition, however, subjects were faster the more facts they had learned about Alan. The more facts they knew about Alan, the more ways there were to judge a particular fact plausible. Thus, plausibility judgment did not have to depend on retrieval of a particular fact.

◆
People will often judge what plausibly might be true rather than try to retrieve exact facts.

The Interaction of Elaboration and Inferential Reconstruction

In the previous chapter, we discussed how people tend to display better memories if they elaborate the material at study. We also discussed there how semantic elaborations were particularly beneficial. Such semantic elaborations should facilitate the process of inference by providing more things from which to infer. Thus, we expect elaborative processing to lead to both an increased recall of what was studied and an increase in the number of inferences recalled. An experiment by Owens, Bower, and Black (1979) confirms this prediction. Subjects studied a story that followed the principal character, a college student, through a day in her life: making a cup of coffee in the morning, visiting a doctor, attending a lecture, going shopping for groceries, and attending a party. The following is a passage from the story:

> *Nancy went to see the doctor. She arrived at the office and checked in with the receptionist. She went to see the nurse, who went through the usual procedures. Then Nancy stepped on the scale and the nurse recorded her weight. The doctor entered the room and examined the results. He smiled at Nancy and said, "Well, it seems my expectations*

have been confirmed." When the examination was finished, Nancy left the office.

Two groups of subjects studied the story. The only difference between the groups was that the theme group had read the following additional information at the beginning:

Nancy woke up feeling sick again and she wondered if she really were pregnant. How would she tell the professor she had been seeing? And the money was another problem.

College students who read this additional passage characterized Nancy as an unmarried student who is afraid she is pregnant as a result of an affair with a college professor. Subjects in the neutral condition who had not read this opening passage had no reason to suspect that there is anything special about Nancy. We would expect subjects in the theme condition to make many more theme-related elaborations of the story than subjects in the neutral condition.

Subjects were asked to recall the story twenty-four hours after studying it. Those in the theme condition introduced a great many more inferences that had not actually been studied. For instance, many subjects reported that the doctor told Nancy she was pregnant. Intrusions of this variety are expected if subjects reconstruct the story on the basis of their elaborations. Table 7.4 reports some of the results from the study. As can be seen, many more inferences are added in recall for the theme condition than for the neutral condition. However, a second important observation is that subjects in the theme condition also recalled more of the propositions they had actually studied. Thus, because of the additional elaborations made by subjects in the theme condition, they were able to recall more of the story.

We might question whether subjects really benefited from their elaborations, since they also "misrecalled" many things that did not occur in the story. However, it is wrong to characterize the intruded inferences as errors. Given the theme information, subjects were perfectly right to make inferences and to recall them. In a nonexperimental setting, such as

Table 7.4 Number of Propositions Recalled		
	Theme Condition	Neutral Condition
Studied propositions	29.2	20.3
Inferred propositions	15.2	3.7

Adapted from Owens et al., 1979.

recalling information on an exam, we would expect these subjects to recall such inferences as easily as material they had actually read.

Advertisers often capitalize on our tendency to embellish what we hear with plausible inferences. Consider the following portion of a Listerine commercial:

> *"Wouldn't it be great," asks the mother, "if you could make him cold-proof? Well, you can't. Nothing can do that." [Boy sneezes.] "But there is something that you can do that may help. Have him gargle with Listerine Antiseptic. Listerine can't promise to keep him coldfree, but it may help him fight off colds. During the cold-catching season, have him gargle twice a day with full-strength Listerine. Watch his diet, see he gets plenty of sleep, and there's a good chance he'll have fewer colds, milder colds this year."*

A verbatim text of this commercial, with the product name changed to "Gargoil," was used by Harris (1977). After hearing this commercial, all fifteen of his subjects checked that "gargling with Gargoil Antiseptic helps prevent colds," although this assertion was clearly not made in the commercial. The Federal Trade Commission explicitly forbids advertisers from making false claims, but does the Listerine ad make a false claim? In a potentially landmark case, the courts ruled against Warner-Lambert, makers of Listerine, for implying false claims in this commercial.

◆

When subjects elaborate on material at study, they tend to recall more of what they studied but also tend to recall inferences that they did not study.

Memory Errors

The ability to elaborate inferentially on our memories at study and test is essential to success in using our memory in everyday life. Inferences at study allow us to go from what we actually heard and saw to what is probably true. When we hear that someone found out that she was pregnant in a doctor's visit, it is a reasonable inference that she was told by the doctor. So, such inferences usually lead to a much more coherent and accurate understanding of the world. However, there are circumstances where we need to be able to separate what we actually saw and heard from our inferences. The difficulty in doing so can lead to harmful false memories of which the Gargoil example above is only the tip of the iceberg.

One situation in which it is critical to separate inference from actual experience is the case of eyewitness testimony. It has been shown that eyewitnesses are often quite inaccurate in the testimony that they give, even though their testimony is given high weight by jurors. One of the reasons for their low accuracy is because people confuse what they actually observe about an incident with what they hear from other sources. Loftus (1975, 1979; Loftus, Miller, & Burns, 1978) showed that subsequent information can change a subject's memory of an event they observed. For instance, one study by Loftus asked subjects who had witnessed a traffic accident about the car's speed when it passed a *yield* sign. Although there was no yield sign, many subjects subsequently remembered having seen one. Another interesting example involves the testimony given by John Dean regarding events in the Nixon White House during the Watergate cover-up (Neisser, 1981). After Dean gave his testimony about conversations in the Oval Office, it was discovered that Nixon had recorded these conversations. While Dean was substantially accurate in gist, it turns out that he confused many details, including the order in which these conversations took place.

Another case of memory confusion that has produced a great deal of recent notoriety is the false memory syndrome. This concerns memories of childhood abuse that appear to be "recovered" by various psychotherapeutic techniques. There is evidence, however, that some of these recovered memories never happened and were created by the strong suggestions of the therapists. A number of researchers have shown that it is possible to create false memories by these techniques. For instance, Loftus and Pickerall (1995) succeeded in convincing about 25 percent of adult subjects that they had been lost in a mall as a child, although this had never happened. In another study, Ceci, Loftus, Leichtman, and Bruck (1995) succeeded in creating such false memories in children from age three to six. The process by which we distinguish between memory and imagination is quite fragile, and it is easy to become confused about the source of information.

◆

Serious errors of memory can occur because people fail to separate what they actually experienced from what they inferred or imagined.

Associative Structure and Retrieval

An implication of the spreading activation theory described in the previous chapter is that we can improve our memory by providing prompts to our memory that are closely associated with these memories. You may find yourself practicing this when you try to remember the name of an old classmate. You may find yourself prompting your memory with names of other classmates or memories of things you did with that classmate. Often, the name does appear to come to mind as a consequence of such efforts. An experiment by Tulving and Pearlstone (1966) provides one experimental demonstration of this. They had subjects learn lists of forty-eight words that contained categories like *dog,*, *cat, horse,* and *cow,* which form a domestic mammal category. Subjects were asked to try to recall all the words in the list. They displayed better memory for the word lists when they were given prompts such as *mammal*, which would serve to cue memory for members of the categories.

Organization and Recall

Numerous manipulations have been shown to improve subjects' memory in recalling a long list of items by providing some mechanism for cueing memory of the individual items in the list. Many such devices involve organizing the material in such a way that subjects can systematically search their memories for the items. A nice demonstration of this use of organization is an experiment by Bower, Clark, Lesgold, and Winzenz (1969). These investigators asked subjects to learn all the words in four hierarchies such as the one in Figure 7.7. Two conditions of learning were compared. In the organized condition, the four hierarchies were presented in upside-down trees, one of which is in the figure. In the random condition, subjects saw four trees, but the positions in the trees were filled by random combinations of words from the four categories. Thus, instead of seeing separate trees for animals, clothing, transportation, and minerals, subjects saw four trees, each containing some items from each category. Subjects were given a minute to study each tree, and after studying all four trees, they were asked to recall all the words in the four trees in any order. This study-test sequence was repeated four times. The performance of the two groups over the four trials is given in Table 7.5 in terms of number of words recalled. The maximum possible recall was 112. The organized group was shown to have an enormous advantage. Analysis of the order in which the

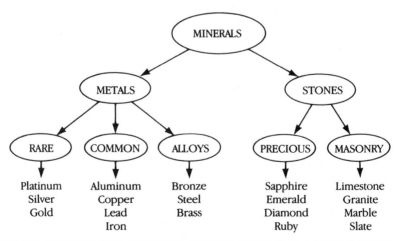

Figure 7.7 A hierarchical tree presented to subjects in the free-recall experiment of Bower et al. (From Bower et al., 1969.)

Table 7.5 Average Number of Words Recalled over Four Trials as a Function of Organization

	Trials			
Conditions	1	2	3	4
Organized	73.0	106.1	112.0	112.0
Random	20.6	38.9	52.8	70.1

Adapted from Bower et al., 1969.

organized group recalled the words indicated that subjects had organized their recall according to the tree hierarchies and recalled the words going down a tree from the top—for example, using Figure 7.7, first they would recall *minerals* and then *metals*. The advantage of the organized group is that they had a systematic way to go through and cue their memories for the elements. For instance, *minerals* cues the recall of *metals*, which cues the recall of *alloys* which cues the recall of *brass*.

The implication of the results in Bower et al. for study habits is both important and clear. Course material can often be organized into hierarchies just as word lists can. Table 7.6 is a hierarchical organization for the material up to this point in the chapter. (In actually studying this material, students would be better off deriving their own organizations, since doing so will force deeper processing of the material.) For readability, levels of the hierarchy are represented by levels of indentation. By organizing material this way, one has placed it in a structure that will facilitate its retrieval when one needs the information in a task such as writing an essay answer.

◆ Retrieval of information is facilitated if it is organized hierarchically.

The Method of Loci

A classic mnemonic technique, the **method of loci**, also has its effect by promoting good organization for purposes of retrieval. This technique, used extensively in ancient times when speeches were given without written notes or teleprompters, is still used today. Cicero (in *De Oratore*) credits the method to a Greek poet, Simonides, who had delivered a lyric poem at a banquet. Following his delivery, he was called from the banquet hall by the gods Castor and Pollux, whom he had praised in this poem. While he was absent, the roof fell in, killing all the participants at the banquet. The corpses were so mangled that relatives could not identify them. However, Simonides was able to identify each corpse according to where each person had been sitting in the banquet hall. This feat of total

---

Table 7.6 Chapter Organization to This Point

Retention
The retention function
    The power law of retention
    Bahrick's study
    Long-term potentiation
Interference effects
    Paired-associate paradigm
    The fan effect
        Anderson (1974a) experiment
        Network interpretation
    Preexperimental memories
    Relationship to decay
    Effects of redundancy

Retrieval
Role of inference
    Bransford, Barclay, and Franks (three turtles)
    Dooling's studies with the Helen Keller passage
    Plausible retrieval (Reder)
    Interaction with elaboration processing
        Owens, Bower, and Black
        Harris's Gargoil experiment
        Memory errors
Role of associative structure
    Effects of organization
        Hierarchies
        Bower, Clark, Lesgold, and Winzenz
        This example

---

recall convinced Simonides of the usefulness of an orderly arrangement of locations into which a person could place objects to be remembered. This story may be rather fanciful, but whatever its true origin, the method of loci, is well documented (e.g., Christen & Bjork, 1976; Ross & Lawrence, 1968) as a useful technique for remembering an ordered sequence of items, such as the points a person wants to make in a speech.

Basically, to use the method of loci the individual imagines a fixed path through a familiar area with some fixed locations along the path. For instance, if there were such a path on campus from the bookstore to the library, we might use it. To remember a series of objects, we simply mentally walk along the path, associating the objects with the fixed locations. As an example, consider a grocery list of six items—milk, hot dogs, dog food, tomatoes, bananas, and bread. To associate the milk with the bookstore, we might imagine a puddle of milk in front of the bookstore with books fallen into the milk. To associate hot dogs with the record shop (the next location in the path from the bookstore), we might imagine a package of hot dogs spinning on a record player turntable. The pizza shop is next, and to associate this with dog food we might imagine a pizza with dog food on it (well, some people even like anchovies). Then, we come to the intersection; to associate this with tomatoes we can imagine an over-turned vegetable truck and tomatoes splattered everywhere. Next we come to the administration building—and an image of the president coming out, wearing only a hula-type skirt made of bananas. Finally, we reach the library and associate it with bread by imagining a huge loaf of bread serving as a canopy under which we must pass to enter. To re-create the list, we need only take an imaginary walk down this path, reviving the associations to each location. This technique works well even with very much longer lists; we only need more locations. There is considerable evidence (e.g., Christen & Bjork, 1976) that the same loci can be used over and over again in the learning of different lists.

Two important principles underlie this method's effectiveness. First, the technique imposes organization on an otherwise unorganized list. We are guaranteed that if we follow the mental path at time of recall, we will pass all the locations for which we created associations. The second principle is that generating imaginal connections between the locations and the items forces us to process the material meaningfully, elaboratively, and by use of visual imagery.

◆

The method of loci works by using a fixed sequence of locations to cue retrieval of memories.

The Effects of Encoding Context

Among the cues that can become associated with a memory are cues from the context in which the memory was formed. If at test such contextual cues could be revived, the subject would have additional ways to reactivate the target memory. There is ample evidence that context can greatly influence memory. This section will review some of the ways in which context influences memory. These context effects are often referred to as encoding effects because the context is affecting what is encoded into the memory trace that records the event.

Smith, Glenberg, and Bjork (1978) performed an experiment that showed the importance of physical context. In their experiment, subjects learned two lists of paired associates on different days and in different physical settings. On day 1, subjects learned the paired associates in a windowless room in a building near the University of Michigan campus. The experimenter was neatly groomed, dressed in a coat and a tie, and the paired associates were shown on slides. On day 2, subjects learned the paired associates in a tiny room with windows on the main campus. The experimenter was dressed sloppily in a flannel shirt and jeans (it was the same experimenter, but some subjects did not recognize him) and presented the paired associates via a tape recorder. A day later, subjects made their recall of half the paired associates in one setting and half in the other setting. Subjects could recall 59 percent of the list learned in the same setting as tested, but only 46 percent of the list learned in the other setting. Thus, it seems that recall is better if the context at test is the same as the context at study.

Perhaps the most dramatic manipulation of context was performed by Godden and Baddeley (1975). They had divers learn a list of forty unrelated words either on the shore or twenty feet under the sea. The divers were then asked to recall the list in either the same or a different environment. Figure 7.8 displays the results of this study. Subjects clearly showed superior memory when they were asked to recall in the same context in which they studied. So, it seems that contextual elements get associated to memories, and that memory is improved when subjects are provided with these contextual elements again.

The degree to which such contextual effects are obtained has proved to be quite variable from experiment to experiment. Fernandez and Glenberg (1985) report a number of failures to find any context dependence; and Saufley, Otaka, and Bavaresco (1985) report a failure to find such effects in a classroom situation. Eich (1985) argues that the magnitude of such contextual effects depends on the degree to which the subject integrates the context with the memories. In his experiment, he read lists to two groups of subjects. In one condition, subjects were instructed to imagine the referents of the nouns alone, and in the other condition subjects were

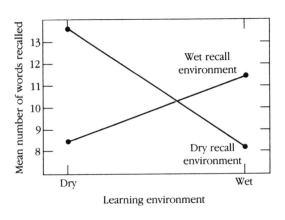

Figure 7.8 Mean number of words recalled as a function of environment in which learning took place. Word lists were recalled better in the same environment in which they were learned than in a different environment. (Data from Godden & Baddeley, 1975.)

asked to imagine the referents integrated with the context. Eich found a much larger effect of a change of context when subjects were instructed to imagine the referent integrated with the context.

Research by Bower, Monteiro, and Gilligan (1978) shows that emotional context can have the same effect as physical context. They also instructed subjects to learn two lists. For one list they hypnotically induced a positive state by having subjects review a pleasant episode in their lives, and for the other list they hypnotically induced a negative state by having subjects review a traumatic event. A later recall test was given under either a positive or a negative emotional state (again hypnotically induced). Better memory was obtained when the emotional state at test matched the emotional state at study.[2]

Such mood-dependent effects are not always obtained. For instance, Bower and Mayer (1985) failed to replicate the Bower et al. (1978) result. Eich and Metcalfe (1989) have found that such mood-dependent effects tend to be obtained only when subjects integrated their memories at study with the mood information. Thus, like effects of physical context, mood-dependent effects only occur in special study situations.

Perhaps a more robust effect is what is called **mood congruence**. This refers to the fact that it is easier to remember happy memories in a happy state and sad memories in a sad state. This is an effect of the content of the memories rather than the emotional state of the subject during study. For instance, Teasdale and Russell (1983) had subjects learn a list of positive, negative, and neutral words in a normal state. Then, at test, they either induced positive or negative states. Their results are illustrated in Figure 7.9. As can be seen, subjects recalled more of the words that matched their mood at test. When mood elements are present at test, they will prime memories that share these mood elements. These elements will include memories whose inherent content matches the mood, as in the Teasdale and Russell experiment, and memories that have such mood elements integrated as part of the study procedure (as in Eich and Metcalfe).

A related phenomenon is referred to as **state-dependent learning**. People find it easier to recall information if they can return to the same emotional and physical state they were in when they learned the information. For instance, it is often casually claimed that heavy drinkers when sober are unable to remember where they hid their alcohol when drunk, and when drunk they are unable to remember where they hid their money

---

[2]As an aside, it is worth commenting that, despite popular reports, the best evidence is that hypnosis per se does nothing to improve memory (see Hilgard, 1968; Smith, 1982), although it can help memory to the extent that it can be used to re-create the contextual factors at the time of test. However, much of a learning context can also be re-created by nonhypnotic means, such as through free association about the circumstances of the to-be-remembered event (e.g., Geiselman, Fisher, Mackinnon, & Holland, 1985).

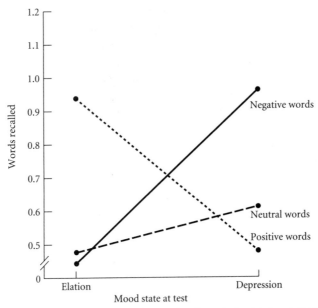

Figure 7.9 Recall of positive, negative, and neutral trait words in elated and depressed mood states. (From Teasdale & Russell, 1983. Reprinted by permission of the British Psychological Society.)

when sober. In fact, some experimental evidence does exist for this state dependency of memory with respect to alcohol, but the more important factor seems to be that alcohol has a general debilitating effect on the acquisition of information (Parker, Birnbaum, & Noble, 1976). Marijuana has been shown to have similar state-dependent effects. In one experiment (Eich, Weingartner, Stillman, & Gillin, 1975), subjects learned a free-recall list after smoking either a marijuana cigarette or an ordinary cigarette. Subjects were tested 4 hours later—again after smoking either a marijuana cigarette or a regular cigarette. Table 7.7 shows the results from this study. Two effects are shown in this table, typical of the research on the effects of

Table 7.7 Interaction between Effects of Drugged State at Study and Test

| | Test | | |
Study	Ordinary Cigarette	Marijuana Cigarette	Average
Ordinary cigarette	25%	20%	23%
Marijuana cigarette	12%	23%	18%

From Eich, Weingartner, Stillman, and Gillin, 1975.

psychoactive drugs on memory. First, there is a state-dependent effect reflected by higher recall when state at test matched the state at study. Second, there is an overall higher level of recall when the material was studied in a nonintoxicated state.

—◆————————————————————————————

People show better memory if their external contexts and internal states match at study and test.

Effects of Other Materials in the Context

Memory for to-be-learned material can also be heavily dependent on the context of other *to-be-learned* material in which it is embedded. Consider a recognition-memory experiment by Thompson (1972). Thompson's subjects studied pairs of words such as *sky blue*. Subjects were told that they were responsible only for the second item of the pair—in this case *blue*; the first word represented context. Later, they were tested by being presented with either *blue* or *sky blue*. In either case, they were asked whether they had originally seen *blue*. In the single-word case, they recognized *blue* 76 percent of the time, while in the pair condition their recognition rate was 85 percent. Thus, even though they were only tested for *blue*, their memories were better in the context of the other word.

A series of experiments (e.g., Tulving & Thompson, 1973; Watkins & Tulving, 1975) has dramatically illustrated how memory for a word can depend on how well the test context matches the original study context. There were three phases to the experiment:

(1) **Original Study:** Watkins and Tulving had subjects learn pairs of words such as *train black* and told them that they were responsible only for the second word, referred to as the to-be-remembered word.

(2) **Generate and Recognize:** Subjects were given words such as *white* and asked to generate four free associates to the word. So, a subject might generate *snow*, *black*, *wool*, and *pure*. The stimuli for the associate task were chosen to have a high probability of eliciting the to-be-remembered word. For instance, *white* has a high probability of eliciting *black*. After they had generated their associates, subjects were told to indicate which of the four associates was the one they had studied. In cases where the to-be-remembered word was generated, subjects correctly chose it only 54 percent of the time. Since subjects were always forced to indicate a choice, some of these correct choices must have been lucky guesses. Thus, true recognition was even lower than 54 percent.

(3) Cued Recall: Subjects were presented with the original context words (e.g., *train*) and asked to recall the to-be-remembered words (i.e., *black*). Subjects recalled 61 percent of the words — higher than their recognition rate without any correction for guessing. Moreover, Watkins and Tulving found that 42 percent of the words recalled had not been recognized earlier when the subjects gave them as free associates.[3]

Recognition is usually superior to recall. Thus, we would expect that if subjects could not recognize a word, they would be unable to recall it. Usually, we expect to do better on a multiple-choice test than on a recall-the-answer test. Experiments such as the one just described provided very dramatic reversals of such standard expectations. The results can be understood in terms of the similarity of the test context to the study context. The test context with the word *white* and its associates was quite different from that in which *black* had originally been studied. In contrast, in the cued-recall test context, subjects were given the original context (*train*) with which they had studied the word. Thus, if the contextual factors are sufficiently weighted in favor of recall, as they were in these experiments, recall can be superior to recognition. Tulving interprets these results as illustrating what he calls the **encoding-specificity principle**: The probability of recalling an item at test depends on the similarity of its encoding at test to its original encoding at study.

◆

Subjects show better word memory if the words are tested in the context of the same words as they were studied.

The Hippocampal Formation and Amnesia

Insight concerning the nature of memory can be obtained by studying patients who suffer from memory loss because of damage to neural structures. There is a great deal of evidence pointing to the hippocampal formation as critical for the establishment of permanent memories. The hippocampal formation is a brain structure embedded within the temporal cortex. In animal studies (typically rats or primates; for a review, see Eichenbaum & Bunsey, 1995, and Squire, 1992), it has been shown that lesions to the hippocampal formation produce severe impairments in the ability of animals to learn new associations, particularly those that require remembering combinations or configurations of elements. Damage to the

---

[3]A great deal of research has been done on this phenomenon. For a review, read Nilsson & Gardiner (1993).

hippocampal area also produces severe **amnesia** (memory loss) in humans. One of the most studied amnesic patients is a patient known as H. M. He had large parts of his temporal lobes removed in an operation to cure epilepsy. He has one of the most profound amnesias and for more than forty years has been almost totally unable to remember new events. His surgical operation involved complete removal of the hippocampus and surrounding structures, and this is considered to be the reason for his profound memory deficits (Squire, 1992).

Only rarely is there a reason for surgically removing the hippocampal formation from humans. However, for various reasons humans can suffer severe damage to this structure and the surrounding temporal lobe. One common cause is a severe blow to the head, but other common causes include brain infections, such as encephalitis, and chronic alcoholism, which can result in a condition called **Korsakoff syndrome**. Such damage will result in two types of amnesia: **retrograde amnesia**, which refers to loss of memories before the injury; and **anterograde amnesia**, which refers to an inability to learn new things.

Often, in the case of blows to the head, the amnesia is not permanent but displays a particular pattern of recovery. Figure 7.10 displays the pattern of recovery for a patient who was in a coma for seven weeks following a closed head injury. Tested five months after the injury, the patient showed total anterograde amnesia, not remembering what had happened since the injury. The patient also displayed total retrograde amnesia for the two years preceding the injury and substantial disturbance of memory beyond that. When tested eight months after the injury, the patient now showed some ability to remember new experiences, and the period of total retrograde amnesia had shrunk to one year. When tested sixteen months after injury, the patient now had full ability to remember new events and only had a permanent two-week period before the injury when he could remember nothing. It is characteristic that retrograde amnesia is for events close in time to the injury and that events just before the injury are never recovered. In general, anterograde and retrograde amnesia show this pattern of occurring and recovering together, although in different patients either the retrograde or the anterograde symptoms can be more severe.

There are a number of striking features that characterize cases of amnesia. One feature is that there can be anterograde amnesia in the face of some preserved long-term memories. This is particularly the case for H. M., who remembers many things from his youth, but is unable to learn anything new. This indicates that the neural structures involved in forming new memories are distinct from those involved in maintaining old ones. It is thought the hippocampal formation is particularly important in creating new memories, but old memories are maintained in the cerebral cortex. It is thought that events just prior to the injury are particularly susceptible in retrograde amnesia because they still require the hippocampus for support.

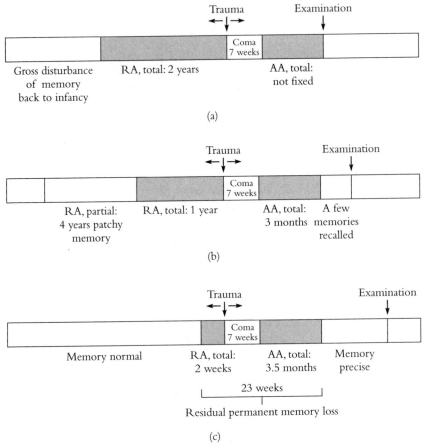

Figure 7.10 Recovery of a patient from amnesia (a) after 5 months; (b) after 8 months, (c) after 16 months. From Barbizet (1970).

A second striking feature of these amnesia cases is that the memory deficit is not complete, and that there are certain kinds of memories the patient is still capable of acquiring. This will be discussed in the next section on implicit and explicit memory. A third striking feature of amnesia is that patients can remember things for short periods but then forget them. Thus, H. M. will be introduced to a person and be told the person's name, use that name for a short while, and then forget it after a half minute. Thus, the problem in anterograde amnesia is retaining the memories for more than five or ten seconds.

◆
Patients with damage to the hippocampal formation show both retrograde amnesia and anterograde amnesia.

Implicit versus Explicit Memory

So far this chapter has focused on memories that people have conscious access to. However, some of the most interesting research in the field of memory concerns memories that we are not conscious we have. Occasionally, we will become aware that we know things which we cannot describe. One example that some people can relate to is memory for the keyboard of a typewriter. Many accomplished typists cannot recall the arrangement of the keys except by imagining themselves typing. Clearly, their fingers know where the keys are, but they just have no conscious access to this knowledge. Such implicit memory demonstrations highlight the significance of retrieval conditions in assessing memory. If we asked the typists to tell us where the keys were, we would conclude they had no knowledge of the keyboard. If we tested their typing, we could conclude that they have perfect knowledge. This section is concerned with such contrasts between explicit and implicit memory. Such contrasts are referred to as **dissociations**. That is, they involve showing that implicit and explicit memory behave differently. In the keyboard example above, explicit memory shows no knowledge, while implicit memory shows total knowledge. **Explicit memory** is the term used to describe knowledge that we can consciously recall. **Implicit memory** is the term used to describe knowledge that we cannot recall but that nonetheless manifests itself in our improved performance on some task.

Cases of total dissociation of implicit and explicit knowledge, such as the typing example, are rare with normal humans. However, such cases are more common in patients who suffer from certain amnesias. Amnesic patients will display implicit memories of many experiences that they cannot consciously recall. For instance, Graf, Squire, and Mandler (1984) compared amnesic versus normal subjects with respect to their memories for a list of words like *banana*. After studying these words, subjects were asked to recall the words. The results are shown in Figure 7.11. Amnesic subjects did much worse than normal subjects. Then subjects were given a word-completion task. They were shown the first three letters of a word they had studied and were asked to make an English word out of it. For instance, subjects might be asked to complete *ban_____*. By chance, there is a less than 10 percent probability that subjects can generate the word (*banana*) that they studied, but as shown in the figure, subjects in both groups were coming up with the studied word more than 50 percent of the time. Moreover, there was no difference between the amnesic and the normal subjects in the word-completion task. So, the amnesic subjects clearly did have memory for the word list. However, they could not gain conscious access to these memories in a free-recall task. Rather, they displayed implicit memory in the word-completion task. The patient H. M.,

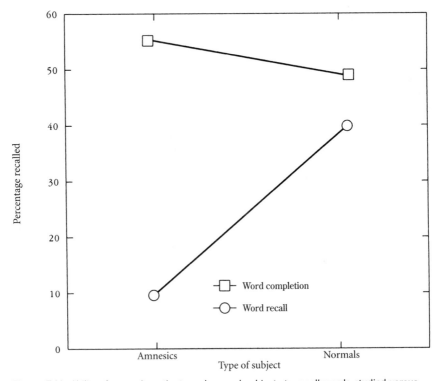

Figure 7.11 Ability of amnesic patients and normal subjects to recall words studied versus ability to complete fragments of words studied. (From Graf, Squire, & Mandler, 1984.)

discussed in the previous section, has also been shown capable of implicit learning. For example, he is able to improve on various perceptual-motor tasks across days, although each day he has no memory of the task from the previous day (Milner, 1962).

◆ ──

Amnesic patients are often unable to consciously recall some event but will show in implicit ways that they have some sort of memory for the event.

──

Implicit versus Explicit Memory in Normal Subjects

A great deal of recent research (for reviews, read Schacter, 1987; Richardson-Klavehn & Bjork, 1988) has looked at dissociations between implicit and explicit memory in normal subjects. With this population it is often not possible to obtain the dramatic dissociations we see in amnesic subjects, where there is no conscious memory in the presence of normal implicit memory. However, it has been possible to demonstrate that certain variables have different effects on tests of explicit memory than on tests of implicit memory. For instance, Jacoby (1983) had subjects either just study a word such as *woman* alone (the no-context condition), or study it in the presence of an antonym *man-woman* (the context condition), or generate the word as an antonym. In this last condition, subjects would see *man-* and have to say *woman*. Jacoby then tested the subjects in two ways, which were designed to tap either explicit memory or implicit memory. The explicit memory test involved presenting subjects with a list of words, some studied and some not, and asking them to recognize the old words. The implicit memory test involved presenting the word to subjects for a brief period (40 milliseconds) and asking them to identify the word. Figure 7.12 shows the results from these two tests as a function of study condition. As can be seen, performance on the explicit memory test is best in the condition that involves more semantic and generative processing—in line with earlier research we reviewed on elaborative processing. In contrast, performance on the implicit perceptual identification test gets worse. All three conditions show better perceptual identification than if the subject had not studied the word at all (only 60 percent). This enhancement of perceptual

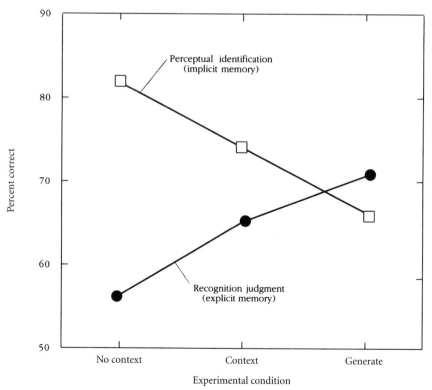

Figure 7.12 Ability to recognize a word in a memory test versus ability to identify it in a perceptual test as a function of how the word was originally studied. (From Jacoby, 1983.)

recognition is referred to as **priming**. Jacoby argues that subjects show greatest priming in the no-context condition because this is the study condition in which they had to rely most on a perceptual encoding to identify the word. In the generate condition, subjects did not even have a word to read.[4]

In another experiment, Jacoby and Witherspoon (1982) asked the question of whether subjects would display more priming for those words they could recognize than for words they could not. Subjects first studied a set of words. Then, in one phase of their experiment, subjects had to try to explicitly recognize whether they had studied the words, and in another phase subjects had to identify the words after a brief presentation. Subjects showed better ability to perceptually identify words they had studied given a brief presentation. However, Jacob, and Witherspoon found no difference between success in perceiving recognized words and success in perceiving nonrecognized words. Thus, exposure to a word improves normal subjects' ability to perceive that word even though they cannot recall seeing the word.

◆
Elaborative processing facilitates explicit memories but not implicit memories.

Procedural Memory

Implicit memory is defined as memory without conscious awareness. By this definition, rather different things can be considered implicit memories. Sometimes, implicit memories involve things like the spelling of words or perceptual information relevant to recognizing the words. These memories result in the priming effects we saw in experiments such as Jacoby's. In other cases, implicit memories involve knowledge about how to perform tasks. A classic example of such an implicit memory is riding a bike. Most of us have learned to ride a bike with no conscious ability to say what it is we have learned. Amnesic subjects show spared memory for procedural information as well as for the sort of information that underlies priming effects.

An experiment by Berry and Broadbent (1984) involved a procedural learning task that has a more cognitive character than riding a bike. They asked subjects to try to control the output of a hypothetical sugar factory (which was simulated by a computer program) by manipulating the size of the workforce. Subjects would see the month's output of the sugar factory

---

[4]Not all research has found poorer implicit memory in the no-context condition. However, all research finds an interaction between study condition and type of memory test. See Masson and MacLeod (1992) for further discussion.

♦

Table 7.8 An Illustrative Series of Inputs and Outputs for Sugar Production

Workforce (W) Input	Sugar Output (S) in Tons
	6,000
700	
	8,000
900	
	10,000
800	
	7,000
1,000	
	12,000
900	
	6,000
1,000	
	13,000
1,000	
	8,000

in thousands of tons (e.g., 6,000 tons) and then have to choose the next month's workforce in hundreds of workers (e.g., 700). They would then see the next month's output of sugar (e.g., 8,000 tons) and have to pick the workforce for the following month. Table 7.8 shows a series of interactions with the hypothetical sugar factory. The subject's goal was to keep sugar production within the range of 8,000 to 10,000 tons.

One can try to infer what the rule is relating sugar output to labor force in Table 7.8. It is not particularly obvious. The sugar output in thousands (S) was related to the workforce in hundreds (W) and the previous month's sugar output in thousands (S_1) by the following formula $S = 2 \times W - S_1$. (In addition, there is sometimes added a random fluctuation of 1,000 tons of sugar.) Oxford undergraduates were given sixty trials at trying to control the factory. Over those sixty trials, they got quite good at controlling the output of the sugar factory. However, they were unable to state what the rule was and claimed they made their responses on the basis of "some sort of intuition" or because it "felt right." Thus, subjects were able to acquire implicit knowledge of how to operate such a factory without corresponding explicit knowledge. Amnesic subjects have also been shown capable of learning this information (Phelps, 1989).

A frequent distinction in psychology (e.g., Anderson, 1976; Cohen & Squire, 1980; and Schacter, 1987) is between declarative and procedural knowledge. **Declarative knowledge** is explicit knowledge that we can report and of which we are consciously aware. **Procedural knowledge** is knowledge of how to do things, and it is often implicit (although, as we noted, there are other kinds of implicit memory, such as that found in priming experiments). The research in this chapter and in Chapter 6 has been mainly concerned with declarative memory. In the next two chapters, we will focus mainly on procedural memory.

◆
Subjects can develop effective procedures for performing tasks without any ability to explain what they are doing.

Remarks and Suggested Readings

The topics of this chapter are discussed more fully in a number of sources. Rubin and Wenzel (1996) provide a review of the retention function. Healy and Bourne (1995) provide a number of reports looking at the high levels of retention for some kinds of knowledge. There has been some discussion of the proper interpretation of the fan effect (see Radvansky & Zacks, 1991; Anderson & Reder, in press). Reder (1996) has edited a book on implicit memory. Squire (1992) provides a review of the role of the hippocampus and related structures in memory. Schacter (1996) makes a popular presentation of recent research on memory. Tulving and Craik (in press) have edited a *Handbook of Memory*, which covers these topics and many more.

8

Problem Solving

This chapter represents a watershed in the book. To this point, we have concerned ourselves with how knowledge about the world gets into the memory system, how this knowledge is represented, and how it is stored in and retrieved from long-term memory. As discussed at the end of the last chapter, this kind of knowledge is frequently referred to as **declarative knowledge**—knowledge about facts and things. In this chapter we begin to consider **procedural knowledge**—knowledge about how to perform various cognitive activities. This chapter focuses on the knowledge underlying problem-solving activities. Later chapters will be concerned with the knowledge underlying reasoning, decision making, language comprehension, and language generation.

Procedural Knowledge and Problem Solving

In understanding procedural knowledge, we start with problem solving because it seems that all cognitive activities are fundamentally problem solving in nature. The basic argument (Anderson, 1983; Newell, 1980; Tolman, 1932) is that human cognition is always purposeful, directed to achieving goals and to removing obstacles to those goals. In order to understand what this claim means, it is useful to understand what we mean when we say that a behavior is an instance of problem solving.

To get a perspective on what is meant by problem solving, we will look at one of the classic studies of problem solving in another species— chimpanzees (Köhler, 1927). Köhler, a famous German gestalt psychologist who came to America in the 1930s, found himself trapped on Tenerife in the Canary Islands during World War I. On this island, he found a colony of captive chimpanzees, which he studied, taking particular interest in the problem-solving behavior of the animals. His prize subject was a chimpanzee named Sultan. One problem posed to Sultan was to get some bananas that were outside his cage. Sultan had no difficulty if he was given a stick that could reach the bananas. He simply used the stick to pull the bananas into his cage. However, the critical problem occurred when Sultan

Figure 8.1 Köhler's ape solving the two-stick problem: He combines two short sticks to form a pole long enough to reach the food. (From Köhler, 1956.)

was provided with two poles, neither of which would reach the food. After vainly reaching with the poles, the frustrated ape sulked in his cage. Suddenly, he went over to the poles and put one inside the other, creating a pole long enough to reach the food; with this extended pole, he was able to reach his prize (see Figure 8.1). This was clearly a creative problem-solving act on the part of Sultan.

What are the essential features that qualify this episode as an instance of problem solving? There seem to be three essential features:

1. **Goal directedness.** The behavior is clearly organized toward a goal—in this case, of getting the food.

2. **Subgoal decomposition.** If the ape could have gotten the food by simply reaching for it, the behavior would have been problem solving but only in the most primitive sense. The essence of the problem solution is that the ape had to decompose the original goal into subtasks, or subgoals, such as getting the poles and putting them together.

3. **Operator application.** Decomposing the overall goal into subgoals such as putting the sticks together is useful because the ape knows operators that can help him achieve these subgoals. The term **operator** refers to an action that will transform the problem state into another problem state. The solution of the overall problem is a sequence of these known operators.

An interesting question is what would have happened had Sultan been required to solve the same problem over and over again? Eventually, the whole solution would have become packaged as a single operation, and Sultan would simply breeze through the sequence of steps required to achieve the goal. It might no longer appear intuitively to be problem solving but rather that the animal was simply executing a learned procedure. However, this just makes the point that all procedural knowledge has its origins in problem solving. In common usage, we tend to reserve the term *problem solving* for the original difficult episodes, such as Sultan's first effort to solve the problem. However, the later, more automated episodes are no less problem solving. Newell (1980) argues that we would see this when something goes wrong. For instance, if one of the sticks were clogged with dirt, Sultan might have reverted back to setting subgoals such as cleaning the dirt out so that he could put one stick into the other.

◆───

Procedural knowledge originates in problem-solving activity in which a goal is decomposed into subgoals for which the problem solver possesses operators.

The Problem Space and Search

Frequently, problem solving is described in terms of searching a **problem space**, which consists of various states of the problem. A **state** is a representation of the problem in some degree of solution. The initial situation of the problem solver is referred to as the initial state, the situations on the way to the goal as intermediate states, and the goal as the **goal state**. Starting from the initial state, there are many ways the problem solver can choose to change his or her state. Sultan could reach for a stick, stand on his head, or sulk, and so on. Suppose the ape reaches for the stick. Now, he is in a new state. He can transform this into another state, for example, by letting go of the stick (thereby returning to the earlier state), reaching with the stick for the food, throwing the stick at the food, or reaching for the other stick. Suppose he reaches for another stick. Again, he is in a new state. From this state, Sultan can choose to try, say, walking on the sticks, putting them together, or eating the sticks. Suppose he chooses to put the sticks together. He can then choose to reach for the food, throw the sticks away, or undo them. If he reaches for the food, he will achieve his goal state.

The various states that the problem solver can achieve are referred to as defining a problem space, or state space. Problem-solving operators can be conceived of as changing one state in the space into another. The problem is to find some possible sequence of operators that goes from the initial state to the goal state in the problem space. We can conceive of the problem space as a maze of states and of the operators as paths for moving among the states. In this conception, the solution to a problem is achieved through **search**; that is, the problem solver must find an appropriate path through a maze of states. This conception of problem solving as a search through a state space was developed by Allen Newell and Herbert Simon of Carnegie Mellon University and has become the dominant analysis of problem solving, in both cognitive psychology and artificial intelligence.

A problem-space characterization consists of a set of states and operators for moving among the states. A good problem for illustrating the problem-space characterization is the eight-tile puzzle, consisting of eight numbered, movable tiles set in a 3 × 3 frame. One cell of the frame is always empty, making it possible to move an adjacent numbered tile into the empty cell and thereby to "move" the empty cell as well. The goal is to achieve a particular configuration of tiles, starting from a different configuration. For instance, a problem might be to transform

2	1	6
4	•	8
7	5	3

into

1	2	3
8	•	4
7	6	5

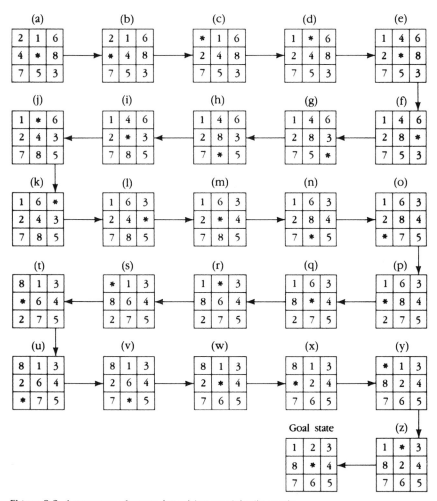

Figure 8.2 A sequence of moves for solving an eight-tile puzzle.

The possible states of this problem are represented as configurations of tiles in the eight-tile puzzle. So, the first configuration shown is the initial state, and the second is the goal state. The operators that change the states are movements of tiles into empty spaces. Figure 8.2 reproduces an attempt of mine to solve this problem. This solution involved 26 moves, each move being an operator that changed the state of the problem. This sequence of operators is considerably longer than necessary. Try to find a shorter sequence of moves. (The shortest sequence possible is given at the end of the chapter, in Figure 8.17.)

Often, discussions of problem solving involve the use of search graphs or **search trees**. Figure 8.3 gives a partial search tree for the following,

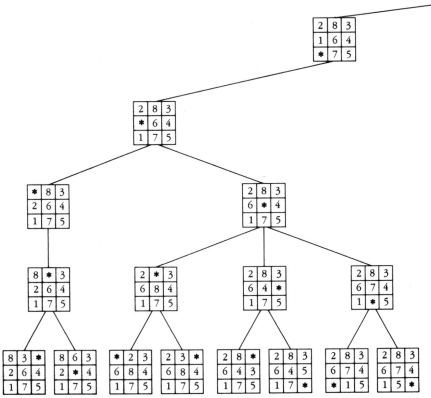

Figure 8.3 Part of the search tree, five moves deep, for an eight-tile problem.
(From Nilsson, 1971.)

simpler eight-tile problem:

2	8	3
1	6	4
7	•	5

into

1	2	3
8	•	4
7	6	5

Figure 8.3 is like an upside-down tree with a single trunk and branches leading out from that. This tree begins with the start state, represents all states reachable from this state, then all states reachable from those states, and so on. Any path through such a tree represents a possible sequence of moves that a problem solver might make. By generating a complete

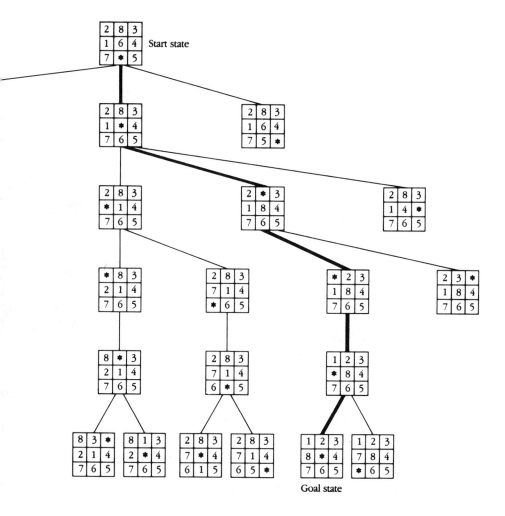

Goal state

tree, we can also find the shortest sequence of operators between the start state and the goal state. Figure 8.3 illustrates some of the problem space. Frequently, in discussions of such examples, only the path through the problem space that leads to the solution is presented (for instance, in Figure 8.2). Figure 8.3 gives a better idea of the size of the space of possible moves that exist for a problem.

This search-space terminology is a descriptive way of characterizing possible steps that the problem solver might take. It leaves open two important questions that we need to answer before we can predict the behavior of a particular problem solver. First, what determines the operators that the problem solver has available? Second, how does the problem solver select a particular operator when there are multiple operators available? An answer to the first question determines the search space in which the problem solver is working. An answer to the second question determines which path the problem solver takes. We will discuss these questions in the next two sections, first focusing on the issue of the origins of the problem-solving operators and then focusing on the issue of operator selection.

◆

Problem-solving operators generate a space of possible states through which the problem solver must search in looking for a path to the goal.

Problem-Solving Operators

Acquisition of Operators

There are at least three ways to acquire new problem-solving operators. One of these is by discovery. For instance, we may find a new service station has opened near us and so learn a new operator for repairing our car. Or a child may learn that its parents are particularly susceptible to temper tantrums and so learn a new way to get what it wants. Or we may learn how a new microwave oven works by playing with it and so learn a new means of preparing food. Or a scientist might discover a new drug that kills bacteria and so invent a new way of combating infections. Each of these examples involves a variety of reasoning processes. These reasoning processes will be the topic of Chapter 10.

This section will discuss in some detail the two other ways we acquire new problem-solving operators—by being told or by observing a solution by someone else. The first method, acquiring problem-solving operators by instruction, seems a uniquely human accomplishment since it depends on language. The second, acquiring problem-solving operators by imitating solutions of others is a capacity particularly associated with primates—monkey see, monkey do. Both might seem rather mundane and straightforward ways of acquiring new operators, but as we will see neither is so transparent.

It might seem that the most efficient way to learn new problem-solving operators would be simply by being told. However, it is not always that straightforward, and sometimes examples, which we can imitate, serve as better means of instruction. Reed and Bolstad (1991) had subjects learn to solve problems such as:

An expert can complete a technical task in five hours but a novice requires seven hours to do the same task. When they work together, the novice works two hours more than the expert. How long does the expert work?

Subjects received instruction on how to use the following equation to solve the problem:

$$\text{Rate}_1 \times \text{Time}_1 + \text{Rate}_2 \times \text{Time}_2 = \text{Tasks}$$

The problem-solving operators that the student needed to acquire concerned the method of assigning values to the terms in this equation. The student either received abstract instruction on how to make these assignments or saw a simple example of how these assignments were made. There was also a condition where subjects saw both the abstract instruction and the example. Subjects given the abstract instruction were able to solve only 13 percent of a set of later problems; subjects given an example solved 28 percent of the problems; subjects given both were able to solve 40 percent of the problems.

Why would giving examples be better for learning problem-solving operators than directly telling a subject what to do? The problem with direct instruction is that it can often be difficult to understand what quantities like Rate_1 refer to. This information can be clearer in the context of an example. On the other hand, it can be difficult to see how to extend an example solution from one problem to another problem. Thus, experiments like that of Reed and Bolstad indicate that best learning occurs when subjects have access to both. Similar results have been obtained by Fong, Krantz, and Nisbett (1986) in the domain of statistics, and by Cheng, Holyoak, Nisbett, and Oliver (1986) in the domain of logic.

◆
Problem-solving operators can be acquired by discovery, by analogy to an example problem solution, or by direct instruction.

Analogy and Imitation

Analogy is the process by which a problem solver maps the solution for one problem into a solution for another problem. Sometimes, the analogy process can be rather straightforward as when a student takes the structure of an example worked out in a section of a mathematics text and maps it into the solution for a problem in the exercises at the end of the section. Other times, the transformations can be more complex as when Rutherford used the solar system as a model for the structure of the atom in which electrons revolved around the atom in the way that the planets revolved around the sun (Koestler, 1964; Gentner, 1983). In any act of analogy, it is necessary to map the elements from the source to the target. Table 8.1 shows the mapping between the solar system and the atom.

An example of the power of analogy in problem solving is provided in an experiment of Gick and Holyoak (1980). They presented their subjects with the following problem, which is adapted from Duncker (1945):

◆

Table 8.1 The Solar System/Atom Analogy

Base Domain: Solar System	Target Domain: Atom
The sun attracts the planets.	The nucleus attracts the electrons.
The sun in larger than the planets.	The nucleus is larger than the electrons.
The planets revolve around the sun.	The electrons revolve around the nucleus.
The planets revolve around the sun because of the attraction and weight difference.	The electrons revolve around the nucleus because of the attraction and weight difference.
The planet Earth has life on it.	No transfer.

Adapted from Gentner, 1983, with permission from LEA, Ltd. —Quarterly Journal of Experimental Psychology.

> *Suppose you are a doctor faced with a patient who has a malignant tumor in his stomach. It is impossible to operate on the patient, but unless the tumor is destroyed the patient will die. There is a kind of ray that can be used to destroy the tumor. If the rays reach the tumor all at once at a sufficiently high intensity, the tumor will be destroyed. Unfortunately, at this intensity the healthy tissue that the rays pass through on the way to the tumor will also be destroyed. At lower intensities the rays are harmless to healthy tissue, but they will not affect the tumor either. What type of procedure might be used to destroy the tumor with the rays, and at the same time avoid destroying the healthy tissue? (pp. 307–308)*

This is a very difficult problem, and few subjects are able to solve it. However, Gick and Holyoak presented their subjects with the following story as an analogy for solution:

> *A small country was ruled from a strong fortress by a dictator. The fortress was situated in the middle of the country, surrounded by farms and villages. Many roads led to the fortress through the countryside. A rebel general vowed to capture the fortress. The general knew that an attack by his entire army would capture the fortress. He gathered his army at the head of one of the roads, ready to launch a full-scale direct attack. However, the general then learned that the dictator had planted mines on each of the roads. The mines were set so that small bodies of*

men could pass over them safely, since the dictator needed to move his troops and workers to and from the fortress. However, any large force would detonate the mines. Not only would this blow up the road, but it would also destroy many neighboring villages. It therefore seemed impossible to capture the fortress. However, the general devised a simple plan. He divided his army into small groups and dispatched each group to the head of a different road. When all was ready he gave the signal and each group marched down a different road. Each group continued down its road to the fortress so that the entire army arrived together at the fortress at the same time. In this way, the general captured the fortress and overthrew the dictator. (p. 351)

Told to use this story as model for a solution, most subjects were able to develop an analogous operation to solve the tumor problem.

An interesting example of problem solving by analogy that did not quite work is a problem encountered by one geometry student whom we have studied. Part a of Figure 8.4 illustrates the steps of a geometry solution that the text gave as an example, and part b illustrates the student's attempts to use that worked-out proof to guide his solution to a homework problem. In part a, two segments of a line are given as equal length, and the goal is to prove that two larger segments have equal length. In part b the student was given two segments with *AB* longer than *CD*, and his task was to prove the same inequality for two larger segments, *AC* and *BD*.

Our subject noted the obvious similarity between the two problems and proceeded to develop the apparent analogy. He thought he could simply substitute points on one line for points on another, and inequality for equality. That is, he tried the following, simply substituting *A* for *R*, *B* for *O*, *C* for *N*, *D* for *Y*, and > for = . With these substitutions he got the first

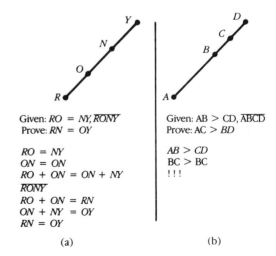

Given: $RO = NY$, $\overline{RONY}$
Prove: $RN = OY$

$RO = NY$
$ON = ON$
$RO + ON = ON + NY$
$\overline{RONY}$
$RO + ON = RN$
$ON + NY = OY$
$RN = OY$

(a)

Given: $AB > CD$, $\overline{ABCD}$
Prove: $AC > BD$

$AB > CD$
$BC > BC$
$!\,!\,!$

(b)

Figure 8.4 (a) A worked-out proof problem given in a geometry text; (b) one student's attempt to use the structure of this problem's solution to guide his solution of a similar problem.

line correct: Analogous to $RO = NY$, he wrote $AB > CD$. Then he had to write something analogous to $ON = ON$. He wrote $BC > BC!$ This example illustrates both how analogy can be used to create operators for problem solving, and that it requires a little sophistication to use analogy correctly.

Another difficulty with analogy is in finding the appropriate examples from which to analogize operators. Often, subjects do not notice when an analogy is possible. Gick and Holyoak did an experiment in which they read subjects the general and the dictator story and then Duncker's ray problem (both given earlier). Very few subjects spontaneously noticed the relevance of the first story to solving the second. To achieve success, subjects had to be explicitly told to use the general and dictator story as an analogy for solving the ray problem.

When subjects do spontaneously use previous examples to solve a problem, they are often guided by superficial similarities in their choice of examples. For instance, Ross (1984, 1987) taught subjects several methods for solving probability problems. These methods were taught with respect to specific examples, such as finding the probability that a pair of tossed dice will sum to 7. Subjects were then tested with new problems that were superficially similar to prior examples. This superficial similarity took the form of both example and problem involving the same content (e.g., dice) but not necessarily the same principle of probability. Subjects tried to solve the new problem by using the operators illustrated in the superficially similar prior example. When that prior example illustrated the same principle as required in the current problem, subjects were able to solve the problem. When it did not, they were unable to solve the current problem. Reed (1987) has found similar results with algebra story problems.

In solving school problems, students use proximity as a cue to what examples to use in analogy. For instance, a student working physics problems at the end of a chapter expects that problems solved as examples in the chapter will use the same methods and so tries analogy to these (Chi, Bassok, Lewis, Riemann, & Glaser, 1989).

◆ ───

Analogy involves both noticing that a past problem solution is relevant and then mapping the elements from that solution to produce an operator for the current problem.

───

Production Rules

Cognitive scientists have devised different ways to formally represent problem-solving operators. There is a general theoretical construct, called **production systems**, that has proved to be particularly useful. Production systems consist of a set of **productions**, which are rules for solving a problem. A typical problem-solving production (Anderson, 1983; Brown & Van Lehn, 1980; Card, Moran, & Newell, 1983) consists of a goal, some application tests, and an action. The following is a fairly simple production rule:

> *If* the goal is to drive a standard transmission car
> and the car is in first gear
> and the car is going more than 10 miles an hour,
> *Then* shift the car into second gear

Such a production is organized into a condition (the *if* part) and an action (the *then* part). The condition consists of a statement of the goal (i.e., to drive a standard transmission car) and of certain tests to determine whether the rule is applicable. If these tests are met, the rule will apply and the action (i.e., shifting the car into second gear) will be performed.

Table 8.2 shows a set of production rules like those proposed in Brown and Van Lehn (1980) for modeling multicolumn subtraction. These

---

Table 8.2 Production Rules for Multicolumn Subtraction

If the goal is to solve a subtraction problem,
Then make the subgoal to process the rightmost column.

If there is an answer in the current column
and there is a column to the left,
Then make the subgoal to process the column to the left.

If the goal is to process a column
and there is no bottom digit,
Then write the top digit as the answer.

If the goal is to process a column
and the top digit is not smaller than the bottom digit,
Then write the difference between the digits as the answer.

If the goal is to process a column
and the top digit is smaller than the bottom digit,
Then add 10 to the top digit
and set as a subgoal to borrow from the column to the left.

If the goal is to borrow from a column
and the top digit in that column is not zero,
Then decrement the digit by 1.

If the goal is to borrow from a column
and the top digit in that column is zero,
Then replace the zero by 9
and set as a subgoal to borrow from the column to the left.

---

productions illustrate some of the critical features of such rules:

1. **Conditionality:** Each production rule consists of a condition that describes when it should apply and an action that describes what to do in that situation.

2. **Modularity:** The overall problem-solving competence is broken up into a number of productions, one for each operator.

3. **Goal factoring:** Each production is relevant to a particular goal such as borrowing from a column.

4. **Abstractness:** Each rule applies to a class of situations. For instance, the fourth production handles all pairs of digits where the top digit is greater than or equal to the bottom digit.

Such production rules are encodings of what might be referred to as "crystallized" problem-solving operators in that they reflect the nature of the problem-solving skill after it has been well mastered. The next chapter, on the development of expertise, will have more to say about the acquisition of such rules.

◆
Production rules encode crystallized problem-solving operators as condition-action rules.

Operator Selection

As noted earlier, in any particular state, multiple problem-solving operators can be applicable, and a critical task is to select the one to apply. In principle, there are numerous ways that a problem solver may select operators, and the field of artificial intelligence has succeeded in enumerating various powerful methods. However, it seems that most methods are not particularly natural as human problem-solving methods. Here we will review three criteria that humans use for operator selection. The simplest criterion humans use for guiding operator selection is avoidance of operators that undo the effect of the previous operators. Thus, for instance, in the eight-tile puzzle people show great reluctance to take back a step even if this might be necessary to solve the problem. However, by itself, **backup avoidance** provides little guidance for operator selection. It biases the problem solver against any operator that returns to the previous state but provides no basis for choosing among the remaining operators.

Humans tend to select the nonrepeating operator that reduces the greatest difference between their current state and the goal. **Difference**

reduction is a very general principle of behavior and describes the behavior of many creatures. For instance, Köhler (1927) describes how a chicken will move directly toward desired food and will not go around a fence that is blocking it. The poor creature is effectively paralyzed, not being able to move forward and unwilling to back up and undo its approach to the fence. It does not seem to have any principles for selection of operators but difference reduction and backup avoidance. This leaves it without a solution to the problem.

On the other hand, Sultan (see Figure 8.1) did not just claw at his cage trying to get the food. He sought to create a new tool to enable the food to be obtained. In effect, his new goal became the creation of a new means for achieving the old goal. **Means-ends analysis** is the term used to describe the creation of a new goal (end) to enable an operator (means) to apply. Humans and other higher primates use means-ends analysis to be more planful in achieving a goal than they could be if they used only difference reduction. In this section, we will discuss both the role of difference reduction and means-ends analysis in operator selection.

◆

People use backup avoidance, difference reduction, and means-ends analysis to guide their selection of operators.

The Difference-Reduction Method

A frequent method of problem solving, particularly in unfamiliar domains, is to try to reduce the difference between the current state and the goal state. For instance, consider my solution to the eight-tile puzzle in Figure 8.2. There were four options possible for the first move. One possible operator was to move the 1 tile into the empty square, another was to move the 8, a third was to move the 5, and the fourth was to move the 4. I chose the last operator. Why? The answer is that it seemed to get me closer to my end goal. I was moving the 4 tile closer to its final destination. Human problem solvers are often strongly governed by difference reduction or equivalently by the converse, similarity. That is, they choose operators that transform the current state into a new state that reduces a difference and resembles the goal state more closely than the current state. Difference reduction is sometimes called **hill climbing**. If we imagine the goal as the highest point of land, one way to try to reach it is always to take steps that go up. By reducing the difference between the goal and the current state the problem solver is taking a step "higher" toward the goal. Hill climbing has a potential problem in that by following it we might reach the top of some hill that is lower than the highest point of land that is the goal. Thus, difference reduction is not guaranteed to work. It is myopic in that it considers only whether the next step is an improvement and not whether the larger plan will work. Means-ends analysis, which we will discuss later, is an attempt to introduce a more global perspective into the problem solving.

One of the ways problem solvers improve is by using more sophisticated measures of similarity. My move above was intended simply to get a tile closer to its final destination. After working with many tile problems, we begin to notice the importance of what is called sequence—that is, whether noncentral tiles are followed by their appropriate successors. For instance, in state 0 of Figure 8.2, the 3 and 4 tiles are in sequence because they are followed by their successors 4 and 5, but the 5 is not in sequence because it is followed by 7 rather than 6. Trying to move tiles first into sequence proves to be more important than trying to move them to their final destinations right away. Thus, using sequence as a measure of increasing similarity leads to more effective problem solving based on difference reduction (see Nilsson, 1971, for further discussion).

The difference-reduction technique relies on evaluations of the similarity between the current state and the goal state. Although difference reduction probably works more often than not, it can also lead the problem solver astray. In some problem-solving situations, a correct solution involves going against the grain of similarity. A good example is called the hobbits and orcs problem:

> On one side of a river are three hobbits and three orcs. They have a boat on their side that is capable of carrying two creatures at a time across the river. The goal is to transport all six creatures across to the other side of the river. At no point on either side of the river can orcs outnumber hobbits (or the orcs would eat the outnumbered hobbits). The problem, then, is to find a method of transporting all six creatures across the river without the hobbits ever being outnumbered.

Stop reading and try to solve this problem. Figure 8.5, shows a correct sequence of moves for solution of this problem. Illustrated there are the locations of hobbits (H), orcs (O), and the boat (b). The boat, the three hobbits, and the three orcs all start on one side of the river. This condition is represented in state 1 by the fact that all are above the line. Then, a hobbit, an orc, and the boat proceed to the other side of the river. The outcome of this action is represented in state 2 by placement of the boat (b), the hobbit (H), and the orc (O) on the other side of the line. In state 3 one hobbit has taken the boat back, and the diagram continues in the same way. Each state in the figure represents another configuration of hobbits, orcs, and boat. Subjects have a particular problem with the transition from state 6 to state 7. In a study by Jeffries, Polson, Razran, and Atwood (1977), about a third of all subjects choose to back up to a previous state 5 rather than moving on to state 7 (see also Greeno, 1974). One reason for this difficulty is that the action involves moving two creatures back to the wrong

Figure 8.5 A diagram of the successive states in a solution to the hobbits and orcs problem.

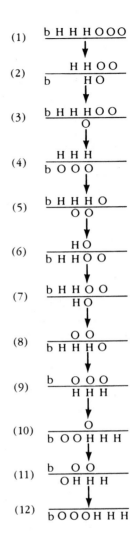

side of the river. The move seems to be away from a solution. At this point, subjects will go back to state 5, even though this undoes their last move. They would rather undo a move than take a step that moves them to a state that appears further from the goal.

Atwood and Polson (1976) provide another experimental demonstration of subjects' reliance on similarity and how that reliance can be sometimes harmful as well as sometimes beneficial. Subjects were given the following water jug problem:

> *You have three jugs, which we will call A, B, and C. Jug A can hold exactly 8 cups of water, B can hold exactly 5 cups, and C can hold exactly 3 cups. Jug A is filled to capacity with 8 cups of water. B and C*

are empty. We want you to find a way of dividing the contents of A equally between A and B so that both have 4 cups. You are allowed to pour water from jug to jug.

Figure 8.6 illustrates two paths of solution to this problem. (Please note that the only way to get exact measures of the water is to fill the jugs to capacity.) At the top of the figure all the water is in jug A—represented by A(8); no water is in jugs B or C—represented by B(0) C(0). The two

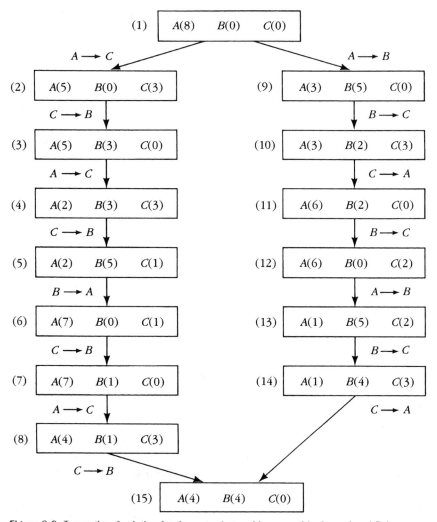

Figure 8.6 Two paths of solution for the water jug problem posed in Atwood and Polson (1976). Each state is represented in terms of the contents of the three jugs. The transitions between states are labeled in terms of which jug is poured into which.

possible actions are to pour A into C, in which case we get A(5) B(0) C(3), or to pour A into B, in which case we get A(3) B(5) C(0). From these two states, more moves can be made. Numerous other sequences of moves are possible besides the two paths illustrated in the figure. However, it does illustrate the two shortest sequences to the goal.

Atwood and Polson used the representation in Figure 8.6 to analyze subjects' behavior. For instance, they asked which move subjects would prefer in starting from the initial state 1. That is, would they prefer to pour jug A into C and get state 2, or jug A into B and get state 9? The answer is that subjects preferred the latter move. More than twice as many subjects moved to state 9 as moved to state 2. Note that state 9 is quite similar to the goal. The goal is to have 4 cups in both A and B, and state 9 has 3 cups in A and 5 cups in B. In contrast, state 2 has no cups of water in B. Throughout the problem, Atwood and Polson found a strong tendency for subjects to move to states that were similar to the goal state. Usually, similarity was a good heuristic, but there are critical cases where similarity is misleading. For instance, the transitions from state 5 to state 6 and from state 11 to state 12 both lead to significant decreases in similarity to the goal. However, both transitions are critical to their solution paths. Atwood and Polson found that more than 50 percent of the time subjects deviated from the correct sequence of moves at these critical points. Rather, subjects chose some move that seemed closer to the goal but actually took them away from the solution.[1]

It is worth noting that people do not get stuck in suboptimal states just while solving puzzles. Hill climbing can get us stuck in serious life choices. A classic example is when people are trapped in a suboptimal job because they are unwilling to get the education needed for a better job. They are unwilling to endure the temporary deviation from their goal (of earning as much as they can) to get the skills to earn an even higher salary.

◆

People experience difficulty in solving a problem at points where the correct solution involves increasing the differences between the current state and the goal.

Means-Ends Analysis

A more sophisticated method of operator selection is referred to as means-ends analysis. This method has been extensively studied by Newell and Simon, who used it in a computer simulation program (called the **General Problem Solver—GPS**) that modeled human problem solving. The following is their description of means-ends analysis.

◆

[1]For instance, moving back to state 9 from either state 5 or state 11.

Means-ends analysis is typified by the following kind of commonsense argument:

I want to take my son to nursery school. What's the difference between what I have and what I want? One of distance. What changes distance? My automobile. My automobile won't work. What is needed to make it work? A new battery. What has new batteries? An auto repair shop. I want the repair shop to put in a new battery; but the shop doesn't know I need one. What is the difficulty? One of communication. What allows communication? A telephone . . . and so on.

This kind of analysis—classifying things in terms of the functions they serve and oscillating among ends, functions required, and means that perform them—forms the basic system of GPS (Newell & Simon, 1972; p. 416).

Means-ends analysis can be viewed as a more sophisticated version of difference reduction. Like difference reduction, it tries to eliminate the differences between the current state and the goal state. For instance, in the example above, it tried to reduce the distance between the home and the nursery school. Means-ends analysis will also identify the biggest difference first and try to eliminate it. Thus, in the example above, the focus is on difference in the general location of home and nursery school. The difference between where the car will be parked and the classroom has not been considered.

The major contrast with difference reduction is that means-ends analysis will not abandon an operator if it cannot be applied immediately. If the car did not work, difference reduction would have one start walking to the nursery school. Rather, the essential feature of means-ends analysis is that it will focus on enabling blocked operators. The means temporarily becomes the end. In the example above, a subgoal has been set of repairing the automobile, which was the means of achieving the original goal of getting the child to nursery school. New operators can be selected to achieve this subgoal. For instance, installing a new battery is chosen. If this operator is blocked, enabling it can become yet another subgoal.

Figure 8.7 displays in flowchart form the procedures used in the means-ends analysis employed by GPS. A general feature of this means-ends analysis is that it breaks a larger goal into subgoals. GPS creates subgoals in two ways. First, in flowchart I, GPS breaks the current state into a set of differences and sets the reduction of each difference as a separate subgoal. It chooses to try to eliminate first what it perceives as the most important difference. Second, in flowchart II, GPS tries to find an operator that will eliminate the difference. However, this operator may be unable to apply immediately because a difference exists between the operator's condition

Flowchart I Goal: Transform current state into goal state

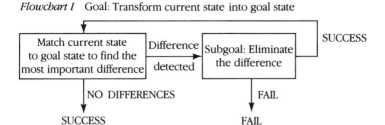

Flowchart II Goal: Eliminate the difference

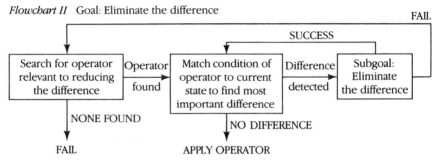

Figure 8.7 The application of means-ends analysis by Newell and Simon's General Problem Solving (GPS). Flowchart I breaks a problem down into a set of differences and tries to eliminate each. Flowchart II searches for an operator relevant to eliminating a difference.

and the state of the environment. Thus, before the operator can be applied, eliminating another difference may be necessary. To eliminate the difference that is blocking the operator's application, flowchart II will have to be called again to find another operator relevant to eliminating that difference. The term *operator subgoal* is used to refer to a subgoal whose purpose is to eliminate a difference that is blocking application of an operator.

◆

Means-ends analysis involves creating subgoals to eliminate the difference between the current state and the condition for applying a desired operator.

The Tower of Hanoi Problem

Means-ends analysis has proved to be an extremely general and powerful method of problem solving. Ernst and Newell (1969) discuss its applications to the modeling of monkey and bananas problems (such as Sultan's predicament described at the beginning of the chapter), algebra problems, calculus problems, and logic problems. However, we will illustrate means-ends analysis here by applying it to the **Tower of Hanoi problem**. A simple version of this problem is illustrated in Figure 8.8. There are three pegs and three disks of differing sizes, *A*, *B*, and *C*. The disks have holes in

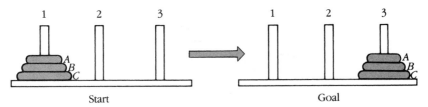

Figure 8.8 The three-disk version of the Tower of Hanoi problem.

them so they can be stacked on the pegs. The disks can be moved from any peg to any other peg. Only the top disk on a peg can be moved, and it can never be placed on a smaller disk. The disks all start out on peg 1, but the goal is to move them all to peg 3, one disk at a time, by means of transferring disks among pegs.

Figure 8.9 traces out the application of the GPS techniques to this problem. The first line gives the general goal of moving disks A, B, and C to peg 3. This goal leads us to the first flowchart of Figure 8.7. One difference between the goal and the current state is that disk C is not on peg 3. This difference is chosen first because GPS tries to remove the most important difference first, and we are assuming that the largest misplaced disk will be viewed as the most important difference. Therefore, a subgoal is set up to eliminate this difference. This takes us to the second flowchart of Figure 8.7, which tries to find an operator to reduce the difference. The operator chosen is to move C to peg 3. The condition for applying a move operator is that nothing be on the disk. Since A and B are on C, there is a difference between the condition of the operator and the current state. Therefore, a new subgoal is created to reduce one of the differences—B on C. This subgoal gets us back to the start of flowchart II, but now with the goal of removing B from C (line 6 in Figure 8.9).[2]

The operator chosen the second time in flowchart II is to move disk B to peg 2. However, we cannot immediately apply the operator of moving B to 2, since B is covered by A. Therefore, another subgoal is set up—that of removing A—and flowchart II is used to remove this difference. The operator relevant to achieving this is to move disk A to peg 3. There are no differences between the conditions for this operator and the current state. Finally, we have an operator we can apply (line 12 in Figure 8.9). Thus, we achieve the subgoal of moving A to 3. Now we return to the earlier intention of moving B to 2. There are no more differences between

---

[2]Note that we have gone from use of flowchart I to the use of II to a *new* use of II. This action is called recursion because to apply flowchart II to find a way to move C to 3 we need to apply flowchart II to find a way to remove disk B from C. Thus, one procedure is using itself as a subprocedure.

1. Goal: Move A, B, and C to Peg 3
2.   :Difference is that C is not on 3
3.   :Subgoal: Make C on 3
4.   :Operator is to move C to 3
5.   :Difference is that A and B are on C
6.   :Subgoal: Remove B from C
7.   :Operator is to move B to 2
8.   :Difference is that A is on B
9.   :Subgoal: Remove A from B
10.   :Operator is to move A to 3
11.   :No difference with operator's condition
12.   :Apply operator (move A to 3)
13.   :Subgoal achieved
14.   :No differences with operator's condition
15.   :Apply operator (move B to 2)
16.   :Subgoal achieved
17.   :Difference is that A is on 3
18.   :Subgoal: Remove A from peg 3
19.   :Operator is to move A to 2
20.   :No difference with operator's condition
21.   :Apply operator (move A to 2)
22.   :Subgoal achieved
23.   :No difference with operator's condition
24.   :Apply operator (move C to 3)
25.   :Subgoal achieved
26.   :Difference is that B is not on 3
27.   :Subgoal: Make B on 3
28.   :Operator is to move B to 3
29.   :Difference is that A is on B
30.   :Subgoal: Remove A from B
31.   :Operator is to move A to 1
32.   :No difference with operator's condition
33.   :Apply operator (move A to 1)
34.   :Subgoal achieved
35.   :No difference with operator's condition
36.   :Apply operator (move B to 3)
37.   :Subgoal achieved
38.   :Difference is that A is not on 3
39.   :Subgoal: Make A on 3
40.   :Operator is to move A to 3
41.   :No difference with operator's condition
42.   :Apply operator (move A to 3)
43.   :Subgoal achieved
44.   :No difference
45.   Goal Achieved

Figure 8.9 A trace of the application of GPS, as shown in Figure 8.7, to the Tower of Hanoi problem in Figure 8.8.

the condition for this operator and the current state, and so the action takes place. The subgoal of removing B from C is then satisfied (line 16 in Figure 8.9).

We have now returned to the original intention of moving disk C to peg 3. However, disk A is now on peg 3, which prevents the action. Thus, we have another difference to be eliminated between the now-current state and the operator's condition. We move A onto peg 2 to remove this difference. Now the original operator of moving C to 3 can be applied (line 24 in Figure 8.9).

The state at this point is that disk C is on peg 3 and disks A and B are on peg 2. At this point, GPS returns to its original goal of moving the three disks to 3. It notes that another difference is that B is not on 3 and sets another subgoal of eliminating this difference. It achieves this subgoal by first moving A to 1 and then B to 3. This gets us to line 37 in the trace of Figure 8.9. The remaining difference is that A is not on 3. This difference is eliminated in lines 38 through 42. With this step, no more differences exist and the original goal is achieved.

Note that subgoals are created in service of other subgoals. For instance, to achieve the subgoal of moving the largest disk, a subgoal is created of moving the second-largest disk, which is on top of it. We indicated this logical dependency of one subgoal on another in Figure 8.9 by indenting the processing of the dependent subgoal. Before the first move in line 12 of the figure, three subgoals had to be created. It appears that creating such goals and subgoals can be quite costly. Both Anderson, Kushmerick, and Lebiere (1993) and Ruiz (1987) found that the time to make one of the moves is a function of the number of subgoals that must be created. For instance, before disk A is moved to peg 3 in Figure 8.9 (the first move), three subgoals have to be created whereas no subgoals have to be created before the next move is taken—moving B to peg 2. Correspondingly, Anderson et al. found it took 8.95 seconds to make the first move and 2.46 seconds to make the second move.

There are two problem-solving methods that subjects could bring to bear in solving the Tower of Hanoi problem. They could use a means-ends approach as illustrated in Figure 8.9 or they could use the simple difference-reduction method, in which case subjects never set as a subgoal to move a disk that currently cannot be moved. In the Tower of Hanoi problem, such a simple difference-reduction method would not be effective, because one needs to look beyond what is currently possible and have a more global plan of attack on the problem. The only step difference reduction could take in Figure 8.8 would be to move the top disk (A) to the target peg, but then it would provide no further guidance because no other move would reduce the difference between the current state and the goal state. Subjects would have to make a random move. Kotovsky, Hayes, and Simon (1985) did a study of the way subjects actually approached the solution of the Tower of Hanoi problem. They found that there was an initial problem-solving period when subjects did adopt this fruitless difference-reduction strategy. Subjects then switched to a means-ends strategy, after which the solution to the problem came quickly.

◆
The Tower of Hanoi task is solved by adopting a means-ends strategy in which subgoals are created.

Goal Structures and Prefrontal Cortex

It is significant that complex goal structures, particularly those involving operator subgoaling, have only been observed with any frequency in humans and higher primates. We have already discussed one instance of Sultan's problem solving with respect to Figure 8.1. Novel tool building, a clear instance of operator subgoaling, is almost unique to the higher apes (Beck, 1980). It has been speculated (Anderson, 1993) that the process of handling complex subgoals is performed by the prefrontal cortex (see Figure 1.6), which is greatly expanded in the higher primates over most mammals, and in humans over most apes. Chapter 6 discussed the role of the prefrontal cortex in holding information in working memory. One of the major prerequisites to developing complex goal structures is the ability to maintain these goal structures in working memory.

Goel and Grafman (1995) looked at performance of frontal patients in the Tower of Hanoi task. These are patients who have suffered severe damage to their prefrontal cortex. Many were veterans of the Vietnam War who had suffered serious losses of brain tissue because of penetrating missile wounds. While these patients were of normal IQ, they showed much worse performance than normal subjects on the Tower of Hanoi task. It is interesting to note the moves where these patients found the task difficult to solve. As we noted in discussing how means-ends analysis applies to the Tower of Hanoi problem, it is necessary to make moves that deviate from the prescriptions of hill climbing. One might have a disk at the correct position but have to move the disk away to enable another disk to be moved to that position. It was just at these points where the patients had to move "backward" that they had their problems. It is only by maintaining a set of goals that one can see that a backward move is necessary for a solution.

More generally, frontal patients have been noted as having difficulty in inhibiting a "prepotent" response (e.g., Roberts, Hager, & Heron, 1994). For instance, in the Stroop task (see Chapter 3) patients have difficulty in not saying the word when they are supposed to say the color of the word. That is, they have a difficulty in keeping in mind that their goal is to say the color and not the word.

There is increased blood flow in the prefrontal cortex in many tasks that involve organizing novel and complex behavior (Gazzaniga, Ivry, & Mangun, 1998). As we will discuss more in the next chapter, prefrontal lobe activation is high in a novel problem-solving task but decreases as students master the problem. All of these results point to the conclusion that the prefrontal lobes play a major role in maintaining the goal structures that enable human problem solving.

◆
The prefrontal cortex plays a critical role in maintaining goal structures.

Problem Representation

The Importance of the Correct Representation

We have analyzed a problem solution into problem states and operators for changing states. So far, we have discussed problem solving as if the only problem were acquiring operators and selecting the appropriate ones. However, the way in which states of the problem are represented also has significant effects. A famous example illustrating the importance of representation is the mutilated-checkerboard problem (Kaplan & Simon, 1990). Suppose we have a checkerboard in which the two diagonally opposite corner squares have been cut out. Figure 8.10 illustrates this mutilated checkerboard, on which 62 squares remain. Now suppose that we have 31 dominos, each of which covers exactly two squares of the board. Can you find some way of arranging these 31 dominos on the board so that they cover all 62 squares? If it can be done, explain how. If it cannot be done, prove that it cannot. Perhaps you would like to ponder this problem before reading on. Relatively few people are able to solve this problem without some hints, and very few see the answer quickly.

The answer is that the checkerboard cannot be covered by the dominos. The trick to seeing this is to include in your representation of the problem the fact that each domino must cover one black and one red

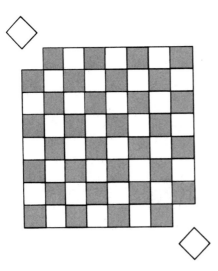

Figure 8.10 The mutilated checkerboard. (Adapted from W. A. Wickelgren, *How to solve problems.* W. H. Freeman and Company. Copyright © 1974.)

square, not just any two squares. There is just no way to place a domino on two squares of the checkerboard without having it cover one black and one red square. This means that with 31 dominos we can cover 31 black squares and 31 red squares. But the mutilation has removed two red squares. Thus, there are 30 red squares and 32 black. It follows that the mutilated checkerboard cannot be covered by 31 dominos.

Why is the mutilated-checkerboard problem easier to solve when we represent each domino as covering a red and a black square? The answer is that in so representing the problem we are encouraged to compare the number of red and black squares on the board. Thus, the effect of the problem representation is that it allows the critical operators to apply (i.e., checking for parity).

Another problem that depends on correct representation is the 27 apples problem. Imagine 27 apples packed together in a crate 3 apples high, 3 apples wide, and 3 apples deep. A worm is in the center apple. Its life's ambition is to eat its way through all the apples in the crate, but it does not want to waste time by visiting any apple twice. The worm can move from apple to apple only by going from the side of one into the side of another. This means it can only move into the apples directly above, below, or to a side. It cannot move diagonally. Can you find some path by which the worm, starting from the center apple, can reach all the apples without going through any apple twice? If not, can you prove it is impossible? The solution is left to you. (*Hint*: The solution is based on a partial three-dimensional analogy to the solution for the mutilated-checkerboard problem; it is given at the end of the chapter.)

Inappropriate problem representations often cause students to fail to solve the problems even though they have been taught the appropriate knowledge. This is a fact that often frustrates teachers. Bassok (1990) and Bassok and Holyoak (1989) studied high-school students who had learned to solve physics problems like:

> *What is the acceleration (increase in speed each second) of a train, if its speed increased uniformly from 15 m/s at the beginning of the 1st second, to 45 m/s at the end of the 12th second.*

Students were taught such physics problems and became very effective at solving them. However, they showed almost no transfer to solving "algebra" problems like:

> *Juanita went to work as a teller in a bank at a salary of $12,400 per year and received constant yearly increases, coming up with a $16,000 salary during her 13th year of work. What was her yearly salary increase?*

These subjects failed to see that their experience with the physics problems was relevant to solving these problems, which are actually isomorphic. This is because students did not appreciate that knowledge associated with rate-like quantities like speed (m/s) was relevant to problems posed in terms of discrete quantities such as dollars.

◆ Successful problem solving depends on representing problems in such a way that appropriate operators can apply.

Functional Fixedness

Sometimes solutions to problems depend on the solver's ability to represent the objects in his or her environment in novel ways. This fact has been demonstrated in a series of studies by different experimenters. A typical experiment in the series is the two-string problem of Maier (1931), illustrated in Figure 8.11. Two strings hanging from the ceiling are to be tied together, but they are so far apart that the subject cannot grasp both at once. Among the objects in the room are a chair and a pair of pliers. Subjects try various solutions involving the chair, but these do not work. The only solution that

Figure 8.11 The two-string problem used by Maier (1931).

works is to tie the pliers to one string and set that string swinging like a pendulum, and then to get the second string, bring it to the center of the room, and wait for the first string to swing close enough to grasp. Only 39 percent of Maier's subjects were able to see this solution within 10 minutes. The difficulty is that subjects do not perceive the pliers as a weight that can be used as a pendulum. This phenomenon is called **functional fixedness**. It is so named because subjects are fixed on representing the object according to its conventional function and fail to represent its novel function.

Another demonstration of functional fixedness is an experiment by Duncker (1945). The task he posed to subjects is to support a candle on a door, ostensibly for an experiment on vision. The problem is illustrated in Figure 8.12. On the table are a box of tacks, some matches, and the candle. The correct solution is to tack the box to the door and use the box as a platform for the candle. This task is difficult for subjects because they see the box as a container, not as a platform. Subjects have greater difficulty with the task if the box is filled with tacks, reinforcing the perception of the box as a container.

These demonstrations of functional fixedness are consistent with the interpretation that representation has its effect on operator selection. For instance, to solve Duncker's candle problem, subjects needed to represent the tack box so that it could be used by the problem-solving operators that

Figure 8.12 The candle problem used by Duncker. (Adapted from Glucksberg & Weisberg, 1966. Copyright © 1966 by the American Psychological Association. Reprinted by permission.)

were looking for a support for the candle. When the box was conceived of as a container and not as a support, it was not available to the support-seeking operators.

◆ Functional fixedness refers to people's tendency to represent objects as serving conventional problem-solving functions, thus failing to see them as serving novel functions.

Set Effects

Problem solvers can become biased by their experiences to prefer certain problem-solving operators in solving a problem. Such biasing of the problem solution is referred to as a **set effect**. A good illustration involves the water jug problem studied by Luchins (1942; Luchins & Luchins, 1959). In Luchins's water jug problems (which are different than the Atwood and Polson problem in Figure 8.6), a subject was given a set of jugs of various capacities and unlimited water supply. The subject's task was to measure out a specified quantity of water. Two examples are given below:

Problem	Capacity of Jug A	Capacity of Jug B	Capacity of Jug C	Desired Quantity
1	5 cups	40 cups	18 cups	28 cups
2	21 cups	127 cups	3 cups	100 cups

Assume that subjects have a tap and a sink so that they can fill jugs and empty them. The jugs start out empty. Subjects are allowed only to fill the jugs to capacity, empty them completely, and pour water from one jug to another. In problem 1, subjects are told that they have three jugs—jug A, with a capacity of 5 cups; jug B, with a capacity of 40 cups; and jug C, with a capacity of 18 cups. To solve this problem, subjects would fill jug A and pour it into B, fill A again and pour it into B, and fill C and pour it into B. The solution to this problem is denoted by $2A + C$. The solution for the second problem is to first fill jug B with 127 cups; fill A from B so that 106 cups are left in B; fill C from B so that 103 cups are left in B; empty C; and fill C again from B so that the goal of 100 cups in jug B is achieved. The solution to this problem can be denoted by $B - A - 2C$. The first solution is called an addition solution because it involves adding the contents of the jugs together; the second solution is referred to as a subtraction solution because it involves subtracting the contents of one jug from another. Luchins studied the effect of giving subjects a series of problems, all of which could be solved by addition. This created an "addition set" such that subjects solved new addition problems faster than control subjects, who had no practice, and solved subtraction problems more slowly.

Table 8.3 Luchins's 1942 Water Jug Problems

Problems	Capacity of Jug A	Capacity of Jug B	Capacity of Jug C	Desired Quantity
1	21	127	3	100
2	14	163	25	99
3	18	43	10	5
4	9	42	6	21
5	20	59	4	31
6	23	49	3	20
7	15	39	3	18
8	28	76	3	25
9	18	48	4	22
10	14	36	8	6

Note: All volumes are in cups.

The set effect that Luchins is most famous for demonstrating is the **Einstellung effect**, or *mechanization of thought*, which is illustrated by the series of problems in Table 8.3. Subjects were given these problems in this order and were required to find solutions for each. Take time out from reading this text and try to solve each problem.

All problems except 8 can be solved by using the $B - 2C - A$ method (i.e., filling B, twice pouring B into C, and once pouring B into A). For problems 1 through 5, this solution is the simplest, but for problems 7 and 9 the simpler solution of $A + C$ also applies. Problem 8 cannot be solved by the $B - 2C - A$ method, but can be solved by the simpler solution of $A - C$. Problems 6 and 10 are also solved more simply as $A - C$ than $B - 2C - A$. Of Luchins's subjects who received the whole setup of ten problems, 83 percent used the $B - 2C - A$ method on problems 6 and 7, 64 percent failed to solve problem 8, and 79 percent used the $B - 2C - A$ method for problems 9 and 10. The performance of subjects who worked on all ten problems was compared with the performance of control subjects who saw only the last five problems. These control subjects did not see the biasing $B - 2C - A$ problems. Fewer than 1 percent of the control subjects used $B - 2C - A$ solutions, and only 5 percent failed to solve problem 8. Thus, the first five problems can create a powerful bias for a particular solution. This bias hurt solutions of problems 6 through 10. While these effects are quite dramatic, they are relatively easy to reverse with the exercise of cognitive control. Luchins found that simply by warning subjects by saying, "Don't be blind," after problem 5, more than 50 percent of them overcame the set for the $B - 2C - A$ solution.

Another kind of set effect in problem solving has to do with the influence of general semantic factors. This effect is nicely illustrated in the experiment of Safren (1962) on anagram solutions. Safren presented subjects with lists such as the following in which each set of letters was to be unscrambled and made into a word:

kmli   graus   teews   recma   foefce   ikrdn

This is an example of an organized list, in that the individual words are all associated with drinking coffee. Safren compared solution times for organized lists such as this with those for unorganized lists. Median solution time was 12.2 seconds for anagrams from unorganized lists but 7.4 seconds for anagrams from organized lists. Presumably, the facilitation evident with the organized lists occurred because the earlier items in the list associatively primed, and so made more available, the later words. Note that this anagram experiment contrasts with the water jug experiment in that no particular procedure is being strengthened. Rather, what is being strengthened is part of the subject's factual (declarative) knowledge about spellings of associatively related words.

In general, set effects occur when some knowledge structures become more available at the expense of others. These knowledge structures can be either procedures, as in the water jug problem, or declarative information, as in the anagram problem. If the available knowledge is what subjects need for solving the problem, their problem solving will be facilitated. If the available knowledge is not what is needed, problem solving will be inhibited. It is good to realize that set effects can sometimes be easily dissipated (as with Luchins's "Don't be blind" instruction). If you find yourself stuck on a problem and you keep generating similar unsuccessful approaches, it is often useful to force yourself to back off, change set, and try a different kind of solution.

◆───

Set effects result when the knowledge relevant to a particular type of problem solution is strengthened.

───

Sensitivity to Success of Problem-Solving Operators

Set effects such as those in Luchins's water jug problems show that subjects tend to try what has been successful in the past. Lovett (1998) has studied how this tendency interacts with other factors like hill climbing. She used "building-sticks" problems like the one illustrated in Figure 8.13. Participants are given an unlimited supply of building sticks of three lengths (a, b, and c) and are told that their goal is to create a target stick of a particular desired length. There are two basic strategies they can select—they can either start with a stick smaller (a or c) than the desired length and add

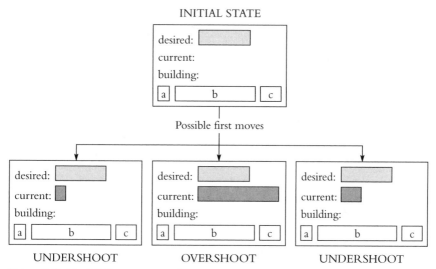

Figure 8.13 The initial state (top) and three possible first moves (bottom) for a problem in the building-sticks task.

sticks (like the addition strategy in Luchins's water jugs) or they can start with a stick that is too long (stick *b*) and "saw off" lengths equal to various sticks until they reach the desired length (like the subtraction strategy). The first is called the undershoot strategy, and the second is called the overshoot strategy. Figure 8.13 shows the three first choices subjects have from their start state—two undershoot choices and one overshoot choice. Subjects show a strong tendency to hill-climb and choose as their first stick a stick that will get them closest to the target stick. So, in the example in Figure 8.13 they will usually choose the overshoot strategy, since the resulting current stick gets them closest to the desired target.

In these problems, only one of the two operators (overshoot and undershoot) works, and subjects cannot achieve a stick of the desired length by the other operator. Lovett either gave subjects experience where the overshoot operator solved 83 percent of the problems or where the undershoot operator solved 83 percent of the problems. Figure 8.14 shows their percent use of the more successful operator as a function of problem bias. Problem bias refers to whether that operator got the student closer to the target problem. The curve labeled 0 shows subject choice at the beginning of the experiment before solving any problem. Subjects show a strong hill climbing bias and tend to select the operator that gets them closest to the goal. However, as they learn which operator is more successful they come to use it more and more; curves 30 (after 30 problems) and 90 (after 90 problems) show more and more use of this successful strategy. Initially,

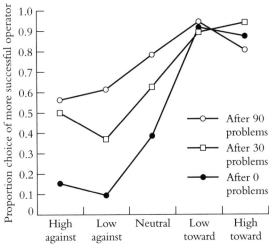

Hill climbing bias with respect to operators

Figure 8.14 Problem solvers' choice proportions as a function of the test problem type (plotted on the abscissa) and amount of experience in the task. Solvers were tested before solving any problems, after solving 30 problems, and after solving 90 problems.

on problems where the less successful operator got them closer to the goal, subjects used the more successful operator only 10 percent of the time, but by the end of the experiment they were using the more successful operator 60 percent of the time on these problems.

Lovett also finds that subjects are sensitive to their very recent experience. Thus, even if one operator has been solving most of the problems in the experiment, subjects will often switch to the other operator if they experience a string of two problems on which it is most successful. Lovett argues that this bias is highly adaptive in enabling people to solve problems rapidly. In the real world, such set effects usually help people solve problems because usually what has worked in the recent past will work in the future. Situations like Luchins's water jug problems, in which subjects are hurt by this bias, are exceptions created in the laboratory.

◆

People develop a bias to choose problem-solving operators that have worked recently.

Incubation Effects

Problem solvers frequently report that after trying and getting nowhere on a problem, they can put the problem aside for hours, days, or weeks and then, upon returning to it, can see the solution quickly. Numerous examples of this pattern were reported by the famous French mathematician

Poincaré (1929), including, for instance, the following:

Then I turned my attention to the study of some arithmetical questions apparently without much success and without a suspicion of any connection with my preceding researches. Disgusted with my failure, I went to spend a few days at the seaside, and thought of something else. One morning, walking on the bluff, the idea came to me, with just the same characteristics of brevity, suddenness, and immediate certainty, that the arithmetic transformations of indeterminate ternary quadratic forms were identical with those of non-Euclidean geometry. (p. 388)

Such phenomena are referred to as **incubation effects**. An incubation effect was nicely demonstrated in an experiment by Silveira (1971). The problem she posed to subjects, called the cheap-necklace problem, is illustrated in Figure 8.15. Subjects were given the following instructions:

You are given four separate pieces of chain that are each three links in length. It costs 2¢ to open a link and 3¢ to close a link. All links are closed at the beginning of the problem. Your goal is to join all 12 links of chain into a single circle at a cost of no more than 15¢.

Try to solve this problem yourself. (A solution is provided at the end of this chapter.) Silveira tested three groups. A control group worked on the problem for half an hour; 55 percent of these subjects solved the problem. For one experimental group, their half hour spent on the problem was interrupted by a half-hour break in which they performed other activities; 64 percent of these subjects solved the problem. A third group had a 4-hour break; and 85 percent of these subjects solved the problem. Silveira

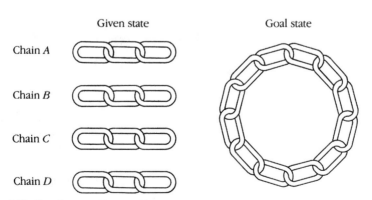

Figure 8.15 The cheap-necklace problem. (Figure 4.5 from W. A. Wickelgren, How to solve problems. W. H. Freeman and Company. Copyright © 1974.)

required her subjects to talk aloud as they solved the cheap-necklace problem. She found that subjects did not come back to the problems with solutions completely worked out. Rather, they started out trying to work out the problem much as before. This is evidence against a common misbelief that people are subconsciously solving the problem in the period that they are away from the problem.

The best explanation for incubation effects relates them to set effects. During initial attempts on a problem, subjects set themselves to think about the problem in certain ways and bring to bear certain knowledge structures. If this initial set is appropriate, subjects will solve the problem. If the initial set is not appropriate, however, they will be stuck throughout the session with inappropriate procedures. By going away from the problem, the activation of the inappropriate knowledge structures will dissipate and subjects will be able to take a fresh approach to the problem.

The basic argument is that incubation effects occur because people "forget" inappropriate ways of solving problems. Smith and Blakenship (1989, 1991) performed a fairly direct test of this hypothesis. They had subjects solve problems like those in Figure 8.16. They provided half of their subjects, the fixation group, with inappropriate ways to think about the problems. For instance, with respect to the third problem they told subjects to think about chemicals. Thus, they deliberately induced incorrect sets in the fixation condition. Not surprisingly, the fixation subjects solved fewer of the problems than control subjects. However, the interesting issue concerned how much incubation effect these two populations of

Puzzles Used in a Study of Incubation

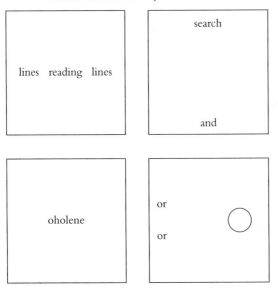

Figure 8.16 Subjects had to figure out what familiar phrase was represented by each picture. For example, the first picture represents the phrase "reading between the lines"; the second represents the phrase "search high and low"; the third represents "a hole in one"; the fourth represents "double or nothing." (After Smith & Blakenship, 1989, 1991.)

subjects showed. Half of both the fixation and control subjects worked on the problems for a continuous period of time, while the other half had an incubation period inserted in the middle of their problem-solving efforts. The fixation subjects showed a greater benefit of the incubation period. Thus, Smith and Blakenship were able to show a greater incubation effect in subjects who had started with an inappropriate way of solving the problem. Second, when they asked the fixation subjects what the clue was, they found that, indeed, more of the subjects with an incubation period had forgotten what the inappropriate clue was.

◆
───

Incubation effects occur when subjects forget the inappropriate strategies they were using to solve a problem.

───

Insight

A common misbelief about learning and problem solving is that there are magical moments of insight when everything falls into place and we suddenly see a solution. This is called the "aha" experience and many of us can report uttering that exact exclamation after a long struggle with a problem that we suddenly solve. The incubation problems discussed in the previous section are one class of problems that have been used to argue for this role of insight. The argument goes that during the incubation periods the subconscious is deriving this insight. However, as we saw, what happens is simply that subjects come to let go of poor ways of solving problems.

Metcalfe and Wiebe (1987) came up with an interesting way of identifying insight problems. The insight problems they used included ones like the cheap-necklace problem. Their non-insight problems required multistep solutions, as in the Tower of Hanoi problem (see Figure 8.8). They asked subjects to judge every 15 seconds how close they felt they were to the solution. Fifteen seconds before they actually solved a non-insight problem, subjects were fairly confident they were close to a solution. In contrast, on the insight problems, subjects had little idea they were close to a solution, even 15 seconds before they actually solved the problem. Metcalfe and Wiebe suggest that we use this difference as a definition of insight problems. That is, an insight problem is one where people are not aware that they are close to a solution.

This definition would seem to support the notion that a solution comes in a single moment. However, what Metcalfe and Wiebe showed was that subjects did not know when they were close to a solution in an insight problem. They did not show that the solution came in a single moment. Kaplan and Simon (1990) studied subjects solving the mutilated checkerboard problem in Figure 8.10, which is another insight problem. They found that some subjects early on noticed key features of the solution to the problem, such as that a domino covers one square of each color. However, sometimes subjects did not judge this to be critical and went off and tried other methods of solution, and only came back to this feature later. So, it is not that solutions to insight problems cannot come in pieces, but rather that subjects do not recognize which pieces are key until they see the final solution. It reminds me of the time that I tried to find my way through a maze cut off from all cues as to where the exit was. I searched for a very long time, was quite frustrated and was wondering if I was ever going to get out, and then I made a turn and there was the exit. I believe I even exclaimed "aha." It was not that I solved the maze in a single turn; it was that I did not appreciate which turns were on the way to the solution until I made that final turn.

Sometimes, insight problems only require a single step (or turn) to solve, and it is just a matter of finding that step. What is so difficult about these problems is just finding that one step, which can be a bit like trying to find a needle in a haystack. As an example of such a problem, consider the following:

What is greater than God

More evil than the Devil

The poor have it

The rich want it

And if you eat it you'll die.

Reportedly, this is a problem that schoolchildren find easier than college undergraduates. If so, it is because they consider fewer possibilities as an answer.

◆

Insight problems are problems where solvers cannot recognize when they are getting close to the solution.

Summary

This chapter has been built around the Newell and Simon model of problem solving as a search through a state space defined by operators. We have looked at problem-solving success as determined by the operators available and the methods used to guide that search. This analysis is particularly appropriate for first-time problems, whether they be Sultan's predicament (Figure 8.1) or a human's predicament when shown a Tower of Hanoi problem for the first time (Figure 8.8). The next chapter will concern itself with the other factors that come into play with repeated problem-solving practice.

Remarks and Suggested Readings

Newell and Simon (1972) is the classic reference on problem solving. A very detailed discussion of GPS is to be found in Ernst and Newell (1969). Recent work on analogy includes Gentner (1989), Hummel and Holyoak (1997), and Keane, Ledgeway, and Duff (1994). Newell (1991) describes his SOAR production-system theory, and Anderson and Lebiere (1998) describe the ACT-R production-system theory. A great deal of research in artificial intelligence could be classified under the topic of problem solving. This work has had a particularly strong influence on the thinking of cognitive psychologists, partly because of the efforts of Newell and Simon. The text by Russell and Norvig (1995) discusses this work. Shallice and Burgess (1991) discuss the role of the prefrontal cortex in problem solving. Lovett (1998) presents a modern discussion of set effects in problem solving.

Appendix

A number of problems were presented in this chapter without solution. Figure 8.17 gives the minimum-path solution to the problem solved less efficiently in Figure 8.2.

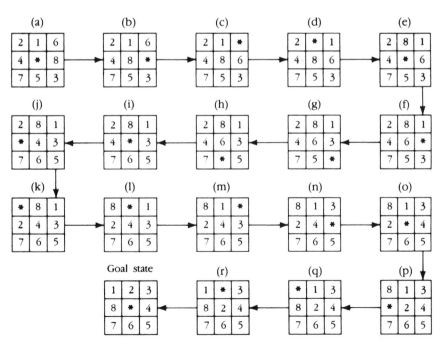

Figure 8.17 The minimum-path solution for the eight-tile problem that was solved less efficiently in Figure 8.2.

With regard to the problem of the 27 apples, the worm cannot succeed. To see that this is the case, imagine that the apples alternate in color, green and red, in a three-dimensional checkerboard pattern. If the center apple, from which the worm starts, is red, there are 13 red apples and 14 green apples in all. Every time the worm moves from one apple to another, he must change colors. Since the worm starts from the red, this means that it cannot reach more green apples than red apples. Thus, it cannot visit all 14 green apples if it also visits each of the 13 red apples just once.

Solve the cheap-necklace problem in Figure 8.15 by opening all three links in one chain (at a cost of 6¢) and then using the three open links to connect together the remaining three chains (at a cost of 9¢).

9

Development of Expertise

While it may seem that we are constantly confronted with new problems to solve, in truth, we most often solve problems in domains that are highly familiar. In performing such commonplace actions as speaking a language, driving a car, or solving a column of addition, our behavior is generally so automatic that it is difficult to recognize that we are solving problems. However, if we look at a novice—someone trying to communicate in an unfamiliar language, a person behind the wheel of a car for the first time, or a child learning addition—we can see that these can be difficult and quite novel problem domains. It is through extensive practice that we have become relatively expert in these domains. The skills just mentioned are ones at which a large fraction of the population becomes expert. There are other skills at which only a small fraction becomes expert— playing chess, doing science, hitting major league pitching, and so on.

Nevertheless, it appears that development of expertise in these specialized areas is really no different from that in the more general areas.

William G. Chase, late of Carnegie Mellon University, was one of our local experts on expertise. He had two mottos that summarize much of the nature of expertise and its development:

- No pain, no gain.
- When the going gets tough, the tough get going.

The first motto reflects the fact that no one develops expertise without a great deal of hard work. John R. Hayes (1985), another Carnegie Mellon faculty member, has studied geniuses in fields varying from music to science to chess. He found that no one reached genius levels of performance without at least ten years of practice. Chase's second motto reflects the fact that the difference between relative novices and relative experts increases as we look at more difficult problems. For instance, there are many chess duffers who could play a credible, if losing, game against a master when they are given unlimited time to choose moves. However, they would lose embarrassingly if forced to play lightning chess, where they are permitted only five seconds per move.

Chapter 8 reviewed some of the general principles governing problem solving, particularly in novel domains. This research has provided a framework for analyzing the development of expertise in problem solving. Research on expertise has been one of the major developments in cognitive science over the last twenty-five years. This is particularly exciting because it has important contributions to make to the instruction of technical or formal skills in areas such as mathematics, science, and engineering, as we will review at the end of this chapter.

This chapter begins with a look at the general characteristics of the development of expertise in a skill. After that we will consider what factors might underlie the development of expertise. We will then move on to the vexing question of how skill might transfer from one domain of expertise to another. Finally, we will discuss the implications of this research for education in various domains.

◆ ──

Through extensive practice we develop the high levels of expertise that are particularly important in dealing with demanding problems.

───

General Characteristics of Skill Acquisition

Three Stages of Skill Acquisition

It is typical to distinguish among three stages in the development of a skill (Anderson, 1983; Fitts & Posner, 1967). Fitts and Posner call the first stage the **cognitive stage**. In this stage, subjects develop a declarative encoding (see the distinction between declarative and procedural representations at the beginning of Chapter 8) of the skill; that is, they commit to memory a set of facts relevant to the skill. Learners typically rehearse these facts as they first perform the skill. For instance, when I was first learning to shift gears in a standard transmission car, I memorized the location of the gears (e.g., "up, left") and the correct sequence of engaging the clutch and moving the stick shift. I rehearsed this information as I performed the skill.

The information that I had learned about the location and function of the gears amounted to a set of problem-solving operators for driving the car. For instance, if I wanted to get the car into reverse, there was the operator of moving the gear to the upper left. Despite the fact that the knowledge about what to do next was unambiguous, one would hardly have judged my driving performance as skilled. My use of the knowledge was very slow because it was still in a declarative form. I had to retrieve specific facts and interpret them to solve my driving problems. I did not have the knowledge in a procedural form.

The second stage of skill acquisition is called the **associative stage**. Two main things happen in this second stage. First, errors in the initial understanding are gradually detected and eliminated. So, I slowly learned to coordinate the release of the clutch in first gear with the application of gas in order not to kill the engine. Second, the connections among the various elements required for successful performance are strengthened. Thus, I no longer had to sit for a few seconds trying to remember how to get to second gear from first. Basically, the outcome of the associative stage is a successful procedure for performing the skill. However, it is not always the case that the procedural representation of the knowledge replaces the declarative. Sometimes, the two forms of knowledge can coexist side by side, as when we can speak a foreign language fluently and still remember many rules of grammar. However, it is the procedural, not the declarative, knowledge that governs the skilled performance.

The procedures, which are the output of the associative stage, can be described by production rules. The use of production rules to represent problem-solving operators was introduced in the previous chapter. So, for instance, rather than use the general problem-solving methods to guide the application of declarative knowledge, the learner may develop a special production for moving into reverse:

If the goal is to go in reverse,
Then set as subgoals:
    1. To disengage the clutch
    2. Then to move the gear to the upper left
    3. Then to engage the clutch
    4. Then to push down on the gas

The third stage in the standard analysis of skill acquisition is the **autonomous stage**. In this stage, the procedure becomes more and more automated and rapid. The concept of automaticity was discussed in Chapter 3 with respect to simple perceptual-motor tasks that could become so automatic that they required few attentional resources. More complex skills like driving a car or playing chess also develop gradually in the direction of becoming more automated and requiring fewer processing resources. For instance, driving a car can become so automatic that people will engage in conversation with no memory for the traffic that they have driven through.

Two of the dimensions of improvement with practice are speed and accuracy. The procedures come to apply more rapidly and more appropriately. Anderson (1982) and Rumelhart and Norman (1978) refer to the increasing appropriateness of the procedures as tuning. For instance, consider our production for moving into reverse. It is only applicable to an ordinary three-speed gear. The process of tuning would result in a production that had additional tests for the appropriateness of this operation. Such a production might be described like this:

> *If* the goal is to go in reverse,
>   and there is a three-speed standard transmission,
> *Then* set as subgoals:
>   1. To disengage the clutch
>   2. Then to move the gear to the upper left
>   3. Then to engage the clutch
>   4. Then to push down on the gas

◆

The three stages of skill acquisition are the cognitive stage, the associative stage, and the autonomous stage.

Power-Law Learning

Chapter 6 documented the way retrieval of simple associations improved according to a power law. It turns out that performance of complex skills, involving the coordination of many such associations, also improves according to a power law. Figure 9.1 illustrates one of the most famous instances of such skill acquisition. This study followed the development of cigar-making ability of a worker in a factory over a period of ten years. The figure plots the time to make a cigar against number of years of practice. Both scales use log-log coordinates to expose a power law (recall from Chapters 6 and 7 that a linear function on log-log coordinates implies a power function in the original scale). The data in this graph show an approximately linear function until about the fifth year, at which point the improvement appears to stop. It turns out that the worker was approaching the cycle

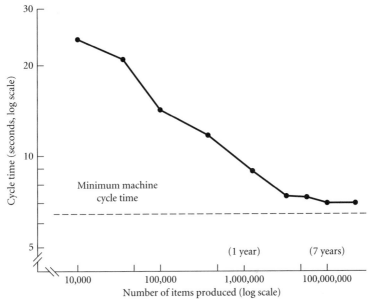

Figure 9.1 Time to produce a cigar as a function of amount of experience. (From Crossman, 1959. Reprinted by permission from Taylor & Francis.)

time of the machinery and could improve no more. There is usually some limit to how much improvement can be achieved, determined by the equipment, the capability of musculature involved, age, and so on. However, except for these physical limits, there is no limit on how much a skill can speed up. The time taken by the cognitive component of a skill will go to zero given enough practice.

Recall from Chapter 6 that a linear relationship between log time T and log practice P can be expressed as:

$$\log(T) = A - b \log(P)$$

which can be transformed into

$$T = aP^{-b}$$

where $a = 10^A$. In Chapter 6, we discussed such power functions in memory (see Figures 6.10 and 6.11). Basically, these are functions where the decrease in processing time with further practice becomes small very rapidly.

Effects of practice have also been studied in domains involving complex problem solving, such as giving justifications for geometrylike proofs (Neves & Anderson, 1981). Figure 9.2 shows a power function for that

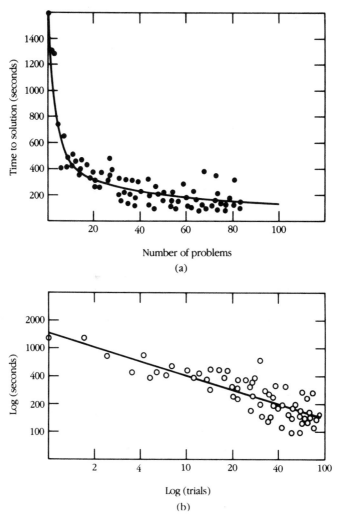

Figure 9.2 Time to generate proofs in a geometrylike proof system as a function of the number of proofs already done: (a) function on a normal scale, $RT = 1410P^{-.55}$; (b) function on a log-log scale.

domain, in terms of both a normal scale and a log-log scale. Such functions illustrate that the benefit of further practice rapidly diminishes, but that no matter how much practice we have had, further practice will help a little.

Kolers (1979) investigated the acquisition of reading skills, using materials such as those illustrated in Figure 9.3. The first type of text (N) is normal, but the others have been transformed in various ways. In the R transformation, the whole line has been turned upside down; in the I transformation, each letter has been inverted; in the M transformation, the

Factors Affecting Practice

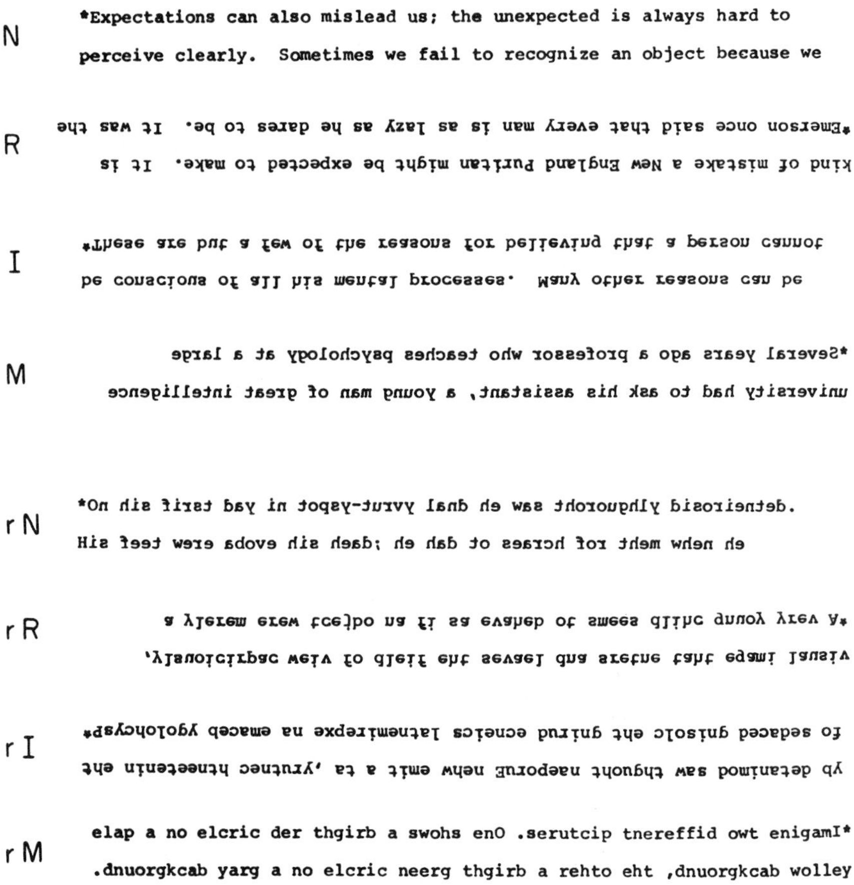

N

*Expectations can also mislead us; the unexpected is always hard to
perceive clearly. Sometimes we fail to recognize an object because we

R

*Emerson once said that every lazy man is as lazy as he dares to be. It was the
kind of mistake a New England Puritan might be expected to make. It is

I

*These are but a few of the reasons for believing that a person cannot
be conscious of all his mental processes. Many other reasons can be

M

*Several years ago a professor who teaches psychology at a large
university had to ask his assistant, a young man of great intelligence

r N

*On his first day in hospital he was thoroughly disoriented.
His feet were above his head; he had of course for them when he

r R

*A very young child was as it an object of sense little to view abstractly,
visual images that leave and retain that grasp that make usual

r I

*the detained saw thought near emit a ta a young when reporting thought was determined by
to sedaeb the stoic guring the latnemirepxe scenece during the emaced ygolohcysp

r M

*Imagine two different pictures. One shows a bright red circle on a pale
yellow background, the other a bright green circle on a gray background.

Figure 9.3 Some examples of the spatially transformed texts used in Kolers's studies of the acquisition of reading skills. The asterisks indicate the starting point for reading. (From Kolers & Perkins, 1975.)

sentence has been set as a mirror image of standard type. The rest are combinations of the several transformations. In one study, Kolers looked at the effect of massive practice on reading inverted (I) text. Subjects took more than 16 minutes to read their first page of inverted text as compared with 1.5 minutes for normal text. Following the initial test of reading speed, subjects practiced on 200 pages of inverted text. Figure 9.4 provides a log-log plot of reading time against amount of practice. In this figure, practice is measured in terms of number of pages read. The change in speed with practice is given by the curve labeled "Original training on inverted text." Kolers interspersed a few tests on normal text; data for these are given by the curve labeled "Original tests on normal text." We see the same kind of improvement for inverted text as in Figures 9.1 and 9.2 (i.e., a straight-line function on a log-log plot). After reading 200 pages, Kolers's subjects were reading at the rate of 1.6 minutes per page—almost the same rate as subjects reading normal text.

Kolers brought his subjects back a year later and had them read inverted text again. These data are given by the curve in Figure 9.4 labeled "Retraining on inverted text." Subjects now took about three minutes to read the first page of the inverted text. Compared with their performance of sixteen minutes on their first page a year earlier, subjects were displaying an enormous savings, but it was now taking them almost twice as long to read the text as it did after their 200 pages of training a year earlier. They had clearly forgotten something. As the figure illustrates, subjects' improvement on the retraining trials showed a log-log relationship between practice and performance, as had their original training. Subjects took 50 pages to reach the same level of performance that they had initially reached after 200 pages of training. It is a general characteristic that skills show very high levels of retention. In many cases, such skills can be maintained over years with no retention loss. When someone comes back to a skill—skiing, for example—after many years of absence, there is often just

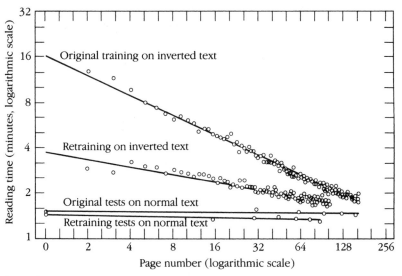

Figure 9.4 The results for readers in Kolers's reading-skills experiment (1976) on two tests more than a year apart. Subjects were trained with 200 pages of inverted text with occasional pages of normal text interspersed. A year later, they were retrained with 100 pages of inverted text, again with normal text occasionally interspersed. The results show the effect of practice on the acquisition of the skill. Both reading time and number of pages practiced are plotted on a logarithmic scale. (From Kolers, 1976. Copyright by the American Psychological Association. Reprinted by permission.)

a short warmup period during which the skill is reestablished, and then performance returns to nearly the same level as before (Schmidt, 1988).

◆
Performance of a cognitive skill improves as a power function of practice and only shows modest declines over long retention intervals.

The Nature of Expertise

We have discussed so far in this chapter some of the phenomena associated with skill acquisition. An understanding of the mechanisms behind these phenomena has come from examining the nature of expertise in various fields of endeavor. Since the mid-1970s, there has been a great deal of research looking at expertise in such domains as mathematics, chess, computer programming, and physics. This research compares people at various levels of development of their expertise. Sometimes this research is truly longitudinal and will follow students from their introduction to a field to their development of some expertise. More typically, such research samples people at different levels of expertise. For instance, research on medical expertise might look at students just beginning medical school, at residents, and at doctors with many years of medical practice. This research has begun to identify some of the ways that problem solving becomes more effective with experience. Below, we will review some of these dimensions of the development of expertise.

Proceduralization

There are dramatic changes in the degree to which subjects rely on declarative versus procedural knowledge. This is illustrated in my own work on the development of expertise in geometry (Anderson, 1982). One student had just learned the side-side-side (SSS) and side-angle-side (SAS) postulates for proving triangles congruent. The side-side-side postulate states that if three sides of one triangle are congruent to the corresponding sides of another triangle, the triangles are congruent. The side-angle-side postulate states that if two sides and the included angle of one triangle are congruent to the corresponding parts of another triangle, the triangles are congruent. Figure 9.5 illustrates the first problem the student had to solve. The first thing he did in trying to solve this problem was to decide which postulate to use. The following is a portion of his thinking-aloud protocol, during which he decided on the appropriate postulate:

> *If you looked at the side-angle-side postulate (long pause) well RK and RJ could almost be (long pause) what the missing (long pause) the missing side. I think somehow the side-angle-side postulate works its*

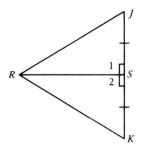

Figure 9.5 The first geometry proof problem encountered by a student after studying the side-side-side and side-angle-side postulates.

Given: ∠1 and ∠2 are right angles
 JS̄ ≅ K̄S̄
Prove: △RSJ ≅ △RSK

way into here (long pause). Let's see what it says: "Two sides and the included angle." What would I have to have to have two sides. JS and KS are one of them. Then you could go back to RS = RS. So that would bring up the side-angle-side postulate (long pause). But where would Angle 1 and Angle 2 are right angles fit in (long pause) wait I see how they work (long pause). JS is congruent to KS (long pause) and with Angle 1 and Angle 2 are right angles that's a little problem (long pause). OK, what does it say—check it one more time: "If two sides and the included angle of one triangle are congruent to the corresponding parts." So I have got to find the two sides and the included angle. With the included angle you get Angle 1 and Angle 2. I suppose (long pause) they are both right angles, which means they are congruent to each other. My first side is JS is to KS. And the next one is RS to RS. So these are the two sides. Yes, I think it is the side-angle-side postulate. (Anderson, 1982, pp. 381–382)

After reaching this point the student still went through a long process of actually writing out the proof, but this is the relevant portion in terms of assessing what goes into recognizing the relevance of the SAS postulate. After a series of four more problems (two solved by SAS and two by SSS), we came to the student's application of the SAS postulate for the problem illustrated in Figure 9.6. The method-recognition portion of the protocol follows:

Right off the top of my head I am going to take a guess at what I am supposed to do: Angle DCK is congruent to Angle ABK. There is only one of two and the side-angle-side postulate is what they are getting to. (Anderson, 1982, p. 382)

A number of things seem striking about the contrast between these two protocols. One is that there has been a clear speedup in the application of

Figure 9.6 The sixth geometry proof problem encountered by a student after studying the side-side-side and side-angle-side postulates.

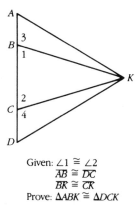

Given: $\angle 1 \cong \angle 2$
$\overline{AB} \cong \overline{DC}$
$\overline{BK} \cong \overline{CK}$
Prove: $\triangle ABK \cong \triangle DCK$

the postulate. A second is that there is no verbal rehearsal of the statement of the postulate in the second case. The student is no longer calling a declarative representation of the postulate into working memory. Note also in the first protocol that there are a number of failures of working memory—points where the student had to recover information that he had forgotten. The third feature of difference is that in the first protocol there is a piecemeal application of the postulate by which the student is separately identifying every element of the postulate. This is absent in the second protocol. It appears that the postulate is being matched in a single step.

These transitions are like the ones that Fitts and Posner characterized as belonging to the associative stage of skill acquisition. The student is no longer relying on verbal recall of the postulate but has advanced to the point where he can simply recognize the application of the postulate as a pattern. We can represent this ability by the following production rule:

> *If* the goal is to prove triangle 1 is congruent to triangle 2
>   and triangle 1 has two sides and an included angle that
>   appear congruent to two sides and an included angle
>   of triangle 2,
> *Then* set as subgoals to prove the corresponding sides and angles congruent
>   and then to use the side-angle-side postulate
>   to prove triangle 1 congruent to triangle 2

Thus, the student has converted the verbal or declarative knowledge of the postulate into procedural knowledge as embodied in the production rule above. The process of conversion is called **proceduralization**.

A similar result in physics is reported by Sweller, Mawer, and Ward (1983). These investigators studied the development of expertise in solving simple kinematics problems and looked at how often subjects wrote down basic formulas involving velocity, distance, and acceleration such as $v = at$, where v is velocity, a is acceleration, and t is time. They found that initially subjects would write these formulas down to remind themselves of them, but that later on they would only write these equations with constants from the problem substituted for some of the variables—for example, $v = 2 * 10 = 20$. Thus, the formula was only implicit in their problem solving rather than being explicitly recalled.

◆
───

Proceduralization refers to the process by which people switch from explicit use of declarative knowledge to direct application of procedural knowledge.

───

Tactical Learning

As students practice problems, they come to learn the sequences of actions required to solve the problem or portions of the problem. Learning to execute such sequences of actions is referred to as **tactical learning** in that a tactic refers to a method that accomplishes a particular goal. For instance, Greeno (1974) found that it took only about four repetitions of the hobbits and orcs problem (see discussion surrounding Figure 8.5 on page 255) before subjects could solve the problem perfectly. Subjects were learning in this experiment the sequence of moves to get the creatures across the river. Once learned, they could simply recall the sequence without further search.

Logan (1988) has argued that the general mechanism of skill acquisition involves people recalling solutions to problems that they formerly had to figure out. A nice illustration of this comes from a domain called alpha-arithmetic. It involves solving problems like $F + 3$ in which the subject is supposed to say the letter that is that many letters forward in the alphabet—so $F + 3 = I$. Logan and Klapp (1991) performed an experiment where they gave subjects problems that involved addends from 2 (e.g., $C + 2$), through 5 (e.g., $G + 5$). Figure 9.7 shows the time subjects took to answer these problems initially and then after twelve sessions of practice. Initially, subjects took 1.5 seconds longer on the 5-addend problems than the 2-addend problems, because it takes longer to count five letters forward in the alphabet than two letters forward. However, the problems were repeated again and again across the sessions. With repeated, continued practice, subjects became faster on all problems, reaching the point where they could solve the 5-addend problems as quickly as the 2-addend problems. They had come to memorize the answers to these problems and were not going through the procedure of solving the problems by counting.[1]

There is evidence that, as people become more practiced at a task and shift from computation to retrieval, there is a shift in brain activation from the prefrontal cortex to more posterior areas of the cortex. For instance,

◆
───

[1]Rabinowitz and Goldberg (1995) report a study making a similar point.

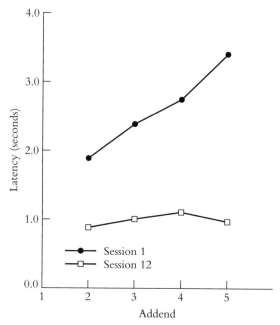

Figure 9.7 After twelve sessions it took subjects considerably less time to solve alpha-arithmetic problems with various-sized addends. (From Logan & Klapp, 1991).

Jenkins, Brooks, Nixon, Frackowiak, and Passingham (1994) looked at subjects learning to key out various sequences of finger presses like "ring, index, middle, little, middle, index, ring, index." They compared subjects initially learning these sequences with subjects practiced in these sequences. They used PET imaging studies and found that early in the learning there was more activation in frontal areas than late in the learning. This early learning activation included the anterior cingulate gyrus, which is actually a medial frontal structure ("medial" means that it is not on the surface of the cortex but a cortical structure interior to the frontal cortex). They also found more activation early in learning in the cerebellum, which is a structure known for motor learning. On the other hand, later there was more activation in the hippocampus, which is a structure associated with memory. As we noted in Chapter 1, we have found similar results with fMRI imaging looking at a much more complex problem-solving task. Such results are consistent with the perspective that early in a task there is significant involvement of the prefrontal cortex in organizing the behavior, but that late in learning subjects are just recalling the answers from memory. Thus, this neurophysiological data is consistent with Logan's proposal.

◆

Tactical learning refers to a process by which people learn specific procedures for solving specific problems.

Strategic Learning

The prior subsection was concerned with how students learn tactics by memorizing sequences of actions to solve problems. Many small problems repeat so often that we can solve them this way. However, as problems get large and complex, they do not repeat exactly, but they still have similar structures, and one can learn how to organize one's solution to the overall problem. Learning how to organize one's problem solving is referred to as **strategic learning**. One of the clearest demonstrations of such strategic changes has been in the domain of physics problem solving. Larkin (1981) compared novice and expert solutions on problems like the one in Figure 9.8. A block is sliding down an inclined plane of length l where θ is the angle between the plane and the horizontal. The coefficient of friction is μ. The subject's task is to find the velocity of the block when it reaches the bottom of the plane. Table 9.1 shows a typical novice's solution to the problem, while Table 9.2 shows a typical expert's solution.

The novice's solution typifies the reasoning backward method, which starts with the unknown, which in this case is the velocity v. Then the novice finds an equation to calculate v. However, to calculate v by this equation it is necessary to calculate a, the acceleration. So an equation is found involving a; and the novice chains backward until a set of equations is found that enable solution of the problem.

The expert, on the other hand, uses similar equations but in the completely opposite order. The expert starts with quantities that can be directly computed, such as gravitational force, and works toward the desired velocity. It is also apparent that the expert is speaking a bit like the physics teacher he is, leaving the final substitutions for the student.

Larkin has shown that on such problems, experts and novices typically apply physics principles in just the opposite order. She developed a computer model that is able to simulate the development from novice to expert with practice. This was done within a production-system framework. Novices start out with productions for reasoning backward and slowly develop productions that make forward inferences. Novice students are

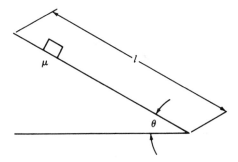

Figure 9.8 A sketch of a sample physics problem. (From Larkin, 1981.)

Table 9.1 Typical Novice Solution to a Physics Problem

To find the desired final speed v requires a principal with v in it, say

$$v = v_0 + 2at$$

But both a and t are unknown, so that seems hopeless. Try instead

$$v^2 - v_0^2 = 2ax$$

In that equation, v_0 is zero and x is known, so it remains to find a. Therefore try

$$F = ma$$

In that equation m is given, and only F is unknown, therefore use

$$F = \Sigma F\text{'s}$$

which in this case means

$$F = F_g'' - f$$

where F_g'' and f can be found from

$$F_g'' = mg \sin \theta$$
$$f = \mu N$$
$$N = mg \cos \theta$$

With a variety of substitutions, a correct expression for speed,

$$v = \sqrt{2(g \sin \theta - \mu g \cos \theta)l}$$

can be found.

Adapted from Larkin, 1981.

simulated by means-ends productions such as:

> *If* the goal is to calculate quantity x
> and there is a physics principle that involves x,
> *Then* try to use that principle to calculate x

Therefore, given the goal of calculating the acceleration, a, this production might invoke the use of the equation $v = v_0 + at$ (velocity equals initial velocity plus acceleration times time). With experience, however, her computer model developed productions that modeled expert students:

> *If* the quantities v, v_0, and t are known,
> *Then* the acceleration a can be calculated

Table 9.2 Skilled Solution to a Physics Problem

The motion of the block is accounted for by the gravitational force,

$$F_g'' = mg \sin \theta$$

directed downward along the plane, and the frictional force,

$$f = \mu mg \cos \theta$$

directed upward along the plane. The block's acceleration a is then related to the (signed) sum of these forces by

$$F = ma$$

or

$$mg \sin \theta - \mu mg \cos \theta = ma$$

Knowing the acceleration a, it is then possible to find the block's final speed v from the relations

$$l = \frac{1}{2} at^2$$

and

$$v = at$$

Adapted from Larkin, 1981.

A similar shift from backward reasoning to forward reasoning also occurs in a number of other domains like theorem proving in geometry. There are real advantages to be had by forward reasoning in such domains as geometry and physics. Reasoning backward involves setting goals and subgoals and keeping track of them. For instance, the student must remember that he or she is calculating F so that a can be calculated and hence so that v can be calculated. This puts a severe strain on working memory and can lead to errors. Reasoning forward eliminates the need to keep track of subgoals. However, to successfully reason forward, one must know which of the many possible forward inferences are relevant to the final solution. This is what the expert learns with experience. He or she learns to associate various inferences with various patterns of features in the problems.

Not all domains see this shift from backward to forward problem solving. A good counterexample is computer programming (Anderson, Farrell, & Sauers, 1984; Jeffries, Turner, Polson, & Atwood, 1981). Both novice and expert programmers develop programs in what is called a top-down manner; that is, they work from the statement of the problem to subproblems

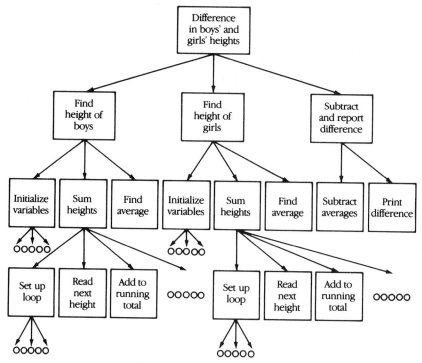

Figure 9.9 A partial representation of the plan for a program to calculate the difference in mean height between boys and girls in a classroom.

to subsubproblems, and so on, until they solve the problem. For instance, Figure 9.9 illustrates part of the development of a plan for a program to calculate the difference in mean height between boys and girls in a classroom. First, the problem is developed into the subproblems of (1) calculating the mean height of the boys, (2) calculating the mean height of the girls, and (3) subtracting the two. The problem of calculating the mean height of the boys is divided into the goals of adding up the heights and dividing by the number of boys. And so the program development continues until we get down to statements in the language such as:

$$Average = Total/Number$$

This top-down development is basically the same thing as what is called reasoning backward in the context of geometry or physics. It is noteworthy that there is not a change to forward problem solving as programmers become more expert (forward problem solving would be working from individual program statements to the larger program structure). This is in sharp contrast to geometry and physics, where experts do change to working forward. This contrast can be understood by considering the differences in the problem domains. Physics and geometry problems have a rich set of givens that are more predictive of solutions than is the goal. In contrast, in the typical statement of a programming problem (that corresponds to the givens) there is nothing that would guide a working forward or bottom-up solution. The typical problem statement only describes the goal and often does so with information that will guide a top-down solution. Thus, we see that development of expertise does not follow the same course in all domains. Rather, experts adapt themselves to the characteristics of a particular domain.

While one does not see this backward-to-forward shift in programming, another difference has been noted between expert and novice development of computer programs (Anderson, 1983; Jeffries, Turner, Polson, & Atwood, 1981). Experts tend to develop problem solutions breadth first, whereas novices develop their solutions depth first. The differences are not striking with a simple problem like the one illustrated in Figure 9.9, but they can become quite dramatic with more complex programs that have more complex plans. The expert tends to expand a full level of the plan tree before going down to expand the next level, whereas the novice will expand the first problem down to its lowest levels. Thus, an expert will have decided on a basic plan of calculating both the boys' and the girls' heights for the problem in Figure 9.9 before working out all the details of calculating the boys' heights, while the novice will completely work out the plan for the boys' heights before considering the plan for the girls' heights. The expert's approach is called breadth-first because a whole layer of tree is created at a time. The novice's approach is called depth-first because of his or her tendency to first complete the leftmost branch of the tree all the way to the bottom. There are good reasons for the expert's approach. Different parts of programming problems are typically not independent. Therefore, the solution of a later problem can often impact the solution of an earlier problem. For instance, you might want to write a program to calculate the boys' heights in such a way that the same program could be used to calculate the girls' heights. Experts, because of breadth-first expansion, are likely to see these dependencies among subproblems.

In summary, it is not the case that the transition from novices to experts involves the same changes in strategy in all domains. Different problem domains have different structures that make different strategies optimal. What we see in the development of expertise in a domain is the discovery of those strategies that are optimal for that domain. Physics experts learn to reason forward, while programming experts learn breadth-first expansion.

◆
Strategic learning involves acquiring a way of organizing one's problem solving that is optimally suited to problems in a particular domain.

Problem Perception

Another dimension of expertise is that problem solvers learn to perceive problems in ways that enable more effective problem-solving procedures to apply. This can be nicely demonstrated in the domain of physics. Physics, being an intellectually deep subject, has principles that are only implicit in the surface features of a physics problem. Experts learn to see these implicit principles and represent problems in terms of them.

Chi, Feltovich, and Glaser (1981) asked subjects to classify a large set of problems into similar categories. Figure 9.10 shows sets of problems that novices thought were similar and the novices' explanations for the similarity groupings. As can be seen, the novices chose surface features, such as rotations or inclined planes, as their bases for classification. Being a physics novice myself, I have to admit that these seem very intuitive bases for similarity. Contrast these classifications with pairs of problems in Figure 9.11 that the expert subjects saw as similar. Problems that are completely

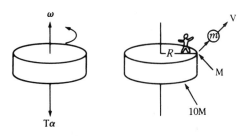

Novice 2: "*Angular* velocity, *momentum,* circular things"

Novice 3: "*Rotational* kinematics, *angular* speeds, *angular* velocities"

Novice 6: "Problems that have something *rotating: angular* speed"

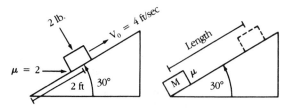

Novice 1: "These deal with blocks on an *incline plane*"

Novice 5: "*Inclined plane* problems, coefficient of *friction*"

Novice 6: "Blocks on *inclined planes* with angles"

Figure 9.10 Diagrams depicting pairs of problems categorized by novices as similar and samples of their explanations for the similarity. (Adapted from Chi et al., 1981.)

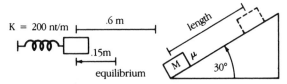

Expert 2: "Conservation of energy"

Expert 3: "Work-energy theorem.
They are all straightforward
problems."

Expert 4: "These can be done from energy
considerations. Either you should
know the *principle of conservation
of energy*, or work is lost somewhere."

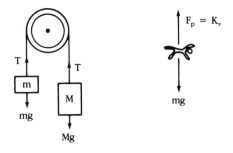

Expert 2: "These can be solved by *Newton's
second law*"

Expert 3: "F = ma; *Newton's second law*"

Expert 4: "Largely use F = ma; *Newton's
second law*"

Figure 9.11 Diagrams depicting pairs of problems categorized by experts as similar and samples of their explanations for the similarity. (Adapted from Chi et al., 1981.)

different on the surface were seen as similar because they both involved conservation of energy or they both used Newton's second law. Thus, experts have the ability to map surface features of a problem onto these deeper principles. This is very useful because the deeper principles are more predictive of the method of solution. This shift in classification from reliance on simple features to more complex features has been found in a number of domains, including mathematics (Silver, 1979; Schoenfeld & Herrmann, 1982), computer programming (Weiser & Shertz, 1983), and medical diagnosis (Lesgold, Rubinson, Feltovich, Glaser, Klopfer, & Wang, 1988).

A good example of this shift in processing of perceptual features occurs in interpreting X-rays. Figure 9.12 is a schematic of one of the X-rays diagnosed by subjects in the research by Lesgold et al. The sail-like area in the

Figure 9.12 Schematic of film showing collapsed right middle lung lobe. (From Lesgold et al. 1988.)

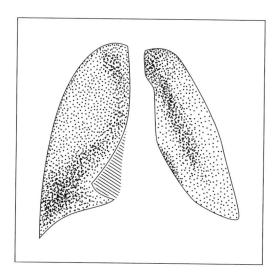

right lung is a shadow (shown on the left-side of the X-ray) caused by a collapsed lobe of the lung that created a denser shadow in an X-ray than other parts of the lung. Medical students interpreted this shadow as indication of a tumor since tumors are the most common cause of shadows on the lung. Radiological experts, on the other hand, were able to correctly interpret this as a collapsed lung. They saw counterindicative features such as the size of the sail-like region. Thus, experts no longer have a simple association between a shadow on the lungs and tumors, but rather can see the X-rays in terms of a richer set of features.

◆

One important dimension of growing expertise is the development of a set of richer perceptual features for encoding problems.

Pattern Learning and Memory

One of the surprising discoveries about expertise is that experts seem to display a special enhanced memory for information about problems in their domain of expertise. This was first discovered in the research of de Groot (1965, 1966), who was attempting to determine what separated master chess players from weaker chess players. It turns out that chess masters are not particularly more intelligent in domains other than chess. De Groot found hardly any differences between expert players and weaker players — except, of course, that the expert players chose much better moves. For instance, chess masters consider about the same number of possible moves before selecting their move. In fact, if anything, masters consider fewer moves than chess duffers.

However, de Groot did find one intriguing difference between masters and weaker players. He presented chess masters with chess positions (i.e., chessboards with pieces in a configuration that occurred in a game) for just five seconds and then removed the chess pieces. The chess masters were able to reconstruct the positions of more than twenty pieces after just five seconds of study. In contrast, the chess duffers could reconstruct only four or five pieces—an amount much more in line with the traditional capacity of working memory (see Chapter 6). It appears that chess masters have built up patterns of four or five pieces that reflect common board configurations as a function of the massive amount of experience they have had with the task. Thus, they remember not individual pieces but these patterns. In line with this analysis, if the players are presented with random chessboard positions rather than ones that are actually encountered in games, no difference is demonstrated between masters and duffers—both reconstruct only a few chess positions. The masters also complain about being very uncomfortable and disturbed by such chaotic board positions.

This basic phenomenon of superior expert memory for meaningful problems has been demonstrated in a large number of domains, including the game of Go (Reitman, 1976), electronic circuit diagrams (Egan & Schwartz, 1979), bridge hands (Engle & Bukstel, 1978; Charness, 1979), and computer programming (McKeithen, Reitman, Rueter, & Hirtle, 1981; Schneiderman, 1976).

Chase and Simon (1973) examined the nature of the patterns or chunks used by chess masters, using a chessboard-reproduction task as illustrated in Figure 9.13. The subjects' task was simply to reproduce the positions of pieces of a target chessboard on a test chessboard. In this task, subjects glanced at the target board, placed some pieces on the test board,

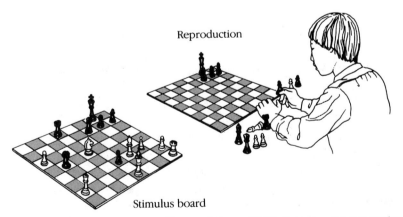

Reproduction

Stimulus board

Figure 9.13 The reproduction task in Chase and Simon (1973). Subjects were to reproduce the configuration of pieces on the reproduction board. (Adapted from Klatzky, 1979.)

glanced back to the target board, placed some more pieces on the test board, and so on. Chase and Simon defined a chunk to be a group of pieces that subjects moved following one glance. They found that these chunks tended to define meaningful game relations among the pieces. For instance, more than half of the masters' chunks were pawn chains (configurations of pawns that occur frequently in chess).

Simon and Gilmartin (1973) estimate that masters have acquired on the order of 50,000 different chess patterns, that they can quickly recognize such patterns on a chessboard, and that this ability is what underlies their superior memory performance in chess. This 50,000 figure is not unreasonable when one considers the years of devoted study that becoming a chess master requires.

What might be the relationship between memory for so many chess patterns and superior performance in chess? Newell and Simon (1972) speculated that, in addition to learning many patterns, masters have also learned what to do in the presence of such patterns. Basically, they must have something on the order of 50,000 productions in which the condition (the *if* part) of a production is a chess pattern and its action (the *then* part) is the appropriate response to that pattern. For instance, if the chunk pattern is symptomatic of a weak side, the response of the production might be to suggest an attack on the weak side. Thus, masters effectively "see" possibilities for moves; they do not have to think them out. This explains why chess masters do so well at lightning chess, in which they have only a few seconds to move.

To summarize, chess experts have stored the solutions to many problems that duffers must solve as novel problems. Duffers have to analyze different configurations, try to figure out their consequences, and act accordingly. Masters have all this information stored in memory, thereby claiming two advantages. First, they do not risk making errors in solving these problems, since they have stored the correct solution. Second, because they have stored correct analyses of so many positions, they can focus their problem-solving efforts on more sophisticated aspects and strategies of chess. Thus, the experts' pattern learning and better memory for board positions is a part of the tactical learning that we discussed earlier.

◆

Experts can recognize chunks in problems, which are patterns of elements that repeat over problems.

Long-Term Memory and Expertise

One might think that the memory advantage shown by experts is just a working-memory advantage, but research has shown that their advantage extends to long-term memory. Charness (1976) compared experts' memory for chess positions immediately after they had viewed the positions or after a 30-second delay filled with an interfering task. Class A chess players show no loss in recall over the 30-second interval, unlike weaker subjects, who show a great deal of forgetting. Thus, expert chess players, unlike duffers, have an increased capacity to store information about the domain. Interestingly, these subjects show the same poor memory for three-letter trigrams as ordinary subjects. Thus, their increased long-term memory is only for the domain of expertise.

There is reason to believe that the memory advantage goes beyond experts' ability to encode the problem in terms of familiar patterns. Experts appear to be able to remember more patterns as well as larger patterns. Some evidence for this was provided by an experiment by Chase and Simon, who had subjects recall chessboards in a similar manner to de Groot (but in contrast to the reproduction task illustrated in Figure 9.13). They tried to identify the patterns that their subjects used to recall the chessboards. They found that subjects would tend to recall a pattern, pause, recall another pattern, pause, and so on. They found that they could use a two-second pause to identify boundaries between patterns. With this objective definition of what a pattern is, they could then explore how many patterns were recalled. In comparing a master chess player with a beginner, they found large differences in both measures. The pattern size of the master averaged 3.8 pieces, whereas it was only 2.4 for the beginner. Moreover, the master also recalled an average of 7.7 patterns per board while the beginner recalled only an average of 5.3. Thus, it seems that the experts' memory advantage is based not only on larger patterns but also on the ability to recall more of them.

The strongest evidence that expertise involves the ability to remember more patterns as well as larger patterns comes from Chase and Ericsson (1982), who studied the development of a simple but remarkable skill. They watched a subject, S. F., increase his digit span, which is the number of digits that he could repeat back after one presentation. As discussed in Chapter 6, the normal digit span is about 7 or 8 items, just enough to accommodate a telephone number. After about 200 hours of practice, S. F. was able to recall 81 random digits presented at the rate of 1 digit per second. Figure 9.14 illustrates how his memory span grew with practice.

What was behind this apparent superhuman feat of memory? In part, S. F. was learning to chunk the digits into meaningful patterns. He was a long-distance runner, and part of his technique was to convert digits into running times. So, he would take four digits, like 3492, and convert them into "Three minutes, 49.2 seconds—near world-record mile time." Using such a strategy, he could convert a memory span for 7 digits into a memory span for 7-digit patterns of length 3 or 4. This would get him to a digit span over 20, far short of his eventual performance. In addition to this chunking, he developed what Chase and Ericsson called a retrieval structure, which

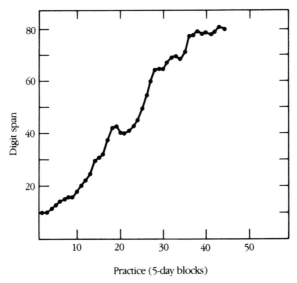

Figure 9.14 The growth in the memory span of the subject S. F. with practice. Notice how the number of digits he can recall increases gradually but continually with the number of practice sessions. (From Chase & Ericsson, 1982.)

enabled him to recall 22 such patterns. This retrieval structure was very specific; it did not generalize to retrieving letters rather than digits. Chase and Ericsson hypothesize that part of what underlies development of expertise in other domains such as chess is development of retrieval structures, which allows superior recall for past patterns.

◆───

As people become more expert in a domain, they develop a better ability to store problem information in long-term memory and to retrieve it.

───

The Role of Deliberate Practice

One of the implications of all the research that we have reviewed is that expertise only comes with the investment of a great deal of time to learn the patterns, the problem-solving rules, and the appropriate problem-solving organization for a domain. We mentioned earlier John Hayes's finding that geniuses in various fields only produce their best work after ten years of apprenticeship in a field. Ericsson, Krampe, and Tesch-Romer (1993) compared the best violinists at a music academy in Berlin with those who were only very good. They looked at diaries and self-estimates to determine how much the two populations had practiced, and estimated that the best violinists had practiced over 7000 hours before coming to the academy, while the very good had practiced only 5000 hours. Ericsson et al. reviewed a great many fields like music where time spent practicing is critical. Time on task is not only important at the highest levels of performance, but it is an essential aspect to school success. Anderson, Reder, and Simon (1998) note that one of the major reasons for the higher achievement in mathematics of students in Asian countries is that those students spend twice as much time practicing mathematics.

Ericsson et al. make the strong claim that almost all of expertise is to be accounted for by amount of practice and there is virtually no role for natural talent. They point to the research of Bloom (1985a, 1985b), who looked at the histories of children who became great in fields like music. Bloom found that most of these children got started by playing around, but after a relatively short time they typically showed promise and were encouraged by their parents to start serious training with a teacher. However, the early natural abilities of these children were surprisingly modest and did not predict ultimate success in the domain (Ericsson et al., 1993). Rather, it seems what is critical is that parents come to believe that a child is talented and consequently pay for their child's instruction and equipment as well as support their time-consuming practice. Ericsson et al. speculate that the resulting training is sufficient to account for development of children's success. There is almost certainly some role for talent (and we will discuss some of this evidence for talent in the last chapter of the book), but all the evidence indicates that genius is 90% perspiration and 10% inspiration.

Ericsson et al. are careful to note, however, that not all practice leads to the development of expertise. They note the many cases of people who spend a lifetime playing chess or some sport without ever getting any better. What is critical according to Ericsson et al. is what they call **deliberate practice**. In deliberate practice, the learners are motivated to learn, not just perform; the learners are given feedback on their performance; and they carefully monitor how well their performance corresponds to the correct performance and where the deviations occur. The learners focus on eliminating these points of discrepancy. The importance of deliberate practice is similar to the importance we saw in the memory chapters on deep and elaborative processing of the to-be-learned material. Those chapters (6 and 7) showed that passive study brought relatively little memory benefits.

◆ ───

A great deal of deliberate practice is necessary to develop expertise in any field.

Transfer of Skill

Expertise can often be quite narrow. As noted, Chase and Ericsson's subject S. F. was unable to transfer memory span skill from digits to letters. This is an almost ridiculous extreme of what is a frequent pattern in the development of cognitive skills — that these skills can be quite narrow and fail to transfer to other activities. Chess grand masters do not appear to be better thinkers for all their genius in chess. An amusing example of the narrowness of expertise is a study by Carraher, Carraher, and Schliemann (1985). These researchers investigated the mathematical strategies used by Brazilian schoolchildren who also worked as street vendors. On the job, these children used quite sophisticated strategies for calculating the total cost of orders involving different numbers of different objects (e.g., the total cost of four coconuts and twelve lemons), and what's more, they could perform such calculations reliably in their heads. Carraher et al. actually went to the trouble of going to the streets and posing as customers for these children, making certain kinds of purchases, and recording the percentage of correct calculations. The experimenters then asked the children to come with them to the laboratory, where they were given written mathematics tests that involved the same numbers and mathematical operations that had been manipulated successfully in the streets. For example, if a child had correctly calculated the total cost of five lemons at 35 cruzeiros apiece on the street, the child was given the following written problem:

$$5 \times 35 = ?$$

The results showed that, whereas children solved 98 percent of the problems presented in the situated context, they solved only 37 percent of the problems presented in the laboratory context. It needs to be stressed that these problems involved the exact same numbers and mathematical operations. Interestingly, if the problems were stated in the form of word problems in the laboratory, performance improved to 74 percent. This runs counter to the usual finding, which is that word problems are more difficult than equivalent "number" problems (Carpenter & Moser, 1982). Apparently, the additional context provided by the word problem allowed the children to make contact with their pragmatic strategies.

The study of Carraher et al. showed a curious failure of expertise in real life to transfer to the classroom, but the typical concern of educators is whether anything taught in one class will transfer to other classes and the real world. At the turn of the century, educators were fairly optimistic on this issue. A number of educational psychologists subscribed to what has been called the doctrine of formal discipline (Angell, 1908; Pillsbury, 1908; Woodrow, 1927), which held that studying such esoteric subjects as Latin and geometry was of significant value because it served to discipline the mind. Formal discipline subscribed to the faculty view of mind, which extends back to Aristotle and was first formalized by Thomas Reid in the late eighteenth century (Boring, 1950). The faculty position held that the mind was composed of a collection of general faculties, such as observation, attention, discrimination, and reasoning, which were exercised in much the same way as a set of muscles. The content of the exercise made little difference; most important was the level of exertion (hence the fondness for Latin and geometry). Transfer in such a view is broad and takes place at a general level, sometimes spanning domains that share no content.

While it might be nice to believe that such general transfer is possible, such as envisioned by the doctrine of formal discipline, there has been effectively no evidence for it, despite a century of research on the topic. Some of the earliest research on this topic was performed by Thorndike (e.g., Thorndike & Woodworth, 1901). In one study, no correlation was found between memory for words and memory for numbers. In another, accuracy in spelling was not correlated with accuracy in arithmetic. Thorndike interpreted these results as evidence against the general faculties of memory and accuracy.

◆ ───
There is often failure to transfer skills to similar domains and virtually no transfer to very different domains.
───

Theory of Identical Elements

In place of the doctrine of formal discipline, Thorndike proposed his **theory of identical elements**. According to Thorndike, the mind was not composed of general faculties but rather of specific habits and associations, which provided a person with a variety of narrow responses to very specific stimuli. In fact, the mind was regarded as just a convenient name for countless special operations or functions (Stratton, 1922). Thorndike's theory stated that training in one kind of activity would transfer to another only if the activities shared common situation-response elements:

> One mental function or activity improves others in so far as and because they are in part identical with it, because it contains elements common to them. Addition improves multiplication because multiplication is largely addition; knowledge of Latin gives increased ability to learn French because many of the facts learned in the one case are needed in the other. (Thorndike, 1906, p. 243)

Thus, Thorndike was happy to accept transfer between diverse skills as long as it could be shown that the transfer was mediated by identical elements. Generally, however, he concluded that

> The mind is so specialized into a multitude of independent capacities that we alter human nature only in small spots, and any special school training has a much narrower influence upon the mind as a whole than has commonly been supposed. (p. 246)

Although the doctrine of formal discipline was too broad in its predictions of transfer, it turns out that Thorndike formulated his theory of identical elements in what proved to be an overly narrow manner. For instance, he argued that if you solved a geometry problem that involved one set of letters to label the points in a diagram, you would not be able to transfer to a geometry problem with a different set of letters. The research that we examined on analogy in the previous chapter indicated that this is not true. Transfer is not tied to identity of surface elements. There is in some cases very large positive transfer between two skills that have the same logical structure even if they have different surface elements (see Singley & Anderson, 1989, for a review). Thus, for instance, there is large positive transfer between different word-processing systems, between different programming languages, and between using calculus to solve economics problems and using calculus to solve problems in solid geometry. However, all the available evidence is that there are very definite bounds on how far skills will transfer and that becoming an expert in one domain will have little positive benefit on becoming an expert in a very different area. There will be positive transfer only to the extent that the two domains involve use of the same facts, productions, and patterns—i.e., the same knowledge. Thus, Thorndike was right in saying that there would be transfer between two skills to the extent that they shared the same elements. However, he was wrong in identifying these "elements" with stimulus-response bonds. Modern cognitive psychology has identified these elements as rather abstract knowledge structures that enjoy a wider range of transfer.

There is a positive side to this specificity in transfer of skill: there seldom seems to be **negative transfer**, in which learning one skill makes a person worse at learning another skill. Interference, such as that which occurs in memory for facts (see Chapter 7), is almost nonexistent in skill acquisition. Polson, Muncher, and Kieras (1987) provide a good demonstration of lack of negative transfer in the domain of text editing on a computer. They asked subjects to learn one text editor and then learn a second, which was designed to be maximally confusing. Whereas the command to go down a line of text might be n and the command to delete a character might be k in one text editor, n would mean to delete a character in another text editor and k would mean to go down a line. However, subjects experienced overwhelming positive transfer in going from one text editor to the other because the two text editors worked in the same way, even though the surface commands had been scrambled. There is only one clearly documented kind of negative transfer in the case of cognitive skills. This is the *Einstellung* effect discussed in the previous chapter. Students can learn ways of solving problems in one domain that are no longer optimal for solving problems in another domain. So, for instance, someone may learn tricks in algebra to avoid having to perform difficult arithmetic computations. These tricks may no longer be necessary when one goes to an environment where there are calculators to perform these calculations.

Still, students show a tendency to continue to perform these unnecessary simplifications in their algebraic manipulations. This is really not a case of failure to transfer. This is a case of transferring knowledge that is no longer useful.

◆

There is transfer between skills only when these skills involve the same abstract knowledge elements.

Educational Implications

With this analysis of skill acquisition, we can ask the question: What are the implications for the training of such skills? One of the implications concerns the importance of problem decomposition. It has been estimated (Anderson, 1992) that traditional high school algebra involves acquiring many thousands of production rules. Instruction can be improved by an analysis of what these individual elements are. Approaches to instruction that begin with an analysis of the elements to be taught are called **componential analyses.** Anderson (2000) describes the application of componential approaches to the instruction of a number of topics in reading and mathematics. Generally, higher achievement is obtained in programs that involve such componential analysis.

A particularly effective part to such componential programs is **mastery learning.** The basic idea in mastery learning is to follow students' performance on each of the components underlying the cognitive skill, and ensure that all components are mastered. Typical instruction, without mastery learning, leaves some students not knowing some of the material. This can snowball in a course when mastery of earlier material is a prerequisite for mastery of later material. There is a good deal of evidence that mastery learning leads to higher achievement (Guskey & Gates, 1986; Kulik, Kulik, & Bangert-Downs, 1986).

◆

Instruction is improved by approaches that identify the underlying knowledge elements and bring students to mastery of them all.

Intelligent Tutoring Systems

Probably the most extensive use of such componential analysis occurs in **intelligent tutoring systems** (Sleeman & Brown, 1982). These are computer systems that interact with students while they are learning and solving problems, much as a human tutor would. One example of such a tutor is the LISP tutor that we have developed (Anderson, Conrad, & Corbett, 1989; Corbett & Anderson, 1990; Anderson & Reiser, 1985), which teaches

LISP, the main programming language used in artificial intelligence. The LISP tutor has continuously taught LISP to students at Carnegie Mellon University since the fall of 1984, and has served as a prototype for a generation of intelligent tutors, many of which have been focused on teaching high school mathematics. Currently, these tutors are improving the mathematics achievements of thousands of students in about 100 schools around the country (Anderson, Corbett, Koedinger, & Pelletier, 1995; Koedinger, Anderson, Hadley, & Mark, 1997).

One of the motivations for research on intelligent tutoring is the evidence showing that private human tutoring is very effective. Studies have shown that giving students a private human tutor enables 98 percent of them to do better than the average student in a standard classroom (Bloom, 1984). An ideal private tutor is one who is with you at all times while studying a particular subject matter. To use the terms of Ericsson et al. (1993), a private tutor guarantees the deliberate practice that is essential for learning. It is particularly important to have the tutor present while solving problems in domains like LISP and mathematics that require complex problem-solving skills. In LISP, problem solving takes the form of writing computer programs, or functions, as they are often called in LISP. Therefore, in developing the LISP tutor, we chose to focus on providing students with tutoring while they are writing computer programs. Table 9.3 presents a short dialogue between a student and the LISP tutor on an early problem in the curriculum. Note how carefully the tutor monitors the student's performance in solving the problem. It can do this because it knows how to write LISP functions. As the student is writing the function, the tutor is simultaneously trying to solve the same problem the student is working on. As soon as it sees the student making a mistake, the tutor can intervene with some remedial instruction.

Underlying the tutor's ability to solve problems and monitor the student's problem solving is a set of production rules that can solve the same LISP programming problems that we expect students to be able to solve. In all, there are about 500 production rules that encode the knowledge relating to LISP. A typical production rule in the LISP tutor is:

> *If* the goal is to multiply one number by another,
> *Then* use * and set subgoals to code the two numbers

The basic goal of the LISP tutor is to communicate these 500 production rules to the student, monitor the performance to see if he or she possesses these rules in correct form, and provide the student with practice on these rules. The success of the LISP tutor is one piece of evidence that these 500 rules are indeed what underlie coding skill in LISP.

Table 9.3 An Interaction Between the LISP Tutor and the Student

The student is working on a piece of code to satisfy the problem description below. Before each point where the tutor and student interact, the partial code that the student has written is printed out.

The Problem Description

Define a function called ctof that takes a degree reading in Celsius degrees and converts it to Fahrenheit degrees. First, you need to change the scale by multiplying the argument by 1.8. Then you need to translate the scale by adding 32, since 0 Celsius = 32 Fahrenheit. For example,
   (ctof 20) returns 68.

Cycles in which the tutor communicates with the student

Code: *(defun ctof (cdeg)*

   ((*)

Tutor: Yes, you will need to call "*" to get the degree on the enlarged scale, but you are ultimately trying to get the Fahrenheit equivalent of the Celsius degree. So you need to code a different function here that takes a call to "*" as an argument.

Code: *(defun ftoc (cdeg)*

   (+<NUM> <NUM2>))

Student: Help

Tutor: You need to multiply together the Celsius degree reading and the size of Fahrenheit degrees using the function *. When you multiply these numbers you will get the degree on the enlarged scale, which is 36 in our example.

Code: *(defun ctof (cdeg)*

   (+(*1.8 cdge) <NUM2>))

Tutor: Did you mean cdeg?

Student: Yes

Code: *(defun ctof (cdeg)*

   (+(*1.8 cdeg) 32))

Tutor: You are done. Type next to go on after testing the function you have defined.

Besides providing an instructional tool, the LISP tutor is a research tool for studying the course of skill acquisition. The tutor can monitor how well the student is doing on each of the 500 production rules, recording statistics such as the number of errors a student is making and the time it takes a student to type the code corresponding to each of these production rules. These data have indicated that students acquire the skill of LISP by independently acquiring each of the 500 rules. Figure 9.15 displays the learning curves for these rules. The two dependent measures in the figure are the number of errors made on a production rule and the time to write the code corresponding to a rule (when that rule is correctly coded). These statistics are plotted as a function of learning opportunities, which occur each time the student comes to a point in a problem where that rule can be applied. As can be seen, performance on these rules dramatically improves from first to second learning opportunity and more gradually improves thereafter. These learning curves are similar to those we identified in Chapter 6 for the learning of simple associations.

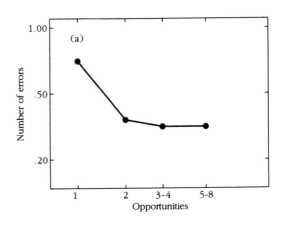

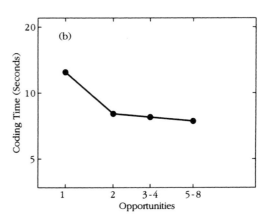

Figure 9.15 Data from the LISP tutor: (a) number of errors (maximum is 3) per production as a function of the number of opportunities for practice; (b) time to correctly code productions as a function of the amount of practice.

We have also pursued the issue of individual differences in the learning of these rules. Students who have learned a prior programming language are at a considerable advantage compared to students for whom this is their first programming language. This advantage can be accounted for in terms of the "identical elements model" of transfer, in which rules for programming in one language transfer to programming in another language.

We also did an analysis of the performance of individual students in the LISP tutor and found evidence for two factors. Some students were able to learn new productions in a lesson quite rapidly, whereas other students had more difficulty. More or less independent of this acquisition factor, students could be classified according to how well they retained productions from earlier lessons.[2] Thus, students differ in how rapidly they learn with the LISP tutor. However, the tutor employs a mastery learning system in which slower students are given more practice, and so are brought to the same level of mastery of the material.

Students emerge from their interactions with the LISP tutor having acquired a complex and sophisticated skill. Their enhanced programming abilities make them appear more intelligent among their peers. However, when we examine what underlies that newfound intelligence, we find that it is the methodical acquisition of some 500 rules of programming. Some students can acquire these rules more easily because of past experience and specific abilities. However, when they graduate from the LISP course, all students have learned the 500 new production rules. Having acquired these rules, there are few remaining differences among the students with respect to ability to program in LISP. Thus, we see that in the end, what is important with respect to individual differences is how much information students have learned, not their native ability. We will be exploring further in Chapter 13 the roles of knowledge and ability in determining individual differences in cognition.

◆

By carefully monitoring individual components of a skill and providing feedback on learning, intelligent tutors can bring students to rapid mastery of complex skills.

Remarks and Suggested Readings

Ericsson (1996) and Ericsson and Lehmann (1996) review recent research on expertise and exceptional performers. While this chapter has focused mainly on the development of cognitive skills, considerable research has also been done on the development of motor skills. Such research is

◆

[2]These acquisition and retention factors were strongly related to math SATs but not to verbal SATs.

reviewed in Rosenbaum (1991) and Schmidt (1988). Singley and Anderson (1989) provide a review of research of transfer and a modern version of Thorndike's theory of identical elements cast in terms of production systems. Work on intelligent tutoring systems can be followed through the proceedings of the biannual International Conference on Intelligent Tutoring Systems.

10

Reasoning and Decision Making

R easoning refers to the processes by which people infer new knowledge from what they already know. Thus, if I know that my children's school closes when four inches of snow falls, and I know that there has been a six-inch snowfall, then I can infer that my children's school will be closed. Or if I discover that if I press "fifteen" and "start" that the microwave will run for fifteen seconds, then I have reason to suppose that if I press "thirty" and "start" that the microwave will run for thirty seconds. Frequently, the information we are told is not adequate in itself to allow us to make the decisions and take the actions that we need to. However, we can often reason from what we are given to get the extra information that we need.

Psychological research on reasoning has had a long and complex relationship to the study of logic. **Logic** is a subdiscipline of philosophy and mathematics that tries to formally specify what it means for an argument to be correct. To understand the psychological research on reasoning, we have to understand the relationship of this research to logic. Until the twentieth century, logic and the psychology of thought were often considered one and the same. The famous Irish mathematician George Boole (1854) called his book on logical calculus *An investigation of the laws of thought,* and designed it "in the first place, to investigate the fundamental laws of those operations of the mind by which reasoning is performed." Of course, humans did not always operate according to the prescriptions of logic, but such lapses were seen as the malfunctioning of mental machinery that was logical when it worked properly. In trying to improve the mind, people tried to train themselves to be logical. A hundred years ago, a section on "cognitive processes" in a psychology text would have been about "logical thinking." The fact that only one chapter in this book is on reasoning reflects the current understanding that a large portion of human thought cannot be considered logical reasoning in any useful sense.

Much of the research on deductive reasoning has been explicitly designed to compare human performance with the prescriptions of logic. In such experiments, the reasoning problems presented to subjects are analyzed in the terms used in logic. This connection between logic and reasoning has been at best a mixed blessing. Research on logic is concerned with the validity of arguments and is valuable in understanding domains such as mathematics and science, whose foundations depend on logical inference. However, there is no reason to suppose that logic has a close relationship to the cognitive processes underlying human reasoning.

This chapter will also discuss research on decision making, which is concerned with how we make choices among alternatives. Just as logic has served as a prescriptive norm for evaluating reason, so there exist prescriptions for decision making that have been developed by mathematicians, statisticians, philosophers, and economists. Again, we will see that humans often fail when measured by these norms. However, again the question will arise as to how much this says about the quality of human thought and how much it says about the appropriateness of the norms.

◆

Psychological research has compared human reasoning and decision making with the prescriptions of various normative models such as logic.

Reasoning about Conditionals

We will begin this chapter with a discussion of **deductive reasoning**, which is to be distinguished from **inductive reasoning**. Deductive reasoning is concerned with conclusions that follow with certainty from their premises, whereas inductive reasoning is concerned with conclusions that probabilistically follow from their premises. To illustrate the distinction, suppose someone is told "Fred is the brother of Mary" and "Mary is the mother of Lisa." Then, one might conclude that "Fred is the uncle of Lisa" and that "Fred is older than Lisa." The first conclusion, "Fred is the uncle of Lisa," would be a correct deductive inference, given the definition of familial relations. On the other hand, the second conclusion, "Fred is older than Lisa," is a good inductive inference, since it is probably true, but not a correct deductive inference, since it is not necessarily true.

Our first topic will concern human deductive reasoning involving the conditional connective *if*. A **conditional statement** is an assertion, such as "If you read this chapter, you will be wiser." The *if* part (*you read this chapter*) is called the **antecedent** and the *then* part (*you will be wiser*) is called the **consequent**. A particularly central rule of inference in the logic of the conditional is known in logic as *modus ponens*. It allows us to infer the consequent of a conditional if we are given the antecedent. Thus, given both the proposition *If A, then B* and the proposition *A*, we can infer *B*. So, suppose we are told the following:

1. If Joan understood this book, then she would get a good grade.

2. Joan understood this book.

From premises 1 and 2 we can infer 3 by *modus ponens*:

3. Joan got a good grade.

This example is an instance of valid deduction. By valid, we mean that if premises 1 and 2 are true, the conclusion 3 must be true. This example also illustrates the artificiality of applying logic to real-world situations. How is one to really know if Joan understands the book? One can only assign a certain probability to this. Even if Joan does understand the book, at best it is only likely—not certain—that she will get a good grade. However, subjects are asked to suspend their knowledge about such matters and treat these facts as if they were certainties. Or more precisely, they are asked to reason what would follow for certain if these facts were certain.[1] Subjects do not find these particularly strange instructions to follow, but, as we will see, they are not always able to make logically correct inferences.

Another rule of inference is known in logic as *modus tollens*. This rule states that if we are given the proposition *A implies B* and the fact that *B is*

---

[1] Interestingly, the mathematical theory of probability involves conditional statements. In this case the objects of the conditional statement are statements about probabilities. This illustrates the fact that precise mathematics requires the formal logic of the conditional; it should not be taken as an illustration of a way of incorporating the formal logic of the conditional into a theory of everyday reasoning.

false, then we can infer that *A is false*. The following is an inference exercise that requires *modus tollens*. Suppose we are given the following premises:

4. If Joan understood this book, then she would get a good grade.

5. Joan did not get a good grade.

Then it follows from premises 4 and 5 by *modus tollens* that

6. Joan did not understand this book.

This conclusion might strike the reader as less than totally compelling, but this is because, again, in the real world such statements are not typically treated as certain.

◆

Modus ponens infers the consequent from the antecedent; *modus tollens* infers the negation of the antecedent from the negation of the consequent.

Evaluation of Conditional Syllogisms

A fair amount of research has been concerned with the way subjects reason with such conditional statements (e.g., Marcus & Rips, 1979; Rips & Marcus, 1977; Staudenmayer, 1975; Taplin, 1971; Taplin & Staudenmayer, 1973). Typical statements are presented to subjects with rather bland content to prevent prior beliefs from having an impact on the outcome. For example:

1. If the ball rolls left, then the green lamp will come on.
The ball rolls left.
Therefore, the green lamp will come on.

2. If the ball rolls left, then the lamp will come on.
The ball does not roll left.
Therefore, the lamp will not come on.

These are called **conditional syllogisms**. Subjects are asked to judge whether the conclusions of the syllogisms are correct or not. In the examples above, 1 is correct and 2 is not.

Abstractly, we may represent these syllogisms according to the following notation:

$$\textbf{1.}\ P \supset Q \qquad\qquad \textbf{2.}\ P \supset Q$$
$$\underline{P} \qquad\qquad\qquad \underline{\sim P}$$
$$\therefore Q \qquad\qquad\qquad\quad \therefore \sim Q$$

where the $\supset$ symbol stands for implication, and the $\sim$ stands for negation.

Consider a representative experiment, by Rips and Marcus (1977), in which undergraduates from the University of Chicago were asked to evaluate eight types of syllogisms in Table 10.1. Though the syllogisms are presented abstractly in Table 10.1, the subjects were actually tested with concrete propositions like the ones given earlier. Subjects were asked to judge whether the conclusion was always true, sometimes true, or never

◆

Table 10.1 Percentage of Total Responses for Eight Types of Conditional Syllogism

Syllogism	Always	Sometimes	Never
1. $P \supset Q$ P $\therefore Q$	100^a	0	0
2. $P \supset Q$ P $\therefore \sim Q$	0	0	100^a
3. $P \supset Q$ $\sim P$ $\therefore Q$	5	79^a	16
4. $P \supset Q$ $\sim P$ $\therefore \sim Q$	21	77^a	2
5. $P \supset Q$ Q $\therefore P$	23	77^a	0
6. $P \supset Q$ Q $\therefore \sim P$	4	82^a	14
7. $P \supset Q$ $\sim Q$ $\therefore P$	0	23	77^a
8. $P \supset Q$ $\sim Q$ $\therefore \sim P$	57^a	39	4

[a]The correct response.
Adapted from Rips & Marcus, 1977.

true given the premises. The table gives the percentage of responses in each category for each type of syllogism.

Syllogisms 1 and 2 in the table indicate that subjects could apply *modus ponens* quite successfully. However, they had much greater difficulty with *modus tollens*, which is required to derive valid inferences for syllogisms 7 and 8. Averaging syllogisms 7 and 8 together, more than 30 percent of the subject population failed to realize that we can reason from the negation of the second term in a conditional to the negation of the first term. Subjects also displayed a certain tendency to accept fallacies — conclusions that do not follow from the premises. Syllogisms 3 and 4 display evidence for a fallacy in conditional reasoning known as **denial of the antecedent**. Almost 20 percent of the subject population believed that we can conclude that Q is not true if we know that *If P, then Q* and that P is not true. Syllogisms 5 and 6 display a tendency for a fallacy known as **affirmation of the consequent**. On these problems, almost 20 percent of the subject population believed that we can conclude that P is true from knowing *If P, then Q* and Q.

It seems that one source of the fallacies displayed in problems 3 through 6 is that subjects do not interpret conditionals in the same way that logicians do. This discrepancy has been demonstrated in a series of experiments by Taplin (1971), Taplin and Staudenmayer (1973), and Staudenmayer (1975). They showed that many subjects interpreted the conditional as being what logicians would call the **biconditional**. The biconditional is rendered in English unambiguously by the rather awkward construction *if and only if*: For instance,

- Israel will use atomic weapons if and only if it is faced with annihilation.

With the biconditional, if either the first or second premise is true, the other will be true. Similarly, if either the first or second premise is false, the other will be false.

◆ Subjects are good at evaluating conditional syllogisms that reflect *modus ponens* but poorer at judging other forms of conditional syllogisms.

Alternatives to the Logical Model

The argument that subjects interpret the conditional as the biconditional is one example of an effort to argue that human subjects actually reason according to the prescriptions of formal logic but do not interpret the premises as expected. However, there is an alternative explanation (e.g., Haviland, 1974; Rips, 1990), which is that subjects do not reason logically but rather reason probabilistically. That is to say, they treat *If P, then Q* to simply mean that Q is probable if P occurs. The details of such probabilistic

Table 10.2 A Probabilistic Interpretation of the P ⊃ Q Rule

a. Probabilities

	Q	$\sim Q$
P	.4	.1
$\sim P$	.2	.3

b. Conditional Probabilities

Modus ponens	$\text{Prob}(Q\mid P) = .80$	$\text{Prob}(\sim Q\mid P) = .20$
Denial of antecedent	$\text{Prob}(\sim Q\mid\sim P) = .60$	$\text{Prob}(Q\mid\sim P) = .40$
Affirmation of consequent	$\text{Prob}(P\mid Q) = .67$	$\text{Prob}(\sim P\mid Q) = .33$
Modus tollens	$\text{Prob}(\sim P\mid\sim Q) = .75$	$\text{Prob}(P\mid\sim Q) = .25$

models have not been well worked out, but Table 10.2 shows a made-up probabilistic model that might be an interpretation of the *If P, then Q* implication. Part *a* of the table classifies the four possible states of the world that can be obtained by crossing the outcomes of P or $\sim P$ with the outcomes of Q or $\sim Q$. If P occurs, the probability is high that Q will also occur. Note we also have designed the probabilities such that when P does not occur, the probability is somewhat higher that Q will not occur. Table 10.2*b* also reproduces the conditional probabilities that various events will occur given other events. For instance, the conditional probability $\text{Prob}(Q\mid P)$ means that the probability Q will occur if P occurs. Corresponding to the choice behavior in Table 10.1, the highest conditional probability occurs for $\text{Prob}(Q\mid P)$, which corresponds to *modus ponens*, the next highest conditional probability occurs with $\text{Prob}(\sim P\mid\sim Q)$, which corresponds to *modus tollens*, the next highest with $\text{Prob}(P\mid Q)$, which corresponds to affirming the consequent, and the next highest with $\text{Prob}(\sim Q\mid\sim P)$, which corresponds to denial of antecedent. The remaining conditional probabilities are all below .5 and correspond to the rows with near-zero acceptances in Table 10.1. Thus, subjects' tendency to accept logical arguments in Table 10.1 could reflect the conditional probabilities in Table 10.2.

The conditional probabilities in Table 10.2*b* correspond quite well with the acceptance rates in Table 10.1. However, this correspondence depends on the exact probabilities that we assumed in Table 10.2*a*. The conditional probabilities would have been different had we assumed different probabilities. The problem with probabilistic explanations is that it is hard to know what are appropriate probabilities.

The probabilistic model assumes that people's tendency to accept a conclusion depends on how probable the conclusion is, given the premises.

The Wason Selection Task

A very striking demonstration of failure to apply *modus tollens* comes from a series of experiments performed by Wason (for a review of the early research, see Wason & Johnson-Laird, 1972, Chapters 13 and 14). In a typical experiment from this research, four cards showing the following symbols were placed in front of subjects:

Subjects were told that a letter appeared on one side of each card and a number on the other. The task was to judge the validity of the following rule, which referred only to these four cards:

- If a card has a vowel on the one side, then it has an even number on the other side.

The subjects' task was to turn over only those cards that had to be turned over for the correctness of the rule to be judged. This task, typically referred to as the **selection task**, has received a great deal of research.

Averaging over a large number of experiments (Oaksford & Chater, 1994), it has been found that 89 percent of subjects select E, which is a logically correct choice since an odd number on the other side would disconfirm the rule. However, 62 percent of the subjects also choose to turn over the 4, which is not logically informative since neither a vowel nor a consonant on the other side would have falsified the rule. Only 25 percent elect to turn over the 7, which is a logically informative choice since a vowel behind the 7 would have falsified the rule. Only 16 percent elect to turn over the K which would not be an informative choice.

Thus, subjects displayed two types of logical errors in the task. First, they often turned over the 4, another example of the fallacy of affirming the consequent. Again, this response might just have reflected an interpretation by subjects of the conditional as a biconditional. However, even more striking was the failure to take the *modus tollens* step of disconfirming the consequent and determining whether the antecedent was also disconfirmed (in other words, to turn over the 7).

This failure to apply *modus tollens* cannot be explained by the logical interpretation of the task. Under the logical interpretation, one simply has to assume that humans do not know the rule of *modus tollens*. However, recently Oaksford and Chater have argued that subjects are not reasoning deductively in this task but rather are reasoning inductively. In their view, subjects are trying to discriminate between a probabilistic model like the one in Table 10.2 and a null model like the one in Table 10.3 that does not

Table 10.3 A Probabilistic Interpretation of a Null Rule

a. Probabilities

	Q	$\sim Q$
P	.16	.24
$\sim P$	.24	.36

b. Conditional Probabilities

Modus ponens	$\mathrm{Prob}(Q\|P) = .40$	$\mathrm{Prob}(\sim Q\|P) = .60$
Denial of antecedent	$\mathrm{Prob}(\sim Q\|\sim P) = .60$	$\mathrm{Prob}(Q\|\sim P) = .40$
Affirmation of consequent	$\mathrm{Prob}(P\|Q) = .40$	$\mathrm{Prob}(\sim P\|Q) = .60$
Modus tollens	$\mathrm{Prob}(\sim P\|\sim Q) = .60$	$\mathrm{Prob}(P\|\sim Q) = .40$

have any probabilistic contingency between P and Q. Table 10.3 continues the standard of using P's and Q's to refer to events. Therefore, it is important to see how they map into choices in the Wason experiment:

P:	A vowel occurs on one side of a card (e.g., the E).
$\sim P$:	A consonant occurs on one side of a card (e.g., the K).
Q:	An even number occurs on one side of a card (e.g., the 4).
$\sim Q$:	An odd number occurs on one side of a card (e.g., the 7).

According to Oaksford and Chater, what subjects are doing is selecting cards that are going to be informative in a statistical sense. A card is informative when the expectation associated with it under the model $P \supset Q$ (Table 10.2) is different from the expectation under the null rule (Table 10.3). Consider selecting card E, which corresponds to conditionalizing on P in the tables. Under the conditional model (Table 10.2), there is a 80 percent chance of a Q (an even number), and under the null model (Table 10.3) there is a 40 percent chance—a large difference, and so this proves to be an informative card. Consider selecting 4, which in the logical model is not informative. This corresponds to conditionalizing on Q in the tables. In the probabilistic model (Table 10.2), there is a 67 percent chance of a P (a vowel), whereas in the null model (Table 10.3) there is a 40 percent chance—a considerable difference. Consider selecting the 7, which is the *modus tollens* step in the logical model. This corresponds to conditionalizing on $\sim Q$. In the probabilistic model (Table 10.2) there is a 75 percent chance of $\sim P$ (a consonant), whereas in the null model there is a 60 percent chance—a small difference. Finally, consider selecting the K, which corresponds to conditionalizing on $\sim P$ in the tables. In the probabilistic model (Table 10.2), there is a 60 percent chance of a $\sim Q$

(an odd number), and in the null model (Table 10.3) there is a 60 percent chance—in this case, no difference. To summarize these cases, the differences in the probabilities of outcomes under the two models perfectly replicate the frequencies of choices by subjects.

The exact details of the Oaksford and Chater explanation depend rather precariously on the probabilities being just right in Tables 10.2 and 10.3. Their argument will be valid when the probabilities of P and Q are low. This is what they refer to as the rarity condition. For instance, suppose you were interested in whether a rare drug tended to cause a rare rash. Since the purported relationship was probabilistic, and since the rash was rare, it would be wise for you to check people who had taken the drug (P) and see if they had the rash, and check people who had the rash (Q) and see if they had taken the drug. Since the rash is so rare and the drug was so rare, it might not be that informative to check people who did not have the rash ($\sim Q$)— because almost all of them would not have taken the drug ($\sim P$).

◆
The behavior in the Wason card selection task can be explained if we assume that subjects select cards that will be informative under a probabilistic model.

Permission Interpretation of the Conditional

It is possible to interpret the connective *if* in ways other than as a logical statement or as a probabilistic statement. Consider the following statement: *If a person is drinking beer, then the person must be over 19.* This is most naturally interpreted as neither a logical assertion nor a probabilistic assertion but rather as a statement about what ought to be the case. This has sometimes been called the **permission schema** for the logical connective (Cheng & Holyoak, 1985). Griggs and Cox (1982) studied subject behavior with this rule in a paradigm that is formally equivalent to the Wason card selection task. Subjects were instructed to imagine that they were police officers responsible for ensuring that a regulation was being followed. They were presented with four cards that represented people sitting around a table. On one side of each card was the age of the person and on the other side was the substance that the person was drinking. The cards were labeled "Drinking beer," "Drinking Coke," "16 years of age," and "22 years of age." The task was to select those people (cards to turn over) from whom further information was needed to determine whether the drinking law was being violated. In this situation, 74 percent of subjects selected the logically correct cards (namely, "Drinking beer" and "16 years of age").

Perhaps the better performance of subjects in this experiment just reflects the familiarity of the rule. The subjects were Florida undergraduates, and this was a rule about drinking that was in force in Florida at the time. Perhaps the subjects would not be able to reason about a similar unfamiliar law. To discriminate between these two possibilities, Cheng and Holyoak (1985) performed the following experiment. One group of subjects was asked to evaluate the following senseless rule against a set of instances: "If the form says 'entering' on one side, then the other side includes cholera among the list of diseases." Another group was given the same rule but also the rationale behind it, which made explicit contact with the idea of permission. The rationale was that, in order to satisfy immigration officials upon entering a particular country, one must have been vaccinated for cholera. The forms indicated on one side whether the passenger was entering the country or in transit, while the other side listed the names of diseases for which he or she was vaccinated. Subjects were presented with a set of forms that said "Transit," or "Entering," or "cholera, typhoid, hepatitis," or "typhoid, hepatitis." The performance of the group given the rationale was much better than that of the group given just the senseless rule—i.e., they knew to check the "Entering" form and the "typhoid, hepatitis" form. Since this was not a familiar rule to the subjects, it is apparent that subjects' good performance depends on evoking the concept of permission and not on practice with the specific rule.

Cosmides (1989) and Gigerenzer and Hug (1992) have argued that our good performance with such rules (which they call social contract rules) depends on the skill with which we have learned to detect cheaters. Gigerenzer and Hug had subjects evaluate the following rule:

- If a student is assigned to Grover High School, then that student must live in Grover City.

In the cheating condition, subjects were asked to take the perspective of a member of the Grover City School Board looking for students who were illegally attending the high school. In the no-cheating condition, subjects were asked to take the perspective of a visiting official from the German government who just wants to find out if this is the rule in effect at Grover High School. Gigerenzer and Hug were interested in the frequency with which subjects would choose to both check students going to Grover High School and check students who did not live in Grover City, which are the logically correct choices. In the cheating condition, where they took the perspective of a school board member, 80 percent of the subjects chose just these two, replicating other results with permission rules. In the no-cheating condition, where they took the perspective of a disinterested visitor, only 45 percent of the subjects chose these two.

◆

When subjects take the perspective of detecting whether a social contract has been violated, they make a large proportion of logically correct choices in the Wason card selection task.

Conclusions

It seems that the logical connective "if" can evoke rather different interpretations. We have discussed evidence for the probabilistic interpretation of it and the permission interpretation of it. People are capable of adopting the logician's interpretation of it as well. Not surprisingly, this is the interpretation that logicians and logic students take of it when doing logic. Studies of their reasoning (Lewis, 1985; Scheines & Sieg, 1994) with the connective find it to be similar to mathematical reasoning such as in the domain of geometry discussed in the previous chapter. Basically, they take a problem-solving approach to formal reasoning with the connective. People take a problem-solving approach to the other interpretations as well, but these other interpretations imply different problem-solving operators.

One of the amusing results is that training in logic does not necessarily result in better behavior when faced with the original Wason selection task. In a study by Cheng, Holyoak, Nisbett, and Oliver (1986), college students who had just taken a semester course in logic did only 3 percent better on the card selection task than those who had no formal logic training. It was not that they did not know the rules of logic; it was rather that they did not bring them to bear in this logical task. They chose to adopt some nonlogical interpretation of the rule.

◆

People use different problem-solving operators, depending on their interpretation of the logical connective *if*.

Reasoning about Quantifiers

Much of human knowledge is cast with **logical quantifiers** such as *all* or *some*. Witness Lincoln's famous statement: "You may fool all the people some of the time; you can even fool some of the people all the time; but you can't fool all of the people all the time." Scientific laws such as Newton's third law, "For every action there is always an opposite and equal reaction," try to identify what is always the case. It is important to understand how we reason with such quantifiers. This section will report research on how people reason about such quantifiers when they occur in simple sentences. As was the case for the logical connective *if*, we will see that there are differences between the logician's interpretation of quantifiers and the way people frequently reason about them.

The Categorical Syllogism

Modern logic is greatly concerned with analyzing the meaning of quantifiers such as *all, no,* and *some,* as in, for example:

- All philosophers read some books.

This might be a statement most of us would believe is true. The logician would say that this would then mean we were committed to the belief that we could not find a philosopher who did not read books, but most of us have no trouble accepting the idea that there were philosophers in societies before there were books or that one still might find somewhere in the world an illiterate person who professed sufficiently profound ideas to deserve the title of "philosopher." This illustrates the fact that frequently when we use *all* in real life, we mean "most" or "with high probability." Similarly, when we use *no* as in

- No doctors are poor.

we often mean "hardly any" or "with small probability." However, as with conditionals, research on human reasoning has been concerned with the logician's interpretation. Most subjects are certainly aware of the strict logical interpretation, and instructions to the subjects have asked them to take this perspective.

By the turn of this century, the sophistication with which such quantified statements were analyzed by logicians increased considerably (see Church, 1956, for a historical discussion). This more advanced treatment of quantifiers is covered in most modern logic courses. However, most of the research on quantifiers in psychology has focused on a simpler and older kind of quantified deduction, called the **categorical syllogism**. Much of Aristotle's writing on reasoning concerned the categorical syllogism. Extensive discussion of these types of syllogisms can be found in older textbooks on logic such as Cohen and Nagel (1934).

Categorical syllogisms involve statements containing the quantifiers *some, all, no,* and *some not.* Examples of such categorical statements are:

1. All doctors are rich.

2. Some lawyers are dishonest.

3. No politician is trustworthy.

4. Some actors are not handsome.

In experiments, the categories (e.g., doctors, rich people, lawyers, dishonest people) in such statements are frequently represented by letters, say, A, B, C, and so on. This system serves as a handy shorthand for describing the material. Thus, the statements might be rendered in this way:

1′. All A's are B's.

2′. Some C's are D's.

3'. No E's are F's.

4'. Some G's are not H's.

A categorical syllogism typically contains two premises and a conclusion. The following is a typical example:

1. All A's are B's.
   All B's are C's.
   ∴All A's are C's.

This syllogism, incidentally, is one that most people correctly recognize as valid. On the other hand, many people accept the following invalid syllogism:

2. Some A's are B's.
   Some B's are C's.
   ∴Some A's are C's.

(To see that this is invalid, consider replacing A with women, B with lawyers, and C with men.)

◆
Research on reasoning with quantifiers has focused on categorical syllogisms.

The Atmosphere Hypothesis

The general problem subjects seem to have with categorical syllogisms is that they are too willing to accept false conclusions. However, subjects are not completely indiscriminate in their acceptance of syllogisms. For instance, even though they will accept example 2 above, they will not accept example 3:

3. Some A's are B's.
   Some B's are C's.
   ∴No A's are C's.

To account for the pattern of what subjects accept and what they reject, Woodworth and Sells (1935) proposed the **atmosphere hypothesis**. This hypothesis states that the logical terms (*some, all, no,* and *not*) used in the premises of a syllogism create an "atmosphere" that predisposes subjects to accept conclusions with the same terms. There are two parts to the atmosphere hypothesis. One part asserts that subjects would tend to accept a positive conclusion to positive premises and a negative conclusion to negative premises. When the premises are mixed, subjects would prefer a negative. Thus, they would tend to accept the following invalid syllogism:

4. No *A*'s are *B*'s.
   All *B*'s are *C*'s.
   ∴No *A*'s are *C*'s.

(To see that this is invalid, consider replacing *A* with men, *B* with women, and *C* with humans.)

The other part of the atmosphere hypothesis concerns a subject's response to particular statements (*some* or *some not*) versus universal statements (*all* or *no*). As example 4 above illustrates, subjects will accept a universal conclusion if the premises are universal. They will tend to accept a particular conclusion if the premises are particular. This accounts for their acceptance of syllogism 2 given earlier. When one premise is particular and the other universal, subjects prefer a particular conclusion. Thus they will accept the following invalid syllogism.

5. All *A*'s are *B*'s.
   Some *B*'s are *C*'s.
   ∴Some *A*'s are *C*'s.

(To see that this is invalid, consider replacing *A* with men, *B* with humans, and *C* with women.)

◆ ───

The atmosphere hypothesis claims that subjects are biased to accept conclusions with the same quantifiers as the premises.

───

Limitations of the Atmosphere Hypothesis

The atmosphere hypothesis provides a very succinct characterization of subject behavior with the various syllogisms, but it tells us little about what the subjects are actually doing or why. Its characterization of subject behavior is also only approximately correct. For one thing, according to the atmosphere hypothesis, subjects would be just as likely to accept the atmosphere-favored conclusion when it was not valid as when it was valid. That is, it predicts that subjects would be just as likely to accept

6. All *A*'s are *B*'s.
   Some *B*'s are *C*'s.
   ∴Some *A*'s are *C*'s.

which is not valid, as they would be to accept

7. Some *A*'s are *B*'s.
All *B*'s are *C*'s.
∴Some *A*'s are *C*'s.

which is valid. In fact, subjects are more likely to accept the conclusion in the valid case. Thus, subjects do display some ability to evaluate a syllogism accurately.

Another limitation of the atmosphere hypothesis is that it fails to predict the effects that the form of a syllogism will have on subjects' validity judgments. For instance, the hypothesis predicts that subjects would be no more likely to erroneously accept

8. Some *A*'s are *B*'s.
Some *B*'s are *C*'s.
∴Some *A*'s are *C*'s.

than they would be to erroneously accept

9. Some *B*'s are *A*'s.
Some *C*'s are *A*'s.
∴Some *A*'s are *C*'s.

In fact, it has been established (Johnson-Laird and Steedman, 1978) that subjects are more willing to erroneously accept the conclusion in the former case. In general, subjects are more willing to accept a conclusion from *A* to *C* if they can find a chain leading from *A* to *B* in one premise and from *B* to *C* in the second premise. Other effects of the form of the argument rather than the quantifiers have been shown by Dickstein (1978).

Another problem with the atmosphere hypothesis is that it does not really handle what subjects do in the presence of two negatives. If subjects are given the following two premises,

No *A*'s are *B*'s.
No *B*'s are *C*'s.

the atmosphere hypothesis would predict that subjects should tend to accept the invalid conclusion:

∴No *A*'s are *C*'s.

In fact, most subjects refuse to accept any conclusion when both premises are negative, which is the correct thing to do (Dickstein, 1978).

When subjects do accept a wrong premise, it tends to be the negative conclusion predicted by the atmosphere hypothesis, but this is definitely a minority of the cases.

◆

Subjects only approximate the predictions of the atmosphere hypothesis and are often more accurate than it would predict.

Process Explanations

There have been a number of more recent attempts to explain what subjects are doing with categorical syllogisms in terms of the underlying cognitive processes. One explanation of subjects' reasoning behavior, developed by Johnson-Laird (Johnson-Laird & Steedman, 1978; Johnson-Laird, 1983), proposed that subjects create a mental model of a world that satisfies the premises of the syllogism and inspect that model to see if the conclusion is satisfied. (A similar idea has been proposed by Guyote and Sternberg, 1981.) This explanation is called **mental model theory**. Consider these premises:

All the squares are striped.
Some of the striped objects have bold borders.

Figure 10.1a illustrates what subjects might imagine, according to Johnson-Laird, as an instantiation of these premises. The subject has imagined a group of objects, some of which are square while others are round, some of

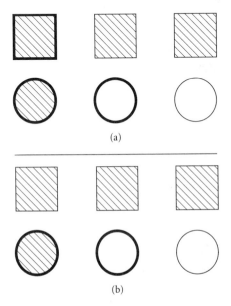

(a)

(b)

Figure 10.1 Two possible models subjects might form for the premises of the categorical syllogism above.

which are striped while others are clear, and some of which have bold borders while others do not. This world represents one possible interpretation of these premises. When the subject is asked to judge a conclusion like the following:

∴Some of the squares have bold borders.

the subject inspects the diagram and concludes that it is true. The problem is that, in this case, there are other interpretations of the premises like Figure 10.1b where this conclusion does not hold. Johnson-Laird claims that subjects have considerable difficulty developing alternative models. Thus, the subject is building a specific model for the premises and is inspecting this to see what is true in that model. This kind of reasoning pattern is a fairly good heuristic but will lead to errors, as in this example. Johnson-Laird (1983) has developed a computer simulation of this theory that reproduces many of the errors that subjects make. Johnson-Laird (1995) also argues that there is neurological evidence in favor of the mental model explanation. He notes that patients with right hemisphere damage are more impaired in reasoning tasks than patients with left hemisphere damage. He notes that the right hemisphere tends to be involved in spatial processing of things like mental images.

Basically, Johnson-Laird's argument is that errors in reasoning occur because people overlook possible explanations of the premises. That is, a subject imagines Figure 10.1a as an explanation and overlooks the possibility of Figure 10.1b. Johnson-Laird (personal communication) argues that a great many errors in human reasoning are produced by failures to consider possible explanations of the data. For instance, one of the problems in the Chernobyl disaster was that for several hours engineers failed to consider the possibility that the reactor was no longer intact.

A number of other theories (e.g., Ceraso & Provitera, 1971; Chapman & Chapman, 1959; Chater & Oaksford, in press; Erickson, 1974; Henle, 1962; Wetherick, 1989) attempt to explain why subjects make errors in reasoning about categorical syllogisms. What all these theories have in common is the assumption that subjects do not treat the task as a logician would prescribe. Many, like Johnson-Laird, assume that subjects reason about a syllogism by applying a very specific and concrete interpretation to it. This research is often described as showing that subjects reason in terms of mental models. Rather than reasoning according to formal rules, they build up a specific model of a situation and determine what is true of that specific situation.

In the previous section of this chapter, we discussed how subjects sometimes treated conditionals as probabilistic statements. There is also evidence that subjects also sometimes treat categorical statements as probabilistic assertions (Chapman & Chapman, 1959; Henle, 1962). Suppose someone is told

> Some of the blue dishes are large.
> Some of the large dishes are dirty.

This might be read as saying about 50 percent of the blue dishes are large and about 50 percent of the large dishes are dirty. Assuming independence, the reader might conclude that about 50 percent of the blue dishes that are large are dirty and therefore at least about 25 percent of the blue dishes are dirty. Therefore, the conclusion would follow that

> ∴Some of the blue dishes are dirty.

In fact, it is probably the case that in most situations in the real world where these two premises are true, the conclusion would also be true. In general, it is the case that people's reasoning errors with categorical syllogisms are of the form that people are accepting conclusions that are not necessarily true but in fact would tend to be true in real situations.

◆
Errors in evaluating syllogisms can be explained by assuming that subjects adopt various specific or probabilistic interpretations of the premises.

Inductive Reasoning

We saw considerable evidence that subjects' behavior in deductive reasoning tasks can sometimes be understood as reflecting a more probabilistic sort of reasoning. Inductive reasoning is the term used to describe the processes by which one comes to conclusions that are probable rather than certain. This would seem to be much more useful in our everyday encounters where very little is for certain and, at best, things are just very likely. It turns out that mathematicians and philosophers have developed a prescriptive model for the way people should reason in inductive situations. This is based on a mathematical result called **Bayes's theorem**. Much of the research in the field has been concerned with how well human subjects match up with the prescriptions of Bayes's theorem.

Bayes's Theorem

As an example of where Bayes's theorem can be applied, suppose I come home and find the door to my house ajar. I am interested in the hypothesis that this might be the work of a burglar. How do I evaluate this hypothesis?

One might treat it as a conditional syllogism of the following sort:

If a burglar is in the house, then the door will be ajar.
The door is ajar.
∴A burglar is in the house.

As a conditional syllogism this would be judged as reflecting the error of affirming the consequent. However, it does have a certain plausibility as an inductive argument. Bayes's theorem provides a way of assessing just how plausible it is. It combines what is called a prior probability and conditional probabilities to produce what is called a posterior probability, which is a measure of the strength of the conclusion.

A **prior probability** is the probability that a hypothesis is true before considering the evidence (e.g., the door is ajar). The less likely the hypothesis was before the evidence, the less likely it should be after the evidence. Let us refer to the hypothesis that my house has been burglarized as H. Suppose that I know from police statistics that the probability of a house in my neighborhood being burglarized on any particular day is 1 in 1000. This probability is expressed as:

$$\text{Prob}(H) = .001$$

This equation expresses the prior probability of the hypothesis, or the probability that the hypothesis is true before the evidence. The other prior probability needed for application of Bayes's theorem is the probability that the house has not been burglarized. This alternate hypothesis is denoted $\sim H$. This value is 1 minus $\text{Prob}(H)$ and is expressed:

$$\text{Prob}(\sim H) = .999$$

A **conditional probability** is the probability that a particular type of evidence is true if a particular hypothesis is true. Let us consider what the conditional probabilities of the evidence (door ajar) would be under the two hypotheses. Suppose I believe that the probability of the door's being ajar is quite high if I have been burglarized; say, 4 out of 5. Let E denote the evidence, or the event of the door being ajar. Then, we will denote this conditional probability of E given that H is true as:

$$\text{Prob}(E|H) = .8$$

Second, we determine the probability of E if H is not true. Suppose I know that chances are only 1 out of 100 that the door would be ajar if no burglary had occurred (e.g., by accident, neighbors with a key). This we denote by:

$$\text{Prob}(E|{\sim}H) = .01$$

the probability of E given that H is not true.

The **posterior probability** is the probability that a hypothesis is true after considering the evidence. The notation $\text{Prob}(H|E)$ is the posterior probability of hypothesis H given evidence E. According to Bayes's theorem, we can calculate the posterior probability of H, that the house has been burglarized given the evidence thus:

$$\text{Prob}(H|E) = \frac{\text{Prob}(E|H) \cdot \text{Prob}(H)}{\text{Prob}(E|H) \cdot \text{Prob}(H) + \text{Prob}(E|{\sim}H) \cdot \text{Prob}({\sim}H)}$$

Given our assumed values, we can solve for $\text{Prob}(H|E)$ by substituting into the equation above:

$$\text{Prob}(H|E) = \frac{(.8)(.001)}{(.8)(.001) + (.01)(.999)} = .074$$

Thus, the probability that my house has been burglarized is still less than 8 in 100. Note that the posterior probability is this low even though an open door is good evidence for a burglary and not for a normal state of affairs: $\text{Prob}(E|H) = .8$ versus $\text{Prob}(E|{\sim}H) = .01$. The posterior probability is still quite low because the prior probability of H — $\text{Prob}(H) = .001$ — was very low to begin with. Relative to that low start, the posterior probability has been drastically revised upward.

Table 10.4 offers an illustration of Bayes's theorem as applied to the burglary example. There are four possible states of affairs, determined by whether the burglary hypothesis is true or not and by whether there is the evidence of an open door or not. The probability of each state of affairs is

Table 10.4 An Analysis of Bayes's Theorem

	Burglarized	Not Burglarized	Sum of Probabilities
Door open	$\text{Prob}(E|H)\text{Prob}(H)$ $=.00080$	$\text{Prob}(E|{\sim}H)\text{Prob}({\sim}H)$ $=.00999$	.01079
Door not open	$\text{Prob}({\sim}E|H)\text{Prob}(H)$ $=.00020$	$\text{Prob}({\sim}E|{\sim}H)(\text{Prob}{\sim}H)$ $=.98901$	.98921
Sum of probabilities	.00100	.99900	1.00000

Adapted from Hayes, 1984.

set forth in the four cells of the table. The probability of each state is the prior probability of that hypothesis times the conditional probability of the event given the hypothesis. For instance, consider the upper-left cell. Since $Prob(H)$ is .001 and $Prob(E|H)$ is .8, the probability in that cell is .0008. The four probabilities in these cells must sum to 1. Given the evidence that the door is open, we can eliminate the two cells in the lower row of the table. Since one of the two remaining states of affairs must be the case, the posterior probabilities of the two remaining states must sum to 1. Bayes's theorem provides us with a means of recalculating the probabilities of the states in light of evidence that makes impossible one row of the matrix. What we have done in calculating the posterior probability is to take the probability of the upper-left cell of Table 10.4, where hypothesis H is true, and divide it by the sum of the probabilities in the two upper cells, which represent the only two possible states of affairs, i.e., .00080/.01079 = .074.

Bayes's theorem rests on a mathematical analysis of the nature of probability. The formula can be proven to evaluate hypotheses correctly; thus, it enables us to determine precisely the posterior probability of a hypothesis given the prior and conditional probabilities. The theorem serves as a **prescriptive model**, or normative model, specifying the means of evaluating the probability of a hypothesis. Such a model contrasts with a **descriptive model**, which specifies what people actually do. People normally do not perform the calculations we have just gone through any more than they follow the steps prescribed by formal logic. Nonetheless, they do hold various strengths of beliefs in assertions such as that their house has been burglarized. Moreover, their strength of belief does vary with evidence such as whether the door has been found ajar. The interesting question is whether the strengths of their beliefs change in accord with Bayes's theorem.

◆

Bayes's theorem specifies how to combine the prior probability of a hypothesis with the conditional probabilities of the evidence, to come up with a posterior probability of a hypothesis.

Base Rate Neglect

Many people are surprised in the previous example that the open door does not provide as much evidence for a burglary as some might have expected. This is because they do not appreciate the importance of the prior probabilities. People sometimes ignore prior probabilities. Kahneman and Tversky (1973) told one group of subjects that an individual had been chosen at random from a set of 100 individuals consisting of 70 engineers and 30 lawyers. This group of subjects was termed the engineer-high group. A second group, the engineer-low group, was told that the individual came from a set of 30 engineers and 70 lawyers. Both groups were asked to determine the probability that the individual chosen at random from the group would be an engineer given no information about the individual. Subjects were able to respond with the right prior probabilities: The engineer-high group estimated .70 and the engineer-low group estimated .30. Then subjects were told that another person was chosen from the population and they were given the following description:

> Jack is a 45-year-old man. He is married and has four children. He is generally conservative, careful, and ambitious. He shows no interest in political and social issues and spends most of his free time on his many hobbies, which include home carpentry, sailing, and mathematical puzzles.

Subjects in both groups gave a .90 probability estimate to the hypothesis that this person was an engineer. No difference was displayed between the two groups, which had been given different prior probabilities for an engineer hypothesis. But Bayes's theorem prescribes that prior probability should have a strong effect, resulting in a higher posterior probability from the engineer-high group than from the engineer-low group. The following sample description was also used by Kahneman and Tversky:

> Dick is a 30-year-old man. He is married with no children. A man of high ability and high motivation, he promises to be quite successful in his field. He is well liked by his colleagues.

This example was designed to provide no diagnostic information either way with respect to Dick's profession. According to Bayes's theorem, the posterior probability of the engineer hypothesis should be the same as the prior probability, since this description is not informative. However, both the engineer-high and the engineer-low groups estimated that the probability was .50 that the individual described was an engineer. Thus, they allowed a completely uninformative event to change their probabilities. Again, subjects were shown to be completely unable to use prior probabilities in assessing the posterior probability of a hypothesis.

The failure to take prior probabilities into account can lead an individual to make some totally unwarranted conclusions. For instance, suppose you take a test for cancer. It is known that a particular type of cancer will result in a positive test 95 percent of the time. On the other hand, if a person does not have the cancer, there is only a 5 percent probability of a positive result. Suppose you are informed that your result is positive. If you are like most people, you will assume that your chances of dying of cancer are about 95 out of 100 (Hammerton, 1973). You would be overreacting in assuming that the cancer would be fatal, but you would also be making a fundamental error in probability estimation. What is the error?

You would have failed to consider the base rate (prior probability) for the particular type of cancer in question. Suppose only 1 in 10,000 people have this cancer. This would be your prior probability. Now, with this information you would be able to determine the posterior probability of your having the cancer. Bringing out the Bayesian formula, you would express the problem this way:

$$\text{Prob}(H|E) = \frac{\text{Prob}(H) \cdot \text{Prob}(E|H)}{\text{Prob}(H) \cdot \text{Prob}(E|H) + \text{Prob}(\sim H) \cdot \text{Prob}(E|\sim H)}$$

where the prior probability of the cancer hypothesis is $\text{Prob}(H) = .0001$, and $\text{Prob}(\sim H) = .9999$, $\text{Prob}(E|H) = .95$, and $\text{Prob}(E|\sim H) = .05$. Thus,

$$\text{Prob}(H|E) = \frac{(.0001)(.95)}{(.0001)(.95) + (.9999)(.05)} = .0019$$

That is, the posterior probability of your having the cancer would still be less than 1 in 500.

◆
People often fail to take base rates into account in making probability judgments.

Conservatism

The previous examples have shown that people pay too much attention to the evidence. However, there are also situations where people do not weigh evidence enough, particularly as the evidence pointing to a conclusion accumulates. Ward Edwards (1968) extensively investigated how people use new information to adjust their estimates of the probabilities of various hypotheses. In one experiment, he presented subjects with two bags, each containing 100 poker chips. One of the bags contained 70 red chips and 30 blue, and the other contained 70 blue chips and 30 red. The experimenter chose one of the bags at random and the subjects' task was to decide which bag had been chosen.

In the absence of any prior information, the probability of either bag being chosen was 50 percent. Thus:

$$\text{Prob}(H_R) = .50 \text{ and } \text{Prob}(H_B) = .50$$

where H_R is the hypothesis of a predominantly red bag and H_B is the hypothesis of a predominantly blue bag. To obtain further information, subjects sampled chips at random from the bag. Suppose the first chip drawn was red. The conditional probability of a red chip drawn from each bag is:

$$\text{Prob}(R|H_R) = .70 \text{ and } \text{Prob}(R|H_B) = .30$$

Now, we can calculate the posterior probability of the bag's being predominantly red given the red chip by applying equation 1 to this situation:

$$\text{Prob}(R \mid H_R) = \frac{\text{Prob}(R \mid H_R) \cdot \text{Prob}(H_R)}{\text{Prob}(R \mid H_R) \cdot \text{Prob}(H_R) + \text{Prob}(R \mid H_B) \cdot \text{Prob}(H_B)}$$

$$= \frac{(.70) \cdot (.50)}{(.70) \cdot (.50) + (.30) \cdot (.50)} = .70$$

This result seems, to both naive and sophisticated observers, to be a rather sharp increase in probabilities. Typically, subjects do not increase their probability of a red-majority bag to .70; rather, they make a more conservative revision to a value such as .60.

After this first drawing, the experiment continues: The poker chip is put back in the bag and a second chip is drawn at random. Suppose this chip too is red. Again, by applying Bayes's theorem, we can show that the posterior probability of a red bag is now .84. Suppose our observations continued for ten more trials and after all twelve we have observed 8 reds and 4 blues. By continuing the Bayesian analysis, we could show that the new posterior probability of the hypothesis of a red bag is .97. Subjects who see this sequence of twelve trials only estimate subjectively a posterior probability of .75 or less for the red bag. Edwards has used the term *conservative* to refer to subjects' tendency to underestimate the force of evidence. He estimates that they use between a half and a fifth of the available evidence from each chip.

◆

People frequently underestimate the cumulative force of evidence in making probability judgments.

___

Correspondence to Bayes's Theorem with Experience

The previous examples all showed that subjects can be quite far off in terms of their judgments of probability. One possibility is that subjects really do not understand probabilities or how to reason with respect to them. Certainly, it is a rare subject in these experiments who could reproduce Bayes's theorem, let alone who would report engaging in Bayesian calculation. There is evidence that, although subjects cannot articulate the correct probabilities, many aspects of their behavior are in accordance with Bayesian principles. To return to the explicit-implicit distinction cited in Chapter 7, it appears that people often display implicit knowledge of Bayesian principles even if they do not display any explicit knowledge and make errors when asked to make explicit judgments.

One such experiment was performed by Gluck and Bower (1988). Subjects were given records of fictitious patients who could display one to four symptoms (bloody nose, stomach cramps, puffy eyes, and discolored gums), and they made discriminative diagnoses as to which of two hypothetical diseases the patients had. One of these diseases had a base rate three times that of the other. Also, the conditional probabilities of displaying the various symptoms given the diseases were varied. Subjects were not told directly about these base rates or conditional probabilities. They merely looked at a series of 256 patient records, chose the disease they thought the patient had, and were given feedback on the correctness of their judgments.

There are fifteen possible combinations of one to four symptom patterns that a patient might have. Gluck and Bower calculated the probability of each disease for each pattern using Bayes's theorem and arranged it so that each disease occurred with that probability when the symptoms were present. Thus, the subjects experienced the base probabilities and conditional probabilities implicitly in terms of the frequencies of symptom-disease combinations. Of interest is the probability with which they assigned the rarer disease to various symptom combinations. Gluck and Bower compared the subject probabilities to the true Bayesian probabilities. This correspondence is displayed by the scatterplot in Figure 10.2. There we have for each symptom combination the Bayesian probability and the proportion of times that subjects assign the rare disease to that symptom combination. As can be seen, these points fall very close to a straight diagonal line with a slope of 1. This indicates that the proportion of the subjects' choices were very close to the true probabilities. Thus, implicitly, the subjects had become quite good Bayesians in this experiment. The behavior of choosing among alternatives in proportion to their success is called **probability matching**.

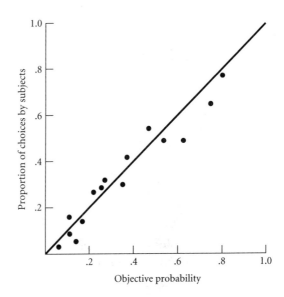

Figure 10.2 Subjects' proportion of choices correspond closely to the objective probabilities as determined by Bayes's theorem.

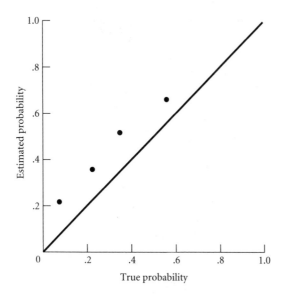

Figure 10.3 Subjects' estimated probabilities systematically overestimated the frequency of the rare disease, showing base-rate neglect.

After the experiment, Bower and Gluck presented the subjects with the four symptoms individually and asked them how frequently each symptom had occurred with the rare disease. This result is presented in Figure 10.3 in a similar format to Figure 10.2. As can be seen, here subjects show some neglect of the base rate, consistently overestimating the frequency of the rare disease. Still, their judgments show some influence of base rate in that their average estimated probability of the rare disease is less than 50 percent.

Gigerenzer and Hoffrage (1995) showed that base rate neglect also goes down if events are stated in terms of frequencies rather than in term of probabilities. Some of their subjects were given a description in terms of probabilities such as below:

> *The probability of breast cancer is 1 percent for women at age forty who participate in routine screening. If a woman has breast cancer, the probability is 80 percent that she will get a positive mammography. If a woman does not have breast cancer, the probability is 9.6 percent that she will also get a positive mammography. A woman in this age group had a positive mammography in a routine screening. What is the probability that she actually has breast cancer? _____ percent.*

Less than 20 percent of the subjects given such statements calculated the correct Bayesian answer (which is about 8 percent). In the other condition subjects were given descriptions in terms of frequencies such as below:

> *Ten out of every 1,000 women at age forty who participate in routine screening have breast cancer. Eight of every 10 women with breast cancer will get a positive mammography. Ninety-five out of every 990 women without breast cancer will also get a positive mammography. Here is a new representative sample of women at age forty who got a positive mammography in routine screening. How many of these women do you expect to actually have breast cancer?* _____ *percent*

Almost 50% of the subjects given such statements calculated the correct Bayesian answer. Gigerenzer and Hoffrage argue that we can reason better with frequencies than probabilities because it is frequencies of events not probabilities that we experience in our daily lives.

There is also evidence that people become more statistically tuned with experience. In a study of medical diagnosis, Weber, Böckenholt, Hilton, and Wallace (1993) found that doctors were quite sensitive both to base rates and the diagnosticity of symptoms. Moreover, the more clinical experience the doctors had, the more tuned were their judgments.

◆
While subjects' processing of probabilities often does not correspond with Bayes's theorem, their behavior based on experience often does.

Judgments of Probability

What are subjects doing when they report probabilities of an event such as the probability that someone who has bloody gums has a particular disease? The evidence is that what subjects are trying to report is the relative proportion of such events among the relevant population. Thus, what they are trying to do is to figure out what proportion of the patients that they saw with bloody gums had that particular disease. People are reasonably accurate at making such proportionate judgments when they do not have to rely on memory (Robinson, 1964; Shuford, 1961). Consider an experiment by Shuford (1961). He presented arrays such as that shown in Figure 10.4 to subjects for 1 second. He then asked subjects to judge the proportion of vertical bars relative to horizontal bars. The numbers of vertical bars varied from 10 to 90 percent in different matrices. Shuford's results are shown in Figure 10.5. As can be seen, subjects' estimates are quite close to the true proportions.

The situations just described are those in which the subjects can see the relevant events and make a proportion judgment. When subjects cannot see the events, but must recall them from memory, they can give

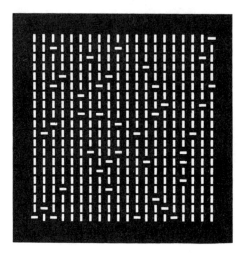

Figure 10.4 A random matrix composed of 90 percent vertical bars and 10 percent horizontal bars presented to subjects to determine their accuracy in judging proportions. (From Shuford, 1961. Copyright ©1961 by the American Psychological Association. Reprinted by permission.)

distorted judgments if they recall too many of one kind from memory. In the Gluck and Bower experiment, subjects were recalling relatively too many of the rare disease patients and so were overestimating the frequency of the association of that disease with various patients.

A fair amount of research has been devoted to the way subjects can be biased in their estimation of the relative frequency of various events in the population. Consider the following experiment reported by Tversky and Kahneman (1974), which demonstrates that judgments of proportion can be biased by differential availability of examples. These investigators asked subjects to judge the proportion of words in the language that fit certain characteristics. For instance, they asked subjects to estimate the proportion

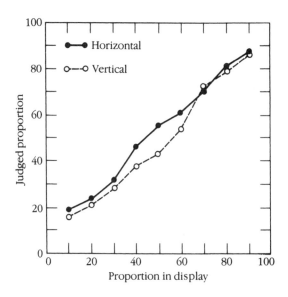

Figure 10.5 Mean estimated proportion as a function of the true proportion. Subjects exhibited a fairly accurate ability to estimate the proportions of vertical and horizontal bars in Figure 10.4. (From Shuford, 1961. Copyright © 1961 by the American Psychological Association. Reprinted by permission.)

of English words that begin with the letter k versus words with a k in the third position. How might subjects perform this task? One obvious heuristic is to briefly try to think of words that satisfy the specification and words that do not and to estimate the relative proportion of target words. How many words can you think of that begin with the letter k? How many words can you think of that do not? What is your estimate of their proportion? Now how many words can you think of that have k in the third position? How many words can you think of that do not? What is their relative proportion? Subjects estimated that more words begin with letter k than have k in the third position. In actual fact, three times as many words have k in the third position as begin with k. Generally, subjects overestimate the frequency with which words begin with various letters.

As in this experiment, many real-life circumstances require that we estimate probabilities without having direct access to the population that these probabilities describe. In such cases, we must rely on memory as the source for our estimates. The memory factors we studied in Chapters 6 and 7 serve to explain how such estimates can be biased. Under the reasonable assumption that words are more strongly associated to their first letter than to their third letter, the bias exhibited in the experimental results can be explained in terms of the spreading-activation theory (Chapter 6). In the case of these gross overestimates of words beginning with particular letters, with the focus of attention on say, k, activation will spread from that letter to words beginning with it. This process will tend to make words beginning with k more available than other words. Thus, these words will be overrepresented in the sample that subjects take from memory to estimate the true proportion in the population. The same overestimation does not occur for words with k in the third position, since words are unlikely to be directly associated to the letters that occur in the third position. Therefore, it is not possible to associatively prime these words and make them more available.

Other factors besides memory lead to biases in probability estimates. Consider another example from Tversky and Kahneman (1974). Which of the following sequences of six tosses from a fair coin is more likely (where H denotes heads and T tails): H T H T T H or H H H H H H? Many people think the first sequence is more probable, but both sequences are actually equally probable. The probability of the first sequence is the probability of H on the first toss (which is .50) times the probability of T on the second toss (which is .50), times the probability of H on the third toss (which is .50), and so on. The probability of the whole sequence is $.50 \times .50 \times .50 \times .50 \times .50 \times .50 = .016$. Similarly, the probability of the second sequence is the product of the probabilities of each coin toss, and the probability of a head on each coin toss is .50. Thus, the final probability again is also $.50 \times .50 \times .50 \times .50 \times .50 \times .50 = .016$. Why do some people have the illusion that the first sequence is more probable? It is because the first event seems similar to a lot of other events, for example, H T H T H T or H T T H T H. These similar events serve to bias upward a person's probability estimate of the target event. On the other hand, H H H H H H, straight heads, seems unlike any other event, and its probability will therefore not be biased upward by other similar sequences. In conclusion, a person's estimate of the probability of an event will be biased by other events that are similar to it.

A related phenomenon is what is called the **gambler's fallacy**. The fallacy is the belief that if an event has not occurred for a while, then it is more likely, by the "law of averages," to occur in the near future. This phenomenon can be demonstrated in an experimental setting, for instance, where subjects see a sequence of coin tosses and must guess whether each toss will be a head or a tail. If they see a string of heads, they become more and more likely to guess that tails will come up on the next trial. Casino operators count on this fallacy to help them make money. Players who have had a string of losses at a table will keep playing, assuming that by the "law of averages" they will experience a compensating string of wins. However, the game is set in favor of the house. The dice do not know or care whether a gambler has had a string of losses. The consequence is that players tend to lose more as they try to recoup their losses. The "law of averages" is a fallacy.

The gambler's fallacy can be used to advantage in certain situations — for instance, at the racetrack. Most racetracks operate by a pari-mutuel system, in which the odds on a horse are determined by the number of people betting on the horse. By the end of the day, if favorites have won all the races, people tend to doubt that another favorite can win, and they switch their bets to the long shots. As a consequence, the betting odds on the favorite deviate from what they should be, and a person can sometimes make money by betting on the favorite.

◆

People can be biased in their estimates of probabilities when they must rely on factors like memory and similarity judgments.

Decision Making

An extension of the research on probabilistic reasoning involves research on decision making. Decision-making research is concerned with the way people make choices. Sometimes, the choices we have to make are easy. If we are offered the choice between $400 and $1000, most of us would not have much difficulty in figuring out which to accept. However, what if we were faced with the choice of a certainty of $400 but only a 50 percent chance of $1000, which would we select then? Something like this might happen if we inherited a risky stock that we could cash in for $400 or that we could hold on to and see whether the company would take off or fold. A great deal of research on decision making under uncertainty has involved requiring subjects to make choices among gambles. For instance, a subject might be asked to choose between the following two gambles:

A. $8 with 1/3 probability

B. $3 with 5/6 probability

Sometimes, subjects are just asked for their opinion, and in other cases they actually get to play the gamble they choose. As an example of the latter possibility, they might roll a die and win in case A if they get a 5 or 6 and win in case B if they get a number other than 1. Which gamble would you choose?

As in the other domains of reasoning, decision making has its own standard prescriptive theory for the way people should behave in such situations (von Neumann & Morgenstern, 1944). This theory says that they should choose the alternative with highest expected value. The expected value of an alternative is to be calculated by multiplying the probability by the value. Thus, the expected value of alternative A above is $8 × 1/3 = $2.67, whereas the expected value of alternative B is $3 × 5/6 = $2.50. Thus, the normative theory says that subjects should select gamble A. On the other hand, most subjects will select gamble B.

Subjects' behavior in situations like these can be explained by assuming that the value they place on money is not linear with the face value of the money. The value a person puts on something is referred to as its **subjective utility**. Figure 10.6 shows a typical function proposed for the relationship of subjective utility to money. It has a couple of properties. One is that it is curvilinear such that it takes more than a doubling in the amount of money to double its utility. Thus, in the example above a subject may value $8 only twice as much as $3. Let us say that the utility of $3 is U and that the utility of $8 is $2U$. Then, the expected value of gamble

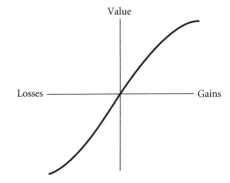

Figure 10.6 A function that relates subjective value to magnitude of gain and loss. (From Kahneman & Tversky, 1984. Reprinted by permission from the American Psychological Association.)

A is $1/3 \times 2U = .67U$, and the expected value of gamble B is $5/6 \times 1U = .83U$. Thus, in terms of subjective utility, gamble B is more valuable and is to be preferred.

The second property of this utility function is that it is steeper in the loss region than in the gain region. Thus, subjects given the following choice of gambles:

A: Gain $10 with 1/2 probability and lose $10 with 1/2 probability

B: Nothing with certainty

prefer B since they weight the loss of $10 more strongly than the gain of $10.

Kahneman and Tversky (1984) also argue that people's subjective probabilities are not identical with objective probabilities. They proposed the function in Figure 10.7 to relate subjective probability to objective probability. According to this function, very low probabilities are over-weighted relative to high probabilities, producing a bowing in the function. Thus, a subject might prefer a 1 percent chance of $400 to a 2 percent chance of $200 because 1 percent is not represented as half of 2 percent. Insurance policies depend on this fact. We are willing to spend $100 to avoid a loss of $100,000 where the probability of that loss is less than 1 in a 1000. The reason is that we overrepresent the probability of such a loss. Kahneman and Tversky (1979) show that a great deal of human decision making can be explained by assuming that subjects are responding in terms of these subjective probabilities and utilities.

It is an interesting question whether the subjective functions in Figures 10.6 and 10.7 represent nonrational tendencies or not. Generally, it is thought that the utility function in Figure 10.6 is reasonable. As we get more money, it seems less and less important to get a little more. Certainly, the amount of happiness that a billion dollars can buy is not 1000 times the

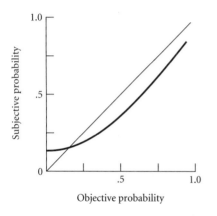

Figure 10.7 A function that relates subjective probability to objective probability. (From Kahneman & Tversky, 1984. Reprinted by permission from the American Psychological Association.)

amount of happiness that a million dollars can buy. It should be noted that the utility functions of different individuals are not all like Figure 10.6, which represents sort of an average. One can imagine someone needing $10,000 for an important medical procedure. Then, all sums under $10,000 would be rather useless, and all sums above would be relatively equally good. Thus, such a person might have a step in the utility function at $10,000.

There is less agreement about how we should assess the subjective probability function in Figure 10.7. I (Anderson, 1990) have argued that it might actually make sense to discount the extremity of low probabilities in the way that function does. The argument is that sometimes when we are told that probabilities are extreme, we are being misinformed. (For instance, the passengers on the *Titanic* were informed that the probability of the ship sinking was zero.) However, there is little consensus in the field about how to evaluate the subjective probability function.

◆
People make decisions under uncertainty in terms of subjective utilities and subjective probabilities.

Framing Effects

While one might view the functions in Figures 10.6 and 10.7 as relatively reasonable, there is evidence that they can lead people to do rather strange things. These demonstrations involve what are called **framing effects**. These effects refer to the fact that people's decisions vary depending on where they perceive themselves to be on the utility curve in Figure 10.6. One example from Kahneman and Tversky compares someone who must purchase a $15 item versus a $125 item. If another store offers a $5 discount off the $15, the person is likely to make the effort to go to the other store, whereas they are not likely to do so if the same $5 discount is offered on the $125 item. However, in both cases it is the same $5 savings, and the issue is simply whether one's time is worth the $5. However, the two contexts place the person on different points of the utility curve, which is negatively accelerated. According to that curve, the difference between $15 and $10 is larger than the difference between $125 and $120. Thus, in the first case the savings seem worth it, but in the second case it does not.

Another example has to do with betting behavior. Consider someone who has lost $140 at the racetrack and has the opportunity to bet $10 on a horse that will pay 15 to 1. The bettor can view this choice in one of two ways. In one way it becomes this choice:

A. Refuse the bet and accept a certainty of losing $140.

B. Make the bet and face a good chance of losing $150 and a poor chance of breaking even.

Because the subjective difference between losing $140 and $150 is small, the person will likely choose B and make the bet. On the other hand, the bettor could view it as the following choice:

C. Refuse the bet and face a certainty of having nothing change.

D. Make the bet and face a good chance of losing an additional $10 and a poor chance of gaining $140.

In this case, because of the greater weight on losses than gains and because of the negatively accelerated utility function, the bettor is likely to avoid the bet. The only difference is whether one places oneself at the −$140 point or the 0 point on the curve in Figure 10.6. However, depending on where one places oneself, one gets a different evaluation of the two outcomes.

As an example that appears to be more consequential, consider this situation described by Kahneman and Tversky (1984):

Problem 1: Imagine that the U.S. is preparing for the outbreak of an unusual Asian disease, which is expected to kill 600 people. Two alternative programs to combat the disease have been proposed. Assume that the exact scientific estimates of the consequences of the programs are as follows:

If Program A is adopted, 200 people will be saved.

If Program B is adopted, there is a one-third probability that 600 people will be saved and a two-thirds probability that no people will be saved.

Which of the two programs would you favor?

Seventy-two percent of the subjects preferred program A, which guarantees lives, over dealing with the risk of program B. However, consider what happens when, rather than describing the two programs in terms of saving lives, the two programs are described as follows:

If Program C is adopted, 400 people will die.

If Program D is adopted, there is a one-third probability nobody will die and a two-thirds probability that 600 people will die. (p. 343)

Now, only 22 percent preferred program C, which the reader will recognize as equivalent to A (and D is equivalent to B). Both of these choices can be understood in terms of a negatively accelerated utility function for lives. In the first case, the subjective value of 600 lives saved is less than three times the subjective value of 200 lives saved, whereas, in the second case, the subjective value of 400 deaths is more than two-thirds the subjective value of 600 deaths. McNeil, Pauker, Cox, and Tversky (1982) found that this tendency extended to actual medical treatment. What treatments a doctor will choose depends on whether the treatment is described in terms of odds of living or odds of dying.

Situations in which framing effects are most prevalent tend to have one thing in common—there is not a clear basis for choice. This is true of the three examples we have reviewed. In the case where the shopper had an opportunity for a savings, it is unclear whether $5 is worth going to another store. In the gambling example, there is not a clear basis for making a decision.[2] The stakes are very high in the third case, but it is unfortunately one of those social policy decisions that defies a clear analysis. Thus, these are cases which are hard to decide on their merits alone.

Shafir (1993) has suggested that in such situations we may make a decision, not on the basis of which is actually the best decision, but on the basis of which will be easiest to justify (to oneself or to others). Different framings make it easier or harder to justify an action. In the disease case above, the first framing focuses one on saving lives and the second framing focuses one on avoiding deaths. In the first case, one would justify the action by pointing to the people whose lives have been saved (therefore it is critical that there be some people to point to). In the second case, a justification would focus on the people who died (and it would be better if there were no such people).

This need to justify one's action can lead a person to pick the same alternative whether asked to pick something to accept or something to reject. Consider the case in Table 10.5 from Shafir where two parents are described in a divorce case and subjects are asked to play the role of a judge who must decide which parent to award custody of the child to. In the award condition, subjects are asked to decide who gets awarded the child, and in the deny condition they are asked to decide who gets denied the child. The parents are overall rather equivalent, but parent B has rather more extreme positive and negative factors. Asked to make an award decision, more subjects choose to award custody to parent B, and asked to make a deny decision they tend to deny custody again to parent B. The reason, Shafir argues, is that parent B offers reasons, such as the close relationship with the child, that can be used to justify the awarding of custody,

---

[2]That is, there is no basis for deciding that would not have rejected gambling as irrational in the first place.

Table 10.5 Problem from Shafir (1993)

Imagine that you serve on the jury of an only-child sole-custody case following a relatively messy divorce. The facts of the case are complicated by ambiguous economic, social, and emotional considerations, and you decide to base your decision entirely on the following few observations. (To which parent would you award sole custody of the child?/To which parent would you deny sole custody of the child?

		Condition	
		Award	Deny
Parent A	Average income	36%	45%
	Average health		
	Average working hours		
	Reasonable rapport with the child		
	Relatively stable social life		
Parent B	Above-average income	64%	55%
	Very close relationship with the child		
	Extremely active social life		
	Lots of work-related travel		
	Minor health problems		

Reprinted by permission from the Psychonomic Society, Inc.

but parent B also has reasons, such as time away from home, to justify denying custody of the child to that parent.

◆

In cases where there is not a clear basis for making a decision, people are influenced by the way the problem is framed.

Conclusions

Most of the research on human reasoning has compared it to various prescriptive models from logic and mathematics. It is the nature of such models that they are content-free. In the case of deductive reasoning, they are concerned with the form of the premises and conclusions, not with what they are about. In the case of inductive reasoning, the Bayesian model is concerned with the probabilities of various states of affairs, not their identity. In the case of decision making, the expected utility model just multiplies utilities and probabilities, and does not consider the framing of the alternatives. Although people can be trained to reason according to such formal rules in logic and statistics classrooms, this is not the way they reason in everyday life. Rather, reasoning in everyday life is better captured by the schema-based inference processes that we studied in Chapter 5. Here, we saw that people could naturally reason about what was likely to be true of birds or restaurants, but that their reasoning was tied to such specific content. We saw in this chapter that one of the reasons why subjects deviate from normative principles is that they slip into these schematic ways of reasoning. We also saw that they can become more normative in their reasoning when they lock into the right schema, as was the case with the permission schema for the Wason selection task. It seems that humans tend to reason more concretely than the normative models. Far from normative models describing what humans do (which is what Boole thought 150 years ago), they provide a reference point for comparison with what humans actually do.

Many people leave a review of research on human reasoning and decision making concerned with how "fragile" the human mind seems to be and how prone it seems to so many fallacies. However, it is good to keep in mind the limitations of the situations in which these demonstrations are made. Researchers in artificial intelligence have been trying to build intelligent agents that would display the kind of commonsense reasoning people do in everyday life. These artificial intelligence programs have been endowed with flawless logical and statistical reasoning. However, it is these programs and not the humans that are fragile and are always displaying problems in coming to the right conclusions in specific situations. This is because people reason in terms of these more concrete schema in which are embedded their experiences in particular situations. Success in the real world depends much more on deploying content-specific knowledge than on being able to correctly apply *modus tollens*.

◆
Human reasoning and decision making is fairly robust in the context of real-world problems.

Remarks and Suggested Readings

There are basically four positions that attempt to explain the way people engage in deductive reasoning. One position is that people use what are called natural laws of deduction, which are somewhat like the logician's rules. For expositions of this viewpoint, read Braine, Reiser, and Rumain (1984) and Rips (1994). The second, represented in Cheng and Holyoak (1985, 1989) and Cosmides (1989) is that people reason by rules that are specific to certain content. The third, represented in Johnson-Laird (1983) and Johnson-Laird and Byrne (1991), is that people reason by reference to concrete situations. The fourth, represented by Chater and Oaksford (in press) and Oaksford and Chater (1994), is that people treat the premises they are given as probabilistic statements.

Nisbett and Ross (1980) is an extensive discussion of the failures of human inference. The Holland, Holyoak, Nisbett, and Thagard (1986) book is basically devoted to producing an information-processing model of induction. There is a current debate about whether human reasoning should be viewed as robust or fragile. One such exchange occurred between Kahneman and Tversky (1996) and Gigerenzer (1996). Oaksford and Chater (1998) edited a recent book of articles presenting the optimistic view of human cognition. Klein (1998) discusses how real people make decisions when faced with real problems.

11

Language Structure

O f all human cognitive abilities, the use of language is among the most impressive. The difference between human language and the natural communication systems of other species is enormous. More than anything else, language is responsible for the current advanced state of human civilization. It is the principal means by which knowledge is recorded and transmitted from one generation to the next. Without language, there would be little technology. Language is the principal medium for establishing religions, laws, and moral conventions. Therefore, without language no means would exist for establishing rules to govern groups ranging in size from tennis partners to nations. Language also provides people with the principal means of assessing what another person knows. So, without language, human beings would experience countless more misunderstandings than they currently do. Language provides an important medium for art, a means of getting to know people, and a valuable aid to courtship. Therefore, without language much of the joy of living would be lost. In its written form, language enables humans to communicate over spatial distance and through time. So without language you would not be reading this book.

This chapter will provide a general overview of the structure of language and its consequences for human cognition. We will review some of the basic ideas developed in linguistics about the structure of language and some evidence for their psychological reality. We will review research and speculation about the relationship between language and thought. Some researchers have claimed that language is quite different from other cognitive faculties. Much of the evidence for and against this claim of uniqueness comes from research on the way children learn the structure of language. Therefore, we will conclude with a review of child language acquisition. This chapter will not contain detailed analyses of how language is processed. Considerable research has focused on this topic, and Chapter 12 of this book will be devoted to language processing.

The Field of Linguistics

Productivity and Regularity

The academic field of **linguistics** attempts to characterize the nature of language. It is distinct from psychology in that it studies the structure of natural languages rather than the way people process natural languages. Despite this difference, the work from linguistics has been extremely influential in the psychology of language. As we will see, concepts from linguistics play an important role in theories of language processing. As noted in Chapter 1, the influence from linguistics was important to the decline of behaviorism and the rise of modern cognitive psychology.

The linguist focuses on two aspects of language: its productivity and its regularity. The term **productivity** refers to the fact that an infinite number of utterances are possible in any language. **Regularity** refers to the fact that these utterances are systematic in many ways. It has been argued (Anderson & Bower, 1973; Chomsky, 1959) that it was impossible to account simultaneously for the productive and regular character of language using the theoretical terminology of behaviorism.

We need not seek far to convince ourselves of the highly productive and creative character of language. We have only to pick up a book and select a sentence from it at random. Suppose that, having chosen a sentence, an individual were instructed to go to the library and search for a repetition of the sentence in a different book! Obviously, no sensible person would take up this challenge. But, were a person to try, it is very unlikely that he or she would find the sentence repeated among the billions of sentences in the library. And yet it is important to realize that the components which make up sentences are quite small in number: English only uses twenty-six letters, forty phonemes (see the discussion in the Speech Recognition section of Chapter 3), and some tens of thousands of words. Nevertheless, with these components we can and do generate trillions of novel sentences.

A look at the structure of sentences makes clear why this productivity is possible. Natural language has facilities for endlessly embedding structure within structure and coordinating structure with structure. A mildly amusing party game starts with a simple sentence and requires participants to keep adding to the sentence:

- The girl hit the boy.

- The girl hit the boy and he cried.

- The big girl hit the boy and he cried.

- The big girl hit the boy and he cried loudly.

- The big girl hit the boy who was misbehaving and he cried loudly.

- The big girl with authoritarian instincts hit the boy who was misbehaving and he cried loudly.

And so on until someone can no longer extend the sentence.

The fact that an infinite number of word strings can be generated would not be particularly interesting in itself. If we have tens of thousands of words for each position and if sentences can be of any length, it is not hard to see that a very large (in fact, an infinite) number of word strings is possible. However, if we merely combine words at random we get "sentences" such as

- From runners physicians prescribing miss a states joy rests what thought most.

In fact, very few of the possible word combinations are acceptable sentences. The speculation is often jokingly made that, given enough monkeys working at typewriters for a long enough time, some monkey will type a best-selling book. It should be clear that it would take a lot of monkeys a long time to type just one acceptable *R@!#s.

So, balanced against the productivity of language is its highly regular character. One goal of linguistics is to discover a set of rules that will account for both the productivity and the regularity of natural language.

Such a set of rules is referred to as a **grammar**. A grammar should be able to prescribe or generate all the acceptable utterances of a language and be able to reject all the unacceptable sentences in the language. A grammar consists of three types of rules—syntactic, semantic, and phonological. **Syntax** is concerned with word order and inflection. As examples of sentences that violate syntax, consider the following:

- The girls hits the boys.
- Did hit the girl the boys?
- The girl hit a boys.
- The boys were hit the girl.

These sentences are fairly meaningful but contain some mistakes in word combinations or word forms.

Semantics is concerned with the meaning of sentences. Consider the following sentences that contain semantic violations, even though the words are correct in form and syntactic position:

- Colorless green ideas sleep furiously.
- Sincerity frightened the cat.

These constructions are called anomalous sentences in that they are syntactically well formed but nonsensical.

Phonology is concerned with the sound structure of sentences. Sentences can be correct syntactically and semantically but be mispronounced. Such sentences are said to contain phonological violations. Consider this example:

> *The Inspector opened his notebook. "Your name is Halcock, is't no?"*
> *he began. The butler corrected him. "H'alcock," he said, reprovingly.*
> *"H,a,double-l?" suggested the Inspector. "There is no h'aich in the*
> *name, young man. H'ay is the first letter, and there is h'only one h'ell."*
> *(Sayers, 1968, p. 73)*

The butler, wanting to hide his cockney dialect, which drops the letter h, is systematically mispronouncing every word that begins with a vowel.

◆
The goal of linguistics is to discover a set of rules that captures the structural regularities in a language.

Linguistic Intuitions

A major goal of linguistics is to explain the **linguistic intuitions** of speakers of the language. Linguistic intuitions are judgments about the nature of linguistic utterances or about the relationships between linguistic utterances. Speakers of the language are often able to make these judgments without knowing how they do so. As such, this is another example of implicit knowledge, a concept we introduced in Chapter 7. Among these linguistic intuitions are judgments about whether sentences are ill-formed and if ill-formed, why. For instance, we can judge that some sentences are ill-formed because they have bad syntactic structure and that other sentences are ill-formed because they lack meaning. Linguists require that a grammar capture this distinction and clearly express the reasons for it. Another kind of intuition is about paraphrase. A speaker of English will judge that the following two sentences are very similar in meaning, and hence are paraphrases:

- The girl hit the boy.
- The boy was hit by the girl.

Yet another kind of intuition is about ambiguity. The following sentence has two meanings:

- They are cooking apples.

This sentence can either mean that some people are cooking some apples or that the apples can be used for cooking. Moreover, speakers of the language can distinguish this type of ambiguity, which is called structural ambiguity, from lexical ambiguity, as in

- I am going to the bank.

where *bank* can refer either to a monetary institution or a riverbank. Lexical ambiguities arise when a word has two or more distinct meanings; structural ambiguities arise when an entire phrase or sentence has two or more meanings.

◆

Linguists try to account for intuitions about the well-formedness of sentences and intuitions about paraphrase and ambiguity.

Competence versus Performance

Our everyday use of language does not always correspond to the prescriptions of linguistic theory. We generate sentences in conversation that, in a more reflective situation, we would judge to be ill-formed and unacceptable. We hesitate, repeat ourselves, stutter, and make slips of the tongue. We misunderstand the meaning of sentences. We hear sentences that are ambiguous but do not note their ambiguity.

Another complication is that linguistic intuitions are not always clear-cut. For instance, we find the linguist Lakoff (1971) telling us that the first sentence below is not acceptable but that the second is:

- Tell John where the concert's this afternoon.

- Tell John that the concert's this afternoon.

People are not always reliable in their judgments of such sentences and certainly do not always agree with Lakoff.

Considerations about the unreliability of human linguistic behavior and judgment led the linguist Noam Chomsky (1965) to make a distinction between linguistic **competence**, a person's abstract knowledge of the language, and linguistic **performance**, the actual application of that knowledge in speaking or listening. In Chomsky's view, the linguist's task is to develop a theory of competence; the psychologist's task is to develop a theory of performance.

The exact relationship between a theory of competence and a theory of performance is unclear and can be the subject of heated debates. Chomsky has argued that a theory of competence is central to performance—that our linguistic competence underlies our ability to use language, if indirectly. Others believe that the concept of linguistic competence is based on a rather unnatural activity (making linguistic judgments) and has very little to do with everyday language use.

◆
Linguistic performance does not always reflect linguistic competence.

Syntactic Formalisms

A major contribution of linguistics to the psychological study of language has been to provide a set of concepts for describing the structure of language. The most frequently used ideas from linguistics involve descriptions of the syntactic structure of language.

Phrase Structure

A great deal of emphasis in linguistics has been given to understanding the syntax of natural language. One central linguistic concept is **phrase structure**. Phrase structure analysis is not only significant in linguistics, but is also very important to an understanding of language processing. Therefore, our coverage of this topic here is partially a preparation for material in the next chapter. Those of you who have had a certain kind of training in high school English will find the analysis of phrase structure to be similar to parsing exercises. For the rest of you, the analysis will be more novel.

The phrase structure of a sentence is the hierarchical division of the sentence into units called phrases. Consider this sentence:

- The brave dog saved the drowning child.

If asked to divide this sentence into two major parts in the most natural way, most people would provide the following division:

- (The brave dog)(saved the drowning child).

The parentheses distinguish the two separate parts. The two parts of the sentence correspond to what are traditionally called subject and predicate, or noun phrase and verb phrase. If asked to divide the second part, the verb phrase, further, most people would give

- (The brave dog) (saved (the drowning child)).

Often, analysis of a sentence is represented as an upside-down tree, as in Figure 11.1. In this phrase structure tree, *sentence* points to its subunits, the *noun phrase* and the *verb phrase,* and each of these units points to its subunits. Eventually, the branches of the tree terminate in the individual words. Such tree structure representations are very common in linguistics. In fact, it is common to use the term *phrase structure* to refer to such tree structures.

An analysis of phrase structure can point up structural ambiguities. Consider again the sentence

- They are cooking apples.

Depending on the meaning, *cooking* is either part of the verb with *are* or part of the noun phrase with *apples.* Figure 11.2 illustrates the phrase

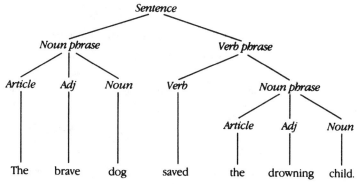

Figure 11.1 An example of the phrase structure of a sentence. The tree structure illustrates the hierarchical division of the sentence into phrases.

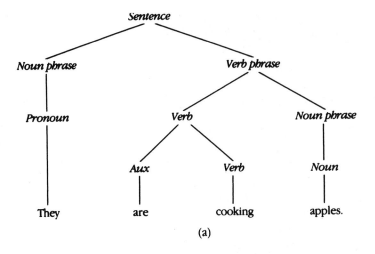

(a)

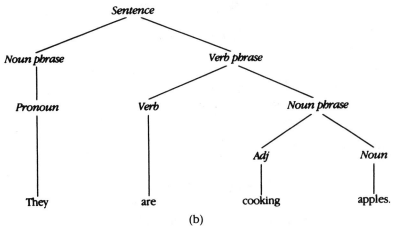

(b)

Figure 11.2 The phrase structures illustrating the two possible meanings of the ambiguous sentence they are cooking apples: (a) that those people (they) are cooking apples; (b) that those apples are for cooking.

structure for these two interpretations. In part a *cooking* is part of the verb, while in part b it is part of the noun phrase.

◆

Phrase structure analysis is concerned with the way sentences are broken up into constituents.

Rewrite Rules

Note that the various nodes in the trees showing phrase structure have meaningful labels, such as *sentence, noun phrase, verb phrase, verb, noun,* and *adj* (for *adjective*), which indicate the character of these sentence units,

Table 11.1 Rewrite Rules for Generating a Fragment of English

	Symbol	Rewrite As
1.	Sentence	→ noun phrase + verb phrase
2A.	Noun phrase	→ (article) + (adj) + noun
2B.		→ pronoun
3A.	Verb phrase	→ verb + noun phrase
3B.		→ verb + prep phrase
4.	Prep phrase	→ preposition + noun phrase
5A.	Verb	→ aux + verb
5B.		→ hit, saved, cooking, danced
6.	Noun	→ dog, child, boy, girl, apples, river
7.	Article	→ the, a
8.	Adj	→ brave, drowning, cooking
9.	Pronoun	→ he, she, they
10.	Preposition	→ in, by
11.	Aux	→ was, were

or constituents. Such labels can be used to form **rewrite rules** for actually generating sentences. Linguists formulate grammars for languages in terms of such rewrite rules. Table 11.1 consists of a set of rewrite rules indicating ways of rewriting these labels, or symbols. The symbol on the left can be rewritten as the symbols on the right. Thus, rule 1 says that *sentence* may be rewritten as *noun phrase* plus *verb phrase*. Rule 2A indicates that a *noun phrase* can be rewritten as an optional *article*, an optional *adjective*, and a *noun*. The parentheses indicate that the *article* and *adjective* are optional. Rule 2B indicates that another way to rewrite a *noun phrase* is as a *pronoun*.

It is possible to derive a sentence through these rewrite rules. For instance, consider the following sequence.

$$Sentence \rightarrow noun\ phrase + verb\ phrase \tag{1}$$
$$\rightarrow article + adj + noun + verb$$
$$+ prep\ phrase \tag{2}$$
$$\rightarrow article + adj + noun + verb$$
$$+ preposition + noun\ phrase \tag{3}$$
$$\rightarrow article + adj + noun + verb$$
$$+ preposition + article + noun \tag{4}$$
$$\rightarrow the + brave + boy + danced$$
$$+ in + the + river \tag{5}$$

In line 1, we rewrote *sentence* as *noun phrase* plus *verb phrase* according to rewrite rule 1. In line 2, we rewrote *noun phrase* into *article* plus *adj*

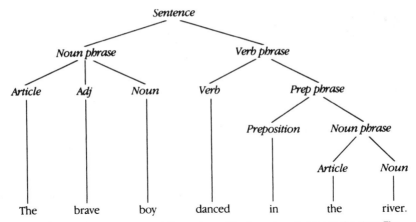

Figure 11.3 The phrase structure of the sentence <u>The brave boy danced in the river.</u> The branches in this tree derive from the rewrite rules in Table 11.1.

plus *noun* (according to rewrite rule 2A) and *verb phrase* into *verb* plus *prep phrase* (according to rule 3B). In line 3, we rewrote *prep phrase* into *preposition* plus *noun phrase* (according to rule 4). In line 4, we rewrote the *noun phrase* from line 3 into *article* plus *noun* (rule 2A). Finally, in line 5 we replaced each of the symbols with words, according to rules 5B, 6, 7, 8, and 10.

The tree representation of the phrase structure of a sentence serves to illustrate derivation of the sentence through the rewrite rules. Figure 11.3 illustrates the phrase structure of the sentence derived above. In such a tree structure, a symbol is connected below to the symbols into which it is rewritten. For instance, the symbol *verb phrase* is connected below to *verb* and *prep phrase*, according to rule 3B.

A set of rewrite rules constitutes one way of specifying the acceptable sentences of the language. As such, they provide a means of achieving one important goal of linguistics—to devise a grammar that (1) generates all the acceptable sentences of the language, (2) avoids generating any unacceptable sentences, and (3) represents intuitions about the structure of such sentences. Can you find ways in which the simple set of rewrite rules in Table 11.1 fails to achieve each of these criteria? Although linguists have come up with rewrite rules that are much more complex and comprehensive than the ones in Table 11.1, they have not yet come close to specifying a set that completely satisfies criteria 1 and 2 stated above. Many issues in the field remain unresolved, including whether these two goals are realistic.

◆

Rewrite rules are formal specifications for generating sentences and their phrase structures.

Pause Structure in Speech

There is abundant evidence that phrase structures play a key role in the generation of sentences.[1] When people produce a sentence they tend to generate it a phrase at a time, pausing at the boundaries between large phrase units. For instance, although no tape recorders were available in Lincoln's time, one might guess he produced the first sentence of "The Gettysburg Address" with brief pauses at the end of each of the major phrases as indicated below:

Four score and seven years ago (pause)
our forefathers brought forth on this continent (pause)
a new nation (pause)
conceived in liberty (pause)
and dedicated to the proposition (pause)
that all men are created equal (pause)

Although Lincoln's speeches are not available for analysis, Boomer (1965) analyzed examples of spontaneous speech and found that pauses did occur more frequently at junctures between major phrases and that these pauses were longer than pauses at other locations. The average pause time at a grammatical juncture was 1.03 seconds, while the average pause within grammatical clauses was 0.75 seconds. This finding suggests that speakers tend to produce sentences a phrase at a time and often need to pause after one phrase to plan the next. Other researchers (Cooper & Paccia-Cooper, 1980; Grosjean, Grosjean, & Lane, 1979) have looked at subjects producing prepared sentences rather than spontaneous speech. The pauses of such subjects tend to be much shorter, around 0.2 seconds. Still, the same pattern holds, with longer pauses at the major phrase boundaries.

As Figures 11.1 to 11.3 illustrate, there are multiple levels of phrases within phrases within phrases. What level do speakers choose for breaking up their sentence into pause units? Gee and Grosjean (1983) argue that speakers tend to choose the smallest level above the word that bundles together coherent semantic information. In English this tends to be noun phrases (e.g., the young woman), verbs plus pronouns (e.g., will have been reading it), and prepositional phrases (e.g., in the house).

◆
People tend to pause briefly after each meaningful unit of speech.

---

[1]In Chapter 12, we will examine the role phrase structures play in language comprehension.

Speech Errors

Other research has found evidence for phrase structure by looking at errors in speech. Maclay and Osgood (1959) analyzed spontaneous recordings of speech and found a number of speech errors that suggested that phrases do have a psychological reality. They found that when speakers repeated themselves or corrected themselves, they tended to repeat or correct a whole phrase. For instance, the following is the kind of repeat that is found:

- Turn on the heater/the heater switch.

And the pair below constitutes a common type of correction:

- Turn on the stove/the heater switch.

In the preceding example, the noun phrase is repeated. In contrast, speakers do not produce repetitions in which part, but not all, of the verb phrase is repeated, such as

- Turn on the stove/on the heater switch.

Other kinds of speech errors also provide evidence for the psychological reality of constituents as major units of speech generation. For instance, some research has analyzed slips of the tongue in speech (Fromkin, 1971, 1973; Garrett, 1975). One kind of speech error is called a spoonerism, after the English clergyman William A. Spooner to whom are attributed some colossal and clever errors of speech. The following are among the errors of speech attributed to Spooner:

- You have hissed all my mystery lectures.
- I saw you fight a liar in the back quad; in fact, you have tasted the whole worm.
- I assure you the insanitary spectre has seen all the bathrooms.
- Easier for a camel to go through the knee of an idol.
- The Lord is a shoving leopard to his flock.
- Take the flea of my cat and heave it at the louse of my mother-in-law.

As illustrated above, spoonerisms involve exchanges of sound between words. There is some reason to suspect that the errors above were deliberate attempts at humor by Spooner. However, people do generate genuine spoonerisms, although they are seldom so funny.

By patient collecting, researchers have gathered a large set of errors made by friends and colleagues. Some of these involve simple sound anticipations and some involve sound exchanges as in spoonerisms:

- Take my bike → bake my bike [an anticipation]
- night life → nife lite [an exchange]
- beast of burden → burst of beaden [an exchange].

One that gives me particular difficulty is

- coin toss → toin coss

The first error listed above is an example of an anticipation, where an early phoneme is changed to a later phoneme. The others are examples of exchanges in which two phonemes switch. The interesting feature about these kinds of errors is that they tend to occur within a single phrase rather than across phrases. So, we are unlikely to find the following anticipation:

- The dancer took my bike. → The bancer took my bike.

where an anticipation occurs between subject and object noun phrases. Also unlikely are sound exchanges where an exchange occurs between the initial prepositional phrase and the final noun phrase, as in

- At night John lost his life. → At nife John lost his lite.

Garrett (1990) distinguishes between errors that involve simple sounds and those that involve whole words. Sound errors occur at what he calls the positional level, which basically corresponds to a single phrase, while word errors occur at what he calls a functional level, which corresponds to a larger unit of speech such as a full clause. Thus, the following word error has been observed:

- That kid's mouse makes a great toy. → That kid's toy makes a great mouse.

whereas, the following sound error would be unlikely:

- That kid's mouse makes a great toy. → That kid's touse makes a great moy.

In Garrett's (1980) corpus, 83% of all word exchanges extended beyond phrase boundaries but only 13% of sound errors do.

It is generally thought that word and sound errors occur at different levels in the speech production process. Words are inserted into the speech plan at a higher level of planning, and so a larger distance is possible for the substitution.

◆
Speech errors involving substitutions of sounds and words suggest that words are selected at the clause level while sounds are inserted at a lower phrase level.

Transformations

A phrase structure describes a sentence hierarchically as pieces within larger pieces. There are certain types of linguistic constructions that some linguists think violate this strictly hierarchical structure. Consider the following pair of sentences:

1. The dog is chasing Bill down the street.

2. Whom is the dog chasing down the street?

In sentence 1, *Bill*, the object of the chasing, occurs as part of the verb phrase. On the other hand, in sentence 2, *whom*, the object of the verb phrase, occurs at the beginning of the sentence. The object is no longer part of the verb phrase structure to which it would seem to belong. Some linguists have proposed that, formally, such questions are generated by starting with a phrase structure which has the object *whom* in the verb phrase, as

3. The dog is chasing whom down the street?

This is a somewhat strange sentence but with the right questioning intonation of the *whom* it can be made to sound reasonable. In some languages, such as Japanese, it is normal to leave the interrogative pronoun in the verb phrase as in sentence 3. However, in English the proposal is that there is a movement transformation that moves the *whom* into its more normal position. Note that this is a linguistic proposal as to the formal structure of language and may not describe the actual process of producing the question.

Many linguists believe that it is necessary to propose such **transformations**, which move elements from one part of the sentence to another part. Transformations can also operate on more complicated sentences. For instance, we can apply it to sentences of the form:

4. John believes that the dog is chasing Bill down the street.

The corresponding question forms are

5. John believes that the dog is chasing whom down the street?

6. Whom does John believe that the dog is chasing down the street?

Sentence 5 is strange even with a questioning intonation for *whom*, but still some linguists believe that sentence 6 is transformationally derived from it, even though we would never produce sentence 5.

One of the intriguing issues to linguists is that there seem to be real limitations on just what things can be moved by transformations. For instance, consider the following set of sentences:

7. John believes the fact that the dog is chasing Bill down the street.

8. John believes the fact that the dog is chasing whom down the street?

9. Whom does John believe the fact that the dog is chasing down the street?

As sentence 7 illustrates, the basic sentence form is acceptable, but one cannot move *whom* from question form 8 to produce question form 9. Sentence 9 just sounds very bizarre. We will return later to the issue of what restrictions there are on movement transformations.

In contrast to the abundant evidence for phrase structure in language processing, the evidence is very poor that people actually compute anything analogous to transformations in understanding or producing sentences. It remains very much an open question how people process such transformationally derived sentences. It is also the case that there is a lot of controversy within linguistics as to how to conceive of transformations. The role of transformations has been deemphasized in some proposals (for a review, see Wasow, 1989).

◆

Transformations move elements from their normal positions in the phrase structure of a sentence.

The Relationship between Language and Thought
The Behaviorist Proposal

We have now reviewed the structure of language as it is seen by the linguist. The question that naturally arises is what effect does the structure of language have on cognition. A wide variety of proposals have been put forth as to the connection between language and thought. The strongest was advanced by John B. Watson, the father of behaviorism. It was one of the tenets of Watson's behaviorism (Watson, 1930) that no such thing as internal mental activity existed. All that humans did, Watson argued, was to emit responses that had been conditioned to various stimuli. This radical proposal, which, as noted in Chapter 1, held sway in America for some time, seemed to fly in the face of the abundant evidence that humans can engage in thinking behavior (e.g., do mental arithmetic) which involves no response emission. To deal with this obvious counter, Watson proposed that thinking was just subvocal speech, that when people were engaged in such "mental" activities they were really talking to themselves. Hence, Watson's proposal was that a very important component of thought was simply subvocal speech. (The philosopher Herbert Feigl once said that Watson "made up his windpipe that he had no mind.")

This proposal was a stimulus for a research program that engaged itself in taking recordings to see if evidence could be found for subvocal activity of the speech apparatus during thinking. Indeed, often when a subject is engaged in thought, it is possible to get recordings of subvocal speech activity. However, the more important observation is that in some situations people engage in various silent thinking tasks with no detectable vocal activity. This finding did not upset Watson. He claimed that we think with our whole bodies—for instance, with our arms. He cited the fascinating evidence that deaf mutes actually make signs while asleep. (Speaking people who have done a lot of communication in sign language also sign while sleeping.)

The decisive experiment addressing Watson's hypothesis was performed by Smith, Brown, Toman, and Goodman (1947). They used a curare derivative that paralyzed the entire human musculature. Smith was the subject for the experiment and had to be kept alive by means of an artificial respirator. Because his entire musculature was completely paralyzed, it was impossible for him to engage in subvocal speech or any other body movement. Nonetheless, under curare, Smith was able to observe what was going on around him, comprehend speech, remember these events, and think about them. Thus, it seems clear that thinking can proceed in the absence of any muscle activity. For our current purposes the relevant additional observation is that thought is not just implicit speech but is truly an internal, nonmotor activity.

Additional evidence that thought is not to be equated with language comes from the research on memory for meaning that was reviewed in Chapter 5. There we discussed the fact that people tend to retain not the exact words of a linguistic communication, but rather some more abstract representation of the meaning of the communication. Thought should be identified, at least in part, with this abstract, nonverbal propositional code.

Still more information comes from the occasional cases of individuals who have no apparent language at all but who certainly give evidence of being able to think. Also, it seems hard to claim that nonverbal animals such as apes are unable to think. Recall, for instance, the problem-solving exploits of Sultan in Chapter 8. It is always hard to determine the exact character of the "thought processes" of nonverbal subjects and the way these processes differ from the thought processes of verbal subjects, since there is no language with which nonverbal subjects can be interrogated. Thus, the apparent dependence of thought on language may be an illusion that derives from the fact that it is hard to obtain evidence about thought without using language.

◆
The behaviorists believed that thought involved covert speech and other implicit motor actions.

The Whorfian Hypothesis of Linguistic Determinism

Linguistic determinism is the claim that language determines or strongly influences the way a person thinks or perceives the world. This proposal is much weaker than Watson's position, because it does not claim that language and thought are identical. The hypothesis has been advanced by a good many linguists but has been most strongly associated with Whorf (1956). Whorf was quite an unusual character himself. He was trained as a chemical engineer at MIT, spent his life working for the Hartford Fire Insurance Company, and studied North American Indian languages as a hobby. He was very impressed by the fact that different languages emphasize in their structure rather different aspects of the world. He believed that these emphases must have a great influence on the way language speakers think about the world. For instance, he claimed that Eskimos have many different words for snow, each of which refers to snow in a different state (wind-driven, packed, slushy, and so on), whereas English speakers have only a single word for snow.[2] Many other examples exist at the vocabulary level: The Hanunoo people in the Philippines supposedly have ninety-two different names for varieties of rice. The Arabic language has many different ways of naming camels. Whorf felt that such a rich variety of terms would cause the speaker of the language to perceive the world differently from a person who had only a single word for a particular category.

Deciding how to evaluate the Whorfian hypothesis is very tricky. Nobody would be surprised to learn that Eskimos know more about snow

◆
[2]There have been challenges to Whorf's claims about the richness of Eskimo vocabulary for snow (Martin, 1986; Pullman, 1989). In general, there is a feeling that Whorf exaggerated the variety of words in various languages.

than average English speakers. After all, snow is a more important part of their life experience. The question is whether their language has any effect on the Eskimos' perception of snow over and above the effect of experience. If speakers of English went through the Eskimo life experience, would their perception of snow be any different than that of the Eskimo-language speakers? (Indeed, ski bums have a life experience that involves a great deal of exposure to snow and have a great deal of knowledge about snow.)

One fairly well researched test of the issue involves color words. English has eleven basic color words—*black, white, red, green, yellow, blue, brown, purple, pink, orange,* and *gray*—a relatively large number. These words are called basic color words because they are short and are used frequently, in contrast to such terms as *saffron, turquoise,* or *magenta.* At the other extreme is the language of the Dani, a stone age agricultural people of Indonesian New Guinea. This language has just two basic color terms: *mili* for dark, cold hues and *mola* for bright, warm hues. If the categories in language determine perception, the Dani should perceive color in a less refined manner than English speakers do. The relevant question is whether this speculation is true.

Speakers of English, at least, judge a certain color within the range referred to by each basic color term to be the best—for instance, the best red, the best blue, and so on (see Berlin & Kay, 1969). Each of the eleven basic color terms in English appears to have one generally agreed-upon best color, called a focal color. English speakers find it easier to process and remember focal colors than nonfocal colors (e.g., Brown & Lenneberg, 1954). The interesting question is whether the special cognitive capacity for identifying focal colors evolved because English speakers have special words for these colors. If so, this would be a case of language influencing thought.

To test whether the special processing of focal colors was an instance of language influencing thought, Rosch (who has published some of this work under her former name, Heider) performed an important series of experiments on the Dani. The point was to see whether the Dani processed focal colors differently from English speakers. One experiment (Rosch, 1973) compared the ability of the Dani to learn nonsense names for focal versus nonfocal colors. English speakers find it easier to learn arbitrary names for focal colors. Dani subjects also found it easier to learn arbitrary names for focal colors than for nonfocal colors, even though they have no names for these colors. In another experiment (Heider, 1972), subjects were shown a color chip for 5 seconds; 30 seconds after the presentation ended, they were required to select the color from among 160 color chips. English speakers perform better at this task when the chip they are to remember is a focal color rather than a nonfocal color. The Dani also perform better at this task for focal colors.

Thus, it appears that despite the differences in their linguistic terminology for colors, the Dani and English speakers see colors in much the same way. It appears that the eleven focal colors are processed specially by all people regardless of language. In fact, the physiology of color vision suggests that many of these focal colors are specially processed by the visual system (de Valois & Jacobs, 1968). The fact that many languages develop basic color terms for just these colors can be seen as an instance of thought determining language.[3]

Another test of the Whorfian hypothesis was performed by Carroll and Casagrande (1958). The Navajo language requires different verb forms depending on the nature of the thing being acted upon, particularly regarding its shape, rigidity, and material. Carroll and Casagrande presented Navajo-speaking children with three objects, such as a yellow stick, a piece of blue rope, and a yellow rope. The children had to say which of the two objects went with the third. Since Navajo requires that a different verb form be used for sticks (rigid) than ropes (flexible), the experimenters predicted that the Navajo-speaking subjects would tend to match the ropes and not match on color. They found that Navajo-speaking children preferred form and that English-speaking Navajo children preferred color. However, in another study they found that English-speaking children from Boston exhibited an even greater tendency to match on the basis of form. It seems that the Boston children's experience with toys (for which shape and rigidity are critical) was more important than the Navajo-language experience, although the language experience may have had some effect.

To conclude, the evidence tends not to support the hypothesis that language has any significant effect on the way we think or on the way we perceive the world. It is certainly true that language can influence us (or else there would be little point in writing this book), but its effect is to communicate ideas, not to determine the kinds of ideas we can think about.

◆

While language clearly influences thought, it does not seem to determine the types of concepts we can think about.

Does Language Depend on Thought?

The alternative possibility is that the structure of language is determined by the structure of thought. Aristotle argued 2500 years ago that the categories of thought determined the categories of language. There are some reasons for believing that he was correct, but most of these reasons were not available to Aristotle. So, although the hypothesis has been around for 2500 years, we have better reasons for holding it today.

There are numerous reasons to suppose that humans' ability to think (i.e., to engage in nonlinguistic cognitive activity such as remembering and

◆
_____

[3]For further research on this topic, read Lucy & Shweder (1979, 1988) and Garro (1986).

problem solving) appeared earlier evolutionarily and occurs sooner developmentally than the ability to use language. Many species of animals without language appear to be capable of complex cognition. Children, before they are effective at using their language, give clear evidence of relatively complex cognition. If we accept the idea that thought occurred before language, it seems natural to suppose that language arose as a tool whose function was to communicate thought. It is generally true that tools are shaped to fit the objects on which they must operate. Analogously, it seems reasonable to suppose that language has been shaped to fit the thoughts it must communicate. In addition to general arguments for the view that the structure of thought shaped the structure of language, a number of pieces of evidence to support the notion have been generated in cognitive psychology and related fields. I will review a few of the lines of evidence.

We saw in Chapter 5 that propositional structures constituted a very important type of knowledge structure in representing information both derived from language and derived from pictures. This propositional structure is reflected in the phrase structure of language. The basic phrase units of a language tend to convey propositions. For instance, *the tall boy* conveys the proposition that the boy is tall. This phenomenon itself—the existence of a linguistic structure, the phrase, designed to accommodate a thought structure, the proposition—seems to be a clear example of the dependence of language on thought.

Another example of the way in which thought shapes language comes from Rosch's research on focal colors. As stated earlier, the human visual system is maximally sensitive to certain colors. As a consequence, languages have special, short, high-frequency words with which to designate these colors. We noted that in English these basic color words are *black, white, red, yellow, green, blue, brown, purple, pink, orange,* and *gray.* Thus, the visual system has determined how the English language divides up the color space.

We find additional evidence for the influence of thought on language when we consider word order. Every language has a preferred word order for expressing subject (S), verb (V), and object (O). Consider this sentence, which exhibits the preferred word order in English:

- Lynne petted the Labrador.

English is referred to as an SVO language. In a study of a diverse sample of the world's languages, Greenberg (1963) found that only four of the six possible orders of S, V, and O are used in natural languages, and one of these four orders is rare. Below are the six possible word orders and the frequency with which each order occurs in the world's languages (the percentages are from Ultan, 1969):

SOV	44 percent	VOS	2 percent
SVO	35 percent	OVS	0 percent
VSO	19 percent	OSV	0 percent

The important feature is that the subject almost always precedes the object. This order makes good sense when we think about cognition. An action starts with the agent and then affects the object. It is natural therefore that the subject of a sentence, when it reflects its agency, occurs first.

◆

In many ways the structure of language reflects the structure of how our minds process the world.

Modularity of Language

We have considered the possibility that thought might depend on language and the possibility that language might depend on thought. There is a third logical possibility, which is that language and thought might be independent. A special version of this independence principle is what is called the **modularity** position (Chomsky, 1980; Fodor, 1983). This position holds that language is a separate cognitive component that functions separately from the rest of cognition. Fodor has argued that there is a separate linguistic module that first analyzes incoming speech and then passes this analysis on to general cognition. Similarly, in language generation the linguistic module takes the intentions to be spoken and produces the speech. This position does not deny that the linguistic module may have been shaped to communicate thought. However, it argues that it operates according to different principles from the rest of cognition and is "encapsulated" such that it cannot be influenced by general cognition. It can only communicate with general cognition by passing its products to general cognition and receiving the products of general cognition.

The modularity hypothesis has turned out to be a major dividing issue in the field with different researchers lining up in support or in opposition. Two domains of research have played a major role evaluating the modularity proposal. One concerns language acquisition. Here, the issue is whether language is acquired according to unique learning principles or whether it is acquired like other cognitive skills. The second domain is language comprehension. Here, the issue is whether major aspects of language processing occur without utilization of any general cognitive processes. We will discuss some of the issues with respect to comprehension in the next chapter. In this chapter, we will look at what is known about language acquisition. We will first overview the general course of language acquisition by young children and then turn to the implications for the uniqueness of language.

◆

The modularity position holds that the acquisition and processing of language is independent from other cognitive systems.

Language Acquisition

Having watched my two children acquire a language, I understand how easy it is to lose sight of what a remarkable feat it is. Days and weeks go by with little apparent change in their linguistic abilities. Progress seems slow. However, something remarkable is happening. With very little and often no deliberate instruction, children by the time they reach age 10 have accomplished implicitly what generations of Ph.D. linguists have not accomplished explicitly. They have internalized all the major rules of a natural language, and there appear to be thousands of such rules with subtle interactions. No linguist in a lifetime has been able to formulate a grammar for any language that will identify all and only the grammatical sentences. However, as children we internalize such a grammar. Unfortunately, our knowledge of the grammar of our language is not something that we can articulate. It is implicit knowledge (see Chapter 7), which we can only display in using the language.

The process by which children acquire a language has some characteristic features that seem to hold no matter what their native language is (and languages around the world differ in marked ways): Children are notoriously noisy creatures from birth. At first, the variety in their sounds is quite impoverished. Their vocalizations consist almost totally of an "ah" sound (although they can produce it at different intensities and with different emotional tones). In the months following birth, children's vocal apparatus matures and by the end of the first year they have articulated a great variety of speech sounds, including some that may not be part of the language spoken by their linguistic community. At about six months, a change takes place in children's utterances. They begin to engage in what is called babbling. Babbling consists of generating a rich variety of speech sounds with interesting intonation patterns. However, the sounds are generally totally meaningless to the listeners.

When the child is about a year old the first words appear, always a point of great excitement to the child's parents. The very first words are there only to the ears of very sympathetic parents and caretakers, but soon the child develops a considerable repertoire of words, which are recognizable to the untrained ear and which the child uses effectively to make requests and to describe what is happening. The early words are concrete and refer to the here and now. Among my children's first words were *Mommy, Daddy, Rogers* (for Mister Rogers), *cheese, puter* (for computer), *eat, hi, bye, go,* and *hot.* One remarkable feature of this stage is that the speech consists only of one-word utterances. Even though children know

Table 11.2 Two-Word Utterances

Kendall swim	pillow fell
doggie bark	Kendall book
see Kendall	Papa door
writing book	Kendall turn
sit pool	towel bed
shoe off	there cow

From Bowerman, 1973.

many words, they never put them together to make multiple-word phrases. Children's use of single words is quite complex. They often use a single word to communicate a whole thought. Children will also overextend their words. Thus, the word *dog* might be used to refer to any furry four-legged animal.

The one-word stage, which lasts about six months, is followed by a stage in which children will put two words together. I can still remember our excitement as parents when our son said his first two-word utterance at eighteen months—*more gee*, which meant for him "more brie"—he was a connoisseur of cheese. Table 11.2 illustrates some of the typical two-word utterances generated by children at this stage. All their utterances are one or two words. Once their utterances extend beyond two words, there are many different lengths of utterances. There is no corresponding three-word stage. The two-word utterances reflect about a dozen or so semantic relationships, including agent-action, agent-object, action-object, object-location, object-attribute, possessor-object, negation-object, and negation-event. The order in which the children place these words usually corresponds to one of the orders that would be correct in adult speech in the children's linguistic community.

Even when children leave the two-word stage and speak in sentences ranging from three to eight words, their speech retains a peculiar quality, which is sometimes referred to as telegraphic. Table 11.3 contains some of these longer multiword utterances. The children speak somewhat as people used to write in telegraphs, omitting unimportant function words like *the* and *is*. In fact, it is rare to find in early-childhood speech any utterance that would be considered to be a well-formed sentence. Yet it is out of this beginning that grammatical sentences eventually appear. One might expect that children would learn to speak some kinds of sentences perfectly, then learn to speak other kinds of sentences perfectly, and so on. However, it seems that children start out speaking all kinds of sentences and all of them imperfectly. Their language development is not characterized by learning more kinds of sentences but by their sentences becoming gradually better approximations of adult sentences.

Table 11.3 Multiword Utterances

Put truck window	My balloon pop
Want more grape juice	Doggie bit me mine boot
Sit Adam chair	That Mommy nose right there
Mommy put sack	She's wear that hat
No I see truck	I like pick dirt up firetruck
Adam fall toy	No pictures in there

From Brown, 1973.

Besides the missing words, there are other dimensions in which children's early speech is incomplete. A classic example of this concerns the rules for pluralization in English. Initially, children do not distinguish in their speech between singular and plural, using a singular form for both. Then, they will learn the *add s* rule for pluralization but overextend it, producing *foots* or even *feets*. Gradually, they learn the pluralization rules for the irregular words. This goes on into adulthood. Cognitive scientists had to learn that the plural of *schema* was *schemata* (a fact I spared the reader from having to deal with when schemas were discussed in Chapter 5).

Another dimension in which children have to perfect their language concerns word order. They have particular difficulties with those aspects of language that involve transformational movements of terms from their natural position in the phrase structure (see the earlier discussion in this chapter). So, for instance, there is a point where children form questions without moving the verb auxiliary from the verb phrase:

- What me think?

- What the doggie have?

Even later, when children's spontaneous speech seems to be well formed, they will display errors in comprehension that reveal they have not yet captured all the subtleties in their language. For instance, Chomsky (1970) found that children had difficulty comprehending sentences such as *John promised Bill to leave*, interpreting Bill as the one who leaves. The verb *promise* is unusual in this respect—for instance, compare *John told Bill to leave*, which children will properly interpret.

By the time children are six, they have mastered most of their language although they continue picking up details at least until the age of ten. In that time, they have learned tens of thousands of special case rules and tens of thousands of words. Studies of the rate of word acquisition by children estimate that they are learning more than five words a day (Carey, 1978; Clark, 1983). A natural language requires more knowledge to be acquired for mastery than any of the domains of expertise we considered in Chapter 9. Of course, children also put an enormous amount of time into the language acquisition process—easily 10,000 hours must have been spent practicing speaking and understanding speech before a child is six.

◆

Children gradually approximate adult speech by producing ever larger and more complex constructions.

The Issue of Rules and the Case of Past Tense

One of the controversies in the study of language acquisition concerns the issue of whether children are learning what might be considered rules such as those that are part of linguistic theory. For instance, when the child learning English begins to inflect a verb like *kick* with *ed* to indicate past tense, is that child learning a past-tense rule or is the child just learning to associate *kick* and *ed*? The young child certainly cannot explicitly articulate the add *ed* rule, but this just may mean that this knowledge is implicit.

Some of the interesting evidence on this score concerns how children learn to deal with irregular past tenses—for instance, the past tense of *sing* is *sang*. The order in which children learn to inflect verbs to indicate past tense follows the same characteristic sequence that we noted for pluralization. First, children will use the irregular correctly, generating *sang*; then they will overgeneralize the past-tense rule and generate *singed*; finally, they will get it right for good and return to *sang*. The existence of this intermediate stage of overgeneralization has been used to argue for the existence of rules, since there is no way the child could have learned from direct experience to associate *ed* to *sing*. Rather, the argument goes, the child must be overgeneralizing a rule that has been learned.

This conventional interpretation of the acquisition of past tense has come in for a severe challenge by Rumelhart and McClelland (1986a). Using their general connectionist PDP model (see the discussion in Chapter 1), these researchers noted that connectionist nets trained on associations naturally produce such generalizations. (We discussed how such generalizations occurred with respect to the Jets and Sharks example in Figure 1.10.) They created the connectionist network illustrated in Figure 11.4 to learn the past tenses of verbs. In the network, one inputs the root form of a verb (e.g., kick, sing), and after passing through a number of layers of association, the past-tense form should appear.

The computer model was trained with a set of 420 pairs of the root with the past tense. A standard connectionist learning system was used. The model mirrored the standard developmental sequence of children, first generating correct irregulars, then overgeneralizing, and finally getting it right. It went through the intermediate stage of generating past-tense forms like *singed* because of generalization from regular past-tense forms.

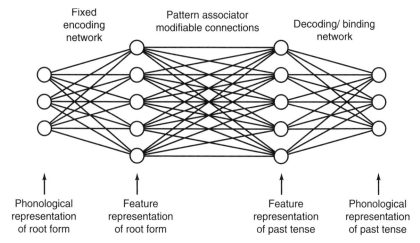

Figure 11.4 A network for past tense. The phonological representation of the root is converted into a distributed feature representation. This is converted into the distributed feature representation of the past tense, which is then mapped onto a phonological representation of the past tense. (Rumelhart & McClelland, 1986a).

With enough practice, the model, in effect, memorized the past-tense forms and was not using generalization. Rumelhart and McClelland concluded:

> We have, we believe, provided a distinct alternative to the view that children learn the rules of English past-tense formation in any explicit sense. We have shown that a reasonable account of the acquisition of past tense can be provided without recourse to the notion of a "rule" as anything more than a description of the language. We have shown that, for this case, there is no induction problem. The child need not figure out what the rules are, nor even that there are rules. (p. 267)

Their claims drew a major counterresponse from Pinker and Prince (1988). Pinker and Prince pointed out that the ability to produce the initial stage of correct irregulars depended on Rumelhart and McClelland's using a disproportionately large number of irregulars at first—more so than the child experiences. They had a number of other criticisms of the model, including the fact that it sometimes produced utterances that children never produce—for instance, it produced *membled* as the past tense of *mail*.

Another of their criticisms had to do with whether it was even possible to really learn past tense as the process of associating root form with past-tense form. It turns out that the way a verb is inflected for past tense does not just depend on its root form but also on its meaning. For instance, the word *ring* has two meanings as a verb—to make a sound or to encircle. Although it is the same root, the past tense of the first is *rang*, whereas the past tense of the latter is *ringed*, as in

- He rang the bell.
- They ringed the fort with soldiers.

It is unclear how fundamental any of these criticisms are, and there are now a number of more adequate attempts to come up with such connectionist models (e.g., MacWhinney & Leinbach, 1991; Daugherty, MacDonald, Petersen, & Seidenberg, 1993, and for a rejoinder see Marcus, Brinkman, Clahsen, Wiese, Woest, & Pinker, 1995).

Marslen-Wilson and Tyler (1998) argue that the debate between rule-based and associative accounts will not be settled by just focusing on children's language acquisition. They suggest that more decisive evidence will come from examining properties of the neural system that implements adult processing of past tense. They cite two sorts of such evidence, which seem to converge in their implications about the nature of the processing of past tense. First, they cite evidence from patients with aphasias (which are deficits in linguistic processing resulting from brain injury—see Chapter 1). They show that some patients have deficient processing of regular past tense, while others have deficient processing of irregular past tenses. The patients with deficient processing of regular past tense have severe damage to Broca's area, which is generally associated with syntactic processing. In contrast, the patients with deficient processing of irregular past tenses have damage to their temporal lobes, which are generally associated with associative learning. Secondly, they cite the PET imaging data of Jaeger, Lockwood, Kemmerer, Valin, Murphy, and Khalak (1996) studying the processing of past tense by unimpaired adults. Jaeger et al. found activation in the region of Broca's area only in the processing of regular past tense and found temporal activation during the processing of irregular past tenses. Based on the data, Marslen-Wilson and Tyler conclude that regular past tense may be processed in a rule-based manner while the irregular may be processed in an associative manner.

◆

Irregular past tenses are produced associatively, and there is debate about whether regular past tenses are produced associatively or by rules.

Quality of Input

An important difference between children's first-language acquisition and the acquisition of many skills (including typical second-language acquisition) is that children receive little if any instruction in acquiring their first language. Thus, the child's task is one of inducing the structure of natural language from listening to parents, caretakers, and older children. In addition to not receiving any direct instruction, the child does not get much information about what are incorrect forms in natural language. Many parents do not correct their children's speech at all, and those who do correct their children's speech appear to do so without any effect. Consider this following famous interaction recorded between a parent and a child (McNeill, 1966):

Child: Nobody don't like me.
Mother: No, say "Nobody likes me."
Child: Nobody don't like me.
Mother: No, say "Nobody likes me."
Child: Nobody don't like me.

[dialogue repeated eight times]

Mother: Now listen carefully, say "Nobody likes me."
Child: Oh! Nobody don't likeS me.

This lack of negative information is puzzling to theorists of natural language acquisition. We have seen that children's early speech is full of errors. If they are never told about their errors, why do children ever abandon these incorrect ways of speaking and adopt the correct forms?

Since children do not get much instruction on the nature of language and ignore most of what they get, their learning task is one of induction — they must infer from the utterances they hear what are the acceptable utterances in their language. This is a very difficult task under the best of conditions, and children often do not operate under the best of conditions. For instance, children hear ungrammatical sentences mixed in with the grammatical. How are they to avoid being misled by these sentences? Some parents and caregivers are careful to make their utterances to children simple and clear. This kind of speech involving short sentences with exaggerated intonation is called motherese (Snow and Ferguson, 1977). However, all children do not receive the benefit of such speech, and still all children learn their native languages. Some parents only speak to their children in adult sentences, and the children learn (Kaluli, studied by Schieffelin, 1979), and other parents do not speak to their children at all and still the children learn by overhearing adults speak (Piedmont Carolinas, studied by Heath, 1983). Moreover, among more typical parents there is no correlation between degree to which motherese is used and rate of linguistic developments (Gleitman, Newport, & Gleitman, 1984). So the quality of the input cannot be that critical.

Another curious fact is that children appear to be capable of learning a language in the absence of any input. Goldin-Meadow, Butcher, Mylander, and Dodge (1994) studied a deaf child who had speaking parents who chose to teach him by the oral method. It is very difficult for deaf children to learn to speak but quite easy for children to learn sign language, which is a perfectly fine language. Despite the fact that this child's parents were not teaching him sign language, he proceeded to invent his own sign language to communicate with his parents. In his invented language, he had nouns and verbs, and he created his own inflections to indicate syntactic roles. Thus, it appears likely children are born with a propensity to communicate and will learn a language no matter what.

The very fact that young children learn a language so successfully in almost all circumstances has been used to argue that the way we learn language must be in some way different from the way we learn other cognitive skills. It is also pointed out that children learn their first language successfully at a point in development when their general intellectual abilities are still weak.

◆

Children master language at a very young age and with little direct instruction.

A Critical Period for Language Acquisition

A related argument has to do with the claim that young children appear to acquire a second language much faster than older children or adults. It is claimed that there is a certain critical period, from two to about eleven years of age, when it is easiest to learn a language. Until the last couple of decades, the claim that children learn second languages more readily was based on informal observations of children of various ages and of adults in new linguistic communities, for example, when families are moved to a foreign country in response to a corporate assignment or when immigrants come to a country permanently. Young children are said to acquire a facility to get along in the new language more quickly than older children or adults. However, there are a great many differences among adults versus the older children versus younger children in terms of amount of linguistic exposure, type of exposure (e.g., whether stocks, history, or Nintendo are being discussed), and willingness to try to learn (McLaughlin, 1978; Nida, 1971). In careful studies in which situations have been selected that controlled for these factors, a positive relationship is exhibited between children's ages and rate of language development (Ervin-Tripp, 1974). That is, older children (older than 11 years) learn faster than younger children.

Even though older children and adults may learn a new language more rapidly than younger children initially, they seem not to acquire the same level of final mastery of the fine points of language, such as the phonology and morphology (Lieberman, 1984; Newport, 1986). For instance, the ability to speak a second language without an accent severely deteriorates with age (Oyama, 1978). In one study, Johnson and Newport (1989) looked at the degree of proficiency in speaking English achieved by Koreans and Chinese as a function of the age at which they arrived in America. They all had been in the United States for about ten years. Figure 11.5 shows the relationship between age of arrival and performance on an aggregate test of

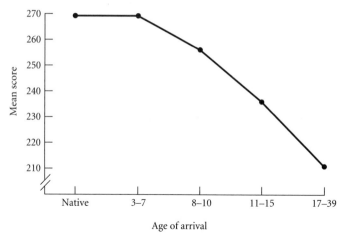

Figure 11.5 The relationship between age of arrival in the United States and total score correct on the test of English grammar. (Johnson & Newport, 1989. Reprinted by permission from Academic Press.)

mastery of English grammar. As can be seen, there is a decline in ultimate performance for people who came to America after about the ages of 8 to 10. Thus, while it is not true that language learning is fastest for the youngest, it is true that the greatest eventual mastery of the fine points of language will be achieved by those who start very young.

Most studies on the effect of age of acquisition have naturally involved second languages. However, an interesting study of first-language acquisition has been performed by Newport and Supalla (1990). They looked at the acquisition of American sign language, one of the few languages that is acquired as a first language in adolescence or adulthood. Deaf children of speaking parents are sometimes not exposed to the sign language until late in life and consequently acquire no language in their early years. Adults who acquire sign language achieve a poorer ultimate mastery of it than children.

◆

At about the age of ten, children start losing the ability to acquire a new language to high levels of proficiency.

Language Universals

Chomsky (1965) has argued that special innate mechanisms underlie the acquisition of language. Specifically, his claim is that the number of formal possibilities for a natural language is so great that learning the language would simply be impossible unless we possessed some innate information about the possible forms of natural human languages. It is possible to prove formally that Chomsky is correct in his claim. While the formal analysis is beyond the scope of this book, an analogy might help. In Chomsky's view, the problem that child learners face is to discover the grammar of their language when only given instances of utterances of the language. The task can be compared to trying to find a matching sock (language) from a pile of socks. One can use various features (utterances) of the sock in hand to determine if any particular sock in the pile is the matching one. If the pile of socks is big enough and the socks are similar enough, this would prove an impossible task. Likewise, enough formally possible grammars are similar enough to one another to make impossible the learning of any formal language. However, since language learning obviously occurs, we must, according to Chomsky, have special innate knowledge that allows us to restrict substantially the number of possible grammars we have to consider. In the sock analogy, this would be like knowing ahead of time which part of the pile to inspect.

Chomsky proposes that **language universals** exist, which limit the possible characteristics of a natural language and a natural grammar. He assumes that children can learn a natural language because they possess innate knowledge of these language universals. A language that violated these universals would simply be unlearnable. This means that there are hypothetical languages that no humans could learn. Languages that humans can learn are referred to as **natural languages**.

As noted above, we can prove formally that Chomsky's assertion is correct—that is, constraints on the possible forms of a natural language must exist. However, the critical issue is whether these constraints reflect any linguistic-specific knowledge on the part of children or whether they simply reflect general cognitive constraints on learning mechanisms. Chomsky would argue that the constraints are language-specific. It is this claim that is open to serious question. Stated as a question the issue is: Are the constraints on the form of natural languages universals of language or universals of cognition?

In speaking of language universals, Chomsky is concerned with a competence grammar. Recall that a competence analysis is concerned with an abstract specification of what a speaker knows about a language; in contrast, a performance analysis is concerned with the way a speaker uses language. Thus, Chomsky is claiming that children possess innate constraints about the types of phrase structures and transformations that might be found in a natural language. Because of the abstract, nonperformance-based character of these purported universals, one cannot simply evaluate Chomsky's claim by observing the details of acquisition of any particular language. Rather, the strategy is to look for properties that are true of all languages or of the acquisition of all languages. These universal properties would be the reflection of the language universals that Chomsky postulates.

Although languages can be quite different from one another, some clear uniformities, or near-uniformities, exist. For instance, as we saw earlier, virtually no language favors the word order object-before-subject. However, as we noted, this constraint appears to have a cognitive explanation (as do many other limits on language form).

Often, the uniformities among languages seem so natural that we do not realize that other possibilities might exist. One such language universal is that adjectives occur near the nouns they modify. Thus, we translate *The brave woman hit the cruel man* into French as

- La femme brave a frappé l'homme cruel

and not as

- La femme cruel a frappé l'homme brave

although a language in which the adjective beside the subject noun modified the object noun and vice versa would be logically possible. However, it is clear that such a language design would be absurd in terms of its cognitive demands. It would require that listeners hold the adjectives from the beginning of the sentence until the noun at the end. No natural language has this perverse structure. If it really needed showing, I have shown with artificial languages that adult subjects were unable to learn such a language (Anderson, 1978b). Thus, many of the universals of language seem cognitive in origin and so do not really support Chomsky's position. In the next subsections, we will consider some universals that seem more language-specific.

◆
There are universal constraints on the kinds of languages that humans can learn.

The Constraints on Transformations

There are a set of peculiar constraints on movement transformations (refer back to the subsection on Transformations on page 366) that have been used to argue for the existence of linguistic universals. One of the more extensively discussed of these is called the A-over-A constraint. Compare sentence 1 with sentence 2:

1. Which woman did John meet who knows the senator?

2. Which senator did John meet the woman who knows?

Linguists would consider sentence 1 to be acceptable but not sentence 2. Sentence 1 can be derived by a transformation from sentence 3 below. This transformation moves *which woman* forward:

3. John met which woman who knows the senator?

4. John met the woman who knows which senator?

Sentence 2 can be derived by a similar transformation operating on *which senator* in sentence 4, but apparently such a transformation cannot move a noun phrase like *which senator* if it is embedded within another noun phrase (in this case, *which senator* is part of the clause modifying *the woman* and so is part of the noun phrase associated with *the woman*). Transformations can move deeply embedded nouns if these nouns are not in clauses modifying other nouns. So, for instance, sentence 5, which is acceptable, is derived transformationally from sentence 6:

5. Which senator does Mary believe that Bill said that John likes?

6. Mary believes that Bill said that John likes which senator?

Thus, we see that there is a very arbitrary constraint on the transformation that forms *which* questions. It can apply to any embedded noun unless that noun is part of another noun phrase. The arbitrariness of this constraint makes it hard to imagine how a child would ever figure it out—unless the child already knew it as a universal of language. Certainly, the child is never explicitly told this fact about language.

The existence of such constraints on the form of language offers a challenge to any theory of language acquisition. They are so peculiar that it is hard to imagine how they could be learned unless the child were especially prepared to deal with them.

◆

There are rather arbitrary constraints on the movements that transformations can produce.

Parameter Setting

With all this discussion about language universals, one might get the impression that all languages are basically alike. Far from it. On many dimensions, the languages of the world are radically different. There are some abstract properties, such as the A-over-A constraint, that they might have in common, but there are many properties on which they differ. We have already mentioned how different languages prefer different orders for subject, verb, and object. Languages also differ in how strict they are about word order. English is very strict, but some highly inflected languages, such as Finnish, allow people to say their sentences with almost any word order they choose. There are languages that do not mark verbs for tense and languages that do mark verbs for the flexibility of the thing being acted upon.

Another example of a difference, which has been a focus of discussion, is that some languages, such as Italian or Spanish, are what are called *pro-drop* languages: they allow one to optionally drop the pronoun when it appears in the subject position. Thus, while in English we would say *I go to the cinema tonight*, Italians can say *Vado al cinema stasera* and Spaniards *Voy al cine esta noche*—in both cases just starting with the verb and omitting the first-person pronoun. It has been argued that pro-drop is a parameter on which natural languages vary, and, while children cannot be born knowing whether their language is pro-drop or not, they can be born knowing it is one way or the other. Thus, knowledge that the pro-drop parameter exists is one of the purported universals of natural language.

Knowledge of a parameter like pro-drop is useful because a number of features are determined by it. For instance, if a language is not pro-drop, it requires what are called expletive pronouns. In English, a non-pro-drop language, the expletive pronouns are *it* and *there* when they are used in sentences such as *It is raining* or *There is no money*. English requires these rather semantically empty pronouns since by definition a non-pro-drop language cannot have empty slots in the subject position. Pro-drop languages such as Spanish and Italian lack such empty pronouns because they are not needed.

Hyams (1986) has argued that children starting to learn any language, including English, will treat it as a pro-drop language and optionally drop pronouns even though this may not be correct in the adult language. She notes that young children learning English tend to omit subjects. They will also not use expletive pronouns, even when they are part of the adult language. When children in a non-pro-drop language start using expletive pronouns, they simultaneously stop optionally dropping pronouns in the subject position. Hyams argues that this is the point at which they learn that their language is not a pro-drop language. For further discussion of Hyams's proposal and alternative formulations, read Bloom (1994).

It is argued that much of the variability among natural languages can be accommodated by setting a hundred or so parameters, such as the pro-drop parameter, and that a major part of learning a language is learning the setting of these parameters (of course, there is a lot more to be learned than just this—for instance, an enormous vocabulary). This theory of language acquisition is called the **parameter setting** proposal. It is quite controversial, but it provides us with one picture of what it might mean for a child to be prepared to learn a language with innate, language-specific knowledge.

◆
It has been proposed that learning the structure of language involves learning the setting of one hundred or so parameters on which natural languages vary.

The Uniqueness of Language: A Summary

With respect to the issue of whether language is really a system different from other human cognitive systems, it is fair to say that the jury is still out. The status of language is a major issue for cognitive psychology. The issue will be resolved by empirical and theoretical efforts more detailed than those reviewed in this chapter. The ideas here have served to define the context for the investigation. The next chapter will review the current state of our knowledge about the details of language comprehension. Careful experimental research on such topics will finally resolve the question of the uniqueness of language.

Remarks and Suggested Readings

There are a number of textbooks on the psychology of language, sometimes called psycholinguistics. Two "classics" are Clark and Clark (1977) and Fodor, Bever, and Garrett (1974). More recent books include Gernsbacher (1993), Gleason and Ratner (1993), Osherson and Lasnik (1990), Singer (1990), and Taylor and Taylor (1990). Pinker (1994) has written a popular discussion of language. Gernsbacher (1994) edited a set of articles reviewing research in psycholinguistics.

12

Language
Comprehension

A favorite device in science fiction is the computer or robot that can
understand and speak language—whether evil, like HAL in *2001,* or
beneficient, like C3PO in *Star Wars.* Workers in artificial intelligence have
been trying to develop computers that understand and generate language.
Progress is being made, but it is clear that Stanley Kubrick was incorrect
when he projected HAL for the year 2001. An enormous amount of knowledge and intelligence underlies the successful use of language. This chapter
will look at language use and, in particular, at language comprehension (as
distinct from language generation). In choosing this focus, we are choosing
to look where the light is—more is known about language comprehension
than language generation.

In discussing language comprehension, we will be treating comprehension as it is involved in both listening and reading. It is often thought that

of the two, the listening process is the more basic. However, it seems that many of the same factors are involved in both listening and reading. Researchers' choice of whether to use written or spoken material is determined by considerations of experimental tractability. More often than not, this has meant presenting subjects with written material.

Comprehension can be analyzed into three stages. The first stage comprises the perceptual processes by which the acoustic or written message is originally encoded. The second stage is termed the *parsing* stage. **Parsing** is the process by which the words in the message are transformed into a mental representation of the combined meaning of the words. The third stage is the **utilization** stage, in which comprehenders actually use the mental representation of the sentence's meaning. If the sentence is an assertion, listeners may simply store the meaning in memory; if it is a question, they may answer; if it is an instruction, they may obey. However, listeners are not always so compliant. They may use an assertion about the weather to make an inference about the speaker's personality, they may answer a question with a question, or they may do just the opposite of what the speaker asks. These three stages—perception, parsing, and utilization—are by necessity partially ordered in time; however, they also partly overlap. Listeners can be making inferences from the first part of a sentence while they are already perceiving a later part. This chapter will focus on the two higher-level processes—parsing and utilization. (The perceptual stage was already discussed in Chapter 2.)

◆

Comprehension involves a perceptual stage, followed by a parsing stage, followed by a utilization stage.

Parsing

Constituent Structure

Language is structured according to a set of rules that tell us how to go from a particular string of words to an interpretation of that string's meaning. For instance, in English we know that if we hear a sequence of the form *A noun action a noun*, the speaker means that an instance of the first noun performed the action on an instance of the second noun. In contrast, if the sentence is of the form *A noun was action by a noun,* the speaker means that an instance of the second noun performed the action on an instance of the first noun. Thus, our knowledge of the structure of English allows us to appreciate the difference between *A doctor shot a lawyer* and *A doctor was shot by a lawyer.*

In learning to comprehend a language, we acquire a great many rules that encode the various linguistic patterns in the language and relate these patterns to meaning interpretations. However, we cannot possibly learn rules for every possible sentence pattern—sentences can be very long and complex. A very large (probably infinite) number of patterns would be required to encode all possible sentence forms. Although we have not learned to interpret all possible full sentence patterns, we have learned to interpret subpatterns, or phrases, of these sentences and to combine, or concatenate, the interpretations of these subpatterns. These subpatterns correspond to basic phrases, or units, in a sentence's structure. These phrase units are also referred to as **constituents**. In the previous chapter, we discussed the evidence for the psychological reality of such phrase structure in language generation. Below, we review some of the evidence for the psychological reality of this constituent structure in comprehension.

We might expect that the more clearly identifiable the constituent structure of a sentence is, the more easily understandable the sentence would be. Graf and Torrey (1966) presented sentences to subjects a line at a time. The passages could be presented in form A, in which each line corresponded with a major constituent boundary, or in form B, in which this was not the case. Examples of the two types of passages follow:

Form A	*Form B*
During World War II,	During World War
even fantastic schemes	II even fantastic
received consideration	schemes received
if they gave promise	consideration if they gave
of shortening the conflict.	promise of shortening the conflict.

Subjects showed better comprehension of passages in form A. This finding demonstrates that the identification of constituent structure is important to the parsing of a sentence.

When people read such passages, they naturally pause at boundaries between clauses. Aaronson and Scarborough (1977) asked subjects to read sentences word by word displayed on a computer screen. Subjects would press the key each time they wanted to read another word. Figure 12.1 illustrates the pattern of reading times for a sentence that subjects were reading for later recall. Notice the U-shaped patterns with prolonged pauses at the phrase boundaries. It appears that with the completion of each major phrase, subjects need time to process it.

Once one has processed a constituent or phrase, there is no need to make further reference to the exact words of the constituent. This is because such constituents are natural units of meaning, and the interpretation of the words can be completed by the end of the constituent. Thus, we would predict that subjects will show poorer memory for the exact wording of a constituent after it has been parsed and the parsing of another constituent has begun. An experiment by Jarvella (1971) confirms this predic-

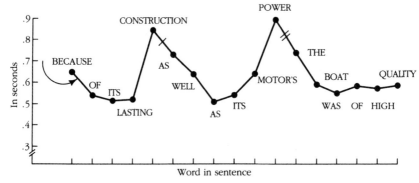

Figure 12.1 Word-by-word reading times for a sample sentence. The short-line markers on the graphs indicate breaks between phrase structures. (From Aaronson & Scarborough, 1977.)

tion. He read subjects passages that were interrupted at various points. At the points of interruption, subjects were instructed to write down as much of the passage as they could remember. Of interest were passages that ended with thirteen-word sentences such as the following:

1	2	3	4	5	6	
Having	failed	to	disprove	the	charges,	

7	8	9	10	11	12	13
Taylor	was	later	fired	by	the	president.

After hearing the last word, subjects were prompted with the first word of the sentence and asked to recall the remaining words. Each sentence was composed of a six-word subordinate clause followed by a seven-word main clause. Figure 12.2 plots the probability of recall for each of the remaining twelve words in the sentence (excluding the first, which was used as a prompt). Note the sharp rise in the function at word 7, the beginning of the main clause. These data show that subjects have best memory for the last major constituent, a result consistent with the hypothesis that they retain a verbatim representation of the last constituent only.

An experiment by Caplan (1972) also presents evidence for the use of constituent structure, but this study uses a reaction-time methodology. Subjects were presented aurally first with a sentence and then with a probe word; they then had to indicate as quickly as possible whether the probe word was in the sentence. Caplan contrasted pairs of sentences such as the following:

1. Now that artists are working fewer hours oil prints are rare.

2. Now that artists are working in oil prints are rare.

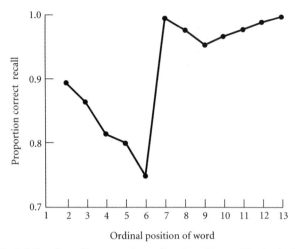

Figure 12.2 Probability of recalling a word as a function of its position in the last twelve words in a passage. (Adapted from Jarvella, 1971.)

Interest focused on how quickly subjects would recognize *oil* in these two sentences when probed at the ends of the sentences. The sentences were cleverly constructed so that in both sentences the word *oil* was fourth from the end and was followed by the same words. In fact, by splicing tape, Caplan arranged the presentation so that subjects heard the same recording of these last four words whichever full sentence they heard. However, in sentence 1 *oil* is part of the last constituent, *oil prints are rare,* whereas in sentence 2 it is part of the first constituent, *now that artists are working in oil.* Caplan predicted that subjects would recognize *oil* more quickly in sentence 1 because they would still have active in memory a representation of this constituent. As he predicted, the probe word was recognized more rapidly if it occurred in the last constituent.

◆ ──

Subjects process the meaning of a sentence a phrase at a time and maintain access to a phrase only while processing its meaning.

──

Immediacy of Interpretation

One of the important principles to emerge in studies of language processing is called the principle of **immediacy of interpretation**. Basically, this principle says that people try to extract as much meaning out of each word as it arrives, and they do not wait until the ends of sentences or even the ends of phrases to decide on how to interpret a word. For instance, Just and Carpenter (1980) studied the eye movements of subjects as they read a sentence. While reading a sentence, subjects will typically fixate on almost every word. Just and Carpenter find that the time subjects spend fixating

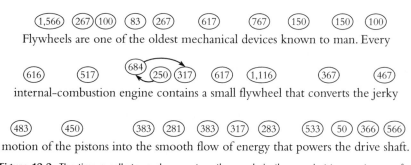

Figure 12.3 The time a college reader spent on the words in the opening two sentences of a technical article about flywheels. The times, indicated above the fixated word, are expressed in milliseconds. This reader read the sentences from left to right with one regressive fixation to an earlier part. (Adapted from Just & Carpenter, 1980.)

on a word is basically proportional to the amount of information provided by the word. Thus, if a sentence contains a relatively unfamiliar or a surprising word, subjects pause on that word. They also pause longer at the end of the phrase involving that word. Figure 12.3 illustrates the eye fixations of one of their college students reading a scientific passage. Gazes within each sentence are indicated by circles above the point where the gaze occurred. The order of the gazes is left to right except for the three gazes above *engine contains*, where the order of gazes is indicated. Note that unimportant function words like *the* and *to* may be skipped, and if not skipped, receive relatively little processing. Note the amount of time spent on the word *flywheels*. The subject is not waiting until the end of the sentence to think about this word. Again, look at the amount of time spent on the highly informative adjective *mechanical*—the subject is not waiting until the end of the noun phrase to think about it.

This immediacy of processing implies that we will begin to attribute an interpretation to the sentence even before we encounter the main verb. This certainly is the experience of speakers of languages such as German, which tend to have the verb in the final position. It is also the experience in English in those rare constructions in which the verb is put last. Consider what happens as we process the following sentence:

- It was the president whom the terrorist from the Middle East shot.

Before we get to *shot* we have already built up a partial model of what might be happening between the president and the terrorist.

If people do process a sentence as each word comes in, it might seem strange that we reviewed so much evidence for the importance of phrase structure boundaries. What this evidence reflects is just the fact that the meaning of a sentence is defined in terms of the phrase structure, and even if listeners try to extract all they can from each word, there will be some things that they are only able to put into place when they reach the end of a phrase. Thus, people will pause at a phrase boundary because some of the information cannot be processed until the phrase is complete. People have to maintain a representation of the current phrase in memory because their interpretation of it may be wrong, and they may have to reinterpret the beginning of the phrase. Manipulations like those of Graf and Torrey are important because they signal the end of the phrase, perceptually, to the reader. Just and Carpenter in their study of reading times found that subjects tend to spend extra time at the end of each phrase wrapping up the meaning conveyed by that phrase. While Figure 12.3 is just one subject's reading and has idiosyncratic complications, it does contain some evidence for wrap-up times. For instance, the various noun phrases like "the oldest mechanical devices," "a small flywheel," and "the drive shafts" all have a longer pause over the last noun.

◆

In processing a sentence, we try to extract as much information as possible from each word and spend some additional wrap-up time at the end of each phrase.

The Use of Syntactic Cues

The basic task in parsing a sentence is to combine the meanings of the individual words to come up with some meaning for the overall sentence. Two basic sources of information can guide us in this task. One is word order. Thus, the following two sentences, although they have identical words, have very different meanings:

- The dog bit the cat.
- The cat bit the dog.

Another cue to sentence meaning comes from the use of function words, such as *a* and *who*, which are important to parsing because they signal the various types of constituents, such as noun phrase or relative clause. Consider the following set of sentences:

1. The boy whom the girl liked was sick.

2. The boy the girl liked was sick.

3. The boy the girl and the dog were sick.

Sentences 1 and 2 are equivalent except that in 2 *whom* is deleted. Sentence 2 is a shorter sentence, but the cost of shortening is the loss of a cue as to the way the sentence should be analyzed. At the point of *The boy the girl,* it is ambiguous whether we have a relative clause, as in sentence 1, or a conjunction, as in sentence 3. If it is true that function words such as *whom* are used to indicate how to parse the sentence, then constructions such as sentence 2 should be more difficult to parse than those similar to sentence 1.

Hakes and Foss (1970; Hakes, 1972) tested this prediction using what has been called the phoneme-monitoring task. They used double-embedded sentences such as the following:

4. The zebra which the lion that the gorilla chased killed was running.

5. The zebra the lion the gorilla chased killed was running.

Sentence 5 lacks the relative pronouns and so is easily confused with sentences having a noun-conjunction structure. Subjects were required to perform two simultaneous tasks. One task was to comprehend and paraphase the sentence. The second task was to listen for a particular phoneme—in this case a [g] (in gorilla).

Hakes and Foss predicted that the more difficult a sentence was to comprehend, the more time subjects would take to detect the target phoneme, since they would have less attention left over from the comprehension task with which to perform the monitoring. In fact, the prediction was borne out; subjects did take longer to indicate hearing [g] when presented with sentences such as sentence 5, which lacked relative pronouns.

The dominant syntactic cue in English is word order. For instance, a person appearing before an action verb is usually the agent. Other languages rely less on word order and instead use inflections of words to indicate semantic role. There is a small remnant of such an inflectional system in some English pronouns. For instance, *he* versus *him,* *I* versus *me,* and so on, signal agent versus object. McDonald (1984) compared English with German, which has a richer inflectional system. She asked her English subjects to interpret sentences such as

6. Him kicked the girl.

7. The girl kicked he.

The word order cue in these sentences suggests one interpretation while the inflection cue suggests an alternative interpretation. English speakers use the word order cue, interpreting sentence 6 with *him* as the agent and the *girl* as the object. German speakers, judging comparable sentences in German, do just the opposite. Interestingly, bilingual speakers of both German and English tend to interpret the English sentences more like German sentences—i.e., assigning *him* in sentence 6 to the object role and *girl* to the agent role.

◆

Comprehenders use the syntactic cues of word order and inflection to help interpret a sentence.

Semantic Considerations

It is clear that people use syntactic patterns, such as those illustrated above, for understanding sentences, but they can also make use of the meanings of the words involved. An individual can determine the meaning of a string of words simply by considering how they can be put together in order to make sense. Thus, when Tarzan says, *Jane fruit eat,* we know what he means even though this sentence does not correspond to the syntax of English. We realize that a relationship is being asserted between someone capable of eating and something edible.

Considerable evidence suggests that people use such semantic strategies in language comprehension. Strohner and Nelson (1974) had two- and three-year-old children act out with animal dolls the following two sentences:

- The cat chased the mouse.

- The mouse chased the cat.

In both cases, the children interpreted the sentence to indicate that the cat chased the mouse, a meaning that corresponded to their prior knowledge about cats and mice. Thus, these young children were relying more heavily on semantic patterns than on syntactic patterns.

Fillenbaum (1971, 1974) had adults paraphrase sentences, among which were "perverse" items such as

- John was buried and died.

More than 60 percent of the subjects paraphrased the sentences in a way that gave them a more conventional meaning; for example, that John died first and then was buried. However, the normal syntactic interpretation of such constructions would be that the first activity occurred before the second, as in

- John had a drink and went to the party.

as opposed to

- John went to the party and had a drink.

So it seems that when a semantic principle is placed in conflict with a syntactic principle, the semantic principle will sometimes (but not always) determine the interpretation of the sentence.

Sometimes people rely on the plausible semantic interpretation of words in a sentence.

Integration of Syntax and Semantics

It appears that a listener combines both syntactic and semantic information in comprehending a sentence. Tyler and Marslen-Wilson (1977) asked subjects to try to continue fragments such as

1. If you walk too near the runway, landing planes are

2. If you've been trained as a pilot, landing planes are

The phrase *landing planes,* by itself, is ambiguous. It can mean either "planes that are landing" or "to land planes." Followed by the plural verb *are,* however, it must have the first meaning. Thus, the syntactic constraints determine a meaning for the ambiguous phrase. The prior context in fragment 1 is consistent with this meaning, whereas the prior context in fragment 2 is not. Subjects took less time to continue 1, which suggests that they were using both the semantics of the prior context and the syntax of the current phrase to disambiguate *landing planes.* When these factors are in conflict, the subject's comprehension is hurt.[1]

Bates, McNew, MacWhinney, Devesocvi, and Smith (1982) looked at the issue of combining syntax and semantics in a different paradigm. They had subjects interpret word strings such as

- Chased the dog the eraser

If you were forced to, what meaning would you assign to this word string? The syntactic fact that objects follow verbs seems to imply that it was the dog who was being chased and the eraser that did the chasing. The semantics, however, suggest the opposite. In fact, American speakers prefer to go with the syntax, but sometimes will adopt the semantic interpretation— that is, most say *The eraser chased the dog,* but some say *The dog chased the eraser.* On the other hand, if the word string is

- Chased the eraser the dog

---

[1]The original Tyler and Marslen-Wilson experiment drew methodological criticisms from Townsend and Bever (1982) and Cowart (1983). For a response, read Marslen-Wilson and Tyler (1987).

listeners agree on the interpretation—that is, that *the dog chased the eraser.*

Another interesting part of the study by Bates et al. compared Americans with Italians. When syntactic cues were put in conflict with semantic cues, Italians tended to go with the semantic cues, whereas Americans preferred the syntactic cues. The most critical case concerned sentences such as

- The eraser bites the dog

or its Italian translation:

- La gomma morde il cane

Americans almost always followed the syntax and interpreted this sentence to mean that the eraser is doing the biting. In contrast, Italians preferred to use the semantics and interpret that the dog is doing the biting. Like English, however, Italian has a subject-verb-object syntax.

Thus, we see that listeners combine both syntactic and semantic cues in interpreting the sentence. Moreover, the weighting of these two types of cues can vary from language to language. This and other evidence indicates that speakers of Italian weight semantic cues more heavily than do speakers of English.

◆
People integrate both semantic and syntactic cues to come up with an interpretation for a sentence.

Neural Indicants of Syntactic and Semantic Processing

ERP studies (see Chapter 1) have found evidence for separate processing of semantics and syntax in what are called the N400 and P600 waves. The N400 wave (Kutas and Hillyard, 1980a, b) occurs when subjects hear a semantically anomalous sentence like "He spread the warm bread with socks." About 400 milliseconds after the anomalous word (socks) ERP recordings show a large negative amplitude shift. On the other hand, there is evidence for what is called the P600 wave in response to syntactic violations. For instance, Osterhout and Holcomb (1992) presented their subjects with sentences like "The broker persuaded to sell the stock" and found a positive wave at about 600 milliseconds after the word *to* which violated the syntax.

Ainsworth-Darnell, Shulman, and Boland (1998) studied how these two effects combined when subjects heard sentences like

Control: Jill entrusted the recipe to friends before she suddenly disappeared.

Syntactic Anomaly: Jill entrusted the recipe friends before she suddenly disappeared.

Semantic Anomaly: Jill entrusted the recipe to platforms before she suddenly disappeared.

Double Anomaly: Jill entrusted the recipe platforms before she suddenly disappeared.

The last sentence combines a semantic and a syntactic anomaly. Figure 12.4 contrasts the ERP waveforms obtained to the various types of sentences from midline versus parietal sites. An arrow in the ERPs points to the onset of the critical word (*friends* or *platforms*). The two types of sentences that

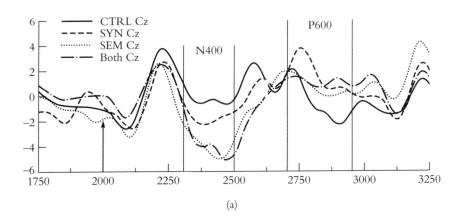

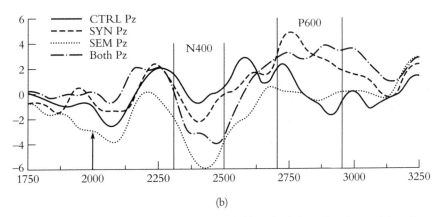

Figure 12.4 ERP recordings from (a) central and (b) parietal sites. (From Ainsworth-Darnell, Shulman, & Boland, 1998.) The arrows point to the onset of the critical word.

involved a semantic anomaly evoked a negative shift at the midline site about 400 milliseconds after the critical word. In contrast, the two types of sentences that involved a semantic anomaly were associated with a positive shift in the parietal area about 600 milliseconds after the onset of the critical word. Ainsworth et al. use the fact that each process—syntactic and semantic—comes from a different brain region to argue that the syntactic and semantic processes are separable.

◆

ERP recordings indicate different responses in different locations to syntactic versus semantic violations.

Ambiguity

Many sentences can be interpreted in two or more ways because of either ambiguous words or ambiguous syntactic constructions. Examples of such sentences are the following:

- John went to the bank.

- Flying planes can be dangerous.

It is also useful to distinguish between transient ambiguity and permanent ambiguity. The examples above are permanently ambiguous. That is, the ambiguity remains to the end of the sentence. **Transient ambiguity** refers to ambiguity that occurs in a sentence but is resolved by the end of the sentence, for example:

- The old train the young.

Following the word *train*, it is unclear whether *old* is a noun or an adjective. The sentence could have continued to yield a sentence in which *train* was a noun:

- The old train left the station.

This ambiguity is resolved by the end of the sentence.

Transient ambiguity is quite prevalent in language, and it leads to a serious interaction with the principle of immediacy of processing that we described earlier. Immediacy of processing implies that we need to commit to an interpretation of a word or a phrase right away, but transient ambiguity implies that we cannot always know the correct interpretation immediately. Consider the sentence:

- The horse raced past the barn fell.

Most people experience a double take on this sentence: they first read one interpretation and then a second. Such sentences are called **garden-path sentences** because we commit to one interpretation at a certain point only to discover that it is wrong at another point. For instance, in the sentence above most readers interpret *raced* as the main verb of the sentence. The existence of such garden-path sentences is considered to be one of the important pieces of evidence for the principle of immediacy of interpretation. People could postpone interpreting such sentences at points of ambiguity until the ambiguity is resolved, but they do not.

When one comes upon a point of syntactic ambiguity in a sentence, what determines its interpretation? A powerful principle seems to be what is called the **principle of minimal attachment**. This principle basically says that one interprets a sentence in a way that involves minimal complication to its phrase structure. Since all sentences must have a main verb, this means that the simpler interpretation would be to include *raced* in the main sentence rather than creating a relative clause to modify the noun *horse*.

It is interesting that many times ambiguities occur that we are not aware of. For instance, consider the following sentence:

- The woman painted by the artist fell.

As we will see in a later subsection, people seem to have difficulty with this sentence (temporarily interpreting the woman as the one doing the painting), just like the earlier *horse raced* sentence. However, people tend not be aware of taking a garden path in the way they are with the *horse raced* sentence.

Why are we aware of a reinterpretation in some sentences, like the *horse raced* example, but not in others, like the *woman painted* example? It seems that if a syntactic ambiguity is resolved within the phrase that involves it, we are not aware of ever considering two interpretations. Only if resolution is postponed beyond the ambiguous phrase are we aware of the need to reinterpret it. Thus, in the *woman painted* example above, the ambiguity is resolved before the clause is complete, and thus most people are not aware of the ambiguity. In contrast, in the *horse raced* example, the phrase seems to successfully complete—*the horse raced past the barn*—only to be later contradicted.

◆ ───────────────────────────────────

When comprehenders come to a point of ambiguity in a sentence, they adopt one interpretation which they will have to retract if it is later contradicted.

───────────────────────────────────

Lexical Ambiguity

The preceding discussion was concerned with how subjects dealt with syntactic ambiguity. In the case of lexical ambiguity, where a single word has two meanings, there often is no structural difference in the two interpretations of the sentence, and principles like minimal attachment cannot serve to select a meaning. A series of experiments by Swinney (e.g., Swinney, 1979) has been useful in revealing how ambiguous words are disambiguated. Swinney asked subjects to listen to sentences such as the following:

- The man was not surprised when he found several spiders, roaches, and other bugs in the corner of the room.

Swinney was concerned with the ambiguous word *bugs* (meaning either insects or electronic listening devices). Just after hearing the word, subjects would be presented with a string of letters on the screen, and their task was to judge whether that string made a correct word or not. Thus, if they saw *ant*, they would say yes; but if they saw *ont*, they would say no. This is the lexical decision task that we described in Chapter 6 in discussing the mechanisms of spreading activation. Swinney was interested in the way the word *bugs* in the passage would prime the lexical judgment.

The critical contrasts involved having subjects judge words such as *spy*, *ant*, or *sew*, following *bugs*. The word *ant* is related to the primed meaning of *bugs*, while *spy* is related to the unprimed meaning. The word *sew* defines a neutral control condition. Swinney found that recognition of both *spy* and *ant* was speeded if the to-be-judged word is presented within 400 milliseconds (ms) of the prime, *bugs*. Thus, the presentation of *bugs* immediately activates both of its meanings and their associations. If Swinney waited more than 700 milliseconds, however, there was facilitation only for the related word *ant*. It appears that a correct meaning is selected in this time and the other meaning becomes deactivated. Thus, two meanings of an ambiguous word are momentarily active, but context operates very rapidly to select the appropriate meaning.

◆

When an ambiguous word is presented, subjects select a particular meaning within 700 milliseconds.

Modularity versus Interactive Processing

There are two bases by which people can disambiguate ambiguous sentences. One is by means of semantics, which is the basis for disambiguating the word *bugs* in the prior sentence. The other possibility is use of syntax. Advocates of the position of language modularity (see the discussion from the previous chapter) have argued that there is an initial phase in which we merely process syntax, and only later do we bring semantic factors to bear. Thus, initially only syntax is available for disambiguation. This is because syntax is part of a language-specific module that can operate quickly by itself. In contrast, to bring semantics to bear requires using all of one's world knowledge, and this goes far beyond anything that is language-specific. Opposing the modularity position is the **interactive processing** position, the proponents of which argue that syntax and semantics are combined at all levels of processing.

Much of the debate between these two positions has involved processing of transient syntactic ambiguity. In the initial study of what has become a long series of studies, Ferreira and Clifton (1986) asked subjects to read sentences such as

1. The woman painted by the artist was very attractive to look at.

2. The woman that was painted by the artist was very attractive to look at.

3. The sign painted by the artist was very attractive to look at.

4. The sign that was painted by the artist was very attractive to look at.

Sentences 1 and 3 are called reduced relatives because the relative pronoun *that* is missing. There is no local syntactic basis for deciding whether the noun-verb combination is a relative clause construction or an agent-action combination. Ferreira and Clifton argue that because of the principle of minimal attachment, people have a natural tendency to encode noun-verb combinations like *The woman painted* as agent-action combinations. Evidence for this is that subjects take longer to read *by the artist* in the first sentence than in the second. The reason is that they discover their agent-action interpretation is wrong in the first sentence and have to recover, while the syntactic cue *that was* in the second sentence prevents them from ever making this misinterpretation.

The real interest in the Ferreira and Clifton experiments is in sentences 3 and 4. Semantic factors should rule out the agent-action interpretation of sentence 3, since a sign cannot be an animate agent and engage in painting. Nonetheless, subjects took just as long to read *by the artist* in sentence 3 as in 1 and longer than in unambiguous 2 or 4. Thus, argue Ferreira and Clifton, subjects first use only syntactic factors and so misinterpret the phrase *The sign painted* and use the syntactic cues in the phrase *by the artist* to correct that misinterpretation. Thus, while semantic factors could have done the job and avoided the misinterpretation, it seems that subjects do all their initial processing using syntactic cues.

Experiments of this sort have been used to argue for the modularity of language. The argument is that our initial processing of language makes use of something specific to language, namely syntax, and ignores other general, nonlinguistic knowledge we have of the world, such as that signs cannot paint. However, Trueswell, Tannehaus, and Garnsey (1994) argued that many of the sentences in the Ferreira and Clifton study were not like sentence 3. Specifically, while the sentences were supposed to have a semantic basis for disambiguation, many did not. For instance, among the Ferreira and Clifton sentences were sentences like

5. The car towed from the parking lot was parked illegally.

Here *car towed* was supposed to be unambiguous, but it is possible for *car* to be the subject of *towed* as in

6. The car towed the smaller car from the parking lot.

When Trueswell et al. used sentences that avoided these problems, they found that subjects did not have any difficulty with the sentences. For instance, subjects showed no more difficulty with

7. The evidence examined by the lawyer turned out to be unreliable.

than with

8. The evidence that was examined by the lawyer turned out to be unreliable.

Thus, it does seem that people are able to select the correct interpretation when it is not semantically possible to interpret the noun (*evidence*) as an agent of the verb. Thus, the initial syntactic decisions are not made without reference to semantic factors.

Also, McRae, Spivey-Knowlton, and Tannehaus (1998) show that the relative plausibility of the noun as agent of the verb affects the difficulty of the construction. They compared the following pairs of sentences:

9. The cop arrested by the detective was guilty of taking bribes.

10. The cop that was arrested by the detective was guilty of taking bribes.

and

11. The crook arrested by the detective was guilty of taking bribes.

12. The crook that was arrested by the detective was guilty of taking bribes.

They found that subjects suffered much greater difficulty with the reduced relatives in the case of sentence 9, where the subject is plausible as the agent for arresting, than in the case of sentence 11, where it is not.

◆
Subjects appear to be able to use semantic information immediately to guide syntactic decisions.

Propositional Representation

So far, we have mainly focused on the processes by which a comprehender goes from a string of words to a meaningful interpretation of that string. We have shown that factors that affect the complexity of this interpretation (ambiguity, presence of syntactic cues) affect the comprehension process. However, it should also be the case that comprehension will be affected by the complexity of the resulting interpretation. One way to measure this is in terms of the number of propositions in the representation of its meaning. For instance, Kintsch and Keenan (1973) compared the comprehension of the following two sentences:

1. Romulus, the legendary founder of Rome, took the women of the Sabine by force.

2. Cleopatra's downfall lay in her foolish trust in the fickle political figures of the Roman world.

According to Kintsch's propositional analysis (see Chapter 5), sentence 1 consists of four propositions:

- (took, Romulus, women, by force)
- (found, Romulus, Rome)
- (legendary, Romulus)
- (Sabine, women)

Sentence 2 consists of eight propositions:

- (because, α, β)[2]
- (fell down, Cleopatra) = α
- (trust, Cleopatra, figures) = β

◆
[2] The α and β indicate that the second and third proposition occur as arguments to the first. See the discussion of the hierarchical organization of propositions on pp. 149–150.

- (foolish, trust)
- (fickle, figures)
- (political, figures)
- (part-of, figures, world)
- (Roman, world)

While these two sentences differ in number of propositions, they are similar in terms of length and other factors. Kintsch and Keenan found that subjects took longer to read the second sentence, reflecting the fact that there were more propositions to extract from it.

◆
***

Comprehension time increases with the number of propositions communicated in the sentence.

***

Utilization

Once a sentence has been parsed and mapped into a representation of its meaning, what then? A listener seldom simply passively records the meaning. If the sentence is a question or an imperative, the speaker expects the listener to take some action in response. However, even for declarative sentences there is usually more to be done than simply registering the sentence. Consider the sentence from earlier:

- Cleopatra's downfall lay in her foolish trust in the fickle political figures of the Roman world.

We indicated earlier the propositional representation that might result from a parsing of that sentence. However, it is likely that a reader in comprehending the sentence would go beyond this propositional representation. The reader might well embellish this with information about the romance of Anthony and Cleopatra, wonder if Mark Anthony was one of the political figures being referenced, elaborate on the downfall with Cleopatra's suicide, and so on. Really understanding a sentence requires making such inferences and connections. In Chapter 6, we discussed how such elaborative processing led to better memory. Here, we will discuss some of the mechanisms by which people go from the literal meaning of a sentence to something that will be useful.

In understanding a sentence, the comprehender must make a good number of inferences. Inferences require going beyond what is stated to things implied by the text. Researchers typically distinguish between what they call **backward inferences** and **forward inferences**. Backward inferences connect the current sentence with prior sentences or to general background knowledge. Forward inferences anticipate things not yet asserted. Thus, if the sentence about Cleopatra had occurred in a text where Mark Anthony had been mentioned but her suicide had not yet been discussed, then the Mark Anthony inference would be a case of a backward inference, while the suicide inference would be a case of a forward inference. As we will review in subsequent subsections, comprehenders typically make the backward inferences that are necessary to make the text coherent. However, they only sometimes make obvious forward inferences.

To illustrate the difference between forward and backward inferences, contrast the following pairs of sentences used by Singer (1994):

1. **Direct Statement:** The dentist pulled the tooth painlessly. The patient liked the method.

2. **Backward Inference:** The tooth was pulled painlessly. The dentist used a new method.

3. **Forward Inference:** The tooth was pulled painlessly. The patient liked the new method.

After all these sentence pairs subjects were asked whether it was true that *A dentist pulled the tooth.* This is explicitly stated in the case of 1, but it is also highly probable in the case of 2 and 3 even though it is not stated. The inference that the dentist pulled the tooth in 2 is required to connect *dentist* in the second sentence to the first and so would be classified as a backward inference. Example 3 is an elaboration (since a dentist is not mentioned in either sentence) and so would be classified as a case of a forward inference. Singer found that subjects were about a quarter of a second slower to verify *A dentist pulled the tooth* in the forward inference case than the other two cases. This pattern of results implies that subjects had made the backward inference in 2 because it was no slower than the direct condition 1, but they had not made the forward inference in 3 because it was slower.

◆ ──

In understanding a sentence, listeners are more likely to make backward inferences to connect it to prior sentences than forward inferences to anticipate future consequences.

──

Inference of Reference

One important aspect of backward inference involves recognizing when an expression in the sentence refers to something that we already should know. Various linguistic cues indicate that an expression is referring to something we already know. One cue in English turns on the difference between the definite article *the* and the indefinite article *a*. *The* tends to be used to signal that the comprehender should know the reference of the noun phrase, while *a* tends to be used to introduce a new object. Compare the difference in meaning of these sentences:

1. Last night I saw the moon.

2. Last night I saw a moon.

Sentence 1 indicates a rather uneventful fact—seeing the same old moon as always—but 2 carries the clear implication of having seen a new moon. There is considerable evidence that language comprehenders are quite sensitive to the meaning communicated by this small difference in the sentences. Haviland and Clark (1974) report an experiment directed at this issue. They compared subjects' comprehension time for two-sentence pairs such as the following:

3. Ed was given an alligator for his birthday. The alligator was his favorite present.

4. Ed wanted an alligator for his birthday. The alligator was his favorite present.

Both pairs have the same second sentence. Pair 3 introduces in its first sentence a specific antecedent for the *alligator*. On the other hand, although in pair 4 *alligator* is mentioned in the first sentence, a specific alligator is not posited. Thus, no antecedent occurs in the first sentence of pair 4 for *the alligator*. The definite article *the* in the second sentence of both pairs supposes a specific antecedent. Therefore, we would expect that subjects would have difficulty with the second sentence in pair 4 but not in pair 3. In the Haviland and Clark experiment, subjects saw pairs of such sentences one at a time. After they comprehended each sentence, they pressed a button. The time was measured from the presentation of the second sentence until subjects pressed a button indicating that they understood that sentence. Subjects took an average of 1031 milliseconds to comprehend the second sentence in pairs such as 3 above, in which an antecedent was given, but they took an average of 1168 milliseconds to comprehend the second sentence in pairs such as 4 above, in which no antecedent for the definite noun phrase occurred. Thus, comprehension took more than a tenth of a second longer when no antecedent occurred.

Loftus and Zanni (1975) did an experiment that showed that choice of articles could impact on listeners' beliefs. These experimenters showed subjects a film of an automobile accident and asked them a series of questions. Some subjects were asked

5. Did you see a broken headlight?

Other subjects were asked

6. Did you see the broken headlight?

In fact, there was no broken headlight in the film, but question 6 uses a definite article, which supposes the existence of a broken headlight. Subjects were more likely to respond yes when asked the question in form 6. As Loftus and Zanni note, this finding has important implications for the interrogation of eyewitnesses.

◆ Comprehenders take the definite article *the* to imply the existence of a reference for the noun.

Pronominal Reference

Another aspect of processing reference concerns the interpretation of pronouns. When one hears a pronoun such as *she,* it is critical to decide who is being referred to. A number of people may already have been mentioned, and they are all candidates for the reference of the pronoun. As Just and Carpenter (1987) discuss, there are a number of bases for resolving the reference of pronouns:

1. One of the most straightforward is to use number or gender cues. Consider

- Melvin, Susan, and their children left when (he, she, they) became sleepy.

Each possible pronoun would have a different referent.

2. A syntactic cue to pronominal reference is that pronouns tend to refer to objects in the same grammatical role (e.g., subject versus object). Consider

- Floyd punched Bert and then he kicked him.

Most people would agree that the subject *he* refers to *Floyd* and the object *him* refers to *Bert.*

3. There is also a strong recency effect such that the most recent candidate referent is preferred. Consider

- Dorothea ate the pie; Ethel ate cake; later she had coffee.

Most people would agree that *she* probably refers to Ethel.

4. Finally, people can use their knowledge of the world to determine reference. Compare

- Tom shouted at Bill because he spilled the coffee.
- Tom shouted at Bill because he had a headache.

Most people would agree that *he* in the first sentence refers to *Bill* because you tend to scold people who make mistakes, while *he* in the second sentence refers to *Tom* because people tend to be cranky when they have headaches.

In keeping with the immediacy-of-interpretation principle articulated earlier, people tend to try to assign a referent to a pronoun immediately upon encountering it. For instance, in studies of eye fixations (Carpenter & Just, 1977; Ehrlich & Rayner, 1983; Just & Carpenter, 1987) researchers find that people pause longer while the pronoun is being fixated than they do on the previous fixation. Ehrlich and Rayner (1983) also found that subjects' resolution of the reference tends to spill over into the next fixation. Their evidence for this was that subjects spent longer on the next fixation after the pronoun the further back in the sentence was the referent for the pronoun.

Corbett and Chang (1983) have found evidence that subjects consider multiple candidates for a referent. They had subjects read sentences such as

- Scott stole the basketball from Warren and he sank a jumpshot.

After reading the sentence, subjects saw a probe word and had to decide whether the word occurred in the sentence. Corbett and Chang found that time to recognize either Scott or Warren was decreased after reading such a sentence. They also asked subjects to read the following control sentence, which did not require the referent of a pronoun to be determined:

- Scott stole the basketball from Warren and Scott sank a jumpshot.

In this case only recognition of Scott was facilitated. Warren was facilitated only in the first sentence because in that sentence subjects had to consider it as the referent of *he*.

Both the Corbett and Chang study and the Ehrlich and Rayner study indicate that resolution of pronoun reference lasts beyond the reading of the pronoun itself. This indicates that processing is not always so immediate as the immediacy-of-processing principle might seem to imply. Processing of pronominal reference spills over into later fixations (Ehrlich & Rayner), and there is still priming for the unselected reference at the end of the sentence (Corbett & Chang).

◆

Comprehenders consider multiple possible candidates for the referent of a pronoun and use syntactic and semantic cues to select a referent.

Negatives

Negative sentences appear to suppose a positive sentence and then ask us to infer what must be true if the positive sentence is false. For instance, the sentence *John is not a crook* supposes that it is reasonable to assume *John is a crook* but asserts that this is false. As another example, imagine the following four replies from a normally healthy friend to the question *How are you feeling?*

1. I am well.

2. I am sick.

3. I am not well.

4. I am not sick.

Replies 1 through 3 would not be regarded as unusual linguistically, but reply 4 does seem peculiar. By using the negative, it is supposing that thinking of our friend as sick is reasonable. Why would we think our friend is sick, and what is our friend really telling us by saying it is not so? In contrast, the negative in reply 3 is easy to understand, since supposing that the friend is normally well is reasonable and our friend is telling us this is not so.

Clark and Chase (e.g., Chase & Clark, 1972; Clark & Chase, 1972; Clark, 1974) conducted a series of experiments on the verification of negatives (see also Trabasso, Rollins, & Shaughnessy, 1971; Carpenter & Just, 1975). In a typical experiment, they presented subjects with a card like that shown in Figure 12.5 and asked them to verify one of four sentences about this card:

1. The star is above the plus—true affirmative.

2. The plus is above the star—false affirmative.

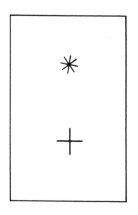

Figure 12.5 A card such as that presented to subjects in Clark and Chase's sentence-verification experiments. Subjects were to say whether simple affirmative and negative sentences correctly described these patterns.

3. The plus is not above the star—true negative.

4. The star is not above the plus—false negative.

The terms *true* and *false* refer to whether the sentence is true of the picture; the terms *affirmative* and *negative* refer to whether the sentence structure has a negative element. Sentences 1 and 2 involve a simple assertion, but sentences 3 and 4 involve a supposition plus a negation of the supposition. Sentence 3 supposes that the plus is above the star and asserts that this supposition is false; sentence 4 supposes that the star is above the plus and asserts that this supposition is false. Clark and Chase assume that subjects will check the supposition first and then process the negation. In sentence 3, the supposition does not match the picture, but in sentence 4 the supposition does match the picture. Assuming that mismatches will take longer to process, Clark and Chase predict that subjects will take longer to respond to sentence 3, a true negative, than to sentence 4, a false negative. In contrast, subjects should take longer to process sentence 2, the false affirmative, than sentence 1, the true affirmative, because sentence 2 does not match the picture. In fact, the difference between sentences 2 and 1 should be identical to the difference between sentences 3 and 4, because both differences reflect the extra time due to a mismatch between the sentence and the picture.

Clark and Chase developed a simple and elegant mathematical model for such data. They assumed that processing sentences 3 and 4 took N time units longer than processing sentences 1 and 2 because of the more complex supposition-plus-negation structure of 3 and 4. They also assumed that processing sentence 2 took M time units longer than processing 1 because of the mismatch between picture and assertion, and similarly that processing sentence 3 took M time units longer than processing 4 because of the mismatch between picture and supposition. Finally, they assumed that processing a true affirmative such as sentence 1 took T time units. The time T reflects the time used in processes not involving negation nor the picture

Table 12.1 Observed and Predicted Reaction Times in Experiment Verification

Condition	Observed Time	Equation	Predicted Time
True affirmative	1463 ms	T	1469 ms
False affirmative	1722 ms	$T + M$	1715 ms
True negative	2028 ms	$T + M + N$	2035 ms
False negative	1796 ms	$T + N$	1789 ms

mismatch. Let us consider the total time subjects should spend processing a sentence such as 3. This sentence has a complex supposition-and-negation structure, which costs N time units, and a supposition mismatch, which costs M time units. Therefore, total processing time should be $T + M + N$. Table 12.1 shows both the observed data and the reaction-time predictions that can be derived for the Clark and Chase experiment. The best predicting values for T, M, and N for this experiment can be estimated from the data as $T = 1469$ ms, $M = 246$ ms, and $N = 320$ ms. As you can confirm, the predictions match the observed time remarkably well. In particular, the difference between true negatives and false negatives is close to the difference between false affirmatives and true affirmatives. This finding supports the hypothesis that subjects do extract the suppositions of negative sentences and match these to the picture.

◆ Comprehenders process a negative by first processing its embedded supposition and then the negation.

Text Processing

So far, we have focused on the comprehension of single sentences in isolation. Sentences are more frequently processed in larger contexts; for example, in the reading of a textbook. Texts, like sentences, are structured according to certain patterns, although these patterns are perhaps more flexible than those associated with sentences. Researchers have noted that a number of recurring relationships serve to organize sentences into larger portions of a text. Some of the relations that have been identified are listed in Table 12.2. These structural relations specify the way a sentence should be related to the overall text. For instance, the first text structure (response) in the table directs the reader to relate one set of sentences as part of the solution to problems posed by other sentences. These relations can occur at any level of a text. That is, the main relation organizing a paragraph might be any of the eight in the table. Subpoints in a paragraph may also be organized according to any of these relations.

Table 12.2 Some Possible Types of Relationships among Sentences in a Text

Type of Relationship	Description
1. Response	A question is presented and an answer follows, or a problem is presented and a solution follows.
2. Specific	Some specific information is given following a more general point.
3. Explanation	An explanation is given for a point.
4. Evidence	Evidence is given to support a point
5. Sequence	Points are presented in their temporal sequence as a set.
6. Cause	An event is presented as the cause of another event.
7. Goal	An event is presented as the goal of another event.
8. Collection	A loose structure of points is presented. (This is perhaps a case where there is no real organizing relation.)

To see how the relations in Table 12.2 might be used, consider Meyer's (1974) now-classic analysis of the following paragraph:

Parakeet Paragraph

The wide variety in color of parakeets that are available on the market today resulted from careful breeding of the color mutant offspring of green-bodied and yellow-faced parakeets. The light green body and yellow face color combination is the color of the parakeets in their natural habitat, Australia. The first living parakeets were brought to Europe from Australia by John Gould, a naturalist, in 1840. The first color mutation appeared in 1872 in Belgium; these birds were completely yellow. The most popular color of parakeets in the United States is sky-blue. These birds have sky-blue bodies and white faces; this color mutation occurred in 1878 in Europe. There are over 66 different colors of parakeets listed by the Color and Technical Committee of the Budgerigar Society. In addition to the original green-bodied and yellow-faced birds, colors of parakeets include varying shades of violets, blues, grays, greens, yellows, and whites. (p. 61)

Her analysis of this paragraph is approximately reproduced in Table 12.3. Note that this analysis tends to organize various facts as more or less major points. The highest-level organizing relationship in this paragraph is

Table 12.3 Analysis of the Parakeet Paragraph

1. A explains B.
  A. There was careful breeding of color mutants of green-bodied and yellow-faced parakeets. The historical sequence is
    1. Their natural habitat was Australia. Specific detail:
      a. Their color here is a light-green body and yellow-face combination.
    2. The first living parakeets were brought to Europe from Australia by John Gould in 1840. Specific detail:
      a. John Gould was a naturalist.
    3. The first color mutation appeared in 1872 in Belgium. Specific detail:
      a. These birds were completely yellow.
    4. The sky-blue mutation occurred in 1878 in Europe. Specific details:
      a. These birds have sky-blue bodies and white faces.
      b. This is the most popular color in America.

  B. There is a wide variety in color of parakeets that are on the market today. Evidence for this is
    1. There are over 66 different colors of parakeets listed by the Color and Technical Committee of the Budgerigar Society.
    2. There are many available colors. A collection of these is
      a. The original green-bodies and yellow-faced birds
      b. Violets
      c. Blues
      d. Grays
      e. Greens
      f. Yellows
      g. Whites

From Meyer, 1974.

explanation (see item 3, Table 12.2). Specifically, the major points in this explanation are that (point A) there has been careful breeding of color mutants and (point B) there is a wide variety of parakeet color, and point A is given as an explanation of point B. Organized under A are some events from the history of parakeet breeding. This organization is an example of a sequence relationship. Organized under these events are specific details. So, for instance, organized under A2 is the fact that John Gould was a naturalist. Organized under point B is evidence supporting the assertion about the wide color variety and some details about the variation in color available.

◆
⎯⎯⎯⎯⎯⎯⎯⎯⎯⎯⎯⎯⎯⎯⎯⎯⎯⎯⎯⎯⎯⎯⎯⎯⎯⎯⎯⎯⎯⎯⎯⎯⎯⎯⎯⎯⎯

The propositions in a larger text can be organized hierarchically according to various semantic relationships.

⎯⎯⎯⎯⎯⎯⎯⎯⎯⎯⎯⎯⎯⎯⎯⎯⎯⎯⎯⎯⎯⎯⎯⎯⎯⎯⎯⎯⎯⎯⎯⎯⎯⎯⎯⎯⎯

Text Structure and Memory

A great deal of research has demonstrated the psychological significance of text structure. A number of theories have been proposed, which differ as to exactly what system of relations should be used in the analysis of texts, but they generally agree that some sort of hierarchical structure organizes the propositions of a text. Memory experiments have yielded evidence that subjects do, to some degree, respond to that hierarchical structure.

The kind of hierarchical structure exemplified in Meyer's analysis is reminiscent of the hierarchical structures we studied in Chapter 7 on memory. From the data cited in that chapter, we would expect such hierarchies to have large effects on memory—if the subjects use these hierarchies in comprehension. Meyer and others have shown that subjects do display better memory for the major points in such a structure (propositions higher in the structure). For instance, subjects are more likely to remember that there was careful breeding of color mutants (point A) than that John Gould was a naturalist (point A2a).

Meyer, Brandt, and Bluth (1978) studied students' perception of the high-level structure of a text—that is, the structural relations at the higher levels of hierarchies like that in Table 12.3. They found considerable variation in subjects' ability to recognize the high-level structure that organized a text. Moreover, they found that subjects' ability to identify the top-level structure of a text was an important predictor of their memory for the text. In another study, on ninth-graders, Bartlett (1978) found that only 11 percent of subjects consciously identified and used high-level structure to remember text material. This select group did twice as well as other students on their recall scores. Bartlett also showed that training students to identify and use top-level structure more than doubled recall performance.

In addition to its hierarchical structure, a text tends to be held together by causal and logical structures. This is clearest in narratives where there are sequences of events in which one event in the sequence causes the next. The scripts we discussed in Chapter 5 are one kind of knowledge structure that is designed to encode such causal relationships. Often the causal links are not explicitly stated but rather have to be inferred. For instance, we might hear on a newscast:

- There is an accident on the Parkway East. Traffic is being rerouted through Wilkinsburg.

It is left to the listener to infer that the first fact is the cause of the second fact. Keenan, Baillet, and Brown (1984) did a study of the effect of the probability of the causal relationship connecting two sentences on the processing of the second sentence. They asked subjects to read pairs of sentences, of which the first might be one of the following:

1a. Joey's big brother punched him again and again.

1b. Racing down the hill, Joey fell off his bike.

1c. Joey's crazy mother became furiously angry with him.

1d. Joey went to a neighbor's house to play.

Keenan et al. were interested in the effect of the first sentence on time to read a second sentence such as

2. The next day, his body was covered with bruises.

Sentences 1a through 1d are ordered in decreasing probability of a causal connection to the second sentence. Correspondingly, Keenan et al. found that subjects' reading times for sentence 2 increased from 2.6 seconds when preceded by high probable causes like 1a to 3.3 seconds when preceded by low probable causes like 1d. It takes longer to create a more distant causal relationship.

There are also effects of causal relatedness on recall. Those parts of a story that are more central to its causal structure are more likely to be recalled (Black & Bern, 1981; Trabasso, Secco, & van den Broek, 1984). For instance, Black and Bern had subjects study stories that included pairs of sentences such as

- The cat leapt up on the kitchen table.
- Fred picked up the cat and put it outside.

which are causally related. They contrasted these with pairs of sentences such as the following:

- The cat rubbed against the kitchen table.
- Fred picked up the cat and put it outside.

which are less plausibly connected by a causal relation. Although the second sentence is identical in both cases, subjects displayed better memories for the first sentence of a causally related pair.

Thorndyke (1977) has also shown that memory for a story is poorer if the organization of the text conflicts with what would be considered its "natural" structure. Some subjects studied an original story while other subjects studied the story with its sentences presented in a scrambled order. Subjects were able to recall 85 percent of the facts in the original story, but only 32 percent of the facts in the scrambled story. This is clearly what we would expect given the results of Chapter 7 (consider, for instance, the experiment of Bower et al., 1969, in that chapter).

Mandler and Johnson (1977) showed that children have much more difficulty than adults when recalling the causal structure of a story. Adults recall events and the outcomes of those events together, whereas children recall the outcomes but tend to forget how they were achieved. For instance, children might recall from a particular story that the butter melted but might forget that this occurred because the butter was out in the sun. Adults do not have trouble with such simple causal structures, but they may have difficulty perceiving the more complex relationships connecting portions of a text. For instance, how easy is it for you to specify the relationship that connects this paragraph to the preceding text?

Palinscar and Brown (1984) have developed a training program that specifically trains children to identify and formulate questions about things such as the causal structure of text. They were able to raise poor-performing seventh-graders from the 20th to the 56th percentile in reading comprehension. This is reminiscent of the results of Bartlett (1978), who improved reading performance by training students to identify the hierarchical structure of text.

◆

Memory for textual material is sensitive to the hierarchical and causal structure of that text and tends to be better when people attend to that structure.

Kintsch and van Dijk's Text Comprehension Model

Kintsch and van Dijk (1978) have brought many of the ideas we have discussed into an overall information-processing model of how one comprehends and remembers a text. Their model assumes that parsing processes have been applied to analyze the text into a set of propositions, and their analysis focuses on the further processing of the text after the initial set of propositions has been identified. As a simple example, consider this short text from Kintsch (1979):

The Swazi tribe was at war with a neighboring tribe because of a dispute over cattle. Among the warriors were two unmarried men, Kakra and his younger brother Gum. Kakra was killed in battle. (p. 6)

This would be analyzed into the following propositions:

1. (name, tribe1, Swazi)

2. (neighbor, tribe2, tribe1)

3. (at-war, tribe1, tribe2) = α

4. (cause, α, β)

5. (dispute, tribe1, tribe2, cattle) = β

6. (among, warriors, men)

7. (number, men, two)

8. (unmarried, men)

9. (name, men, [Kakra, Gum])

10. (younger-brother-of, Kakra, Gum)

11. (killed, Kakra, battle)

In the Kintsch and van Dijk model, as the propositions are processed, the comprehender must relate new propositions to previous ones. This is done by overlap of terms. Thus, proposition 2 above can be easily related to proposition 1 because they overlap in the term *tribe1*. It is usually easy to relate the propositions within a sentence. Difficulties frequently arise when one must relate propositions across sentence boundaries. In the example above, there is a difficulty relating proposition 6 to the preceding. To relate the proposition, comprehenders have to make what is called a **bridging inference** (Haviland & Clark, 1974). In this case, the bridging inference is that the warriors in proposition 6 were the people from the Swazi tribe. According to Kintsch and van Dijk, one of the things that makes comprehension difficult is the need to make such bridging inferences.

Kintsch and van Dijk propose that there is a capacity limit (which they estimate to be four, on average) on the number of propositions one can keep active in working memory (see Chapter 6). There are two important consequences of this capacity limit. One is that the comprehender may fail to relate a new proposition to the previous text because the previous proposition with the shared term is no longer active. We noted earlier in our discussion of reference that subjects need more time to process a referring expression the farther back in the text that referring expression occurred. According to Kintsch and van Dijk, this is because of a reinstatement search in which comprehenders reactivate past propositions from long-term memory looking for a proposition that overlaps in terms with the current proposition.

The second consequence of this limitation on the number of active propositions involves recall. Referring to previous research on memory (see Chapter 6), Kintsch and van Dijk argue that the longer a proposition is held active, the greater the strength of its long-term encoding and the higher the probability of its eventual recall. Since there is a limitation on the number of propositions a person can keep active in working memory, one has to select which propositions will stay in working memory and which propositions will be dropped. Depending on what one picks, different propositions will enjoy different levels of recall.

Kintsch and van Dijk propose that comprehenders use some combination of recency and importance to select which propositions to keep active. They propose what has been called the **leading-edge strategy**, in which subjects keep active the most recent proposition that has been processed and the propositions that are superior to it in a hierarchical representation of a text (e.g., see Table 12.3). Thus, upon reading proposition 5 about the cattle dispute, they would keep it active; they would do the same with proposition 4, which relates it to the war proposition. Fletcher (1986) has shown, by examining subjects' protocols while reading, that subjects keep active not only those propositions that are high in the hierarchy, but also those propositions that are causally important. This is consistent with the earlier evidence that both position in the text structure and causal centrality are important in text processing. One consequence of such strategies for keeping the more central propositions active is that the Kintsch and van Dijk model predicts that the hierarchically and causally central facts from a text are the better recalled. We reviewed the evidence for this prediction in the previous subsection.

Kintsch and van Dijk propose that there are two kinds of elaborations a reader makes to embellish on the propositions in the text. The first are the bridging inferences that we have already discussed, in which the comprehender adds inferences to relate otherwise unrelated terms. The other is the formation of what Kintsch and van Dijk called macropropositions, which are summaries of the gist of the text. So, for instance, one summary proposition for the text we read at the beginning of this subsection is *A soldier is killed in war*. The formation of these macropropositions also leads to the observed phenomenon of better recall for the main points of a text in contrast to the details.

Kintsch and Vipond (1979) describe an interesting application of this analysis to the speeches of Eisenhower and Stevenson from the presidential campaign of 1952. It has been argued that Stevenson lost the election because his speeches were hard to understand. However, if one does a comparison of the speeches using standard readability measures that consider features such as word length, word frequency, and sentence length,

Eisenhower's speeches are rated as more complex. On the other hand, if one applies the Kintsch and van Dijk comprehension model to Stevenson's speeches, one finds that they required a number of bridging inferences and reinstatement searches to determine reference, whereas Eisenhower's speeches did not. The implication is that listeners found it too taxing to try to integrate the references in Stevenson's speeches.

◆

According to Kintsch and van Dijk, comprehenders process a text one proposition at a time, trying to relate new propositions to a leading edge of propositions that they are keeping active.

Conclusions

The number and diversity of topics covered in this chapter give witness to the impressive cumulative progress that has been made in the area of language comprehension. It is fair to say we knew almost nothing about language processing when cognitive psychology emerged from the collapse of behaviorism forty years ago. Now, we have a rather articulate picture of what is happening in scales that range from 100 milliseconds after a word is heard to the integration of large stretches of complex text. The field of language processing turns out to harbor a number of theoretical controversies, some of which have been discussed in our review of the field (e.g., whether early syntactic processing is separate from the rest of cognition). Such controversies should not blind us to the impressive progress that has been made. The heat in the field has also generated much light.

Remarks and Suggested Readings

The 1997 April/June edition of *Language and Cognitive Processes* is a collection of recent papers on parsing. Singer (1994) reviews research on inference in language processing. Fletcher (1994) discusses the role of the text representations. Van den Broek (1994) discusses both inference and text processing. These three articles are all part of a *Handbook of Psycholinguistics* edited by Gernsbacher (1994). Kintsch (1998) describes his construction-integration theory of language comprehension.

13

Individual Differences in Cognition

Clearly all people do not think alike. There are many dimensions of difference in cognition, but humans, naturally being an evaluative species, tend to focus on ways in which some people perform "better" on cognitive tasks than others. This is often identified with the word *intelligence*—some people are perceived to be more intelligent than others. The first chapter identified intelligence as the defining feature of the human species. So, to call some members of the species more intelligent than others can be a potent claim. As we will see, human cognition is too complex to try to place people on a unidimensional evaluative scale of intelligence.

This chapter will explore the issue of individual differences both because of its inherent interest and because it sheds some light on the general nature of human cognition. This chapter will first look at the way human cognition changes as we change chronologically from young children to young adults to old adults. Then, it will examine how cognition varies among people of a particular chronological age.

The big debate that will be with us throughout this chapter is the nurture-versus-nature debate. Are some people better at some cognitive tasks because they are innately endowed with more capacity for those kinds of tasks or because they have learned more knowledge relevant to these tasks? The answer is that it is some of both, and we will discuss some of the ways in which basic capacities and experiences contribute to human intelligence.

Cognitive Development

Part of the uniqueness of the human species concerns the way children are brought into the world and develop to become adults. Humans have very large brains in relation to their body size, which eventuated in a major evolutionary problem: How was the birth of such large-brained babies to be effected? One way was through progressive enlargement of the birth canal, which is now as large as is considered possible given the constraints of mammalian skeletons (Geschwind, 1980). In addition, children are born with a skull that is sufficiently pliable for it to be compressed into a cone shape in order to fit through the birth canal. Still, the human birth process is particularly difficult compared to that of most other mammals.

Not even the evolutionary modifications just mentioned would suffice, however, if humans were born with fully developed brains. Compared with many other mammals, human infants are born with particularly immature brains. At birth a human brain occupies a volume of about 350 cubic centimeters (cm^3). During the first year it doubles to 700 cm^3, and before a human being reaches puberty, the size of its brain doubles again. Most other mammals do not have as much growth in brain size after birth (Gould, 1977). Since the human birth canal has been expanded to its limits, much of our neural development has been postponed until after birth.

Even though they spend nine months developing in the womb, human infants are quite helpless at birth and spend an extraordinarily long time growing to adult stature—around 15 years, which is about a fifth of our life span. Contrast this with a puppy: After a gestation period of just nine weeks, it is born more capable than a newborn. In less than a year, less than a tenth of its life span, it has reached full size and reproductive capability.

Childhood is prolonged more than would be needed to develop large brains. Indeed, most neural development is complete by age 2 and almost all by age 5. Humans are kept children by the slowness of their physical development. It has been speculated (de Beer, 1959) that the function of this slow physical development has been to keep children in a dependency relationship to adults. There is much that has to be learned in order to become a competent adult, and staying a child so long gives the human time enough to acquire that knowledge. Childhood is an apprenticeship for adulthood.

Modern society is so complex that we cannot learn all that is needed by simply associating with our parents for 15 years. To provide the needed training, society has created social institutions such as high schools, colleges, and postcollege professional schools. It is not unusual for people to spend more than 25 years, almost as long as their professional lives, preparing for their roles in society.

◆
Human development is delayed relative to that of other mammals to enable growth of a large brain and acquisition of a large amount of knowledge.

Piaget's Stages of Development

Developmental psychologists have tried to understand the intellectual changes that occur as we grow from infancy through adulthood. They have been particularly influenced by the Swiss psychologist Jean Piaget, who studied and theorized about child development for more than half a century. Much of the recent information-processing work in cognitive development has been concerned with correcting and restructuring Piaget's theory of cognitive development. Despite these revisions, his research has organized a large set of qualitative observations about cognitive development spanning the period from birth to adulthood. Therefore, it is worth reviewing these to get a picture of the general nature of cognitive development during childhood.

According to Piaget, a child enters the world lacking virtually all the basic cognitive competencies of the adult but gradually develops these competencies by passing through a series of stages of development. Piaget distinguishes four major stages. The **sensory-motor stage** occupies the first two years. During this stage, children develop schemes for thinking about the physical world—for instance, they develop the notion of an object as a permanent thing in the world. The second stage is the **preoperational stage**, which is characterized as spanning the period from two to seven years. Unlike the younger child, a child in this period can engage in internal thought about the world, but these mental processes are intuitive and lack systematicity. For instance, a four-year-old who was asked to describe his painting of a farm and some animals said, "First over here is a house where the animals live. I live in a house. So do my mommy and daddy. This is a horse. I saw horses on TV. Do you have a TV?"

The next stage is the **concrete-operational stage**, which spans the period from seven to eleven years. In this period, children develop a set of mental operations that allow them to treat the physical world in a systematic way. However, children still have major limitations on their capacity to reason formally about the world. The capacity for formal reasoning emerges during Piaget's fourth period, the **formal-operational stage**, spanning the years from eleven to fifteen. After emerging from this period, the child has become an adult conceptually and is capable of scientific reasoning—which Piaget takes as the paradigm case of mature intellectual functioning.

Piaget's concept of a stage has always been a sore point in developmental psychology. Obviously, a child does not suddenly change on an eleventh birthday from the stage of concrete operations to the stage of formal operations. There are large differences among children and cultures, and the ages given are just rough figures. However, careful analysis of the development within a single child also fails to find abrupt changes at any age. One response to this gradualness has been to break down the stages into smaller substages. Another response has been to interpret stages as simply ways of characterizing what is inherently a gradual and continuous process. Siegler (1996) has argued that upon careful analysis all cognitive development is continuous and gradual. He characterizes belief in stages as "the myth of the immaculate transition."

Just as important as Piaget's stage analysis is his analysis of children's performance in specific tasks within these stages. These task analyses provide the empirical substance to back up his broad and abstract characterization of the stages. Probably his most famous task analysis is his research on conservation, which we will discuss next.

◆

Piaget proposed that children progress through four stages of increasing intellectual sophistication: sensory-motor, preoperational, concrete-operational, and formal-operational.

Conservation

The term **conservation** most generally refers to knowledge of what properties of the world are preserved under various transformations. Children's appreciation of this develops as the child progresses through the Piagetian stages.

Conservation in the sensory-motor stage: One of the first things a child must come to appreciate is that objects continue to exist over transformations in time and space. If a cloth is placed over a toy that a six-month-old is reaching for, the infant stops reaching and appears to lose interest in the toy (see Figure 13.1). It is as if the object ceases to exist for the child when it is no longer in view. Piaget concluded from his experiments that children do not come into the world with this knowledge but rather develop a concept of object permanence during the first year.

According to Piaget, the concept of object permanence develops slowly and is one of the major intellectual developments in the sensory-motor

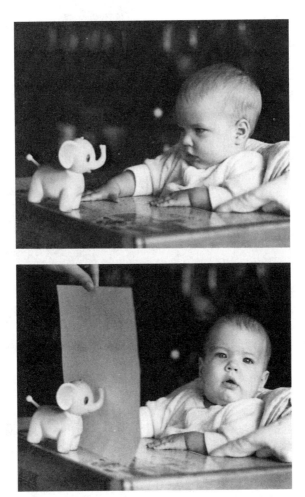

Figure 13.1 An illustration of a child's apparent inability to understand the permanence of an object. (Monkmeyer Press Photo Service, Inc. From John W. Santrock and Steven R. Yussen, <u>Child development: An introduction,</u> 4th Edition. Copyright © 1989 Wm. C. Brown Publishers, Dubuque, IA. All Rights Reserved. Reprinted by permission.)

stage. An older infant will search for an object that has been hidden, but more demanding tests reveal failings in the older infant's understanding of a permanent object. In one experiment, an object is put under cover A, and then, in front of the child, it is removed and put under cover B. The child will often look for the object under cover A. Piaget argues that the child does not understand that the object will still be in location B. It is only after the age of twelve months that the child can succeed consistently at this task.

Conservation in the preoperational and concrete-operational stages: A number of important advances in conservation occur around the age of six, which, according to Piaget, is the transition between the preoperational and concrete-operational stages. Before this age, children can be shown to have some glaring errors in their reasoning. These errors start to correct themselves at this point in time. There has been considerable controversy about the cause of this change, with different theorists pointing to language (Bruner, 1964) and the advent of schooling (Cole & D'Andrade, 1982), among other possible causes. Here, we will content ourselves with describing the changes involving the child's understanding of conservation of quantity.

As adults we can almost instantaneously recognize that there are four apples in a bowl and can confidently know that these apples will remain four when dumped into a bag. Piaget was interested in how a child develops the concept of quantity and learns that quantity is something that is preserved under various transformations, such as moving the objects from a bowl to a bag. Figure 13.2 illustrates a typical conservation problem that has been posed by psychologists in many variations to preschool children in countless

Figure 13.2 A typical experimental situation to test for conservation of number. (Monkmeyer Press Photo Service, Inc. From John W. Santrock and Steven R. Yussen, Child development: An introduction, 4th edition. Copyright © 1989 Wm. C. Brown Publishers, Dubuque, IA. All Rights Reserved. Reprinted by permission.)

experiments. A child is presented with two rows of objects, such as checkers. The two rows contain the same number of objects and have been lined up so as to correspond. The child is asked whether the two rows have the same amount and responds that they do. The child can be asked to count the objects in the two rows to confirm that conclusion. Now, before the child's eyes, one row is compressed so that it is shorter than the other row, but no checkers are added or removed. Again asked which row has more objects, the child now says that the longer row has more. The child appears not to know that quantity is something that is preserved under transformations such as compression of space. If asked to count the two rows, the child expresses great surprise that they have the same number.

A general feature in demonstrations of lack of conservation is that children are distracted by the irrelevant physical features of a display. Another example of this is the liquid conservation task, which is illustrated in Figure 13.3. A child is shown two identical beakers containing identical amounts of water and also an empty, tall, thin beaker. When asked whether the two identical beakers hold the same amount of water, the child agrees that they do. The water from one beaker is then poured into the tall, thin beaker. When asked whether the amount of water in the two containers is the same, the child now says that the tall beaker holds more. The young children are distracted by physical appearance and do not relate their having seen the water poured from one beaker into the other to the unchanging quantity of liquid. Bruner (1964) demonstrated that a child is less likely to fail to conserve if the tall beaker is hidden from sight while it is filled; then the child does not see the high column of water and so is not distracted by physical appearance. Thus, it is a case of being overwhelmed by physical appearance. It is not that the child does not know at all that water preserves its quantity after being poured.

Failure of conservation has also been shown with weight and volume of solid objects (for a discussion of studies of conservation see Brainerd, 1978; Flavell, 1985; Ginsburg & Opper, 1980). It was once thought that failure of conservation in the preoperational period was a more or less unitary problem. Now, however, it is clear that successful conservation appears earlier on some tasks than on others. For instance, conservation of number usually appears before conservation of liquid. Also, children in transition will show conservation of number in one experimental situation but not another.

Conservation in the formal operational period: Once children reach the formal-operational period, their appreciation of conservation reaches new levels of abstraction. They are able to understand the idealized conservations that are part of modern science. These include concepts like the conservation of energy and conservation of motion. In a frictionless world, an object once set in motion continues. This is something the child never experiences, but the child comes to appreciate this abstraction and the way the abstraction relates to experiences in the real world.

Figure 13.3 A typical experimental situation to test for conservation of liquid. (Monkmeyer Press Photo Service, Inc. From John W. Santrock and Steven R. Yussen, <u>Child development: An introduction,</u> 4th edition. Copyright ©1989 Wm. C. Brown Publishers, Dubuque, IA. All Rights Reserved. Reprinted by permission.)

◆

As children develop, they gain increasingly sophisticated appreciation about what properties of objects are conserved under which transformations.

What Develops?

Clearly, as Piaget and others have documented, major intellectual changes occur during childhood. However, there are serious questions concerning what underlies these changes. There are two ways of explaining why children perform better on various intellectual tasks as they get older: One is that they "think better," and the other is that they "know better." The think-better option holds that children's basic cognitive processes become better. Perhaps they can hold more information in working memory or process information faster. The know-better option holds that children have learned more and better facts and methods as they get older. I refer to this as "know better," not "know more," because it is not just a matter of adding knowledge but also a matter of eliminating erroneous facts and inappropriate methods (such as relying on appearance in the conservation tasks). Perhaps this superior knowledge enables them to perform the tasks more efficiently. A computer metaphor is apt here: A computer system (e.g., for doing deduction) can be made to perform better by running the same program on a faster machine that has more memory or by running a better program on the same machine. Which is it in the case of child development—better machine or better program?

Of course, this is not an either-or situation. The child's improvement is due to both factors, but this leaves open the relative contributions of the two. Siegler (1998) argues that many of the developmental changes that take place over the first two years are to be understood in terms of neural changes. The neural changes that occur in the first two years are considerable. An infant is actually born with more neurons than it will have at a later age. While the number of neurons decrease there is a dramatic tenfold increase in the number of synaptic connections over the first two years. Figure 13.4 illustrates the dramatic changes in synaptic density over the first two years. The number of synapses actually reaches a peak at about age two after which it declines. The earlier pruning of neurons and later pruning of synaptic connections is thought of as a process by which the brain can fine-tune itself. The initial overproduction guarantees that there will be enough neurons and synapses to process the required information. When some neurons or synapses are not used, and so are proven unnecessary, they wither away (Huttenlocher, 1994). After age two, there is not much further growth of neurons or their synaptic connections, but the brain continues to grow because of the proliferation of other cells. In particular, the glial cells increase, including those that provide the myelinated sheaths around the axons of neurons. As reviewed in Chapter 1, myelina-

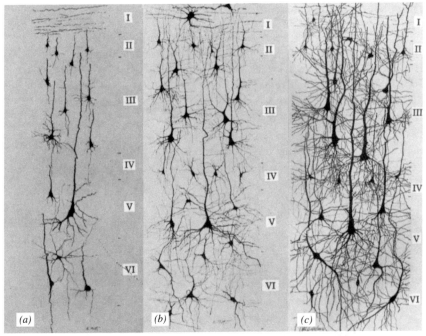

Figure 13.4 Postnatal development of human cerebral cortex around Broca's Area:
a: newborn; b: 3 months; c: 24 months. (From Lenneberg, 1967.)

tion enables the axon to conduct brain signals much more rapidly. The process of myelination continues into the late teens but at an increasingly gradual pace. The effects of this gradual myelination can be considerable. For instance, the time for a nerve impulse to cross the hemispheres in an adult is about 5 milliseconds, which is four to five times faster than in a four-year-old (Salamy, 1978).

It is tempting to emphasize the improvement in processing capacity as the basis for improvement after age two. After all, consider the physical difference between a two-year-old and an adult. When my son was two, he had difficulty mastering the undoing of his pajama buttons. If his muscles and coordination had so much maturation ahead, why not his brain? This analogy, however, does not hold: A two-year-old has reached only 20 percent of his adult body weight, whereas the brain has already reached 80 percent of its final size. We might argue that cognitive development after age two will, to an approximation, depend on the knowledge an individual puts in his or her brain rather than on any physical improvement in the capacities of the brain.

◆

Neural development is a more important contributor to cognitive development before the age of two than after.

Increased Mental Capacity

A number of developmental theories have argued that an important component of development is a trend of increasing mental capacity that continues through the teenage years (Case, 1985; Fischer, 1980; Halford, 1982; Pascual-Leone, 1980). These are often called neo-Piagetian theories of development. I will review here the memory-space theory of Case, whose proposal is that a growing working-memory capacity is the key to the developmental sequence. The basic idea is that more advanced cognitive performance requires that more information be held in working memory.

As an example of this analysis, consider Case's (1978) description of how children solve Noelting's (1975) juice problems. The child is given two empty pitchers, A and B, and is told that several tumblers of orange juice and water will be poured into each. The child's task is to predict which pitcher will taste most strongly of orange juice. Figure 13.5 illustrates the problems that children can solve at various ages. At the youngest age, children can reliably solve only problems where all orange juice goes into one pitcher and all water into another. At ages four to five, they can count the number of tumblers of orange juice going into a pitcher and choose the pitcher that holds the larger number—not considering the number of tumblers of water. At ages seven to eight, they notice whether there is more orange juice or more water going into a pitcher. If pitcher A has more orange juice than water and pitcher B has more water than orange juice, they will choose pitcher A even if the absolute number of glasses of orange juice is fewer. Finally, at age nine or ten, children compute the difference between the amount of orange juice and the amount of water (still not a perfect solution).

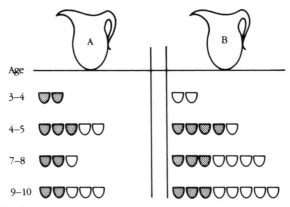

Figure 13.5 The Noelting juice problem that children can solve at various ages. The problem is to tell which pitcher will taste more strongly of orange juice after subjects observe the tumblers of water and juice that will be poured into each pitcher.

Case argues that the working-memory requirements differ for the various types of problems represented in Figure 13.5. For the simplest problems the child has to keep only one fact in memory—which set of tumblers has the orange juice. Children at ages three to four can keep only one such fact in mind. If both sets of tumblers have orange juice, the child cannot solve the problem. For the second type of problem the child needs to keep two things in memory—the number of orange juice tumblers in each array. In the third type of problem, the child needs to keep additional partial products in mind to determine which side has more orange juice. To solve the fourth type of problem, the child needs four facts to make a judgment:

1. The absolute difference in tumblers going into pitcher A

2. The sign of the difference for pitcher A (i.e., whether there is more water or more orange juice going into pitcher)

3. The absolute difference in tumblers going into pitcher B

4. The sign of the difference for pitcher B.

Case argues that children's developmental sequences are controlled by their working-memory capacity for the problem. Only when they can keep four facts in memory will they achieve the fourth stage in the developmental sequence. Case's theory has been criticized (e.g., Flavell, 1978) because it is hard to decide how to count the working-memory requirements.

Another question concerns what controls the growth in working memory. Case argues that a major factor in the increase of working memory is increased speed of neural function. He cites the evidence that the degree of myelination increases with age, with spurts approximately at those points where he postulates major changes in working memory. On the other hand, he also argues that practice plays a significant role as well. He argues that with practice we learn to perform our mental operations more efficiently, so that they do not require so much working-memory capacity.

The research of Kail (1988) can be viewed as consistent with this proposal. This investigator looked at a number of cognitive tasks, including the mental rotation task we examined in Chapter 4. He presented subjects with pairs of letters in different orientations and asked them to judge whether the letters were the same or were mirror images of one another. As we discussed in Chapter 4, subjects tend to mentally rotate an image of one object into congruence with the other in order to make this judgment. Kail observed people from the ages of eight to twenty-two performing this task-and found that they got systematically faster with age. He was interested in rotation rate, which he measured as the num-

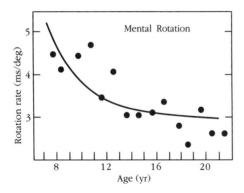

Figure 13.6 Rates of mental rotation, estimated from the slope of the function relating response time to the orientation of the stimulus. (Kail, 1988.)

ber of milliseconds to rotate one degree of angle (ms/deg). Figure 13.6 shows these data, plotting rate of rotation as a function of age. It turns out that the time to rotate a degree of angle decreases as a function of age.

In some of his writings, Kail has argued that this is evidence for an increase in basic mental speed as a function of age. However, an alternative hypothesis is that this merely reflects increased processing speed as a function of years of practice at performing these elemental mental operations. Kail and Park (1990) put this hypothesis to the test by giving eleven-year-old children and adults over 3000 trials of practice at mental rotation. They found that both groups sped up but that adults started out faster. However, Kail and Park showed that all their data could be fit by a single power function that assumed that the adults came into the experiment with what amounted to an extra 1800 trials of practice (Chapters 6 and 9 showed that learning curves tended to be fit by power functions). Figure 13.7 shows the resulting data, with the children's learning function superimposed on the adult's learning function. The practice curve for the children assumes that they start with about 150 trials of prior practice and that the adults start with 1950 trials of prior practice. However, after 3000 trials of practice, children are a good bit faster than beginning adults. Thus, while rate of information processing increases with development, this increase may have a practice and not a biological explanation.

◆

Qualitative and quantitative developmental changes occur in cognitive development because of increases in both working memory capacity and rate of information processing.

Increased Knowledge

Chi (1978) has demonstrated that developmental differences may be knowledge-related. Her domain of demonstration was memory. Not sur-

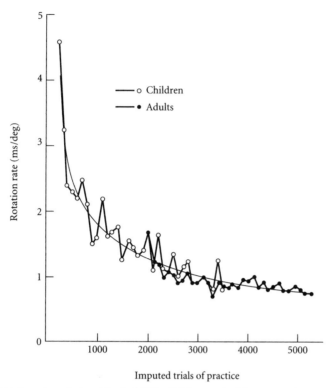

Figure 13.7 Data from Kail and Park (1990): Children and adults are on the same learning curve but children are advanced in 1800 trials.

prisingly, children do worse than adults on almost every memory task. Is this because their memories have less capacity, or is it because they know less about what they are being asked to remember? To address this question, she compared the memory performance of ten-year-olds to that of adults on two tasks—a standard digit-span task and a chess memory task (see the discussion of these tasks in Chapters 6 and 9). The ten-year-olds were skilled chess players, whereas the adults were novices at chess. The chess task was the one illustrated earlier in Figure 9.13 on page 300—a chessboard was presented for ten seconds and then withdrawn, and subjects were then asked to reproduce the chess pattern.

Figure 13.8 illustrates the number of chess pieces recalled by children and adults. The figure also contrasts these results with the number of digits recalled in the digit-span task. As Chi predicted, the adults were better on the digit-span task, but the children were better on the chess task. The children's superior chess performance was attributed to their greater knowledge of chess. The adults' superior digit performance was due to their greater familiarity with digits—the dramatic digit-span performance

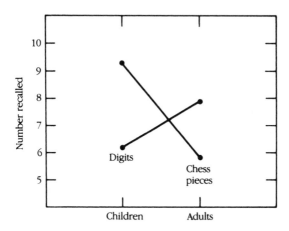

Figure 13.8 Number of chess pieces and number of digits recalled by children versus adults. (From Chi, 1978.)

of subject S.F. in Chapter 9 shows just how much digit knowledge can lead to improved memory performance.

The novice-expert contrasts from Chapter 9 are often used to explain developmental phenomena. We saw that a great deal of experience in a domain is required if a person is to become an expert. Chi's argument is that children, because of their lack of knowledge, are near universal novices but they can become more expert than adults through concentrated experience in one domain, like chess.

The Chi experiment contrasted child experts with adult novices. Schneider, Körkel, and Weinert (1988) looked at the effect of expertise at various age levels. They categorized German schoolchildren as either experts or novices with respect to soccer. They did this separately for grade levels 3, 5, and 7. The students at each grade level were asked to recall a story about soccer. Table 13.1 illustrates the amount of recall displayed as a function of grade level and expertise. The effect of expertise was much greater than that of grade level. On a recognition test, there was no effect of grade level, only an effect of expertise. They also classified each group of subjects into high-ability and low-ability subjects on the basis of their performance on intelligence tests. Although such tests generally predict mem-

Table 13.1 Mean Percentages of Idea Units Recalled as a Function of Grade and Expertise

Grade	Soccer Experts	Soccer Novices
3	54	32
5	52	33
7	61	42

From Körkel, 1987.

ory for stories, Schneider et al. found no effect of general ability level but only of knowledge for soccer. They argue that high-ability students are just those who know a lot about a lot of domains and consequently generally do well on memory tests. However, when tested on a story about a specific domain like soccer, a high-ability student who knows nothing about that domain will do worse than a low-ability student who knows a lot about the domain.

In addition to lack of relevant knowledge, children have difficulty on memory tasks because they do not know the strategies that lead to improved memory. The clearest case of this concerns rehearsal. If you were asked to dial a novel seven-digit telephone number, I would hope you would rehearse it until you were confident you had it memorized or until you had dialed the number. It would not occur to young children that they should rehearse the number. In one study comparing five-year-olds with ten-year-olds, Keeney, Cannizzo, and Flavell (1967) found that ten-year-olds almost always verbally rehearsed a set of objects to be remembered, whereas five-year-olds seldom did. Young children's performance often improves if they are instructed to follow a verbal rehearsal strategy, although very young children are simply unable to execute such a rehearsal strategy.

Chapter 7 emphasized the importance of elaborative strategies for good memory performance. Particularly for long-term retention, elaboration appears to be much more effective than rote rehearsal. There also appear to be sharp developmental trends with respect to the use of elaborative encoding strategies. For instance, Paris and Lindauer (1976) looked at the elaborations that children use to relate two paired-associate nouns such as *lady* and *broom*. Older children are more likely to generate interactive sentences such as *The lady flew on the broom* than static sentences such as *The lady had a broom*. Such interactive sentences will lead to better memory performance. Young children are also poorer at drawing the inferences that improve memory for a story (Stein & Trabasso, 1981).

◆
Younger children often do worse on tasks than older children because they have less relevant knowledge and poorer strategies.

Cognition and Aging

Changes in cognition do not cease when we reach adulthood. As we get older, we continue to learn more things, but human cognitive ability does not uniformly increase with added years, as one might expect if intelligence were just a matter of what one knows. Figure 13.9 shows data compiled by Salthouse (1992) on two components of the WAIS-R intelligence tests. One component involves verbal intelligence, which involves elements such as vocabulary and language comprehension. As you can see, this component maintains itself quite constantly across the years. On the other hand,

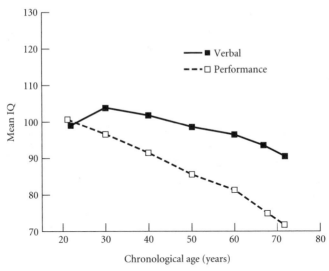

Figure 13.9 Mean verbal and performance IQs from the WAIS-R standardization sample as a function of age. (From Salthouse, 1992. Reprinted by permission from LEA, Inc.)

there is a very dramatic decrease in the performance component, which is involved with abilities like reasoning and problem solving.

It is easy to exaggerate the importance of these declines in basic measures of cognitive ability. Such tests are typically speeded, and older adults do better on slower tests. Also, such tests tend to be like school tests, and young adults have had more recent experience with such tests. When it comes to relevant job-related behavior, one finds older adults often doing better than younger adults (e.g., Perlmutter, Kaplan, & Nyquist, 1990), both reflecting their greater accumulation of knowledge and a more mature approach to job demands.

There are substantial age-related declines in brain function. Brain cells gradually die. Some areas are particularly susceptible to cell death. The hippocampus, which, as we reviewed in Chapter 7, is particularly important to memory, loses about 5 percent of its cells every decade (Selkoe, 1992). Other cells, while they might not die, have been observed to shrink and atrophy. On the other hand, there is some evidence for compensatory growth. Cells remaining in the hippocampus will grow to compensate for the age-related deaths of their neighbors. In addition to this gradual loss, adults can suffer various brain-related disorders. The most common of these is Alzheimer's disease, which is associated with substantial impairment of brain function.

It seems that as we get older there is a race going on between growth in knowledge and loss of neural function. It is interesting that people in many professions (artists, scientists, philosophers) tend to produce their

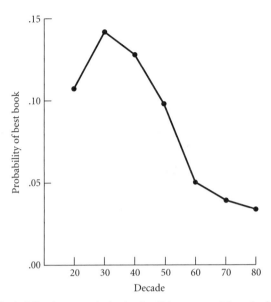

Figure 13.10 Probability that a particular book will become a philosopher's best as a function of the age at which the philosopher wrote the book. (Adapted from Lehman, 1953.)

best work during their mid-thirties. Figure 13.10 shows some interesting data from Lehman (1953). He examined the works of 182 famous deceased philosophers who collectively wrote some 1,785 books. Figure 13.10 plots the probability that a book was considered that philosopher's best book as a function of the age at which it was written. These philosophers remained prolific, publishing many books in their seventies. However, as Figure 13.10 displays, a book written in this decade is unlikely to be considered that philosopher's best.[1] Lehman reviews data from a number of fields consistent with the hypothesis that the decade of the thirties tends to be the time of peak intellectual performance. However, as Figure 13.10 shows, relatively high intellectual performance is often maintained into the forties and fifties.

The evidence for an age-related correlation between brain function and cognition makes it clear that there is a contribution of biology to intelligence that knowledge cannot always overcome. Salthouse (1992) argues that in information-processing terms, people lose their ability to hold information in working memory with age. He contrasted subjects of different ages on the reasoning problems in Figure 13.11. These problems differ in the number of premises that need to be combined to come to a particular solution. Figure 13.11 shows how people at various ages perform in these tasks. As can be seen, people's ability to solve these problems generally declines with the number of premises that need to be combined. However, this dropoff is much steeper for older adults. He argues that this is because

Q and R do the OPPOSITE
If Q INCREASES, what will happen to R?

D and E do the OPPOSITE
C and D do the SAME
If C INCREASES, what will happen to E?

R and S do the SAME
Q and R do the OPPOSITE
S and T do the OPPOSITE
If Q INCREASES, what will happen to T?

U and V do the OPPOSITE
W and X do the SAME
T and U do the SAME
V and W do the OPPOSITE
If T INCREASES, what will happen to X?

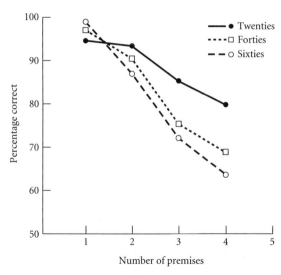

Figure 13.11 Illustration of integrative reasoning trials hypothesized to vary in working-memory demands (top panel), and mean performance of adults in their twenties, forties, and sixties with each trial type (bottom panel).

older people are slower in their information processing than younger adults, and this inhibits their ability to maintain information in working memory.

────◆────

Age-related declines in rates of information processing are sometimes compensated for by increased knowledge and maturity.

────◆────

[1] It is important to note that this graph denotes the probability of a specific book being the best, and so the outcome is not an artifact of the number of books written during a decade.

Summary

With respect to the nature-versus-nurture issue, the developmental data paint a mixed picture. A person's brain probably is at its best physically in the early twenties and there is some tendency for intellectual capacity to follow brain function. The relationship seems particularly strong in the early years of childhood. However, we saw evidence that practice could overcome age-related differences in speed (Figure 13.7), and knowledge could be a more dominant factor than age (Figure 13.8 and Table 13.1). Also, it appears that the point of peak intellectual output is postponed beyond the twenties (Figure 13.10), reflecting the need for accumulated knowledge. As Chapter 9 reviewed, truly exceptional performance in a field tends to require at least ten years of experience in that field.

Psychometric Studies of Cognition

We now turn from considering how cognition varies as a function of age to considering how cognition varies within a population of a fixed age. All this research has basically the same character. It involves collecting measures of the performances of various individuals on a number of tasks and then looking at the way these performance measures correlate across tests. Such tests are referred to as **psychometric tests**. This research has pretty well established that there is not just a single dimension of "intelligence" on which people vary, but rather that individual differences in cognition are much more complex. We will start our discussions of this research with work on intelligence tests.

Intelligence Tests

Research on intelligence testing has had a much longer sustained intellectual history than cognitive psychology. In 1904, the Minister of Public Instruction in Paris named a commission charged with identifying children in need of remedial education. Alfred Binet set about developing a test that would objectively identify students having intellectual difficulty. In 1916, Terman adapted Binet's test for use with American students. His efforts led to the development of the Stanford-Binet, which is one of the major general intelligence tests in use today in America (Terman & Merrill, 1973). The other major intelligence test used in America is the Wechsler, which has separate scales for children and adults. These tests include measures of digit span, vocabulary, analogical reasoning, spatial judgment, and arithmetic. A typical question for adults on the Stanford-Binet is "Which direction would you have to face so your right hand would be to the north?" A great deal of effort goes into selecting test items that will predict scholastic performance.

Both of these tests produce measures that are called **intelligence quotients (IQs)**. The original definition of IQ involved relating mental ages and chronological ages. The test establishes one's mental age. If a child can solve problems on the test that the average eight-year-old can solve, then the child has a mental age of 8 independent of chronological age. IQ is defined as the ratio of mental age to chronological age times 100 or

$$IQ = 100 \times MA/CA$$

where MA is mental age and CA is chronological age. Thus, if the child's mental age were 8 and chronological age were 6, the IQ would be $100 \times 8/6 = 133$.

This definition of IQ proved unsuitable for a number of reasons. It cannot extend to measurement of adult intelligence since performance on intelligence tests starts to level off in the late teens and declines in later years. To deal with such difficulties, the common way of defining IQ now is in terms of what are called deviation scores. One subtracts the raw score of a person from the mean score for that age group and then transforms this difference score into a measure that will vary around 100, roughly as the earlier IQ scores would. The precise definition is expressed as

$$IQ = 100 + 15 \times \frac{(\text{score} - \text{mean})}{\text{standard deviation}}$$

where standard deviation is a measure of the variability of the scores. IQs so measured tend to be distributed according to a normal distribution. Figure 13.12 shows such a normal distribution of intelligence scores and the percentage of people who have scores in various ranges.

While the Stanford-Binet and the Weschler are two general intelligence tests, there are many others, some of which were developed to

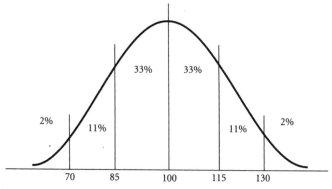

Figure 13.12 A normal distribution of IQ measures.

test specialized abilities, such as spatial ability. These tests partly owe their continued use in our society to the fact that they do predict performance in school with some accuracy, which was one of Binet's original goals. There is, however, considerable controversy about their use for this purpose. In particular, since such tests can be used to determine who can have access to what educational opportunities, there is a great deal of concern that they should be constructed to avoid biases against certain cultural groups. Immigrant groups to America often do poorly on tests of intelligence because of cultural biases on the tests. For instance, immigrant Italians of less than a century ago scored an average of 87 on IQ tests (Sarason & Doris, 1979) while today their descendants have slightly above average IQs (Ceci, 1991).

The very concept of intelligence is culturally relative. What one culture values as intelligent another culture will not. For instance, the Kpelle, an African culture, think the way Westerners sort instances into categories (a basis for some items in intelligence tests) is foolish (Cole, Gay, Glick, & Sharp, 1971). Sternberg (personal communication) notes that some cultures do not even have a word for intelligence. Still, the fact remains that intelligence tests do predict performance in our (Western) schools. It is an extremely subtle question as to when they are doing a valuable service in assessing students for schools and when they are simply enforcing arbitrary cultural beliefs about what is to be valued.

Related to the issue of the fairness of intelligence tests is whether they reflect innate endowment or acquired ability (the nature-versus-nurture issue again). Potentially definitive data would seem to come from studies of identical twins reared apart. Usually, these cases involve twins who have been adopted into different families—they have identical genetic endowment but different environmental experiences. The research on this topic is controversial (Kamin, 1974), but analyses (Bouchard, 1983; Bouchard & McGue, 1981) indicate that identical twins raised apart have IQs much more similar to each other than nonidentical fraternal twins raised in the same family. This certainly seems to be evidence that there is a strong innate component to IQ. It would be a mistake to generalize this to the conclusion that intelligence is largely innate. Intelligence and IQ are by no means the same thing. Because of the goals of intelligence tests, they must predict success across a range of environments, particularly academic. This means that they must discount the contributions of specific experiences to intelligence. We noted in Chapter 9, for instance, that chess masters tend not to have particularly high IQs. This is more a comment on the IQ test than on chess masters. If an IQ test focused on chess experience, it would have little success in predicting academic success generally. Thus, intelligence tests try to measure raw abilities and general knowledge that it is reasonable to expect of everyone in a culture. However, as we saw in Chapter 9, excellence in any specific domain depends on knowledge and experience that are not general in the culture.

Another interesting demonstration of this lack of correlation between expertise and IQ was performed by Ceci and Liker (1986). These researchers looked at the ability of avid horse racing fans to handicap races. They found that handicapping skill was related to developing a complex interactive model of horse racing, but that there was no relationship between this skill and IQ.

While specific experience is clearly important to success in any field, the remarkable fact is that these intelligence tests are able to predict success in certain endeavors. They predict with modest accuracy both performance in school and general success in life (or at least in Western societies). What is it about the mind that they are measuring? Much of the theoretical work in the field has been concerned with trying to answer this question. To understand how this question has been pursued, one must understand a little about a major method of the field, factor analysis.

◆

Standard intelligence tests measure general factors that predict success in school.

Factor Analysis

The general intelligence tests contain a number of subtests that measure individual abilities. Also, as noted, many specialized tests are available for measuring particular abilities. The basic observation is that people who do well on one test or subtest tend to do well on another test or subtest. The degree to which people perform comparably on two subtests is measured by a correlation coefficient. If all the same people who did well on one test did just as well on another, the correlation between the two tests would be 1. If all the people who did well on one test did proportionately badly on another, the correlation coefficient would be -1. If there was no relationship between how people did on one test and how they did on another test, the correlation coefficient would be zero. Typical correlations between tests are positive but not 1, indicating a less-than-perfect relationship between performance on one test and another.

As an example of this, Hunt (1985) looked at the relationships among the seven tests described in Table 13.2. Table 13.3 shows the intercorrelations among these test scores. As can be seen, some pairs of tests are more correlated than others. For instance, there is a relatively high (.67) correlation between reading comprehension and vocabulary but a relatively low (.14) correlation between reading comprehension and spatial reasoning. **Factor analysis** is a way of trying to make sense of these correlational patterns. The basic idea is to try to place these tests into some dimensional space such that the distance among the tests reflects the correlation. Items close together will have high correlations and so are measuring the same thing. Figure 13.13 shows an attempt to organize the tests in

Table 13.2 Description of Some of the Tests on the Washington Pre-College Test Battery

Test Name	Description
1. Reading comprehension	Answer questions about paragraph
2. Vocabulary	Choose synonyms for a word
3. Grammar	Identify correct and poor usage
4. Quantitative skills	Read word problems and decide whether problem can be solved
5. Mechanical reasoning	Examine a diagram and answer questions about it; requires knowledge of physical and mechanical principles
6. Spatial reasoning	Indicate how two-dimensional figures will appear if they are folded through a third dimension
7. Mathematics achievement	A test of high school algebra

From Hunt, 1985.

Table 13.2 into a two-dimensional space. The reader may confirm that the closer the items are in this space, the higher the correlation they have in Table 13.3.

The interesting question is how to make sense of this space. As we go from the bottom to the top, we get more and more symbolic and linguistic. One might refer to this dimension as a linguistic factor. Second, one might argue that as we go from the left to the right, the tests become more computational in character. We might consider this a reasoning factor.

Table 13.3 Intercorrelations Between Results of the Tests Listed in Table 13.2

Test no.	1	2	3	4	5	6	7
1	1.00	.67	.63	.40	.33	.14	.34
2		1.00	.59	.29	.46	.19	.31
3			1.00	.41	.34	.20	.46
4				1.00	.39	.46	.62
5					1.00	.47	.39
6						1.00	.46
7							1.00

From Hunt, 1985.

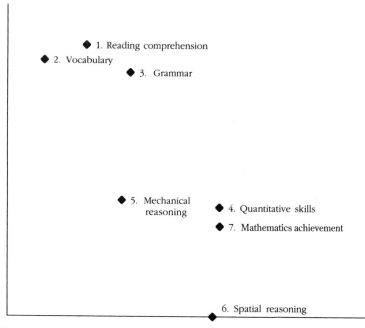

Figure 13.13 A representation of the tests in Table 13.2 in a two-dimensional space such that the distance between points decreases with increases in the intercorrelations from Table 13.3.

High correlations are now to be explained in terms of students having similar values of these factors. Thus, there is a high correlation between quantitative skills and mathematics achievement because they both have an intermediate degree of linguistic involvement and require substantial reasoning. People who are high on reasoning ability and not too low on verbal ability will tend to do well on these tests.

Factor analysis is basically an effort to go from a set of intercorrelations like those in Table 13.3 to a small set of factors that explain those intercorrelations. Unfortunately, there has been considerable debate about what the underlying factors are. Perhaps you can see other ways to explain the correlations in Table 13.3. For instance, one might argue that there is a linguistic factor linking tests 1 through 3, a reasoning factor linking tests 4, 5, and 7, and a separate spatial factor for test 6. Indeed, we will see that there have been many proposals for separate linguistic, reasoning, and spatial factors, although, as shown by the data in Table 13.3, it is a little difficult to separate the spatial and reasoning factors.

The difficulty of interpreting such data is reflected in the wide variety of positions that have been taken as to what the underlying factors of human intelligence are. Spearman (1904) argued that there was only one general factor that underlay performance across tests. He called his factor *g*.

In contrast, Thurstone (1938) argued that there were a number of separate factors, including the verbal, spatial, and reasoning we mentioned above. Guilford (1982) proposed no less than 120 distinct intellectual abilities. Cattell (1963) proposed a distinction between fluid and crystallized intelligence; **crystallized intelligence** referred to acquired knowledge, while **fluid intelligence** referred to the ability to reason or problem-solve in novel domains. (In Figure 13.9 it is the fluid intelligence that is showing the age-related decay, not the crystallized intelligence.) Horn (1968), elaborating on Cattell's theory, argued that there is a spatial intelligence that can be separated from fluid intelligence. Table 13.3 can be interpreted in terms of the Horn-Cattell theory, where crystallized intelligence maps into the linguistic factor (tests 1 to 3), fluid intelligence into the reasoning factor (tests 4, 5, and 7), and spatial intelligence into the spatial factor (test 6). Fluid intelligence tends to be tapped strongly in mathematical tests, but it is probably better referred to as a reasoning ability than a mathematical ability per se. As we noted with respect to Figure 13.13 and as is generally true, it is a bit difficult to separate the fluid and spatial intelligences in factor analytical studies, but it appears possible (Horn & Stankov, 1982).

It is hard to come away from this debate with any very firm conclusions, but it seems clear that in fact there is some differentiation in human intelligence as it appears on intelligence tests. Probably, the Horn-Cattell theory or the Thurstone theory offer the best analyses, producing what we will call a verbal factor, a spatial factor, and a reasoning factor. The rest of this chapter will provide further evidence for the division of the human intellect into various abilities. This is a significant conclusion because it indicates that there is some specialization in achieving human cognitive function.

In a survey of virtually all data sets, Carroll (1993) proposed a theory of intelligence that combines the Horn-Cattell and Thurstone perspectives. He proposed what he called a three-stratum theory. At the lowest stratum are very specific abilities like the ability to be a physicist. Such abilities Carroll thinks are largely not inheritable. At the next stratum are broader abilities like the verbal factor (or crystallized intelligence), the reasoning factor (or fluid intelligence), and the spatial factor. Finally, Carroll noted that these factors tend to correlate together to define something like Thurstone's g at the highest stratum.

In the last few decades, there has been considerable interest in the way these measures of individual differences relate to the kinds of theories of information processing that are found in cognitive psychology. For instance, how do subjects with high versus low spatial abilities differ in terms of the processes involved in the spatial imagery tasks discussed in Chapter 4? Makers of intelligence tests have tended to ignore such questions because their major goal is to predict scholastic performance. We will look at some information-processing studies that try to understand the reasoning factor, the verbal factor, and the spatial factor.

◆ ───

Factor analysis methods identify that a reasoning ability, a verbal ability, and a spatial ability underlie performance on various intelligence tests.

Reasoning Ability

Typical tests used to measure reasoning include mathematical problems, analogy problems, series extrapolation problems, deductive syllogisms, and problem-solving tasks. These are the kinds of tasks that we analyzed in great detail in Chapters 8 to 10. In the context of this book, such abilities might better be called problem-solving abilities. Most of the research in psychometric tests has focused only on whether a person gets a question right or not. In contrast, information-processing analyses try to examine the steps by which a person decides on an answer to such a question and the time necessary to perform each step.

The research of Sternberg (1977; Sternberg & Gardner, 1983) is an attempt to connect the psychometric research tradition with the information-processing tradition. He analyzed how people process a wide variety of reasoning problems. Figure 13.14 illustrates one of his analogy problems. Subjects were asked to solve the analogy "A is to B as C is to D_1 or D_2?" Sternberg analyzed the process of making such analogies into a number of stages. Two critical stages in his analysis are called reasoning and

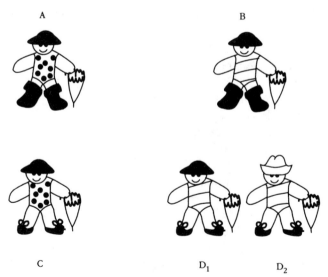

Figure 13.14 An example of an analogy problem used by Sternberg and Gardner, 1983. (Copyright © 1983 by the APA. Adapted by permission.)

comparison. Reasoning involves finding each feature that changes between A and B and applying it to C. Thus, A and B differ in the figure by a change in costume from spotted to striped. Thus, one predicts that C will change from spotted to striped to yield D. Comparison involves comparing the predicted version of D to the two choices, D_1 and D_2. Each feature is compared until one is found that enables a choice. Thus, the subject may first check that both D_1 and D_2 have an umbrella (which they do), then that they have a striped suit (which they do), and then that they have a dark hat (which only D_1 has). The dark hat feature will allow the subjects to reject D_2 and so accept D_1.

Sternberg was interested in the time subjects needed to make these judgments. He theorized that they would take a certain amount longer for each feature that A differed from B because this feature would have to be changed to derive D from C. Sternberg and Gardner (1983) estimated a time of about 0.28 seconds for each such feature. This is the *reasoning parameter*. They also estimated 0.60 seconds to compare a feature predicted of D with the features of D_1 and D_2. This is the *comparison parameter*. The values 0.28 and 0.60 are just averages; the actual values of these reasoning and comparison times varied across subjects. Sternberg and Gardner looked at the correlations between the values of these parameters for individual subjects and the psychometric measures of subjects' reasoning abilities. They found a correlation of .79 between the reasoning parameter and a psychometric measure of reasoning and a correlation of .75 between the comparison parameter and the psychometric measure. This means that subjects who are slow in reasoning or comparison do poorly in psychometric tests of reasoning. Thus, they were able to show that measures of speed identified in an information-processing analysis are critical to psychometric measures of intelligence.

◆
Subjects who score high on reasoning ability are able to perform individual steps of reasoning more rapidly.

Verbal Ability

Probably the most robust factor to emerge from intelligence tests is the verbal factor. There has been considerable interest in determining what processes distinguish people with strong verbal abilities. Goldberg, Schwartz, and Stewart (1977) compared people with high and low verbal ability with respect to the way they make various kinds of word judgments. One kind of word judgment concerned simply whether pairs of words were identical. Thus, they would say yes to a pair such as

- bear, bear

Other subjects were asked to judge whether pairs of words sounded alike. Thus, they would say yes to a pair such as

- bare, bear

A third group of subjects were asked to judge whether pairs of words were in the same category. Thus, they would say yes to a pair such as

- lion, bear

Figure 13.15 shows the difference between subjects with high and low verbal abilities in terms of the time needed to make these three kinds of judgments. As can be seen, subjects with high verbal ability enjoy only a small advantage on the identity judgments but show much larger advantages on the sound and meaning matches. This and other studies (e.g., Hunt, Davidson, & Lansman, 1981) have convinced researchers that a major advantage of subjects with high verbal ability is the speed with which they can go from a linguistic stimulus to information about it—in the case of the

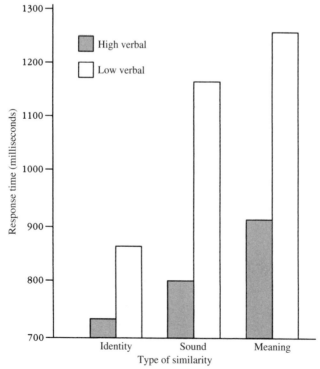

Figure 13.15 Response time to judge the similarity of pairs of words for subjects with high and low verbal abilities, and three types of similarity. (From Goldberg, Schwartz, & Stewart, 1977.)

study above, subjects were going from the visual word to information about its sound and meaning. Thus, as in the Sternberg studies in the previous section, speed of processing is related to intellectual ability.

There is also evidence for a fairly strong relationship between working-memory capacity for linguistic material and for verbal ability. Daneman and Carpenter (1980) developed the following test of individual differences in working-memory capacity. Subjects would read or hear a number of unrelated sentences such as

- When at last his eyes opened, there was no gleam of triumph, no shade of anger.

- The taxi turned up Michigan Avenue where they had a clear view of the lake.

After reading or hearing these sentences, subjects had to recall the last word of each sentence. They were tested with two to seven such sentences. The largest group of sentences for which they could recall the last words was defined as the reading span or listening span. College students had spans from 2 to 5.5. It turns out that these spans are very strongly related to their comprehension scores and to tests of verbal ability. These reading and listening spans are much more strongly related than are measures of simple digit span. Daneman and Carpenter argue that a larger reading and listening span indicates the ability to store a larger portion of the text during comprehension. The Kintsch and van Dijk model, reviewed in Chapter 12, illustrated how holding a larger portion of the text in working memory might enhance comprehension.

♦
People of high verbal ability are able to rapidly retrieve meanings of words and have larger working memories for verbal information.

Spatial Ability

There have also been efforts to relate measures of spatial ability to research on mental rotation, such as that discussed in Chapter 4. Just and Carpenter (1985) compared subjects with low spatial ability and those with high spatial ability performing the Shepard and Metzler mental rotation tasks (see Figure 4.4). Figure 13.16 plots the speed with which these two types of subjects can rotate figures of differing angular disparity. As can be seen, subjects with low spatial ability were not only performing the task more slowly but were also more affected by angle of disparity. This means that the rate of mental rotation is slower for subjects with low spatial ability.

Spatial ability has often been set in contrast with verbal ability. Although some people rate high on both abilities or low on both, interest often focuses

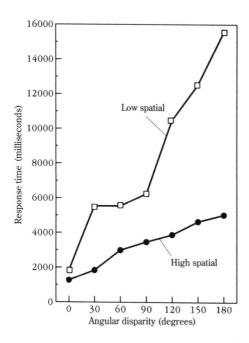

Figure 13.16 Mean time to determine that two objects have the same three-dimensional shape as a function of the angular difference in their portrayed orientations. Separate functions are plotted for subjects with high and low spatial ability. (From Just & Carpenter, 1985. Copyright © 1985 by the APA. Adapted by permission.)

on people who display a relative imbalance of the abilities. MacLeod, Hunt, and Matthews (1978) found evidence that these different types of people will solve a cognitive task differently. They looked at performance on the Clark and Chase sentence verification task that we considered in Chapter 12. Recall that this task involves presenting subjects with sentences such as *The plus is above the star* or *The star is not above the plus* and asking them to determine whether the sentence accurately describes the picture. Typically, subjects are slower when there is a negative like *not* in the sentence and when the supposition of the sentences mismatches the picture.

MacLeod et al. speculated, however, that there were really two groups of subjects—those who took a representation of the sentence and matched it against a picture and those who first converted the sentence to an image of a picture and then matched that against the picture. They speculated that the first group would be high in verbal ability while the second group would be high in spatial ability. In fact, they did find two groups of subjects. Figure 13.17 shows the judgment times of these two groups as a function of whether the sentence was true or not and whether it involved a negative. As can be seen, one group of subjects showed no effect of whether the sentence involved a negative, whereas the other group showed a very substantial effect. The group of subjects not showing the effect of a negative had higher scores on tests of spatial ability than the other group. This was the group of subjects that compared an image formed from the sentence against the picture. Such an image would not have a negative in it.

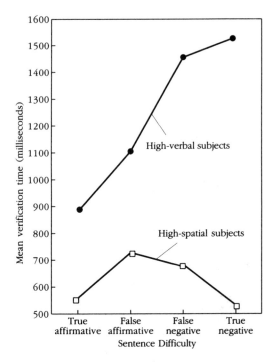

Figure 13.17 Mean time to judge a sentence as a function of sentence type for subjects with high verbal ability compared to those with high spatial ability. (From MacLeod, Hunt, & Mathews, 1978.)

◆

People with high spatial ability can perform elementary spatial operations quite rapidly and often choose to solve a task spatially rather than verbally.

Conclusions from Information-Processing Studies

One of the major outcomes of the research relating psychometric measures to cognitive tasks has been to reinforce the distinction between verbal and spatial ability. The reader will recall from Chapter 4 that there is considerable nonpsychometric evidence for this distinction as well. A second outcome of this research has been to indicate that differences in an ability (reasoning, linguistic, or spatial) may result from differences in rates of processing and working-memory capacities. A number of researchers (e.g., Salthouse, 1992; Just & Carpenter, 1992) have argued that the working-memory differences may be derivative of processing speed differences, in that people can maintain more information in working memory when they can process it more rapidly.

Research on the neural correlates of individual differences (Haier, Siegel, Nuechterlein, Hazlett, Wu, Paek, Browning, & Buchsbaum, 1988) is interesting in this regard. These researchers looked at PET recordings (see Chapter 1) during an abstract reasoning task. They found that the better-performance subjects showed less PET activity. This suggests that poorer-performance subjects have to work harder at the same task. Like the information-processing work pointing to processing speed, this suggests that differences in intelligence may reflect very basic processes. There is a tendency to see such results as favoring a nativist view, but in fact they are neutral to the nature-versus-nurture controversy. Some people may take longer and may need to expend more effort to solve a problem, either because they have practiced less or because they have inherently less efficient neural structures. We saw earlier in the chapter that, with practice, children could become faster than adults at processes like mental rotation.

◆
Individual differences on general factors like verbal, reasoning, and spatial abilities appear to reflect the speed and ease with which basic cognitive processes are performed.

Gardner's Multiple Intelligences

In his 1983 book, Howard Gardner argued for the existence of at least six types of intelligence — linguistic, musical, mathematical, spatial, bodily kinesthetic, and personal. His book juxtaposes a wide variety of evidence on these issues. He supplements the traditional psychometric evidence for such traits with a large number of other criteria: He uses evidence that there are separate neural centers underlying these various types of intelligence, that people can be found who are exceptionally talented in just one of these dimensions, that information-processing research has found evidence for such abilities, that there are separate developmental histories for each intelligence, that there are cross-cultural universals in the display of such abilities, and that distinct representational systems have emerged for each of these intelligences. He cannot apply each of his criteria to produce convincing evidence for each type of intelligence, but enough criteria apply to each to present a rather convincing picture.

Clearly, the strongest case exists for linguistic intelligence. As we noted in Chapters 1, 4, and 11, there is good evidence for separate neural centers for language processing. Gardner regards the great poets and writers as people with truly exceptional linguistic talent. We have already discussed in this chapter and in Chapters 11 and 12 the rather distinctive cognitive processes that underlie language. In Chapter 11, we also discussed the cross-linguistic universals of language and the rather distinctive developmental history of language acquisition. Finally, language does have a distinctive symbol system, which is its written form.

There is also a fairly strong case for a separate spatial intelligence. Again, we noted in Chapter 4 the evidence for separate neural centers for spatial processing both in perception and imagery. We have reviewed the psychometric and experimental data pointing to a separate ability for spatial processing. Gardner takes the ubiquity of visual art across cultures to be further evidence for the existence of a special spatial intelligence.

Psychometrically, measures of mathematical ability tend to be strongly correlated with spatial ability. In general, Gardner's case for a separate cross-cultural mathematical ability is somewhat weak. Part of the problem is definitional. All cultures have counting systems, but much of what psychometric tests measure under mathematical abilities is unique to modern societies. It is hard to make the case that there are universals of modern algebra in the way that there are universals of natural language. There may be universals of simpler abilities with numbers, such as counting. Gardner points to a syndrome called the Gerstmann syndrome, which is associated with damage to the left parietal lobes and to the temporal and occipital association areas contiguous to them. People with damage to these neural centers will suffer problems in arithmetic calculation, in left-right orientation, and in identifying their fingers. However, there is not much consensus about the nature of this problem. Probably it would be wise to read Gardner's case for mathematical ability as not specific to mathematics but rather as a more general reasoning factor, as discussed earlier.[2]

The other three intelligences Gardner mentions are not typically thought of as cognitive, and many researchers question Gardner's use of the term *intelligence* to describe them. Nonetheless, his discussion makes the point that individual differences go beyond the purely cognitive. The case for a musical ability would seem to be quite good. There are indeed striking individual differences in musical ability, with the existence of such remarkably precocious children as Mozart. Music is certainly a cultural universal. Gardner argues that musical ability is localized in the right hemisphere in contrast to language, which is localized in the left hemisphere.

By bodily-kinesthetic intelligence Gardner refers to skilled use of the body, regarding a mime like Marcel Marceau as someone who is especially skilled in this way. We reviewed in Chapter 1 the evidence for special neural centers for body movement. Gardner views the universality of tool building and dance as evidence for a universal human-specific ability involving body movement.

Gardner distinguishes between two types of personal intelligence, one concerned with self-understanding and one associated with the capacity for social success. He argues that humans around the world reflect a very

---

[2] McCloskey (1992) reports a study of two patients with difficulty in retrieval of multiplication facts. However, these patients do not seem to fit Gardner's pattern. At least one has damage to the frontal lobe, not the parietal. Also, both patients suffered deficits more general than just arithmetic.

distinctive and universal developmental history in the unfolding of their personalities, starting with the strong infant attachments to mothers and progressing through the rebellious teenage years during which independence is established.

One of the implications of Gardner's view of multiple intelligences is that it does not make sense to talk about one person as being more intelligent than another. Intelligence is not a unitary concept like height. As Horn, a well-known psychometrician, has put it: "Although the word intelligence (as a unitary concept) continues to be useful in everyday life, this does not represent a good scientific concept" (Horn, 1986, p. 69).

◆

Gardner has argued that there are biological bases for a wide variety of different types of intelligence.

Conclusions

This concludes our discussion of human intelligence (this chapter) and human cognition (this book). One recurring theme throughout the book has been the relative diversity of the components of the mind. The first chapter reviewed evidence for different specializations in the nervous system. The early chapters reviewed the evidence for different levels of processing as the information entered the system. We presented the different types of knowledge representation and the distinction between procedural and declarative knowledge. Then, we discussed the distinct status of language. Many of these distinctions have been reinforced in this chapter on individual differences.

A second dimension of discussion has been rate of processing. Latency data has been the most frequently used measure of cognitive functioning in this book. Often, when we reported error measures (the second most common dependent measure), this was just the reflection of slow processing. We have seen evidence in this chapter that individuals vary in their rate of processing, and this book has stressed that that rate can be increased with practice.

In addition to the quantitative component of speed, there is a qualitative component to individual differences. People can differ in terms of where their strengths lie. They can also differ according to what strategies they use to solve problems. We saw evidence in Chapter 9 that one dimension of growing expertise is the development of more effective strategies.

One might view the human mind in analogy to a large corporation that consists of many interacting components. Different corporations have different strengths, reflecting the relative strengths of their components. With practice, different components tend to become more efficient at doing their tasks. Another way to achieve improvement is by strategic reorganizations of parts of the corporation. However, there is more to a successful company than just the sum of its parts. These pieces have to interact together smoothly to achieve the overall goals of the organization. Some researchers (e.g., Anderson, 1983; Newell, 1991) have complained about the rather fragmented picture of the human mind that emerges from current research in cognitive psychology. One agenda for future research will be to understand how all the pieces fit together to achieve a human mind.

Remarks and Suggested Readings

Piaget and his coauthors have written a great many books on child development that have been translated from the original French. These include *The Origins of Intelligence in Children* (1952a), *The Child's Conception of Number* (1952b), and by Inhelder and Piaget, *The Growth of Logical Thinking from Childhood to Adolescence* (1958). Siegler (1998) is a text on cognitive development. Kuhn and Siegler (1998) is a general review. Four Carnegie Symposia on Cognition (Siegler, 1978; Sophian, 1984; Granrud, 1993; McClelland & Siegler, in press) contain a large number of papers presenting information-processing approaches to cognition. A number of people have written on cognition and aging, including Salthouse (1991) and Perlmutter (1988). Simonton (1997) describes his theory of productivity across a lifetime and presents further data consistent with Figure 13.10. Sternberg (1985) describes his triarchic theory of intelligence and has been highly critical of traditional approaches to intelligence (e.g., Sternberg, in press). A considerable I.Q. controversy was stirred by the publication of Herrnstein and Murray's (1994) *The Bell Curve*. A report of a task force of the American Psychological Association on the issues behind the controversies is contained in the February 1996 issue of the *American Psychologist*.

✦ Glossary

2 1/2-D sketch: Marr's proposal for a visual representation that identified where surfaces were in space. (p. 46)

3-D model: Marr's proposal for an object-centered representation. (p. 46)

abstraction theories: Theories that hold that concepts are represented as abstract descriptions of their central tendencies. (p. 164)

ACT: Anderson's theory of the way declarative and procedural knowledge interact in complex cognitive processes. (p. 181)

action potential: The sudden change in electric potential that travels down the axon of a neuron. (p. 18)

activation: A state of memory traces that determines both the speed and probability of access to the memory trace. (p. 181)

affirmation of the consequent: The logical fallacy that one can reason from the validation of the consequent of a conditional statement to the validation of its antecedent: *If A, then B* and *B is true* can be thought (falsely) to always imply *A is true.* (p. 319)

agnosia: See visual agnosia.

AI: Abbreviation for artificial intelligence. (pp. 2,11)

amnesia: A memory deficit that occurs as a result of brain damage. (p. 231)

analogy: The process by which a problem solver maps the solution for one problem into a solution for another problem. (p. 247)

antecedent: The condition of a conditional statement: It is the *A* in *If A, then B.* (p. 316)

anterograde amnesia: Loss of ability to remember events after an injury. (p. 231)

aphasia: An impairment in speech that results from a brain injury. (p. 25)

apperceptive agnosia: Inability to recognize simple shapes such as circles or triangles. (p. 37)

argument: An element of a propositional representation that corresponds to a time, place, person, or object. (p. 146) *articulatory loop:* Baddeley's proposed system for rehearsing verbal information. (p. 176)

artificial intelligence (AI): A field of computer science that attempts to develop intelligently behaving machines. (pp. 2, 11)

associative agnosia: Inability to recognize complex objects such as an anchor, even though one can recognize simple shapes and copy the drawings of complex objects. (p. 37)

associative priming: Facilitation in access to information when closely related items are presented. (p. 185)

associative stage: The second of Fitts's stages of skill acquisition, in which the declarative representation of the skill is converted into a procedural representation. (p. 281)

atmosphere hypothesis: The proposal by Woodworth and Sels that when faced with a categorical syllogism, subjects tend to accept conclusions with the same quantifiers as the premises. (p. 327)

attention: The allocation of cognitive resources among ongoing processes. (p. 104)

attenuation theory: Treisman's theory of attention, which proposed that we weaken some incoming sensory signals on the basis of their physical characteristics. (p. 79)

automatic process: A process that does not require attention to execute. (pp. 92–99)

autonomous stage: The third of Fitts's stages of skill acquisition, in which the performance of the skill becomes automated. (p. 282)

axon: The portion of a neuron that carries information from one region of the brain to another. (p. 18)

backup avoidance: The tendency in problem solving to avoid operators that take one back to a state already visited. (p. 252)

backward inferences: Inferences in sentence comprehension that connect the sentence to the prior context. (p. 406)

bar detectors: Cells in the visual cortex that respond maximally to bars in their visual field. (p. 41)

Bayes's theorem: A theorem that prescribes how to combine the prior probability of a hypothesis with the conditional probability of the evidence given the hypothesis to assess the posterior probability of the hypothesis. (p. 332)

behaviorism: The theoretical viewpoint that psychological theory should be concerned only with behavior and should not refer to mental constructs. (p. 9)

biconditional: A logical assertion consisting of two parts that each imply the other: *A if and only if B.* (p. 319) *bottom-up processing:* Information from the physical stimulus is used to help recognize a stimulus. Contrast with top-down processing. (p. 63)

bridging inference: An inference that is necessary to connect two portions of a text. (p. 419)

Broca's area: A region in the left frontal cortex that is important for processing language, particularly syntax in speech. (p. 25)

categorical perception: The phenomenon of perceiving stimuli in distinct categories without graded boundaries. (p. 62)

categorical syllogism: A syllogism involving statements with logical quantifiers where one premise relates A to B, another relates B to C, and the conclusion relates A to C. (p. 326)

central executive: Baddeley's proposed system for controlling various slave rehearsal systems, such as the articulatory loop and the visuospatial sketchpad. (p. 177)

chunk: A term introduced by Miller to refer to a unit of knowledge that organizes together a few subitems. (p. 123)

cognitive architecture: A theory of mind which involves general principles that organize cognition across a wide variety of domains. (p. 15)

cognitive maps: Mental representations of the locations of objects and places in the environment. (p. 124)

cognitive neuroscience: The study of the neural basis of cognition. (p. 16)

cognitive stage: The first of Fitts's stages of skill acquisition, in which a declarative encoding of the skill is developed and used. (p. 281)

competence: A term in linguistics that refers to a person's abstract knowledge of a language, which is not always reflected in performance. (p. 358)

componential analyses: An approach to instruction that involves analyzing a competence into the individual elements that need to be learned. (p. 308)

concrete-operational stage: The third part of Piaget's four stages of development, during which a child has systematic schemes for thinking about the physical world. (p. 424)

conditional probability: In the context of Bayes's theorem, this is the probability that a particular piece of evidence will be found if a hypothesis is true. (p. 333)

conditional statement: An assertion that if an antecedent is true, then a consequent must be true: A statement of the form *If A, then B*. (p. 316)

conditional syllogisms: Arguments consisting of a conditional statement and a related assertion as premises and a conclusion that is supposed to follow. (p. 317) *connectionism:* The viewpoint that cognition is to be explained in terms of the interactions of connected neuronlike components. (p. 31)

consequent: The result of a conditional statement: It is the *B* in *If A, then B.* (p. 316)

conservation: Used by Piaget to refer to which properties of objects are preserved under certain transformations. (p. 425)

consonantal feature: A consonantlike quality in a phoneme. (p. 59)

constituents: Subpatterns that correspond to basic phrases, or units, in a sentence's surface structure. (p. 390)

corpus callosum: A broad band of fibers that enables communication between the left and right hemispheres. (p. 24)

crystallized intelligence: Cattell's term for the factor in intelligence that depends on acquired knowledge. (p. 447)

decay theory: The theory that forgetting is caused by the spontaneous decay of memory traces over time. (p. 206)

declarative knowledge: Explicit knowledge of various facts. (pp. 238, 239)

deductive reasoning: Reasoning in situations where the conclusions can be determined to follow with certainty from the premises. (p. 315)

default values: Typical values for slots in a schema representation. (p. 155)

deliberate practice: The kind of practice postulated by Ericsson to be critical for development of expertise. This practice is highly motivated and involves careful self-monitoring. (p. 304)

delta rule: A rule for neural learning that changes strengths of associations in proportion to the activation of input and to the difference between desired and target activation of the output. (p. 166)

dendrite: The branching portion of a neuron that receives synapses from the axons of other neurons. (p. 18)

denial of the antecedent: The logical fallacy that one can reason from the denial of the antecedent of a conditional statement to the denial of its consequent: *If A, then B* and *Not A* together are thought to imply *Not B.* (p. 319)

depth of processing: The theory that memory for information is improved if the information is processed at deeper levels of analysis. (p. 175)

descriptive model: A model that states how people actually behave, in contrast to a prescriptive model. (p. 335)

dichotic listening task: A task in which subjects are presented with two messages to two ears over headphones and are instructed to shadow one. (p. 75) *difference reduction:* The tendency in problem solving to select operators that eliminate a difference between the current state and the goal. (pp. 252–253)

dissociations: Situations in which different tests of memory show different results. Such demonstrations are thought to be important in arguing for different memory systems. (p. 233)

dual-code theory: Paivio's theory that there are separate visual and verbal representations for knowledge. (p. 106)

edge detectors: Cells in the visual cortex that respond maximally to edges in their visual field. (p. 41)

Einstellung effect: The term used by Luchins to refer to the set effect in which subjects will repeat a solution that has worked for previous problems, even when a simpler solution is possible. (p. 269)

elaborative processing: Embellishing a to-be-remembered item with additional information. (p. 190)

empiricism: The position that knowledge is acquired through experience in the world. (p. 6)

encoding-specificity principle: Tulving's principle that memory is better when the encoding of an item at study matches the encoding at test. (p. 230)

ERP: Abbreviation for event-related potential. (p. 28)

event-related potential (ERP): Measurement of changes in electrical activity at the scalp in response to an external event. (p. 28)

excitatory postsynaptic potential: A measure of the decrease in the difference in electric potential between the outside and inside of the neuron. This is used as a measure in studies of long-term potentiation. (p. 189)

excitatory synapses: Synapses where the neurotransmitters decrease the potential difference across the membrane of the neuron. (p. 18)

explicit memories: Memories that a subject can consciously recall. (p. 233)

factor analysis: A statistical method that, in the context of intelligence tests, tries to find a set of factors that will account for performance across a range of tests. (p. 444)

fan effect: The phenomenon that retrieval of memories is slower the more additional material is associated with the items composing the original memories. (p. 210)

feature analysis: A theory of pattern recognition that claims that we extract primitive features and then recognize their combinations. (p. 51)

feature integration theory: Treisman's proposal that one must focus attention on a set of features before they can be synthesized into a pattern. (p. 89) *feature map:* A representation of the spatial locations of a particular feature. (p. 44)

filter theory: Broadbent's theory of attention that sensory information has to pass through some bottleneck, at which point only some of the information is selected for further processing. (p. 76)

flashbulb memories: Particularly good memory for events that are very important and traumatic. (p. 197)

FLMP (fuzzy logical model of perception): Massaro's theory of perception, which claims that stimulus features and context combine independently to determine perception. (pp. 68–69)

fluid intelligence: Cattell's term for the factor in intelligence that reflects the ability to reason or solve problems. (p. 447)

formal-operational stage: The fourth of Piaget's four stages of development, during which the child has abstract schemes for reasoning about the world. (p. 425)

forward inferences: Inferences in sentence comprehension that anticipate things not yet asserted. (p. 406)

fovea: The area of the retina of the eye with highest visual acuity. When one fixates on an object, one moves the eye so that the image of the object falls on the fovea. (p. 39)

framing effects: The tendency for people to make different choices among the same alternatives, depending on the statement of the alternatives. (p. 347)

frontal lobe: The region at the front of the cerebral cortex that includes the motor cortex and the prefrontal cortex. (p. 23)

functional fixedness: The tendency to represent objects as serving conventional problem-solving functions and thus failing to see that they can serve novel functions. (p. 267)

functional magnetic resonance imaging (fMRI): Measurement of metabolic activity by measuring the magnetic field produced by the iron in oxygenated blood. (p. 28)

gambler's fallacy: The belief that if a string of probabilistic events has turned out one way, there is an increased probability that the next event will now turn out the other way. (p. 344)

garden-path sentence: A sentence with a transient ambiguity where we make the wrong interpretation initially and have to correct ourselves. (p. 401)

General Problem Solver (GPS): A problem-solving simulation created by Newell and Simon that embodied means-ends analysis. (p. 257) *geons:* The primitive objects in terms of which Biederman proposed larger objects were perceived. (p. 54)

gestalt principles of organization: Principles that determine how a scene is organized into components. (p. 47)

goal state: A state in a problem space where the goal is satisfied. (p. 242)

grammar: A set of rules that prescribe all the acceptable utterances of a language. A grammar consists of syntax, semantics, and phonology. (p. 355)

hill climbing: The tendency to choose operators in problem solving that yield states more similar to the goal. (p. 253)

hippocampus: The subcortical area that plays a critical role in the formation of permanent memories. (p. 22)

icon: The name used by Neisser for the information representation in visual sensory memory. (p. 88)

immediacy of interpretation: The principle of language processing that people commit to an interpretation of a word and its role in a sentence as soon as they process the word. (p. 392)

implicit memories: Memories that cannot be displayed in tests that call for explicit recall, but that can be demonstrated by performance on various tasks. (p. 233)

incubation effect: The phenomenon that sometimes solutions to a particular problem come easier after a period of time in which one has ignored trying to solve the problem. (p. 273)

inductive reasoning: Reasoning in situations in which the conclusions follow only probabilistically from the premises. (p. 315)

information-processing approach: An analysis of human cognition into a set of steps in which abstract information is processed. (p. 12)

inhibition of return: Decreased ability to return attention to a location or object that has already been attended. (p. 95)

inhibitory synapses: Synapses where the neurotransmitters increase the potential difference across the membrane of a neuron. (p. 18)

insight problems: Problems whose solution depend on one key insight. (p. 275)

instance theories: Theories that hold that our knowledge of concepts comes by retrieving specific instances of the concepts. (p. 164)

intelligence quotient (IQ): A measure of general intellectual performance, which is normed to have a mean of 100 and a standard deviation of 15. (p. 442)

intelligent tutoring systems: Computer systems that combine cognitive models with techniques from artificial intelligence to create instructional interactions with students. (p. 308) *interactive processing:* The position that semantic and syntactic cues are simultaneously brought to bear in interpreting a sentence. Contrasts with the modularity position. (p. 403)

interference theory: The theory that forgetting is caused by other memories interfering with the retention of the target memory. (p. 206)

introspection: A methodology much practiced at the turn of the century in Germany. It involved trying to analyze thought into its components through self-analysis. (p. 7)

isa link: A particular link in a semantic network or schema representation that indicates the superset of the category. (p. 152)

knowledge representations: Proposals that attempt to explain how different types of information are encoded and processed. (p. 105)

Korsakoff syndrome: An amnesia that occurs as a result of chronic alcoholism and nutritional deficit. (p. 231)

language universals: Properties that all natural languages satisfy. (p. 383)

late selection theory: Deutsch and Deutsch's theory of attention, which proposed that all sensory information could be processed but that attentional limitations occurred in our ability to respond to that information. (pp. 75, 79)

leading-edge strategy: The proposal in the Kintsch and van Dijk text-processing model that subjects maintain in working memory a subset of the propositions from the text. (p. 420)

linguistic determinism: The proposal that the structure of one's language strongly influences the way one thinks. (p. 369)

linguistic intuitions: Judgments by the speakers of a language about whether sentences are well formed and about other properties of sentences. (p. 356)

linguistics: An academic field that attempts to characterize the structure of language. (p. 354)

link: A connection between elements in a network. (p. 148)

logic: A subdiscipline of philosophy and mathematics that tries to formally specify what it means for an argument to be correct. (p. 314)

logical quantifiers: Elements like *all, no, some,* and *some not* that appear in statements like *All A are B.* (p. 325)

long-term potentiation (LTP): The increase in responsiveness of a neuron as a function of past stimulation. (p. 189)

LTP: Abbreviation for long-term potentiation. (p. 189)

mastery learning: The effort to bring students to mastery of each element in a curriculum before promoting them to new material in the curriculum. (p. 308) *meaning-based representation:* A knowledge representation that attempts to abstract out some significant aspects of an experience. (pp. 105, 137)

means-ends analysis: The creation of a new goal to enable a problem-solving operator to apply. (p. 253)

memory span: The amount of information that can be perfectly retained in an immediate test of memory. (p. 172)

mental images: Internal representations of visual and spatial information. (p. 111)

mental model theory: Johnson-Laird's theory that subjects judge a syllogism by imagining a world that satisfies the premises and seeing if the conclusion is satisfied in that world. (p. 330)

mental rotation: The process of continuously transforming the orientation of a mental image. (p. 111)

method of loci: A mnemonic technique that involves associating to-be-remembered items with locations along a well-known path. (p. 223)

mnemonic technique: A technique to enhance memory performance. (p. 144)

modularity: The proposal that language is a separate component from the rest of cognition. It further argues that language comprehension involves an initial phase in which only syntactic considerations are brought to bear. (p. 373)

modus ponens: The rule of logic that says that if a conditional statement is true and its antecedent is true, then its consequent must be true: *If A, then B* and *A* together imply *B*. (p. 316)

modus tollens: The rule of logic that says that if a conditional statement is true and its consequent is false, then its antecedent must be false: *If A, then B* and *Not B* together imply *Not A*. (p. 317)

mood congruence: The result that one's memory is better for material whose emotional content matches one's mood at test. (p. 227)

nativism: The position that children are born knowing significant elements of knowledge. (p. 6)

natural language: A language that can be acquired and spoken by a human. (p. 383)

negative transfer: Poorer learning of a second task as a function of having learned a first task. (p. 307)

neuron: The cell in the nervous system responsible for information processing. Neurons accumulate and transmit electrical activity. (p. 16)

neurotransmitter: A chemical that crosses the synapse from the axon of one neuron to alter the electric potential of the membrane of another neuron. (p. 18) *node:* An element of a propositional or semantic network. (p. 148)

occipital lobe: The region at the back of the cerebral cortex that is mainly devoted to vision. (p. 23)

operator: A term used in problem-solving research to refer to knowledge of a particular action that will produce a particular state of affairs. (p. 241)

parallel distributed processing (PDP): A theory of neural information processing that emphasizes interactions between patterns of activation among connected neural elements. (p. 31)

parameter setting: The proposal that children learn a language by learning the setting of a hundred or so parameters that define a natural language. (p. 386)

parietal lobe: The region at the top of the cerebral cortex that is involved in attention and higher-level sensory functions. (p. 23)

parsing: The process by which the words in a linguistic message are transformed into a mental representation of their combined meaning. (p. 389)

partial-report procedure: An experimental procedure in which subjects are cued to report only some of the items from a display. (p. 86)

PDP: Abbreviation for parallel distributed processing. (p. 31)

perception-based representation: A knowledge representation that attempts to preserve much of the structure of a perceptual experience. (p. 105)

performance: A term in linguistics that refers to the way a person speaks. This behavior is thought to be only an imperfect reflection of that person's linguistic competence. (p. 358)

permission schema: An interpretation of a conditional statement in which the antecedent specifies the situations in which the consequent is permitted. (p. 323)

PET: Abbreviation for positron emission tomography. (p. 28)

phoneme restoration effect: The tendency to hear phonemes that make sense in the speech context even if no phoneme occurred. (p. 64)

phonemes: The basic units of speech that make up words. (p. 57)

phonology: Grammatical rules for assigning sound structure to sentences (p. 356).

phrase structure: The hierarchical organization of a sentence into a set of units called phrases, sometimes represented as a tree structure. (p. 358)

place of articulation: The place at which the vocal tract is closed or constricted in the production of a phoneme. (p. 59) *positron emission tomography (PET):* Measurement of metabolic activity on different regions of the brain using a radioactive tracer. (p. 28)

posterior probability: In Bayes's theorem, the probability that a hypothesis is true after considering the evidence. (p. 334)

power function: A function in which the independent variable X is raised to a power to obtain the dependent variable Y, as in $Y = AX^b$. (p. 188)

power law of forgetting: The phenomenon that memory performance deteriorates as a power function of the retention interval. (p. 203)

power law of learning: The phenomenon that memory performance improves as a power function of practice. (p. 188)

prefrontal cortex: The region at the front of the frontal cortex that is involved in planning and other higher-level cognition. (p. 23)

preoperational stage: The second of Piaget's four stages of development, during which a child has unsystematic schemes for thinking about the physical world. (p. 424)

prescriptive model: A model that specifies how people ought to behave to be considered rational, in contrast to a descriptive model. (p. 335)

primal sketch: Level of visual processing in Marr's model in which the visual features have been extracted. (p. 72)

priming: An enhancement of the processing of a stimulus as a function of prior exposure. (p. 236)

principle of minimal attachment: A principle of parsing that interprets a sentence in a way that involves the minimal complication to the phrase structure. (p. 401)

prior probability: In Bayes's theorem, the probability that a hypothesis is true before considering the evidence. (p. 333)

probability matching: The tendency to choose an alternative with a probability that matches the frequency with which it occurs in experience. (p. 339)

problem space: A representation of the various sequences of problem-solving operators that lead among various states of a problem. (p. 242)

procedural knowledge: Knowledge of how to perform various tasks. (pp. 238, 239)

proceduralization: The process by which declarative knowledge is converted into procedural knowledge. (p. 289)

production systems: Systems that represent problem-solving competencies as sets of productions. (p. 250)

productions: Condition-action rules that encode the situations in which it is appropriate to take a particular problem-solving operator. (p. 250) *productivity:* The fact that natural languages have an infinite number of possible utterances. (p. 354)

proposition: The smallest unit of knowledge that can stand as a separate assertion. (p. 145)

propositional network: A propositional representation in which the relation and arguments of the proposition are linked in a network. (p. 148)

propositional representation: A representation of meaning in terms of a set of propositions. (p. 144)

psychometric tests: Tests of different aspects of an individual's intellectual performance. (p. 441)

rate of firing: The rate at which nerve impulses are generated along axons. (p. 19)

recognition-by-components theory: Biederman's proposal that we recognize objects by first identifying the geons that correspond to their subobjects. (p. 53)

regularity: The fact that natural languages have very systematic rules that determine the possible forms of utterances. (p. 354)

relation: The element that organizes the arguments of a propositional representation. (p. 145)

representation: See knowledge representation.

retrograde amnesia: Loss of memories for things that occurred before an injury. (p. 231)

rewrite rules: Rules for expanding nonterminal symbols in a phrase structure into other symbols. Such rules will generate a complete sentence and its phrase structure. (p. 361)

route maps: Representation of the environment consisting of the paths between locations (contrast with survey maps). (p. 125)

SAM: The theory of memory proposed by Shiffrin that claims that the availability of memories is a function of their familiarity, which in turn is a function of their strength of association to cues in the environment. (p. 181)

schema: A representation of members of a category in terms of what type of objects they are, what parts they tend to have, and what their typical properties are. A slot-value structure is used to represent this information. (p. 154)

scripts: A schema representation proposed by Schank and Abelson for event concepts. (p. 161)

search: The process by which a problem solver finds a sequence of operators to solve a problem. (p. 242) *search tree:* A representation of the set of states that can be reached by applying operators to a start state. (p. 243)

selection task: A subject is given a conditional statement of the form *If A, then B* and must choose which situations among *A*, *B*, *Not A*, and *Not B* need to be checked to test the truth of the conditional. (p. 321)

self-reference effect: Better memory that people often show for information about themselves. (p. 198)

semantics: Grammatical rules for assigning meaning to a sentence. (p. 356)

sensory-motor stage: The first of Piaget's four stages of development, during which a child lacks basic schemes for thinking about the physical world. (p. 424)

serial bottleneck: The point in the path from perception to action at which people cannot process all the information in parallel. (p. 75)

serial-order information: Representation of the position of information in a sequence. (pp. 130–135)

set effect: The biasing of a solution to a problem as a result of past experiences in solving that kind of problem. (p. 268)

short-term memory: A proposed intermediate memory system in which information had to reside on its journey from sensory memory to long-term memory. (p. 172)

slots: Elements of a schema representation that indicate different aspects of a concept. (p. 155)

split-brain patients: Patients who have had an operation that surgically severed the corpus callosum that connects left and right hemispheres. (p. 24)

spotlight metaphor: A theory of visual attention which holds that we can move our attention to focus on various areas of the visual field. (pp. 82–84)

spreading activation: The proposal that activation spreads from sources to other parts of the memory network, activating the memory traces that reside there. (p. 183)

state: A term in problem solving used to refer to a representation of the problem at a point in its solution. (p. 242)

state-dependent learning: The phenomenon that memory performance is better when we are tested in the same state that we were in when we learned the material. (p. 227)

Sternberg paradigm: An experimental paradigm in which subjects are presented with a memory set consisting of a few items and must decide whether various probe items are in the memory set. (p. 12) *strategic learning:* Learning how to organize one's problem solving for a specific class of problems. (p. 292)

strength: The property of a memory trace that determines how active the trace can become. Strength increases with practice and decays with time. (p. 187)

Stroop effect: The tendency to name a word will interfere with the ability to say the color in which the word is printed. (p. 100)

subjective utility: The value someone places on something. (p. 345)

survey maps: Representation of the environment consisting of the position of locations in space (contrast with route maps). (p. 125)

syllogism: A logical argument consisting of two premises and a conclusion. (pp. 317, 325)

synapse: The location where the axon of one neuron almost makes contact with another neuron. (p. 18)

syntax: Grammatical rules for specifying correct word order and inflectional structure in a sentence. (p. 356)

tactical learning: Learning of sequences of actions that help solve a problem. (p. 290)

template matching: A theory of pattern recognition which claims that an object is recognized as a function of its overlap with various pattern templates. (p. 49)

temporal lobe: The region at the side of the cerebral cortex that contains the primary auditory areas and that is involved in the recognition of objects. (p. 23)

theory of identical elements: The theory that there will be transfer from one skill to another only to the extent that the skills share the same knowledge elements. (p. 306)

top-down processing: Information from the general context is used to help recognize a stimulus. Contrast with bottom-up processing. (p. 63)

topographic organization: A principle of neural organization in which adjacent neural areas process information from adjacent parts of the world. (p. 25)

Tower of Hanoi problem: A problem-solving task studied in the laboratory, which involves moving disks among pegs. (p. 259)

transformation: A linguistic rule that moves a term from one part of a sentence to another part. (p. 366)

transient ambiguity: A temporary ambiguity within a sentence that is resolved by the end of the sentence. (p. 400) *unilateral visual neglect:* A tendency to ignore one side of the visual field; found in patients who have had damage to the parietal lobe on the opposite side of the brain. (p. 93)

utilization: The process by which language comprehenders respond to the meaning of a linguistic message. (p. 389)

visual agnosia: An inability to recognize visual objects that is a function neither of general intellectual loss nor of loss of basic sensory abilities. (p. 37)

visual sensory store: A memory system that effectively holds all the information in a visual array for a very brief period of time. (p. 88)

visuospatial sketchpad: Baddeley's proposed system for rehearsing visual information. (p. 177)

voicing: The property of a phoneme produced by vibration of the vocal cords. (p. 59)

Wernicke's area: A region of the left temporal lobe important to language, particularly the semantic content of speech. (p. 25)

whole-report procedure: A procedure in which subjects are asked to report all the items from a display. (p. 86)

word-superiority effect: Superior recognition of letters in a word context than alone. (p. 63)

✦ References

Aaronson, D., & Scarborough, H. S. (1977). Performance theories for sentence coding: Some quantitative models. *Journal of Verbal Learning and Verbal Behavior, 16,* 277–304.

Ainsworth-Darnell, K., Shulman, H. G., & Boland, J. E. (1998). Dissociating brain responses to syntactic and semantic anomalies: Evidence from event-related potentials. *Journal of Memory and Language, 38,* 112–130.

Albert, M. L. (1973). A simple test of visual neglect. *Neurology, 23,* 658–664.

Alkire, M. T., Haier, R. J., Fallon, J. H., & Cahill, L. (1998, Nov. 24). Hippocampal, but not amygdala, activity at encoding correlates with long-term, free recall of non-emotional information. *Proceedings of the National Academies of Science, 95,* 24, 14506–14510.

Anderson, J. R. (1972). *Recognition confusions in sentence memory.* Unpublished manuscript.

Anderson, J. R. (1974a). Retrieval of propositional information from long-term memory. *Cognitive Psychology, 6,* 451–474.

Anderson, J. R. (1974b). Verbatim and propositional representation of sentences in immediate and long-term memory. *Journal of Verbal Learning and Verbal Behavior, 13,* 149–162.

Anderson, J. R. (1976). *Language, memory, and thought.* Hillsdale, NJ: Erlbaum.

Anderson, J. R. (1978a). Arguments concerning representations for mental imagery. *Psychological Review, 85,* 249–277.

Anderson, J. R. (1978b). Computer simulation of a language acquisition system: A second report. In D. LaBerge & S. J. Samuels (Eds.), *Perception and comprehension.* Hillsdale, NJ: Erlbaum.

Anderson, J. R. (1982). Acquisition of cognitive skill. *Psychological Review, 89,* 369–406.

Anderson, J. R. (1983). *The architecture of cognition.* Cambridge, MA: Harvard University Press.

Anderson, J. R. (1990). *The adaptive character of thought.* Hillsdale, NJ: Erlbaum.

Anderson, J. R. (1991). The adaptive nature of human categorization. *Psychological Review, 98,* 409–429.

Anderson, J. R. (1992). Intelligent tutoring and high school mathematics. *Proceedings of the Second International Conference on Intelligent Tutoring Systems* (pp. 1–10). Montreal: Springer-Verlag.

Anderson, J. R. (1993). *Rules of the mind.* Hillsdale, NJ: Erlbaum.

Anderson, J. R. (2000). *Learning and memory.* New York, NY: Wiley & Sons.

Anderson, J. R., Bothell, D., Lebiere, C., & Matessa, M. (1998). An integrated theory of list memory. *Journal of Memory and Language, 38*, 341–380.

Anderson, J. R., & Bower, G. H. (1972). Configural properties in sentence memory. *Journal of Verbal Learning and Verbal Behavior, 11*, 594–605.

Anderson, J. R., & Bower, G. H. (1973). *Human associative memory.* Washington, DC: Winston.

Anderson, J. R., Conrad, F. G., & Corbett, A. T. (1989). Skill acquisition and the LISP Tutor. *Cognitive Science, 13*, 467–506.

Anderson, J. R., Corbett, A. T., Koedinger, K., & Pelletier, R. (1995). Cognitive tutors: Lessons learned. *The Journal of Learning Sciences, 4*, 167–207.

Anderson, J. R., Farrell, R., & Sauers, R. (1984). Learning to program in LISP. *Cognitive Science, 8*, 87–129.

Anderson, J. R., & Fincham, J. M. (1994). Acquisition of procedural skills from examples. *Journal of Experimental Psychology: Learning, Memory, and Cognition, 20*, 1322–1340.

Anderson, J. R., Kushmerick, N., & Lebiere, C. (1993). Navigation and conflict resolution. In J. R. Anderson (Ed.), *Rules of the mind.* Hillsdale, NJ: Erlbaum.

Anderson, J. R., & Lebiere, C. (1998) (Eds.), *Atomic components of thought.* Mahwah, NJ: Erlbaum.

Anderson, J. R., Matessa, M., & Lebiere, C. (1997). ACT-R: A theory of higher level cognition and its relation to visual attention. *Human Computer Interaction, 12*, 439–462.

Anderson, J. R., & Reder, L. M. (1999). The size of the fan effect: Process, not representation. *Journal of Experimental Psychology: General, 128*, 186–187.

Anderson, J. R., Reder, L. M., & Simon, H. (1998). Radical constructivism and cognitive psychology. In D. Ravitch (Ed.) *Brookings papers on education policy,* 227–278. Washington, DC: Brookings Institute Press.

Anderson, J. R., & Reiser, B. J. (1985). The LISP tutor. *Byte, 10*, 159–175.

Anderson, J. R., & Schooler, L. J. (1991). Reflections of the environment in memory. *Psychological Science, 2*, 396–408.

Anderson, T. H. (1978). *Another look at the self-questioning study technique.* (Technical Education Report No. 6). Champaign: University of Illinois, Center for the Study of Reading.

Angell, J. R. (1908). The doctrine of formal discipline in the light of the principles of general psychology. *Educational Review, 36*, 1–14.

Atkinson, R. C., & Shiffrin, R. M. (1968). Human memory: A proposed system and its control processes. In K. Spence & J. Spence (Eds.), *The psychology of learning and motivation* (Vol. 2). New York: Academic Press.

Atwood, M. E., & Polson, P. G. (1976). A process model for water jug problems. *Cognitive Psychology, 8*, 191–216.

Ausubel, D. P. (1968). *Educational psychology: A cognitive view.* New York: Holt, Rinehart, & Winston.

Baddeley, A. D. (1976). *The psychology of memory.* New York: Basic Books.

Baddeley, A. D. (1986). *Working memory.* Oxford: Oxford University Press.

Baddeley, A. D. (1998). *Human memory: Theory and practice.* Boston: Allyn and Bacon.

Baddeley, A. D., Thompson, N., & Buchanan, M. (1975). Word length and the structure of short-term memory. *Journal of Verbal Learning and Verbal Behavior, 14*, 575–589.

Baddeley, A. D., Wilson, B. A., & Watts, F. N. (1995). *Handbook of memory disorders*. New York: Wiley.

Bahrick, H. P. (1984). Semantic memory content in permastore: Fifty years of memory for Spanish learned in school. *Journal of Experimental Psychology: General, 113,* 1–24.

Banich, M. T. (1997). *Neuropsychology: The neural bases of mental function.* Boston, MA: Houghton Mifflin Company.

Barbizet, J. (1970). *Human memory and its pathology.* San Francisco: Freeman.

Barnes, C. A. (1979). Memory deficits associated with senescence: A neurophysiological and behavioral study in the rat. *Journal of Comparative Physiology, 43,* 74–104.

Bartlett, B. J. (1978). *Top-level structure as an organizational strategy for recall of classroom text.* Unpublished doctoral dissertation. Arizona State University.

Bassok, M. (1990). Transfer of domain-specific problem-solving procedures. *Journal of Experimental Psychology: Learning, Memory, and Cognition, 16,* 522–533.

Bassok, M., & Holyoak, K. J. (1989). Interdomain transfer between isomorphic topics in algebra and physics. *Journal of Experimental Psychology: Learning, Memory, and Cognition, 15,* 153–166.

Bates, A., McNew, S., MacWhinney, B., Devesocvi, A., & Smith, S. (1982). Functional constraints on sentence processing: A cross-linguistic study. *Cognition, 11,* 245–299.

Beck, B. B. (1980). *Animal tool behavior: The use and manufacture of tools by animals.* New York: Garland STPM Press.

Behrmann, M., & Moscovitch, M. (1994). Object-centered neglect in patients with unilateral neglect: Effects of left-right coordinates of objects. *Journal of Cognitive Neuroscience, 6,* 1–16.

Behrmann, M., Zemel, R. S., & Mozer, M. C. (1998). Object-based attention and occlusion: Evidence from normal participants and computational model. *Journal of Experimental Psychology: Human Perception and Performance, 24,* 1011–1036.

Benson, D. F., & Greenberg, J. P. (1969). Visual form agnosia. *Archives of Neurology, 20,* 82–89.

Berbaum, K., & Chung, C. P. (1981). Mueller-Lyer illusion induced by imagination. *Journal of Mental Imagery, 5,* 125–128.

Berlin, B., & Kay, P. (1969). *Basic color terms: Their universality and evolution.* Berkeley: University of California Press.

Berry, D. C., & Broadbent, D. E. (1984). On the relationship between task performance and associated verbalizable knowledge. *Quarterly Journal of Experimental Psychology, 36A,* 209–231.

Biederman, I. (1987). Recognition-by-components: A theory of human image understanding. *Psychological Review, 94,* 115–147.

Biederman, I., & Ju, G. (1988). Surface vs. edge-based determinants of visual recognition. *Cognitive Psychology, 20,* 38–64.

Biederman, I., Beiring, E., Ju, G., & Blickle, T. (1985). *A comparison of the perception of partial vs. degraded objects.* Unpublished manuscript, State University of New York at Buffalo.

Biederman, I., Glass, A. L., & Stacy, E. W. (1973). Searching for objects in real world scenes. *Journal of Experimental Psychology, 97,* 22–27.

Black, J. B., & Bern, H. (1981). Causal coherence and memory for events in narratives. *Journal of Verbal Learning and Verbal Behavior, 20,* 267–275.

Blackburn, J. M. (1936). *Acquisition of skill: An analysis of learning curves.* IHRB Report No. 73.

Blake, R., & Sekuler, R. (1994). *Perception.* New York, NY: McGraw-Hill.

Bloom, B. S. (1984). The 2 sigma problem: The search for methods of group instruction as effective as one-to-one tutoring. *Educational Researcher, 13,* 3–16.

Bloom, B. S. (Ed.). (1985a). *Developing talent in young people.* New York: Ballantine Books.

Bloom, B. S. (1985b). Generalizations about talent development. In B. S. Bloom (Ed.), *Developing talent in young people* (pp. 507–549). New York: Ballantine Books.

Bloom, R. (1994). Recent controversies in the study of language acquisition. In M. A. Gernsbacher (Ed.), *Handbook of psycholinguistics.* San Diego, CA: Academic Press.

Boden, M. (1996). *Artificial intelligence.* San Diego, CA: Academic Press.

Boole, G. (1854). *An investigation of the laws of thought.* London: Walton and Maberly.

Boomer, D. S. (1965). Hesitation and grammatical encoding. *Language and Speech, 8,* 148–158.

Boring, E. G. (1950). *A history of experimental psychology.* New York: Appleton Century.

Bouchard, T. J. (1983). Do environmental similarities explain the similarity in intelligence of identical twins reared apart? *Intelligence, 7,* 175–184.

Bouchard, T. J., & McGue, M. (1981). Familial studies of intelligence: A review. *Science, 212,* 1055–1059.

Bower, G. H., Black, J. B., & Turner, T. J. (1979). Scripts in memory for text. *Cognitive Psychology, 11,* 177–220.

Bower, G. H., Clark, M. C., Lesgold, A. M., & Winzenz, D. (1969). Hierarchical retrieval schemes in recall of categorical word lists. *Journal of Verbal Learning and Verbal Behavior, 8,* 323–343.

Bower, G. H., Karlin, M. B., & Dueck, A. (1975). Comprehension and memory for pictures. *Memory & Cognition, 3,* 216–220.

Bower, G. H., & Mayer, J. D. (1985). Failure to replicate mood-dependent retrieval. *Bulletin of the Psychonomic Society, 23,* 39–42.

Bower, G. H., Monteiro, K. P., & Gilligan, S. G. (1978). Emotional mood as a context for learning and recall. *Journal of Verbal Learning and Verbal Behavior, 17,* 573–587.

Bowerman, M. (1973). Structural relationships in children's utterances: Syntactic or semantic. In T. E. Moore (Ed.), *Cognitive development and the acquisition of language.* New York: Academic Press.

Bradshaw, G. L., & Anderson, J. R. (1982). Elaborative encoding as an explanation of levels of processing. *Journal of Verbal Learning and Verbal Behavior, 21,* 165–174.

Braine, M. D. S., Reiser, B. J., & Rumain, B. (1983) Some empirical justification for a theory of natural propositional logic. In G. H. Bower (Ed.), *The psychology of learning and motivation* (Vol. 18). New York: Academic Press.

Brainerd, C. J. (1978). *Piaget's theory of intelligence.* Englewood Cliffs, NJ: Prentice-Hall.

Bransford, J. D., Barclay, J. R., & Franks, J. J. (1972). Sentence memory: A constructive versus interpretive approach. *Cognitive Psychology, 3,* 193–209.

Bransford, J. D., & Franks, J. J. (1971). The abstraction of linguistic ideas. *Cognitive Psychology, 2*, 331–380.

Brewer, W. F., & Treyens, J. C. (1981). Role of schemata in memory for places. *Cognitive Psychology, 13*, 207–230.

Broadbent, D. E. (1958). *Perception and communication.* New York: Pergamon.

Broadbent, D. E. (1975). The magical number seven after fifteen years. In R. A. Kennedy & A. Wilkes (Eds.), *Studies in long-term memory.* New York: Wiley.

Brodman, K. (1909). *Vergleichende Lokalisationslehre der Grosshirnrinde in ihren Prinzipien dargestellt auf Grund des Zellenbaues.* Leipzig: J. A. Barth. In G. von Bonin, Some papers on the cerebral cortex. Translated as, *"On the comparative localization of the cortex."* Springfield, IL: Charles C. Thomas, 1960. pp. 201–230.

Brooks, L. R. (1968). Spatial and verbal components of the act of recall. *Canadian Journal of Psychology, 22*, 349–368.

Brown, J. S., & Van Lehn, K. (1980). Repair theory: A generative theory of bugs in procedural skills. *Cognitive Science, 4*, 397–426.

Brown, R. (1973). *A first language.* Cambridge, MA: Harvard University Press.

Brown, R., & Kulik, J. (1977). Flashbulb memories. *Cognition, 5*, 73–99.

Brown, R., & Lenneberg, E. H. (1954). A study in language and cognition. *Journal of Abnormal and Social Psychology, 49*, 454–462.

Bruce, C. J., Desimone, R., & Gross, C. G. (1981). Visual properties of neurons in a polysensory area in superior temporal sulcus of the macaque. *Neurophysiology, 46*, 369–384.

Bruner, J. S. (1964). The course of cognitive growth. *American Psychologist, 19*, 1–15.

Buckner, R. L., & Koustal, W. (1998). Functional neuroimaging studies of encoding, priming, and explicit memory retrieval. *Proceedings of the National Academy of Science, USA, 95*, 891–898.

Caplan, D. (1972). Clause boundaries and recognition latencies for words in sentences. *Perception and Psychophysics, 12*, 73–76.

Card, S. K., Moran, T. P., & Newell, A. (1983). *The psychology of human-computer interaction.* Hillsdale, NJ: Erlbaum.

Carey, S. (1978). The child as word learner. In M. Halle, J. Bresnan, & G. Miller (Eds.), *Linguistic theory and psychological reality.* Cambridge, MA: MIT Press.

Carpenter, P. A., & Just, M. A. (1975). Sentence comprehension: A psycholinguistic processing model of verification. *Psychological Review, 82*, 45–73.

Carpenter, P. A., & Just, M. A. (1977). Reading comprehension as eyes see it. In M. A. Just & P. A. Carpenter (Eds.), *Cognitive processes in comprehension.* Hillsdale, NJ: Erlbaum.

Carpenter, T. P., & Moser, J. M. (1982). The development of addition and subtraction problem-solving skills. In T. P. Carpenter, J. M. Moser, & T. Romberg (Eds.), *Addition and subtraction: A cognitive perspective.* Hillsdale, NJ: Erlbaum.

Carraher, T. N., Carraher, D. W., & Schliemann, A. D. (1985). Mathematics in the streets and in the schools. *British Journal of Developmental Psychology, 3*, 21–29.

Carroll, J. B. (1993). *Human cognitive abilities: A survey of factor-analytic studies.* Cambridge: Cambridge University Press.

Carroll, J. B., & Casagrande, J. B. (1958). The function of language classifications in behavior. In E. E. Maccoby, T. M. Newcomb, & E. L. Hartley (Eds.), *Readings in social psychology* (3rd ed.). New York: Holt, Rinehart, & Winston.

Case, R. (1978). Intellectual development from birth to adulthood: A neo-Piagetian approach. In R. S. Siegler (Ed.), *Children's thinking: What develops?* Hillsdale, NJ: Erlbaum.

Case, R. (1985). *Intellectual development: A systematic reinterpretation.* New York: Academic Press.

Cattell, R. B. (1963). Theory of fluid and crystallized intelligence: A critical experiment. *Journal of Educational Psychology, 54,* 1–22.

Ceci, S. J. (1991). How much does schooling influence general intelligence and its cognitive components? A reassessment of the evidence. *Developmental Psychology, 27,* 703–722.

Ceci, S. J., & Liker, J. K. (1986). A day at the races: A study of IQ, expertise, and cognitive complexity. *Journal of Experimental Psychology: General, 115,* 255–266.

Ceci, S. J., Loftus, E. F., Leichtman, M. D., & Bruck, M, (1994). The possible role of source misattributions in the creation of false beliefs among preschoolers. *International Journal of Clinical and Experimental Hypnosis, 42,* 304–320.

Ceraso, J., & Provitera, A. (1971). Sources of error in syllogistic reasoning. *Cognitive Psychology, 2,* 400–410.

Chambers, D., & Reisberg, D. (1985). Can mental images be ambiguous? *Journal of Experimental Psychology: Human Perception and Performance, 11,* 317–328.

Chapman, L. J., & Chapman, J. P. (1959). Atmosphere effect reexamined. *Journal of Experimental Psychology, 58,* 220–226.

Charness, N. (1976). Memory for chess positions: Resistance to interference. *Journal of Experimental Psychology: Human Learning and Memory, 2,* 641–653.

Charness, N. (1979). Components of skill in bridge. *Canadian Journal of Psychology, 33,* 1–16.

Chase, W. G., & Clark, H. H. (1972). Mental operations in the comparisons of sentences and pictures. In L. W. Gregg (Ed.), *Cognition in learning and memory.* New York: Wiley.

Chase, W. G., & Ericsson, K. A. (1982). Skill and working memory. In G. H. Bower (Ed.), *The psychology of learning and motivation* (Vol. 16). New York: Academic Press.

Chase, W. G., & Simon, H. A. (1973). The mind's eye in chess. In W. G. Chase (Ed.), *Visual information processing.* New York: Academic Press.

Chater, N., & Oaksford, M. (in press). The probability heuristics model of syllogistic reasoning. *Cognitive Psychology.*

Chen, S., Swartz, K. B., & Terrace, H. S. (1997). Knowledge of the original position of list items in rhesus monkeys. *Psychological Science, 8,* 80–86.

Cheng, P. W., & Holyoak, K. J. (1985). Pragmatic reasoning schemas. *Cognitive Psychology, 17,* 391–416.

Cheng, P. W., & Holyoak, K. J. (1989). On the natural selection of reasoning theories. *Cognition, 33,* 285–313.

Cheng, P. W., Holyoak, K. J., Nisbett, R. E., & Oliver, L. M. (1986). Pragmatic versus syntactic approaches to training deductive reasoning. *Cognitive Psychology, 18,* 293–328.

Cherry, E. C. (1953). Some experiments on the recognition of speech with one and with two ears. *Journal of the Acoustical Society of America, 25,* 975–979.

Chi, M. T. H. (1978). Knowledge structures and memory development. In R. S. Siegler (Ed.), *Children's thinking: What develops?* Hillsdale, NJ: Erlbaum.

Chi, M. T. H., Bassok, M., Lewis, M., Reimann, P., & Glaser, R. (1989). Self-explanations: How students study and use examples in learning to solve problems. *Cognitive Science, 13,* 145–182.

Chi, M. T. H., Feltovich, P. J., & Glaser, R. (1981). Categorization and representation of physics problems by experts and novices. *Cognitive Science, 5,* 121–152.

Chomsky, C. (1970). *The acquisition of syntax in children from 5 to 10.* Cambridge, MA: MIT Press.

Chomsky, N. (1959). Review of Skinner's verbal behavior. *Language, 35,* 26–58.

Chomsky, N. (1965). *Aspects of the theory of syntax.* Cambridge, MA: MIT Press.

Chomsky, N. (1980). Rules and representations. *Behavioral and Brain Sciences, 3,* 1–61.

Chomsky, N., & Halle, M. (1968). *The sound pattern of English.* New York: Harper.

Christen, F., & Bjork, R. A. (1976). *On updating the loci in the method of loci.* Paper presented at the seventeenth annual meeting of the Psychonomic Society, St. Louis, MO.

Church, A. (1956). *Introduction to mathematical logic.* Princeton: Princeton University Press.

Clark, E. V. (1983). Meanings and concepts. In P. H. Mussen (Ed.), *Handbook of child psychology.* New York: Wiley.

Clark, H. H. (1974). Semantics and comprehension. In R. A. Sebeok (Ed.), *Current trends in linguistics* (Vol. 12). The Hague: Mouton.

Clark, H. H., & Chase, W. G. (1972). On the process of comparing sentences against pictures. *Cognitive Psychology, 3,* 472–517.

Clark, H. H., & Clark, E. V. (1977). *Psychology and language.* New York: Harcourt Brace Jovanovich.

Cohen J. D., & Servan-Schreiber, D. (1992). Context, cortex and dopamine: A connectionist approach to behavior and biology in schizophrenia. *Psychological Review, 99,* 45–77.

Cohen, M. R., & Nagel, E. (1934). *An introduction to logic and scientific method.* New York: Harcourt, Brace.

Cohen, N. J., & Squire, L. R. (1980). Preserved learning and retention of pattern analyzing skills in amnesia: Dissociation of knowing how and knowing that. *Science, 210,* 207–210.

Cole, M., & D'Andrade, R. (1982). The influence of schooling on concept formation; some preliminary conclusions. *Quarterly Newsletter of the Laboratory of Comparative Human Cognition, 4,* 19–26.

Cole, M., Gay, J., Glick, J., & Sharp, D. (1971). *The cultural context of learning and thinking.* New York: Basic Books.

Collins, A. M., & Quillian, M. R. (1969). Retrieval time from semantic memory. *Journal of Verbal Learning and Verbal Behavior, 8,* 240–247.

Coltheart, M. (1983). Iconic memory. *Philosophical Transactions of the Royal Society, London B, 302,* 283–294.

Conrad, C. (1972). Cognitive economy in semantic memory. *Journal of Experimental Psychology, 92,* 149–154.

Conrad, R. (1964). Acoustic confusions in immediate memory. *British Journal of Psychology, 55,* 75–84.

Conway, M. A., Anderson, S. J., Larsen, S. F., Donnelly, C. M., McDaniel, M. A., McClelland, A. G. R., Rawles, R. E., & Logie, R. H. (1994). The formation of flashbulb memories. *Memory & Cognition, 22*, 326–343.

Cooper, W. E., & Paccia-Cooper, J. (1980). *Syntax and speech.* Cambridge, MA: Harvard University Press.

Corbett, A. T., & Anderson, J. R. (1990). The effect of feedback control on learning to program with the LISP tutor. *Proceedings of the 12th Annual Conference of the Cognitive Science Society,* 796–803.

Corbett, A. T., & Chang, F. R. (1983). Pronoun disambiguation: Accessing potential antecedents. *Memory & Cognition, 11*, 283–294.

Cosmides, L. (1989) The logic of social exchange: Has natural selection shaped how humans reason? Studies with the Wason selection task. *Cognition, 31*, 187–276.

Cowart, W. (1983). *Reference relations and syntactic processing: Evidence of pronoun's influence on a syntactic decision that affects naming.* Indiana University Linguistics Club.

Craik, F. I. M., & Lockhart, R. S. (1972). Levels of processing: A framework for memory research. *Journal of Verbal Learning and Verbal Behavior, 11*, 671–684.

Crick, F. H. C., & Asanuma, C. (1986). Certain aspects of the anatomy and physiology of the cerebral cortex. In J. L. McClelland & D. E. Rumelhart (Eds.), *Parallel distributed processing: Explorations in the microstructure of cognition* (Vol. 2). Cambridge, MA: MIT Press/Bradford Books.

Crossman, E. R. F. W. (1959). A theory of the acquisition of speed-skill. *Ergonomics, 2*, 153–166.

Daneman, M., & Carpenter, P. A. (1980). Individual differences in working memory and reading. *Journal of Verbal Learning and Verbal Behavior, 19*, 450–466.

Daugherty, K. G., MacDonald, M. C., Petersen, A. S., & Seidenberg, M. S. (1993). Why no mere mortal has ever flown out to center field but people often say they do. *Proceedings of the Fifteenth Annual Conference of the Cognitive Science Society,* 383–388.

de Beer, G. R. (1959). Paedomorphesis. *Proceedings of the 15th International Congress of Zoology,* 927–930.

de Groot, A. D. (1965). *Thought and choice in chess.* The Hague: Mouton.

de Groot, A. D. (1966). Perception and memory versus thought. In B. Kleinmuntz (Ed.), *Problem-solving.* New York: Wiley.

DeValois, R. L., & Jacobs, G. H. (1968). Primate color vision. *Science, 162*, 533–540.

Desimone, R., Albright, T. D., Gross, C. G., & Bruce, C. (1984). Stimulus-selective properties of inferior temporal neurons in the macaque. *Neuroscience, 4*, 2051–2062.

Deutsch, G., Bourbon, W. T., Papanicolaou, A. C., & Eisenberg, H. M. (1988). Visuospatial experiments compared via activation of regional cerebral blood flow. *Neuropsychologia, 26*, 445–452.

Deutsch, J. A., & Deutsch, D. (1963). Attention: Some theoretical considerations. *Psychological Review, 70*, 80–90.

Diamond, A. (1991). Frontal lobe involvement in cognitive changes during the first year of life. In K. R. Gibson & A. C. Petersen (Eds.), *Brain maturation and cognitive development: Comparative and cross-cultural perspectives* (pp. 127–180). New York: Aldine de Gruyter.

Dickstein, L. S. (1978). The effect of figure on syllogistic reasoning. *Memory & Cognition, 6,* 76–83.

Dooling, D. J., & Christiaansen, R. E. (1977). Episodic and semantic aspects of memory for prose. *Journal of Experimental Psychology: Human Learning and Memory, 3,* 428–436.

Driver, J., & Halligan, P. W. (1991). Can visual neglect operate in object-centered coordinates: An affirmative study. *Cognitive Neuropsychology, 8,* 475–496.

Driver, J., Baylis, G. C., Goodrich, S., & Rafal, R. D. (1994). Axis-based neglect of visual shape. *Neuropsychologia, 32,* 1353–1365.

Dunbar, K., & MacLeod, C. M. (1984). A horse race of a different color: Stroop interference patterns with transformed words. *Journal of Experimental Psychology: Human Perception and Performance, 10,* 622–639.

Duncan, J. (1984). Selective attention and the organization of visual information. *Journal of Experimental Psychology: General, 113,* 501–517.

Duncan, J., & Humphreys, G. W. (1989). Visual search and stimulus similarity. *Psychological Review, 96,* 433–458.

Duncker, K. (1945). On problem-solving (translated by L. S. Lees). *Psychological Monographs, 58,* No. 270.

Ebbinghaus, H. (1885). *Memory: A contribution to experimental psychology* (translated by H. A. Ruger & C. E. Bussenues, 1913). New York: Teachers College, Columbia University.

Edwards, W. (1968). Conservatism in human information processing. In B. Kleinmuntz (Ed.), *Formal representations of human judgment.* New York: Wiley.

Egan, D. E., & Schwartz, B. J. (1979). Chunking in recall of symbolic drawings. *Memory & Cognition, 7,* 149–158.

Ehrlich, K., & Rayner, K. (1983). Pronoun assignment and semantic integration during reading: Eye movements and immediacy of processing. *Journal of Verbal Learning and Verbal Behavior, 22,* 75–87.

Eich, E. (1985). Context, memory, and integrated item/context imagery. *Journal of Experimental Psychology: Learning, Memory, and Cognition, 11,* 764–770.

Eich, E., & Metcalfe, J. (1989). Mood dependent memory for internal versus external events. *Journal of Experimental Psychology: Learning, Memory, and Cognition, 15,* 443–455.

Eich, J., Weingartner, H., Stillman, R. C., & Gillin, J. C. (1975). State-dependent accessibility of retrieval cues in the retention of a categorized list. *Journal of Verbal Learning and Verbal Behavior, 14,* 408–417.

Eichenbaum, H., & Bunsey, M. (1995). On the binding of associations in memory: Clues from studies on the role of the hippocampal region in paired-associate learning. *Current Directions in Psychological Science, 4,* 19–23.

Eimas, P. D., & Corbit, J. (1973). Selective adaptation of linguistic feature detectors. *Cognitive Psychology, 4,* 99–109.

Ekstrand, B. R. (1972). To sleep, perchance to dream. In C. P. Duncan, L. Sechrest, & A. W. Melton (Eds.), *Human memory: Festschrift in honor of Benton J. Underwood* (pp. 58–82). New York: Appleton-Century Crofts.

Elio, R., & Anderson, J. R. (1981). The effects of category generalizations and instance similarity on schema abstraction. *Journal of Experimental Psychology: Human Learning and Memory, 7,* 397–417.

Ellis, A. W., & Young, A. W. (1988). *Human Cognitive Neuropsychology.* Hillsdale, NJ: Erlbaum.

Engle, R. W., & Bukstel, L. (1978). Memory processes among bridge players of differing expertise. *American Journal of Psychology, 91*, 673–689.

Erickson, J. R. A. (1974). A set analysis theory of behavior in formal syllogistic reasoning tasks. In R. L. Solso (Ed.), *Theories in cognitive psychology: The Loyola Symposium.* Hillsdale, NJ: Erlbaum.

Ericsson, K. A. (Ed.) (1996). *The road to excellence: The acquisition of expert performance in the arts and sciences, sports, and games.* Mahwah, NJ: Erlbaum.

Ericsson, K. A., Krampe, R. T., & Tesch-Römer, C. (1993). The role of deliberate practice in the acquisition of expert performance. *Psychological Review, 100*, 363–406.

Ericsson, K. A., & Lehmann, A. C. (1996). Expert and exceptional performance: Evidence of maximal adaptation to task constraints. *Annual Review of Psychology, 47*, 273–305.

Erikson, B. A., & Erikson, C. W. (1974). Effects of noise letters upon the identification of a target letter in a nonsearch task. *Perception and Psychophysics, 1*, 143–149.

Erikson, C. W., & Hoffman, J. E. (1972). Temporal and spatial characteristics of selective encoding from visual displays. *Perception and Psychophysics, 12*, 201–204.

Erikson, C. W., & St. James, J. D. (1986). Visual attention within and around the field of focal attention: A zoom lens model. *Perception and Psychophysics, 40*, 225–240.

Erikson, C. W., & Yeh, Y. Y. (1987). Allocation of attention in the visual field. *Journal of Experimental Psychology: Human Perception and Performance, 11*, 583–597.

Ernst, G., & Newell, A. (1969). *GPS: A case study in generality and problem solving.* New York: Academic Press.

Ervin-Tripp, S. M. (1974). Is second language learning like the first? *TESOL Quarterly, 8*, 111–127.

Estes, W. K. (1991). Cognitive architectures from the standpoint of an experimental psychologist. *Annual Review of Psychology, 42*, 1–28.

Farah, M. J. (1990). *Visual agnosia: Disorders of object recognition and what they tell us about normal vision.* Cambridge, MA: MIT Press.

Farah, M. J. (1995). The neural bases of mental imagery. In M. S. Gazzaniga (Ed.), *The cognitive neurosciences*, 963–976. Cambridge, MA: MIT Press.

Farah, M. J., Hammond, K. M., Levine, D. N., & Calvanio, R. (1988). Visual and spatial mental imagery: Dissociable systems of representation. *Cognitive Psychology, 20*, 439–462.

Farah, M. J., & McClelland, J. (1991). A computational model of semantic memory impairment: Modality specificity and emergent category specificity. *Journal of Experimental Psychology: General, 120*, 339–357.

Fernandez, A., & Glenberg, A. M. (1985). Changing environmental context does not reliably affect memory. *Memory & Cognition, 13*, 333–345.

Ferreira, F., & Clifton, C. (1986). The independence of syntactic processing. *Journal of Memory and Language, 25*, 348–368.

Fillenbaum, S. (1971). On coping with ordered and unordered conjunctive sentences. *Journal of Experimental Psychology, 87*, 93–98.

Fillenbaum, S. (1974). Pragmatic normalization: Further results for some conjunctive and disjunctive sentences. *Journal of Experimental Psychology, 103*, 913–921.

Finke, R. A., Pinker, S., & Farah, M. J. (1989). Reinterpreting visual patterns in mental imagery. *Cognitive Science, 13*, 51–78.

Fischer, K. W. (1980). A theory of cognitive development: The control and construction of hierarchies of skills. *Psychological Review, 87*, 477–531.

Fitts, P. M., & Posner, M. I. (1967). *Human performance*. Belmont, CA: Brooks Cole.

Flavell, J. H. (1978). Comment. In R. S. Siegler (Ed.), *Children's thinking: What develops?* Hillsdale, NJ: Erlbaum.

Flavell, J. H. (1985). *Cognitive development*. Englewood Cliffs, NJ: Prentice-Hall.

Fletcher, C. R. (1986). Strategies for the allocation of short-term memory during comprehension. *Journal of Memory and Language, 25*, 43–58.

Fletcher, C. R. (1994). Levels of representation in memory for discourse. In M. A. Gernsbacher (Ed.), *Handbook of psycholinguistics*. San Diego, CA: Academic Press.

Flowers, J. H., Warner, J. L., & Polansky, M. L. (1979). Response and encoding factors in ignoring irrelevant information. *Memory & Cognition, 7*, 86–94.

Fodor, J. A. (1983). *The modularity of mind*. Cambridge, MA: MIT/Bradford Books.

Fodor, J. A., Bever, T. G., & Garrett, M. F. (1974). *The psychology of language*. New York: McGraw-Hill.

Fong, G. T., Krantz, D. H., & Nisbett, R. E. (1986). The effects of statistical training on thinking about everyday problems. *Cognitive Psychology, 18*, 253–292.

Franklin, N., & Tversky, B. (1990). Searching imagined environments. *Journal of Experimental Psychology: General, 119*, 63–76.

Frase, L. T. (1975). Prose processing. In G. H. Bower (Ed.), *The psychology of learning and motivation* (Vol. 9). New York: Academic Press.

Frederiksen, C. H. (1975). Representing logical and semantic structure of knowledge acquired from discourse. *Cognitive Psychology, 7*, 371–458.

Fromkin, V. (1971). The non-anomalous nature of anomalous utterances. *Languages, 47*, 27–52.

Fromkin, V. (1973). *Speech errors as linguistic evidence*. The Hague: Mouton.

Funahashi, S., Bruce, C. J., & Goldman-Rakic, P. S. (1991). Neural activity related to saccadic eye movements in the monkey's dorsolateral prefrontal cortex. *Journal of Neurophysiology, 65*, 1464–1483.

Gagné, E., Yekovich, C. W., & Yekovich, F. R. (1993). *The cognitive psychology of school learning*. New York: Harper Collins College Publishers.

Gardner, H. (1975). *The shattered mind: The person after brain damage*. New York: Knopf.

Gardner, H. (1983). *Frames of mind: The theory of multiple intelligences*. New York: Basic Books.

Garrett, M. F. (1975). The analysis of sentence production. In G. H. Bower (Ed.), *The psychology of learning and motivation* (Vol. 9). New York: Academic Press.

Garrett, M. F. (1980). Levels of processing in sentence production. In B. Butterworth (Ed.), *Language production* (Vol. 1, pp. 177–220). London: Academic Press.

Garrett, M. F. (1990). Sentence processing. In D. N. Osherson & H. Lasnik (Eds.), *Language: An invitation to cognition science*. Cambridge, MA: MIT Press.

Garro, L. (1986). Language, memory, and focality: A reexamination. *American Anthropologist, 88*, 128–136.

Gazzaniga, M. S. (1995). *The cognitive neurosciences*, Cambridge, MA: MIT Press.

Gazzaniga, M. S., Ivry, R. B., & Mangun, G. R. (1998). *Cognitive neuroscience: The biology of the mind*. New York: W. W. Norton.

Gee, J. P., & Grosjean, F. (1983). Performance structures: A psycholinguistic and linguistic appraisal. *Cognitive Psychology, 15*, 411–458.

Geiselman, E. R., Fisher, R. P., MacKinnon, D. P., & Holland, H. L. (1985). Eyewitness memory enhancement in the police interview: Cognitive retrieval mnemonics versus hypnosis. *Journal of Applied Psychology, 70*, 401–412.

Gentner, D. (1983) Structure-mapping: A theoretical framework for analogy. *Cognitive Science, 7*, 155–170.

Gentner, D. (1989). The mechanisms of analogical learning. In S. Vosniadou & A. Ortony (Eds.), *Similarity and analogical reasoning.* Cambridge: Cambridge University Press.

Georgopoulos, A. P., Lurito, J. T., Petrides, M., Schwartz, A. B., & Massey, J. T. (1989). Mental rotation of the neuronal population vector. *Science, 243*, 234–236.

Gernsbacher, M. A. (1985). Surface information loss in comprehension. *Cognitive Psychology, 17*, 324–363.

Gernsbacher, M. A. (1993). *Language comprehension as structure building.* Hillsdale, NJ: Erlbaum.

Gernsbacher, M. A. (1994). *Handbook of psycholinguistics.* San Diego, CA: Academic Press.

Geschwind, N. (1980). Neurological knowledge and complex behaviors. *Cognitive Science, 4*, 185–194.

Gibson, J. J. (1950). *Perception of the visual world.* Boston: Houghton Mifflin.

Gibson, J. J. (1966). *The senses considered as perceptual systems.* Boston: Houghton Mifflin.

Gibson, J. J. (1979). *The ecological approach to visual perception.* Boston: Houghton Mifflin.

Gick, M. L., & Holyoak, K. J. (1980). Analogical problem solving. *Cognitive Psychology, 12*, 306–355.

Gigerenzer, G. (1996). On narrow norms and vague heuristics: A reply to Kahneman and Tversky (1996). *Psychological Review, 103*, 592–596.

Gigerenzer, G., & Hoffrage, U. (1995). How to improve Bayesian reasoning without instruction: Frequency formats. *Psychological Review, 102*, 684–704.

Gigerenzer, G., & Hug, K. (1992) Domain-specific reasoning: Social contracts, cheating, and perspective change. *Cognition, 43*, 127–171.

Gillund, G., & Shiffrin, R. M. (1984). A retrieval model for both recognition and recall. *Psychological Review, 91*, 1–67.

Ginsburg, H. J., & Opper, S. (1980). *Piaget's theory of intellectual development.* Englewood Cliffs, NJ: Prentice-Hall.

Glass, A. L., & Holyoak, K. J. (1986). *Cognition.* New York: Random House.

Gleason, J. B., & Ratner, N. B. (1993). *Psycholinguistics.* Fort Worth, TX: Harcourt Brace Jovanovich.

Gleitman, L. R., Newport, E. L., & Gleitman, H. (1984). The current status of the motherese hypothesis. *Journal of Child Language, 11*, 43–80.

Glenberg, A. M., Smith, S. M., & Green, C. (1977). Type I rehearsal: Maintenance and more. *Journal of Verbal Learning and Verbal Behavior, 16*, 339–352.

Gluck, M. A., & Bower, G. H. (1988). From conditioning to category learning: An adaptive network model. *Journal of Experimental Psychology: General, 8*, 37–50.

Glucksberg, S., & Cowan, G. N., Jr. (1970). Memory for nonattended auditory material. *Cognitive Psychology, 1*, 149–156.

Glucksberg, S., & Weisberg, R. W. (1966). Verbal behavior and problem solving: Some effects of labelling in a functional fixedness problem. *Journal of Experimental Psychology, 71*, 659–666.

Godden, D. R., & Baddeley, A. D. (1975). Context-dependent memory in two natural environments: On land and under water. *British Journal of Psychology, 66*, 325–331.

Goel, V., & Grafman, J. (1995) Are the frontal lobes implicated in "planning" functions? Interpreting data from the Tower of Hanoi. *Neuropsychologica, 33*, 623–642.

Goldberg, R. A., Schwartz, S., & Stewart, M. (1977). Individual differences in cognitive processes. *Journal of Educational Psychology, 69*, 9–14.

Goldin-Meadow, S., Butcher, C., Mylander, C., & Dodge, M. (1994). Nouns and verbs in a self-styled gesture system: What's in a name? *Cognitive Psychology, 27*, 259–319.

Goldman-Rakic, P. S. (1987). Circuitry of primate prefrontal cortex and regulation of behavior by representational memory. In *Handbook of physiology. The nervous system. Higher functions of the brain.* Bethesda, MD: American Physiology Society (Vol. 5, pp. 373–417).

Goldman-Rakic, P. S. (1988). Topography of cognition: Parallel distributed networks in primate association cortex. *Annual Review of Neuroscience, 11*, 137–156.

Goldman-Rakic, P. S. (1992). Working memory and mind. *Scientific American, 267*, 111–117.

Goldstein, E. B. (1999). *Sensation and perception* (5th ed.). Belmont, CA: Wadsworth.

Goldstein, M. N. (1974). Auditory agnosia for speech ("pure word deafness"): A historical review with current implications. *Brain and Language, 1*, 195–204.

Gould, S. J. (1977). *Ontogeny and phylogeny.* Cambridge, MA: Belknap.

Graf, P., Squire, L. R., & Mandler, G. (1984). The information that amnesic patients do not forget. *Journal of Experimental Psychology: Learning, Memory, and Cognition, 10*, 164–178.

Graf, P., & Torrey, J. W. (1966). Perception of phrase structure in written language. *American Psychological Association Convention Proceedings*, 83–88.

Granrud, C. E. (1986). Binocular vision and spatial perception in 4- and 5-month-old infants. *Journal of Experimental Psychology: Human Perception and Performance, 12*, 36–49.

Granrud, C. E. (1987). Visual size constancy in newborn infants. *Investigative Ophthalmology & Visual Science, 28* (Suppl. 5).

Granrud, C. E. (Ed.) (1993). *Visual perception and cognition in infancy.* Hillsdale, NJ: Erlbaum.

Gray, J. A., & Wedderburn, A. A. I. (1960). Grouping strategies with simultaneous stimuli. *Quarterly Journal of Experimental Psychology, 12*, 180–184.

Greenberg, J. H. (1963). Some universals of grammar with particular reference to the order of meaningful elements. In J. H. Greenberg (Ed.), *Universals of language.* Cambridge, MA: MIT Press.

Greeno, J. G. (1974). Hobbits and orcs: Acquisition of a sequential concept. *Cognitive Psychology, 6*, 270–292.

Greenwald, A. G., & Banjeri, M. R. (1989). The self as a memory system: Powerful, but ordinary. *Journal of Personality and Social Psychology, 57*, 41–54.

Griggs, R. A., & Cox, J. R. (1982). The elusive thematic-materials effect in Wason's selection task. *British Journal of Psychology, 73*, 407–420.

Grosjean, F., Grosjean, L., & Lane, H. (1979). The patterns of silence: Performance structures in sentence production. *Cognitive Psychology, 11*, 58–81.

Grossberg, S. (1987). *The adaptive brain, 1: Cognition learning, reinforcement and rhythm.* Amsterdam: North-Holland, Elsevier.

Guilford, J. P. (1982). Cognitive psychology's ambiguities: Some suggested remedies. *Psychological Review, 89*, 48–59.

Guskey, T. R., & Gates, S. (1986). Synthesis of research on the effects of mastery learning in elementary and secondary classrooms. *Educational Leadership, 43*, 73–80.

Guyote, M. J., & Sternberg, R. S. (1981). A transitive-chain theory of syllogistic reasoning. *Cognitive Psychology, 13*, 461–525.

Haber, R. N. (1983). The impending demise of the icon: A critique of the concept of iconic storage in visual information processing. *Behavioral and Brain Sciences, 6*, 1–11.

Haier, R. J., Siegel, B. V., Jr., Nuechterlein, K. H., Hazlett, E., Wu, J. C., Paek, J., Browning, H. L., & Buchsbaum, M. S. (1988). Cortical glucose metabolic rate correlates of abstract reasoning and attention studied with positron emission tomography. *Intelligence, 12*, 199–217.

Hakes, D. T. (1972). Effects of reducing complement constructions on sentence comprehension. *Journal of Verbal Learning and Verbal Behavior, 11*, 278–286.

Hakes, D. T., & Foss, D. J. (1970). Decision processes during sentence comprehension: Effects of surface structure reconsidered. *Perception and Psychophysics, 8*, 413–416.

Halford, G. S. (1982). *The development of thought.* Hillsdale, NJ: Erlbaum.

Hammerton, M. (1973). A case of radical probability estimation. *Journal of Experimental Psychology, 101*, 252–254.

Harris, R. J. (1977). Comprehension of pragmatic implications in advertising. *Journal of Applied Psychology, 62*, 603–608.

Hart, R. A., & Moore, G. I. (1973). The development of spatial cognition: A review. In R. M. Downs & D. Stea (Eds.). *Image and environment.* Chicago: Aldine.

Haviland, S. E. (1974) *Nondeductive strategies in reasoning.* Unpublished doctoral dissertation, Stanford University.

Haviland, S. E., & Clark, H. H. (1974). What's new? Acquiring new information as a process in comprehension. *Journal of Verbal Learning and Verbal Behavior, 13*, 512–521.

Hayes, J. R. (1984). *Problem solving techniques.* Philadelphia: Franklin Institute Press.

Hayes, J. R. (1985). Three problems in teaching general skills. In J. Segal, S. Chipman, & R. Glaser (Eds.), *Thinking and learning* (Vol. 2). Hillsdale, NJ: Erlbaum.

Hayes-Roth, B., & Hayes-Roth, F. (1977). Concept learning and the recognition and classification of exemplars. *Journal of Verbal Learning and Verbal Behavior, 16*, 321–338.

Healy, A. F., & Bourne, Jr., L. E. (1995). *Learning and memory of knowledge and skills: Durability and specificity.* Thousand Oaks, CA: Sage Publications.

Healy, A. F., & McNamara, D. S. (1996). Verbal learning and memory: Does the modal model still work? In J. T. Spence, J. M. Darley, & D. J. Foss (Eds.), *Annual Review of Psychology, 47*, 143–172.

Heath, S. B. (1983). *Ways with words: Language, life and work in communities and classrooms.* New York: Cambridge University Press.

Heathcote, A., Brown, S., & Mewhort, D. J. K. (in press). The power law repealed: The case for an exponential law of practice. *Psychonomic Bulletin & Review.*

Heider, E. (1972). Universals of color naming and memory. *Journal of Experimental Psychology, 93,* 10–20.

Henle, M. (1962). On the relation between logic and thinking. *Psychological Review, 69,* 366–378.

Herrnstein, R. J., & Murray, C. (1994). *The bell curve: Intelligence and class structure in American life.* New York: Free Press.

Hilgard, E. R. (1968). *The experience of hypnosis.* New York: Harcourt Brace Jovanovich.

Hockey, G. R. J., Davies, S., & Gray, M. M. (1972). Forgetting as a function of sleep at different times of day. *Experimental Psychology, 24,* 386–393.

Hoffman, D. D., & Richards, W. (1985). Parts of recognition. *Cognition, 18,* 65–96.

Holland, J. H., Holyoak, K., Nisbett, R. E., & Thagard, P. R. (1986). *Induction: Processes of inference, learning, and discovery.* Cambridge, MA: MIT Press.

Horn, J. L. (1968). Organization of abilities and the development of intelligence. *Psychological Review, 75,* 242–259.

Horn, J. L. (1986). Intellectual ability concepts. In R. J. Sternberg (Ed.), *Advances in the psychology of human abilities* (Vol. 1). Hillsdale, NJ: Erlbaum.

Horn, J. L., & Stankov, L. (1982). Auditory and visual intelligence. *Intelligence, 6,* 165–185.

Horton, J. C. (1984). Cytochrome oxidase patches: A new cytoarchitectonic feature of monkey visual cortex. *Philos. Trans. Royal Society of London, 304,* 199–253.

Hubel, D. H., Henson, C. D., Rupert, A., & Galambos, R. (1959). Attention units in the auditory cortex. *Science, 129,* 1279–1280.

Hubel, D. H., & Wiesel, T. N. (1977). Functional architecture of macaque monkey visual cortex. *Philos. Trans. Royal Society of London, 198,* 1–59.

Hubel, D. H., & Wiesel, T. N. (1962). Receptive fields, binocular interaction, and functional architecture in the cat's visual cortex. *Journal of Physiology, 166,* 106–154.

Hummel, J. E., & Holyoak, K. J. (1997). Distributed representations of structure: A theory of analogical access and mapping. *Psychological Review, 104,* 427–466.

Hunt, E. B. (1985). Verbal ability. In R. J. Sternberg (Ed.), *Human abilities: An information-processing approach.* New York: W. H. Freeman.

Hunt, E. B., Davidson, J., & Lansman, M. (1981). Individual differences in long-term memory access. *Memory & Cognition, 9,* 599–608.

Huttenlocher, P. R. (1994). Synaptogenesis in human cerebral cortex. In G. Dawson & K. W. Fischer (Eds.), *Human behavior and the developing brain* (pp. 137–152). New York: Guilford Press.

Hyams, N. M. (1986). *Language acquisition and the theory of parameters.* Dordrecht: D. Reidel.

Hyde, T. S., & Jenkins, J. J. (1973). Recall for words as a function of semantic, graphic, and syntactic orienting tasks. *Journal of Verbal Learning and Verbal Behavior, 12,* 471–480.

Inhelder, B., & Piaget, J. (1958). *The growth of logical thinking from childhood to adolescence.* New York: Basic Books.

Jacobsen, C. F. (1935). Functions of frontal association areas in primates. *Archives of Neurology & Psychiatry, 33,* 558–560.

Jacobsen, C. F. (1936). Studies of cerebral functions in primates. I. The function of the frontal association areas in monkeys. *Comparative Psychology Monographs, 13,* 1–60.

Jacoby, L. L. (1983). Remembering the data: Analyzing interactive processes in reading. *Journal of Verbal Learning and Verbal Behavior, 22,* 485–508.

Jacoby, L. L., & Witherspoon, D. (1982). Remembering without awareness. *Canadian Journal of Psychology, 36,* 300–324.

Jaeger, J. J., Lockwood, A. H., Kemmerer, D. L., Van Valin, R. D., Jr., Murphy, B. W., & Khalak, H. G. (1996). A positron emission tomographic study of regular and irregular verb morphology in English. *Language, 72,* 451–497.

James, W. (1890). *The principles of psychology* (Vols. 1 and 2). New York: Holt.

Jarvella, R. J. (1971). Syntactic processing of connected speech. *Journal of Verbal Learning and Verbal Behavior, 10,* 409–416.

Jeffries, R. P., Polson, P. G., Razran, L., & Atwood, M. E. (1977). A process model for missionaries—Cannibals and other river-crossing problems. *Cognitive Psychology, 9,* 412–440.

Jeffries, R. P., Turner, A. A., Polson, P. G., & Atwood, M. E. (1981). The processes involved in designing software. In J. R. Anderson (Ed.), *Cognitive skills and their acquisition.* Hillsdale, NJ: Erlbaum.

Jenkins, I. H., Brooks, D. J., Nixon, P. D., Frackowiak, R. S. J., & Passingham, R. E. (1994). Motor sequence learning: A study with positron emission tomography. *Journal of Neuroscience, 14,* 3775–3790.

Johnson, D. M. (1939). Confidence and speed in the two-category judgment. *Archives of Psychology, 241,* 1–52.

Johnson, J. S., & Newport, E. L. (1989). Critical period effects in second language learning: The influence of maturational state on the acquisition of English as a second language. *Cognitive Psychology, 21,* 60–99.

Johnson, N. F. (1970). The role of chunking and organization in process of recall. In G. H. Bower (Ed.), *Psychology of language and motivation* (Vol. 4). New York: Academic Press.

Johnson-Laird, P. N. (1983). *Mental models.* Cambridge, MA: Harvard University Press.

Johnson-Laird, P. N. (1995). Mental models, deductive reasoning, and the brain. In M. S. Gazzaniga (Ed.), *The cognitive neurosciences,* 999–1008. Cambridge, MA; MIT Press.

Johnson-Laird, P. N., & Byrne, R. M. J. (1991). *Deduction.* Hove, Sussex: Erlbaum.

Johnson-Laird, P. N., & Steedman, M. (1978). The psychology of syllogisms. *Cognitive Psychology, 10,* 64–99.

Johnston, W. A., & Heinz, S. P. (1978). Flexibility and capacity demands of attention. *Journal of Experimental Psychology: General, 107,* 420–435.

Just, M. A., & Carpenter, P. A. (1980). A theory of reading: From eye fixations to comprehension. *Psychological Review, 87,* 329–354.

Just, M. A., & Carpenter, P. A. (1985). Cognitive coordinate systems: Accounts of mental rotation and individual differences in spatial ability. *Psychological Review, 92,* 137–172.

Just, M. A., & Carpenter, P. A. (1987). *The psychology of reading and language comprehension.* Boston: Allyn and Bacon.

Just, M. A., & Carpenter, P. A. (1992). A capacity theory of comprehension: Individual differences in working memory. *Psychological Review, 99,* 122–149.

Kahneman, D., & Tversky, A. (1973). On the psychology of prediction. *Psychological Review, 80,* 237–251.

Kahneman, D., & Tversky, A. (1979). Prospect theory: An analysis of decisions under risk. *Econometrica, 97,* 263–291.

Kahneman, D., & Tversky, A. (1984). Choices, values, and frames. *American Psychologist, 80,* 341–350.

Kahneman, D., & Tversky, A. (1996). On the reality of cognitive illusions. *Psychological Review, 103,* 582–591.

Kail, R. (1988). Developmental functions for speeds of cognitive processes. *Journal of Experimental Child Psychology, 45,* 339–364.

Kail, R., & Park, Y. (1990). Impact of practice on speed of mental rotation. *Journal of Experimental Child Psychology, 49,* 227–244.

Kamin, L. J. (1974). *The science and politics of IQ.* Potomac, MD: Erlbaum.

Kandel, E. R., & Hawkins, R. D. (1992). The biological basis of learning and individuality. *Scientific American, 267,* 78–87.

Kandel, E. R., & Schwartz, J. H. (1984). *Principles of neural science* (2nd Ed.). New York: Elsevier.

Kandel, E. R., Schwartz, J. H., & Jessell, T. M. (Eds.). (1991). *Principles of neural science.* New York: Elsevier.

Kaplan, C. A., & Simon, H. A. (1990). In search of insight. *Cognitive Psychology, 22,* 374–419.

Kapur, S., Craik, F. I. M., Tulving, E., Wilson, A. A., Houle, S., & Brown, G. M. (1994). Neuroanatomical correlates of encoding in episodic memory: Levels of processing effect. *Proceedings of National Academy of Science, USA, 91,* 2008–2011.

Karlin, L., & Kestenbaum, R. (1968). Effects of the number of alternatives on the psychological refractory period. *Quarterly Journal of Experimental Psychology, 20,* 167–178.

Katz, B. (1952). The nerve impulse. *Scientific American, 187,* 55–64.

Keane, M. T., Ledgeway, T., & Duff, S. (1994). Constraints on analogical mapping: A comparison of three models. *Cognitive Science, 18,* 387–438.

Keenan, J. M., Baillet, S. D., & Brown, P. (1984). The effects of causal cohesion on comprehension and memory. *Journal of Verbal Learning and Verbal Behavior, 23,* 115–126.

Keeney, T. J., Cannizzo, S. R., & Flavell, J. H. (1967). Spontaneous and induced verbal rehearsal in a recall task. *Child Development, 38,* 953–966.

Keeton, W. T. (1980). *Biological science.* New York: Norton.

Keppel, G. (1968). Retroactive and proactive inhibition. In T. R. Dixon & D. L. Horton (Eds.), *Verbal behavior and general behavior theory* (pp. 172–213). Englewood Cliffs, NJ: Prentice-Hall.

Kinney, G. C., Marsetta, M., & Showman, D. J. (1966). Studies in display symbol legibility, part XXI. *The legibility of alphanumeric symbols for digitized television* (ESD-TR-66–117). Bedford, MA: The Mitre Corporation.

Kintsch, W. (1974). *The representation of meaning in memory.* Hillsdale, NJ: Erlbaum.

Kintsch, W. (1979). On modeling comprehension. *Educational Psychologist, 14,* 3–14.

Kintsch, W. (1998). *Comprehension: A paradigm for cognition.* Cambridge, MA: Cambridge University Press.

Kintsch, W., & Keenan, J. (1973). Reading rate and retention as a function of the number of propositions in the base structure of sentences. *Cognitive Psychology, 5,* 257–274.

Kintsch, W., & van Dijk, T. A. (1978). Toward a model of text comprehension and reproduction. *Psychological Review, 85,* 363–394.

Kintsch, W., & Vipond, P. (1979). Reading comprehension and readability in educational practice and psychological theory. In L. G. Nilsson (Ed.), *Perspectives on memory research.* Hillsdale, NJ: Erlbaum.

Kirsh, D., & Maglio, P. (1994) On distinguishing epistemic from pragmatic action. *Cognitive Science, 18,* 513–549.

Klahr, D., Chase, W. G., & Lovelace, E. A. (1983). Structure and process in alphabetic retrieval. *Journal of Experimental Psychology: Learning, Memory, and Cognition, 9,* 462–477.

Klatzky, R. L. (1975). *Human memory,* 1st Edition. New York: W. H. Freeman.

Klatzky, R. L. (1979). *Human memory,* 2nd Edition. New York: W. H. Freeman.

Klein, G. A. (1998). *Sources of power: How people make decisions.* Cambridge, MA: MIT Press.

Koedinger, K. R., Anderson, J. R., Hadley, W. H., & Mark, M. (1997). Intelligent tutoring goes to school in the big city. *International Journal of Artificial Intelligence in Education, 8,* 30–43.

Koestler, A. (1964). *The action of creation.* London: Hutchinson.

Köhler, W. (1927). *The mentality of apes.* New York: Harcourt, Brace.

Köhler, W. (1956). *The mentality of apes.* London: Routledge & Kegan Paul.

Kolb, B., & Wishaw, I. Q. (1996). Fundamentals of human neuropsychology, (4th Ed.), New York: W. H. Freeman.

Kolers, P. A. (1976). Reading a year later. *Journal of Experimental Psychology: Human Learning and Memory, 2,* 554–565.

Kolers, P. A. (1979). A pattern analyzing basis of recognition. In L. S. Cermak & F. I. M. Craik (Eds.), *Levels of processing in human memory.* Hillsdale, NJ: Erlbaum.

Kolers, P. A., & Perkins, P. N. (1975). Spatial and ordinal components of form perception and literacy. *Cognitive Psychology, 7,* 228–267.

Körkel, J. (1987). *Die Entwicklung von Gedächtnis- und Metagedächtnisleistungen in Abhängigkeit von bereichsspezifischen Vorkenntnissen.* Frankfurt: Lang.

Kosslyn, S. M. (1995) Mental imagery. In S. M. Kosslyn & N. D. Osherson (Eds.), *Visual cognition.* Cambridge, MA: MIT Press.

Kosslyn, S. M., Alpert, N. M., Thompson, W. I., Maljkovic, V., Weise, S. B., Chabris, C. F., Hamilton, S. E., Raunch, S. L., & Buonanno, F. S. (1993). Visual mental imagery activates topographically organized visual cortex: PET investigation. *Journal of Cognitive Neuroscience, 5,* 263–287.

Kosslyn, S. M., & Koenig, O. (1992). *Wet mind: The new cognitive neuroscience.* New York: Free Press.

Kosslyn, S. M., & Osherson, N. D. (1995). *Visual cognition.* Cambridge, MA: MIT Press.

Kosslyn, S. M., & Pomerantz, J. P. (1977). Imagery, propositions, and the form of internal representations. *Cognitive Psychology, 9,* 52–76.

Kotovsky, K., Hayes, J. R., & Simon, H. A. (1985). Why are some problems hard? Evidence from Tower of Hanoi. *Cognitive Psychology, 17,* 248–294.

Kruschke, J. K. (1992). ALCOVE: An exemplar-based connectionist model of category learning. *Psychological Review, 99,* 22–44.

Kuffler, S. W. (1953). Discharge pattern and functional organization of mammalian retina. *Journal of Neurophysiology, 16,* 37–68.

Kuhn, D., & Siegler, R. S. (1998). *Handbook of Child Psychology* (Vol. 2: Cognition, Perception, and Language). New York: Wiley.

Kulik, C., Kulik, J., & Bangert-Downs, R. (1986). *Effects of testing for mastery on student learning.* Paper presented at the annual meeting of the American Educational Research Association, San Francisco.

Kutas, M., & Hillyard, S. A. (1980a). Reading senseless sentences: Brain potentials reflect semantic incongruity. *Science, 207,* 203–205.

Kutas, M., & Hillyard, S. A. (1980b). Event-related brain potentials to semantically inappropriate and surprisingly large words. *Biological Psychology, 11,* 539–550.

LaBerge, D. (1983). Spatial extent of attention to letters and words. *Journal of Experimental Psychology: Human Perception and Performance, 9,* 371–379

Labov, W. (1973). The boundaries of words and their meanings. In C.-J. N. Bailey & R. W. Shuy (Eds.), *New ways of analyzing variations in English.* Washington, DC: Georgetown University Press.

Lakoff, G. (1971). On generative semantics. In D. Steinberg & L. Jakobovits (Eds.), *Semantics—An interdisciplinary reader in philosophy, linguistics, anthropology, and psychology.* London: Cambridge University Press.

Langley, P. W., Simon, H. A., Bradshaw, G. L., & Zytkow, J. (1987). *Scientific discovery: Computational explorations of the cognitive processes.* Cambridge, MA: MIT Press.

Larkin, J. H. (1981). Enriching formal knowledge: A model for learning to solve textbook physics problems. In J. R. Anderson (Ed.), *Cognitive skills and their acquisition.* Hillsdale, NJ: Erlbaum.

Le Bihan, D., Turner, R., Zeffiro, T. A., Cuenod, C. A., Jezzard, P., & Bonnerot, V. (1993). Activation of human primary visual cortex during visual recall: A magnetic resonance imaging study. *Proceedings of the National Academy of Science. USA.*

Lehman, H. G. (1953). *Age and achievement.* Princeton, NJ: Princeton University Press.

Lenneberg, E. H. (1967). *Biological foundations of language.* New York: Wiley.

Lesgold, A., Rubinson, H., Feltovich, P., Glaser, R., Klopfer, D., & Wang, Y. (1988). Expertise in a complex skill: Diagnosing x-ray pictures. In M. T. H. Chi, R. Glaser, & M. J. Farr (Eds.), *The nature of expertise.* Hillsdale, NJ: Erlbaum.

Lewis, C. H., & Anderson, J. R. (1976). Interference with real world knowledge. *Cognitive Psychology, 7,* 311–335.

Lewis, M. W. (1985). *Context effects on cognitve skill acquisition.* Unpublished doctoral dissertation, Carnegie-Mellon University.

Liberman, A. M. (1970). The grammars of speech and language. *Cognitive Psychology, 1,* 301–323.

Lieberman, P. (1984). *The biology and evolution of language.* Cambridge, MA: Harvard University Press.

Lindsay, P. H., & Norman, D. A. (1977). *Human information processing.* New York: Academic Press.

Lisker, L., & Abramson, A. (1970). The voicing dimension: Some experiments in comparative phonetics. *Proceedings of Sixth International Congress of Phonetic Sciences, Prague, 1967.* Prague: Academia.

Livingstone, M., & Hubel, D. (1988). Segregation of form, color, movement, and depth: Anatomy, physiology, and perception. *Science, 240,* 740–749.

Loftus, E. F (1974). Activation of semantic memory. *American Journal of Psychology, 86,* 331–337.

Loftus, E. F. (1975). Leading questions and the eyewitness report. *Cognitive Psychology, 7,* 560–572.

Loftus, E. F. (1979). *Eyewitness testimony.* Cambridge, MA: Harvard University Press.

Loftus, E. F., Miller, D. G., & Burns, H. J. (1978). Misinformation and memory: The creation of new memories. *Journal of Experimental Psychology: General, 118,* 100–104.

Loftus, E. F., & Pickerall, J. (1995). The formation of false memories. *Psychiatric Annals, 25,* 720–725.

Loftus, E. F., & Zanni, G. (1975). Eyewitness testimony: The influence of the wording of a question. *Bulletin of the Psychonomic Society, 5,* 86–88.

Logan, G. D., & Klapp, S. T. (1991). Automatizing alphabet arithmetic: I. Is extended practice necessary to produce automaticity. *Journal of Experimental Psychology: Learning, Memory, and Cognition, 17,* 179–195.

Logan, G. D. (1988). Toward an instance theory of automatization. *Psychological Review, 95,* 492–527.

Lovett, M. C. (1998). *Choice.* In J. R. Anderson & C. Lebiere, (Eds.), *The atomic components of thought,* 255–296. Mahwah, NJ: Erlbaum.

Luchins, A. S. (1942). Mechanization in problem solving. *Psychological Monographs, 54,* No. 248.

Luchins, A. S., & Luchins, E. H. (1959). *Rigidity of behavior: A variational approach to the effects of Einstellung.* Eugene, OR: University of Oregon Books.

Lucy, J., & Shweder, R. (1979). Whorf and his critics: Linguistic and non-linguistic influences on color memory. *American Anthropologist, 81,* 581–615.

Lucy, J., & Shweder, R. (1988). The effect of incidental conversation on memory for focal colors. *American Anthropologist, 90,* 923–931.

Lynch, G., & Baudry, M. (1984). The biochemistry of memory: A new and specific hypothesis. *Science, 224,* 1057–1063.

Maclay, H., & Osgood, C. E. (1959). Hesitation phenomena in spontaneous speech. *Word, 15,* 19–44.

MacLeod, C. M., & Dunbar, K. (1988). Training and Stroop-like interferences: Evidence for a continuum of automaticity. *Journal of Experimental Psychology: Learning, Memory, and Cognition, 14,* 126–135.

MacLeod, C. M., Hunt, E. B., & Matthews, N. N. (1978). Individual differences in the verification of sentence-picture relationships. *Journal of Verbal Learning and Verbal Behavior, 17,* 493–507.

MacWhinney, B., & Leinbach, J. (1991). Implementations are not conceptualizations: Revising the verb learning model. *Cognition, 29,* 121–157.

Maier, N. R. F. (1931). Reasoning in humans: II. The solution of a problem and its appearance in consciousness. *Journal of Comparative Psychology, 12,* 181–194.

Mandler, J. M., & Johnson, N. S. (1977). Remembrance of things parsed: Story structure and recall. *Cognitive Psychology, 9,* 111–151.

Mandler, J. M., & Ritchey, G. H. (1977). Long-term memory for pictures. *Journal of Experimental Psychology: Human Learning and Memory, 3,* 386–396.

Mangun, G. R., Hillyard, S. A., & Luck, S. J. (1993). Electrocortical substrates of visual selective attention. In D. Meyer & S. Kornblum (Eds.), *Attention and Performance* (Vol. 14, pp. 219–243). Cambridge MA: MIT Press.

Marcus, G. F., Brinkman, U., Clahsen, H., Wiese, R., Woest, A., & Pinker, S. (1995). German inflection: The exception that proves the rule. *Cognitive Psychology, 29,* 189–256.

Marcus, S. L., & Rips, L. J. (1979). Conditional reasoning. *Journal of Verbal Learning and Verbal Behavior, 18,* 199–223.

Marr, D. (1982). *Vision.* San Francisco: W. H. Freeman.

Marr, D., & Nishihara, H. K. (1978). Representation and recognition of the spatial organization of three-dimensional shapes. *Proceedings of the Royal Society, London, B, 200,* 269–294.

Marslen-Wilson, W., & Tyler, L. K. (1987). Against modularity. In J. L. Garfield (Ed.), *Modularity in knowledge representation and natural-language understanding.* Cambridge, MA: MIT Press.

Marslen-Wilson, W., & Tyler, L. K. (1998). Rules, representations, and the English past tense. *Trends in Cognitive Science, 2,* 428–435.

Martin, L. (1986). Eskimo words for snow: A case study on the genesis and decay of an anthropological example. *American Anthropologist, 88,* 418–423.

Massaro, D. W. (1979). Letter information and orthographic context in word perception. *Journal of Experimental Psychology: Human Perception and Performance, 5,* 595–609.

Massaro, D. W. (1989). Testing between the TRACE model and the fuzzy logical model of speech perception. *Cognitive Psychology, 21,* 398–421.

Massaro, D. W. (1992). Broadening the domain of the fuzzy logical model of perception. In H. L. Pick, Jr., P. Van den Broek, & D. C. Knill (Eds.), *Cognition: Conceptual and methodological issues* (pp. 51–84). Washington, DC: American Psychological Association.

Massaro, D. W. (1996). Modeling multiple influences in speech perception. In A. Dijkstra, & K. de Smedt (Eds.), *Computational psycholinguistics: AI and connectionist models of human language processing,* 85–113. London, England: Taylor and Francis.

Massaro, D. W., & Cohen, M. M. (1991). Integration versus interactive activation: The joint influence of stimulus and context in perception. *Cognitive Psychology, 23,* 558–614.

Masson, M. E. J., & MacLeod, C. M. (1992). Reenacting the route to interpretation: Enhanced identification without prior perception. *Journal of Experimental Psychology: General, 121,* 145–176.

Mayer, A., & Orth, I. (1901). Zur qualitativen Untersuchung der Association. *Zeitschrift für Psychologie, 26,* 1–13.

Mazoyer, B. M., Tzourio, N., Frak, V., Syrota, A., Murayama, N., Levrier, G., Salamon, A., Dehaene, S., Cohen, L., & Mehler, J. (1993). The cortical representation of speech. *Journal of Cognitive Neuroscience, 5,* 467–479.

McClelland, J. L. (1981). Retrieving general and specific knowledge from stored knowledge of specifics. *Proceedings of the Third Annual Conference of the Cognitive Science Society,* Berkeley, CA.

McClelland, J. L. (1991). Stochastic interactive processes and the effect of context on perception. *Cognitive Psychology, 23,* 1–44.

McClelland, J. L., & Elman, J. L. (1986). The TRACE model of speech perception. *Cognitive Psychology, 18,* 1–86.

McClelland, J. L., & Johnston, J. C. (1977) The role of familiar units in perception of words and nonwords. *Perception and Psychophysics, 22,* 249–261.

McClelland, J. L., & Rumelhart, D. E. (1981). An interactive model of context effects in letter perception: I. An account of basic findings. *Psychological Review, 88*, 375–407.

McClelland, J. L., & Rumelhart, D. E. (Eds.). (1986). *Parallel distributed processing. Explorations in the microstructure of cognition* (Vol. 2). Cambridge, MA: MIT Press/Bradford Books.

McClelland, J. L., Rumelhart, D. E., & Hinton, G. E. (1986). The appeal of parallel distributed processing. In D. E. Rumelhart & J. L. McClelland (Eds.), *Parallel distributed processing: Explorations in the microstructure of cognition* (Vol. 1). Cambridge, MA: MIT Press/Bradford Books.

McClelland, J., & Siegler, R. S. (in press) (Eds.). *Mechanisms of cognitive development: Behavioral and neural perspectives.* Mahwah, NJ: Erlbaum.

McCloskey, M. (1992). Cognitive mechanisms in numerical processing: Evidence from acquired dyscalculia. *Cognition, 44*, 107–157.

McCloskey, M., & Glucksberg, S. (1978). Natural categories. Well-defined or fuzzy sets? *Memory & Cognition, 6*, 462–472.

McCloskey, M., Wible, C. G., & Cohen, N. J. (1988). Is there a special flashbulb-memory mechanism? *Journal of Experimental Psychology: General, 117*, 171–181.

McDonald, J. L. (1984). *The mapping of semantic and syntactic processing cues by first and second language learners of English, Dutch, and German.* Unpublished doctoral dissertation, Carnegie-Mellon University.

McKeithen, K. B., Reitman, J. S., Rueter, H. H., & Hirtle, S. C. (1981). Knowledge organization and skill differences in computer programmers. *Cognitive Psychology, 13*, 307–325.

McKoon, G., & Ratcliff, R. (1992). Inference during reading. *Psychological Review, 99*, 440–466.

McLaughlin, B. (1978). *Second-language acquisition in childhood.* Hillsdale, NJ: Erlbaum.

McNamara, T. P. (1992). Priming and constraints it places on theories of memory and retrieval. *Psychological Review, 99*, 650–662.

McNamara, T. P. (1994). Priming and theories of memory: A reply to Ratcliff and McKoon. *Psychological Review, 101*, 185–187.

McNamara, T. P., Hardy, J. K., & Hirtle, S. C. (1989). Subjective hierarchies in spatial memory. *Journal of Experimental Psychology: Learning, Memory, and Cognition, 15*, 211–227.

McNeil, B. J., Pauker, S. G., Cox, H. C., Jr., & Tversky, A. (1982). On the elicitation of preferences for alternative therapies. *New England Journal of Medicine, 306*, 1259–1262.

McNeill, D. (1966). Developmental psycholinguistics. In F. Smith & G. A. Miller (Eds.), *The genesis of language: A psycholinguistic approach.* Cambridge, MA: MIT Press.

McRae, K., Spivey-Knowlton, M. J., & Tannehaus, M. K. (1998). Modeling the influence of thematic fit (and other constraints) in on-line sentence comprehension. *Journal of Memory and Language, 38*, 283–312.

Medin, D. L., & Heit, E., (in press). Categorization. In D. Rumelhart & B. Martin (Eds.), *Cognition and perception: Cognitive science.* San Diego, Academic Press.

Medin, D. L., & Ross, B. H. (1996). *Cognitive Psychology* (2nd Ed.). Orlando, FL: Harcourt Brace College Publishers.

Medin, D. L., & Schaffer, M. M. (1978). A context theory of classification learning. *Psychological Review, 85,* 207–238.

Metcalfe, J., & Wiebe, D. (1987). Intuition in insight and non-insight problem solving. *Memory & Cognition, 15,* 238–246.

Metzler, J., & Shepard, R. N. (1974). Transformational studies of the internal representations of three-dimensional objects. In R. L. Solso (Ed.), *Theories of cognitive psychology: The Loyola Symposium.* Hillsdale, NJ: Erlbaum.

Meyer, B. J. F. (1974). The organization of prose and its effect on recall. Unpublished doctoral dissertation, Cornell University.

Meyer, B. J. F., Brandt, D. M., & Bluth, G. J. (1978). *Use of author's textual schema: Key for ninth-grader's comprehension.* Paper presented at the annual conference of the American Educational Research Association, Toronto.

Meyer, D. E., & Kieras, D. E. (1997) A computational theory of executive cognitive processes and multiple-task performance: Part 1. Basic mechanisms. *Psychological Review, 104,* 3–65.

Meyer, D. E., & Schvaneveldt, R. W. (1971). Facilitation in recognizing pairs of words: Evidence of a dependence between retrieval operations. *Journal of Experimental Psychology, 90,* 227–234.

Miller, G. A. (1956). The magical number seven, plus or minus two: Some limits on our capacity for processing information. *Psychological Review, 63,* 81–97.

Miller, G. A., & Nicely, P. (1955). An analysis of perceptual confusions among some English consonants. *Journal of the Acoustical Society of America, 27,* 338–352.

Milner, B. (1962). Les troubles de la memoire accompagnant des lesions hippocampiques bilaterales. In P. Passonant (Ed.), *Physiologie de l'hippocampe.* Paris: Centre National de la Recherche Scientifique.

Moray, N. (1959). Attention in dichotic listening: Affective cues and the influence of instructions. *Quarterly Journal of Experimental Psychology, 9,* 56–90.

Moyer, R. S. (1973). Comparing objects in memory: Evidence suggesting an internal psychophysics. *Perception and Psychophysics, 13,* 180–184.

Neath, I. (1998). *Human memory: An introduction to research, data, and theory.* Pacific Grove, CA: Brooks/Cole Publishing Company.

Neisser, U. (1967). *Cognitive psychology.* New York: Appleton.

Neisser, U. (1976). *Cognition and reality: Principles and implications of cognitive psychology.* New York: W. H. Freeman.

Neisser, U. (1981). John Dean's memory: A case study. *Cognition, 9,* 1–22.

Neisser, U. (1982). Memory: What are the important questions? In U. Neisser (Ed.), *Memory observed.* New York: W. H. Freeman.

Neisser, U., & Becklen, R. (1975). Selective looking: Attending to visually specified events. *Cognitive Psychology, 7,* 480–494.

Nelson, D. L. (1979). Remembering pictures and words: Appearance, significance, and name. In L. S. Cermak & F. I. M. Craik (Eds.), *Levels of processing in human memory* (pp. 45–76). Hillsdale, NJ: Erlbaum.

Nelson, T. O. (1971). Savings and forgetting from long-term memory. *Journal of Verbal Learning and Verbal Behavior, 10,* 568–576.

Nelson, T. O. (1976). Reinforcement and human memory. In W. K. Estes (Ed.), *Handbook of learning and cognitive processes* (Vol. 3). Hillsdale, NJ: Erlbaum.

Nelson, T. O. (1978). Detecting small amounts of information in memory: Savings for nonrecognized items. *Journal of Experimental Psychology: Human Learning and Memory, 4,* 453–468.

Neves, D. M., & Anderson, J. R. (1981). Knowledge compilation: Mechanisms for the automatization of cognitive skills. In J. R. Anderson (Ed.), *Cognitive skills and their acquisition.* Hillsdale, NJ: Erlbaum.

Newell, A. (1973). You can't play 20 questions with nature and win: Projective comments on the papers of this symposium (pp. 283–310). In W. G. Chase (Ed.) *Visual information processing.* New York: Academic Press Inc.

Newell, A. (1980). Reasoning, problem-solving, and decision processes: The problem space as a fundamental category. In R. Nickerson (Ed.), *Attention and performance* (Vol. 8). Hillsdale, NJ: Erlbaum.

Newell, A. (1991). *Unified theories of cognition.* Cambridge, MA: Cambridge University Press.

Newell, A., & Rosenbloom, P. S. (1981). Mechanisms of skill acquisition and the law of practice. In J. R. Anderson (Ed.), *Cognitive skills and their acquisition.* Hillsdale, NJ: Erlbaum.

Newell, A., & Simon, H. (1972). *Human problem solving.* Englewood Cliffs, NJ: Prentice-Hall.

Newport, E. L. (1986). *The effect of maturational state on the acquisition of language.* Paper presented at the Eleventh Annual Boston University Conference on Language Development, October 17–19.

Newport, E. L., & Supalla, T. (1990). *A critical period effect in the acquisition of a primary language.* Unpublished manuscript, University of Rochester, Rochester, NY.

Nida, E. A. (1971). Sociopsychological problems in language mastery and retention. In P. Pimsleur & T. Quinn (Eds.), *The psychology of second language acquisition.* London: Cambridge University Press.

Nilsson, L.-G., & Gardiner, J. M. (1993). Identifying exceptions in a database of recognition failure studies from 1973 to 1992. *Memory & Cognition, 21,* 397–410.

Nilsson, N. J. (1971). *Problem-solving methods in artificial intelligence.* New York: McGraw-Hill.

Nisbett, R. E., & Ross, L. (1980). *Human inference: Strategies and shortcomings of social judgment.* Englewood Cliffs, NJ: Prentice-Hall.

Noelting, G. (1975). *Stages and mechanisms in the development of the concept of proportion in the child and adolescent.* Paper presented at the First Interdisciplinary Seminar on Piagetian Theory and Its Implications for the Helping Professions, University of Southern California, Los Angeles.

Norman, D. A., & Rumelhart, D. E. (1975). *Explorations in cognition.* New York: W. H. Freeman.

Nosofsky, R. M. (1986). Attention, similarity, and the identification-categorization relationship. *Journal of Experimental Psychology: General, 115,* 39–57.

Nosofsky, R. M. (1991). Tests of an exemplar model for relating perceptual classification and recognition in memory. *Journal of Experimental Psychology: Human Perception and Performance, 17,* 3–27.

Nosofsky, R. M., Palmeri, T. J., & McKinley, S. C. (1994). Rule-plus-exception model of classification learning. *Psychological Review, 101,* 53–79.

O'Nuallain, S., McKevitt, P., & MacAogain, E. (1997). *Two sciences of mind.* Philadelphia, PA: John Benjamins North America.

Oaksford, M., & Chater, N. (1994). A rational analysis of the selection task as optimal data selection. *Psychological Review, 101,* 608–631.

Oaksford, M., & Chater, N. (1998). *Rational models of cognition.* Oxford: Oxford University Press.

Okada, S., Hanada, M., Hattori, H., & Shoyama, T. (1963). A case of pure word-deafness. *Studia Phonologica, 3,* 58–65.

Osherson, D. N., & Lasnik, H. (1990). *Language: An introduction to cognitive science* (Vol. 1). Cambridge, MA: MIT Press.

Osterhout, L., & Holcomb, P. J. (1992). Event-related potentials elicited by syntactic anomaly. *Journal of Memory and Language, 31,* 785–806.

Owens, J., Bower, G. H., & Black, J. B. (1979). The "soap opera" effect in story recall. *Memory & Cognition, 7,* 185–191.

Oyama, S. (1978). The sensitive period and comprehension of speech. *Working Papers on Bilingualism, 16,* 1–17.

Paivio, A. (1971). *Imagery and verbal processes.* New York: Holt, Rinehart, & Winston.

Paivio, A. (1975). Perceptual comparisons through the mind's eye. *Memory & Cognition, 3,* 635–647.

Paivio, A. (1986). *Mental representations: A dual coding approach.* New York: Oxford University Press.

Palinscar, A. S., & Brown, A. L. (1984). Reciprocal teaching of comprehension monitoring activities. *Cognition and Instruction, 1,* 117–175.

Palmer, S. E. (1975). The effects of contextual scenes on the identification of objects. *Memory & Cognition, 3,* 519–526.

Palmer, S. E. (1977). Hierarchical structure in perceptual representation. *Cognitive Psychology, 9,* 441–474.

Palmer, S. E. (1978). Fundamental aspects of cognitive representation. In E. Rosch & B. Lloyd (Eds.), *Cognition and categorization.* Hillsdale, NJ: Erlbaum.

Palmer, S. E., Schreiber, G., & Fox., C. (1991, November 22–24). Remembering the earthquake: "Flashbulb" memory of experienced versus reported events. Paper presented at the 32nd annual meeting of the Psychonomic Society, San Francisco.

Paris, S. C., & Lindauer, B. K. (1976). The role of interference in children's comprehension and memory for sentences. *Cognitive Psychology, 8,* 217–227.

Parker, E. S., Birnbaum, I. M., & Noble, E. P. (1976). Alcohol and memory: Storage and state dependency. *Journal of Verbal Learning and Verbal Behavior, 15,* 691–702.

Pascual-Leone, J. (1980). Constructive problems for constructive theories: The current relevance of Piaget's work and a critique of information-processing psychology. In R. H. Kluwe & H. Spada (Eds.), *Developmental models of thinking.* New York: Academic Press.

Pashler, H. E. (1995). Attention and visual perception: Analyzing divided attention. In S. M. Kosslyn & N. D. Osherson (Eds.), *Visual cognition.* Cambridge, MA: MIT Press.

Pashler, H. E. (1998). *The psychology of attention.* Cambridge, MA: MIT Press.

Penfield, W. (1959). The interpretive cortex. *Science, 129,* 1719–1725.

Penfield, W., & Jasper, H. (1954). *Epilepsy and the functional anatomy of the human brain.* Boston: Little and Brown.

Perky, C. W. (1910). An experimental study of imagination. *American Journal of Psychology, 21,* 422–452.

Perlmutter, M. (1988). Cognitive potential throughout life. In J. Birren & V. Bengtson (Eds.), *Theories of aging: Psychological and social perspectives on time, self, and society.* Hillsdale, NJ: Erlbaum.

Perlmutter, M., Kaplan, M., & Nyquist, L. (1990). Development of adaptive competence in adulthood. *Human Development, 33*, 185–197.

Perrett, D. I., Rolls, E. T., & Caan, W. (1982). Visual neurons responsive to faces in the monkey temporal cortex. *Experimental Brain Research, 47*, 329–342.

Peterson, M. A., Kihlstrom, J. F., Rose, P. M., & Gilsky, M. L. (1992). Mental images can be ambiguous: Reconstruals and reference-frame reversals. *Memory & Cognition, 20*, 107–123.

Peterson, S. B., & Potts, G. R. (1982). Global and specific components of information integration. *Journal of Verbal Learning and Verbal Behavior, 21*, 403–420.

Peterson, S. E., Robinson, D. L., & Morris, J. D. (1987). Contributions of the pulvinar to visual spatial attention. *Neuropsychologia, 25*, 97–105.

Petrides, M., Alvisatos, B., Evans, A. C., & Meyer, E. (1993). Dissociation of human mid-dorsolateral from posterior dorsolateral frontal cortex in memory processing. *Proceedings of the National Academy of Science, 90*, 873–877.

Phelps, E. A. (1989). *Cognitive skill learning in amnesiacs.* Doctoral dissertation, Princeton University.

Piaget, J. (1952a). *The origins of intelligence in children.* New York: International Universities Press.

Piaget, J. (1952b). *The child's conception of number.* New York: Humanities Press.

Pillsbury, W. B. (1908). The effects of training on memory. *Educational Review, 36*, 15–27.

Pinker, S. (1994). Language acquisition. In M. I. Posner (Ed.), *Foundations of cognitive science.* Cambridge, MA: MIT Press.

Pinker, S., & Prince, A. (1988). On language and connectionism: Analysis of a parallel distributed processing model of language acquisition. *Cognition, 28*, 73–193.

Pirolli, P. L., & Card, S. K. (in press). Information foraging. *Psychological Review.*

Pirolli, P. L., & Anderson, J. R. (1985). The role of practice in fact retrieval. *Journal of Experimental Psychology: Learning, Memory, and Cognition, 11*, 136–153.

Plaut, D. C., & Farah, M. J. (1990). Visual object representation: Interpreting neurophysiological data within a computational framework. *Journal of Cognitive Neuroscience, 2*, 320–343.

Poincaré, H. (1929). *The foundations of science.* New York: Science House.

Polson, P. G., Muncher, E., & Kieras, D. E. (1987). *Transfer of skills between inconsistent editors.* (MCC Technical Report Number ACA-HI-395-87.) Microelectronics and Computer Technology Corporation, Austin, TX.

Posner, M. I. (1988). Structures and functions of selective attention. In T. Boll & B. Bryant (Eds.), *Master lectures in clinical neuropsychology.* Washington, DC: American Psychological Association.

Posner, M. I., & Raichle, M. E. (1994). *Images of mind.* New York: W. H. Freeman.

Posner, M. I., Cohen, Y., & Rafal, R. D. (1982). Neural systems control of spatial orienting. *Philosophical Transactions of the Royal Society* (London), *B298*, 187–198.

Posner, M. I., Nissen, M. J., & Ogden, W. C. (1978). Attended and unattended processing modes: The role of set for spatial location. In H. L. Pick, Jr., & I. J. Saltzman (Eds.), *Modes of perceiving and processing information.* Hillsdale, NJ: Erlbaum.

Posner, M. I., Peterson, S. E., Fox, P. T., & Raichle, M. E. (1988). Localization of cognitive operations in the human brain. *Science, 240*, 1627–1631.

Posner, M. I., Rafal, R. D., Chaote, L. S., & Vaughn, J. (1985). Inhibition of return: Neural basis and function. *Cognitive Neuropsychology, 2,* 211–228.

Posner, M. I., Snyder, C. R. R., & Davidson, B. J. (1980). Attention and the detection of signals. *Journal of Experimental Psychology: General, 109,* 160–174.

Posner, M. I., Walker, J. A., Friederich, F. J., & Rafal, R. D. (1984). Effects of parietal injury on covert orienting of attention. *Journal of Neuroscience, 4,* 1863–1874.

Postman, L. (1964). Short-term memory and incidental learning. In A. W. Melton (Ed.), *Categories of human learning.* New York: Academic Press.

Pressley, M., McDaniel, M. A., Turnure, J. E., Wood, E., & Ahmad, M. (1987). Generation and precision of elaboration: Effects on intentional and incidental learning. *Journal of Experimental Psychology: Learning, Memory, and Cognition, 13,* 291–300.

Pritchard, R. M. (1961). Stabilized images on the retina. *Scientific American, 204,* 72–78.

Pullman, G. K. (1989). The great Eskimo vocabulary hoax. *National Language and Linguistic Theory, 7,* 275–281.

Pylyshyn, Z. W. (1973). What the mind's eye tells the mind's brain: A critique of mental imagery. *Psychological Bulletin, 80,* 1–24.

Quillian, M. R. (1966). *Semantic memory.* Cambridge, MA: Bolt, Beranak and Newman.

Raaijmakers, J. G. W., & Shiffrin, R. M. (1981). Search of associative memory. *Psychological Review, 88,* 93–134.

Rabinowitz, M., & Goldberg, N. (1995). Evaluating the structure-process hypothesis. In F. E. Weinert & W. Schneider (Eds.), *Memory Performance and Competencies: Issues in Growth and Development.* Hillsdale, NJ: Lawrence Erlbaum.

Radvansky, G. A., & Zacks, R. T. (1991). Mental models and the fan effect. *Journal of Experimental Psychology: Learning, Memory, and Cognition, 17,* 940–953.

Ratcliff, R. A., & McKoon, G. (1978). Priming in item recognition: Evidence for the propositional structure of sentences. *Journal of Verbal Learning and Verbal Behavior, 17,* 403–417.

Ratcliff, R. A., & McKoon, G. (1981). Does activation really spread? *Psychological Review, 88,* 454–462.

Ratcliff, R. A., & McKoon, G. (1994). Retrieving information from memory: Spreading-activation theories versus compound-cue theories. *Psychological Review, 101,* 177–184.

Ratcliff, G., & Newcombe, F. (1982). Object recognition: Some deductions from the clinical evidence. In A. W. Ellis (Ed.), *Normality and pathology in cognitive functions.* London: Academic Press.

Reder, L. M. (1982). Plausibility judgment versus fact retrieval: Alternative strategies for sentence verification. *Psychological Review, 89,* 250–280.

Reder, L. M. (Ed.). (1996). *Implicit memory and metacognition.* Mahwah, NJ: Erlbaum.

Reder, L. M., & Ross, B. H. (1983). Integrated knowledge in different tasks: Positive and negative fan effects. *Journal of Experimental Psychology: Human Learning and Memory, 8,* 55–72.

Reed, S. K. (1972). Pattern recognition and categorization. *Cognitive Psychology, 3,* 382–407.

Reed, S. K. (1974). Structural descriptions and the limitations of visual images. *Memory & Cognition, 2*, 329–336.

Reed, S. K. (1987). A structure-mapping model for word problems. *Journal of Experimental Psychology: Learning, Memory, and Cognition, 13*, 124–139.

Reed, S. K., & Bolstad, C. A. (1991). Use of examples and procedures in problem solving. *Journal of Experimental Psychology: Learning, Memory, and Cognition, 17*, 753–766.

Reed, S. K., & Johnsen, J. A. (1975). Detection of parts in patterns and images. *Memory & Cognition, 3*, 569–575.

Reicher, G. (1969). Perceptual recognition as a function of meaningfulness of stimulus material. *Journal of Experimental Psychology, 81*, 275–280.

Reisberg, D. (1992). *Auditory imagery*, Hillsdale, NJ: Erlbaum.

Reitman, J. (1976). Skilled perception in GO: Deducing memory structures from interresponse times. *Cognitive Psychology, 8*, 336–356.

Richardson-Klavehn, A., & Bjork, R. A. (1988). Measures of memory. *Annual Review of Psychology, 39*, 475–543.

Rips, L. J. (1990). Reasoning. *Annual Review of Psychology, 41*, 321–354.

Rips, L. J. (1994). *The psychology of proof*. Cambridge, MA: MIT Press.

Rips, L. J., & Marcus, S. L. (1977). Supposition and the analysis of conditional sentences. In M. A. Just & P. A. Carpenter (Eds.), *Cognitive processes in comprehension*. Hillsdale, NJ: Erlbaum.

Roberts, R. J., Hager, L. D., & Heron, C. (1994). Prefrontal cognitive processes: Working memory and inhibition in the Antisaccade task. *Journal of Experimental Psychology: General, 123*, 374–393.

Robinson, G. H. (1964). Continuous estimation of a time-varying probability. *Ergonomics, 7*, 7–21.

Rogers, T. B., Kuipers, N. A., & Kirker, W. S. (1977). Self-reference and the encoding of personal information. *Journal of Personality and Social Psychology, 35*, 677–688.

Roland, P. E., & Friberg, L. (1985). Localization of cortical areas activated by thinking. *Journal of Neurophysiology, 53*, 1219–1243.

Rosch, E. (1973). On the internal structure of perceptual and semantic categories. In T. E. Moore (Ed.), *Cognitive development and the acquisition of language*. New York: Academic Press.

Rosch, E. (1975). Cognitive representations of semantic categories. *Journal of Experimental Psychology: General, 104*, 192–223.

Rosch, E. (1977). Human categorization. In N. Warren (Ed.), *Advances in crosscultural psychology* (Vol. 1). London: Academic Press.

Rosenbaum, D. A. (1991). *Human motor control*. San Diego: Academic Press.

Ross, B. H. (1984). Remindings and their effects in learning a cognitive skill. *Cognitive Psychology, 16*, 371–416.

Ross, B. H. (1987). This is like that: The use of earlier problems and the separation of similarity effects. *Journal of Experimental Psychology: Learning, Memory, and Cognition, 13*, 629–639.

Ross, J., & Lawrence, K. A. (1968). Some observations on memory artifice. *Psychonomic Science, 13*, 107–108.

Rothkopf, E. Z. (1966). Learning from written instruction materials: An explanation of the control of inspection behavior by test-like events. *American Educational Research Journal, 3*, 241–249.

Rubin, D. C., & Wenzel, A. E. (1996). One hundred years of forgetting: A quantitative description of retention. *Psychological Review, 103,* 734–760

Ruiz, D. (1987). Learning and problem solving: What is learned while solving the Tower of Hanoi? Doctoral dissertation, Stanford University, 1986. *Dissertation Abstracts International, 42,* 3438b.

Rumelhart, D. E., & McClelland, J. L. (1986a). On learning the past tenses of English verbs. In J. L. McClelland & D. E. Rumelhart (Eds.), *Parallel distributed processing: Explorations in the microstructure of cognition* (Vol. 2). Cambridge, MA: MIT Press/Bradford Books.

Rumelhart, D. E., & McClelland, J. L. (Eds.) (1986b). *Parallel distributed processing: Explorations in the microstructure of cognition* (Vol. 1). Cambridge, MA: MIT Press/Bradford Books.

Rumelhart, D. E., & Norman, D. A. (1978). Accretion, tuning, and restructuring: Three modes of learning. In J. W. Cotton & R. Klatzky (Eds.), *Semantic factors in cognition.* Hillsdale, NJ: Erlbaum.

Rumelhart, D. E., & Ortony, A. (1976). The representation of knowledge in memory. In R. C. Anderson, R. J. Spiro, & W. E. Montague (Eds.), *Semantic factors in cognition.* Hillsdale, NJ: Erlbaum.

Rumelhart, D. E., & Siple, P. (1974). Process of recognizing tachistoscopically presented words. *Psychological Review, 81,* 99–118.

Rundus, D. J. (1971). Analysis of rehearsal processes in free recall. *Journal of Experimental Psychology, 89,* 63–77.

Russell, S., & Norvig, P. (1995). *Artificial intelligence: A modern approach.* Upper Saddle River, NJ: Prentice-Hall.

Sacks, O. W. (1985). *The man who mistook his wife for a hat and other clinical tales.* New York: Summit Books.

Saffran, E. M., & Schwartz, M. F. (1994). Of cabbages and things: semantic memory from a neuropsychological perspective—A tutorial review. In C. Umilta & M. Moscovitch (Eds.), *Attention and Performance XV.* Hove and London, UK: Churchill Livingstone.

Safren, M. A. (1962). Associations, set, and the solution of word problems. *Journal of Experimental Psychology, 64,* 40–45.

Sakitt, B. (1976). Iconic memory. *Psychological Review, 83,* 257–276.

Salamy, A. (1978). Commissural transmission: Maturational changes in humans. *Science, 200,* 1409–1411.

Salthouse, T. A. (1985). Anticipatory processes in transcription typing. *Journal of Applied Psychology, 70,* 264–271.

Salthouse, T. A. (1986). Perceptual, cognitive, and motoric aspects of transcription typing. *Psychological Bulletin, 99,* 303–319.

Salthouse, T. A. (1991). *Theoretical perspectives on cognitive aging.* Hillsdale, NJ: Erlbaum.

Salthouse, T. A. (1992). *Mechanisms of age-cognition relations in adulthood.* Hillsdale, NJ: Erlbaum.

Santa, J. L. (1977). Spatial transformations of words and pictures. *Journal of Experimental Psychology: Human Learning and Memory, 3,* 418–427.

Sarason, S. B., & Doris, J. (1979). *Educational handicap, public policy, and social history.* New York: Free Press.

Saufley, W. H., Otaka, S. R., & Bavaresco, J. L. (1985). Context effects: Classroom tests and context independence. *Memory & Cognition, 13,* 522–528.

Sayers, D. L. (1968). *Five red herrings.* New York: Avon.

Schacter, D. L. (1987). Implicit memory: History and current status. *Journal of Experimental Psychology: Learning, Memory, and Cognition, 13,* 501–518.

Schacter, D. L. (1996). *Searching for memory.* New York: Basic Books.

Schank, R. C., & Abelson, R. (1977). *Scripts, plans, goals, and understanding.* Hillsdale, NJ: Erlbaum.

Scheines, R., & Sieg, W. (1994). Computer environments for proof construction. In E. Soloway (Ed.), *Interactive learning environments, 4,* 159–169.

Schieffelin, B. (1979). How Kaluli children learn what to say, what to do, and how to feel: An ethnographic study of the development of communicative competence. Doctoral dissertation, Columbia University.

Schmidt, R. A. (1988). Motor and action perspectives on motor behavior. In O. G. Meijer & K. Rother (Eds.), *Complex movement behavior: The motor-action controversy* (pp. 3–44). Amsterdam: Elsevier.

Schneider, W., Körkel, J., & Weinert, F. E. (July 6–8, 1988). Expert knowledge, general abilities, and text processing. *Presentation at the Workshop on Interactions among Aptitudes, Strategies, and Knowledge in Cognitive Performance.*

Schneider, W., & Oliver, W. L. (1991). An instructable connectionist/control architecture: Using rule-based instructions to accomplish connectionist learning on a human-time scale. In K. Van Lehn (Ed.), *Architectures for intelligence* (pp. 113–146). Hillsdale, NJ: Erlbaum.

Schneiderman, B. (1976). Exploratory experiments in programmer behavior. *International Journal of Computer and Information Sciences, 5,* 123–143.

Schoenfeld, A. H., & Herrmann, D. J. (1982). Problem perception and knowledge structure in expert and novice mathematical problem solvers. *Journal of Experimental Psychology: Learning, Memory, and Cognition, 8,* 484–494.

Selfridge, O. G. (1955). Pattern recognition and modern computers. *Proceedings of the Western Joint Computer Conference.* New York: Institute of Electrical and Electronics Engineers.

Selkoe, D. J. (1992). Aging brain, aging mind. *Scientific American* (September), 135–142.

Shafir, E. (1993). Choosing versus rejecting: Why some opinions are both better and worse than others. *Memory & Cognition, 21,* 546–556.

Shallice, T., & Burgess, W. (1991). Deficits in strategy application following frontal lobe damage in man. *Brain, 114,* 727–741.

Shepard, R. N. (1967). Recognition memory for words, sentences, and pictures. *Journal of Verbal Learning and Verbal Behavior, 6,* 156–163.

Shepard, R. N., & Metzler, J. (1971). Mental rotation of three-dimensional objects. *Science, 171,* 701–703.

Shepard, R. N., & Teghtsoonian, M. (1961). Retention of information under conditions approaching a steady state. *Journal of Experimental Psychology, 62,* 302–309.

Shriffrin, R. M. (1997). Attention, automatism, and consciousness. In J. D. Cohen, & J. W. Schooler (Eds.), *25th Symposium on Cognition: Scientific Approaches of Consciousness,* 49–64. Hillsdale, NJ: Erlbaum.

Shuford, E. H. (1961). Percentage estimation of proportion as a function of element type, exposure time, and task. *Journal of Experimenal Psychology, 61,* 430–436.

Siegler, R. S. (1996). *Emerging minds: The process of change in children's thinking.* New York: Oxford University Press.

Siegler, R. S. (1998). *Children's thinking.* Upper Saddle River, NJ: Prentice-Hall.

Siegler, R. S. (Ed.). (1978). *Children's thinking: What develops?* Hillsdale, NJ: Erlbaum.

Silveira, J. (1971). *Incubation: The effect of interruption timing and length on problem solution and quality of problem processing.* Unpublished doctoral dissertation, University of Oregon.

Silver, E. A. (1979). Student perceptions of relatedness among mathematical verbal problems. *Journal for Research in Mathematics Education, 12,* 54–64.

Simon, H. A. (1974). How big is a chunk? *Science, 183,* 482–488.

Simon, H. A. (1989). The scientist as a problem solver. In D. Klahr & K. Kotovsky (Eds.), *Complex information processing: The impact of Herbert Simon.* Hillsdale, NJ: Erlbaum.

Simon, H. A., & Gilmartin, K. (1973). A simulation of memory for chess positions. *Cognitive Psychology, 5,* 29–46.

Simonton, D. K. (1997). Creative productivity: A predictive and explanatory model of career trajectories and landmarks. *Psychological Review, 104,* 66–89.

Singer, M. (1990). *Psychology of language: An introduction to sentence and discourse processes.* Hillsdale, NJ: Erlbaum.

Singer, M. (1994). Discourse inference processes. In M. A. Gernsbacher (Ed.), *Handbook of psycholinguistics.* San Diego, CA: Academic Press.

Singley, K., & Anderson, J. R. (1989). *The transfer of cognitive skill.* Cambridge, MA: Harvard University Press.

Slamecka, N. J., & Graf, P. (1978). The generation effect: Delineation of a phenomenon. *Journal of Experimental Psychology: Human Learning and Memory, 4,* 592–604.

Sleeman, D., & Brown, J. S. (Eds.). (1982). *Intelligent tutoring systems.* New York: Academic Press.

Smith, E. E., & Jonides, J. (1995). Working memory in humans: Neuropsychological evidence. In M. S. Gazzaniga (Ed.), *The cognitive neurosciences,* 1009–1020. Cambridge, MA: MIT Press.

Smith, M. (1982). *Hypnotic memory enhancement of witnesses: Does it work?* Paper presented at the meeting of the Psychonomic Society, Minneapolis.

Smith, S. M., & Blakenship, S. E. (1991). Incubation and the persistence of fixation in problem solving. *American Journal of Psychology, 104,* 61–87.

Smith, S. M., & Blakenship, S. E. (1989). Incubation effects. *Bulletin of the Psychonomic Society, 27,* 311–314.

Smith, S. M., Brown, H. O., Toman, J. E. P., & Goodman, L. S. (1947). The lack of cerebral effects of d-Tubercurarine. *Anesthesiology, 8,* 1–14.

Smith, S. M., Glenberg, A., & Bjork, R. A. (1978). Environmental context and human memory. *Memory & Cognition, 6,* 342–353.

Snow, C., & Ferguson, C. (Eds.) (1977). Talking to children: Language input and acquisition *(Papers from a conference sponsored by the Committee on Sociolinguistics of the Social Science Research Council).* Cambridge, MA: Cambridge University Press.

Sophian, C. (1984). *Origins of cognitive skills.* Hillsdale, NJ: Erlbaum.

Spearman, C. (1904). The proof and measurement of association between two things. *American Journal of Psychology, 15,* 72–101.

Spelke, E., Hirst, W., & Neisser, U. (1976). Skills of divided attention. *Cognition, 4,* 215–230.

Sperling, G. A. (1960). The information available in brief visual presentation. *Psychological Monographs, 74,* Whole No. 498.

Sperling, G. A. (1967). Successive approximations to a model for short-term memory. *Acta Psychologica, 27*, 285–292.

Spiro, R. J. (1977). Constructing a theory of reconstructive memory: The state of the schema approach. In R. C. Anderson, R. J. Spiro, & W. E. Montague (Eds.), *Schooling and the acquisition of knowledge.* Hillsdale, NJ: Erlbaum.

Squire, L. R. (1992). Memory and the hippocampus: A synthesis from findings with rats, monkeys, and humans. *Psychological Review, 99*, 195–232.

Standing, L. (1973). Learning 10,000 pictures. *Quarterly Journal of Experimental Psychology, 25*, 207–222.

Staudenmayer, H. (1975). Understanding conditional reasoning with meaningful propositions. In R. J. Falmagne (Ed.), *Reasoning: Representation and process in children and adults.* Hillsdale, NJ: Erlbaum.

Stein, B. S., & Bransford, J. D. (1979). Constraints on effective elaboration: Effects of precision and subject generation. *Journal of Verbal Learning and Verbal Behavior, 18*, 769–777.

Stein, N. L., & Trabasso, T. (1981). What's in a story? Critical issues in comprehension and instruction. In R. Glaser (Ed.), *Advances in the psychology of instruction* (Vol. 2). Hillsdale, NJ: Erlbaum.

Sternberg, R. J. (1977). *Intelligence, information processing, and analogical reasoning.* Hillsdale, NJ: Erlbaum.

Sternberg, R. J. (1985). *Beyond IQ: A triarchic theory of human intelligence.* New York: Cambridge University Press.

Sternberg, R. J., & Gardner, M. K. (1983). Unities in inductive reasoning. *Journal of Experimental Psychology: General, 112*, 80–116.

Sternberg, S. (1966). High-speed scanning in human memory. *Science, 153*, 652–654.

Sternberg, S. (1969). Memory scanning: Mental processes revealed by reaction time experiments. *American Scientist, 57*, 421–457.

Stevens, A., & Coupe, P. (1978). Distortions in judged spatial relations. *Cognitive Psychology, 10*, 422–437.

Stillings, N. A., Feinstein, M. H., Garfield, J. L., Rissland, E. L., Rosenbaum, D. A., Weisler, S. E., & Baker-Ward, L. (1987). *Cognitive science: An introduction.* Cambridge, MA: MIT Press.

Stratton, G. M. (1922). *Developing mental power.* New York: Houghton Mifflin.

Strohner, H., & Nelson, K. E. (1974). The young child's development of sentence comprehension: Influence of event probability, nonverbal context, syntactic form, and strategies. *Child Development, 45*, 567–576.

Stroop, J. R. (1935) Studies of interference in serial verbal reactions. *Journal of Experimental Psychology, 18*, 643–662.

Studdert-Kennedy, M. (1976). Speech perception. In N. J. Lass (Ed.), *Contemporary issues in experimental phonetics.* Springfield, IL: Charles C. Thomas.

Sulin, R. A., & Dooling, D. J. (1974). Intrusion of a thematic idea in retention of prose. *Journal of Experimental Psychology, 103*, 255–262.

Sweller, J., Mawer, R. F., & Ward, M. R. (1983). Development of expertise in mathematical problem solving. *Journal of Experimental Psychology: General, 112*, 463–474.

Swinney, D. A. (1979). Lexical access during sentence comprehension: (Re)consideration of context effects. *Journal of Verbal Learning and Verbal Behavior, 18*, 645–659.

Taplin, J. E. (1971). Reasoning with conditional sentences. *Journal of Verbal Learning and Verbal Behavior, 10,* 218–225.

Taplin, J. E., & Staudenmayer, H. (1973). Interpretation of abstract conditional sentences in deductive reasoning. *Journal of Verbal Learning and Verbal Behavior, 12,* 530–542.

Taylor, I., & Taylor, M. M. (1990). *Psycholinguistics: Learning and using language.* Englewood Cliffs, NJ: Prentice-Hall.

Taylor, H. A., & Tversky, B. (1992). Spatial mental models derived from survey and route descriptions. *Journal of Memory and Language, 31,* 261–292.

Teasdale, J. D., & Russell, M. L. (1983). Differential effects of induced mood on the recall of positive, negative and neutral words. *British Journal of Clinical Psychology, 22,* 163–171.

Terman, L. M., & Merrill, M. A. (1973). *Stanford-Binet intelligence scales: 1973 norms edition.* Boston: Houghton Mifflin.

Thomas, E. L., & Robinson, H. A. (1972). *Improving reading in every class: A sourcebook for teachers.* Boston: Allyn & Bacon.

Thompson, D. M. (1972). Context effects on recognition memory. *Journal of Verbal Learning and Verbal Behavior, 11,* 497–511.

Thompson, M. C., & Massaro, D. W. (1973). Visual information and redundancy in reading. *Journal of Experimental Psychology, 98,* 49–54.

Thorndike, E. L. (1906). *Principles of teaching.* New York: A. G. Seiler.

Thorndike, E. L., & Woodworth, R. S. (1901). The influence of improvement in one mental function upon the efficiency of other functions. *Psychological Review, 9,* 374–382.

Thorndyke, P. W. (1977). Cognitive structures in comprehension and memory in narrative discourse. *Cognitive Psychology, 9,* 77–110.

Thorndyke, P. W., & Hayes-Roth, B. (1982). Differences in spatial knowledge acquired from maps and navigation. *Cognitive Psychology, 14,* 560–589.

Thurstone, L. L. (1938). *Primary mental abilities.* Chicago: University of Chicago Press.

Tipper, S. P., Driver, J., & Weaver, B. (1991). Object-centered inhibition of return of visual attention. *Quarterly Journal of Experimental Psychology, 43A,* 289–298.

Tolman, E. C. (1932). *Purposive behavior in animals and men.* New York: Appleton-Century-Crofts.

Tootell, R. B. H., Silverman, M. S., Switkes, E., & DeValois, R. L. (1982). Deoxyglucose analysis of retinotopic organization in primate striate cortex. *Science, 218,* 902–904.

Townsend, D. J., & Bever, T. G. (1982). Natural units interact during language comprehension. *Journal of Verbal Learning and Verbal Behavior, 28,* 681–703.

Trabasso, T. R., Rollins, H., & Shaughnessy, E. (1971). Storage and verification stages in processing concepts. *Cognitive Psychology, 2,* 239–289.

Trabasso, T. R., Secco, T., & van den Broek, P. (1984). Causal cohesion and story coherence. In H. Mandl (Ed.), *Learning and comprehension of text.* Hillsdale, NJ: Erlbaum.

Treisman, A. M. (1960). Verbal cues, language, and meaning in selective attention. *Quarterly Journal of Experimental Psychology, 12,* 242–248.

Treisman, A. M. (1964). Monitoring and storage of irrelevant messages and selective attention. *Journal of Verbal Learning and Verbal Behavior, 3,* 449–459.

Treisman, A. M. (1991). Search, similarity, and integration of features between and within dimensions. *Journal of Experimental Psychology: Human Perception and Performance, 17,* 652–676.

Treisman, A. M., & Geffen, G. (1967). Selective attention: Perception or response? *Quarterly Journal of Experimental Psychology, 19,* 1–17.

Treisman, A. M., & Gelade, G. (1980). A feature-integration theory of attention. *Cognitive Psychology, 12,* 97–136.

Treisman, A. M., & Riley, J. (1969). Is selective attention selective perception or selective response? A further test. *Journal of Experimental Psychology, 79,* 27–34.

Treisman, A. M., & Sato, S. (1990). Conjunction search revisited. *Journal of Experimental Psychology: Human Perception and Performance, 16,* 459–478.

Treisman, A. M., & Schmidt, H. (1982). Illusory conjunction in the perception of objects. *Cognitive Psychology, 14,* 107–141.

Trueswell, J. C., Tannehaus, M. K., & Garnsey, S. M. (1994). Semantic influences on parsing: Use of thematic role information in syntactic ambiguity resolution. *Journal of Memory and Language, 33,* 285–318.

Tulving, E., & Craik, F. I. M. (Eds.). (in press). *The Oxford handbook of memory.* New York: Oxford University Press.

Tulving, E., & Pearlstone, Z. (1966). Availability versus accessibility of information in memory for words. *Journal of Verbal Learning and Verbal Behavior, 5,* 381–391.

Tulving, E., & Thompson, D. M. (1973). Encoding specificity and retrieval processes in episodic memory. *Psychological Review, 80,* 352–373.

Tversky, A., & Kahneman, D. (1974). Judgments under uncertainty: Heuristics and biases. *Science, 185,* 1124–1131.

Tversky, B. (in press). Remembering spaces. In E. Tulving & F. I. M. Craik (Eds.), *The Oxford handbook of memory.* New York: Oxford University Press.

Tyler, R., & Marslen-Wilson, W. (1977). The on-line effects of semantic context on syntactic processing. *Journal of Verbal Learning and Verbal Behavior, 16,* 683–692.

Ultan, R. (1969). Some general characteristics of interrogative systems. *Working Papers in Language Universals (Stanford University), 1,* 41–63.

Underwood, G. (1974). Moray vs. the rest: The effect of extended shadowing practice. *Quarterly Journal of Experimental Psychology, 26,* 368–372.

Vallar, G., & Baddeley, A. D. (1982). Short-term forgetting and the articulatory loop. *Quarterly Journal of Experimental Psychology, 34,* 53–60.

Van den Broek, P. (1994). Comprehension and memory of narrative texts: Inferences and coherence. In M. A. Gernsbacher (Ed.), *Handbook of psycholinguistics.* San Diego, CA: Academic Press.

Van Essen, D. C., & DeYoe, E. A. (1995). Concurrent processing in the primitive visual cortex. In M. S. Gazzaniga (Ed.), *The Cognitive neurosciences.* Cambridge, MA: MIT Press.

von Neumann, J., & Morgenstern, O. (1944). *Theory of games and economic behavior.* New York: Wiley.

Wagner, A. D., Schacter, D. L., Rotte, M., Koutstaal, W., Maril, A., Dale, A. M., Rosen, B. R., & Buckner, R. L. (1998). Building memories: Remembering and forgetting of verbal experiences as predicted by brain activity. *Science, 281,* 1188–1191.

Wallace, B. (1984). Apparent equivalence between perception and imagery in the production of various illusions. *Memory & Cognition, 12,* 156–162.

Wanner, H. E. (1968). *On remembering, forgetting, and understanding sentences. A study of the deep structure hypothesis.* Unpublished doctoral dissertation, Harvard University.

Warren, R. M. (1970). Perceptual restorations of missing speech sounds. *Science, 167,* 392–393.

Warren, R. M., & Warren, R. P. (1970). Auditory illusions and confusions. *Scientific American, 223,* 30–36.

Warrington, E. K., & Shallice, T. (1984). Category specific semantic impairments. *Brain, 197,* 829–854.

Wason, P. C., & Johnson-Laird, P. N. (1972). *Psychology of reasoning: Structure and content.* Cambridge, MA: Harvard University Press.

Wasow, T. (1989). Grammatical theory. In M. I. Posner (Ed.), *Foundations of cognitive science.* Cambridge, MA: MIT Press.

Watkins, M. J., & Tulving, E. (1975). Episodic memory: When recognition fails. *Journal of Experimental Psychology: General, 104,* 5–29.

Watson, J. (1930). *Behaviorism.* New York: Norton.

Waugh, N. C., & Norman, D. A. (1965). Primary memory. *Psychological Review, 72,* 89–104.

Weber, E., Böckenholt, U., Hilton, D., & Wallace, B. (1993). Determinants of diagnostic hypothesis generation: Effects of information, base rates and experience. *Journal of Experimental Psychology: Learning, Memory, and Cognition, 19,* 1151–1164.

Weisberg, R. W. (1969). Sentence processing assessed through intrasentence word associations. *Journal of Experimental Psychology, 82,* 332–338.

Weisberg, R. W. (1986). *Creativity: Genius and other myths.* New York: W. H. Freeman.

Weiser, M., & Shertz, J. (1983). Programming problem representation in novice and expert programmers. *International Journal of Man-Machine Studies, 19,* 391–398.

Wertheimer, M. (1912/1932). Experimentelle Studien über das Sehen von Beuegung. *Zeitschrift für Psychologie, 61,* 161–265.

Wetherick, N. (1989). Psychology and syllogistic reasoning. *Philosophical Psychology, 2,* 111–124.

Wheeler, D. D. (1970). Processes in word recognition. *Cognitive Psychology, 1,* 59–85.

Whorf, B. L. (1956). *Language, thought, and reality.* Cambridge, MA: MIT Press.

Wickelgren, W. A. (1974). *How to solve problems.* New York: W. H. Freeman.

Wickelgren, W. A. (1975). Alcoholic intoxication and memory storage dynamics. *Memory & Cognition, 3,* 385–389.

Wickens, C. D. (1992). *Engineering psychology and human performance* (2nd Ed.). New York: HarperCollins.

Winston, P. H. (1970). *Learning structural descriptions from examples.* AI Laboratory, Technical Report-231, MIT, Cambridge, MA.

Wixted, J. T., & Ebbesen, E. B. (1991). On the form of forgetting. *Psychological Science, 2,* 409–415.

Woldorff, M. G., Gallen, C. C., Hampson, S. A., Hillyard, S. A., Pantev, C., Sobel, D., & Bloom, F. E. (1993). Modulation of early sensory processing in human auditory cortex during auditory selective attention. *Proceedings of the National Academy of Science, 90,* 8722–8726.

Wolfe, J. M. (1994). Guided search 2.0: A revised model of visual search. *Psychonomic Bulletin & Review, 1,* 202–238.

Woodrow, H. (1927). The effect of the type of training upon transference. *Journal of Educational Psychology, 18,* 159–172.

Woodworth, R. S., & Sells, S. B. (1935). An atmospheric effect in formal syllogistic reasoning. *Journal of Experimental Psychology, 18,* 451–460.

Wurtz, R. H., Goldberg, M. E., & Robinson, D. L. (1980). Behavioral modulation of visual responses in the monkey: Stimulus selection for attention and movement. *Prog. Psychobiology, Physiology and Psychology, 9,* 43–83.

◆ Name Index

Page references followed by *n* indicate material in footnotes.

Subject Index

ships in the harbour. When the curtain rises, to the accompaniment of a new theme in the orchestra:

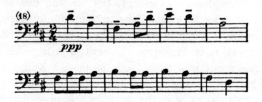

we see the three figures as we left them at the conclusion of the preceding scene.

The day breaks gradually, the orchestra rising to life with it. At last, when the sunshine fills the room, Butterfly rouses herself, wakens Suzuki, and then takes up the baby tenderly. Seeing how weary Butterfly is, Suzuki implores her to go and rest, promising that she will call her when Pinkerton arrives. Butterfly goes off with the child, singing it a sweet little lullaby that has a curious touch of Grieg about it; after each of the final phrases Suzuki breaks in with a sad " Poor Madam Butterfly! "

To the accompaniment of one of Puccini's typically sombre, slow-treading themes:

Suzuki is opening the *shosi* when a knock is heard at the door. Opening it, she finds Pinkerton, who signals to her to be silent. He enters cautiously on tiptoe, followed by Sharpless. Suzuki tells them of Butterfly's vigil, and how for three years she has examined eagerly the flag and the colours of every ship that has crossed the harbour. Pointing to the flowers, Suzuki shows Pinkerton the preparations that have been made for his return. Hearing a noise in the garden she goes to look out, and is surprised to find a lady there. A fear of coming evil strikes into her heart, and she excitedly implores Pinkerton to tell her who this woman is.

At first he tries to evade the question, simply saying, " She came with me "; but Sharpless thinks it better to tell her the truth at once: it is Pinkerton's American wife. The stupefied Suzuki breaks out into a wild cry of despair and falls to the ground. Sharpless raises her, tries to soothe her, and explains that they have come so early in the morning hoping to find her alone and to be able to count upon her discretion and help. To the strain of No. 19 he tells her that for such a trouble as Butterfly's there is no consolation, but the future of the baby must be their first thought; the lady outside dare not enter, but she will give the child a mother's care. He exhorts Suzuki, however, to go and speak to the lady, and induce her to come in even though Butterfly should see her and learn with her own eyes the bitter truth that none dares tell her.

Meanwhile Suzuki is sobbing out her only half-coherent lamentations, and Pinkerton, seeing his own portrait, is touched by the evidence that he has been in Butterfly's mind all these years. He feels himself unequal to the ordeal of meeting her. Giving Sharpless money for the support of Butterfly, and sobbing out his anguish and remorse, he bids farewell to the house in which he had once known such happiness:

and ends his own difficulties by pusillanimous flight. Sharpless, having shaken him by the hand, bows his head sadly.

Kate Pinkerton and Suzuki enter from the garden, and from their conversation we learn that Suzuki has promised to tell Butterfly everything and give her Mrs. Pinkerton's promise that she will tend the child like a son.

Butterfly's voice is now heard calling " Suzuki! Suzuki! Where are you? " from the room above; and soon she appears at the top of the staircase. She is about to descend the stairs when Suzuki rushes forward to prevent her. But Butterfly will not be withheld. Something has told her that Pinkerton has come, and she paces the room joyously and excitedly in search of him. Seeing only Sharpless, she begins to be alarmed.

After a further search she notices Kate Pinkerton, who is weeping. She asks the strange lady who she is, but receiving no answer, begins to understand everything, and shrinks in upon herself like a frightened child. To Suzuki, as the only one she can trust, she turns with the pitiful question, " Say yes, or no, quite softly; does he live? " Suzuki mutters despairingly " Yes," but at first cannot be induced to answer Butterfly's next question, " They have told you that he will come no more? "

When the truth has been wrung from Suzuki, Butterfly's last illusion is gone: at last she understands. She looks fixedly at Kate, both terrified and fascinated; and Kate can say nothing but " Through no fault of my own I am the cause of your trouble. Forgive me." She would approach Butterfly to console her, but the latter shrinks from her. Calmly she asks, " How long ago was it he married you? " Kate answers, " A year." She blunders on with futile expressions of sympathy and offers to do everything for the child, and Butterfly, seemingly filled with a great calm, the calm of utter despair, congratulates her on her happiness and asks her to take Pinkerton a message that to Butterfly also peace will come. She implores them all to leave her. Kate, still not quite sure of the situation, asks Sharpless, " Can he have his son? " Butterfly, who has overheard this, says gravely, " I will give him his son if he will come to fetch him, in half an hour from now."

When they have gone, Butterfly seems to be on the point of

collapsing, but steadies herself. As the light hurts and offends her, she bids Suzuki close the curtains and the doors, so that the room becomes almost completely dark. Butterfly, after having insisted on the weeping Suzuki leaving her, lights the lamp in front of the Buddah, and stands motionless for a time, sunk in bitter thought. Then, from a convulsive movement of her body, we see that an idea has struck her. She takes the white veil from the shrine, throws it across the screen, takes the sacred dagger from the wall, kisses the blade, and softly reads aloud the words engraved on it — "Death with honour is better than life with dishonour."

She is about to thrust the knife into her throat when the door on the left opens, and Suzuki's arm is seen pushing the child towards his mother. Butterfly drops the dagger, runs to meet the little totterer, clasps him in her arms, and kisses him madly. She bids him an anguished farewell:

telling him that it is for him she is making this last great sacrifice. Then she seats him with his back to the audience, blindfolds him, gives him the American flag and a doll to play with, takes up the dagger again, and, with her eyes always on the child, goes behind the screen.

Sombre and heavily-moving chords in the orchestra intensify the sense of tragic strain and foreboding in the air. There is a moment's silence; then the knife is heard falling to the ground, and the veil is plucked from the screen. Butterfly totters into view, the veil round her neck, groping blindly for the child. She finds him at last, embraces him with her last strength, and falls beside him.